FREE Study Skills Videos/DVD Offer

Dear Customer,

Thank you for your purchase from Mometrix! We consider it an honor and a privilege that you have purchased our product and we want to ensure your satisfaction.

As part of our ongoing effort to meet the needs of test takers, we have developed a set of Study Skills Videos that we would like to give you for <u>FREE</u>. These videos cover our *best practices* for getting ready for your exam, from how to use our study materials to how to best prepare for the day of the test.

All that we ask is that you email us with feedback that would describe your experience so far with our product. Good, bad, or indifferent, we want to know what you think!

To get your FREE Study Skills Videos, you can use the **QR code** below, or send us an **email** at studyvideos@mometrix.com with *FREE VIDEOS* in the subject line and the following information in the body of the email:

- The name of the product you purchased.
- Your product rating on a scale of 1-5, with 5 being the highest rating.
- Your feedback. It can be long, short, or anything in between. We just want to know your impressions and experience so far with our product. (Good feedback might include how our study material met your needs and ways we might be able to make it even better. You could highlight features that you found helpful or features that you think we should add.)

If you have any questions or concerns, please don't hesitate to contact me directly.

Thanks again!

Sincerely,

Jay Willis
Vice President
jay.willis@mometrix.com
1-800-673-8175

Mometrix
TEST PREPARATION

Mometrix
TEST PREPARATION

ATI TEAS®

TEAS® 7 Prep Book Secrets Study Guide

Six Full-Length Practice Tests (1,000+ Questions)

Step-by-Step Video Tutorials

[Updated for the 7th Edition]

Written and edited by Matthew Bowling

Printed in the United States of America

This paper meets the requirements of ANSI/NISO Z39.48-1992 (Permanence of Paper).

Mometrix offers volume discount pricing to institutions. For more information or a price quote, please contact our sales department at sales@mometrix.com or 888-248-1219.

ATI TEAS® is a registered trademark of the Assessment Technologies Institute®, which was not involved in the production of, and does not endorse, this product.

Paperback
ISBN 13: 978-1-5167-2000-2
ISBN 10: 1-5167-2000-8

DEAR FUTURE EXAM SUCCESS STORY

First of all, **THANK YOU** for purchasing Mometrix study materials!

Second, congratulations! You are one of the few determined test-takers who are committed to doing whatever it takes to excel on your exam. **You have come to the right place.** We developed these study materials with one goal in mind: to deliver you the information you need in a format that's concise and easy to use.

In addition to optimizing your guide for the content of the test, we've outlined our recommended steps for breaking down the preparation process into small, attainable goals so you can make sure you stay on track.

We've also analyzed the entire test-taking process, identifying the most common pitfalls and showing how you can overcome them and be ready for any curveball the test throws you.

Standardized testing is one of the biggest obstacles on your road to success, which only increases the importance of doing well in the high-pressure, high-stakes environment of test day. Your results on this test could have a significant impact on your future, and this guide provides the information and practical advice to help you achieve your full potential on test day.

Your success is our success

We would love to hear from you! If you would like to share the story of your exam success or if you have any questions or comments in regard to our products, please contact us at **800-673-8175** or **support@mometrix.com**.

Thanks again for your business and we wish you continued success!

Sincerely,
The Mometrix Test Preparation Team

> **Need more help? Check out our flashcards at:**
> **http://MometrixFlashcards.com/TEAS**

TABLE OF CONTENTS

Introduction

Thank you for purchasing this resource! You have made the choice to prepare yourself for a test that could have a huge impact on your future, and this guide is designed to help you be fully ready for test day. Obviously, it's important to have a solid understanding of the test material, but you also need to be prepared for the unique environment and stressors of the test, so that you can perform to the best of your abilities.

For this purpose, the first section that appears in this guide is the **Secret Keys**. We've devoted countless hours to meticulously researching what works and what doesn't, and we've boiled down our findings to the five most impactful steps you can take to improve your performance on the test. We start at the beginning with study planning and move through the preparation process, all the way to the testing strategies that will help you get the most out of what you know when you're finally sitting in front of the test.

We recommend that you start preparing for your test as far in advance as possible. However, if you've bought this guide as a last-minute study resource and only have a few days left before your test, go ahead and skip over the first two Secret Keys since they address a long-term approach.

If you have time to prepare but you're not sure where to begin, we've got you covered! Check out our **Four-Week TEAS Study Plan** and adapt it as necessary to fit the time that you have before your test.

Finally, if you struggle with **test anxiety**, we strongly encourage you to check out our recommendations for how you can overcome it. Test anxiety is a formidable foe, but it can be beaten, and we want to make sure you have the tools you need to defeat it.

TEAS FAQs

Q. Will I be allowed to use a calculator?

A. Yes, you will be provided with a simple four-function calculator to use on the math section of the TEAS. *You may NOT bring your own calculator*. If you are taking a paper version of the TEAS, the school or testing center will provide a calculator for you to use. If you are taking the TEAS on a computer, it will be an on-screen calculator built into the testing software.

Q. What scores do I need to earn on the TEAS?

A. It is left up to each school to set its own cut scores. You will need to check with each school where you plan to apply to see what scores they require.

Q. When will I get my scores?

A. It depends on where and how you will be taking the test. At most testing locations with computer-based testing, you will receive your TEAS scores as soon as you finish taking the test. However, you may have to wait a few days for your score if you are taking a pencil-and-paper test *or* if the school where you are taking it has administratively set a waiting period.

1

Secret Key #1 – Plan Big, Study Small

There's a lot riding on your performance. If you want to ace this test, you're going to need to keep your skills sharp and the material fresh in your mind. You need a plan that lets you review everything you need to know while still fitting in your schedule. We'll break this strategy down into three categories.

Information Organization

Start with the information you already have: the official test outline. From this, you can make a complete list of all the concepts you need to cover before the test. Organize these concepts into groups that can be studied together, and create a list of any related vocabulary you need to learn so you can brush up on any difficult terms. You'll want to keep this vocabulary list handy once you actually start studying since you may need to add to it along the way.

Time Management

Once you have your set of study concepts, decide how to spread them out over the time you have left before the test. Break your study plan into small, clear goals so you have a manageable task for each day and know exactly what you're doing. Then just focus on one small step at a time. When you manage your time this way, you don't need to spend hours at a time studying. Studying a small block of content for a short period each day helps you retain information better and avoid stressing over how much you have left to do. You can relax knowing that you have a plan to cover everything in time. In order for this strategy to be effective though, you have to start studying early and stick to your schedule. Avoid the exhaustion and futility that comes from last-minute cramming!

Study Environment

The environment you study in has a big impact on your learning. Studying in a coffee shop, while probably more enjoyable, is not likely to be as fruitful as studying in a quiet room. It's important to keep distractions to a minimum. You're only planning to study for a short block of time, so make the most of it. Don't pause to check your phone or get up to find a snack. It's also important to **avoid multitasking**. Research has consistently shown that multitasking will make your studying dramatically less effective. Your study area should also be comfortable and well-lit so you don't have the distraction of straining your eyes or sitting on an uncomfortable chair.

The time of day you study is also important. You want to be rested and alert. Don't wait until just before bedtime. Study when you'll be most likely to comprehend and remember. Even better, if you know what time of day your test will be, set that time aside for study. That way your brain will be used to working on that subject at that specific time and you'll have a better chance of recalling information.

Finally, it can be helpful to team up with others who are studying for the same test. Your actual studying should be done in as isolated an environment as possible, but the work of organizing the information and setting up the study plan can be divided up. In between study sessions, you can discuss with your teammates the concepts that you're all studying and quiz each other on the details. Just be sure that your teammates are as serious about the test as you are. If you find that your study time is being replaced with social time, you might need to find a new team.

Secret Key #2 – Make Your Studying Count

You're devoting a lot of time and effort to preparing for this test, so you want to be absolutely certain it will pay off. This means doing more than just reading the content and hoping you can remember it on test day. It's important to make every minute of study count. There are two main areas you can focus on to make your studying count.

Retention

It doesn't matter how much time you study if you can't remember the material. You need to make sure you are retaining the concepts. To check your retention of the information you're learning, try recalling it at later times with minimal prompting. Try carrying around flashcards and glance at one or two from time to time or ask a friend who's also studying for the test to quiz you.

To enhance your retention, look for ways to put the information into practice so that you can apply it rather than simply recalling it. If you're using the information in practical ways, it will be much easier to remember. Similarly, it helps to solidify a concept in your mind if you're not only reading it to yourself but also explaining it to someone else. Ask a friend to let you teach them about a concept you're a little shaky on (or speak aloud to an imaginary audience if necessary). As you try to summarize, define, give examples, and answer your friend's questions, you'll understand the concepts better and they will stay with you longer. Finally, step back for a big picture view and ask yourself how each piece of information fits with the whole subject. When you link the different concepts together and see them working together as a whole, it's easier to remember the individual components.

Finally, practice showing your work on any multi-step problems, even if you're just studying. Writing out each step you take to solve a problem will help solidify the process in your mind, and you'll be more likely to remember it during the test.

Modality

Modality simply refers to the means or method by which you study. Choosing a study modality that fits your own individual learning style is crucial. No two people learn best in exactly the same way, so it's important to know your strengths and use them to your advantage.

For example, if you learn best by visualization, focus on visualizing a concept in your mind and draw an image or a diagram. Try color-coding your notes, illustrating them, or creating symbols that will trigger your mind to recall a learned concept. If you learn best by hearing or discussing information, find a study partner who learns the same way or read aloud to yourself. Think about how to put the information in your own words. Imagine that you are giving a lecture on the topic and record yourself so you can listen to it later.

For any learning style, flashcards can be helpful. Organize the information so you can take advantage of spare moments to review. Underline key words or phrases. Use different colors for different categories. Mnemonic devices (such as creating a short list in which every item starts with the same letter) can also help with retention. Find what works best for you and use it to store the information in your mind most effectively and easily.

Secret Key #3 – Practice the Right Way

Your success on test day depends not only on how many hours you put into preparing, but also on whether you prepared the right way. It's good to check along the way to see if your studying is paying off. One of the most effective ways to do this is by taking practice tests to evaluate your progress. Practice tests are useful because they show exactly where you need to improve. Every time you take a practice test, pay special attention to these three groups of questions:

- The questions you got wrong
- The questions you had to guess on, even if you guessed right
- The questions you found difficult or slow to work through

This will show you exactly what your weak areas are, and where you need to devote more study time. Ask yourself why each of these questions gave you trouble. Was it because you didn't understand the material? Was it because you didn't remember the vocabulary? Do you need more repetitions on this type of question to build speed and confidence? Dig into those questions and figure out how you can strengthen your weak areas as you go back to review the material.

 Additionally, many practice tests have a section explaining the answer choices. It can be tempting to read the explanation and think that you now have a good understanding of the concept. However, an explanation likely only covers part of the question's broader context. Even if the explanation makes perfect sense, **go back and investigate** every concept related to the question until you're positive you have a thorough understanding.

As you go along, keep in mind that the practice test is just that: practice. Memorizing these questions and answers will not be very helpful on the actual test because it is unlikely to have any of the same exact questions. If you only know the right answers to the sample questions, you won't be prepared for the real thing. **Study the concepts** until you understand them fully, and then you'll be able to answer any question that shows up on the test.

It's important to wait on the practice tests until you're ready. If you take a test on your first day of study, you may be overwhelmed by the amount of material covered and how much you need to learn. Work up to it gradually.

On test day, you'll need to be prepared for answering questions, managing your time, and using the test-taking strategies you've learned. It's a lot to balance, like a mental marathon that will have a big impact on your future. Like training for a marathon, you'll need to start slowly and work your way up. When test day arrives, you'll be ready.

Start with the strategies you've read in the first two Secret Keys—plan your course and study in the way that works best for you. If you have time, consider using multiple study resources to get different approaches to the same concepts. It can be helpful to see difficult concepts from more than one angle. Then find a good source for practice tests. Many times, the test website will suggest potential study resources or provide sample tests.

Secret Key #4 – Pace Yourself

Once you're fully prepared for the material on the test, your biggest challenge on test day will be managing your time. Just knowing that the clock is ticking can make you panic even if you have plenty of time left. Work on pacing yourself so you can build confidence against the time constraints of the exam. Pacing is a difficult skill to master, especially in a high-pressure environment, so **practice is vital**.

Set time expectations for your pace based on how much time is available. For example, if a section has 60 questions and the time limit is 30 minutes, you know you have to average 30 seconds or less per question in order to answer them all. Although 30 seconds is the hard limit, set 25 seconds per question as your goal, so you reserve extra time to spend on harder questions. When you budget extra time for the harder questions, you no longer have any reason to stress when those questions take longer to answer.

Don't let this time expectation distract you from working through the test at a calm, steady pace, but keep it in mind so you don't spend too much time on any one question. Recognize that taking extra time on one question you don't understand may keep you from answering two that you do understand later in the test. If your time limit for a question is up and you're still not sure of the answer, mark it and move on, and come back to it later if the time and the test format allow. If the testing format doesn't allow you to return to earlier questions, just make an educated guess; then put it out of your mind and move on.

On the easier questions, be careful not to rush. It may seem wise to hurry through them so you have more time for the challenging ones, but it's not worth missing one if you know the concept and just didn't take the time to read the question fully. Work efficiently but make sure you understand the question and have looked at all of the answer choices, since more than one may seem right at first.

Even if you're paying attention to the time, you may find yourself a little behind at some point. You should speed up to get back on track, but do so wisely. Don't panic; just take a few seconds less on each question until you're caught up. Don't guess without thinking, but do look through the answer choices and eliminate any you know are wrong. If you can get down to two choices, it is often worthwhile to guess from those. Once you've chosen an answer, move on and don't dwell on any that you skipped or had to hurry through. If a question was taking too long, chances are it was one of the harder ones, so you weren't as likely to get it right anyway.

On the other hand, if you find yourself getting ahead of schedule, it may be beneficial to slow down a little. The more quickly you work, the more likely you are to make a careless mistake that will affect your score. You've budgeted time for each question, so don't be afraid to spend that time. Practice an efficient but careful pace to get the most out of the time you have.

Secret Key #5 – Have a Plan for Guessing

When you're taking the test, you may find yourself stuck on a question. Some of the answer choices seem better than others, but you don't see the one answer choice that is obviously correct. What do you do?

The scenario described above is very common, yet most test takers have not effectively prepared for it. Developing and practicing a plan for guessing may be one of the single most effective uses of your time as you get ready for the exam.

In developing your plan for guessing, there are three questions to address:

- When should you start the guessing process?
- How should you narrow down the choices?
- Which answer should you choose?

When to Start the Guessing Process

Unless your plan for guessing is to select C every time (which, despite its merits, is not what we recommend), you need to leave yourself enough time to apply your answer elimination strategies. Since you have a limited amount of time for each question, that means that if you're going to give yourself the best shot at guessing correctly, you have to decide quickly whether or not you will guess.

Of course, the best-case scenario is that you don't have to guess at all, so first, see if you can answer the question based on your knowledge of the subject and basic reasoning skills. Focus on the key words in the question and try to jog your memory of related topics. Give yourself a chance to bring the knowledge to mind, but once you realize that you don't have (or you can't access) the knowledge you need to answer the question, it's time to start the guessing process.

It's almost always better to start the guessing process too early than too late. It only takes a few seconds to remember something and answer the question from knowledge. Carefully eliminating wrong answer choices takes longer. Plus, going through the process of eliminating answer choices can actually help jog your memory.

Summary: Start the guessing process as soon as you decide that you can't answer the question based on your knowledge.

6

How to Narrow Down the Choices

The next chapter in this book (**Test-Taking Strategies**) includes a wide range of strategies for how to approach questions and how to look for answer choices to eliminate. You will definitely want to read those carefully, practice them, and figure out which ones work best for you. Here though, we're going to address a mindset rather than a particular strategy.

Your odds of guessing an answer correctly depend on how many options you are choosing from.

Number of options left	5	4	3	2	1
Odds of guessing correctly	20%	25%	33%	50%	100%

You can see from this chart just how valuable it is to be able to eliminate incorrect answers and make an educated guess, but there are two things that many test takers do that cause them to miss out on the benefits of guessing:

- Accidentally eliminating the correct answer
- Selecting an answer based on an impression

We'll look at the first one here, and the second one in the next section.

To avoid accidentally eliminating the correct answer, we recommend a thought exercise called **the $5 challenge**. In this challenge, you only eliminate an answer choice from contention if you are willing to bet $5 on it being wrong. Why $5? Five dollars is a small but not insignificant amount of money. It's an amount you could afford to lose but wouldn't want to throw away. And while losing

$5 once might not hurt too much, doing it twenty times will set you back $100. In the same way, each small decision you make—eliminating a choice here, guessing on a question there—won't by itself impact your score very much, but when you put them all together, they can make a big difference. By holding each answer choice elimination decision to a higher standard, you can reduce the risk of accidentally eliminating the correct answer.

The $5 challenge can also be applied in a positive sense: If you are willing to bet $5 that an answer choice *is* correct, go ahead and mark it as correct.

Summary: Only eliminate an answer choice if you are willing to bet $5 that it is wrong.

Which Answer to Choose

You're taking the test. You've run into a hard question and decided you'll have to guess. You've eliminated all the answer choices you're willing to bet $5 on. Now you have to pick an answer. Why do we even need to talk about this? Why can't you just pick whichever one you feel like when the time comes?

The answer to these questions is that if you don't come into the test with a plan, you'll rely on your impression to select an answer choice, and if you do that, you risk falling into a trap. The test writers know that everyone who takes their test will be guessing on some of the questions, so they intentionally write wrong answer choices to seem plausible. You still have to pick an answer though, and if the wrong answer choices are designed to look right, how can you ever be sure that you're not falling for their trap? The best solution we've found to this dilemma is to take the decision out of your hands entirely. Here is the process we recommend:

Once you've eliminated any choices that you are confident (willing to bet $5) are wrong, select the first remaining choice as your answer.

Whether you choose to select the first remaining choice, the second, or the last, the important thing is that you use some preselected standard. Using this approach guarantees that you will not be enticed into selecting an answer choice that looks right, because you are not basing your decision on how the answer choices look.

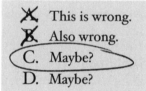

This is not meant to make you question your knowledge. Instead, it is to help you recognize the difference between your knowledge and your impressions. There's a huge difference between thinking an answer is right because of what you know, and thinking an answer is right because it looks or sounds like it should be right.

Summary: To ensure that your selection is appropriately random, make a predetermined selection from among all answer choices you have not eliminated.

8

Test-Taking Strategies

This section contains a list of test-taking strategies that you may find helpful as you work through the test. By taking what you know and applying logical thought, you can maximize your chances of answering any question correctly!

It is very important to realize that every question is different and every person is different: no single strategy will work on every question, and no single strategy will work for every person. That's why we've included all of them here, so you can try them out and determine which ones work best for different types of questions and which ones work best for you.

Question Strategies

☑ READ CAREFULLY

Read the question and the answer choices carefully. Don't miss the question because you misread the terms. You have plenty of time to read each question thoroughly and make sure you understand what is being asked. Yet a happy medium must be attained, so don't waste too much time. You must read carefully and efficiently.

☑ CONTEXTUAL CLUES

Look for contextual clues. If the question includes a word you are not familiar with, look at the immediate context for some indication of what the word might mean. Contextual clues can often give you all the information you need to decipher the meaning of an unfamiliar word. Even if you can't determine the meaning, you may be able to narrow down the possibilities enough to make a solid guess at the answer to the question.

☑ PREFIXES

If you're having trouble with a word in the question or answer choices, try dissecting it. Take advantage of every clue that the word might include. Prefixes can be a huge help. Usually, they allow you to determine a basic meaning. *Pre-* means before, *post-* means after, *pro-* is positive, *de-* is negative. From prefixes, you can get an idea of the general meaning of the word and try to put it into context.

☑ HEDGE WORDS

Watch out for critical hedge words, such as *likely, may, can, sometimes, often, almost, mostly, usually, generally, rarely,* and *sometimes*. Question writers insert these hedge phrases to cover every possibility. Often an answer choice will be wrong simply because it leaves no room for exception. Be on guard for answer choices that have definitive words such as *exactly* and *always*.

☑ SWITCHBACK WORDS

Stay alert for *switchbacks*. These are the words and phrases frequently used to alert you to shifts in thought. The most common switchback words are *but, although,* and *however*. Others include *nevertheless, on the other hand, even though, while, in spite of, despite,* and *regardless of*. Switchback words are important to catch because they can change the direction of the question or an answer choice.

9

⊘ Face Value

When in doubt, use common sense. Accept the situation in the problem at face value. Don't read too much into it. These problems will not require you to make wild assumptions. If you have to go beyond creativity and warp time or space in order to have an answer choice fit the question, then you should move on and consider the other answer choices. These are normal problems rooted in reality. The applicable relationship or explanation may not be readily apparent, but it is there for you to figure out. Use your common sense to interpret anything that isn't clear.

Answer Choice Strategies

⊘ Answer Selection

The most thorough way to pick an answer choice is to identify and eliminate wrong answers until only one is left, then confirm it is the correct answer. Sometimes an answer choice may immediately seem right, but be careful. The test writers will usually put more than one reasonable answer choice on each question, so take a second to read all of them and make sure that the other choices are not equally obvious. As long as you have time left, it is better to read every answer choice than to pick the first one that looks right without checking the others.

⊘ Answer Choice Families

An answer choice family consists of two (in rare cases, three) answer choices that are very similar in construction and cannot all be true at the same time. If you see two answer choices that are direct opposites or parallels, one of them is usually the correct answer. For instance, if one answer choice says that quantity x increases and another either says that quantity x decreases (opposite) or says that quantity y increases (parallel), then those answer choices would fall into the same family. An answer choice that doesn't match the construction of the answer choice family is more likely to be incorrect. Most questions will not have answer choice families, but when they do appear, you should be prepared to recognize them.

⊘ Eliminate Answers

Eliminate answer choices as soon as you realize they are wrong, but make sure you consider all possibilities. If you are eliminating answer choices and realize that the last one you are left with is also wrong, don't panic. Start over and consider each choice again. There may be something you missed the first time that you will realize on the second pass.

⊘ Avoid Fact Traps

Don't be distracted by an answer choice that is factually true but doesn't answer the question. You are looking for the choice that answers the question. Stay focused on what the question is asking for so you don't accidentally pick an answer that is true but incorrect. Always go back to the question and make sure the answer choice you've selected actually answers the question and is not merely a true statement.

⊘ Extreme Statements

In general, you should avoid answers that put forth extreme actions as standard practice or proclaim controversial ideas as established fact. An answer choice that states the "process should be used in certain situations, if…" is much more likely to be correct than one that states the "process should be discontinued completely." The first is a calm rational statement and doesn't even make a definitive, uncompromising stance, using a hedge word *if* to provide wiggle room, whereas the second choice is far more extreme.

⊘ BENCHMARK

As you read through the answer choices and you come across one that seems to answer the question well, mentally select that answer choice. This is not your final answer, but it's the one that will help you evaluate the other answer choices. The one that you selected is your benchmark or standard for judging each of the other answer choices. Every other answer choice must be compared to your benchmark. That choice is correct until proven otherwise by another answer choice beating it. If you find a better answer, then that one becomes your new benchmark. Once you've decided that no other choice answers the question as well as your benchmark, you have your final answer.

⊘ PREDICT THE ANSWER

Before you even start looking at the answer choices, it is often best to try to predict the answer. When you come up with the answer on your own, it is easier to avoid distractions and traps because you will know exactly what to look for. The right answer choice is unlikely to be word-for-word what you came up with, but it should be a close match. Even if you are confident that you have the right answer, you should still take the time to read each option before moving on.

General Strategies

⊘ TOUGH QUESTIONS

If you are stumped on a problem or it appears too hard or too difficult, don't waste time. Move on! Remember though, if you can quickly check for obviously incorrect answer choices, your chances of guessing correctly are greatly improved. Before you completely give up, at least try to knock out a couple of possible answers. Eliminate what you can and then guess at the remaining answer choices before moving on.

⊘ CHECK YOUR WORK

Since you will probably not know every term listed and the answer to every question, it is important that you get credit for the ones that you do know. Don't miss any questions through careless mistakes. If at all possible, try to take a second to look back over your answer selection and make sure you've selected the correct answer choice and haven't made a costly careless mistake (such as marking an answer choice that you didn't mean to mark). This quick double check should more than pay for itself in caught mistakes for the time it costs.

⊘ PACE YOURSELF

It's easy to be overwhelmed when you're looking at a page full of questions; your mind is confused and full of random thoughts, and the clock is ticking down faster than you would like. Calm down and maintain the pace that you have set for yourself. Especially as you get down to the last few minutes of the test, don't let the small numbers on the clock make you panic. As long as you are on track by monitoring your pace, you are guaranteed to have time for each question.

⊘ DON'T RUSH

It is very easy to make errors when you are in a hurry. Maintaining a fast pace in answering questions is pointless if it makes you miss questions that you would have gotten right otherwise. Test writers like to include distracting information and wrong answers that seem right. Taking a little extra time to avoid careless mistakes can make all the difference in your test score. Find a pace that allows you to be confident in the answers that you select.

11

⊘ KEEP MOVING

Panicking will not help you pass the test, so do your best to stay calm and keep moving. Taking deep breaths and going through the answer elimination steps you practiced can help to break through a stress barrier and keep your pace.

Alternative Item Types (New on TEAS 7)

ATI has introduced four new question types on the TEAS 7. Some of them will require a slightly different approach than the standard multiple-choice questions. Note that these new question types will only appear on the computer-based version of the test. If you're taking the TEAS on paper, you shouldn't expect to see anything but standard multiple-choice questions.

⊘ NUMERIC ENTRY

On numeric entry questions, you will not be provided with answer options to choose from. Instead, you will have to solve the question and supply a number for your answer. For obvious reasons, these questions will appear primarily in the Math and Science sections. There are no real shortcuts available on these. You simply have to calculate the correct answer, round it if necessary (the question will specify the decimal place you must round to), and type it in.

⊘ MULTIPLE CORRECT ANSWER (SELECT ALL THAT APPLY)

On these questions, you will be presented with 4-6 possible answer options and asked to select all of the correct answers from the list. What makes these question tricky is that there is no partial credit. If you select only some of the correct answers, it's counted wrong. If you select all of the correct answers plus one incorrect answer, it's counted wrong. The best way to approach these questions is to evaluate each option individually. Treat each one as its own true/false question and decide if it is correct based on the criteria given in the question.

⊘ ORDERING

For ordering questions, you will be provided with a list of things and asked to place them into a designated order. This may be a numerical order (least to greatest), a locational order (distal to proximal), a sequential order (steps in a process), or some other defined order. The approach to take with these questions depends heavily on which type of order is involved. The simplest type is the numerical order. For these, the process is to convert each number into a common form (e.g., convert all to decimals or all to fractions) so their values can be easily compared. For most types of ordering though, there are not any well-defined processes for solving. Just make sure you understand what the question is asking for, and then reason through the placement of each item in the sequence.

⊘ HOT SPOT

Hot spot questions will present you with an image and ask you to click on the part of the image that is specified in the question. This is not as open-ended as it might sound though, because there will be a limited number of areas on the image highlighted as options for you to select. Functionally, these are nothing more than standard multiple-choice questions, so they can be treated in much the same way. If you know exactly what the answer is, you can just go ahead and select it. If you're not sure, you can rule out answer choices and make an educated guess.

Final Notes

The combination of a solid foundation of content knowledge and the confidence that comes from practicing your plan for applying that knowledge is the key to maximizing your performance on test day. As your foundation of content knowledge is built up and strengthened, you'll find that the strategies included in this chapter become more and more effective in helping you quickly sift through the distractions and traps of the test to isolate the correct answer.

Now that you're preparing to move forward into the test content chapters of this book, be sure to keep your goal in mind. As you read, think about how you will be able to apply this information on the test. If you've already seen sample questions for the test and you have an idea of the question format and style, try to come up with questions of your own that you can answer based on what you're reading. This will give you valuable practice applying your knowledge in the same ways you can expect to on test day.

Good luck and good studying!

Four-Week TEAS Study Plan

On the next four pages, we've provided an optional study plan to help you use this study guide to its fullest potential over the course of four weeks. If you only have two weeks to study before your exam, you can double up this four-week timeline, completing two weeks' worth of studying each week. If you have eight weeks available and want to spread it out more, spend two weeks on each section of the plan.

Below is a quick summary of the subjects covered in each week of the plan.

- Week 1: Reading
- Week 2: Mathematics
- Week 3: Science*
- Week 4: English and Language Usage

Please note that not all subjects will take the same amount of time to work through.

*The science chapter in particular is very long, and the content is complex. If science is not a strong subject for you, it may take a long time to read through and absorb all the information that is presented, so make sure to plan enough time for it that week.

Two full-length practice tests are printed in this study guide, and you can access four more practice tests by scanning the QR code to the right or following this link on your computer or mobile device: **mometrix.com/bonus948/teas7**

We recommend saving the four additional practice tests for after you've completed the study plan. Take these last four practice tests timed and without any reference materials in the week or two before the real thing to get yourself in the mode of answering questions at a good pace.

Week 1: Reading

INSTRUCTIONAL CONTENT

First, read carefully through the Reading chapter in this book, checking off your progress as you go:

- ❏ Key Ideas and Details
- ❏ Craft and Structure
- ❏ Integration of Knowledge and Ideas

As you read, do the following:

- Highlight any areas you think are important
- Draw an asterisk (*) next to any areas you are struggling with
- Watch the review videos to gain more understanding of a particular topic
- Take notes in your notebook or in the margins of this book

After you've read through everything, go back and review any sections that you highlighted or that you drew an asterisk next to, referencing your notes along the way.

PRACTICE TEST #1

Now that you've read over the instructional content, it's time to take a practice test. Complete the Reading section of Practice Test #1. Take this test with **no time constraints**, and feel free to reference the applicable sections of this guide as you go. Once you've finished, check your answers against the provided answer key. For any questions you answered incorrectly, review the answer rationale, and then **go back and review** the applicable sections of the book. The goal in this stage is to understand why you answered the question incorrectly, and make sure that the next time you see a similar question, you will get it right.

PRACTICE TEST #2

Next, take the Reading section of Practice Test #2. This time, give yourself **55 minutes** (the amount of time you will have on the real TEAS) to complete all 45 questions. You should again feel free to reference the guide and your notes, but be mindful of the clock. If you run out of time before you finish all 45 questions, mark where you were when time expired, but go ahead and finish taking the practice test. Once you've finished, check your answers against the provided answer key, and as before, review the answer rationale for any that you answered incorrectly and go back and review the associated instructional content. Your goal is still to increase understanding of the content but also to get used to the time constraints you will face on the test.

Week 2: Mathematics

INSTRUCTIONAL CONTENT

First, read carefully through the Mathematics chapter in this book, checking off your progress as you go:

- ❏ Numbers
- ❏ Operations
- ❏ Rational Numbers
- ❏ Proportions and Ratios
- ❏ Expressions, Equations, and Inequalities
- ❏ Measurement Principles
- ❏ Units of Measurement
- ❏ Geometric Quantities
- ❏ Statistics
- ❏ Displaying Information

As you read, do the following:

- Highlight any sections, tables, formulas, etc. you think are important
- Draw an asterisk (*) next to any areas you are struggling with
- Work through the practice problems at the end of each section
- Watch the review videos to gain more understanding of a particular topic
- Take notes in your notebook or in the margins of this book

After you've read through everything, go back and review any sections that you highlighted or that you drew an asterisk next to, referencing your notes along the way.

PRACTICE TEST #1

Now that you've read over the instructional content, it's time to take a practice test. Complete the Mathematics section of Practice Test #1. Take this test with **no time constraints**, and feel free to reference the applicable sections of this guide as you go. Once you've finished, check your answers against the provided answer key. For any questions you answered incorrectly, review the answer rationale, and then **go back and review** the applicable sections of the book. The goal in this stage is to understand why you answered the question incorrectly, and make sure that the next time you see a similar question, you will get it right.

PRACTICE TEST #2

Next, take the Mathematics section of Practice Test #2. This time, give yourself 57 minutes (the amount of time you will have on the real TEAS) to complete all 38 questions. You should again feel free to reference the guide and your notes, but be mindful of the clock. If you run out of time before you finish all 38 questions, mark where you were when time expired, but go ahead and finish taking the practice test. Once you've finished, check your answers against the provided answer key, and as before, review the answer rationale for any that you answered incorrectly and then go back and review the associated instructional content. Your goal is still to increase understanding of the content but also to get used to the time constraints you will face on the test.

Week 3: Science

NOTE: This section contains especially complex material that may require extra studying time.

INSTRUCTIONAL CONTENT

First, read carefully through the Science chapter in this book, checking off your progress as you go:

- ❏ General Anatomy and Physiology
- ❏ Respiratory System
- ❏ Cardiovascular System
- ❏ Gastrointestinal System
- ❏ Nervous System
- ❏ Muscular System
- ❏ Reproductive System
- ❏ Integumentary System
- ❏ Endocrine System
- ❏ Urinary System
- ❏ Immune System
- ❏ Skeletal System

- ❏ Cells
- ❏ Genetic Material
- ❏ Genetic Inheritance
- ❏ Macromolecules
- ❏ Microorganisms and Disease
- ❏ Basic Atomic Structure
- ❏ States of Matter
- ❏ Overview of Chemical Reactions
- ❏ Rate of Reaction
- ❏ Solutions
- ❏ Acid and Base Chemistry
- ❏ Scientific Reasoning

As you read, do the following:

- Highlight any important sections, diagrams, or terms
- Draw an asterisk (*) next to any difficult areas
- Watch the review videos to gain more understanding
- Take notes in your notebook or in the margins of this book

After you've read through everything, go back and review any sections that you highlighted or that you drew an asterisk next to, referencing your notes along the way.

PRACTICE TEST #1

Now that you've read over the instructional content, it's time to take a practice test. Complete the Science section of Practice Test #1. Take this test with **no time constraints**, and feel free to reference the applicable sections of this guide as you go. Once you've finished, check your answers against the provided answer key. For any questions you answered incorrectly, review the answer rationale, and then **go back and review** the applicable sections of the book. The goal in this stage is to understand why you answered the question incorrectly, and make sure that the next time you see a similar question, you will get it right.

PRACTICE TEST #2

Next, take the Science section of Practice Test #2. This time, give yourself 60 minutes (the amount of time you will have on the real TEAS) to complete all 50 questions. You should again feel free to reference the guide and your notes, but be mindful of the clock. If you run out of time before you finish all 50 questions, mark where you were when time expired, but go ahead and finish taking the practice test. Once you've finished, check your answers against the provided answer key, and as before, review the answer rationale for any that you answered incorrectly and then go back and review the associated instructional content. Your goal is still to increase understanding of the content but also to get used to the time constraints you will face on the test.

17

Week 4: English and Language Usage

INSTRUCTIONAL CONTENT

First, read carefully through the English and Language Usage chapter in this book, checking off your progress as you go:

❑ Conventions of Standard English: Spelling
❑ Conventions of Standard English: Punctuation
❑ Conventions of Standard English: Grammar
❑ Conventions of Standard English: Sentence Structure
❑ Knowledge of Language
❑ Using Language and Vocabulary to Express Ideas in Writing

As you read, do the following:

- Highlight any sections, tables, vocabulary words, etc. you think are important
- Draw an asterisk (*) next to any areas you are struggling with
- Watch the review videos to gain more understanding of a particular topic
- Take notes in your notebook or in the margins of this book

After you've read through everything, go back and review any sections that you highlighted or that you drew an asterisk next to, referencing your notes along the way.

PRACTICE TEST #1

Now that you've read over the instructional content, it's time to take a practice test. Complete the English and Language Usage section of Practice Test #1. Take this test with **no time constraints**, and feel free to reference the applicable sections of this guide as you go. Once you've finished, check your answers against the provided answer key. For any questions you answered incorrectly, review the answer rationale, and then **go back and review** the applicable sections of the book. The goal in this stage is to understand why you answered the question incorrectly, and make sure that the next time you see a similar question, you will get it right.

PRACTICE TEST #2

Next, take the English and Language Usage section of Practice Test #2. This time, give yourself 37 minutes (the amount of time you will have on the real TEAS) to complete all 37 questions. You should again feel free to reference the guide and your notes, but be mindful of the clock. If you run out of time before you finish all 37 questions, mark where you were when time expired, but go ahead and finish taking the practice test. Once you've finished, check your answers against the provided answer key, and as before, review the answer rationale for any that you answered incorrectly and then go back and review the associated instructional content. Your goal is still to increase understanding of the content but also to get used to the time constraints you will face on the test.

About the TEAS Test

This study guide includes comprehensive review sections on each of the four TEAS test sections. Following those review sections, you will find two complete TEAS practice tests printed in the guide, and a link where you can find an **additional four practice tests** in online interactive format.

Below is a breakdown of the four sections on the exam, including the subcategories, how many questions are in each section, and how much time will be allotted for you to complete that section. Each section of the test contains more questions for you to answer than will actually be scored. Those extra questions are being evaluated by the test makers for future use.

Content Areas	Time	Test Items	% of Test	Scored Items
Reading	**55 min**	**45**	**26%**	**39**
Key Ideas and Details				15
Craft and Structure				9
Integration of Knowledge and Ideas				15
Mathematics	**57 min**	**38**	**23%**	**34**
Numbers and Algebra				18
Measurement and Data				16
Science	**60 min**	**50**	**29%**	**44**
Human Anatomy and Physiology				18
Biology				9
Chemistry				8
Scientific Reasoning				9
English and Language Usage	**37 min**	**37**	**22%**	**33**
Conventions of Standard English				12
Knowledge of Language				11
Using Language and Vocabulary to Express Ideas in Writing				10
Total	**209 min**	**170**	**100%**	**150**

Reading

Key Ideas and Details

SUMMARIZING A MULTI-PARAGRAPH TEXT
SUMMARIES

Summarizing information you have read in a paragraph or passage format can be quite helpful. This process is similar to creating an effective outline. First, a summary should accurately define the main idea of the passage, though the summary does not need to explain this main idea in exhaustive detail. The summary should continue by laying out the most important supporting details or arguments from the passage. All of the significant supporting details should be included, and none of the details included should be irrelevant or insignificant to the text's overall meaning. Also, the summary should accurately report all of these details. Too often, the desire for brevity in a summary leads to the sacrifice of clarity or accuracy. Summaries are often difficult to read because they omit all of the graceful language, digressions, and asides that distinguish great writing. However, an effective summary should communicate the same overall message as the original text.

TOPICS AND MAIN IDEAS

One of the most important skills in reading comprehension is the identification of **topics** and **main ideas.** There is a subtle difference between these two features. The topic is the **subject** of a text, or what the text is about. The main idea, on the other hand, is the **most important point** being made by the author. The topic is usually expressed in a few words at the most, while the main idea often needs a full sentence to be completely defined. As an example, a short passage might have the topic of penguins and the main idea *Penguins are different from other birds in many ways.* In most nonfiction writing, the topic and the main idea will be stated directly, often in a sentence at the very beginning or end of the text. When being tested on an understanding of the author's topic, the reader can quickly *skim* the passage for the general idea, stopping to read only the first sentence of each paragraph. A paragraph's first sentence is often (but not always) the main topic sentence, and it gives the reader a summary of the content of the paragraph.

However, there are cases in which the reader must figure out an **unstated** topic or main idea. In these instances, the reader must read every sentence of the text and try to come up with an overarching idea that is supported by each of those sentences.

> **Review Video: Topics and Main Ideas**
> Visit mometrix.com/academy and enter code: 407801

SUPPORTING DETAILS

Supporting details, also called key points, provide **evidence** and backing for the main point. In order to show that a main idea is correct, or valid, the author needs to add details that prove their point. All texts contain details, but they are only classified as supporting details when they serve to reinforce some larger point. Supporting details are most commonly found in **informative** and **persuasive** texts. In some cases, they will be clearly indicated with words like *for example* or *for instance*, or they will be enumerated with words like *first, second,* and *last*. However, they may not be indicated with special words. As a reader, it is important to consider whether the author's supporting details really back up his or her **main point**. Supporting details can be factual and correct but still not relevant to the author's point. Conversely, supporting details can seem pertinent but be ineffective because they are based on opinion or assertions that cannot be proven.

Review Video: **Supporting Details**
Visit mometrix.com/academy and enter code: 396297

TOPIC AND SUMMARY SENTENCES

Topic and summary sentences are a convenient way to encapsulate the **main idea** of a text. In some textbooks and academic articles, the author will place a **topic** or **summary sentence** at the beginning of each section as a means of preparing the reader for what is to come. Research suggests that the brain is more receptive to new information when it has been prepared by the presentation of the main idea or some key words. The phenomenon is somewhat akin to the primer coat of paint that allows subsequent coats of paint to absorb more easily. A good topic sentence will be **clear** and not contain any **jargon**. When topic or summary sentences are not provided, good readers can jot down their own so that they can find their place in a text and refresh their memory.

PARAPHRASING

Paraphrasing is a strategy that can be used both to increase reading comprehension and to include information when writing. Paraphrasing involves putting a portion of a text into the reader's own words. This can be done post-reading as a way to encourage readers to actively engage with the text rather than passively receiving the information. Taking the time to put what they have read into their own words helps readers consider the information more fully and is a good check for understanding. Writers can use paraphrasing to include information from sources without adding a direct quote. Paraphrasing can be a useful tool for providing background a writer gained from their research before moving into the body of an essay or text. An important note here is that even paraphrasing someone else's writing requires a citation to provide credit to the original writer.

Review Video: **Summarizing Text**
Visit mometrix.com/academy and enter code: 172903

MAKING INFERENCES

Readers are often required to understand a text that claims and suggests ideas without stating them directly. An **inference** is a piece of information that is implied but not written outright by the author. For instance, consider the following sentence: *After the final out of the inning, the fans were filled with joy and rushed the field.* From this sentence, a reader can infer that the fans were watching a baseball game and their team won the game. Readers should take great care to avoid using information **beyond the provided passage** before making inferences. As you practice drawing inferences, you will find that they require concentration and attention.

Review Video: **Inference**
Visit mometrix.com/academy and enter code: 379203

While being tested on your ability to make correct inferences, you must look for **contextual clues**. An answer can be *true* but not *correct*. The contextual clues will help you find the answer that is the **best answer** out of the given choices. Be careful in your reading to understand the context in which a phrase is stated. When asked for the implied meaning of a statement made in the passage, you should immediately locate the statement and read the **context** in which the statement was made. Also, look for an answer choice that has a similar phrase to the statement in question.

DRAWING CONCLUSIONS

It is important to understand the logical conclusion of the ideas presented in an informational text. **Identifying a logical conclusion** can help you determine whether you agree with the writer or not. Coming to this conclusion is much like making an inference: the approach requires you to combine the information given by the text with what you already know and make a logical conclusion. If the author intended for the reader to draw a certain conclusion, then you can expect the author's argumentation and detail to be leading in that direction. One way to approach the task of drawing conclusions is to make brief **notes** of all the points made by the author. When the notes are arranged on paper, they may clarify the logical conclusion. Another way to approach conclusions is to consider whether the reasoning of the author raises any pertinent questions. Sometimes you will be able to draw several conclusions from a passage. On occasion these will be conclusions that were never imagined by the author. Therefore, be aware that these conclusions must be **supported directly by the text**.

DIRECTLY STATED INFORMATION

A reader should always be drawing conclusions from the text. Sometimes conclusions are **implied** from written information, and other times the information is **stated directly** within the passage. One should always aim to draw conclusions from information stated within a passage, rather than to draw them from mere implications. At times an author may provide some information and then describe a counterargument. Readers should be alert for direct statements that are subsequently rejected or weakened by the author. Furthermore, you should always read through the entire passage before drawing conclusions. Many readers are trained to expect the author's conclusions at either the beginning or the end of the passage, but many texts do not adhere to this format.

IMPLICATIONS

Drawing conclusions from information implied within a passage requires confidence on the part of the reader. **Implications** are things that the author does not state directly, but readers can assume based on what the author does say. Consider the following passage: *I stepped outside and opened my umbrella. By the time I got to work, the cuffs of my pants were soaked.* The author never states that it is raining, but this fact is clearly implied. Conclusions based on implication must be well supported by the text. In order to draw a solid conclusion, readers should have **multiple pieces of evidence**. If readers have only one piece, they must be assured that there is no other possible explanation than their conclusion. A good reader will be able to draw many conclusions from information implied by the text, which will be a great help on the exam.

EXPLICIT AND IMPLICIT EVIDENCE

When informational text states something **explicitly**, the reader is told by the author exactly what is meant, which can include the author's interpretation or perspective of events. For example, a professor writes, "I have seen students go into an absolute panic just because they weren't able to complete the exam in the time they were allotted." This explicitly tells the reader that the students were afraid, and by using the words "just because," the writer indicates their fear was exaggerated out of proportion relative to what happened. However, another professor writes, "I have had students come to me, their faces drained of all color, saying 'We weren't able to finish the exam.'" This is an example of **implicit** meaning: the second writer did not state explicitly that the students were panicked. Instead, he wrote a description of their faces being "drained of all color." From this description, the reader can infer that the students were so frightened that their faces paled.

> **Review Video: Explicit and Implicit Information**
> Visit mometrix.com/academy and enter code: 735771

23

Both explicit and implicit evidence can be used to support a logical conclusion, as long as the evidence is clearly stated or reasonably implied in the text. Explicit information is most commonly used as evidence to support a conclusion because it can be easily found in the text. Implicit information is more difficult to identify or verify in a text. Discerning implied information requires the reader to make a conclusion based on explicit evidence. Implicit evidence can help readers make more conclusions, but it must be sufficiently implied by the text to serve as appropriate evidence for a conclusion.

COMPREHENDING WRITTEN DIRECTIONS

Technical passages often require the reader to **follow a set of directions**. For many people, especially those who are tactile or visual learners, this can be a difficult process. It is important to approach a set of directions differently than other texts. First, it is a good idea to **scan** the directions to determine whether special equipment or preparations are needed. Sometimes in a recipe, for instance, the author fails to mention that the oven should be preheated first, and then halfway through the process, the cook is supposed to be baking. After briefly reading the directions, the reader should return to the first step. When following directions, it is appropriate to **complete each step** before moving on to the next. If this is not possible, it is useful at least to visualize each step before reading the next.

SIGNAL WORDS IN WRITTEN DIRECTIONS

Instructional passages will often use many signal words to tell the reader when each step should be completed and whether the step is essential to the described procedure. Signal words that show the sequence of steps include words like *first*, *next*, *then*, and *last*. These words show the reader the relationship between each step and help the reader better understand the process as a whole. Other signal words describe whether a step is necessary or essential to the whole procedure. For example, a recipe may include words like *to taste* or *as desired* to show which steps are suggested but not required to cook the dish.

MISSING INFORMATION AND CONTRADICTIONS IN WRITTEN DIRECTIONS

Occasionally, an instructional passage may leave out information or include details that are contradictory. When this occurs, the reader must first read carefully to ensure that he or she understands the text and that there is truly an error or inconsistency in the text. The reader should then consider the information provided, prior knowledge, and logic to determine the best response to the contradictory or missing information. The solution for responding to such errors is similar to making conclusions based on a text. The solution must be supported by the information in the text and be logical and compatible with that information.

SELECTING AND FINDING RELEVANT INFORMATION

When approaching an informational text, readers often have a purpose for consulting the text. This purpose may be to find a solution, to answer a question, or simply to become more informed about a topic. To effectively use the text for his or her purpose, the reader must seek out information that is relevant within the text. Many informational texts include tools like a table of contents. Readers can use the headings in a table of contents by identifying key words that are closely related to the information they are seeking and identify where in the text this information is located. When using online sources, users can use tools like search engines to find the information they need. Search engines and digital copies of texts often include search bars. To effectively use these tools, a user should first identify the information he or she is seeking. Next, the user should choose some key terms from this information. When the user enters these terms in the search bar, the search engine or digital text will provide links to sources or sections that are relevant to the key terms.

TEXT FEATURES

HEADINGS AND SUBHEADINGS

Many informative texts, especially textbooks, use **headings** and **subheadings** for organization. Headings and subheadings are printed in larger and bolder fonts than the rest of the text. Sometimes, they are in a different color than the main body of the book. Headings are often larger than subheadings. Also, headings and subheadings are not always complete sentences. A heading gives the **topic** that will be addressed in the paragraphs below. Headings are meant to alert you about what is coming next. Subheadings give the **topics of smaller sections**. For example, the heading of a section in a science textbook might be *AMPHIBIANS*. Within that section, you may have subheadings for *Frogs, Salamanders,* and *Newts*. Pay close attention to headings and subheadings. They make it easy to go back and find specific details in a book.

LEGEND OR KEY OF A MAP

Almost all maps contain a **key**, or **legend**, that defines the **symbols** used on the map for various landmarks. This key is usually placed in a corner of the map. It should contain listings for all of the important symbols on the map. Of course, these symbols will vary depending on the nature of the map. A road map uses different colored lines to indicate roads, highways, and interstates. A legend might also show different dots and squares that are used to indicate towns of various sizes. The legend may contain information about the map's **scale**, though this may be elsewhere on the map. Many legends will contain special symbols, such as a picnic table indicating a campground.

BOLD TEXT AND UNDERLINING

Authors will often incorporate text features like bold text and underlining to communicate meaning to the reader. When text is made **bold**, it is often because the author wants to emphasize the point that is being made. Bold text indicates **importance**. Also, many textbooks place key terms in bold. This not only draws the reader's attention, but also makes it easy to find these terms when reviewing before a test. **Underlining** serves a similar purpose. It is often used to suggest **emphasis**. However, underlining is also used on occasion beneath the **titles** of books, magazines, and works of art. This was more common when people used typewriters, which weren't able to create italics. Now that word processing software is nearly universal, italics are generally used for longer works.

ITALICS

Italics, like bold text and underlines, are used to **emphasize** important words, phrases, and sentences in a text. However, italics have other uses as well. A word is placed in italics when it is being discussed as a word; that is, when it is being **defined** or its use in a sentence is being **described**. For instance, it is appropriate to use italics when saying that *esoteric* is an unusual adjective. Italics are also used for the titles of long or large works, like books, magazines, long operas, and epic poems. Shorter works are typically placed within **quotation marks**. A reader should note how an author uses italics, as this is a marker of style and tone. Some authors use them frequently, creating a tone of high emotion, while others are more restrained in their use, suggesting calm and reason.

FOOTNOTES AND ENDNOTES

Footnotes and endnotes can also be used in word processing programs. A **footnote** is text that is listed at the *bottom of a page* which lists where facts and figures within that document page were obtained. An **endnote** is similar to a footnote, but differs in the fact that it is listed at the *end of paragraphs and chapters* of a document, instead of the bottom of each page of the document.

GLOSSARY

A glossary is a list of terms and their definitions that can be found at the back of certain types of books, such as textbooks or reference books. A glossary does not have the definitions of all words, like a dictionary, but instead gives the definitions of the important terms within that particular book which are either uncommon or newly introduced. One may use a glossary when reading a book about economics or a chapter in a science textbook, for example, to define some of the technical terms within the text.

INDEX

Normally, a nonfiction book will have an **index** at the end. The index is for you to find information about specific topics. An index lists the topics in alphabetical order (i.e., a, b, c, d...). The names of people are listed by last name. For example, *Adams, John* would come before *Washington, George*. To the right of a topic, the page numbers are listed for that topic. When a topic is spread over several pages, the index will connect these pages with a dash. For example, if a topic is said to be on pages 35 to 42 and again on 53, the topic will be labeled as 35–42, 53. Some topics will have **subtopics**. These subtopics are listed below the main topic, indented slightly, and placed in alphabetical order. This is common for subjects that are covered over several pages in the book. For example, if you have a book about Elizabethan drama, William Shakespeare is likely an important topic. Beneath Shakespeare's name in the index, you may find listings for *death of*, *dramatic works of*, *life of*, etc. These specific sub-topics help you narrow your search.

TABLE OF CONTENTS

Most books, magazines, and journals have a **table of contents** at the beginning. The table of contents lists the different **subjects** or **chapter titles** with a page number. This information allows you to find what you need with ease. Normally, the table of contents is found a page or two after the title page in a book or in the first few pages of a magazine. In a book, the table of contents will have the chapters listed on the left side. The page number for each chapter comes on the right side. Many books have a **preface** (i.e., a note that explains the background of the book) or introduction. The preface and introduction come with Roman numerals. The chapters are listed in order from the beginning to the end.

CHARTS, GRAPHS, VISUALS, AND PRINTED COMMUNICATION

PIE CHART

A pie chart, also known as a circle graph, is useful for depicting how a single unit or category is divided. The standard pie chart is a circle with designated wedges. Each wedge is **proportional** in size to a part of the whole. For instance, consider Shawna, a student at City College, who uses a pie chart to represent her budget. If she spends half of her money on rent, then the pie chart will represent that amount with a line through the center of the pie. If she spends a quarter of her money on food, there will be a line extending from the edge of the circle to the center at a right angle to the line depicting rent. This illustration would make it clear that the student spends twice the amount of money on rent as she does on food.

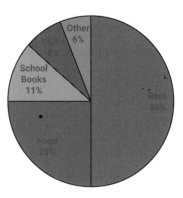

A pie chart is effective at showing how a single entity is divided into parts. They are not effective at demonstrating the relationships between parts of different wholes. For example, an unhelpful use

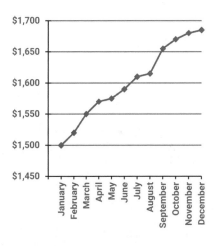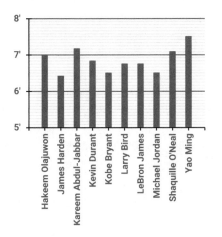

of a pie chart would be to compare the respective amounts of state and federal spending devoted to infrastructure since these values are only meaningful in the context of the entire budget.

BAR GRAPH

The bar graph is one of the most common visual representations of information. **Bar graphs** are used to illustrate sets of numerical **data**. The graph has a vertical axis (along which numbers are listed) and a horizontal axis (along which categories, words, or some other indicators are placed). One example of a bar graph is a depiction of the respective heights of famous basketball players: the vertical axis would contain numbers ranging from five to eight feet, and the horizontal axis would contain the names of the players. The length of the bar above the player's name would illustrate his height, and the top of the bar would stop perpendicular to the height listed along the left side. In this representation, one would see that Yao Ming is taller than Michael Jordan because Yao's bar would be higher.

LINE GRAPH

A line graph is a type of graph that is typically used for measuring trends over time. The graph is set up along a vertical and a horizontal **axis**. The variables being measured are listed along the left side and the bottom side of the axes. Points are then plotted along the graph as they correspond with their values for each variable. For instance, consider a line graph measuring a person's income for each month of the year. If the person earned $1500 in January, there should be a point directly above January (perpendicular to the horizontal axis) and directly to the right of $1500 (perpendicular to the vertical axis). Once all of the lines are plotted, they are connected with a line from left to right. This line provides a nice visual illustration of the general **trends** of the data, if they exist. For instance, using the earlier example, if the line sloped up, then one would see that the person's income had increased over the course of the year.

PICTOGRAPHS

A **pictograph** is a graph, generally in the horizontal orientation, that uses pictures or symbols to represent the data. Each pictograph must have a key that defines the picture or symbol and gives the quantity each picture or symbol represents. Pictures or symbols on a pictograph are not always shown as whole elements. In this case, the fraction of the picture or symbol shown represents the same fraction of the quantity a whole picture or symbol stands for.

TYPES OF PRINTED COMMUNICATION
MEMO

A memo (short for *memorandum*) is a common form of written communication. There is a standard format for these documents. It is typical for there to be a **heading** at the top indicating the author, date, and recipient. In some cases, this heading will also include the author's title and the name of his or her institution. Below this information will be the **body** of the memo. These documents are typically written by and for members of the same organization. They usually contain a plan of action, a request for information on a specific topic, or a response to such a request. Memos are considered to be official documents, so they are usually written in a **formal** style. Many memos are organized with numbers or bullet points, which make it easier for the reader to identify key ideas.

POSTED ANNOUNCEMENT

People post **announcements** for all sorts of occasions. Many people are familiar with notices for lost pets, yard sales, and landscaping services. In order to be effective, these announcements need to *contain all of the information* the reader requires to act on the message. For instance, a lost pet announcement needs to include a good description of the animal and a contact number for the owner. A yard sale notice should include the address, date, and hours of the sale, as well as a brief description of the products that will be available there. When composing an announcement, it is important to consider the perspective of the **audience**—what will they need to know in order to respond to the message? Although a posted announcement can have color and decoration to attract the eye of the passerby, it must also convey the necessary information clearly.

CLASSIFIED ADVERTISEMENT

Classified advertisements, or **ads**, are used to sell or buy goods, to attract business, to make romantic connections, and to do countless other things. They are an inexpensive, and sometimes free, way to make a brief **pitch**. Classified ads used to be found only in newspapers or special advertising circulars, but there are now online listings as well. The style of these ads has remained basically the same. An ad usually begins with a word or phrase indicating what is being **sold** or **sought**. Then, the listing will give a brief **description** of the product or service. Because space is limited and costly in newspapers, classified ads there will often contain abbreviations for common attributes. For instance, two common abbreviations are *bk* for *black*, and *obo* for *or best offer*. Classified ads will then usually conclude by listing the **price** (or the amount the seeker is willing to pay), followed by **contact information** like a telephone number or email address.

SCALE READINGS OF STANDARD MEASUREMENT INSTRUMENTS

The scales used on **standard measurement instruments** are fairly easy to read with a little practice. Take the **ruler** as an example. A typical ruler has different units along each long edge. One side measures inches, and the other measures centimeters. The units are specified close to the zero reading for the ruler. Note that the ruler does not begin measuring from its outermost edge. The zero reading is a black line a tiny distance inside of the edge. On the inches side, each inch is indicated with a long black line and a number. Each half-inch is noted with a slightly shorter line. Quarter-inches are noted with still shorter lines, eighth-inches are noted with even shorter lines, and sixteenth-inches are noted with the shortest lines of all. On the centimeter side, the second-largest black lines indicate half-centimeters, and the smaller lines indicate tenths of centimeters, otherwise known as millimeters.

INTERPRETING EVENTS IN A SEQUENCE

Readers must be able to identify a text's **sequence**, or the order in which things happen. Often, the sequence of steps or events in a text is indicated by signal words like *first, then, next, before,* and *last*. In narratives, adverbs are often used as signal words, and verb tenses are also used to guide the reader through the sequence of events. However, a sequence can be merely implied and must be noted by the reader. Consider the sentence: *He walked through the garden and gave water and fertilizer to the plants*. Clearly, the man did not walk through the garden before he collected water and fertilizer for the plants. So, the implied sequence is that he first collected water, then he collected fertilizer, next he walked through the garden, and last he gave water or fertilizer as necessary to the plants. Texts do not always proceed in an **orderly** sequence from first to last.

Sometimes they begin at the end and start over at the beginning. As a reader, you can enhance your understanding of the passage by taking brief **notes** to clarify the sequence.

> **Review Video: Sequence**
> Visit mometrix.com/academy and enter code: 489027

KEY IDEAS AND DETAILS CHAPTER QUIZ

1. Summaries are difficult to read because they omit all of the following EXCEPT:

a. Supporting details
b. Graceful language
c. Digressions
d. Asides

2. Which of the following describes the text at the conclusion of a page outlining where facts and figures were found?

a. Footnote
b. Endnote
c. Tailnote
d. Lognote

3. Which of the following is most important when drawing conclusions from a text?

a. The conclusions make sense to others.
b. The conclusions are supported directly by the text.
c. The conclusions agree with previous convictions.
d. The conclusions align with the author's purpose for writing the text.

4. What benefit do topic sentences provide for the reader?

a. They organize a text into headings and subheadings.
b. They prepare the reader to receive new information by providing the main idea.
c. They convince the reader with detailed evidence.
d. They give the reader a call to action based on the supporting evidence.

5. What is implied by the following scenario?

I hurried as fast as I could to class, only to find the test had already started when I arrived.

a. I am at the wrong class.
b. I stayed up late and slept past my alarm.
c. I am late for class.
d. The test is too hard.

6. Which type of tool is typically used for measuring trends over time?

a. Line graph
b. Bar graph
c. Pie chart
d. Flow chart

Answers for all of the chapter quiz questions can be found right before Practice Test #1.

Craft and Structure

DISTINGUISHING FACT AND OPINION

Readers must always be conscious of the distinction between **fact** and **opinion**. A fact can be subjected to analysis and can be either **proved or disproved**. An opinion, on the other hand, merely conveys an author's **personal thoughts or feelings**, which may not be based on or even affected by research or evidence. The author who writes "The distance between New York and Boston is about two hundred miles" is stating a fact. The author who writes "New York is too crowded" is giving an opinion because there is no objective standard for *too crowded*.

An opinion is often signaled by words like *believe*, *think*, or *feel*, but opinions can also be stated by the author as though they were facts. Readers should also be aware that opinions may be **supported by facts**. For instance, the author might cite the population density of New York as evidence of an overcrowded population. An opinion that is supported by fact tends to be more convincing than an opinion that is stated without support or that is supported by other opinions. In these latter cases, readers should not be persuaded by the argument to any degree.

> **Review Video: Fact or Opinion?**
> Visit mometrix.com/academy and enter code: 870899

AUTHOR'S POINT OF VIEW

Another element that impacts a text is the writer's point of view. The **point of view** of a text is the perspective from which a passage is told. A writer will always have a point of view about a story or topic before he or she begins planning a composition. A writer will also have an opinion on the topic or series of events which is presented in the composition that is based on their prior experience and beliefs. **First-person** point of view lets narrators express their inner feelings and thoughts. In first person, the writer writes from the perspective of *I*. First person is generally used for personal correspondence, narratives, fiction, or informal writing. Second-person point of view allows the writer to address the reader or audience. Second person is characterized by the use of pronouns that directly address the audience, like *you*.

Third person is another point of view that does not reference the writer or the writer's audience. Third-person point of view uses pronouns like *he, she*, and *they*. There are multiple types of third-person narration in fiction, such as third-person omniscient and third-person limited. Third person is regarded as the most formal point of view, as it removes the subjectivity of first person and the direct audience address of second person. Third-person writing places all of the focus on the meaning of the text and does not clearly share the writer's personal thoughts or feelings. Even in third person, bias or prejudice can be detected in the writing, but they will not be as clearly or directly communicated as they would in first person.

AUTHOR'S TONE

Tone is defined as the writer's **attitude** toward a subject or audience as it is reflected in his use of language, such as word choice. This is similar to the mood of a piece, which is the overall feeling conveyed by a written work. Whereas the mood is about what the reader feels, tone is about how the writer feels about his subject or audience. For instance, a story can have a very serious topic, while describing it in a playful or humorous way. The language a writer uses to describe a topic can reveal the writer's true feelings toward a topic or audience. Readers should keep the tone in mind, as it can often reveal the author's purpose or biases.

TONE AND BIAS

Because tone reflects the writer's attitude, tone can also be a means through which a writer's biases are revealed. The word choice and tone a writer uses when describing or addressing a particular idea, person, or group of people may be discernably positive or negative, communicating a writer's preference or distaste for the subject. Writers should work to establish an appropriate tone for their purpose, but when discussing an idea, a person, or a group, the writer's tone should be without bias.

BIASES AND STEREOTYPES

Every author has a point of view, but authors demonstrate a **bias** when they ignore reasonable counterarguments or distort opposing viewpoints. A bias is evident when an author is purposefully or grossly **unfair** or **inaccurate** in his or her presentation. An overly critical or judgmental tone can be a clue that the author is being unfair because of bias. Bias may be intentional or unintentional, and readers should be skeptical of the author's argument. Remember that a biased author may still be correct; however, the author will be correct in spite of his or her bias, not because of the bias. A **stereotype** is like a bias in that it is a generalization, but a stereotype is applied specifically to a **group** or **place**. Stereotyping is considered to be particularly abhorrent because the practice promotes negative generalizations about people. Readers should be very cautious of authors who stereotype in their writing. These faulty assumptions typically reveal the author's ignorance and lack of curiosity.

> **Review Video: Bias and Stereotype**
> Visit mometrix.com/academy and enter code: 644829

INFERRING WORD MEANING FROM CONTEXT

One of the benefits of reading is the expansion of one's vocabulary. In order to obtain this benefit, however, one needs to know how to identify the definition of a **word from its context**. This means defining a word based on the **words around it** and the way it is **used in a sentence**. Consider the following sentence: *The elderly scholar spent his evenings hunched over arcane texts that few other people even knew existed.* The adjective *arcane* is uncommon, but you can obtain significant information about it based on its use in the sentence. The fact that few other people know of their existence allows you to assume that "arcane texts" must be rare and be of interest to few people. Also, the texts are being read by an elderly scholar. So, you can assume that they focus on difficult academic subjects. Sometimes, words can be defined by **what they are not**. Consider the following sentence: *Ron's fealty to his parents was not shared by Karen, who disobeyed their every command.* Someone who disobeys is not demonstrating *fealty*. So, you can infer that the word means something like *obedience* or *loyalty*.

WORD CHOICE

A writer's word choice is a signature of his or her style. Word choice can also contribute to the tone of a text. Word choice can help a writer evoke emotion from the reader in a way that helps him or her achieve their purpose for writing. Careful thought about the use of words can improve a piece of writing. A passage can be an exciting piece to read when attention is given to the use of vivid or specific nouns rather than general ones.

Example:

General: His kindness will never be forgotten.

Specific: His thoughtful gifts and bear hugs will never be forgotten.

31

DENOTATIVE AND CONNOTATIVE MEANING OF WORDS

The **denotative** meaning of a word is the literal meaning. The **connotative** meaning goes beyond the denotative meaning to include the **emotional reaction** that a word may evoke. The connotative meaning often takes the denotative meaning a step further due to associations the reader makes with the denotative meaning. Readers can differentiate between the denotative and connotative meanings by first recognizing how authors use each meaning. Most non-fiction, for example, is fact-based and authors do not use flowery, figurative language. The reader can assume that the writer is using the denotative meaning of words. In fiction, the author may use the connotative meaning. Readers can determine whether the author is using the denotative or connotative meaning of a word by implementing **context clues**.

> **Review Video: Denotation and Connotation**
> Visit mometrix.com/academy and enter code: 310092

DICTIONARY ENTRY

Dictionaries can be used to find a word's meaning, to check spelling, and to find out how to say or pronounce a word. **Dictionary entries** are in alphabetical order. **Guide words** are the two words at the top of each page. One word is the first word listed on the page and the other word is the last word listed on the page. Using these guide words will help you use dictionaries more effectively. You may notice that many words have more than one definition. These different definitions are numbered. Also, some words can be used as different **parts of speech**. The definitions for each part of speech are separated. A simple entry might look like this:

WELL: (adverb) 1. in a good way | (noun) 1. a hole drilled into the earth

The correct definition of a word depends on how the word is used in a sentence. To know that you are using the word correctly, you can try to replace the dictionary's definitions for the word in the passage. Then, choose the definition that seems to be the best fit.

FIGURATIVE LANGUAGE

There are many types of language devices that authors use to convey their meaning in a descriptive way. Understanding these concepts will help you understand what you read. These types of devices are called **figurative language**—language that goes beyond the literal meaning of a word or phrase. **Descriptive language** that evokes imagery in the reader's mind is one type of figurative language. **Exaggeration** is another type of figurative language. When you compare two things, you are using figurative language. **Similes** and **metaphors** are ways of comparing things, and both are types of figurative language commonly found in poetry. Here is an example of figurative language (a simile in this case): *The child howled like a coyote when her mother told her to pick up the toys*. In this example, the child's howling is compared to that of a coyote and helps the reader understand the sound being made by the child.

> **Review Video: Figurative Language**
> Visit mometrix.com/academy and enter code: 584902

METAPHOR

A **metaphor** is a type of figurative language in which the writer equates something with another thing that is not particularly similar, instead of using *like* or *as*. For instance, *the bird was an arrow arcing through the sky*. In this sentence, the arrow is serving as a metaphor for the bird. The point of a metaphor is to encourage the reader to consider the item being described in a *different way*. Let's continue with this metaphor for a flying bird. You are asked to envision the bird's flight as being

32

similar to the arc of an arrow. So, you imagine the flight to be swift and bending. Metaphors are a way for the author to describe an item *without being direct and obvious*. This literary device is a lyrical and suggestive way of providing information. Note that the reference for a metaphor will not always be mentioned explicitly by the author. Consider the following description of a forest in winter: *Swaying skeletons reached for the sky and groaned as the wind blew through them.* In this example, the author is using *skeletons* as a metaphor for leafless trees. This metaphor creates a spooky tone while inspiring the reader's imagination.

> **Review Video: <u>Metaphor</u>**
> Visit mometrix.com/academy and enter code: 133295

SIMILE

A **simile** is a figurative expression that is similar to a metaphor, yet the expression requires the use of the distancing words *like* or *as*. Some examples: *The sun was like an orange, eager as a beaver*, and *nimble as a mountain goat*. Because a simile includes *like* or *as*, the device creates a space between the description and the thing being described. If an author says that *a house was like a shoebox*, then the tone is different than the author saying that the house *was a shoebox*. In a simile, authors explicitly indicate that the description is **not** the same thing as the thing being described. In a metaphor, there is no such distinction. The decision of which device to use will be made based on the authors' intended **tone**.

> **Review Video: <u>Simile</u>**
> Visit mometrix.com/academy and enter code: 642949

PERSONIFICATION

Another type of figurative language is **personification**. This is describing a non-human thing, like an animal or an object, as if it were human. The general intent of personification is to describe things in a manner that will be comprehensible to readers. When an author states that a tree *groans* in the wind, he or she does not mean that the tree is emitting a low, pained sound from a mouth. Instead, the author means that the tree is making a noise similar to a human groan. Of course, this personification establishes a tone of sadness or suffering. A different tone would be established if the author said that the tree was *swaying* or *dancing*. Alfred Tennyson's poem "The Eagle" uses all of these types of figurative language: "He clasps the crag with crooked hands." Tennyson used alliteration, repeating /k/ and /kr/ sounds. These hard-sounding consonants reinforce the imagery, giving visual and tactile impressions of the eagle.

> **Review Video: <u>Personification</u>**
> Visit mometrix.com/academy and enter code: 260066

AUTHOR'S PURPOSE

Usually, identifying the author's **purpose** is easier than identifying his or her position. In most cases, the author has no interest in hiding his or her purpose. A text that is meant to entertain, for instance, should be written to please the reader. Most narratives, or stories, are written to entertain, though they may also inform or persuade. Informative texts are easy to identify, while the most difficult purpose of a text to identify is persuasion because the author has an interest in making this purpose hard to detect. When a reader discovers that the author is trying to persuade, he or she should be skeptical of the argument. For this reason, persuasive texts often try to establish an entertaining tone and hope to amuse the reader into agreement. On the other hand, an informative tone may be implemented to create an appearance of authority and objectivity.

An author's purpose is evident often in the **organization** of the text (e.g., section headings in bold font points to an informative text). However, you may not have such organization available to you in your exam. Instead, if the author makes his or her main idea clear from the beginning, then the likely purpose of the text is to **inform**. If the author begins by making a claim and provides various arguments to support that claim, then the purpose is probably to **persuade**. If the author tells a story or wants to gain the reader's attention more than to push a particular point or deliver information, then his or her purpose is most likely to **entertain**. As a reader, you must judge authors on how well they accomplish their purpose. In other words, you need to consider the type of passage (e.g., technical, persuasive, etc.) that the author has written and if the author has followed the requirements of the passage type.

> **Review Video: Purpose**
> Visit mometrix.com/academy and enter code: 511819

INFORMATIVE TEXTS

An **informative text** is written to educate and enlighten readers. Informative texts are almost always nonfiction and are rarely structured as a story. The intention of an informative text is to deliver information in the most comprehensible way. So, look for the structure of the text to be very clear. In an informative text, the thesis statement is one or two sentences that normally appears at the end of the first paragraph. The author may use some colorful language, but he or she is likely to put more emphasis on clarity and precision. Informative essays do not typically appeal to the emotions. They often contain facts and figures and rarely include the opinion of the author; however, readers should remain aware of the possibility for bias as those facts are presented. Sometimes a persuasive essay can resemble an informative essay, especially if the author maintains an even tone and presents his or her views as if they were established fact.

> **Review Video: Informative Text**
> Visit mometrix.com/academy and enter code: 924964

PERSUASIVE WRITING

In a persuasive essay, the author is attempting to change the reader's mind or **convince** him or her of something that he or she did not believe previously. There are several identifying characteristics of **persuasive writing**. One is **opinion presented as fact**. When authors attempt to persuade readers, they often present their opinions as if they were fact. Readers must be on guard for statements that sound factual but which cannot be subjected to research, observation, or experiment. Another characteristic of persuasive writing is **emotional language**. An author will often try to play on the emotions of readers by appealing to their sympathy or sense of morality. When an author uses colorful or evocative language with the intent of arousing the reader's passions, then the author may be attempting to persuade. Finally, in many cases, a persuasive text will give an **unfair explanation of opposing positions**, if these positions are mentioned at all.

ENTERTAINING TEXTS

The success or failure of an author's intent to **entertain** is determined by those who read the author's work. Entertaining texts may be either fiction or nonfiction, and they may describe real or imagined people, places, and events. Entertaining texts are often narratives or poems. A text that is written to entertain is likely to contain **colorful language** that engages the imagination and the emotions. Such writing often features a great deal of figurative language, which typically enlivens the subject matter with images and analogies.

Though an entertaining text is not usually written to persuade or inform, authors may accomplish both of these tasks in their work. An entertaining text may *appeal to the reader's emotions* and cause him or her to think differently about a particular subject. In any case, entertaining texts tend to showcase the personality of the author more than other types of writing.

DESCRIPTIVE TEXT

In a sense, almost all writing is descriptive, insofar as an author seeks to describe events, ideas, or people to the reader. Some texts, however, are primarily concerned with **description**. A descriptive text focuses on a particular subject and attempts to depict the subject in a way that will be clear to readers. Descriptive texts contain many adjectives and adverbs (i.e., words that give shades of meaning and create a more detailed mental picture for the reader). A descriptive text fails when it is unclear to the reader. A descriptive text will certainly be informative and may be persuasive and entertaining as well.

> **Review Video: Descriptive Texts**
> Visit mometrix.com/academy and enter code: 174903

EXPOSITORY PASSAGE

An **expository** passage aims to **inform** and enlighten readers. Expository passages are nonfiction and usually center around a simple, easily defined topic. Since the goal of exposition is to teach, such a passage should be as clear as possible. Often, an expository passage contains helpful organizing words, like *first*, *next*, *for example*, and *therefore*. These words keep the reader **oriented** in the text. Although expository passages do not need to feature colorful language and artful writing, they are often more effective with these features. For a reader, the challenge of expository passages is to maintain steady attention. Expository passages are not always about subjects that will naturally interest a reader, so the writer is often more concerned with **clarity** and **comprehensibility** than with engaging the reader. By reading actively, you can ensure a good habit of focus when reading an expository passage.

> **Review Video: Expository Passages**
> Visit mometrix.com/academy and enter code: 256515

NARRATIVE PASSAGE

A **narrative** passage is a story that can be fiction or nonfiction. However, there are a few elements that a text must have in order to be classified as a narrative. First, the text must have a **plot** (i.e., a series of events). Narratives often proceed in a clear sequence, but this is not a requirement. If the narrative is good, then these events will be interesting to readers. Second, a narrative has **characters**. These characters could be people, animals, or even inanimate objects—so long as they participate in the plot. Third, a narrative passage often contains **figurative language** which is meant to stimulate the imagination of readers by making comparisons and observations. For instance, a *metaphor*, a common piece of figurative language, is a description of one thing in terms of another. *The moon was a frosty snowball* is an example of a metaphor. In the literal sense this is obviously untrue, but the comparison suggests a certain mood for the reader.

TECHNICAL PASSAGE

A **technical** passage is written to *describe* a complex object or process. Technical writing is common in medical and technological fields, in which complex ideas of mathematics, science, and engineering need to be explained *simply and clearly*. To ease comprehension, a technical passage usually proceeds in a very logical order. Technical passages often have clear headings and subheadings, which are used to keep the reader oriented in the text. Additionally, you will find that these passages divide sections up with numbers or letters. Many technical passages look more like an outline than a piece of prose. The amount of **jargon** or difficult vocabulary will vary in a technical passage depending on the intended audience. As much as possible, technical passages try to avoid language that the reader will have to research in order to understand the message, yet readers will find that jargon cannot always be avoided.

> **Review Video: A Technical Passage**
> Visit mometrix.com/academy and enter code: 478923

EXPRESSION OF FEELINGS

When an author intends to **express feelings**, he or she may use **expressive and bold language**. An author may write with emotion for any number of reasons. Sometimes, authors will express feelings because they are describing a personal situation of great pain or happiness. In other situations, authors will attempt to persuade the reader and will use emotion to stir up the passions. This kind of expression is easy to identify when the writer uses phrases like *I felt* and *I sense*. However, readers may find that the author will simply describe feelings without introducing them. As a reader, you must know the importance of recognizing when an author is expressing emotion and not to become overwhelmed by sympathy or passion. Readers should maintain some **detachment** so that they can still evaluate the strength of the author's argument or the quality of the writing.

> **Review Video: Emotional Language in Literature**
> Visit mometrix.com/academy and enter code: 759390

STRUCTURE OF TEXTS
PROBLEM-SOLUTION TEXT STRUCTURE

Some nonfiction texts are organized to **present a problem** followed by a **solution**. For this type of text, the problem is often explained before the solution is offered. In some cases, as when the problem is well known, the solution may be introduced briefly at the beginning. Other passages may focus on the solution, and the problem will be referenced only occasionally. Some texts will outline multiple solutions to a problem, leaving readers to choose among them. If the author has an interest or an allegiance to one solution, he or she may fail to mention or describe accurately some of the other solutions. Readers should be careful of the author's **agenda** when reading a problem-solution text. Only by understanding the author's perspective and interests can one develop a proper judgment of the proposed solution.

COMPARISON AND CONTRAST

Authors will use different stylistic and writing devices to make their meaning clear for readers. One of those devices is **comparison and contrast**. As mentioned previously, when an author describes the ways in which two things are **alike**, he or she is comparing them. When the author describes the ways in which two things are **different**, he or she is contrasting them.

> **Review Video: Compare and Contrast**
> Visit mometrix.com/academy and enter code: 171799

The "compare and contrast" essay is one of the most common forms in nonfiction. These passages are often signaled with certain words. A comparison may have indicating terms such as *both*, *same*, *like*, *too*, and *as well*, while a contrast may have terms like *but*, *however*, *on the other hand*, *instead*, and *yet*. Of course, comparisons and contrasts may be implicit without using any such signaling language. A single sentence may both compare and contrast. Consider the sentence *Brian and Sheila love ice cream, but Brian prefers vanilla while Sheila prefers strawberry.* In one sentence, the author has described both a similarity (love of ice cream) and a difference (favorite flavor).

CAUSE AND EFFECT

One of the most common text structures is **cause and effect**. A **cause** is an act or event that makes something happen, and an **effect** is the thing that happens as a **result** of the cause. A cause-and-effect relationship is not always explicit, but there are some terms in English that signal causes, such as *since*, *because*, and *due to*. Furthermore, terms that signal effects include *consequently*, *therefore, this leads to.* As an example, consider the sentence *Because the sky was clear, Ron did not bring an umbrella.* The cause is the clear sky, and the effect is that Ron did not bring an umbrella. However, readers may find that sometimes the cause-and-effect relationship will not be clearly noted. For instance, the sentence *He was late and missed the meeting* does not contain any signaling words, but the sentence still contains a cause (he was late) and an effect (he missed the meeting).

> **Review Video: Rhetorical Strategy of Cause-and-Effect Analysis**
> Visit mometrix.com/academy and enter code: 725944

EVIDENCE THAT SUPPORTS THE AUTHOR'S PURPOSE

If the reader cannot clearly identify the author's purpose by examining the type and structure of the text, he or she can determine the author's purpose using other attributes of the text. If the text presents a discernable bias or uses a tone that makes the text seem less objective, then the text provides evidence about the author's purpose. This also informs the reader of whether or not the author is trustworthy or credible. The same strategies that are used to detect bias and identify tone can be used to discern an author's purpose when it is not clear or when the text does not seem to be aligned with the presented purpose of the text.

EVALUATING CREDIBILITY AND RELEVANCE

There are innumerable primary and secondary sources available in print and online. When finding sources, the reader must know how to evaluate each source for credibility and relevance. Appropriate sources will contribute valuable information and arguments to the writer's thoughts and conclusions, providing useful evidence to bolster the claims in the text. The writer of a text has the freedom to choose which sources they reference and how he or she uses them to support the claims made in the text. However, readers should consider the credibility of the sources a writer uses, but determining a source's credibility is not always easy.

CONSIDERATIONS FOR EVALUATING THE CREDIBILITY OF A SOURCE

- The author and their purpose for writing the source
- The author's qualifications to write on the topic
- Whether the source is peer-reviewed or included in a scholarly publication
- The publisher
- The target audience
- The jargon or dialect the source is written in (e.g., academic, technical)
- The presence of bias or manipulation of information
- The date of publication
- The author's use of other sources to support their claims
- Whether any outside sources are cited appropriately in the source
- The accuracy of information presented

AUTHOR'S PURPOSE AND CREDIBILITY

Knowing who wrote a source and why they wrote it is important to determine whether a source is appropriate and credible. The author should be qualified to write on the subject of the material. Their purpose may be to inform their audience of information, to present and defend an analysis, or even to criticize a work or other argument. The source's container and publisher are important to note because they indicate the source's reputability and whether other qualified individuals have reviewed the information in the source. Credible secondary sources should also reference other sources, primary or secondary, that support or inform the source's content. Evaluating the accuracy of the information or the presence of bias in a source will require careful reading and critical thinking on the part of the reader. However, a source with excellent credentials may still contain pieces of inaccurate information or bias, so writers must take care in their use of each source.

DETERMINING AUTHOR'S POINT OF VIEW AND PURPOSE

In some texts, readers find it easy to identify the author's point of view and purpose, such as when the author explicitly states his or her position and reason for writing. But other texts are more difficult, either because of the content or because the authors give neutral or balanced viewpoints. This is particularly true in scientific texts, in which authors may state the purpose of their research in the report, but never state their point of view except by interpreting evidence or data.

To analyze text and identify point of view or purpose, readers should ask themselves the following four questions:

1. With what main point or idea does this author want to persuade readers to agree?
2. How does this author's word choice affect the way that readers consider this subject?
3. How do this author's choices of examples and facts affect the way that readers consider this subject?
4. What is it that this author wants to accomplish by writing this text?

DETERMINING AN AUTHOR'S POSITION

In order to be an effective reader, one must pay attention to the author's **position** and **purpose**. Even those texts that seem objective and impartial, like textbooks, have a position and **bias**. Readers need to take these positions into account when considering the author's message. When an author uses emotional language or clearly favors one side of an argument, his or her position is clear. However, the author's position may be evident not only in what he or she writes, but also in what he or she doesn't write. In a normal setting, a reader would want to review some other texts on the same topic in order to develop a view of the author's position. If this was not possible, then you would want to at least acquire some background about the author. However, since you are in the middle of an exam and the only source of information is the text, you should look for language and argumentation that seems to indicate a particular stance on the subject.

CRAFT AND STRUCTURE CHAPTER QUIZ

1. Which of the following is an opinion?
- a. Basketball is the best sport because it maintains the most constant action. ✓
- b. Stephen has a meeting after lunch this afternoon. ✗
- c. Mark's favorite color is orange because it reminds him of autumn. ✗
- d. Jim's team hasn't made it to the playoffs in three years. ✗

2. Which of the following is NOT a form of figurative language?
- a. Exaggeration
- b. Simile
- c. Fact ✓
- d. Metaphor·

C

3. Which of the following sentences includes a personification?
- a. She spun with such incredible ferocity; it was hard to believe she wouldn't fall. ✗
- b. The swans danced gracefully across the surface of the water underneath the moonlight. ✓
- c. Unable to be contained any longer, his mirth erupted forth with raucous roars of laughter.
- d. His shout of triumph resounded throughout the stadium as he crossed the finish line.

4. Which of the following sentences contains a simile?
- a. The light faded with each step as the trees grew ever denser.
- b. His eyes began to water as the car quickly pulled away. ✓
- c. He's as stubborn as a mule and twice as ugly.
- d. Without so much as a pause, she deftly darted around the obstacle and continued running.

5. Which of the following sentences contains a metaphor?
- a. She could not remember the last time she felt so lost, perhaps not since before the accident.
- b. The snow blanketed the small town in a pristine white quilt. ✓
- c. Despite his best efforts, the group grew more and more unruly as the party continued.
- d. Without a sound, she returned to the night as quickly as she had come.

B

Answers for all of the chapter quiz questions can be found right before Practice Test #1.

Integration of Knowledge and Ideas

MAKING PREDICTIONS AND DRAWING CONCLUSIONS

PREDICTIONS

A **prediction** is a **guess** about what will happen next. Readers constantly make predictions based on what they have read and what they already know. We can make predictions before we begin reading and during our reading. Consider the following sentence: *Staring at the computer screen in shock, Kim blindly reached over for the brimming glass of water on the shelf to her side.* The sentence suggests that Kim is distracted, and that she is not looking at the glass that she is going to pick up. So, a reader might **predict** that Kim is going to knock over the glass. Of course, not every prediction will be accurate: perhaps Kim will pick the glass up cleanly. Nevertheless, the author has certainly created the expectation that the water might be spilled.

> **Review Video: Predictive Reading**
> Visit mometrix.com/academy and enter code: 437248

DRAWING CONCLUSIONS

In addition to inference and prediction, readers must often **draw conclusions** about the information they have read. When asked for a *conclusion* that may be drawn, look for critical "hedge" phrases, such as *likely, may, can, will often*, among many others. When you are being tested on this knowledge, remember the question that writers insert into these hedge phrases to cover every possibility. Often an answer will be wrong simply because there is no room for exception. Extreme positive or negative answers (such as *always* or *never*) are usually not correct. The reader should not use any outside knowledge that is not gathered from the passage to answer the related questions. Correct answers can be derived *straight from the passage.*

EVIDENCE TO SUPPORT PREDICTIONS, CONCLUSIONS, AND INTERPRETATIONS

When reading a text, readers may need to make a variety of predictions, conclusions, and interpretations. Sometimes, writers leave a text open ended. Readers can make predictions about what the writer would have said next or the next event in a story left on a cliffhanger. Readers can draw conclusions about the author's purpose or beliefs related to what he or she has written in a text. Readers can make interpretations about the purpose, meaning, or best application of a text. No matter which of these the reader chooses to complete, predictions, conclusions, and interpretations must be supported by evidence from the text. This evidence can take many forms, as the genre and form of a text can allude to its purpose. The context of a text may also guide the reader's predictions, conclusions, and interpretations. Evidence can most commonly be found as explicit and implicit information in a text. This information can help readers make inferences, but often, the reader will have to combine this information with their own knowledge or other information to make full conclusions, predictions, or interpretations.

THEME

Themes are seldom expressed directly in a text and can be difficult to identify. A **theme** is *an issue, an idea, or a question raised by the text*. A theme must also be able to be universally understood or applicable to all people. For instance, a theme in *Cinderella* (the Charles Perrault version) is *perseverance*, as the title character serves her step-sisters and step-mother, and the prince seeks to find the girl with the missing slipper. A passage may have many themes. One common characteristic of themes is that they raise more questions than they answer. In a good piece of fiction, authors are trying to elevate the reader's perspective and encourage him or her to consider the themes in a deeper way. In the process of reading, one can identify themes by constantly *asking about the* *general issues that the text is addressing.* A good way to evaluate an author's approach to a theme is to begin reading with a question in mind (e.g., How does this text approach the theme of love?) and to look for evidence in the text that addresses that question.

> **Review Video: Theme**
> Visit mometrix.com/academy and enter code: 732074

VARIATION IN THEMES BETWEEN TWO TEXTS

Two texts may communicate the same theme in different ways. For example, two narrative texts may both communicate the theme of "have hope, even when all is lost." One text may present this theme by having the protagonist be rewarded by his or her hope in the face of trials. The other text may present this theme by leaving the protagonist in his or her troubles and trials and communicating that hope keeps the character going. Additionally, two texts may use the same basic plot and theme, but may present this theme using a different tone, mood, or context. This is especially true if a theme is presented by multiple works of different forms, as each will have different methods for communicating meaning.

SIMILAR THEMES ACROSS CULTURES

A brief study of world literature suggests that writers from vastly different cultures address **similar themes**. For instance, works like the *Odyssey* and *Hamlet* both consider the individual's battle for self-control and independence. In most cultures, authors address themes of *personal growth and the struggle for maturity*. Another universal theme is the *conflict between the individual and society*. Works that are as culturally disparate as *Native Son*, the *Aeneid*, and *1984* dramatize how people struggle to maintain their personalities and dignity in large (sometimes) oppressive groups. Finally, many cultures have versions of the *hero's or heroine's journey* in which an adventurous person must overcome many obstacles in order to gain greater knowledge, power, and perspective. Some famous works that treat this theme are the *Epic of Gilgamesh*, Dante's *Divine Comedy*, and Cervantes' *Don Quixote*.

DIFFERENCES IN THEMES ACROSS CULTURES AND GENRES

Authors from different **genres** and **cultures** may address similar themes, but they do so in different ways. For instance, poets are likely to address subject matter indirectly through the use of *images and allusions*. In a play, the author is more likely to dramatize themes by using characters to express opposing viewpoints; this disparity is known as a *dialectical approach*. In a passage, the author does not need to express themes directly; indeed, they can be expressed through *events and actions*. In some regional literatures, such as Greece or England, authors tend to use more irony. In the 1950s, Latin American authors popularized the use of unusual and surreal events to show themes about real life in the genre of magical realism. Japanese authors use the well-established poetic form of the haiku to organize their treatment of common themes.

EVALUATING AN ARGUMENT

Argumentative and persuasive passages take a **stand** on a debatable issue, seek to explore all sides of the issue, and find the best possible solution. Argumentative and persuasive passages should not be combative or abusive. The word *argument* may remind you of two or more people shouting at each other and walking away in anger. However, an argumentative or persuasive passage should be a calm and reasonable presentation of an author's ideas for others to consider. When an author writes reasonable arguments, his or her goal is not to win or have the last word. Instead, authors want to reveal current understanding of the question at hand and suggest a **solution** to a problem. The purpose of argument and persuasion in a free society is to reach the best solution.

EVIDENCE

The term **text evidence** refers to information that supports a **main point** or **minor points** and can help lead the reader to a conclusion about the text's credibility. Information used as text evidence is precise, descriptive, and factual. A main point is often followed by **supporting details** that provide evidence to back up a claim. For example, a passage may include the claim that winter occurs during opposite months in the Northern and Southern hemispheres. Text evidence for this claim may include examples of countries where winter occurs in opposite months. Stating that the tilt of the Earth as it rotates around the sun causes winter to occur at different times in separate hemispheres is another example of text evidence. Text evidence can come from common knowledge, but it is also valuable to include text evidence from credible, relevant outside sources.

> **Review Video: Text Evidence**
> Visit mometrix.com/academy and enter code: 486236

Evidence that supports the thesis and additional arguments needs to be provided. Most arguments must be supported by facts or statistics. A **fact** is something that is *known with certainty* and has been verified by several independent individuals. **Examples** and **illustrations** add an emotional component to arguments. With this component, writers persuade readers in ways that facts and statistics cannot. There are many other types of evidence that can be effective in supporting a claim or an argument. Regardless of how a writer or speaker uses evidence, the evidence must be appropriate for the writer's purpose. Evidence that is irrelevant is not appropriate, as it clutters a text or argument with distracting information and does not help the writer show the audience why his or her claims are valid.

RELEVANT AND SUFFICIENT EVIDENCE

Evidence must also be sufficient to defend an argument. If the evidence provided does not fully support the argument in the text, then the evidence is insufficient and the writer must continue working to sufficiently support the argument or claim. When comparing two texts or arguments on a subject, examining the evidence each uses is a good starting place for evaluating credibility. Examining bias and rhetorical devices is also useful for determining credibility, but the relevance, sufficiency, and reliability of evidence used by each is a clear indicator of credibility.

CREDIBLE EVIDENCE

The text used to support an argument can be the argument's downfall if the text is not credible. A text is **credible**, or believable, when its author is knowledgeable and objective, or unbiased. The author's **motivations** for writing the text play a critical role in determining the credibility of the text and must be evaluated when assessing that credibility. Reports written about the ozone layer by an environmental scientist and a hairdresser will have a different level of credibility.

> **Review Video: Credible**
> Visit mometrix.com/academy and enter code: 827257

COUNTERARGUMENTS

When authors give both sides to the argument, they build trust with their readers. As a reader, you should start with an undecided or neutral position. If an author presents only his or her side to the argument, then they are not exhibiting credibility and are weakening their argument.

Building common ground with readers can be effective for persuading neutral, skeptical, or opposed readers. Sharing values with undecided readers can allow people to switch positions without giving up what they feel is important. People who may oppose a position need to feel that they can change their minds without betraying who they are as a person. This appeal to having an open mind can be a powerful tool in arguing a position without antagonizing other views. Objections can be countered on a point-by-point basis or in a summary paragraph. Be mindful of how an author points out flaws in counter arguments. If they are unfair to the other side of the argument, then you should lose trust with the author.

ANALYZING THE EFFECTIVENESS OF RHETORICAL DEVICES

First, readers should identify the author's **thesis**—what he or she argues for or against. They should consider the argument's content and the author's reason for presenting it. Does the author offer **solutions** to problems raised? If so, are they realistic? Note all central ideas and evidence supporting the author's thesis. Research any unfamiliar subjects or vocabulary. Readers should then outline or summarize the work in their own words. Identify which types of appeals the author uses. Readers should evaluate how well the author communicated meaning from the reader's perspective: Did they respond to emotional appeals with anger, concern, happiness, etc.? If so, why? Decide if the author's reasoning sufficed for changing the reader's mind. Determine whether the content and presentation were accurate, cohesive, and clear. Readers should also ask themselves whether they found the author believable or not, and why or why not.

RHETORICAL DEVICES

Sometimes, authors will **appeal to the reader's emotion** in an attempt to persuade or to distract the reader from the weakness of the argument. For instance, the author may try to inspire the **pity** of the reader by delivering a heart-rending story. An author also might use the **bandwagon** approach, in which he suggests that his opinion is correct because it is held by the majority. Some authors resort to **name-calling**, in which insults and harsh words are delivered to the opponent in an attempt to distract. In advertising, a common appeal is the **celebrity testimonial**, in which a famous person endorses a product. Of course, the fact that a famous person likes something should not really mean anything to the reader. These and other emotional appeals are usually evidence of poor reasoning and a weak argument.

PRIMARY, SECONDARY, AND INTERNET SOURCES

PRIMARY SOURCES

In literature review, one may examine both primary and secondary sources. Primary sources contain original information that was witnessed, gathered, or otherwise produced by the source's author. **Primary sources** can include firsthand accounts, found in sources such as books, autobiographies, transcripts, speeches, videos, photos, and personal journals or diaries. Primary sources may also include records of information, such as government documents, or personally-conducted research in sources like reports and essays. They may be found in academic books, journals and other periodicals, and authoritative databases. Using primary sources allows researchers to develop their own conclusions about the subject. Primary sources are also reliable for finding information about a person or their personal accounts and experiences. Primary sources such as photos, videos, audio recordings, transcripts, and government documents are often reliable, as they are usually objective and can be used to confirm information from other sources.

SECONDARY SOURCES

Secondary sources are sources that reference information originally provided by another source. The original source may be cited, quoted, paraphrased, or described in a secondary source. **Secondary sources** may be articles, essays, videos, or books found in periodicals, magazines, newspapers, films, databases, or websites. A secondary source can be used to reference another researcher's analysis or conclusion from a primary source. This information can inform the researcher of the existing discussions regarding their subject. These types of sources may also support the researcher's claims by providing a credible argument that contributes to the researcher's argument. Secondary sources may also highlight connections between primary sources or criticize both primary and other secondary sources. These types of secondary sources are valuable because they provide information and conclusions the researcher may not have considered or found, otherwise.

> **Review Video: <u>Primary and Secondary Sources</u>**
> Visit mometrix.com/academy and enter code: 383328

INTERNET SOURCES

The internet was once considered a poor place to find sources for an essay or article, but its credibility has improved greatly over the years. Still, one needs to exercise caution when performing research online. The best sources are those affiliated with **established institutions**, like universities, public libraries, and think tanks. Most newspapers are available online, and many of them allow the public to browse their archives. Magazines frequently offer similar services. When obtaining information from an unknown website, however, one must exercise considerably more caution. A website can be considered trustworthy if it is referenced by other sites that are known to be reputable. Also, credible sites tend to be properly maintained and frequently updated. A site is easier to trust when the author provides some information about him or herself, including some credentials that indicate expertise in the subject matter.

DATA FROM VARIOUS SOURCES AND IN VARIOUS FORMATS

JOURNAL ARTICLES

Although published journal articles listed in library databases have been reviewed and edited to be acceptable for publication, you should still evaluate them by six criteria.

- **Source**: Articles by experts in their subjects, published in scholarly journals, are more *reliable*. They also contain *references* to more publications on the same topic. Try to start your search with a database that includes searching by article type (e.g., reviews, clinical trials, editorials, and research articles).
- **Length**: The citation states an article's number of pages, an indication of its research utility.
- **Authority**: Research sources should be authoritative, written by *experts* affiliated with academic institutions.
- **Date**: Many research fields are constantly changing, so research must be as *current* as possible. In areas with new research breakthroughs, some articles are not up to date.
- **Audience**: If an author wrote an article for professional colleagues, it will include subject-specific language and terminology.
- **Usefulness**: Evaluate whether an article is *relevant* to your own research topic.

> **Review Video: <u>Media</u>**
> Visit mometrix.com/academy and enter code: 785859

ORGANIZING AND SYNTHESIZING DATA

ORGANIZING INFORMATION

Organizing information effectively is an important part of research. The data must be organized in a useful manner so that it can be effectively used. Three basic ways to organize information are:

- **Spatial organization** is useful as it lets the user "see" the information, to fix it in space. This has benefits for those individuals who are visually adept at processing information.
- **Chronological organization** is the most common presentation of information. This method places information in the sequence with which it occurs. Chronological organization is very useful in explaining a process that occurs in a step-by-step pattern.
- **Logical organization** includes presenting material in a logical pattern that makes intuitive sense. Some patterns that are frequently used are illustrated, definition, compare/contrast, cause/effect, problem/solution, and division/classification.

LOGICAL ORGANIZATION

There are six major types of logical organization that are frequently used:

- **Illustrations** may be used to support the thesis. Examples are the most common form of this organization.
- **Definitions** say what something is or is not is another way of organization. What are the characteristics of the topic?
- **Dividing** or **classifying** information into separate items according to their similarities is a common and effective organizing method.
- **Comparing**, focusing on the similarities of things, and contrasting, highlighting the differences between things is an excellent tool to use with certain kinds of information.
- **Cause and effect** is a simple tool to logically understand relationships between things. A phenomenon may be traced to its causes for organizing a subject logically.
- **Problem and solution** is a simple and effective manner of logically organizing material. It is very commonly used and lucidly presents information.

SYNTHESIZING DATA

When you must generate questions about the data that you have collected, you realize whether you understand it and whether you can answer your own questions. You can learn to ask yourself questions which require that you **synthesize** content from different portions of the data, such as asking questions about the data's important information.

Understanding how to **summarize** what you have collected allows you to discern what is important in the data and to be able to express the important content in your own words. When you learn to summarize your data, you are better able to identify the main ideas of the research, and to connect these main ideas. Then, you will be better able to generate central ideas from your research. Also, you will be able to avoid irrelevant information and to remember what you have researched.

INTEGRATION OF KNOWLEDGE AND IDEAS CHAPTER QUIZ

1. An author arguing that his point is correct because everybody else already agrees with it is an example of which type of persuasive technique?

- a. Traditionalism
- b. Bandwagon approach ✓
- c. Testimonials
- d. Generalizations

2. How many major types of logical organization are there?

- a. Three
- b. Four ▷
- c. Five
- d. Six ✓

3. Which of the following factors can be used as evidence for making predictions, conclusions, or interpretations about a text? (Select all that apply)

- a. Genre
- b. Context
- c. Author's name ✗ ✓
- d. Implicit information
- e. Explicit information

4. Which of the following is a primary source?

- a. Bibliography
- b. A review of a movie ✗ ✓
- c. Autobiography
- d. A movie adaptation of real-life events

5. What is the purpose of argument and persuasion in a free society?

- a. To give a space to underrepresented viewpoints free from hostility
- b. To quell insurrection and dangerous ideas ✗
- c. To allow experts to most efficiently debate their ideals ▷
- d. To reach the best solution for a common good ✗

Answers for all of the chapter quiz questions can be found right before Practice Test #1.

Mathematics

Numbers and Algebra

NUMBERS

Numbers are the basic building blocks of mathematics. Specific features of numbers are identified by the following terms:

Integer – any positive or negative whole number, including zero. Integers do not include fractions $\left(\frac{1}{3}\right)$, decimals (0.56), or mixed numbers $\left(7\frac{3}{4}\right)$.

Prime number – any whole number greater than 1 that has only two factors, itself and 1; that is, a number that can be divided evenly only by 1 and itself.

Composite number – any whole number greater than 1 that has more than two different factors; in other words, any whole number that is not a prime number. For example: The composite number 8 has the factors of 1, 2, 4, and 8.

Even number – any integer that can be divided by 2 without leaving a remainder. For example: 2, 4, 6, 8, and so on.

Odd number – any integer that cannot be divided evenly by 2. For example: 3, 5, 7, 9, and so on.

Decimal number – any number that uses a decimal point to show the part of the number that is less than one. Example: 1.234.

Decimal point – a symbol used to separate the ones place from the tenths place in decimals or dollars from cents in currency.

Decimal place – the position of a number to the right of the decimal point. In the decimal 0.123, the 1 is in the first place to the right of the decimal point, indicating tenths; the 2 is in the second place, indicating hundredths; and the 3 is in the third place, indicating thousandths.

The **decimal**, or base 10, system is a number system that uses ten different digits (0, 1, 2, 3, 4, 5, 6, 7, 8, 9). An example of a number system that uses something other than ten digits is the **binary**, or base 2, number system, used by computers, which uses only the numbers 0 and 1. It is thought that the decimal system originated because people had only their 10 fingers for counting.

Rational numbers include all integers, decimals, and fractions. Any terminating or repeating decimal number is a rational number.

Irrational numbers cannot be written as fractions or decimals because the number of decimal places is infinite and there is no recurring pattern of digits within the number. For example, pi (π) begins with 3.141592 and continues without terminating or repeating, so π is an irrational number.

Real numbers are the set of all rational and irrational numbers.

> **Review Video and Practice: Numbers and Their Classifications**
> Visit mometrix.com/academy and enter code: 461071

47

THE NUMBER LINE

A number line is a graph to see the distance between numbers. Basically, this graph shows the relationship between numbers. So, a number line may have a point for zero and may show negative numbers on the left side of the line. Any positive numbers are placed on the right side of the line. For example, consider the points labeled on the following number line:

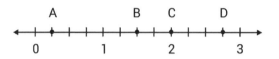

We can use the dashed lines on the number line to identify each point. Each dashed line between two whole numbers is $\frac{1}{4}$. The line halfway between two numbers is $\frac{1}{2}$.

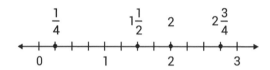

> **Review Video and Practice: The Number Line**
> Visit mometrix.com/academy and enter code: 816439

NUMBERS IN WORD FORM AND PLACE VALUE

When writing numbers out in word form or translating word form to numbers, it is essential to understand how a place value system works. In the decimal or base-10 system, each digit of a number represents how many of the corresponding place value—a specific factor of 10—are contained in the number being represented. To make reading numbers easier, every three digits to the left of the decimal place is preceded by a comma. The following table demonstrates some of the place values:

Power of 10	10^3	10^2	10^1	10^0	10^{-1}	10^{-2}	10^{-3}
Value	1,000	100	10	1	0.1	0.01	0.001
Place	thousands	hundreds	tens	ones	tenths	hundredths	thousandths

For example, consider the number 4,546.09, which can be separated into each place value like this:

4: thousands
5: hundreds
4: tens
6: ones
0: tenths
9: hundredths

This number in word form would be *four thousand five hundred forty-six and nine hundredths*.

> **Review Video and Practice: Number Place Value**
> Visit mometrix.com/academy and enter code: 205433

FACTORS AND GREATEST COMMON FACTOR

Factors are numbers that are multiplied together to obtain a **product**. For example, in the equation $2 \times 3 = 6$, the numbers 2 and 3 are factors. A **prime number** has only two factors (1 and itself), but other numbers can have many factors.

A **common factor** is a number that divides exactly into two or more other numbers. For example, the factors of 12 are 1, 2, 3, 4, 6, and 12, while the factors of 15 are 1, 3, 5, and 15. The common factors of 12 and 15 are 1 and 3.

A **prime factor** is also a prime number. Therefore, the prime factors of 12 are 2 and 3. For 15, the prime factors are 3 and 5.

The **greatest common factor** (**GCF**) is the largest number that is a factor of two or more numbers. For example, the factors of 15 are 1, 3, 5, and 15; the factors of 35 are 1, 5, 7, and 35. Therefore, the greatest common factor of 15 and 35 is 5.

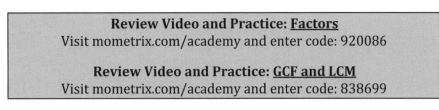

Review Video and Practice: Factors
Visit mometrix.com/academy and enter code: 920086

Review Video and Practice: GCF and LCM
Visit mometrix.com/academy and enter code: 838699

MULTIPLES AND LEAST COMMON MULTIPLE

Often listed out in multiplication tables, **multiples** are integer increments of a given factor. In other words, dividing a multiple by the factor will result in an integer. For example, the multiples of 7 include: $1 \times 7 = 7$, $2 \times 7 = 14$, $3 \times 7 = 21$, $4 \times 7 = 28$, $5 \times 7 = 35$. Dividing 7, 14, 21, 28, or 35 by 7 will result in the integers 1, 2, 3, 4, and 5, respectively.

The least common multiple (**LCM**) is the smallest number that is a multiple of two or more numbers. For example, the multiples of 3 include 3, 6, 9, 12, 15, etc.; the multiples of 5 include 5, 10, 15, 20, etc. Therefore, the least common multiple of 3 and 5 is 15.

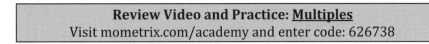

Review Video and Practice: Multiples
Visit mometrix.com/academy and enter code: 626738

PRACTICE

P1. Write the place value of each digit in 14,059.826

P2. Write out each of the following in words:

    (a) 29
    (b) 478
    (c) 98,542
    (d) 0.06
    (e) 13.113

P3. Write each of the following in numbers:

(a) nine thousand four hundred thirty-five
(b) three hundred two thousand eight hundred seventy-six
(c) nine hundred one thousandths
(d) nineteen thousandths
(e) seven thousand one hundred forty-two and eighty-five hundredths

PRACTICE SOLUTIONS

P1. The place value for each digit would be as follows:

Digit	Place Value
1	ten-thousands
4	thousands
0	hundreds
5	tens
9	ones
8	tenths
2	hundredths
6	thousandths

P2. Each written out in words would be:

(a) twenty-nine
(b) four hundred seventy-eight
(c) ninety-eight thousand five hundred forty-two
(d) six hundredths
(e) thirteen and one hundred thirteen thousandths

P3. Each in numeric form would be:

(a) 9,435
(b) 302,876
(c) 0.901
(d) 0.019
(e) 7,142.85

OPERATIONS

OPERATIONS

An **operation** is simply a mathematical process that takes some value(s) as input(s) and produces an output. Elementary operations are often written in the following form: *value operation value*. For instance, in the expression $1 + 2$ the values are 1 and 2 and the operation is addition. Performing the operation gives the output of 3. In this way we can say that $1 + 2$ and 3 are equal, or $1 + 2 = 3$.

ADDITION

Addition increases the value of one quantity by the value of another quantity (both called **addends**). For example, $2 + 4 = 6; 8 + 9 = 17$. The result is called the **sum**. With addition, the order does not matter, $4 + 2 = 2 + 4$.

When adding signed numbers, if the signs are the same simply add the absolute values of the addends and apply the original sign to the sum. For example, $(+4) + (+8) = +12$ and $(-4) + (-8) = -12$. When the original signs are different, take the absolute values of the addends and subtract the smaller value from the larger value, then apply the original sign of the larger value to the difference. For instance, $(+4) + (-8) = -4$ and $(-4) + (+8) = +4$.

SUBTRACTION

Subtraction is the opposite operation to addition; it decreases the value of one quantity (the **minuend**) by the value of another quantity (the **subtrahend**). For example, $6 - 4 = 2; 17 - 8 = 9$. The result is called the **difference**. Note that with subtraction, the order does matter, $6 - 4 \neq 4 - 6$.

For subtracting signed numbers, change the sign of the subtrahend and then follow the same rules used for addition. For example, $(+4) - (+8) = (+4) + (-8) = -4$.

MULTIPLICATION

Multiplication can be thought of as repeated addition. One number (the **multiplier**) indicates how many times to add the other number (the **multiplicand**) to itself. For example, $3 \times$ 2 (three times two) $= 2 + 2 + 2 = 6$. With multiplication, the order does not matter: $2 \times 3 = 3 \times 2$ or $3 + 3 = 2 + 2 + 2$, either way the result (the **product**) is the same.

If the signs are the same, the product is positive when multiplying signed numbers. For example, $(+4) \times (+8) = +32$ and $(-4) \times (-8) = +32$. If the signs are opposite, the product is negative. For example, $(+4) \times (-8) = -32$ and $(-4) \times (+8) = -32$. When more than two factors are multiplied together, the sign of the product is determined by how many negative factors are present. If there are an odd number of negative factors then the product is negative, whereas an even number of negative factors indicates a positive product. For instance, $(+4) \times (-8) \times (-2) = +64$ and $(-4) \times (-8) \times (-2) = -64$.

DIVISION

Division is the opposite operation to multiplication; one number (the **divisor**) tells us how many parts to divide the other number (the **dividend**) into. The result of division is called the **quotient**. For example, $20 \div 4 = 5$; if 20 is split into 4 equal parts, each part is 5. With division, the order of the numbers does matter, $20 \div 4 \neq 4 \div 20$.

Math

The rules for dividing signed numbers are similar to multiplying signed numbers. If the dividend and divisor have the same sign, the quotient is positive. If the dividend and divisor have opposite signs, the quotient is negative. For example, $(-4) \div (+8) = -0.5$.

PARENTHESES

Parentheses are used to designate which operations should be done first when there are multiple operations. For example, $4 - (2 + 1) = 1$; the parentheses tell us that we must add 2 and 1, and then subtract the sum from 4, rather than subtracting 2 from 4 and then adding 1 (this would give us an answer of 3).

EXPONENTS

An **exponent** is a superscript number placed next to another number at the top right. It indicates how many times the base number is to be multiplied by itself. Exponents provide a shorthand way to write what would be a longer mathematical expression. For example, $2^4 = 2 \times 2 \times 2 \times 2$. A number with an exponent of 2 is said to be "squared," while a number with an exponent of 3 is said to be "cubed." The value of a number raised to an exponent is called its power. So 8^4 is read as "8 to the 4th power," or "8 raised to the power of 4."

The properties of exponents are as follows:

Property	Description
$a^1 = a$	Any number to the power of 1 is equal to itself
$1^n = 1$	The number 1 raised to any power is equal to 1
$a^0 = 1$	Any number raised to the power of 0 is equal to 1
$a^n \times a^m = a^{n+m}$	Add exponents to multiply powers of the same base number
$a^n \div a^m = a^{n-m}$	Subtract exponents to divide powers of the same base number
$(a^n)^m = a^{n \times m}$	When a power is raised to a power, the exponents are multiplied
$(a \times b)^n = a^n \times b^n$ $(a \div b)^n = a^n \div b^n$	Multiplication and division operations inside parentheses can be raised to a power. This is the same as each term being raised to that power.
$a^{-n} = \dfrac{1}{a^n}$	A negative exponent is the same as the reciprocal of a positive exponent

ROOTS

A **root**, such as a square root, is the inverse of raising a number to an exponent. Instead of using a superscript, roots use the radical symbol ($\sqrt{}$) to indicate the operation. A radical will have a number underneath the bar, $\sqrt{a}$, read as "the square root of a." When we say that a is the square root of b ($a = \sqrt{b}$), we mean that a multiplied by itself equals b: ($a \times a = b$).

A **perfect square** is a number that has an integer for its square root. There are 10 perfect squares from 1 to 100: 1, 4, 9, 16, 25, 36, 49, 64, 81, 100 (the squares of integers 1 through 10).

> **Review Video and Practice: <u>Roots</u>**
> Visit mometrix.com/academy and enter code: 795655
>
> **Review Video and Practice: <u>Square Root and Perfect Squares</u>**
> Visit mometrix.com/academy and enter code: 648063

ORDER OF OPERATIONS

The order of operations is a set of rules that dictates the order in which we must perform each operation in an expression so that we will evaluate it accurately. If we have an expression that includes multiple different operations, the order of operations tells us which operations to do first. The most common mnemonic for the order of operations is **PEMDAS**, or "Please Excuse My Dear Aunt Sally." PEMDAS stands for parentheses, exponents, multiplication, division, addition, and subtraction. It is important to understand that multiplication and division have equal precedence, as do addition and subtraction, so those pairs of operations are simply worked from left to right in order.

For example, evaluating the expression $5 + 20 \div 4 \times (2 + 3)^2 - 6$ using the correct order of operations would be done like this:

- **P:** Perform the operations inside the parentheses: $(2 + 3) = 5$
- **E:** Simplify the exponents: $(5)^2 = 5 \times 5 = 25$
  - The equation now looks like this: $5 + 20 \div 4 \times 25 - 6$
- **MD:** Perform multiplication and division from left to right: $20 \div 4 = 5$; then $5 \times 25 = 125$
  - The equation now looks like this: $5 + 125 - 6$
- **AS:** Perform addition and subtraction from left to right: $5 + 125 = 130$; then $130 - 6 = 124$

> **Review Video and Practice: <u>Order of Operations</u>**
> Visit mometrix.com/academy and enter code: 259675

SUBTRACTION WITH REGROUPING

A great way to make use of some of the features built into the decimal system would be regrouping when attempting longform subtraction operations. When subtracting within a place value, sometimes the minuend is smaller than the subtrahend, **regrouping** enables you to 'borrow' a unit from a place value to the left in order to get a positive difference. For example, consider subtracting 189 from 525 with regrouping.

> **Review Video and Practice: <u>Subtracting Large Numbers</u>**
> Visit mometrix.com/academy and enter code: 603350

First, set up the subtraction problem in vertical form:

```
   525
 - 189
```

Notice that the numbers in the ones and tens columns of 525 are smaller than the numbers in the ones and tens columns of 189. This means you will need to use regrouping to perform subtraction:

```
    5   2   5
-   1   8   9
```

To subtract 9 from 5 in the ones column you will need to borrow from the 2 in the ten's columns:

```
    5   1   15
-   1   8    9
                6
```

Next, to subtract 8 from 1 in the tens column you will need to borrow from the 5 in the hundred's column:

```
    4   11   15
-   1    8    9
         3    6
```

Last, subtract the 1 from the 4 in the hundred's column:

```
    4   11   15
-   1    8    9
    3    3    6
```

WORD PROBLEMS AND MATHEMATICAL SYMBOLS

When working on word problems, you must be able to translate verbal expressions or "math words" into math symbols. This chart contains several "math words" and their appropriate symbols:

Phrase	Symbol
equal, is, was, will be, has, costs, gets to, is the same as, becomes	=
times, of, multiplied by, product of, twice, doubles, halves, triples	×
divided by, per, ratio of/to, out of	÷
plus, added to, sum, combined, and, more than, totals of	+
subtracted from, less than, decreased by, minus, difference between	−
what, how much, original value, how many, a number, a variable	x, n, etc.

EXAMPLES OF TRANSLATED MATHEMATICAL PHRASES

The phrase four more than twice a number can be written algebraically as $2x + 4$. The phrase half a number decreased by six can be written algebraically as $\frac{1}{2}x - 6$. The phrase the sum of a number and the product of five and that number can be written algebraically as $x + 5x$.

You may see a test question that says something like, "Olivia is constructing a bookcase from seven boards. Two of them are for vertical supports and five are for shelves. The height of the bookcase is twice the width of the bookcase. If the seven boards total 36 feet in length, what will be the height of Olivia's bookcase?" You would need to make a sketch and then create the equation to determine the width of the shelves. The height can be represented as double the width. (If x represents the width of the shelves in feet, then the height of the bookcase is $2x$. Since the seven boards total 36 feet, $2x + 2x + x + x + x + x + x = 36$ or $9x = 36$; $x = 4$. The height is twice the width, or 8 feet.)

RATIONAL NUMBERS
FRACTIONS

A **fraction** is a number that is expressed as one integer written above another integer, with a dividing line between them $\left(\frac{x}{y}\right)$. It represents the **quotient** of the two numbers "x divided by y." It can also be thought of as x out of y equal parts.

The top number of a fraction is called the **numerator**, and it represents the number of parts under consideration. The 1 in $\frac{1}{4}$ means that 1 part out of the whole is being considered in the calculation. The bottom number of a fraction is called the **denominator**, and it represents the total number of equal parts. The 4 in $\frac{1}{4}$ means that the whole consists of 4 equal parts. A fraction cannot have a denominator of zero; this is referred to as "*undefined*."

Fractions can be manipulated, without changing the value of the fraction, by multiplying or dividing (but not adding or subtracting) both the numerator and denominator by the same number. If you divide both numbers by a common factor, you are **reducing** or simplifying the fraction. Two fractions that have the same value but are expressed differently are known as **equivalent fractions**. For example, $\frac{2}{10}, \frac{3}{15}, \frac{4}{20}$, and $\frac{5}{25}$ are all equivalent fractions. They can also all be reduced or simplified to $\frac{1}{5}$.

When two fractions are manipulated so that they have the same denominator, this is known as finding a **common denominator**. The number chosen to be that common denominator should be the least common multiple of the two original denominators. Example: $\frac{3}{4}$ and $\frac{5}{6}$; the least common multiple of 4 and 6 is 12. Manipulating to achieve the common denominator: $\frac{3}{4} = \frac{9}{12}; \frac{5}{6} = \frac{10}{12}$.

PROPER FRACTIONS AND MIXED NUMBERS

A fraction whose denominator is greater than its numerator is known as a **proper fraction**, while a fraction whose numerator is greater than its denominator is known as an **improper fraction**. Proper fractions have values *less than one* and improper fractions have values *greater than one*.

A **mixed number** is a number that contains both an integer and a fraction. Any improper fraction can be rewritten as a mixed number. Example: $\frac{8}{3} = \frac{6}{3} + \frac{2}{3} = 2 + \frac{2}{3} = 2\frac{2}{3}$. Similarly, any mixed number can be rewritten as an improper fraction. Example: $1\frac{3}{5} = 1 + \frac{3}{5} = \frac{5}{5} + \frac{3}{5} = \frac{8}{5}$.

Review Video and Practice: Improper Fractions and Mixed Numbers
Visit mometrix.com/academy and enter code: 211077

Review Video and Practice: Overview of Fractions
Visit mometrix.com/academy and enter code: 262335

Mometrix

ADDING AND SUBTRACTING FRACTIONS

If two fractions have a common denominator, they can be added or subtracted simply by adding or subtracting the two numerators and retaining the same denominator. If the two fractions do not already have the same denominator, one or both of them must be manipulated to achieve a common denominator before they can be added or subtracted. Example: $\frac{1}{2} + \frac{1}{4} = \frac{2}{4} + \frac{1}{4} = \frac{3}{4}$.

> **Review Video and Practice: Adding and Subtracting Fractions**
> Visit mometrix.com/academy and enter code: 378080

MULTIPLYING FRACTIONS

Two fractions can be multiplied by multiplying the two numerators to find the new numerator and the two denominators to find the new denominator. Example: $\frac{1}{3} \times \frac{2}{3} = \frac{1\times2}{3\times3} = \frac{2}{9}$.

DIVIDING FRACTIONS

Two fractions can be divided by flipping the numerator and denominator of the second fraction and then proceeding as though it were a multiplication problem. Example: $\frac{2}{3} \div \frac{3}{4} = \frac{2}{3} \times \frac{4}{3} = \frac{8}{9}$.

> **Review Video and Practice: Multiplying and Dividing Fractions**
> Visit mometrix.com/academy and enter code: 473632

MULTIPLYING A MIXED NUMBER BY A WHOLE NUMBER OR A DECIMAL

When multiplying a mixed number by something, it is usually best to convert it to an improper fraction first. Additionally, if the multiplicand is a decimal, it is most often simplest to convert it to a fraction. For instance, to multiply $4\frac{3}{8}$ by 3.5, begin by rewriting each quantity as a whole number plus a proper fraction. Remember, a mixed number is a fraction added to a whole number and a decimal is a representation of the sum of fractions, specifically tenths, hundredths, thousandths, and so on:

$$4\frac{3}{8} \times 3.5 = \left(4 + \frac{3}{8}\right) \times \left(3 + \frac{1}{2}\right)$$

Next, the quantities being added need to be expressed with the same denominator. This is achieved by multiplying and dividing the whole number by the denominator of the fraction. Recall that a whole number is equivalent to that number divided by 1:

$$= \left(\frac{4}{1} \times \frac{8}{8} + \frac{3}{8}\right) \times \left(\frac{3}{1} \times \frac{2}{2} + \frac{1}{2}\right)$$

When multiplying fractions, remember to multiply the numerators and denominators separately:

$$= \left(\frac{4 \times 8}{1 \times 8} + \frac{3}{8}\right) \times \left(\frac{3 \times 2}{1 \times 2} + \frac{1}{2}\right)$$
$$= \left(\frac{32}{8} + \frac{3}{8}\right) \times \left(\frac{6}{2} + \frac{1}{2}\right)$$

Now that the fractions have the same denominators, they can be added:

$$= \frac{35}{8} \times \frac{7}{2}$$

56

Finally, perform the last multiplication and then simplify:

$$= \frac{35 \times 7}{8 \times 2} = \frac{245}{16} = \frac{240}{16} + \frac{5}{16} = 15\frac{5}{16}$$

DECIMALS

Decimals are one way to represent parts of a whole. Using the place value system, each digit to the right of a decimal point denotes the number of units of a corresponding *negative* power of ten.

For example, consider the decimal 0.24. We can use a model to represent the decimal. Since a dime is worth one-tenth of a dollar and a penny is worth one-hundredth of a dollar, one possible model to represent this fraction is to have 2 dimes representing the 2 in the tenths place and 4 pennies representing the 4 in the hundredths place.

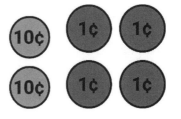

To write the decimal as a fraction, put the decimal in the numerator with 1 in the denominator. Multiply the numerator and denominator by tens until there are no more decimal places. Then simplify the fraction to lowest terms. For example, converting 0.24 to a fraction:

$$0.24 = \frac{0.24}{1} = \frac{0.24 \times 100}{1 \times 100} = \frac{24}{100} = \frac{6}{25}$$

Review Video and Practice: Decimals
Visit mometrix.com/academy and enter code: 837268

OPERATIONS WITH DECIMALS

When adding and subtracting decimals, the decimal points must always be aligned. Adding decimals is just like adding regular whole numbers. Example: $4.5 + 2.0 = 6.5$.

If the problem-solver does not properly align the decimal points, an incorrect answer of 4.7 may result. An easy way to add decimals is to align all of the decimal points in a vertical column visually. This will allow you to see exactly where the decimal should be placed in the final answer. Begin adding from right to left. Add each column in turn, making sure to carry the number to the left if a column adds up to more than 9. The same rules apply to the subtraction of decimals.

Review Video and Practice: Adding and Subtracting Decimals
Visit mometrix.com/academy and enter code: 381101

A simple multiplication problem has two components: a **multiplicand** and a **multiplier**. When multiplying decimals, work as though the numbers were whole rather than decimals. Once the final product is calculated, count the number of places to the right of the decimal in both the multiplicand and the multiplier. Then, count that number of places from the right of the product and place the decimal in that position.

For example, 12.3×2.56 has a total of three places to the right of the respective decimals. Multiply 123×256 to get 31,488. Now, beginning on the right, count three places to the left and insert the decimal. The final product will be 31.488.

Review Video and Practice: How to Multiply Decimals
Visit mometrix.com/academy and enter code: 731574

Every division problem has a **divisor** and a **dividend**. The dividend is the number that is being divided. In the problem $14 \div 7$, 14 is the dividend and 7 is the divisor. In a division problem with decimals, the divisor must be converted into a whole number. Begin by moving the decimal in the divisor to the right until a whole number is created. Next, move the decimal in the dividend the same number of spaces to the right. For example, 4.9 into 24.5 would become 49 into 245. The decimal was moved one space to the right to create a whole number in the divisor, and then the same was done for the dividend. Once the whole numbers are created, the problem is carried out normally: $245 \div 49 = 5$.

> **Review Video and Practice: How to Divide Decimals**
> Visit mometrix.com/academy and enter code: 560690
>
> **Review Video and Practice: Dividing Decimals by Whole Numbers**
> Visit mometrix.com/academy and enter code: 535669

PERCENTAGES

Percentages can be thought of as fractions that are based on a whole of 100; that is, one whole is equal to 100%. The word **percent** means "per hundred." Percentage problems are often presented in three main ways:

- Find what percentage of some number another number is.
  - Example: What percentage of 40 is 8?
- Find what number is some percentage of a given number.
  - Example: What number is 20% of 40?
- Find what number another number is a given percentage of.
  - Example: What number is 8 20% of?

There are three components in each of these cases: a **whole** (W), a **part** (P), and a **percentage** (%). These are related by the equation: $P = W \times \%$. This can easily be rearranged into other forms that may suit different questions better: $\% = \frac{P}{W}$ and $W = \frac{P}{\%}$. Percentage problems are often also word problems. As such, a large part of solving them is figuring out which quantities are what. For example, consider the following word problem:

In a school cafeteria, 7 students choose pizza, 9 choose hamburgers, and 4 choose tacos. What percentage of student choose tacos?

To find the whole, you must first add all of the parts: $7 + 9 + 4 = 20$. The percentage can then be found by dividing the part by the whole $\left(\% = \frac{P}{W} \right): \frac{4}{20} = \frac{20}{100} = 20\%$.

> **Review Video and Practice: Computation with Percentages**
> Visit mometrix.com/academy and enter code: 693099
>
> **Review Video and Practice: Percent Increase vs. Percent of Whole**
> Visit mometrix.com/academy and enter code: 130715

CONVERTING BETWEEN PERCENTAGES, FRACTIONS, AND DECIMALS

Converting decimals to percentages and percentages to decimals is as simple as moving the decimal point. To *convert from a decimal to a percentage*, move the decimal point **two places to the right**. To *convert from a percentage to a decimal*, move it **two places to the left**. It may be helpful to remember that the percentage number will always be larger than the equivalent decimal number. For example:

$$0.23 = 23\% \quad 5.34 = 534\% \quad 0.007 = 0.7\%$$
$$700\% = 7.00 \quad 86\% = 0.86 \quad 0.15\% = 0.0015$$

To convert a fraction to a decimal, simply divide the numerator by the denominator in the fraction. To convert a decimal to a fraction, put the decimal in the numerator with 1 in the denominator. Multiply the numerator and denominator by tens until there are no more decimal places. Then simplify the fraction to lowest terms. For example, converting 0.24 to a fraction:

$$0.24 = \frac{0.24}{1} = \frac{0.24 \times 100}{1 \times 100} = \frac{24}{100} = \frac{6}{25}$$

Fractions can be converted to a percentage by finding equivalent fractions with a denominator of 100. For example,

$$\frac{7}{10} = \frac{70}{100} = 70\% \quad \frac{1}{4} = \frac{25}{100} = 25\%$$

To convert a percentage to a fraction, divide the percentage number by 100 and reduce the fraction to its simplest possible terms. For example,

$$60\% = \frac{60}{100} = \frac{3}{5} \quad 96\% = \frac{96}{100} = \frac{24}{25}$$

> **Review Video and Practice: <u>Converting Fractions to Percentages and Decimals</u>**
> Visit mometrix.com/academy and enter code: 306233
>
> **Review Video and Practice: <u>Converting Percentages to Decimals and Fractions</u>**
> Visit mometrix.com/academy and enter code: 287297
>
> **Review Video and Practice: <u>Converting Decimals to Fractions and Percentages</u>**
> Visit mometrix.com/academy and enter code: 986765

RATIONAL NUMBERS

The term **rational** means that the number can be expressed as a ratio or fraction. That is, a number, r, is rational if and only if it can be represented by a fraction $\frac{a}{b}$ where a and b are integers and b does not equal 0. The set of rational numbers includes integers and decimals. If there is no finite way to represent a value with a fraction of integers, then the number is **irrational**. Common examples of irrational numbers include: $\sqrt{5}, \left(1 + \sqrt{2}\right)$, and π.

> **Review Video and Practice: <u>Rational and Irrational Numbers</u>**
> Visit mometrix.com/academy and enter code: 280645

PRACTICE

P1. What is 30% of 120?

P2. What is 150% of 20?

P3. What is 14.5% of 96?

P4. Simplify the following expressions:

(a) $\left(\frac{2}{5}\right)/\left(\frac{4}{7}\right)$

(b) $\frac{7}{8} - \frac{8}{16}$

(c) $\frac{1}{2} + \left(3\left(\frac{3}{4}\right) - 2\right) + 4$

(d) $0.22 + 0.5 - (5.5 + 3.3 \div 3)$

(e) $\frac{3}{2} + (4(0.5) - 0.75) + 2$

P5. Convert the following to a fraction and to a decimal: **(a)** 15%; **(b)** 24.36%

P6. Convert the following to a decimal and to a percentage. **(a)** 4/5; **(b)** $3\frac{2}{5}$

P7. A patient was given pain medicine at a dosage of 0.22 grams. The patient's dosage was then increased to 0.80 grams. By how much was the patient's dosage increased?

P8. At a hotel, $\frac{3}{4}$ of the 100 rooms are occupied today. Yesterday, $\frac{4}{5}$ of the 100 rooms were occupied. On which day were more of the rooms occupied and by how much more?

P9. At a school, 40% of the teachers teach English. If 20 teachers teach English, how many teachers work at the school?

P10. A patient was given blood pressure medicine at a dosage of 2 grams. The patient's dosage was then decreased to 0.45 grams. By how much was the patient's dosage decreased?

P11. Two weeks ago, $\frac{2}{3}$ of the 60 customers at a skate shop were male. Last week, $\frac{3}{6}$ of the 80 customers were male. During which week were there more male customers?

P12. A patient was given 40 mg of a certain medicine. Later, the patient's dosage was increased to 45 mg. What was the percent increase in his medication?

PRACTICE SOLUTIONS

P1. The word *of* indicates multiplication, so 30% of 120 is found by multiplying 120 by 30%. Change 30% to a decimal, then multiply: $120 \times 0.3 = 36$

P2. The word *of* indicates multiplication, so 150% of 20 is found by multiplying 20 by 150%. Change 150% to a decimal, then multiply: $20 \times 1.5 = 30$

P3. Change 14.5% to a decimal before multiplying. $0.145 \times 96 = 13.92$.

P4. Follow the order of operations and utilize properties of fractions to solve each:

(a) Rewrite the problem as a multiplication problem: $\frac{2}{5} \times \frac{7}{4} = \frac{2\times7}{5\times4} = \frac{14}{20}$. Make sure the fraction is reduced to lowest terms. Both 14 and 20 can be divided by 2.

$$\frac{14}{20} = \frac{14 \div 2}{20 \div 2} = \frac{7}{10}$$

(b) The denominators of $\frac{7}{8}$ and $\frac{8}{16}$ are 8 and 16, respectively. The lowest common denominator of 8 and 16 is 16 because 16 is the least common multiple of 8 and 16. Convert the first fraction to its equivalent with the newly found common denominator of 16: $\frac{7\times2}{8\times2} = \frac{14}{16}$. Now that the fractions have the same denominator, you can subtract them.

$$\frac{14}{16} - \frac{8}{16} = \frac{6}{16} = \frac{3}{8}$$

(c) When simplifying expressions, first perform operations within groups. Within the set of parentheses are multiplication and subtraction operations. Perform the multiplication first to get $\frac{1}{2} + \left(\frac{9}{4} - 2\right) + 4$. Then, subtract two to obtain $\frac{1}{2} + \frac{1}{4} + 4$. Finally, perform addition from left to right:

$$\frac{1}{2} + \frac{1}{4} + 4 = \frac{2}{4} + \frac{1}{4} + \frac{16}{4} = \frac{19}{4} = 4\frac{3}{4}$$

(d) First, evaluate the terms in the parentheses $(5.5 + 3.3 \div 3)$ using order of operations. $3.3 \div 3 = 1.1$, and $5.5 + 1.1 = 6.6$. Next, rewrite the problem: $0.22 + 0.5 - 6.6$. Finally, add and subtract from left to right: $0.22 + 0.5 = 0.72$; $0.72 - 6.6 = -5.88$. The answer is -5.88.

(e) First, simplify within the parentheses, then change the fraction to a decimal and perform addition from left to right:

$$\frac{3}{2} + (2 - 0.75) + 2 =$$

$$\frac{3}{2} + 1.25 + 2 =$$

$$1.5 + 1.25 + 2 = 4.75$$

P5. (a) 15% can be written as $\frac{15}{100}$. Both 15 and 100 can be divided by 5: $\frac{15 \div 5}{100 \div 5} = \frac{3}{20}$

When converting from a percentage to a decimal, drop the percent sign and move the decimal point two places to the left: 15% = 0.15

(b) 24.36% written as a fraction is $\frac{24.36}{100}$, or $\frac{2436}{10,000}$, which reduces to $\frac{609}{2500}$. 24.36% written as a decimal is 0.2436. Recall that dividing by 100 moves the decimal two places to the left.

P6. (a) Recall that in the decimal system the first decimal place is one tenth: $\frac{4\times2}{5\times2} = \frac{8}{10} = 0.8$

Percent means "per hundred." $\frac{4\times20}{5\times20} = \frac{80}{100} = 80\%$

61

Math

(b) The mixed number $3\frac{2}{5}$ has a whole number and a fractional part. The fractional part $\frac{2}{5}$ can be written as a decimal by dividing 5 into 2, which gives 0.4. Adding the whole to the part gives 3.4.

To find the equivalent percentage, multiply the decimal by 100. $3.4(100) = 340\%$. Notice that this percentage is greater than 100%. This makes sense because the original mixed number $3\frac{2}{5}$ is greater than 1.

P7. The first step is to determine what operation (addition, subtraction, multiplication, or division) the problem requires. Notice the keywords and phrases "by how much" and "increased." "Increased" means that you go from a smaller amount to a larger amount. This change can be found by subtracting the smaller amount from the larger amount: 0.80 grams– 0.22 grams = 0.58 grams.

Remember to line up the decimal when subtracting:

$$
\begin{array}{r}
0.80 \\
-\ \ 0.22 \\
\hline
0.58
\end{array}
$$

P8. First, find the number of rooms occupied each day. To do so, multiply the fraction of rooms occupied by the number of rooms available:

$$\text{Number occupied} = \text{Fraction occupied} \times \text{Total number}$$

$$\text{Number of rooms occupied today} = \frac{3}{4} \times 100 = 75$$

$$\text{Number of rooms occupied} = \frac{4}{5} \times 100 = 80$$

The difference in the number of rooms occupied is: $80 - 75 = 5$ rooms

P9. To answer this problem, first think about the number of teachers that work at the school. Will it be more or less than the number of teachers who work in a specific department such as English? More teachers work at the school, so the number you find to answer this question will be greater than 20.

40% of the teachers are English teachers. "Of" indicates multiplication, and words like "is" and "are" indicate equivalence. Translating the problem into a mathematical sentence gives $40\% \times t = 20$, where t represents the total number of teachers. Solving for t gives $t = \frac{20}{40\%} = \frac{20}{0.40} = 50$. Fifty teachers work at the school.

P10. The decrease is represented by the difference between the two amounts:

$$2 \text{ grams} - 0.45 \text{ grams} = 1.55 \text{ grams}.$$

Remember to line up the decimal point before subtracting.

$$
\begin{array}{r}
2.00 \\
-\ \ 0.45 \\
\hline
1.55
\end{array}
$$

P11. First, you need to find the number of male customers that were in the skate shop each week. You are given this amount in terms of fractions. To find the actual number of male customers, multiply the fraction of male customers by the number of customers in the store.

$$\text{Actual number of male customers} = \text{fraction of male customers} \times \text{total customers}$$

$$\text{Number of male customers two weeks ago} = \frac{2}{3} \times 60 = \frac{120}{3} = 40$$

$$\text{Number of male customers last week} = \frac{3}{6} \times 80 = \frac{1}{2} \times 80 = \frac{80}{2} = 40$$

The number of male customers was the same both weeks.

P12. To find the percent increase, first compare the original and increased amounts. The original amount was 40 mg, and the increased amount is 45 mg, so the dosage of medication was increased by 5 mg ($45 - 40 = 5$). Note, however, that the question asks not by how much the dosage increased but by what percentage it increased.

$$\text{Percent increase} = \frac{\text{new amount} - \text{original amount}}{\text{original amount}} \times 100\%$$

$$= \frac{45\text{ mg} - 40\text{ mg}}{40\text{ mg}} \times 100\% = \frac{5}{40} \times 100\% = 0.125 \times 100\% = 12.5\%$$

PROPORTIONS AND RATIOS

PROPORTIONS

A proportion is a relationship between two quantities that dictates how one changes when the other changes. A **direct proportion** describes a relationship in which a quantity increases by a set amount for every increase in the other quantity, or decreases by that same amount for every decrease in the other quantity. Example: Assuming a constant driving speed, the time required for a car trip increases as the distance of the trip increases. The distance to be traveled and the time required to travel are directly proportional.

An **inverse proportion** is a relationship in which an increase in one quantity is accompanied by a decrease in the other, or vice versa. Example: the time required for a car trip decreases as the speed increases and increases as the speed decreases, so the time required is inversely proportional to the speed of the car.

> **Review Video and Practice: Proportions**
> Visit mometrix.com/academy and enter code: 505355

RATIOS

A **ratio** is a comparison of two quantities in a particular order. Example: If there are 14 computers in a lab, and the class has 20 students, there is a student to computer ratio of 20 to 14, commonly written as 20: 14. Ratios are normally reduced to their smallest whole number representation, so 20: 14 would be reduced to 10: 7 by dividing both sides by 2.

> **Review Video and Practice: Ratios**
> Visit mometrix.com/academy and enter code: 996914

CONSTANT OF PROPORTIONALITY

When two quantities have a proportional relationship, there exists a **constant of proportionality** between the quantities. The product of this constant and one of the quantities is equal to the other quantity. For example, if one lemon costs $0.25, two lemons cost $0.50, and three lemons cost $0.75, there is a proportional relationship between the total cost of lemons and the number of lemons purchased. The constant of proportionality is the **unit price**, namely $0.25/lemon. Notice that the total price of lemons, t, can be found by multiplying the unit price of lemons, p, and the number of lemons, n: $t = pn$.

WORK/UNIT RATE

Unit rate expresses a quantity of one thing in terms of one unit of another. For example, if you travel 30 miles every two hours, a unit rate expresses this comparison in terms of one hour: in one hour you travel 15 miles, so your unit rate is 15 miles per hour. Other examples are how much one ounce of food costs (price per ounce) or figuring out how much one egg costs out of the dozen (price per 1 egg, instead of price per 12 eggs). The denominator of a unit rate is always 1. Unit rates are used to compare different situations to solve problems. For example, to make sure you get the best deal when deciding which kind of soda to buy, you can find the unit rate of each. If soda #1 costs $1.50 for a 1-liter bottle, and soda #2 costs $2.75 for a 2-liter bottle, it would be a better deal to buy soda #2, because its unit rate is only $1.375 per 1-liter, which is cheaper than soda #1. Unit rates can also help determine the length of time a given event will take. For example, if you can

64

paint 2 rooms in 4.5 hours, you can determine how long it will take you to paint 5 rooms by solving for the unit rate per room and then multiplying that by 5.

SLOPE

On a graph with two points, (x_1, y_1) and (x_2, y_2), the **slope** is found with the formula $m = \frac{y_2 - y_1}{x_2 - x_1}$; where $x_1 \neq x_2$ and m stands for slope. If the value of the slope is **positive**, the line has an *upward direction* from left to right. If the value of the slope is **negative**, the line has a *downward direction* from left to right. Consider the following example:

A new book goes on sale in bookstores and online stores. In the first month, 5,000 copies of the book are sold. Over time, the book continues to grow in popularity. The data for the number of copies sold is in the table below.

# of Months on Sale	1	2	3	4	5
# of Copies Sold (In Thousands)	5	10	15	20	25

So, the number of copies that are sold and the time that the book is on sale is a proportional relationship. In this example, an equation can be used to show the data: $y = 5x$, where x is the number of months that the book is on sale. Also, y is the number of copies sold. So, the slope of the corresponding line is $\frac{\text{rise}}{\text{run}} = \frac{5}{1} = 5$.

FINDING AN UNKNOWN IN EQUIVALENT EXPRESSIONS

It is often necessary to apply information given about a rate or proportion to a new scenario. For example, if you know that Jedha can run a marathon (26.2 miles) in 3 hours, how long would it take her to run 10 miles at the same pace? Start by setting up equivalent expressions:

$$\frac{26.2 \text{ mi}}{3 \text{ hr}} = \frac{10 \text{ mi}}{x \text{ hr}}$$

Now, cross multiply and solve for x:

$$26.2x = 30$$
$$x = \frac{30}{26.2} = \frac{15}{13.1}$$
$$x \approx 1.15 \text{ hrs } or \text{ 1 hr 9 min}$$

So, at this pace, Jedha could run 10 miles in about 1.15 hours or about 1 hour and 9 minutes.

PRACTICE

P1. Solve the following for x.

(a) $\frac{45}{12} = \frac{15}{x}$

(b) $\frac{0.50}{2} = \frac{1.50}{x}$

(c) $\frac{40}{8} = \frac{x}{24}$

P2. At a school, for every 20 female students there are 15 male students. This same student ratio happens to exist at another school. If there are 100 female students at the second school, how many male students are there?

P3. In a hospital emergency room, there are 4 nurses for every 12 patients. What is the ratio of nurses to patients? If the nurse-to-patient ratio remains constant, how many nurses must be present to care for 24 patients?

P4. In a bank, the banker-to-customer ratio is 1:2. If seven bankers are on duty, how many customers are currently in the bank?

P5. Janice made $40 during the first 5 hours she spent babysitting. She will continue to earn money at this rate until she finishes babysitting in 3 more hours. Find how much money Janice earns per hour and the total she earned babysitting.

PRACTICE SOLUTIONS

P1. Cross multiply, then solve for x:

(a)

$$45x = 12 \times 15$$
$$45x = 180$$
$$x = \frac{180}{45} = 4$$

(b)

$$0.5x = 1.5 \times 2$$
$$0.5x = 3$$
$$x = \frac{3}{0.5} = 6$$

(c)

$$8x = 40 \times 24$$
$$8x = 960$$
$$x = \frac{960}{8} = 120$$

P2. One way to find the number of male students is to set up and solve a proportion.

$$\frac{\text{number of female students}}{\text{number of male students}} = \frac{20}{15} = \frac{100}{\text{number of male students}}$$

Represent the unknown number of male students as the variable x:

$$\frac{20}{15} = \frac{100}{x}$$

Cross multiply and then solve for x:

$$20x = 15 \times 100$$
$$x = \frac{1500}{20}$$
$$x = 75$$

P3. The ratio of nurses to patients can be written as 4 to 12, 4:12, or $\frac{4}{12}$. Because four and twelve have a common factor of four, the ratio should be reduced to 1:3, which means that there is one nurse present for every three patients. If this ratio remains constant, there must be eight nurses present to care for 24 patients.

P4. Use proportional reasoning or set up a proportion to solve. Because there are twice as many customers as bankers, there must be fourteen customers when seven bankers are on duty. Setting up and solving a proportion gives the same result:

$$\frac{\text{number of bankers}}{\text{number of customers}} = \frac{1}{2} = \frac{7}{\text{number of customers}}$$

Represent the unknown number of customers as the variable x: $\frac{1}{2} = \frac{7}{x}$.

To solve for x, cross multiply: $1 \times x = 7 \times 2$, so $x = 14$.

P5. Janice earns $8 per hour. This can be found by taking her initial amount earned, $40, and dividing it by the number of hours worked, 5. Since $\frac{40}{5} = 8$, Janice makes $8 in one hour. This can also be found by finding the unit rate, money earned per hour: $\frac{40}{5} = \frac{x}{1}$. Since cross multiplying yields $5x = 40$, and division by 5 shows that $x = 8$, Janice earns $8 per hour.

Janice will earn $64 babysitting in her 8 total hours (adding the first 5 hours to the remaining 3 gives the 8-hour total). Since Janice earns $8 per hour and she worked 8 hours, $\frac{\$8}{\text{hr}} \times 8 \text{ hrs} = \$64$. This can also be found by setting up a proportion comparing money earned to babysitting hours. Since she earns $40 for 5 hours and since the rate is constant, she will earn a proportional amount in 8 hours: $\frac{40}{5} = \frac{x}{8}$. Cross multiplying will yield $5x = 320$, and division by 5 shows that $x = 64$.

EXPRESSIONS, EQUATIONS, AND INEQUALITIES

TERMS, COEFFICIENTS, AND EXPRESSIONS

Mathematical expressions consist of a combination of one or more values arranged in terms that are added together. As such, an expression could be just a single number, including zero. A **variable term** is the product of a real number, also called a **coefficient**, and one or more variables. Expressions may also include numbers without a variable, called **constants** or **constant terms**. The expression $6s$, for example, is a single term where the coefficient is the real number 6 and the variable part is s. Note that if a term is written as simply a variable, like t, then the coefficient is 1, because $t = 1t$.

A **single variable linear expression** is the sum of a single variable term and a constant, which may be zero. For instance, the expression $2w + 7$ has $2w$ as the variable term and 7 as the constant term. It is important to realize that terms are separated by addition or subtraction. Since an expression is a sum of terms, expressions such as $5x - 3$ can be written as $5x + (-3)$ to emphasize that the constant term is negative. A real-world example of a single variable linear expression is the perimeter of a square, four times the side length, often expressed as $4s$.

LINEAR EQUATIONS

Equations that can be written as $ax + b = 0$, where $a \neq 0$, are referred to as **one variable linear equations**. A solution to such an equation is called a **root**. In the case where we have the equation $5x + 10 = 0$, if we solve for x, we get a solution of $x = -2$. In other words, the root of the equation is -2. This is found by first subtracting 10 from both sides, which gives $5x = -10$. Next, simply divide both sides by the coefficient of the variable, in this case 5, to get $x = -2$. This can be checked by plugging -2 back into the original equation $(5)(-2) + 10 = -10 + 10 = 0$.

The **solution set** is the set of all solutions of an equation. In our example, the solution set would simply be -2. If there were more solutions (there usually are in multivariable equations), then they would also be included in the solution set. When an equation has no true solutions, this is referred to as an **empty set**. Equations with identical solution sets are **equivalent equations**. An **identity** is a term whose value or determinant is equal to 1.

Linear equations can be written many ways. Below is a list of some forms linear equations can take:

- **Standard Form**: $Ax + By = C$; the slope is $\frac{-A}{B}$ and the y-intercept is $\frac{C}{B}$
- **Slope Intercept Form**: $y = mx + b$, where m is the slope and b is the y-intercept
- **Point-Slope Form**: $y - y_1 = m(x - x_1)$, where m is the slope and (x_1, y_1) is a point on the line
- **Two-Point Form**: $\frac{y - y_1}{x - x_1} = \frac{y_2 - y_1}{x_2 - x_1}$, where (x_1, y_1) and (x_2, y_2) are two points on the given line
- **Intercept Form**: $\frac{x}{x_1} + \frac{y}{y_1} = 1$, where $(x_1, 0)$ is the point at which a line intersects the x-axis, and $(0, y_1)$ is the point at which the same line intersects the y-axis

> **Review Video and Practice: <u>Slope-Intercept and Point-Slope Forms</u>**
> Visit mometrix.com/academy and enter code: 113216

SOLVING ONE-VARIABLE LINEAR EQUATIONS

Multiply all terms by the lowest common denominator to eliminate any fractions. Look for addition or subtraction to undo so you can isolate the variable on one side of the equal sign. Divide both sides by the coefficient of the variable. When you have a value for the variable, substitute this value into the original equation to make sure you have a true equation. Consider the following example:

Kim's savings are represented by the table below. Represent her savings, using an equation.

X (Months)	Y (Total Savings)
2	$1,300
5	$2,050
9	$3,050
11	$3,550
16	$4,800

The table shows a function with a constant rate of change, or slope, of 250. Given the points on the table, the slopes can be calculated as $\frac{(2,050-1300)}{(5-2)}$, $\frac{(3,050-2,050)}{(9-5)}$, $\frac{(3,550-3,050)}{(11-9)}$, and $\frac{(4,800-3,550)}{(16-11)}$, each of which equals 250. Thus, the table shows a constant rate of change, indicating a linear function. The slope-intercept form of a linear equation is written as $y = mx + b$, where m represents the slope and b represents the y-intercept. Substituting the slope into this form gives $y = 250x + b$. Substituting corresponding x- and y-values from any point into this equation will give the y-intercept, or b. Using the point, (2, 1,300), gives $1,300 = 250(2) + b$, which simplifies as $b = 800$. Thus, her savings may be represented by the equation, $y = 250x + 800$.

RULES FOR MANIPULATING EQUATIONS

CARRYING OUT THE SAME OPERATION ON BOTH SIDES OF AN EQUATION

When solving an equation, the general procedure is to carry out a series of operations on both sides of an equation, choosing operations that will tend to simplify the equation when doing so. The reason why the same operation must be carried out on both sides of the equation is because that leaves the meaning of the equation unchanged, and yields a result that is equivalent to the original equation. This would not be the case if we carried out an operation on one side of an equation and not the other. Consider what an equation means: it is a statement that two values or expressions are equal. If we carry out the same operation on both sides of the equation—add 3 to both sides, for example—then the two sides of the equation are changed in the same way, and so remain equal. If we do that to only one side of the equation—add 3 to one side but not the other—then that wouldn't be true; if we change one side of the equation but not the other then the two sides are no longer equal.

ADVANTAGE OF COMBINING LIKE TERMS

Combining like terms refers to adding or subtracting like terms—terms with the same variable—and therefore reducing sets of like terms to a single term. The main advantage of doing this is that it simplifies the equation. Often, combining like terms can be done as the first step in solving an equation, though it can also be done later, such as after distributing terms in a product.

For example, consider the equation $2(x + 3) + 3(2 + x + 3) = -4$. The 2 and the 3 in the second set of parentheses are like terms, and we can combine them, yielding $2(x + 3) + 3(x + 5) = -4$. Now we can carry out the multiplications implied by the parentheses, distributing the outer 2 and 3 accordingly: $2x + 6 + 3x + 15 = -4$. The $2x$ and the $3x$ are like terms, and we can add them together: $5x + 6 + 15 = -4$. Now, the constants 6, 15, and –4 are also like terms, and we can combine them as well: subtracting 6 and 15 from both sides of the equation, we get $5x = -4 - 6 - 15$, or $5x = -25$, which simplifies further to $x = -5$.

CANCELING TERMS ON OPPOSITE SIDES OF AN EQUATION

Two terms on opposite sides of an equation can be canceled if and only if they *exactly* match each other. They must have the same variable raised to the same power and the same coefficient. For example, in the equation $3x + 2x^2 + 6 = 2x^2 - 6$, $2x^2$ appears on both sides of the equation and can be canceled, leaving $3x + 6 = -6$. The 6 on each side of the equation *cannot* be canceled, because it is added on one side of the equation and subtracted on the other. While they cannot be canceled, however, the 6 and –6 are like terms and can be combined, yielding $3x = -12$, which simplifies further to $x = -4$.

It's also important to note that the terms to be canceled must be independent terms and cannot be part of a larger term. For example, consider the equation $2(x + 6) = 3(x + 4) + 1$. We cannot cancel the x's, because even though they match each other they are part of the larger terms $2(x + 6)$ and $3(x + 4)$. We must first distribute the 2 and 3, yielding $2x + 12 = 3x + 12 + 1$. Now we see that the terms with the x's do not match, but the 12s do, and can be canceled, leaving $2x = 3x + 1$, which simplifies to $x = -1$.

> **Review Video and Practice: <u>Rules for Manipulating Equations</u>**
> Visit mometrix.com/academy and enter code: 838871

PROCESS FOR MANIPULATING EQUATIONS
ISOLATING VARIABLES

To **isolate a variable** means to manipulate the equation so that the variable appears by itself on one side of the equation and does not appear at all on the other side. Generally, an equation or inequality is considered to be solved once the variable is isolated and the other side of the equation or inequality is simplified as much as possible. In the case of a two-variable equation or inequality, only one variable needs to be isolated; it will not usually be possible to simultaneously isolate both variables.

For a linear equation—an equation in which the variable only appears raised to the first power—isolating a variable can be done by first moving all the terms with the variable to one side of the equation and all other terms to the other side. (*Moving* a term really means adding the inverse of the term to both sides; when a term is *moved* to the other side of the equation, its sign is flipped.) Then combine like terms on each side. Finally, divide both sides by the coefficient of the variable, if applicable. The steps need not necessarily be done in this order, but this order will always work.

WORKING WITH INEQUALITIES

Commonly in algebra and other upper-level fields of math you find yourself working with mathematical expressions that do not equal each other. The statement comparing such expressions with symbols such as < (less than) or > (greater than) is called an *inequality*. An example of an inequality is $7x > 5$. To solve for x, simply divide both sides by 7 and the solution is shown to be $x > \frac{5}{7}$. Graphs of the solution set of inequalities are represented on a number line. Open circles are used to show that an expression approaches a number but is never quite equal to that number.

> **Review Video and Practice: <u>Inequalities</u>**
> Visit mometrix.com/academy and enter code: 347842

DETERMINING SOLUTIONS TO INEQUALITIES

To determine whether a coordinate is a solution of an inequality, you can substitute the values of the coordinate into the inequality, simplify, and check whether the resulting statement holds true. For instance, to determine whether $(-2,4)$ is a solution of the inequality $y \geq -2x + 3$, substitute

70

Math

the values into the inequality, $4 \geq -2(-2) + 3$. Simplify the right side of the inequality and the result is $4 \geq 7$, which is a false statement. Therefore, the coordinate is not a solution of the inequality. You can also use this method to determine which part of the graph of an inequality is shaded. The graph of $y \geq -2x + 3$ includes the solid line $y = -2x + 3$ and, since it excludes the point $(-2,4)$ to the left of the line, it is shaded to the right of the line.

FLIPPING INEQUALITY SIGNS

When given an inequality, we can always turn the entire inequality around, swapping the two sides of the inequality and changing the inequality sign. For instance, $x + 2 > 2x - 3$ is equivalent to $2x - 3 < x + 2$. Aside from that, normally the inequality does not change if we carry out the same operation on both sides of the inequality. There is, however, one principal exception: if we *multiply* or *divide* both sides of the inequality by a *negative number*, the inequality is flipped. For example, if we take the inequality $-2x < 6$ and divide both sides by -2, the inequality flips and we are left with $x > -3$. This *only* applies to multiplication and division, and only with negative numbers. Multiplying or dividing both sides by a positive number, or adding or subtracting any number regardless of sign, does not flip the inequality.

GRAPHICAL SOLUTIONS TO EQUATIONS AND INEQUALITIES

When equations are shown graphically, they are usually shown on a **Cartesian coordinate plane**. The Cartesian coordinate plane consists of two number lines placed perpendicular to each other and intersecting at the zero point, also known as the origin. The horizontal number line is known as the x-axis, with positive values to the right of the origin, and negative values to the left of the origin. The vertical number line is known as the y-axis, with positive values above the origin, and negative values below the origin. Any point on the plane can be identified by an ordered pair in the form (x, y), called coordinates. The x-value of the coordinate is called the abscissa, and the y-value of the coordinate is called the ordinate. The two number lines divide the plane into **four quadrants**: I, II, III, and IV.

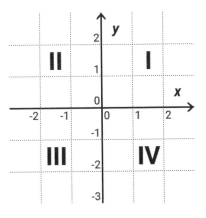

Note that in quadrant I $x > 0$ and $y > 0$, in quadrant II $x < 0$ and $y > 0$, in quadrant III $x < 0$ and $y < 0$, and in quadrant IV $x > 0$ and $y < 0$.

Recall that if the value of the slope of a line is positive, the line slopes upward from left to right. If the value of the slope is negative, the line slopes downward from left to right. If the y-coordinates are the same for two points on a line, the slope is 0 and the line is a **horizontal line**. If the x-coordinates are the same for two points on a line, there is no slope and the line is a **vertical line**.

Two or more lines that have equivalent slopes are **parallel lines**. **Perpendicular lines** have slopes that are negative reciprocals of each other, such as $\frac{a}{b}$ and $\frac{-b}{a}$.

GRAPHING SIMPLE INEQUALITIES

To graph a simple inequality, we first mark on the number line the value that signifies the end point of the inequality. If the inequality is strict (involves a less than or greater than), we use a hollow circle; if it is not strict (less than or equal to or greater than or equal to), we use a solid circle. We then fill in the part of the number line that satisfies the inequality: to the left of the marked point for less than (or less than or equal to), to the right for greater than (or greater than or equal to).

For example, we would graph the inequality $x < 5$ by putting a hollow circle at 5 and filling in the part of the line to the left:

PRACTICE

P1. Seeing the equation $2x + 4 = 4x + 7$, a student divides the first terms on each side by 2, yielding $x + 4 = 2x + 7$, and then combines like terms to get $x = -3$. However, this is incorrect, as can be seen by substituting –3 into the original equation. Explain what is wrong with the student's reasoning.

P2. Describe the steps necessary to solve the equation $2x + 1 - x = 4 + 3x + 7$.

P3. Describe the steps necessary to solve the equation $2(x + 5) = 7(4 - x)$.

P4. Ray earns $10 an hour at his job. Write an equation for his earnings as a function of time spent working. Determine how long Ray has to work in order to earn $360.

PRACTICE SOLUTIONS

P1. As stated, it's easy to verify that the student's solution is incorrect: $2(-3) + 4 = -2$ and $4(-3) + 7 = -5$; clearly $-2 \neq -5$. The mistake was in the first step, which illustrates a common type of error in solving equations. The student tried to simplify the two variable terms by dividing them by 2. However, it's not valid to multiply or divide only one term on each side of an equation by a number; when multiplying or dividing, the operation must be applied to *every* term in the equation. So, dividing by 2 would yield not $x + 4 = 2x + 7$, but $x + 2 = 2x + \frac{7}{2}$. While this is now valid, that fraction is inconvenient to work with, so this may not be the best first step in solving the equation. Rather, it may have been better to first combine like terms. Subtracting $4x$ from both sides yields $-2x + 4 = 7$; subtracting 4 from both sides yields $-2x = 3$; *now* we can divide both sides by –2 to get $x = -\frac{3}{2}$.

P2. Our ultimate goal is to isolate the variable, x. To that end we first move all the terms containing x to the left side of the equation, and all the constant terms to the right side. Note that when we move a term to the other side of the equation its sign changes. We are therefore now left with $2x - x - 3x = 4 + 7 - 1$.

Next, we combine the like terms on each side of the equation, adding and subtracting the terms as appropriate. This leaves us with $-2x = 10$.

At this point, we're almost done; all that remains is to divide both sides by -2 to leave the x by itself. We now have our solution, $x = -5$. We can verify that this is a correct solution by substituting it back into the original equation.

P3. Generally, in equations that have a sum or difference of terms multiplied by another value or expression, the first step is to multiply those terms, distributing as necessary: $2(x + 5) = 2(x) + 2(5) = 2x + 10$, and $7(4 - x) = 7(4) - 7(x) = 28 - 7x$. So, the equation becomes $2x + 10 = 28 - 7x$. We can now add $7x$ to both sides to eliminate the variable from the right-hand side: $9x + 10 = 28$. Similarly, we can subtract 10 from both sides to move all the constants to the right: $9x = 18$. Finally, we can divide both sides by 9, yielding the final answer, $x = 2$.

P4. The number of dollars that Ray earns is dependent on the number of hours he works, so earnings will be represented by the dependent variable y and hours worked will be represented by the independent variable x. He earns 10 dollars per hour worked, so his earnings can be calculated as $y = 10x$. To calculate the number of hours Ray must work in order to earn \$360, plug in 360 for y and solve for x:

$$10x = 360$$
$$x = \frac{360}{10} = 36$$

Measurement and Data

MEASUREMENT PRINCIPLES

PRECISION, ACCURACY, AND ERROR

Precision: How reliable and repeatable a measurement is. The more consistent the data is with repeated testing, the more precise it is. For example, hitting a target consistently in the same spot, which may or may not be the center of the target, is precision.

Accuracy: How close the data is to the correct data. For example, hitting a target consistently in the center area of the target, whether or not the hits are all in the same spot, is accuracy.

Note: it is possible for data to be precise without being accurate. If a scale is off balance, the data may be precise, but will not be accurate. For data to have precision and accuracy, it must be repeatable and correct.

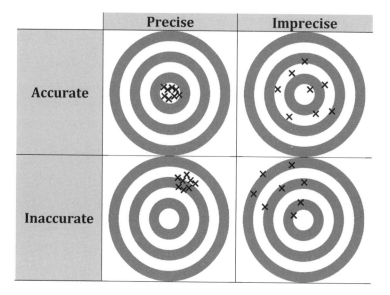

Approximate error: The amount of error in a physical measurement. Approximate error is often reported as the measurement, followed by the $\pm$ symbol and the amount of the approximate error.

Maximum possible error: Half the magnitude of the smallest unit used in the measurement. For example, if the unit of measurement is 1 centimeter, the maximum possible error is $\frac{1}{2}$ cm, written as ± 0.5 cm following the measurement. It is important to apply significant figures in reporting maximum possible error. Do not make the answer appear more accurate than the least accurate of your measurements.

ROUNDING AND ESTIMATION

Rounding is reducing the digits in a number while still trying to keep the value similar. The result will be less accurate but in a simpler form and easier to use. Whole numbers can be rounded to the nearest ten, hundred, or thousand.

When you are asked to estimate the solution to a problem, you will need to provide only an approximate figure or **estimation** for your answer. In this situation, you will need to round each number in the calculation to the level indicated (nearest hundred, nearest thousand, etc.) or to a level that makes sense for the numbers involved. When estimating a sum **all numbers must be**

rounded to the same level. You cannot round one number to the nearest thousand while rounding another to the nearest hundred.

UNITS OF MEASUREMENT
METRIC MEASUREMENT PREFIXES
Giga-: one billion (1 *giga*watt is one billion watts)
Mega-: one million (1 *mega*hertz is one million hertz)
Kilo-: one thousand (1 *kilo*gram is one thousand grams)
Deci-: one-tenth (1 *deci*meter is one-tenth of a meter)
Centi-: one-hundredth (1 *centi*meter is one-hundredth of a meter)
Milli-: one-thousandth (1 *milli*liter is one-thousandth of a liter)
Micro-: one-millionth (1 *micro*gram is one-millionth of a gram)

MEASUREMENT CONVERSION
When converting between units, the goal is to maintain the same meaning but change the way it is displayed. In order to go from a larger unit to a smaller unit, multiply the number of the known amount by the equivalent amount. When going from a smaller unit to a larger unit, divide the number of the known amount by the equivalent amount.

For complicated conversions, it may be helpful to set up conversion fractions. In these fractions, one fraction is the **conversion factor**. The other fraction has the unknown amount in the numerator. So, the known value is placed in the denominator. Sometimes, the second fraction has the known value from the problem in the numerator and the unknown in the denominator. Multiply the two fractions to get the converted measurement. Note that since the numerator and the denominator of the factor are equivalent, the value of the fraction is 1. That is why we can say that the result in the new units is equal to the result in the old units even though they have different numbers.

It can often be necessary to chain known conversion factors together. As an example, consider converting 512 square inches to square meters. We know that there are 2.54 centimeters in an inch and 100 centimeters in a meter, and we know we will need to square each of these factors to achieve the conversion we are looking for.

$$\frac{512 \text{ in}^2}{1} \times \left(\frac{2.54 \text{ cm}}{1 \text{ in}}\right)^2 \times \left(\frac{1 \text{ m}}{100 \text{ cm}}\right)^2 = \frac{512 \text{ in}^2}{1} \times \left(\frac{6.4516 \text{ cm}^2}{1 \text{ in}^2}\right) \times \left(\frac{1 \text{ m}^2}{10000 \text{ cm}^2}\right) = 0.330 \text{ m}^2$$

Common Units and Equivalents

Metric Equivalents

1000 μg (microgram)	1 mg
1000 mg (milligram)	1 g
1000 g (gram)	1 kg
1000 kg (kilogram)	1 metric ton
1000 mL (milliliter)	1 L
1000 μm (micrometer)	1 mm
1000 mm (millimeter)	1 m
100 cm (centimeter)	1 m
1000 m (meter)	1 km

Distance and Area Measurement

Unit	Abbreviation	US equivalent	Metric equivalent
Inch	in	1 inch	2.54 centimeters
Foot	ft	12 inches	0.305 meters
Yard	yd	3 feet	0.914 meters
Mile	mi	5280 feet	1.609 kilometers
Acre	ac	4840 square yards	0.405 hectares
Square Mile	sq. mi. or mi.^{2}	640 acres	2.590 square kilometers

Capacity Measurements

Unit	Abbreviation	US equivalent	Metric equivalent
Fluid Ounce	fl oz	8 fluid drams	29.573 milliliters
Cup	c	8 fluid ounces	0.237 liter
Pint	pt.	16 fluid ounces	0.473 liter
Quart	qt.	2 pints	0.946 liter
Gallon	gal.	4 quarts	3.785 liters
Teaspoon	t or tsp.	1 fluid dram	5 milliliters
Tablespoon	T or tbsp.	4 fluid drams	15 or 16 milliliters
Cubic Centimeter	cc or cm.^{3}	0.271 drams	1 milliliter

Weight Measurements

Unit	Abbreviation	US equivalent	Metric equivalent
Ounce	oz	16 drams	28.35 grams
Pound	lb	16 ounces	453.6 grams
Ton	tn.	2,000 pounds	907.2 kilograms

TEMPERATURE CONVERSION

Converting between Fahrenheit (°F) and Celsius (°C) is slightly more involved than a direct proportion. From the following equations, we can see that a change of one degree Celsius is greater than a change of one degree Fahrenheit.

Conversion	Equation	Example
°F→°C	$°C = \dfrac{5}{9}(°F - 32)$	Convert 200.0 °F to °C $\dfrac{5}{9}(200.0 - 32) = \dfrac{5}{9}(168.0)$ $= 93.33\ °C$
°C→°F	$°F = \dfrac{9}{5}(°C) + 32$	Convert 24.0 °C to °F $\dfrac{9}{5}(24.0) + 32 = 43.2 + 32$ $= 75.2\ °F$

PRACTICE

P1. Perform the following conversions:

(a) 1.4 meters to centimeters

(b) 218 centimeters to meters

(c) 42 inches to feet

(d) 15 kilograms to pounds

(e) 80 ounces to pounds

(f) 2 miles to kilometers

(g) 5 feet to centimeters

(h) 15.14 liters to gallons

(i) 8 quarts to liters

(j) 13.2 pounds to grams

PRACTICE SOLUTIONS

P1. (a) $\frac{100 \text{ cm}}{1 \text{ m}} = \frac{x \text{ cm}}{1.4 \text{ m}}$ Cross multiply to get $x = 140$

(b) $\frac{100 \text{ cm}}{1 \text{ m}} = \frac{218 \text{ cm}}{x \text{ m}}$ Cross multiply to get $100x = 218$, or $x = 2.18$

(c) $\frac{12 \text{ in}}{1 \text{ ft}} = \frac{42 \text{ in}}{x \text{ ft}}$ Cross multiply to get $12x = 42$, or $x = 3.5$

(d) $15 \text{ kilograms} \times \frac{2.2 \text{ pounds}}{1 \text{ kilogram}} = 33 \text{ pounds}$

(e) $80 \text{ ounces} \times \frac{1 \text{ pound}}{16 \text{ ounces}} = 5 \text{ pounds}$

(f) $2 \text{ miles} \times \frac{1.609 \text{ kilometers}}{1 \text{ mile}} = 3.218 \text{ kilometers}$

(g) $5 \text{ feet} \times \frac{12 \text{ inches}}{1 \text{ foot}} \times \frac{2.54 \text{ centimeters}}{1 \text{ inch}} = 152.4 \text{ centimeters}$

(h) $15.14 \text{ liters} \times \frac{1 \text{ gallon}}{3.785 \text{ liters}} = 4 \text{ gallons}$

(i) $8 \text{ quarts} \times \frac{1 \text{ gallon}}{4 \text{ quarts}} \times \frac{3.785 \text{ liters}}{1 \text{ gallon}} = 7.57 \text{ liters}$

(j) $13.2 \text{ pounds} \times \frac{1 \text{ kilogram}}{2.2 \text{ pounds}} \times \frac{1000 \text{ grams}}{1 \text{ kilogram}} = 6000 \text{ grams}$

GEOMETRIC QUANTITIES

PERIMETER, AREA, AND VOLUME

When you have a two- or three-dimensional figure like a square or a cube, it is often useful to determine measurements of perimeter, area, or volume. Regular shapes have well-defined formulas for each of these quantities. The **perimeter** of a two-dimensional shape is the total length of its edges. Finding it can be as simple as adding up all the various side lengths, or it can be a bit more complicated, like when finding the perimeter of a circle (also called the circumference). Either way, the concept is the same.

The **area** of a two-dimensional shape is a measure of how much flat space the shape contains. Again, finding the area may be as simple as multiplying length and width like for a rectangle, or it could be a compound figure with parts that need to be added together. For instance, the area of a square with a semicircle on one edge would require adding the areas of the two separate shapes together.

For three-dimensional figures, also called solids, calculating **volume** is a way to determine how much space is contained within the figure. As with perimeter and area, there are simple formulas, like the one to determine the volume of a rectangular prism or a cube, and more involved ones, like the formula for the volume of a sphere or a cone.

POLYGONS

A **polygon** is a closed, two-dimensional figure with three or more straight line segments called **sides**. The point at which two sides of a polygon intersect is called the **vertex**. In a polygon, the number of sides is always equal to the number of vertices. A polygon with all sides congruent and all angles equal is called a **regular polygon**. Common polygons are:

Triangle = 3 sides

Quadrilateral = 4 sides

Pentagon = 5 sides

Hexagon = 6 sides

Heptagon = 7 sides

Octagon = 8 sides

Nonagon = 9 sides

Decagon = 10 sides

Dodecagon = 12 sides

More generally, an *n*-gon is a polygon that has *n* angles and *n* sides.

> **Review Video and Practice: Polygons**
> Visit mometrix.com/academy and enter code: 271869

Math

TRIANGLES

The **perimeter of any triangle** is found by summing the three side lengths; $P = a + b + c$. For an equilateral triangle, this is the same as $P = 3a$, where a is any side length, since all three sides are the same length.

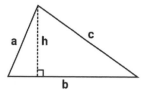

The **area of any triangle** can be found by taking half the product of one side length, referred to as the base and often given the variable b, and the perpendicular distance from that side to the opposite vertex, called the height and given the variable h. In equation form that is $A = \frac{1}{2}bh$.

> **Review Video and Practice: <u>Area and Perimeter of a Triangle</u>**
> Visit mometrix.com/academy and enter code: 853779

QUADRILATERALS

A **quadrilateral** is a closed two-dimensional geometric figure that has four straight sides. Lines that connect opposite corners are called **diagonals**.

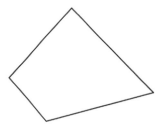

KITE

A **kite** is a quadrilateral with two pairs of adjacent sides that are congruent. A result of this is perpendicular diagonals. A kite can be concave or convex and has one line of symmetry.

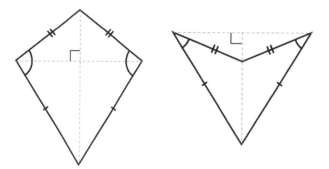

TRAPEZOID

Trapezoid: A trapezoid is defined as a quadrilateral that has at least one pair of parallel sides. There are no rules for the second pair of sides. So there are no rules for the diagonals and no lines of symmetry for a trapezoid.

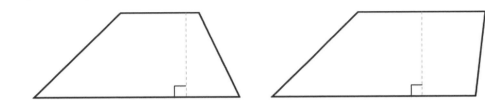

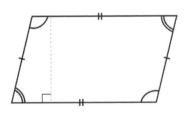

Isosceles trapezoid: A trapezoid with equal base angles. This gives rise to other properties including: the two nonparallel sides have the same length, the two non-base angles are also equal, and there is one line of symmetry through the midpoints of the parallel sides.

The **area of a trapezoid** is found by the formula $A = \frac{1}{2}h(b_1 + b_2)$, where h is the height (segment joining and perpendicular to the parallel bases), and b_1 and b_2 are the two parallel sides (bases). Do not use one of the other two sides as the height unless that side is also perpendicular to the parallel bases.

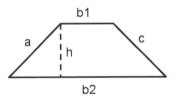

The **perimeter of a trapezoid** is found by the formula $P = a + b_1 + c + b_2$, where a, b_1, c, and b_2 are the four sides of the trapezoid.

> **Review Video and Practice: <u>Area and Perimeter of a Trapezoid</u>**
> Visit mometrix.com/academy and enter code: 587523

PARALLELOGRAM

A **parallelogram** is a quadrilateral that has two pairs of opposite parallel sides. As such it is a special type of trapezoid. The sides that are parallel are also congruent. The opposite interior angles are always congruent, and the consecutive interior angles are supplementary. The diagonals of a parallelogram divide each other. Each diagonal divides the parallelogram into two congruent triangles. A parallelogram has no line of symmetry, but does have 180-degree rotational symmetry about the midpoint.

The **area of a parallelogram** is found by the formula $A = bh$, where b is the length of the base, and h is the height. Note that the base and height correspond to the length and width in a rectangle, so this formula would apply to rectangles as well. Do not confuse the height of a parallelogram with the length of the second side. The two are only the same measure in the case of a rectangle.

The **perimeter of a parallelogram** is found by the formula $P = 2a + 2b$ or $P = 2(a + b)$, where a and b are the lengths of the two sides.

> **Review Video and Practice: <u>Diagonals of Parallelograms</u>**
> Visit mometrix.com/academy and enter code: 320040
>
> **Review Video and Practice: <u>Area and Perimeter of a Parallelogram</u>**
> Visit mometrix.com/academy and enter code: 718313

RECTANGLE

A **rectangle** is a quadrilateral with four right angles. All rectangles are parallelograms and trapezoids, but not all parallelograms or trapezoids are rectangles. The diagonals of a rectangle are congruent. Rectangles have two lines of symmetry (through each pair of opposing midpoints) and 180-degree rotational symmetry about the midpoint.

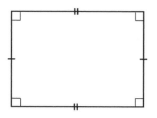

The **area of a rectangle** is found by the formula $A = lw$, where A is the area of the rectangle, l is the length (usually considered to be the longer side) and w is the width (usually considered to be the shorter side). The numbers for l and w are interchangeable.

The **perimeter of a rectangle** is found by the formula $P = 2l + 2w$ or $P = 2(l + w)$, where l is the length, and w is the width. It may be easier to add the length and width first and then double the result, as in the second formula.

RHOMBUS

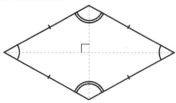

A **rhombus** is a quadrilateral with four congruent sides. All rhombuses are parallelograms and kites; thus, they inherit all the properties of both types of quadrilaterals. The diagonals of a rhombus are perpendicular to each other. Rhombi have two lines of symmetry (along each of the diagonals) and 180-degree rotational symmetry.

The **area of a rhombus** is half the product of the diagonals, $A = \frac{d_1 d_2}{2}$, and the perimeter of a rhombus is $P = 2\sqrt{(d_1)^2 + (d_2)^2}$.

SQUARE

A **square** is a quadrilateral with four right angles and four congruent sides. Squares satisfy the criteria of all other types of quadrilaterals. The diagonals of a square are congruent and perpendicular to each other. Squares have four lines of symmetry (through each pair of opposing midpoints and along each of the diagonals) as well as 90° rotational symmetry about the midpoint.

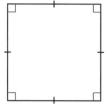

The **area of a square** is found by using the formula $A = s^2$, where s is the length of one side. The **perimeter of a square** is found by using the formula $P = 4s$, where s is the length of one side. Because all four sides are equal in a square, it is faster to multiply the length of one side by 4 than to add the same number four times. You could use the formulas for rectangles and get the same answer.

CIRCLES

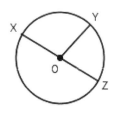

The **center** of a circle is the single point from which every point on the circle is **equidistant**. The **radius** is a line segment that joins the center of the circle and any one point on the circle. All radii of a circle are equal. Circles that have the same center but not the same length of radii are **concentric**. The **diameter** is a line segment that passes through the center of the circle and has both endpoints on the circle. The length of the diameter is exactly twice the length of the radius. Point O in the diagram below is the center of the circle, segments $\overline{OX}$, $\overline{OY}$, and $\overline{OZ}$ are radii; and segment $\overline{XZ}$ is a diameter.

The **area of a circle** is found by the formula $A = \pi r^2$, where r is the length of the radius. If the diameter of the circle is given, remember to divide it in half to get the length of the radius before proceeding. The **circumference** of a circle is found by the formula $C = 2\pi r$, where r is the radius. Again, remember to convert the diameter if you are given that measure rather than the radius.

> **Review Video and Practice: The Diameter, Radius, and Circumference of Circles**
> Visit mometrix.com/academy and enter code: 448988
>
> **Review Video and Practice: Area and Circumference of a Circle**
> Visit mometrix.com/academy and enter code: 243015

SOLIDS

The **volume of any prism** is found by the formula $V = Bh$, where B is the area of the base, and h is the height (perpendicular distance between the bases).

For a **rectangular prism**, the volume can be found by the formula $V = lwh$, where V is the volume, l is the length, w is the width, and h is the height.

The **volume of a cube** can be found by the formula $V = s^3$, where s is the length of a side. This formula is the same as the one used for the volume of a rectangular prism, but simplified since all three quantities (length, width, and height) are the same.

The **volume of a sphere** is given by the formula $V = \frac{4}{3}\pi r^3$, where r is the radius. Both quantities are generally given in terms of π.

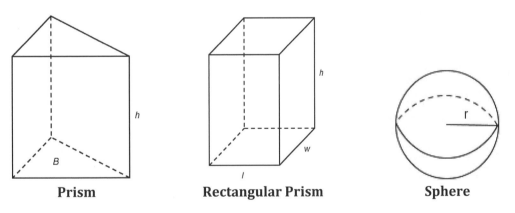

| Prism | Rectangular Prism | Sphere |

The **volume of a cylinder** can be calculated by the formula $V = \pi r^2 h$, where r is the radius, and h is the height.

The **volume of a pyramid** is found by the formula $V = \frac{1}{3}Bh$, where B is the area of the base, and h is the height (perpendicular distance from the vertex to the base). Notice this formula is the same as $\frac{1}{3}$ times the volume of a prism. Like a prism, the base of a pyramid can be any shape.

The **volume of a cone** is found by the formula $V = \frac{1}{3}\pi r^2 h$, where r is the radius, and h is the height. Notice this is the same as $\frac{1}{3}$ times the volume of a cylinder.

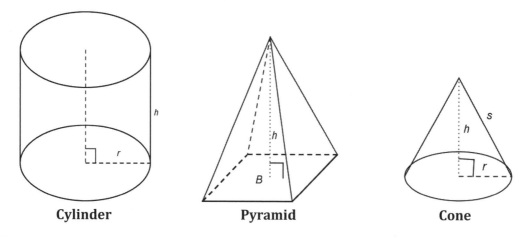

| Cylinder | Pyramid | Cone |

PRACTICE

P1. Find the area and perimeter of the following quadrilaterals:

    (a) A square with side length 2.5 cm.

    (b) A parallelogram with height 3 m, base 4 m, and other side 6 m.

P2. Find the volume of the following solids:

    (a) A cylinder with radius 5 m and height 0.5 m.

    (b) A trapezoidal prism with base area of 254 mm^2, base perimeter 74 mm, and height 10 mm.

PRACTICE SOLUTIONS

P1. (a) $A = s^2 = (2.5 \text{ cm})^2 = 6.25 \text{ cm}^2$; $P = 4s = 4 \times 2.5 \text{ cm} = 10 \text{ cm}$

    (b) $A = bh = (3 \text{ m})(4 \text{ m}) = 12 \text{ m}^2$; $P = 2a + 2b = 2 \times 6 \text{ m} + 2 \times 4 \text{ m} = 20 \text{ m}$

P2. (a) $V = \pi r^2 h = \pi(5 \text{ m})^2(0.5 \text{ m}) = 12.5\pi \text{ m}^3 \approx 39.27 \text{ m}^3$

    (b) $V = Bh = (254 \text{ mm}^2)(10 \text{ mm}) = 2{,}540 \text{ mm}^3$

STATISTICS

MEASURES OF CENTRAL TENDENCY

A **measure of central tendency** is a statistical value that gives a reasonable estimate for the center of a group of data. There are several different ways of describing the measure of central tendency. Each one has a unique way it is calculated, and each one gives a slightly different perspective on the data set. Whenever you give a measure of central tendency, always make sure the units are the same. If the data has different units, such as hours, minutes, and seconds, convert all the data to the same unit, and use the same unit in the measure of central tendency. If no units are given in the data, do not give units for the measure of central tendency.

MEAN

The **statistical mean** of a group of data is the same as the arithmetic average of that group. To find the mean of a set of data, first convert each value to the same units, if necessary. Then find the sum of all the values, and count the total number of data values, making sure you take into consideration each individual value. If a value appears more than once, count it more than once. Divide the sum of the values by the total number of values and apply the units, if any. Note that the mean does not have to be one of the data values in the set, and may not divide evenly.

$$\text{mean} = \frac{\text{sum of the data values}}{\text{quantity of data values}}$$

For instance, the mean of the data set {88, 72, 61, 90, 97, 68, 88, 79, 86, 93, 97, 71, 80, 84, 89} would be the sum of the fifteen numbers divided by 15:

$$\frac{88 + 72 + 61 + 90 + 97 + 68 + 88 + 79 + 86 + 93 + 97 + 71 + 80 + 84 + 88}{15} = \frac{1242}{15}$$
$$= 82.8$$

While the mean is relatively easy to calculate and averages are understood by most people, the mean can be very misleading if it is used as the sole measure of central tendency. If the data set has **outliers** (data values that are unusually high or unusually low compared to the rest of the data values), the mean can be very distorted, especially if the data set has a small number of values. If unusually high values are countered with unusually low values, the mean is not affected as much. For example, if five of twenty students in a class get a 100 on a test, but the other 15 students have an average of 60 on the same test, the class average would appear as 70. Whenever the mean is skewed by outliers, it is always a good idea to include the median as an alternate measure of central tendency.

A **weighted mean**, or weighted average, is a mean that uses "weighted" values. The formula is weighted mean $= \frac{w_1x_1+w_2x_2+w_3x_3\ldots+w_nx_n}{w_1+w_2+w_3+\cdots+w_n}$. Weighted values, such as $w_1, w_2, w_3, \ldots w_n$ are assigned to each member of the set $x_1, x_2, x_3, \ldots x_n$. When calculating the weighted mean, make sure a weight value for each member of the set is used.

MEDIAN

The **statistical median** is the value in the middle of the set of data. To find the median, list all data values in order from smallest to largest or from largest to smallest. Any value that is repeated in the set must be listed the number of times it appears. If there are an odd number of data values, the median is the value in the middle of the list. If there is an even number of data values, the median is the arithmetic mean of the two middle values.

For example, the median of the data set {88, 72, 61, 90, 97, 68, 88, 79, 86, 93, 97, 71, 80, 84, 88} is 86 since the ordered set is {61, 68, 71, 72, 79, 80, 84, **86**, 88, 88, 88, 90, 93, 97, 97}.

The big disadvantage of using the median as a measure of central tendency is that is relies solely on a value's relative size as compared to the other values in the set. When the individual values in a set of data are evenly dispersed, the median can be an accurate tool. However, if there is a group of rather large values or a group of rather small values that are not offset by a different group of values, the information that can be inferred from the median may not be accurate because the distribution of values is skewed.

MODE

The **statistical mode** is the data value that occurs the greatest number of times in the data set. It is possible to have exactly one mode, more than one mode, or no mode. To find the mode of a set of data, arrange the data like you do to find the median (all values in order, listing all multiples of data values). Count the number of times each value appears in the data set. If all values appear an equal number of times, there is no mode. If one value appears more than any other value, that value is the mode. If two or more values appear the same number of times, but there are other values that appear fewer times and no values that appear more times, all of those values are the modes.

For example, the mode of the data set {**88**, 72, 61, 90, 97, 68, **88**, 79, 86, 93, 97, 71, 80, 84, **88**} is 88.

The main disadvantage of the mode is that the values of the other data in the set have no bearing on the mode. The mode may be the largest value, the smallest value, or a value anywhere in between in the set. The mode only tells which value or values, if any, occurred the greatest number of times. It does not give any suggestions about the remaining values in the set.

> **Review Video and Practice: Mean, Median, and Mode**
> Visit mometrix.com/academy and enter code: 286207

DISPERSION

A **measure of dispersion** is a single value that helps to "interpret" the measure of central tendency by providing more information about how the data values in the set are distributed about the measure of central tendency. The measure of dispersion helps to eliminate or reduce the disadvantages of using the mean, median, or mode as a single measure of central tendency, and give a more accurate picture of the dataset as a whole. To have a measure of dispersion, you must know or calculate the range, standard deviation, or variance of the data set.

RANGE

The **range** of a set of data is the difference between the greatest and lowest values of the data in the set. To calculate the range, you must first make sure the units for all data values are the same, and then identify the greatest and lowest values. If there are multiple data values that are equal for the highest or lowest, just use one of the values in the formula. Write the answer with the same units as the data values you used to do the calculations.

> **Review Video and Practice: Statistical Range**
> Visit mometrix.com/academy and enter code: 778541

STANDARD DEVIATION

Standard deviation is a measure of dispersion that compares all the data values in the set to the mean of the set to give a more accurate picture. A larger standard deviation results in greater variance of the data values from the mean.

Small Standard Deviation   **Large Standard Deviation**

When data is distributed normally around the mean, the graph of the data will be in the shape of a bell curve. The less a graph follows this shape, the *larger* the standard deviation, and the further away most data is from the mean. The more a graph follows this shape, the *smaller* the standard deviation, meaning the majority of the values are closer to the mean.

SKEWNESS

Skewness is a way to describe the symmetry or asymmetry of the distribution of values in a dataset. If the distribution of values is symmetrical, there is no skew. In general the closer the mean of a data set is to the median of the data set, the less skew there is. Generally, if the mean is to the right of the median, the data set is *positively skewed*, or right-skewed, and if the mean is to the left of the median, the data set is *negatively skewed*, or left-skewed. However, this rule of thumb is not infallible. When the data values are graphed on a curve, a set with no skew will be a perfect bell curve.

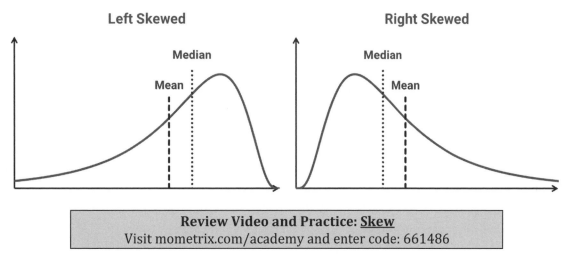

Left Skewed   **Right Skewed**

Review Video and Practice: Skew
Visit mometrix.com/academy and enter code: 661486

UNIMODAL VS. BIMODAL

If a distribution has a single peak, it would be considered **unimodal**. If it has two discernible peaks it would be considered **bimodal**. Bimodal distributions may be an indication that the set of data being considered is actually the combination of two sets of data with significant differences. A **uniform distribution** is a distribution in which there is *no distinct peak or variation* in the data. No values or ranges are particularly more common than any other values or ranges.

PROBABILITY

Probability is the likelihood of a certain outcome occurring for a given event. An **event** is any situation that produces a result. It could be something as simple as flipping a coin or as complex as launching a rocket. Determining the probability of an outcome for an event can be equally simple or complex. As such, there are specific terms used in the study of probability that need to be understood:

- **Compound event**—an event that involves two or more independent events (rolling a pair of dice and taking the sum)
- **Desired outcome** (or success)—an outcome that meets a particular set of criteria (a roll of 1 or 2 if we are looking for numbers less than 3)
- **Independent events**—two or more events whose outcomes do not affect one another (two coins tossed at the same time)
- **Dependent events**—two or more events whose outcomes affect one another (two cards drawn consecutively from the same deck)
- **Certain outcome**—probability of outcome is 100% or 1
- **Impossible outcome**—probability of outcome is 0% or 0
- **Mutually exclusive outcomes**—two or more outcomes whose criteria cannot all be satisfied in a single event (a coin coming up heads and tails on the same toss)
- **Random variable**—refers to all possible outcomes of a single event which may be discrete or continuous.

> **Review Video and Practice: Intro to Probability**
> Visit mometrix.com/academy and enter code: 212374

THEORETICAL AND EXPERIMENTAL PROBABILITY

Theoretical probability can usually be determined without actually performing the event. The likelihood of an outcome occurring, or the probability of an outcome occurring, is given by the formula:

$$P(A) = \frac{\text{Number of acceptable outcomes}}{\text{Number of possible outcomes}}$$

Note that $P(A)$ is the probability of an outcome A occurring, and each outcome is just as likely to occur as any other outcome. If each outcome has the same probability of occurring as every other possible outcome, the outcomes are said to be equally likely to occur. The total number of acceptable outcomes must be less than or equal to the total number of possible outcomes. If the two are equal, then the outcome is certain to occur and the probability is 1. If the number of acceptable outcomes is zero, then the outcome is impossible and the probability is 0. For example, if there are 20 marbles in a bag and 5 are red, then the theoretical probability of randomly selecting a red marble is 5 out of 20, $\left(\frac{5}{20} = \frac{1}{4}, 0.25, \text{ or } 25\%\right)$.

SAMPLE SPACE

The total set of all possible results of a test or experiment is called a **sample space**, or sometimes a universal sample space. The sample space, represented by one of the variables S, Ω, or U (for universal sample space) has individual elements called outcomes. Other terms for outcome that may be used interchangeably include elementary outcome, simple event, or sample point. The number of outcomes in a given sample space could be infinite or finite, and some tests may yield multiple unique sample sets. For example, tests conducted by drawing playing cards from a standard deck would have one sample space of the card values, another sample space of the card suits, and a third sample space of suit-denomination combinations. For most tests, the sample spaces considered will be finite.

An **event**, represented by the variable E, is a portion of a sample space. It may be one outcome or a group of outcomes from the same sample space. If an event occurs, then the test or experiment will generate an outcome that satisfies the requirement of that event. For example, given a standard deck of 52 playing cards as the sample space, and defining the event as the collection of face cards, then the event will occur if the card drawn is a J, Q, or K. If any other card is drawn, the event is said to have not occurred.

For every sample space, each possible outcome has a specific likelihood, or probability, that it will occur. The probability measure, also called the **distribution**, is a function that assigns a real number probability, from zero to one, to each outcome. For a probability measure to be accurate, every outcome must have a real number probability measure that is greater than or equal to zero and less than or equal to one. Also, the probability measure of the sample space must equal one, and the probability measure of the union of multiple outcomes must equal the sum of the individual probability measures.

Probabilities of events are expressed as real numbers from zero to one. They give a numerical value to the chance that a particular event will occur. The probability of an event occurring is the sum of the probabilities of the individual elements of that event. For example, in a standard deck of 52 playing cards as the sample space and the collection of face cards as the event, the probability of drawing a specific face card is $\frac{1}{52} = 0.019$, but the probability of drawing any one of the twelve face cards is $12(0.019) = 0.228$. Note that rounding of numbers can generate different results. If you multiplied 12 by the fraction $\frac{1}{52}$ before converting to a decimal, you would get the answer $\frac{12}{52} = 0.231$.

If two events have no outcomes in common, they are said to be **mutually exclusive**. For example, in a standard deck of 52 playing cards, the event of all card suits is mutually exclusive to the event of all card values. If two events have no bearing on each other so that one event occurring has no influence on the probability of another event occurring, the two events are said to be independent. For example, rolling a standard six-sided die multiple times does not change that probability that a particular number will be rolled from one roll to the next. If the outcome of one event does affect the probability of the second event, the two events are said to be dependent. For example, if cards are drawn from a deck, the probability of drawing an ace after an ace has been drawn is different than the probability of drawing an ace if no ace (or no other card, for that matter) has been drawn.

ADDITION RULE

The **addition rule** for probability is used for finding the probability of a compound event. Use the formula $P(A \text{ or } B) = P(A) + P(B) - P(A \text{ and } B)$, where $P(A \text{ and } B)$ is the probability of both events occurring to find the probability of a compound event. The probability of both events occurring at the same time must be subtracted to eliminate any overlap in the first two probabilities.

CONDITIONAL PROBABILITY AND TWO-WAY FREQUENCY TABLES

Given two events A and B, the **conditional probability** is the probability that event A will occur, given that event B has occurred. For example, a certain store's recent T-shirt sales:

Size / Color	Small	Medium	Large	Total
Blue	25	40	35	100
White	27	25	22	74
Black	8	23	15	46
Total	60	88	72	220

Suppose we want to find the conditional probability that a customer buys a black shirt, given that the shirt he buys is size small. Since we know the shirt is small, the total for our probability will be 60 because $\frac{60}{220}$ of the shirts are small. Then, if we want to find the probability that the small shirt is black, we will compare the number of small black shirts (8) to the total number of small shirts (60): $\frac{8}{60} = \frac{2}{15}$. Therefore, the probability that a customer buys a black shirt, given that he buys a small shirt, is $\frac{2}{15}$.

Conditional probability often arises in everyday situations in, for example, estimating the risk or benefit of certain activities. The conditional probability of having a heart attack given that you exercise daily may be smaller than the overall probability of having a heart attack. The conditional probability of having lung cancer given that you are a smoker is larger than the overall probability of having lung cancer. Note that changing the order of the conditional probability changes the meaning: the conditional probability of having lung cancer given that you are a smoker is a very different thing from the probability of being a smoker given that you have lung cancer. In an extreme case, suppose that a certain rare disease is caused only by eating a certain food, but even then, it is unlikely. Then the conditional probability of having that disease given that you eat the dangerous food is nonzero but low, but the conditional probability of having eaten that food given that you have the disease is 100%!

> **Review Video and Practice: Conditional Probability**
> Visit mometrix.com/academy and enter code: 397924

MULTIPLICATION RULE

The **multiplication rule** can be used to find the probability of two independent events occurring using the formula $P(A \text{ and } B) = P(A) \times P(B)$, where $P(A \text{ and } B)$ is the probability of two independent events occurring, $P(A)$ is the probability of the first event occurring, and $P(B)$ is the probability of the second event occurring.

Use a **combination of the multiplication** rule and the rule of complements to find the probability that at least one outcome of the element will occur. This is given by the general formula $P(\text{at least one event occurring}) = 1 - P(\text{no outcomes occurring})$. For example, to find the probability that at least one even number will show when a pair of dice is rolled, find the probability that two odd numbers will be rolled (no even numbers) and subtract from one. You can always use a tree diagram or make a chart to list the possible outcomes when the sample space is small, such as in the dice-rolling example, but in most cases it will be much faster to use the multiplication and complement formulas.

> **Review Video and Practice: Multiplication Rule**
> Visit mometrix.com/academy and enter code: 782598

PRACTICE

P1. Given the following graph, determine the range of patient ages:

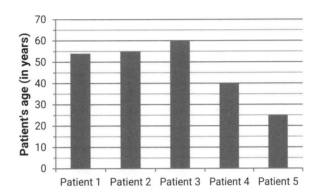

P2. Determine the probability of the following events:

(a) Rolling an even number on a regular 6-sided die.

(b) Not getting a red ball when selecting one from a bag of 3 red balls, 4 black balls, and 2 green balls.

PRACTICE SOLUTIONS

P1. Patient 1 is 54 years old; Patient 2 is 55 years old; Patient 3 is 60 years old; Patient 4 is 40 years old; and Patient 5 is 25 years old. The range of patient ages is the age of the oldest patient minus the age of the youngest patient. In other words, $60 - 25 = 35$. The range of ages is 35 years.

P2. (a) The values on the faces of a regular die are 1, 2, 3, 4, 5, and 6. Since three of these are even numbers (2, 4, 6), The probability of rolling an even number is $\frac{3}{6} = \frac{1}{2} = 0.5 = 50\%$.

(b) The bag contains a total of 9 balls, 6 of which are not red, so the probability of selecting one non-red ball would be $\frac{6}{9} = \frac{2}{3} \cong 0.667 \cong 66.7\%$.

DISPLAYING INFORMATION

INDEPENDENT AND DEPENDENT VARIABLES

When displaying information, it is important to know which of the aspects you are presenting are dependent and which are independent. **Independent variables** are those that determine the grouping or the order of your information, like time or category. **Dependent variables** are those that are of interest when compared across the independent variables, like growth or frequency.

FREQUENCY TABLES

Frequency tables show how frequently each unique value appears in a set. A **relative frequency table** is one that shows the proportions of each unique value compared to the entire set. Relative frequencies are given as percentages; however, the total percent for a relative frequency table will not necessarily equal 100 percent due to rounding. An example of a frequency table with relative frequencies is below.

Favorite Color	Frequency	Relative Frequency
Blue	4	13%
Red	7	22%
Green	3	9%
Purple	6	19%
Cyan	12	38%

LINE PLOTS

A **line plot**, also known as a *dot plot*, has plotted points that are not connected by line segments. In this graph, the horizontal axis lists the different possible values for the data, and the vertical axis lists the number of times the individual value occurs. A single dot is graphed for each value to show the number of times it occurs. This graph is more closely related to a bar graph than a line graph. Do not connect the dots in a line plot or it will misrepresent the data. This method of graphical representation is best suited to relatively small numbers of discrete items. Like the number of various types of fruits cosumed in a given time period.

LINE GRAPHS

Line graphs have one or more lines of varying styles (solid or broken) to show the different values for a set of data. The individual data are represented as ordered pairs, much like on a Cartesian plane. In this case, the x- and y-axes are defined in terms of their units, such as dollars or time. The individual plotted points are joined by line segments to show whether the value of the data is increasing (line sloping upward), decreasing (line sloping downward), or staying the same (horizontal line). Multiple sets of data can be graphed on the same line graph to give an easy visual comparison. An example of this would be graphing achievement test scores for different groups of students over the same time period to see which group had the greatest increase or decrease in performance from year to year (as shown below).

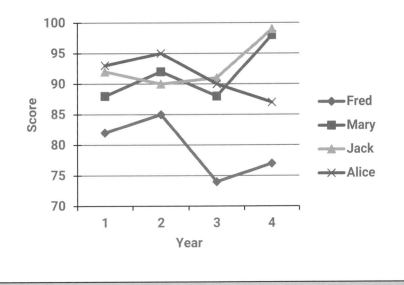

Review Video and Practice: Line Graphs
Visit mometrix.com/academy and enter code: 480147

BAR GRAPHS

A **bar graph** is one of the few graphs that can be drawn correctly in two different configurations – both horizontally and vertically. A bar graph is similar to a line plot in the way the data is organized on the graph. Both axes must have their categories defined for the graph to be useful. Rather than placing a single dot to mark the point of the data's value, a bar, or thick line, is drawn from zero to the exact value of the data, whether it is a number, percentage, or other numerical value. Longer bar lengths correspond to greater data values. To read a bar graph, read the labels for the axes to find the units being reported. Then, look where the bars end in relation to the scale given on the corresponding axis and determine the associated value. Bar graphs are a good way to represent large or small counts in various categories.

The bar chart below represents the responses from our favorite-color survey.

Favorite Color

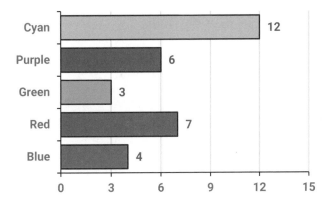

93

HISTOGRAMS

At first glance, a **histogram** looks like a vertical bar graph. The difference is that a bar graph has a separate bar for each piece of data and a histogram has one continuous bar for each *range* of data. For example, a histogram may have one bar for the range 0–9, one bar for 10–19, etc. While a bar graph has numerical values on one axis, a histogram has numerical values on both axes. Each range is of equal size, and they are ordered left to right from lowest to highest. The height of each column on a histogram represents the number of data values within that range. Like a stem and leaf plot, a histogram makes it easy to glance at the graph and quickly determine which range has the greatest quantity of values. A simple example of a histogram is below.

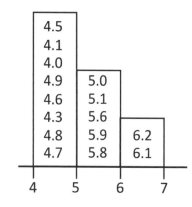

BIVARIATE DATA

Bivariate data is simply data from two different variables. (The prefix *bi-* means *two*.) In a *scatter plot*, each value in the set of data is plotted on a grid similar to a Cartesian plane, where each axis represents one of the two variables. By looking at the pattern formed by the points on the grid, you can often determine whether or not there is a relationship between the two variables, and what that relationship is, if it exists. The variables may be directly proportionate, inversely proportionate, or show no proportion at all. It may also be possible to determine if the data is linear, and if so, to find an equation to relate the two variables. The following scatter plot shows the relationship between preference for brand "A" and the age of the consumers surveyed.

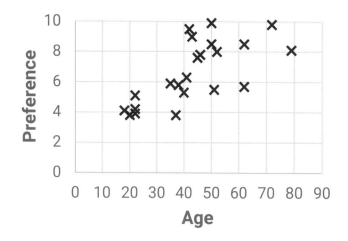

94

SCATTER PLOTS

Scatter plots are also useful in determining the type of function represented by the data and finding the simple regression. Linear scatter plots may be positive or negative, meaning that the variables have a positive or negative correlation, respectively. **Positive correlations** indicate that both variables increase together and are directly proportional. **Negative correlations** show that as one variable increases, the other decreases, so the variables are inversely proportional. Nonlinear scatter plots are generally exponential or quadratic. Below are some common types of scatter plots:

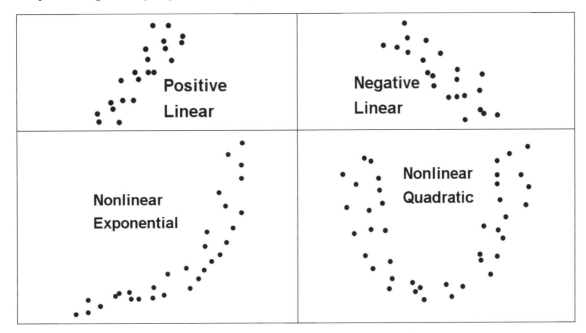

Review Video and Practice: <u>Scatter Plot</u>
Visit mometrix.com/academy and enter code: 596526

Science

Human Anatomy and Physiology

GENERAL ANATOMY AND PHYSIOLOGY
STANDARD ANATOMICAL POSITION

To understand terminology for direction and orientation on the body, the standard anatomical position is used. In this position, the person is standing with feet facing forward about hip width apart. Their legs and torso are completely upright with their arms at their side. Both hands should have the palms facing forward.

THE THREE PRIMARY BODY PLANES

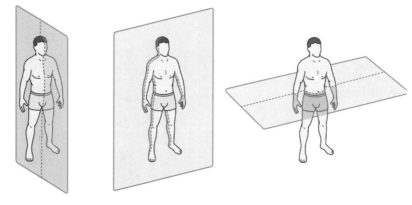

Sagittal/Lateral   Coronal/Frontal   Axial/Transverse

The **sagittal plane** divides the body, or any body part, vertically into right and left sections. The sagittal plane runs parallel to the midline of the body.

The **coronal (or frontal) plane** divides the body, or any body structure, vertically into front and back (*anterior* and *posterior*) sections. The coronal plane runs vertically through the body at right angles to the midline.

The **transverse (or horizontal) plane** divides the patient's body into imaginary upper (*superior*) and lower (*inferior or caudal*) halves.

TERMS OF DIRECTION

- **Medial** means *nearer to the midline* of the body. In anatomical position, the little finger is medial to the thumb.
- **Lateral** is the opposite of medial. It refers to structures *further away from the body's midline*, at the sides. In anatomical position, the thumb is lateral to the little finger.
- **Proximal** refers to structures *closer to the center* of the body. The hip is proximal to the knee.
- **Distal** refers to structures *further away from the center* of the body. The knee is distal to the hip.
- **Anterior** refers to structures in *front*.
- **Posterior** refers to structures *behind*.

96

- **Cephalad** and **cephalic** are adverbs meaning towards the *head*. **Cranial** is the adjective, meaning of the *skull*.
- **Caudad** is an adverb meaning towards the *tail* or posterior. **Caudal** is the adjective, meaning of the *hindquarters*.
- **Superior** means *above*, or closer to the head.
- **Inferior** means *below*, or closer to the feet.

ABDOMINAL REGIONS OF THE BODY AND UNDERLYING ORGANS

Abdominal regions include the following:

- **A: Right hypochondriac**—right kidney, liver, gallbladder, and small intestine
- **B: Epigastric** (Epi = on, above)—stomach, liver, adrenal glands, pancreas, spleen, small intestine
- **C: Left hypochondriac**—left kidney, spleen, pancreas, and colon
- **D: Right lumbar**—ascending colon, liver, gallbladder
- **E: Umbilical**—small intestine, duodenum, umbilicus
- **F: Left lumbar**—descending colon, left kidney
- **G: Right iliac**—cecum, appendix
- **H: Hypogastric** (Hypo = below, beneath, less than normal)—bladder, female internal reproductive organs, sigmoid colon
- **I: Left iliac**—descending and sigmoid colon

Science

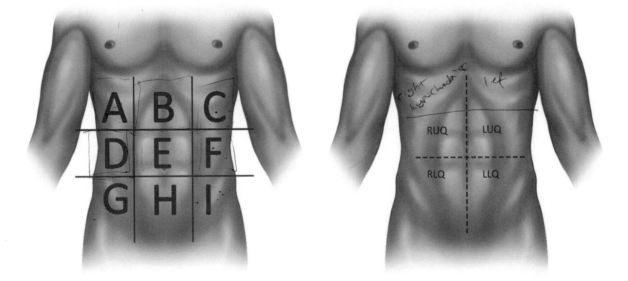

ABDOMINAL QUADRANTS

The abdomen may also be divided into four **quadrants** (sections) with the umbilicus (navel) at the center, helping to identify the position of organs:

- **Right upper quadrant** (RUQ): Duodenum, part of the ascending and transverse colon, hepatic flexure, liver, gallbladder, pancreas (head), right kidney, and right adrenal gland
- **Right lower quadrant** (RLQ): Cecum, appendix, right ureter, right fallopian tube, and right ovary

- **Left upper quadrant** (LUQ): Stomach, liver (left lobe), pancreas (body), left kidney, left adrenal gland, splenic flexure, spleen, part of transverse and descending colon
- **Left lower quadrant** (LLQ): Left ureter, left fallopian tube, left ovary, part of descending colon, and sigmoid colon

VENTRAL CAVITY

The ventral cavity, located on the anterior aspect of the trunk, comprises the thoracic and the abdominopelvic cavities, separated by the diaphragm. The walls of both cavities are comprised of skin, skeletal muscles, and bone. The organs within the cavities are the viscera.

- **Thoracic cavity**: The thoracic cavity is above the diaphragm and contains the lungs and the mediastinum, which separates the cavity into a right and left compartment. The heart, trachea, esophagus, and thymus gland lie within the mediastinum.
- **Abdominopelvic cavity**: The abdominopelvic cavity extends below the diaphragm to the pelvic floor, contains the upper abdominal cavity and the lower pelvic cavity (not physically separated). The organs within the abdominal cavity include the stomach, liver, gallbladder, spleen, kidneys, pancreas, large and small intestines. The pelvic cavity, encased in the pelvic bones, contains the internal reproductive organs, the bladder, and the distal part of the colon.

The cavities are lined with thin serous membranes, which secrete serous fluid that separates the parietal layer (lining the cavity walls) from the visceral layer (lining the organs). The membrane lining the thoracic cavities is referred to as the parietal pleura. The pericardial membrane lines the heart and the peritoneal membrane lines the abdominopelvic cavity.

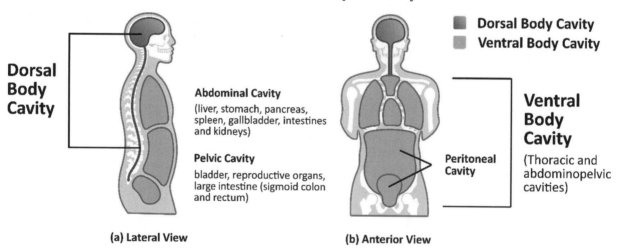

(a) Lateral View

(b) Anterior View

DORSAL CAVITY

The dorsal cavity is located on the posterior (dorsal) aspect of the body and contains the brain and the spinal cord.

Cranial cavity: Encased in cranial bones at the bottom and the skull cap the top, this cavity contains the brain, the 12 cranial nerves, and the pituitary gland. The meninges (comprised of the dura mater, arachnoid mater, and pia mater) line the cavity and surround the brain and the spinal cord and contain cerebrospinal fluid between the arachnoid mater and pia mater in the subarachnoid space. The meninges and cerebrospinal fluid protect and cushion the dorsal cavity. The vascularized pia mater is adhered to the surface of the brain and the spinal cord. The middle layer, the arachnoid mater, contains connective tissue but not nerves or blood vessels. The

98

enervated, vascularized dura mater is the outer layer that lies next to the bones and folds inward in places in the cavity and separates the brain into different compartments. The dura mater has two layers: The endosteal layer lines the cranial bones. The meningeal layer, which lines the endosteal layer within the cranium, lines the vertebral cavity.

Vertebral cavity: The vertebral cavity contains the vertebrae and the spinal cord. The meninges extend from the cranial cavity to enclose the vertebral cavity.

RESPIRATORY SYSTEM

GENERAL FUNCTION

The respiratory system includes the nose, mouth, nasal cavity, sinuses, pharynx, larynx, trachea, bronchial tree, and lungs. These organs facilitate the delivery of oxygen to the cells of the body for use in cellular respiration. The **conductive zone** brings inhaled air to the **respiratory zone** where gas exchange occurs. As oxygen is loaded into the blood, carbon dioxide is removed. Essential to this process are the diaphragm and intercostal muscles which are used to enlarge the chest cavity during pulmonary respiration (breathing). External respiration is the exchange of gas between the lungs and the blood. Internal respiration is the exchange of gas between the blood and tissues. Secondary functions of the respiratory system include pH regulation of the blood, thermoregulation, odor detection, and the production of speech.

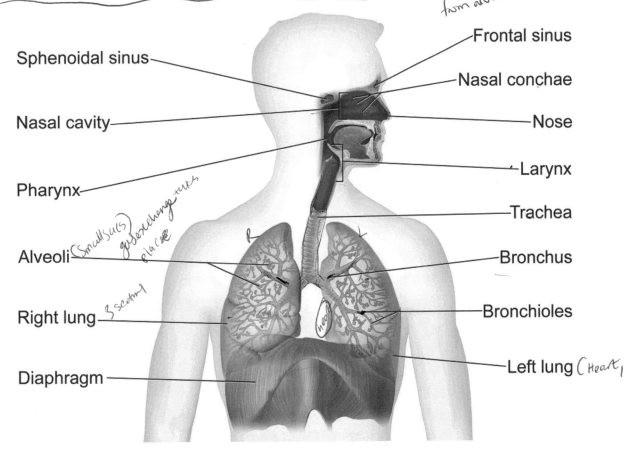

GAS EXCHANGE, THERMOREGULATION

Gas exchange is the loading of oxygen into pulmonary blood, and the removal of carbon dioxide. Inhaled air moves from through the mouth or nose to the pharynx, larynx, trachea, right and left main bronchi, bronchioles, and then the alveoli. It is here that gases diffuse down their partial

99

pressure gradients across a shared membrane between the capillaries and alveoli called the respiratory membrane. Oxygen diffuses into the blood where it is delivered to tissues throughout the body, and carbon dioxide diffuses out of the blood as a waste product of cellular respiration.

The respiratory system is also involved in **thermoregulation**, the regulation of body temperature. Capillaries within the respiratory tract, particularly the nasal passages and trachea, can constrict to conserve heat and dilate to release heat. The exhalation of warm, moistened air also helps to cool the body.

PROTECTION AGAINST DISEASE: PARTICULATE MATTER

A secondary role of the respiratory system is protection against disease and filtration of particulate matter. Some particles are filtered by nostril hairs and others get caught in mucus. Lysozymes within the mucus help to break down the trapped debris, and the cilia that line the respiratory tract then sweep it away. Immunoglobulin A (IgA) is also produced in the mucosal lining, and these antibodies aid in immune defenses by neutralizing pathogens. Mast cells within the respiratory tract release inflammatory chemicals that increase blood flow to the region and alert the immune system to a threat. Large phagocytic cells called macrophages can also help to protect the lungs by engulfing small cells and particulates.

STRUCTURE OF LUNGS AND ALVEOLI

The lungs are spongy, porous organs that occupy most of the thoracic cavity. A serous membrane called the pleura lines the thoracic cavity (**parietal pleura**) as well as the surface of the lungs (**visceral pleura**). The three-lobed right lung is separated from the two-lobed left lung by the **mediastinum**. The trachea forks into primary bronchi which enter the left and right lung (along with blood and lymphatic vessels) at a region called the **hilum**. Each primary bronchus splits repeatedly into secondary bronchi, tertiary bronchi, and bronchioles to form the bronchial tree. The terminal bronchioles further divide into respiratory bronchioles, which are characterized by the presence of some alveoli. The respiratory bronchioles lead into alveolar ducts, which terminate in alveolar sacs.

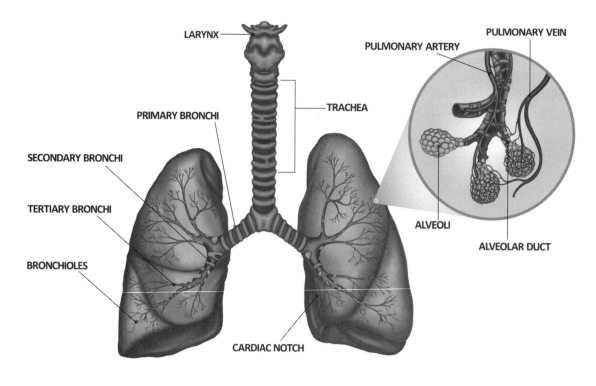

Within the alveolar sacs of the bronchi are clusters of **alveoli**: microscopic pouches where gas exchange occurs. The lungs contain hundreds of millions of these sacs, with a combined surface area that averages 70 m^2. The wall of each alveolus consists of a single layer of epithelial cells, most of which are type I cells. These squamous cells are involved in gas exchange. Type II cells are cuboidal cells that secrete surfactant to prevent the alveoli from collapsing. The alveolar walls are perforated by pores that connect adjacent alveoli, providing an alternate route for the passage of air in case of blocked ducts. The outer surfaces are covered with a network of capillaries. The basement membrane of a capillary fuses with the alveolar basement membrane to form the **respiratory membrane** (which also includes the capillary and alveolar epithelial cells).

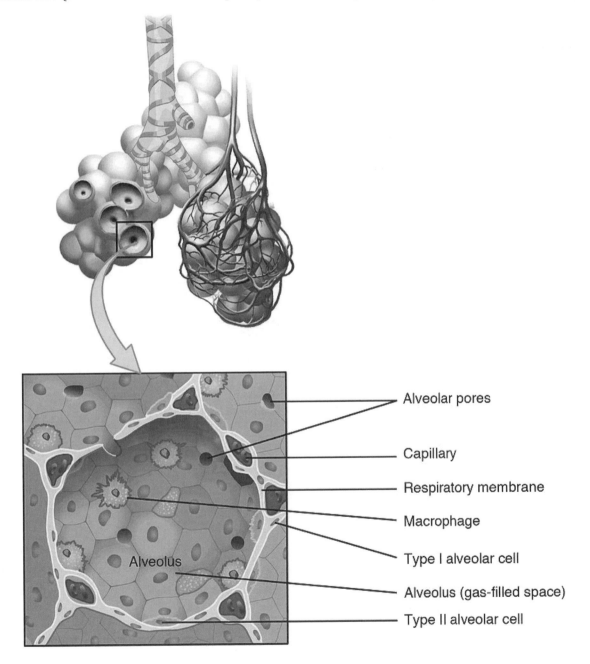

Science

101

BREATHING MECHANISMS

The diaphragm is a thin, dome-shaped muscle that separates the abdominal cavity from the thoracic cavity. This muscle, along with the external and internal intercostal muscles of the rib cage, is responsible for changing the volume, and therefore the pressure, of air in the lungs. This mechanism of breathing follows **Boyle's law**: the pressure and volume of a gas have an inverse relationship, assuming the temperature is constant.

When the diaphragm and external intercostals contract, the volume of the thoracic cavity increases, and the rib cage and sternum elevate and expand outward. The increase in volume results in a decrease in intrapleural pressure, and air enters the lungs in a process called **inspiration**. This is called **negative-pressure breathing** because the pressure in the lungs is lower than atmospheric pressure (and gases move down the pressure gradient). **Expiration** is usually a more passive process, and it is achieved by simply relaxing the same muscles that facilitated inhalation. As the volume of the thoracic cavity decreases, intrapleural pressure increases, and air leaves the lungs. Air can be forcibly pushed out through the contraction of the internal intercostals and abdominal muscles.

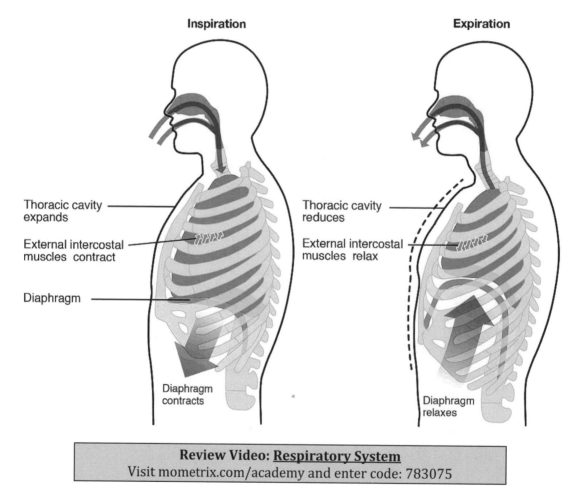

Review Video: Respiratory System
Visit mometrix.com/academy and enter code: 783075

CARDIOVASCULAR SYSTEM

FUNCTIONS

The circulatory system is primarily associated with the transport of oxygen, nutrients, hormones, ions, and fluids throughout the body, as well as the removal of metabolic wastes. In cellular respiration, glucose is burned or combined with oxygen as shown in the following equation:

$$C_6H_{12}O_6 \text{ (glucose)} + 6O_2 \text{ (oxygen)} \rightarrow 6CO_2 \text{ (carbon dioxide)} + 6H_2O \text{ (water)}$$

Oxygen moves down its partial pressure gradient from the air into the blood of the alveolar capillaries, where most of it binds to hemoglobin molecules in the red blood cells. A small amount dissolves in the blood. Without oxygen, cells would be unable to transfer the energy in glucose to ATP during cellular respiration.

The carbon dioxide that is produced during cellular respiration is transported away from tissues and diffuses out of the alveolar capillaries. Like oxygen, carbon dioxide can dissolve in blood or bind to hemoglobin, but most travels in the form of bicarbonate ions. Other metabolic waste products such as urea are brought to the kidneys to be filtered. The kidneys also help to regulate the levels of fluids and ions in the blood.

Digested nutrients such as glucose, amino acids, and fats are circulated to target cells where they are absorbed. Hormones released by endocrine glands also reach their target cells in this way. Lipid-soluble molecules require the use of a carrier protein to be transported in blood.

ROLE IN THERMOREGULATION

The circulatory system plays an important role in thermoregulation. The human body maintains an average temperature of around 98.6 °F (37 °C), which is optimal for metabolic processes and defense against pathogens. Heat exchange occurs at the surface of the skin, where blood vessels can dilate or constrict in response to signals from the brain.

Sensory neurons called thermoreceptors detect changes in temperature and send impulses to the hypothalamus, which then sends signals to the effectors—the smooth muscles that surround cutaneous arterioles. If the body temperature is too warm, the smooth muscle relaxes, and the arterioles dilate. Vasodilation allows more blood to flow through the capillary beds near the surface of the skin, and more heat is lost to the surroundings. If the temperature is too cool, the smooth muscle contracts, and the arterioles constrict. Vasoconstriction reduces the volume of blood that flows near the body's surface, which minimizes heat loss to the surroundings. Sweating and shivering also help to control body temperature.

> **Review Video: Circulatory System**
> Visit mometrix.com/academy and enter code: 376581

THE HEART

The wall of the heart is a composed of three layers of tissue. The outer layer is the **epicardium**, which protects the heart and secretes lubricating serous fluid. The middle layer is the muscular **myocardium**, which contracts to pump blood. The innermost layer is the **endocardium**, which lines the chambers and valves.

The heart is a four-chambered organ. The superior "receiving" chambers are the atria. The **right atrium** receives blood from the vena cava, and the **left atrium** receives blood from the pulmonary veins. The muscular "discharging" chambers are the ventricles. The **right ventricle** pumps blood into the pulmonary trunk, and the **left ventricle** pumps blood into the aorta.

The **tricuspid valve** (also called the right atrioventricular valve, or right AV valve) prevents backflow into the atrium when the ventricle contracts. The **pulmonary semilunar valve** prevents the return of blood into the right ventricle. The **bicuspid valve** (also called the left AV valve, or mitral valve) prevents blood from entering the left atrium when the ventricle contracts. The aortic semilunar valve stops the backflow of blood into the left ventricle as it leaves through the aorta.

The path of blood through the heart is traced in the diagram below:

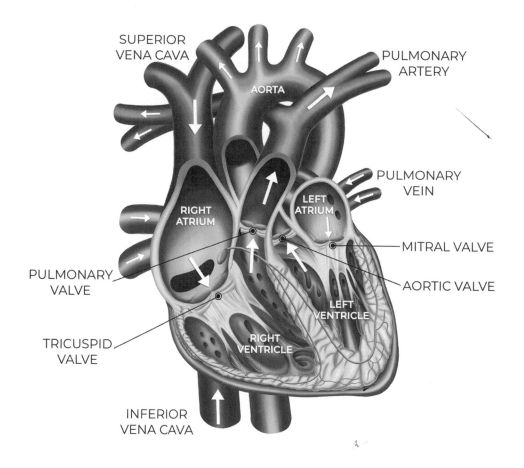

ENDOTHELIAL CELLS

The thin inner lining of blood vessels (and the lymphatic vessels) is called the **endothelium**. This tissue lines the entire circulatory system, including the interior of the heart. It is composed of a single layer of squamous endothelial cells that are connected by tight junctions and adherens junctions. This allows the endothelium to act as a selectively permeable barrier between the blood and the surrounding tissue, though some vessels have pores and gaps that allow the passage of larger molecules. The smoothness of the endothelium reduces friction between the blood and the vessel wall. Endothelial cells also play a role in vasoconstriction by releasing peptides called endothelins that cause the smooth muscle within the vessel walls to contract. They also secrete chemicals that inhibit the coagulation of blood, but if the endothelium is damaged, they release different chemicals required for clot formation.

contracts   *relat*

SYSTOLIC AND DIASTOLIC PRESSURE

Blood pressure is the force per unit area that is exerted by the blood on the walls of the vessels. Unless otherwise indicated, blood pressure refers specifically to the pressure within the major arteries, since arterioles, capillaries, venules, and veins have progressively less pressure. Blood pressure is often expressed as two numbers and in units of millimeters of mercury (mmHg). The first number refers to the **systolic pressure**, or the maximum pressure that is exerted during **systole**. During this time, the ventricles contract, forcing blood into the aorta and pulmonary trunk. As the blood enters the arteries, the elastic walls stretch to accommodate the increased volume, and then return to their normal diameter during **diastole**. Diastole is the period in which the ventricles relax and blood pressure is at its lowest point. The normal average blood pressure for an adult at rest is 120/80 mmHg, where 120 is the systolic bp, and 80 is the diastolic bp. High blood pressure can damage the walls of the blood vessels and increase the risk of heart disease, heart failure, and stroke. Low blood pressure is only concerning if it occurs suddenly, or if it causes noticeable symptoms such as lightheadedness or fainting.

SYSTEMIC AND PULMONARY CIRCULATION

The **systemic circuit** carries blood from the muscular left ventricle of the heart to the aorta, which gives rise to the arteries that eventually branch into arterioles and then the capillary beds within the tissues of the body. Oxygen and nutrients enter the tissues, and carbon dioxide and other wastes enter the blood. Deoxygenated blood leaves the capillary beds through venules, which merge into larger veins. The blood then enters the right atrium through the superior and inferior vena cava. Because this circuit is much longer than the pulmonary circuit, blood pressure is *higher*. Unlike the pulmonary circuit, blood in the arteries carries *more* oxygen than blood in the veins. When oxygen levels are low, vessels dilate to promote blood flow to tissues that need it.

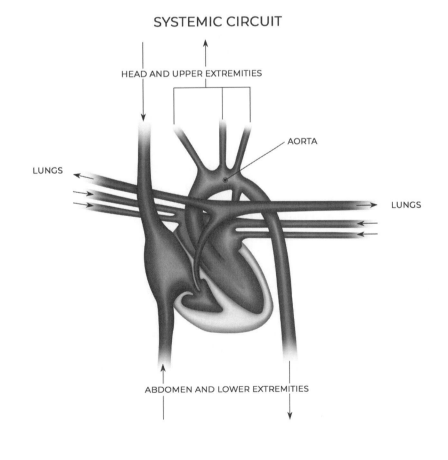

SYSTEMIC CIRCUIT

HEAD AND UPPER EXTREMITIES

AORTA

LUNGS

LUNGS

ABDOMEN AND LOWER EXTREMITIES

Science

The **pulmonary circuit** is the part of the circulatory system that carries blood from the heart to the lungs and back to the heart. When deoxygenated blood is expelled from the right ventricle, it moves through the pulmonary trunk, which bifurcates into the right and left pulmonary arteries. Each branch extends into the lungs, eventually giving rise to arterioles and then the capillaries where gas exchange occurs by diffusion. Oxygenated blood leaves the capillaries through venules which fuse into veins, finally merging into four pulmonary veins that return blood to the left atrium. Note that in the pulmonary circuit, the arteries have *less* oxygen than the veins. Low blood oxygen in the pulmonary circuit triggers vasoconstriction, which redirects blood to better ventilated parts of the lung.

PULMONARY CIRCUIT

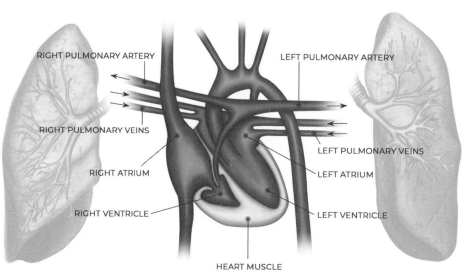

ELECTRICAL CONDUCTION SYSTEM

The electrical conduction system of the heart generates and propagates the electrical impulses that sustain the rhythmic electrical contractions of the heart. The entire system is composed of the sinoatrial (SA) and atrioventricular (AV) nodes and the internodal pathways, the Bundle of His, as well as the right and left bundle branches and the anterior and posterior fascicles. First, the SA node generates a spontaneous electrical impulse that stimulates atrial contraction, corresponding to the P wave on the ECG. Next, the electrical impulse reaches the AV node and slows in velocity. This corresponds to the PR segment on the ECG. The electrical impulse travels through the Bundle of His and the bundle branches, then to the Purkinje fibers. The Purkinje fibers carry the electrical impulse that stimulate the ventricles to depolarize and contract, corresponding to the QRS complex.

ELECTROCARDIOGRAMS

CARDIAC CYCLE AND THE ECG RELATIONSHIP

Each heart beat is seen as three major waves or complexes on an ECG. The heart rhythm begins in the sinoatrial node and leads to atrial depolarization. The P wave represents depolarization of the atria on an ECG. This is followed by the QRS interval, which represents depolarization of the ventricle. Next follows the ST segment and T wave, corresponding to repolarization of the ventricle. A small U wave may follow the T wave and represents further repolarization of the ventricle.

The first phase of the cardiac cycle is seen as the **P wave** on the ECG and corresponds to the wave of depolarization that spreads from the sinoatrial node to the atria, representing activation of the atria. The normal length of the P wave is 0.08 to 0.1 seconds in duration. The appearance of the P wave is smooth and round. The first segment of the P wave represents activation, or contraction, of the right atrium, followed by activation of the left atrium. The activation of the atrioventricular node is represented by the middle of the P wave. Absent P waves may suggest certain arrhythmias.

The **Q wave** is seen as a negative wave on an ECG, marking the beginning of the QRS complex. A normal duration of the Q wave is small, but the actual value will depend on which lead is used to measure the wave in an ECG. However, this value may often be less than 0.03 seconds. An enlarged Q wave suggests abnormal conduction in the ventricles or a myocardial infarction.

The **R wave** is a positive wave on an ECG and is the predominant portion of the QRS complex. It may or may not be preceded by a Q wave. If a second positive wave is seen following the R wave, it is termed the R' wave. The **S wave** is a negative wave that follows the R wave in the QRS complex seen on an ECG. Together with the Q wave, the R and S waves represent ventricular depolarization.

The **T wave** is a positive wave following the S wave on the ECG that represents ventricular repolarization, or recovery of the ventricle. It is the final major wave of the cardiac cycle seen on an ECG. It is longer than the QRS complex, indicating that repolarization takes longer than depolarization during the cardiac cycle. The T wave is smooth and round, similar in shape to the P wave. Abnormal T waves may indicate heart disease or electrolyte imbalances. The T wave may be followed by a small **U wave** that still represents the final repolarization of the ventricles.

PR INTERVAL

The PR interval on an ECG represents the period from the beginning of atrial depolarization to the beginning of ventricular depolarization. The PR interval also includes activation of the bundle of His and bundle branches. The PR interval is measured from the beginning of the P wave to the beginning of the QRS complex. A normal PR interval ranges from 0.12 to 0.20 seconds. If the PR interval is shorter than 0.12 seconds, the heart is said to have "accelerated conduction." If a first-degree AV block or heart block is present, the interval is longer than 0.20 seconds. The PR interval may also vary with heart rate, decreasing in length as heart rate increases. Further, the PR interval increases with age, being short in childhood and lengthening into adulthood.

QRS COMPLEX

Together, the Q, R, and S waves comprise the QRS complex that indicates depolarization, or activation, of both the right and left ventricles. A normal QRS complex is 0.06 to 0.1 seconds in duration. This indicates that ventricular depolarization occurs very rapidly. A long QRS interval suggests impaired conduction in the ventricles. The Q wave precedes the R wave on an ECG and is a negative wave. The R wave is a positive wave.

The S wave is a negative wave, seen after the R wave in an ECG. On an ECG, the shape of the QRS complex will change depending on which recording electrodes are used. In some instances, all three waves (Q, R, and S) are not visible.

ST SEGMENT

The ST segment follows the QRS interval and corresponds to the period in which the ventricle is completely depolarized. It is measured from the end of the QRS complex to the beginning of the T wave. This approximately corresponds to the plateau phase of the action potential. The J point is the junction of the QRS complex and the ST segment. This point is usually a 90° angle with the S wave.

The ST segment may be depressed or elevated and can be used to diagnose ventricular ischemia or hypoxia.

QT Interval

The QT interval represents the entire action potential, the time for both ventricular depolarization and repolarization. The normal QT interval lasts 0.2 to 0.4 seconds. At increased heart rates, this interval shortens. Long QT intervals may be indicative of arrhythmias.

Measuring Heart Rate

Heart rate can easily be calculated on ECG graph paper if the heartbeat occurs at regular intervals. Usually, there are the same number of P waves and QRS complexes and they occur at regular intervals. To calculate the heart rate, simply count the number of horizontal squares on the graph paper between recurring waves or cycles. Counting the number of cardiac cycles in six seconds and multiplying this number by 10 may also determine heart rate.

If the heart rate is less than 100 beats per minute, only the large squares on the ECG graph paper need to be counted to determine time. If, however, the heart rate is greater than 100 beats per minute, it is best to consider the smaller squares when measuring the time interval.

Cardiac Arrhythmias

Cardiac arrhythmias, abnormal heart beats, in adults are frequently the result of damage to the conduction system during major cardiac surgery or as the result of a myocardial infarction.

Bradyarrhythmias are pulse rates that are abnormally slow:

- **Complete atrioventricular block** (AV block) may be congenital or a response to surgical trauma.
- **Sinus bradycardia** may be caused by the autonomic nervous system or a response to hypotension and decrease in oxygenation.
- **Junctional/nodal rhythms** often occur in post-surgical patients when the absence of the P wave is noted but heart rate and output usually remain stable. Unless there is compromise, usually no treatment is necessary.

Tachyarrhythmias are pulse rates that are abnormally fast:

- **Sinus tachycardia** is often caused by fever and infection.
- **Supraventricular tachycardia** (200-300 BPM) may have a sudden onset and result in congestive heart failure.

Conduction irregularities are irregular pulses that often occur post-operatively and are usually not significant.

Premature contractions may arise from the atria or ventricles.

ARTERIAL AND VENOUS SYSTEMS (ARTERIES, ARTERIOLES, VENULES, VEINS)

The walls of all blood vessels (except the capillaries) consist of three layers: the innermost **tunica intima**, the **tunica media** consisting of smooth muscle cells and elastic fibers, and the outer **tunica adventitia**.

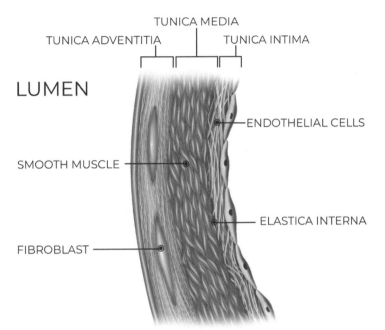

Vessel	Structure	Function
Elastic arteries	Includes the aorta and major branches. Tunica media has more elastin than any other vessels. They are the largest vessels in the arterial system.	Stretch when blood is forced out of the heart, and recoil under low pressure.
Muscular arteries	Includes the arteries that branch off of the elastic arteries. Tunica media has a higher proportion of smooth muscle cells, and fewer elastic fibers as compared to elastic arteries.	Regulate blood flow by vasoconstriction/vasodilation.
Arterioles	Tiny vessels that lead to the capillary beds. Tunica media is thin but composed of almost entirely smooth muscle cells.	Primary vessels involved in vasoconstriction/vasodilation. Control blood flow to capillaries.
Venules	Tiny vessels that exit the capillary beds. Thin, porous walls; few muscle cells and elastic fibers	Empty blood into larger veins.
Veins	Thin tunica media and tunica intima, wide lumen, valves prevent backflow of blood.	Carry blood back to the heart.

PRESSURE AND FLOW CHARACTERISTICS

Blood pressure is highest in the main arteries of the systemic circuit, particularly the aorta. The pressure decreases progressively as blood flows through the arterioles, capillaries, venules, and veins. The blood pressure is lowest in the vena cava. The steepest *drop* in blood pressure (as opposed to absolute pressure) occurs at the arterioles. The large reduction in diameter from artery to arteriole results in an increase in resistance as blood moves against the vessel wall. This slows down the flow of blood, and decreases the pressure.

Blood flow can be described as turbulent or laminar. **Turbulence** is an unsteady, swirling flow of blood that can occur during periods of high velocity, when the blood encounters an obstruction, or when the vessels take a sharp turn or narrow suddenly. Turbulent flow usually produces sounds, while laminar flow is silent. **Laminar flow** is the steady, streamlined flow of blood that occurs throughout most of the circulatory system.

CAPILLARY BEDS
MECHANISMS OF GAS AND SOLUTE EXCHANGE

Capillaries have only a single layer of endothelial cells that rest on a basement membrane. Capillary beds are groups of interconnected capillaries that facilitate the exchange of gas and solutes between the blood and interstitial fluid. Nutrients and oxygen enter the interstitial fluid, and carbon dioxide and other wastes enter the capillary blood. Gases and lipid-soluble substances can cross the endothelial cell membranes by simple diffusion, but ions and large particles often require the help of transport proteins or vesicular transport. Sometimes materials move through **intercellular clefts**: channels between adjacent endothelial cells. Capillaries with a nonporous continuous endothelium are called **continuous capillaries**. These are the most common types of capillaries in the body, and also the most impermeable. **Fenestrated capillaries** have pores that increase their permeability and are found in the kidneys and small intestine. **Sinusoidal capillaries** have a discontinuous endothelium that permits the passage of large particles and even blood cells. They are the most permeable of the capillaries.

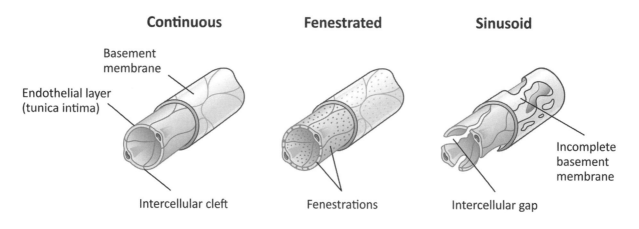

SOURCE OF PERIPHERAL RESISTANCE

Peripheral resistance is the resistance of the vessels to the flow of blood as a result of friction. As resistance increases, the rate of blood flow decreases. The main factors that affect peripheral resistance are diameter and length of the vessel and volume and viscosity of the blood.

Resistance is most affected by changes in the *diameter* of the vessel. The relationship is inverse; as the radius decreases, the resistance increases proportionally to the fourth power of the radius. For example, if the radius of a blood vessel is cut in half due to the buildup of plaque, resistance increases by a factor of 16. As such, vasoconstriction and vasodilation are critical to maintaining the appropriate level of resistance and flow. As *length* of the vessel increases, the resistance increases proportionally due to the increased surface area. As a person gains weight, the new blood vessels that nourish the new adipose tissue cause the total resistance of the system to increase. Blood volume and blood viscosity are usually not subject to sudden changes, but the effects of such changes are fairly intuitive. A decrease in either of these factors results in a decrease in resistance and an increase in flow rate.

COMPOSITION OF BLOOD

PLASMA, CHEMICALS, BLOOD CELLS

Blood is a mixture of plasma, chemicals, and blood cells. The clear, straw-colored liquid portion that makes up 55% of the blood is called plasma, and the remaining 45% consists of formed elements: red and white blood cells and platelets.

Plasma is a solution of water, plasma proteins (albumin, antibodies, clotting proteins), carbohydrates, amino acids, lipids, vitamins, salts, gases, hormones, and waste products. About 92% of plasma is water. Most of the cells in the blood are **red blood cells** (RBCs, or erythrocytes). These biconcave cells lack organelles, leaving room for hemoglobin—a protein to which oxygen and carbon dioxide can bind. The percentage of red blood cells by volume is called **hematocrit** and averages about 42% for women and 46% for men. Less than 1% of blood consists of white blood cells and platelets. White blood cells (WBCs, or leukocytes) are the only blood cells with nuclei. Unlike RBCs, they are not confined to the blood and can move in and out of vessels. There are many types of WBCs, and all are specialized to fight pathogens in different ways. **Platelets** (thrombocytes) are cell fragments that initiate clotting, and they outnumber WBCs about 40:1.

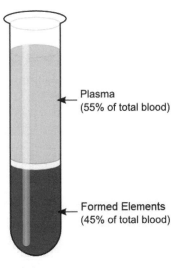

Plasma
(55% of total blood)

Formed Elements
(45% of total blood)

ERYTHROCYTE PRODUCTION AND DESTRUCTION

Erythropoiesis (the production of red blood cells) occurs in the red bone marrow. When oxygen levels are low, the hormone **erythropoietin** (produced by the kidneys and liver) targets the marrow, stimulating **myeloid stem cells** to differentiate into **erythroblasts**. These immature RBCs divide many times, filling up with newly synthesized hemoglobin. The nuclei condense and are ejected along with other organelles until only some endoplasmic reticulum remains. These cells are called **reticulocytes**, and they are released into the blood. After 1-2 days, the rest of the endoplasmic reticulum is lost, and mature **erythrocytes** are formed. Note that these cells are incapable of division.

After about 120 days, old and damaged RBCs are recognized and engulfed by phagocytes that are concentrated in the liver, spleen, and bone marrow. Hemoglobin is broken down into its four globin polypeptide chains and heme groups. Amino acids are released from the chains and enter the blood. The iron within the heme groups is either stored as ferritin in the liver or returned to the marrow to make more hemoglobin. The rest of the heme group is degraded to bilirubin and excreted in the bile.

LEUKOCYTES (WHITE BLOOD CELLS)

Lymphocytes are a special type of white blood cell that play an important role in the immune system. B cells and T cells are the two types of lymphocytes.

A **monocyte** is another type of white blood cell. These cells are characterized by a well-defined nucleus. They play an important role in the body's immune response to pathogens. These cells are also produced in the bone marrow.

A **granulocyte** is a type of white blood cell that has granules in its cytoplasm. These granules are released in response to certain infections and allergens. There are several types of granulocytes: basophils, eosinophils, neutrophils and mast cells. Some categorizations of granulocytes merge mast cells into the basophil category, though they are in fact two separate types of granulocytes.

Approximately 75% of all white blood cells are granulocytes. The types of granulocytes are distinguished by their ability to be stained with various types of stains in the laboratory. Basophils are stained black by basic stains, eosinophils are stained red by acid stains, neutrophils are stained pale lilac by neutral pH stains, and mast cells are stained red/purple by toluidine blue stains. Basophils play an important role in allergies and allergic reactions, as well as in inflammation. Eosinophils play an important part in the defense against infection by parasites in addition to responding to allergens by inducing inflammation, and neutrophils take part in the defense against infection from microorganisms.

Leukocyte	Maturation Series
Granulocytes:	Myeloid progenitor
	Myeloblast (10-20 mm): Oval nucleus with no granules evident in cytoplasm
	Promyelocyte (10-20 mm): Granules in cytoplasm
	Myelocyte (10-18 mm): Large oval nucleus; primary granules evident but secondary more prevalent
	Metamyelocyte (10-18 mm): Kidney-shaped nucleus with primary and secondary (most prevalent) granules
	Band: U-shaped nucleus, secondary or neutrophilic or basophils granules most common
	Segmented cells (14 mm): 2-5 joined lobes
Monocyte:	Myeloid progenitor
	Monoblast (12-20 mm) with large oval nucleus and lymphoid dendritic cells
	Promonocyte (from monoblast)
	Monocyte
	Macrophage and myeloid dendritic cell
Lymphocyte:	Common lymphoid progenitor
	Lymphoblast (10-20 mm) with large round nucleus
	Prolymphocyte
	Small lymphocyte and natural killer cell
	B and T lymphocytes (from small lymphocyte)

BLOOD TYPES

In the ABO blood group, there are 4 main blood types as follows: A, B, O, and AB. These blood types are categorized based on whether or not A and B red cell antigens are present. Individuals with blood type A have A antigens. Individuals with blood type B have B antigens. Individuals with blood type AB have A and B antigens. Individuals with blood type O have neither A nor B antigens. Blood also contains antibodies to the antigens. Individuals with type A blood produce anti-B antibodies. The opposite is true of individuals with type B blood. Individuals with type AB blood produce no antibodies. Those with type O blood produce anti-A and anti-B antibodies. In the Rhesus group of blood types an individual is either positive or negative for the Rh factor. The Rh factor is an antigenic substance.

COAGULATION AND CLOTTING MECHANISMS

When a blood vessel is damaged, the smooth muscle constricts at the site of injury and platelets adhere to the exposed collagen of the vessel wall. The platelets develop spine-like projections and release chemicals to attract other platelets and promote further vasoconstriction. A plug is formed as platelets aggregate, but this is rarely a sufficient fix without the coagulation of the blood.

There are two clotting mechanisms: extrinsic and intrinsic. In the extrinsic clotting mechanism, damaged tissue releases thromboplastin, which triggers a cascade of reactions that results in the production of an enzyme called prothrombin activator. Prothrombin activator is also produced by the slower-acting *intrinsic* clotting mechanism. When blood encounters a foreign substance or tissue, the Hageman factor (also called coagulation factor XII) is activated, leading to the production of prothrombin activator. From here, the clotting pathways are the same. Prothrombin activator converts prothrombin to thrombin using calcium as a cofactor. Thrombin splits fibrinogen to form fibrin but also stimulates its own production (a positive feedback loop). Fibrin is a fibrous protein that forms a mesh-like network that traps more platelets and red blood cells. This forms a clot that seals the injured region of the blood vessel.

> **Review Video: The Coagulation Profile**
> Visit mometrix.com/academy and enter code: 423595

OXYGEN TRANSPORT BY BLOOD

Almost all oxygen is transported by molecules of **hemoglobin** (Hb) that are found within erythrocytes, though 1.5% of blood oxygen is dissolved in the plasma. Hemoglobin has a protein component and a heme component. The protein component consists of four polypeptide chains known as globin (two alpha chains and two beta chains). Associated with each chain is a heme group that gives blood its red color. The heme group consists of a single iron atom surrounded by a complex organic ring called **protoporphyrin**. When blood passes through the capillaries of the lungs, it picks up oxygen. Each iron atom binds a molecule of oxygen—so one hemoglobin can bind up to four molecules of oxygen, and each erythrocyte carries around 250 million molecules of hemoglobin. The oxygenated form of hemoglobin is called **oxyhemoglobin**.

Hemoglobin can also transport up to four carbon dioxide molecules, though CO_2 binds to amino acids within the globin, not iron. Only about 23% of carbon dioxide is transported in this form, known as **carbaminohemoglobin**. Roughly 70% travels in the form of bicarbonate ions (as seen in the bicarbonate buffer system), and the rest is dissolved in the plasma.

NERVOUS AND ENDOCRINE CONTROL

Heart rate and blood pressure are greatly influenced by the nervous and endocrine systems. The sympathetic division of the autonomic nervous system increases the heart rate by releasing norepinephrine (NE), which acts on the SA node of the heart. The parasympathetic division has the opposite effect. The vagus nerves that innervate the heart release acetylcholine (ACh), which slows the heart rate. Central and peripheral chemoreceptors also help to regulate heart rate by monitoring levels of pH, carbon dioxide, and oxygen.

Blood pressure is regulated by baroreceptors in the aortic arch and carotid arteries (both of which detect high blood pressure) and also the venae cavae, pulmonary veins, and atrial walls (all of which detect low blood pressure). When high blood pressure is detected, the blood vessels dilate and heart rate decreases to restore homeostasis. Blood pressure is also regulated by hormones of the endocrine system. When blood pressure drops, the kidneys secrete a hormone called renin which initiates a series of reactions that ultimately cause the release of aldosterone from the adrenal glands. Aldosterone promotes the reabsorption of water, increasing the plasma volume.

DIGESTIVE SYSTEM

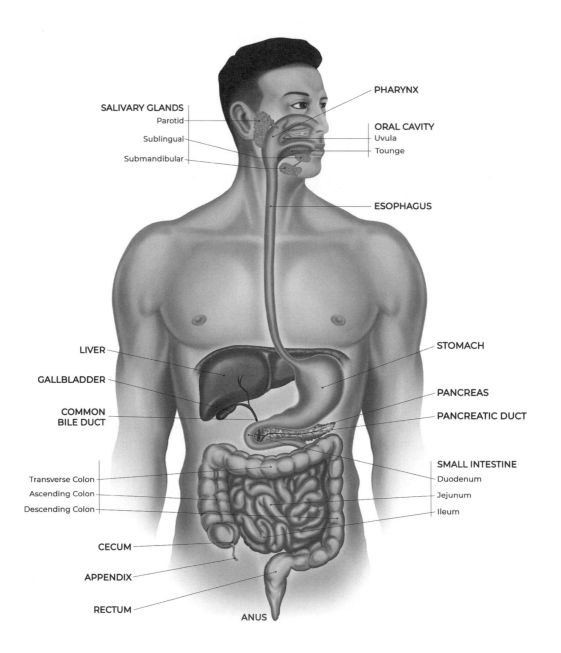

Mechanical digestion begins in the mouth with the voluntary act of chewing (mastication). Skeletal muscles of the mouth and pharynx aid in swallowing (deglutition), which consists of three phases: the voluntary buccal phase and the involuntary pharyngeal and esophageal phases. The muscularis externa of the digestive tract consists two layers of muscle tissue (three in the stomach) that contract radially and then relax to squeeze food in one direction. This involuntary propulsive process is called **peristalsis**. Peristalsis moves food from the pharynx to the esophagus to the stomach where an extra muscle layer helps to churn and mix the food. Another involuntary process called **segmentation** occurs in the intestines, in addition to peristalsis. In segmentation, non-adjacent portions of the digestive tract contract and relax to move the chyme, partly digested food, back and forth. Haustral contractions in the large intestine are a form of segmentation that moves chyme from one haustrum to the next. Mass peristalsis describes the movements that occur two to four times a day to push large amounts of chyme toward the rectum. Movement along the digestive tract is also controlled by the gastroesophageal sphincter, pyloric sphincter, and anal sphincters.

INGESTION

When food is ingested, it is immediately moistened by saliva. This lubricating fluid is secreted by hundreds of minor salivary glands that are scattered throughout the oral cavity and three pairs of major salivary glands: the parotid, submandibular, and sublingual glands.

Saliva contains a variety of solutes, many of which are enzymes. **Salivary amylase** begins the chemical breakdown of polysaccharides into simpler sugars, and **lingual lipase** begins the breakdown of fats. The effects of salivary enzymes are minimal, however, compared to the digestion that occurs later in the stomach and small intestine. Saliva contains antimicrobial agents as well. **Lysozyme** is an enzyme that works together with immunoglobulin A to break down the cell walls of many bacteria. Other components of saliva include bicarbonate ions that help the saliva to maintain a pH that is optimal for salivary enzymes, as well as other ions. **Mucin** is a protein that helps to form a gel-like coating that lubricates the bolus of food.

ESOPHAGUS AND TRANSPORT FUNCTION

The esophagus is a 25-cm tube extending from the pharynx to the stomach that functions as a passageway for food. It is not involved in digestion or absorption of nutrients, but it does secrete mucus to lubricate the esophagus and aid in the transport of food. The esophagus (and the alimentary canal that follows) has a wall that consists of four layers: the mucosa, submucosa, muscularis externa, and adventitia. Most of the digestive tract has a muscularis externa made of smooth muscle tissue, but the upper third of the esophagus is composed of skeletal muscle and is under voluntary control. The middle portion is a mixture of both skeletal and smooth muscle, and the lower third is entirely smooth muscle. Food does not simply "fall" into the stomach; it is pushed along by **peristalsis**, an involuntary process in which the muscles in the wall of the digestive organ rhythmically contract and relax. The upper esophageal sphincter at the superior end of the esophagus and the lower esophageal sphincter at the inferior end control the passage of food by contracting and relaxing.

STOMACH
STORAGE AND CHURNING OF FOOD

The stomach is a muscular organ that can stretch to accommodate a high volume of food. While some chemical digestion does occur, the primary role of the stomach is the storage and mechanical breakdown of food. The inner surface (mucosa) is folded into a series of ridges called rugae that allow the stomach to expand as it fills with food. The stomach holds about 1 liter after a typical meal, but can stretch to accommodate nearly four times that amount. It churns and pummels food for an average of three to four hours with the help of a third muscle layer in the muscularis externa that is unique to the stomach. As the food is mixed with gastric juices, it turns into a creamy paste called chyme. A valve called the pyloric sphincter regulates the passage of chyme into the small intestine.

PRODUCTION OF DIGESTIVE ENZYMES, SITE OF DIGESTION

The mucosa of the stomach contains gastric glands which open into numerous gastric pits. There are four types of cells in these glands: mucous cells, parietal cells, chief cells, and endocrine cells. **Endocrine cells** (G cells) release hormones such as gastrin into the blood and do not contribute to gastric juices. The rest of the glands are exocrine and secrete their products into the stomach.

115

Parietal cells secrete intrinsic factor, which is required for the absorption of vitamin B_{12} in the small intestine. They also release hydrochloric acid (HCl), which lowers the pH of gastric juice to an average range of 1 to 3. This acidic environment is required for the activation of pepsinogen, which is secreted by the **chief cells**. The active form of pepsinogen, called pepsin, is a digestive enzyme that breaks down proteins into smaller peptide chains. Chief cells also secrete gastric lipase, which continues the digestion of fats (though most fat and protein digestion occurs in the small intestine). The **mucous cells** secrete bicarbonate-containing mucus to protect the stomach from the acidity and digestive enzymes.

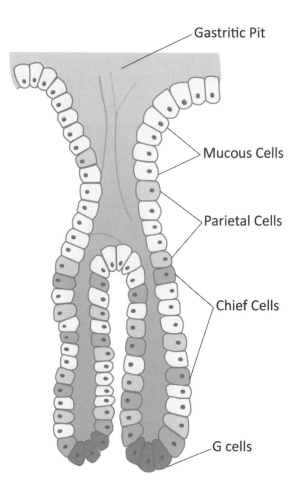

STRUCTURE (GROSS)

The stomach is a muscular organ located in the left superior region of the abdomen. The gastroesophageal sphincter (also called the lower esophageal or cardioesophageal sphincter) found at the junction between the esophagus and stomach helps to prevent the reflux of acidic contents. The stomach itself can be divided into four main parts: the cardiac region, the fundus, the body, and the pylorus. The **cardiac region** is the area where food is emptied into the stomach. The **fundus** is the most superior region of the stomach, and the **body** is the largest, most central region. The body curves toward the right to form a "J" shape, with a lesser curvature and a greater curvature. It then narrows into a funnel-shaped region called the **pylorus**. The wider end of the pylorus is called the pyloric antrum and the narrow portion is the pyloric canal. The pyloric sphincter is the valve that regulates the release of small amounts of chyme into the small intestine. Other features of the stomach include the gastric folds (rugae) of the mucosa that allow the stomach to stretch and

116

expand. The stomach is also characterized by an inner oblique layer of smooth muscle that is not seen in the rest of the alimentary canal.

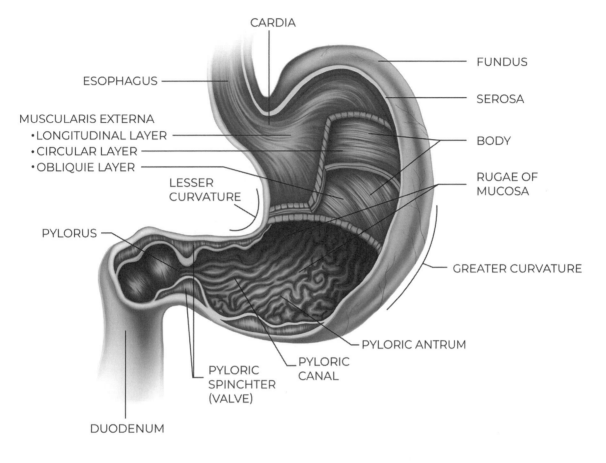

LIVER

ROLE IN THE GASTROINTESTINAL SYSTEM

The liver is an essential component of the gastrointestinal system but is not a part of the alimentary canal. This large, four-lobed organ acts as an accessory organ by performing many functions such as the production of bile, nutrient metabolism, and detoxification.

The primary digestive function of the liver is the synthesis of bile. **Bile** is a yellow-green solution of bile salts, pigments (mainly bilirubin from the breakdown of hemoglobin), cholesterol, and electrolytes. Only the bile salts play a role in digestion, and they do so mechanically (not enzymatically) by emulsifying fats into smaller globules called micelles that can be acted on by lipases in the small intestine. Bile also enhances the absorption of the fat-soluble vitamins A, D, E, and K. Liver cells synthesize bile salts from cholesterol.

Bile is stored and concentrated in the gallbladder. When food enters the small intestine, a hormone called cholecystokinin (CCK) signals the gallbladder to contract, and the bile is squeezed into the common bile duct. This duct joins with the pancreatic duct at the hepatopancreatic ampulla

(ampulla of Vater), and bile spills into the duodenum via the duodenal papilla. Bile can also flow directly from the liver to the duodenum.

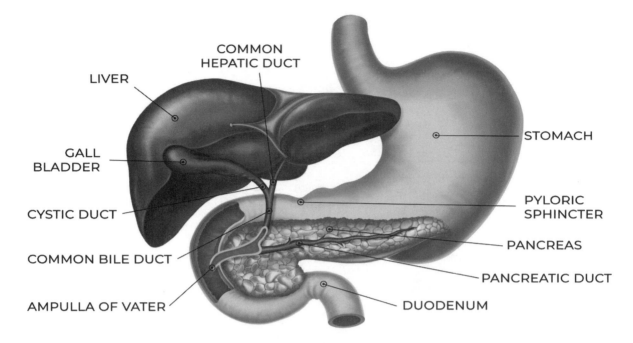

ROLE IN BLOOD GLUCOSE REGULATION, DETOXIFICATION

The liver performs many metabolic functions, including the regulation of blood glucose concentration (which averages 100 mg/dl). Blood from the digestive tract enters the liver through the hepatic portal vein. If the blood sugar is too high, the liver polymerizes glucose to form glycogen in a process called **glycogenesis**. If blood sugar is too low, liver cells break down stored glycogen and release glucose monomers in a process called **glycogenolysis**. In cases of prolonged fasting, the liver can produce glucose from non-carbohydrate sources such as proteins and fats. This is called **gluconeogenesis**.

The liver also has a vital role in detoxification. Ammonia (a toxic waste product of the metabolism of amino acids) is converted to urea in the liver and excreted by the kidneys. Hormones that are circulating in the blood are inactivated by the liver and eliminated by the kidneys as well. The liver also breaks down exogenous compounds, such as drugs and alcohol.

PANCREAS
PRODUCTION OF ENZYMES AND TRANSPORT OF ENZYMES TO SMALL INTESTINE

The **pancreas** is a triangular-shaped organ with both endocrine and exocrine functions. (As an endocrine gland, it releases insulin, glucagon, and somatostatin into the blood.) It is located below the stomach and extends from the duodenum to the spleen. Its role in digestion is the production and secretion of digestive juices. When chyme reaches the duodenum, enteroendocrine cells secrete cholecystokinin (CCK), which stimulates the acinar cells of the pancreas to release enzyme-rich juices. Secretin is secreted as well, which stimulates the duct cells to release a bicarbonate-rich solution that raises the pH. This provides the optimal environment for enzymes released by the pancreas. Pancreatic amylase digests starch, and pancreatic lipase digests fats. Proteases are released in their inactive form but are activated in the small intestine. These activated protein-digesting enzymes include trypsin, carboxypeptidases A and B, and chymotrypsin. Nucleases digest nucleic acids. Pancreatic juice is emptied into the main pancreatic duct, which merges with the common bile duct at the hepatopancreatic ampulla. Juices enter the duodenum at the duodenal papilla. There is also an accessory pancreatic duct that empties directly into the duodenum at the minor papilla.

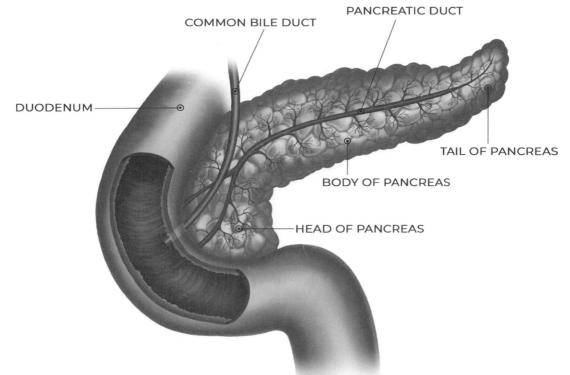

SMALL INTESTINE

The small intestine is a long tube that extends from the pyloric sphincter to the ileocecal valve. Pancreatic enzymes and enzymes of the small intestine continue the digestion of food so the nutrients are small enough to be absorbed. These enzymes (called brush border enzymes) are embedded in the **microvilli**: tiny folds of the apical cell membrane that increase surface area. The core of each microvillus consists of actin filaments that extend out from the cytoplasm. Finger-like projections of the mucosa (villi) and deep circular folds of the mucosa and submucosa (plicae circulares) also increase the surface area available for absorption.

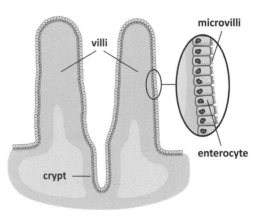

Absorption of water and food molecules occurs mostly in the jejunum and ileum of the small intestine. Amino acids and most sugars are taken into the intestinal cells using cotransport with sodium ions (secondary active transport). Lipid components and water are absorbed into the cells by simple diffusion. Short-chain fatty acids, sugars, amino acids, water, and electrolytes enter the bloodstream by diffusing into capillaries within the villi and traveling to the liver.

PRODUCTION OF ENZYMES, SITE OF DIGESTION AND NEUTRALIZATION OF STOMACH ACID

Most of the chemical digestion of food occurs in the small intestine. Brush border enzymes of the microvilli (as well as pancreatic enzymes) break down carbohydrates, fats, proteins, and nucleic acids into smaller components which are then absorbed. Some mechanical digestion occurs in the small intestine as well. Peristalsis moves chyme toward the small intestine, while segmentation pushes it back and forth to help mix enzymes into the chyme. Brunner's glands in the duodenum secrete bicarbonate-containing fluid that (with the help of alkaline pancreatic juice) neutralizes the acidic chyme, providing the optimal pH for enzyme activity.

Brush border enzymes and the substrates that they break down are summarized in the table below.

Brush border enzyme	Substrate
Dextrinase	Oligosaccharides
Glucoamylase	Oligosaccharides
Maltase	Maltose (disaccharide)
Lactase	Lactose (disaccharide)
Sucrase	Sucrose (disaccharide)
Aminopeptidase	Peptides
Dipeptidase	Dipeptides
Nucleosidase	Nucleotides
Phosphatase	Nucleotides

STRUCTURE (ANATOMIC SUBDIVISIONS)

The small intestine is subdivided into three regions: the duodenum, the jejunum, and the ileum. At about 25 cm, the C-shaped **duodenum** is the shortest segment, but it has the widest diameter. It receives chyme from the stomach and neutralizing digestive juices from the pancreas. Most of the chemical digestion of food occurs here. It does not play a large role in absorption, with the exception of iron. The **jejunum** is the main site of absorption. It averages 2.5 meters in length and is characterized by prominent plicae circulares, long villi, and dense microvilli. The longest segment of the small intestine is the **ileum**. It averages 3.5 meters in length, but is the narrowest in diameter. Small aggregates of lymphatic cells called Peyer's patches are common in this segment, but they can be found throughout the small intestine. The primary role of the ileum is to absorb vitamin B_{12}, bile salts, and any nutrients that were not absorbed by the jejunum. It has few circular folds, and they disappear altogether in the distal region. It terminates at the ileocecal valve, which controls the movement of chyme into the large intestine.

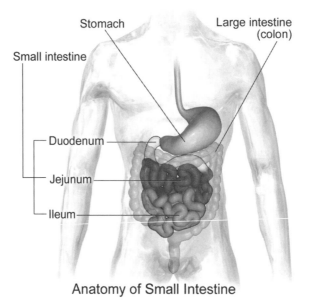

Anatomy of Small Intestine

120

LARGE INTESTINE

ABSORPTION OF WATER

The large intestine specializes in the absorption of vitamin K, biotin, sodium ions, chloride ions, and water. By the time chyme reaches the large intestine, most of the water (approximately 80%) has already been absorbed by the small intestine. As the chyme is pushed through the colon 90% of the remaining liquid is absorbed, leaving a mass of indigestible food, water, and bacteria. If the feces are excreted before enough water is absorbed, they leave as diarrhea. Constipation results when too much water is absorbed.

BACTERIAL FLORA

The large intestine does not secrete digestive enzymes, but there are hundreds of species of resident bacteria that can digest certain materials left in chyme. These beneficial microbes are nourished by small amounts of cellulose and other carbohydrates, and they release gases such as carbon dioxide and methane as waste products of fermentation. The bacteria also release vitamin K, biotin, thiamin, riboflavin, and vitamin B_{12}. Vitamin K (required for the synthesis of clotting proteins) and biotin (a cofactor for many enzymes) are absorbed for use in the body. Resident gut flora also help to keep populations of pathogenic bacteria in check. The appendix *may* serve as a reservoir for beneficial species of bacteria, though it is often infected with harmful microbes.

STRUCTURE (GROSS)

The large intestine is the portion of the alimentary canal that begins at the **ileocecal valve** and terminates at the anus. It is larger in diameter than the small intestine, but much shorter in length—averaging 1.5 meters. The first portion of the large intestine is a pouch called the **cecum**, and it receives chyme from the small intestine. It is also the site of a blind-ended tube called the **appendix**. The middle portion of the large intestine is the **colon**, which can be further subdivided into the ascending colon (right side of the body), transverse colon (extends across the abdominal cavity), descending colon (left side of the body), and sigmoid colon. The sigmoid colon lies in the pelvic cavity and becomes the **rectum**, which opens to the anus. There are no villi in the large intestine, but there are pouch-like sacculations called **haustra** that are separated by folds called plicae semilunares. These pouches are formed by the contraction of smooth muscle within the muscularis layer. The walls of the large intestine are lubricated by mucus, which is secreted by goblet cells.

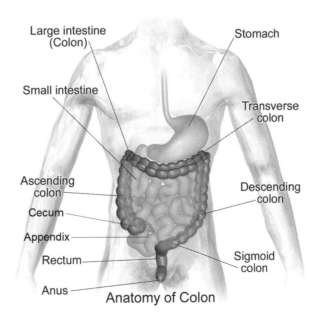

Anatomy of Colon

RECTUM: STORAGE AND ELIMINATION OF WASTE, FECES

The final 12 to 15 cm of the large intestine is called the rectum. In humans, it curves to conform to the shape of the sacrum and coccyx bone. The **anal canal** is the last portion of the rectum, and it ends with an involuntary internal sphincter and a voluntary external sphincter. A dilated region (superior to the anal canal) called the **rectal ampulla** functions as a storage area for feces before they are eliminated in the process of defecation. Feces consist of bacteria, water, undigested material, epithelial cells, and bile (which accounts for the brown coloration). As this material accumulates, the walls of the rectum expand and stretch receptors send signals that cause the rectal muscles to contract, the internal sphincter to relax, and the external sphincter to contract. At this point, the decision can be made to eliminate or delay elimination.

THE ENTERIC NERVOUS SYSTEM

The network of neurons buried in the lining of the gastrointestinal tract that controls the function of the digestive system is called the **enteric nervous system** (ENS). The ENS can operate independently of the brain and spinal cord, and communicates with the CNS through the parasympathetic and sympathetic nervous systems. The parasympathetic nervous system stimulates digestive activities, while the sympathetic nervous system inhibits them.

The ENS is divided into two main parts: the submucosal and myenteric plexuses. The **submucosal plexus** is embedded in the connective tissue of the submucosa. It functions in regulating local secretions, absorption, contraction of submucosal muscle, and blood flow. The **myenteric plexus** is located between the circular and longitudinal layers of the muscularis externa. This network exerts control over the motility of the GI tract. It increases the tone, as well as the rate, intensity, and velocity of contractions.

> **Review Video: Gastrointestinal System**
> Visit mometrix.com/academy and enter code: 378740

NERVOUS SYSTEM
ORGANIZATION OF VERTEBRATE NERVOUS SYSTEM

The nervous system is divided into two main parts: the central nervous system (CNS), which consists of the brain and spinal cord, and the peripheral nervous system (PNS), which consists of nervous tissues (nerves, ganglia) that are outside the CNS. The **CNS** integrates sensory information, and the **PNS** sends information to and from the CNS, allowing it to communicate with the rest of the body. Afferent neurons of the PNS transmit impulses to the CNS, and efferent neurons transmit impulses to effectors.

The PNS is further divided into the autonomic system (ANS) and somatic nervous system (SNS). The **SNS** controls voluntary movements, such as the contraction of skeletal muscles. The **ANS** controls involuntary movements, such as the contraction of smooth and cardiac muscles, and glandular secretions. The ANS has two subdivisions that tend to work antagonistically (though there are exceptions). The **sympathetic division** activates the "fight or flight" response, preparing the body for action by increasing heart rate, dilating pupils and bronchial tubes, and suppressing functions that are not required for immediate survival. The **parasympathetic division** activates the "rest and digest" functions by decreasing heart rate, constricting pupils and bronchial tubes, and promoting digestion.

122

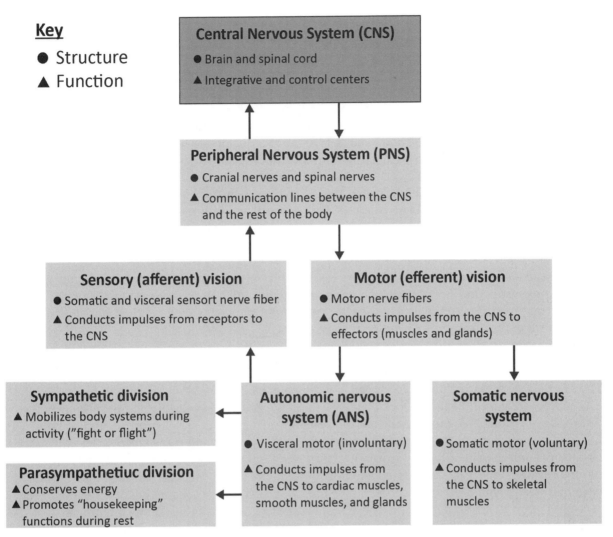

Key
- ● Structure
- ▲ Function

Central Nervous System (CNS)
- ● Brain and spinal cord
- ▲ Integrative and control centers

Peripheral Nervous System (PNS)
- ● Cranial nerves and spinal nerves
- ▲ Communication lines between the CNS and the rest of the body

Sensory (afferent) vision
- ● Somatic and visceral sensort nerve fiber
- ▲ Conducts impulses from receptors to the CNS

Motor (efferent) vision
- ● Motor nerve fibers
- ▲ Conducts impulses from the CNS to effectors (muscles and glands)

Sympathetic division
- ▲ Mobilizes body systems during activity ("fight or flight")

Parasympathetiuc division
- ▲ Conserves energy
- ▲ Promotes "housekeeping" functions during rest

Autonomic nervous system (ANS)
- ● Visceral motor (involuntary)
- ▲ Conducts impulses from the CNS to cardiac muscles, smooth muscles, and glands

Somatic nervous system
- ● Somatic motor (voluntary)
- ▲ Conducts impulses from the CNS to skeletal muscles

Science

SYMPATHETIC AND PARASYMPATHETIC NERVOUS SYSTEMS: ANTAGONISTIC CONTROL

The autonomic nervous system has two divisions, sympathetic and parasympathetic, and they tend to have antagonistic effects when they both innervate the same organ. Both divisions use a two-neuron pathway, consisting of a preganglionic neuron which runs from the CNS to a ganglion and a postganglionic neuron which innervates the effector.

The sympathetic nervous division is responsible for triggering the "fight or flight" response. Preganglionic neurons of the sympathetic nervous system release acetylcholine (ACh), which is the stimulus for the release of norepinephrine from postganglionic neurons. Norepinephrine acts on target tissues, prompting a rapid and unified response. The heart rate increases, respiration rate increases, blood flow to the heart and skeletal muscle increases, pupils dilate, and glycogen is broken down.

The parasympathetic nervous division is responsible for the "rest and digest" response. Both pre- and postganglionic neurons of the parasympathetic nervous system release acetylcholine. The parasympathetic nervous system stimulates events that are slower-paced, and less essential for immediate survival. Heart rate and respiration rate decrease, blood flow is directed to digestive organs, peristalsis is promoted, pupils constrict, and glycogen is synthesized.

SENSORY AND EFFECTOR NEURONS

Sensory neurons are the afferent neurons that deliver impulses to the CNS. They are sometimes classified by the type of stimulus that they respond to. **Mechanoreceptors** respond to changes in pressure or tension. Cutaneous touch receptors such as Meissner's corpuscles, Merkel's disks, Pacinian corpuscles, and Ruffini endings are all mechanoreceptors, as are the muscle spindles that detect stretching of skeletal muscle and the receptors of the inner ear that detect vibrations. **Chemoreceptors** such as olfactory and taste receptors detect the presence of chemicals. **Photoreceptors** such as the rod and cone cells of the eye respond to light. **Thermoreceptors** sense both absolute temperature and changes in temperature. **Nociceptors** detect pain.

Sensory neurons can also be categorized by location. **Exteroceptors** near the body surface transmit information about the external environment. **Proprioceptors** within the inner ear, skeletal muscles, and joints provide information about movement, position, and equilibrium. **Interoceptors** of visceral organs and blood vessels provide information about internal stimuli.

Once the sensory information has been processed, **effector neurons** (motor neurons) transmit the impulse away from the CNS to activate muscles and glands. All motor neurons of the somatic division run directly from the CNS to the effector without synapsing with another neuron. The autonomic division uses two-neuron pathways.

MAJOR FUNCTIONS

The nervous system is responsible for coordinating and controlling all of the activities of the body. It is composed of a complex network of neurons and the neuroglial cells that support them. Neurons are responsible for carrying out the **sensory**, **integrative**, and **motor** functions of the nervous system. Sensory receptors detect changes in the internal and external environment, such as pain, pressure, light, or temperature. During integration, the information is brought to the central nervous system where it is processed and interpreted. The motor function refers to the voluntary or involuntary response that is carried out by effectors, such as the contraction of a muscle, or the secretion of products by gland cells. These rapid responses are essential for the maintenance of homeostasis, heart rate, breathing, regulation of temperature, movement, sensations, memory, emotion, language, and more.

> **Review Video: The Nervous System**
> Visit mometrix.com/academy and enter code: 708428

HIGH LEVEL CONTROL AND INTEGRATION OF BODY SYSTEMS

The nervous system is responsible for the integration of body systems. The central nervous system (CNS) consists of the brain and spinal cord. It is considered the control/integration center because it combines sensory information from various sources. It communicates with the rest of the body via the peripheral nervous system (PNS). The **afferent** division of the PNS brings information *to* the CNS, and the **efferent** division delivers messages *from* the CNS to muscles or glands.

The nervous system works particularly closely with the endocrine system. Nerve impulses send information about the condition of the body to the hypothalamus, which regulates the release of hormones from the pituitary. The pituitary, or "master gland," controls other glands of the endocrine system. All body systems ultimately require direction from the nervous system to function properly and maintain homeostasis. Heart rate, digestion, body temperature, movement, and higher functions such as cognitive ability, memory, emotion, and fine motor skills are under the control of the nervous system.

ADAPTIVE CAPABILITY TO EXTERNAL INFLUENCES

The nervous system is the first body system to respond to changes in the environment. The receptors of afferent neurons (sensory neurons) are specialized to detect certain types of stimuli, and these neurons transmit action potentials to the CNS where a motor response may be called for. Sensory receptors are found nearly everywhere in the body. They can be classified by location, morphology (free vs. encapsulated nerve endings), the nature of the stimuli they detect (pressure, chemicals, light, temperature), and rate of adaptation.

Sensory adaptation refers to the change in sensitivity that occurs when receptors are exposed to a prolonged stimulus. Adaptation rates vary greatly across the different types of receptors, but they can be classified into two main groups. **Phasic** receptors quickly adapt to a constant stimulus, meaning that action potentials decrease over time and eventually stop. This explains the loss of sensation of clothes against the skin, or how an odor seems to disappear when the source is still present. Most tactile and chemoreceptors are phasic. **Tonic** receptors adapt slowly, constantly alerting the CNS of the stimulus with action potentials. Proprioceptors (receptors that provide feedback about position and movement of the body) are tonic receptors, as are photoreceptors (light-detecting receptors) and nociceptors (pain receptors).

CENTRAL NERVOUS SYSTEM

BRAIN

The brain consists of the hindbrain, midbrain, and forebrain. The **hindbrain** includes the medulla oblongata, cerebellum, and pons. The **midbrain** integrates sensory signals and orchestrates responses to these signals. The **forebrain** includes the cerebrum, thalamus, and hypothalamus. The **cerebral cortex** is a thin layer of grey matter covering the cerebrum. The brain is divided into two hemispheres, with each responsible for multiple functions. The brain is divided into four main lobes, the frontal lobe, the parietal lobe, the occipital lobe, and the temporal lobes. The **frontal lobe** located in the front of the brain is responsible for short term and working memory and information processing as well as decision-making, planning, and judgment. The **parietal lobe** is located slightly toward the back of the brain and the top of the head and is responsible for sensory input as well as spatial positioning of the body. The **occipital lobe** is located at the back of the head just above the brain stem. This lobe is responsible for visual input, processing, and output; nerves from the eyes enter directly into this lobe. Finally, the **temporal lobes** are located at the left and right sides of the brain. These lobes are responsible for all auditory input, processing, and output.

The **cerebellum** plays a role in the processing and storing of implicit memories. Specifically, for those memories developed during classical conditioning learning techniques. The role of the cerebellum was discovered by exploring the memory of individuals with damaged cerebellums. These individuals were unable to develop stimulus responses when presented via a classical conditioning technique. Researchers found that this was also the case for automatic responses. For example, when these individuals were presented with a puff of air into their eyes, they did not blink, which would have been the naturally occurring and automatic response in an individual with no brain damage.

The posterior area of the brain that is connected to the spinal cord is known as the **brain stem**. The midbrain, the pons, and the medulla oblongata are the three parts of the brain stem. Information from the body is sent to the brain through the brain stem, and information from the brain is sent to the body through the brain stem. The brain stem is an important part of respiratory, digestive, and circulatory functions.

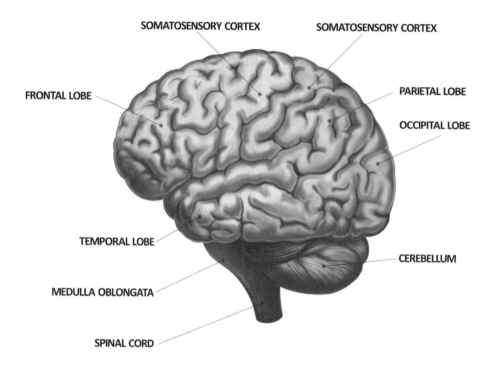

The **midbrain** lies above the pons and the medulla oblongata. The parts of the midbrain include the tectum, the tegmentum, and the ventral tegmentum. The midbrain is an important part of vision and hearing. The **pons** comes between the midbrain and the medulla oblongata. Information is sent across the pons from the cerebrum to the medulla and the cerebellum. The **medulla oblongata** (or medulla) is beneath the midbrain and the pons. The medulla oblongata is the piece of the brain stem that connects the spinal cord to the brain. So, it plays an important role with the autonomous nervous system in the circulatory and respiratory system.

Encased in cranial bones that form of base of the cavity and the skull cap the top, the **cranial cavity** contains the brain, the 12 cranial nerves, and the pituitary gland. The meninges (comprised of the dura mater, arachnoid mater, and pia mater) line the cavity and surround the brain and the spinal cord and contain cerebrospinal fluid between the arachnoid mater and pia mater in the subarachnoid space. The meninges and cerebrospinal fluid protect and cushion the dorsal cavity. The vascularized pia mater is adhered to the surface of the brain and the spinal cord. The middle layer, the arachnoid mater, contains connective tissue but not nerves or blood vessels. The enervated, vascularized dura mater is the outer layer that lies next to the bones and folds inward in places in the cavity and separates the brain into different compartments. The dura mater has two layers: the endosteal layer which lines the cranial bones and the meningeal layer which lines the vertebral cavity and lays beneath the endosteal layer.

CRANIAL NERVES

The cranial nerves are 12 pairs of nerves that come from the brain and brainstem and control the senses, muscles, and internal organs. Cranial nerve names, functions and types are as follows:

Nerve	What It Controls	Sensory/ Motor/Both
I. Olfactory	Smell	S
II. Optic	Sight	S
III. Oculomotor	Moves the eye up, down, left, right and diagonally; adjusts the pupil and lens of the eye	M
IV. Trochlear	Moves the eye up, down, left, right, and diagonally	M
V. Trigeminal	Largest of the cranial nerves; chewing, face sensation.	B
VI. Abducens	Moves the eye up, down, left, right, and diagonally	M
VII. Facial	Facial expression and anterior two-thirds of the tongue	B
VIII. Vestibulocochlear	Sound	S
IX. Glossopharyngeal	Swallowing, saliva, and taste	B
X. Vagus	Control of the peripheral nervous system	B
XI. Accessory	Swallowing and movement of the head and neck	M
XII. Hypoglossal	Speech and swallowing; tongue muscles	M

Mnemonic for nerve names: Oh, Once One Takes The Anatomy Final, Very Good Vacations Are Heavenly.

Mnemonic for whether nerves are sensory/motor/both: Some Say My Mother Bought My Brother Some Bad Beer, My, My.

SPINAL CORD

The spinal cord is a column of nerve fibers that connects the brain to the rest of the body. It is encased in the bony structure of the vertebrae, which protects and supports it. Its nervous tissue functions mainly with respect to limb movement and internal organ activity. Major nerve tracts ascend and descend from the spinal cord to the brain. The vertebrae and spinal cord are contained within the vertebral cavity. The meninges extend from the cranial cavity to enclose the vertebral cavity. The spinal cord is divided into 5 regions: cervical, thoracic, lumbar, sacral, and coccyx.

ROLE OF SPINAL CORD AND SUPRASPINAL CIRCUITS

The spinal cord is a major reflex center that connects the afferent and efferent pathways. It is made of an exterior layer of white matter that surrounds an interior core of grey matter. The white matter consists of glial cells and myelinated bundles of axons that form tracts to and from the brain. There are no cell bodies or dendrites in white matter. Grey matter consists mostly of interneurons, but also contains motor neurons and glial cells. (The axons are mostly unmyelinated, giving the tissue its grey appearance.) The cell bodies of afferent neurons reside in dorsal root ganglia, just outside the spinal cord. Afferent fibers enter into the posterior/dorsal aspect of the spinal cord (a region called the posterior grey horn) through the anterior root, while efferent fibers exit on the anterior/ventral aspect (the anterior grey horn) through the posterior root. Spinal neurons usually innervate structures that are inferior to the neck.

Science

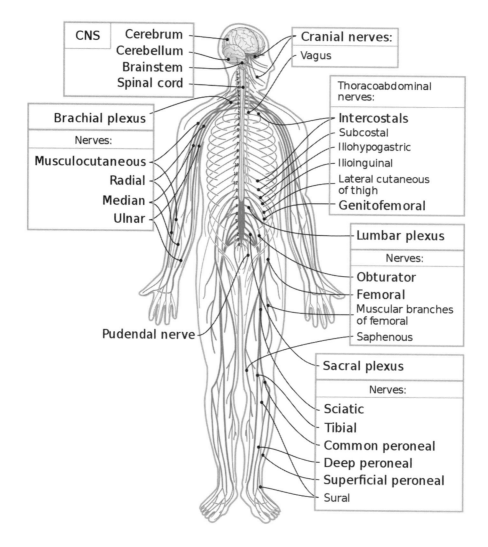

CNS	Cerebrum
	Cerebellum
	Brainstem
	Spinal cord

| Cranial nerves: |
| Vagus |

| Brachial plexus |
| Nerves: |
| Musculocutaneous |
| Radial |
| Median |
| Ulnar |

| Thoracoabdominal nerves: |
| Intercostals |
| Subcostal |
| Iliohypogastric |
| Ilioinguinal |
| Lateral cutaneous of thigh |
| Genitofemoral |

| Lumbar plexus |
| Nerves: |
| Obturator |
| Femoral |
| Muscular branches of femoral |
| Saphenous |

Pudendal nerve

| Sacral plexus |
| Nerves: |
| Sciatic |
| Tibial |
| Common peroneal |
| Deep peroneal |
| Superficial peroneal |
| Sural |

Not all reflexes are mediated by spinal neurons. Supraspinal circuits require input from the brain or brainstem and are involved in actions such as the blinking and gagging reflexes.

Cross section of a spinal cord		
Grey matter	1. Anterior horn	
	2. Posterior horn	
	3. Grey commissure	
White matter	4. Anterior funiculus	
	5. Lateral funiculus	
	6. Posterior funiculus	
	7. Anterior commissure	
	8. Anterior median fissure	
	9. Posterior median sulcus	
Other structures	10. Central canal	
	11. Anterior root	
	12. Posterior root	
	13. Dorsal root ganglion	

REFLEXES

A **reflex** is a nearly instantaneous, unconscious, and involuntary response to a stimulus. The stimulus (for example, the sensation of heat when one touches a hot stove) is detected by the receptors of afferent neurons, and sensory information is sent to interneurons in the spinal cord. (Interneurons are entirely restricted to the central nervous system and act as bridges between sensory and motor neurons.) From here, the signal travels along motor neurons to the effectors (the muscles of the arm and hand). Before the signal for pain has reached the brain, the hand has already been withdrawn. While reflexes do not require conscious thought, some have pathways that involve the brain. The brain can sometimes override reflex actions, such as when you try not to blink during an eye exam. Sometimes, a reflex involves a direct link between the sensory and motor neuron, like the patellar reflex, or knee-jerk reaction. This is referred to as a monosynaptic reflex. Polysynaptic reflexes are more complex because they involve interneurons.

FEEDBACK LOOP, REFLEX ARC

A reflex arc describes a neural pathway that triggers a reflex action. It begins with a **receptor**, the site or organ that receives the stimulus. A **sensory neuron** carries the impulse along the afferent pathway to the **integration center** within the central nervous system. Interneurons process the information and pass the impulse to a **motor neuron**. The impulse travels along the efferent pathway to the **effector**, the responding muscle or gland.

Most reflexes attempt to maintain homeostasis by inhibiting a change in condition; this is called negative feedback. A **negative feedback** process is one in which the response to an imbalance acts to reverse or reduce the change. The maintenance of body temperature is one of many examples. As body temperature changes, thermoreceptors send information to the hypothalamus. If body temperature is too high, a command is sent to dilate blood vessels and release sweat. If the temperature is too low, the body shivers and blood vessels constrict. **Positive feedback** loops are less common, and sometimes harmful because they enhance the stimuli rather than inhibit them. A beneficial form of positive feedback occurs during childbirth. When the cervix is stretched by the descending fetus, impulses are sent to the pituitary, which sends a command to increase uterine contractions. The more the fetus is pushed, the more the cervix stretches. This positive feedback loop continues until birth.

INTEGRATION WITH ENDOCRINE SYSTEM: FEEDBACK CONTROL

The nervous system is closely integrated with the endocrine system. Both systems control the body—the nervous system through electrical impulses and the endocrine system though slower-acting, but longer-lasting hormones. The two systems are linked via the hypothalamus, a region in the brain that controls the autonomic nervous system as well as the pituitary gland. In fact, neurons within the hypothalamus have axons that extend through the infundibulum and terminate in the posterior pituitary. The hypothalamus produces oxytocin and antidiuretic hormone (ADH), but these hormones are stored in and secreted by the posterior pituitary. The release of other important hormones from the anterior pituitary is also regulated by the hypothalamus. Pituitary hormones go on to control other endocrine glands and body functions. Hormones travel through the bloodstream to target tissues, eliciting responses that are important for growth, development, metabolism, and the maintenance of homeostasis. An example of the interaction between the two systems can be seen in the letdown of milk during nursing. As a baby begins to nurse, the stimulus sends an impulse to the hypothalamus, causing the pituitary to release oxytocin into the blood. The hormone targets the mammary gland, inducing it to release milk.

NERVE CELL

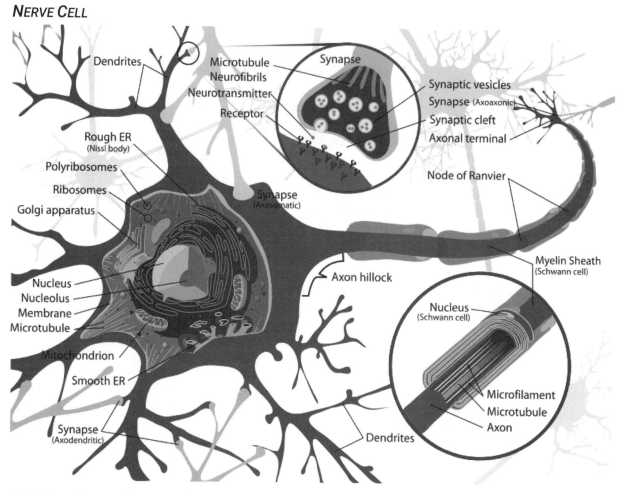

CELL BODY: SITE OF NUCLEUS, ORGANELLES

The cell body, or soma, of a neuron contains the organelles that are responsible for the metabolic activities of the neuron. The interior of the cell body contains a nucleus with a prominent nucleolus. The DNA within the nucleus encodes the information for the many proteins that are needed for the neuron to function. The neuronal cytoplasm contains most of the organelles that are characteristic of animal cells (cytoskeleton, rough and smooth endoplasmic reticulum, Golgi bodies, lysosomes, peroxisomes, and mitochondria). There are relatively high numbers of mitochondria to support the high metabolic needs of the neuron. Granular Nissl bodies (made of rough ER and clusters of free ribosomes) synthesize proteins for use within the cell. Notably absent in mature neurons are centrioles, as differentiated neurons have lost their ability to divide.

Various projections (dendrites and/or an axon) extend from the cell body, and neurons can be classified according to these structural differences.

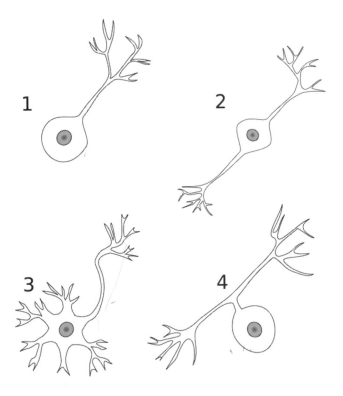

1: Unipolar (many sensory neurons are unipolar)

2: Bipolar (rare, associated with retina and inner ear)

3: Multipolar (most common, interneurons and motor neurons)

4: Pseudounipolar (sensory neurons)

DENDRITES: BRANCHED EXTENSIONS OF CELL BODY

Dendrites are relatively short, branched extensions of the cell body that receive incoming chemical signals (neurotransmitters) from the other neurons. These tree-like projections taper with every branch, maximizing the surface area for synaptic inputs. Many dendrites have tiny protrusions called dendritic spines that synapse with a single axon. The cytoplasm within the dendrites contains the same organelles as the cell body, with the exception of the nucleus.

The neurotransmitters that are released from axon terminals of the presynaptic cell cross the synaptic cleft, where they bind to receptor sites on the dendrites of the postsynaptic cells. These signals may be excitatory or inhibitory, and the net effect of these signals determines whether the neuron is inhibited or triggered to fire (in which case the chemical message will be converted to an electrical impulse that travels down the axon).

AXON: STRUCTURE AND FUNCTION

An axon is a smooth, cable-like nerve fiber that is specialized to conduct electrical impulses away from the soma. Most neurons have one long axon, but the axon's length can vary, and some neurons have no axon at all. The axon emerges from a slightly elevated structure called the **axon hillock** that connects the soma to the axon. The cytoplasm of the axon is called **axoplasm**, and it lacks the Golgi bodies, Nissl bodies, and ribosomes found in dendritic cytoplasm. Since there is little to no translation, proteins must be imported from the soma. The axon often splits into **collaterals** that allow one neuron to interact with more than one cell. At the end of each axon are highly branched structures called **axon terminals**. These club-shaped endings contain synaptic vesicles filled with neurotransmitters. When an action potential is generated at the axon hillock, it propagates along the axon. When it reaches the axon terminals, the neurotransmitters are released to a target cell.

MYELIN SHEATH, SCHWANN CELLS, INSULATION OF AXON

The axons of many neurons are sheathed in a lipid-based coating called **myelin**. Myelin insulates the axon much like the coating on electrical wire. It also increases the rate at which an impulse can travel. There are intermittent gaps in the sheath called nodes of Ranvier that allow the impulse to jump quickly from one node to the next.

Neurons of the peripheral nervous system are myelinated by **Schwann cells**. These glial cells curve around the axon, wrapping their plasma membranes around it like a bandage to form multiple lipid-rich layers. The nucleus and cytoplasm remain outside the myelin sheath, but are encased in the outer **neurilemmal** sheath of the Schwann cell. Axons of very small diameter may be supported by Schwann cells, but are not myelinated by them. These are called non-myelinating Schwann cells. **Oligodendrocytes** are responsible for sheathing the neurons of the central nervous system. Unlike Schwann cells, a single oligodendrocyte can myelinate dozens of axons by extending its membrane in multiple directions and wrapping around the axons. White matter of the CNS is made mostly of myelinated axons, while the axons associated with grey matter are unmyelinated.

Multiple sclerosis, the leukodystrophies, and many other diseases result from damaged myelin. Without the proper insulation, the neurons of affected individuals cannot effectively conduct an impulse.

NODES OF RANVIER: PROPAGATION OF NERVE IMPULSE ALONG AXON

Nodes of Ranvier are uninsulated gaps between myelinated portions of the axon that increase the rate of conduction. These exposed portions are about 1 μm in length, and they contain a high density of voltage gated sodium and potassium channels. The channels open to allow the passage of these ions, depolarizing the membrane. Since ions are unable to diffuse through the myelin, the action potential must jump to the next node. This is called **saltatory propagation**. This type of conduction is faster and more efficient than the continuous conduction that is seen along the entire length of an unsheathed axon. Large-diameter myelinated axons conduct impulses much faster (80-120 m/s) than thin unmyelinated axons (0.5-10 m/s). While rapid conduction has its benefits, myelinated axons have less neuroplasticity than unmyelinated axons; that is, they are more limited in their ability to form new connections with other neurons.

GLIAL CELLS

Glial cells, also called neuroglia, support and protect neurons within the central and peripheral nervous system. Despite their inability to conduct impulses, there are many more glial cells than neurons within nervous tissue. Glial cells also have the ability to divide, and so nearly all brain tumors arise from them.

	Glial Cell	Characteristics	Function
CNS	Astrocytes	The most abundant cells found in neural tissue	Anchor neurons, facilitate exchange of materials between capillaries and neurons, uptake excess ions and neurotransmitters
	Microglia	Relatively few extensions	Phagocytic—immune defense, digest dead neurons and debris
	Oligodendrocytes	Extensions wrap around axons of CNS neurons	Produce myelin sheaths that insulate CNS neurons and speed up neurotransmission
	Ependyma	Form the epithelial lining of the ventricles and central canal of the spinal cord	Circulate cerebrospinal fluid (CSF) and facilitate exchange of materials between the CSF and interstitial fluid of brain and spinal cord

	Glial Cell	Characteristics	Function
PNS	Schwann cells	Extensive lipid membranes wrap around PNS axons to form layers	Produce the myelin sheaths that insulate PNS neurons Speed up neurotransmission
	Satellite cells	Surround the soma of neurons within PNS ganglia	Protect and cushion PNS neurons

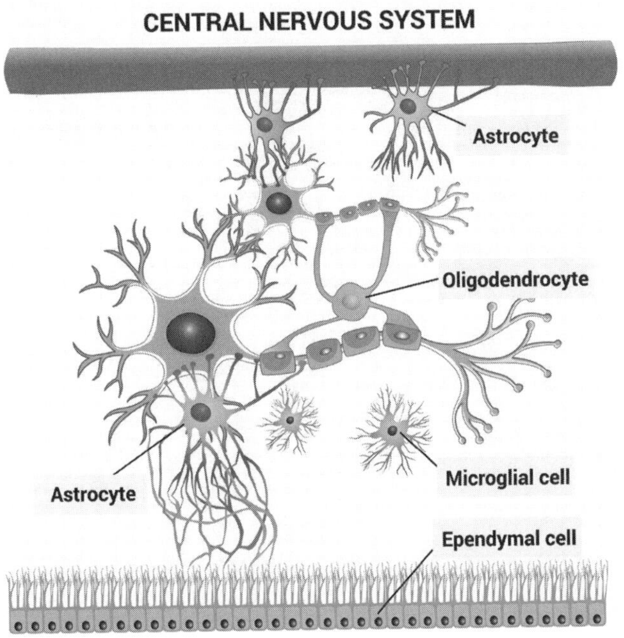

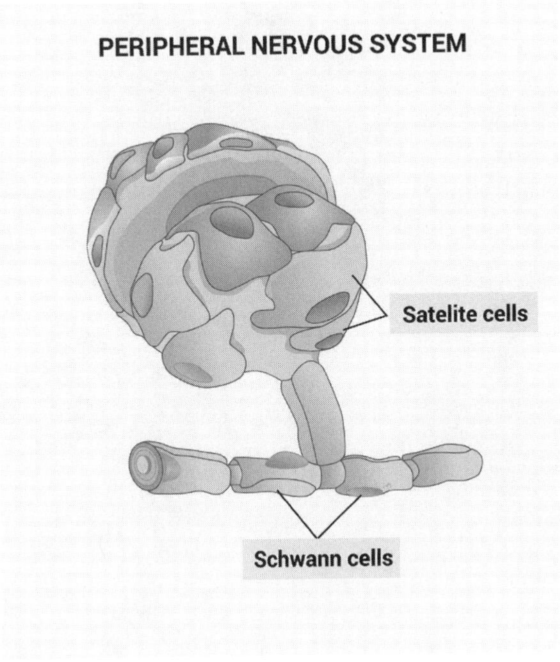

CENTRAL NERVOUS SYSTEM

PERIPHERAL NERVOUS SYSTEM

SYNAPSE: SITE OF IMPULSE PROPAGATION BETWEEN CELLS

A **synapse** is a communicating junction between two neurons, or between a neuron and an effector (muscle or gland). The synapse consists of a presynaptic element, a tiny gap called the synaptic cleft, and a postsynaptic element. Impulses are transmitted across the synaptic cleft through the action of neurotransmitters. Synapses can be classified according to the nature of the postsynaptic element. **Axodendritic** synapses terminate on the dendrites of a postsynaptic neuron. **Axosomatic** synapses terminate on a postsynaptic soma. **Axoaxonic** synapses are rare, terminating on a postsynaptic axon.

They can also be classified by the mode in which the impulse is transmitted. Most synapses are unidirectional **chemical** junctions, using neurotransmitters to send messages to the postsynaptic cell. When the impulse reaches the axon terminals, the vesicles that store the neurotransmitters fuse with the plasma membrane, releasing the signals into the synaptic cleft before they bind to receptors on the postsynaptic target. At this point, the postsynaptic membrane will either be excited (depolarized) or inhibited (hyperpolarized). Bidirectional **electrical** synaptic junctions do

133

not use neurotransmitters. They are linked by gap junctions that allow the flow of ions between cells. Electrical synapses are faster, always excitatory, and more rare.

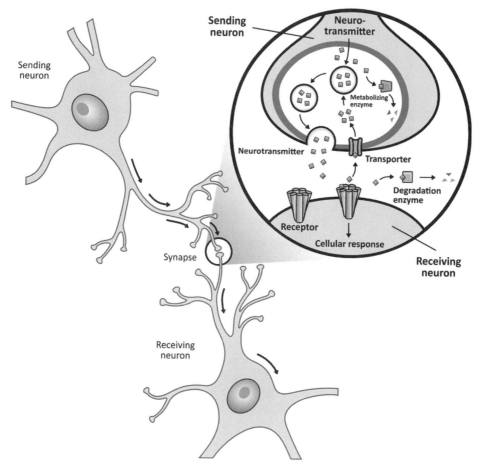

SYNAPTIC ACTIVITY: TRANSMITTER MOLECULES

When an action potential reaches the axon terminal, voltage-gated calcium channels open in response to the depolarization of the membrane. Calcium ions enter, triggering the release of neurotransmitters by exocytosis. The neurotransmitters diffuse across the synaptic cleft, binding to receptors in the target cell and eliciting either an excitatory or an inhibitory response. The neurotransmitters are then recycled back to the presynaptic cell, are degraded by enzymes, or diffuse away from the synaptic cleft to prevent overstimulation.

Common neurotransmitters and their actions are summarized below:

Neurotransmitter	Action
Acetylcholine (ACh)	Stimulates skeletal muscle
Norepinephrine (NE)	Influences mood and sleep patterns
Dopamine	Associated with mood, attention, reward system, and movement
Histamine	Works with the hypothalamus, promotes wakefulness
Serotonin	Many roles—mostly inhibitory. Influences sleep, mood, hunger, arousal
GABA	The major inhibitory neurotransmitter
Glutamate	The major excitatory neurotransmitter

MUSCULAR SYSTEM

IMPORTANT FUNCTIONS

SUPPORT: MOBILITY

The muscle system is made up of skeletal, smooth, and cardiac muscles that contract to produce nearly all body movements. **Skeletal muscles** are used for voluntary actions. Walking, jumping, smiling, eye movements, and the maintenance of posture are all under the control of the somatic nervous system. The muscles that coordinate voluntary movements are attached to bone by tendons, and the bone is moved when the muscle shortens. Skeletal muscles also work with the tendons, ligaments, and bone to support and stabilize the joints.

Contraction of **smooth muscle** is involuntary and therefore under autonomic control. Smooth muscle in the gastrointestinal tract contracts rhythmically to propel food along the gastrointestinal tract. This is called peristalsis. Blood pressure is regulated by contraction and relaxation of the smooth muscle within the vessel wall. Vasoconstriction increases blood pressure and decreases blood flow, while vasodilation decreases blood pressure and increases blood flow. Cardiac muscle of the heart contracts to pump blood throughout the body.

PERIPHERAL CIRCULATORY ASSISTANCE

The return of blood to the heart is assisted by a system called the **skeletal muscle pump**. Large peripheral veins in the legs and arms have valves that prevent the backflow of blood. When the skeletal muscles around these deep veins contract, the vessel is compressed, and blood is forced through the valves in the direction of the heart. Exercising these muscle groups increases the rate of blood flow.

The **thoracic pump** also facilitates venous return. During inspiration, contraction of the diaphragm and intercostal muscles expands the thoracic cavity. The increased volume results in a decrease in pressure, which is transmitted to the right atrium. This drop in pressure helps the blood to return to the heart. Also, when the pressure in the thoracic cavity decreases, the pressure in the abdominal cavity increases, squeezing the blood in the inferior vena cava toward the heart.

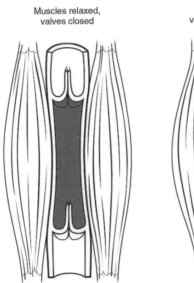
Muscles relaxed, valves closed

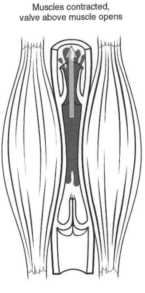
Muscles contracted, valve above muscle opens

THERMOREGULATION (SHIVERING REFLEX)

When thermoreceptors detect a drop in temperature, impulses are sent to the posterior hypothalamus, which then sends signals to the effectors. Smooth muscles in the walls of the

135

Science

cutaneous arterioles contract involuntarily to reduce the blood flow near the surface of the skin. This minimizes heat lost to the environment. Arrector pili muscles also contract, causing hairs to stand on end in an attempt to trap warm air. If the core body temperature drops, the shivering reflex is triggered by the posterior hypothalamus. Shivering is involuntary shuddering, caused by the rapid contracting and relaxing of skeletal muscles. Contraction of these muscles requires the hydrolysis of ATP, and this exothermic reaction releases energy in the form of heat. Some heat is also generated as a result of friction between the sliding filaments of the muscle.

When thermoreceptors detect a rise in temperature, the anterior hypothalamus tells the smooth muscles that surround cutaneous arterioles to relax. Vasodilation allows more blood to flow near the surface of the skin, and heat is lost to the environment.

MOVEMENT

SAGITTAL PLANE OF MOTION

The sagittal plane passes through the body from front to back, dividing the body into left and right sides.

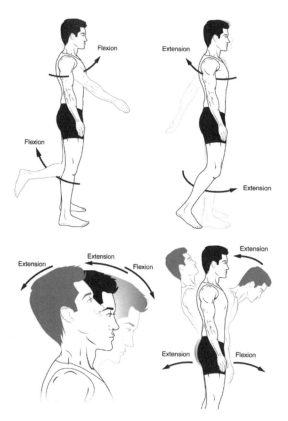

Flexion	Decrease the angle between two body parts (bending the elbow)
Extension	Increasing the angle between two body parts (straightening the elbow)
Dorsiflexion	Ankle flexion (moving the toes toward the shin)
Plantar flexion	Ankle extension (moving the toes toward the ground/pointing the toes)

FRONTAL PLANE OF MOTION

The frontal plane passes through the body from left to right, dividing the body into anterior and posterior.

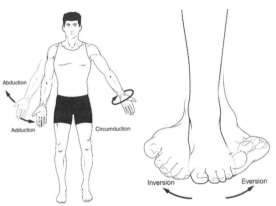

Adduction	Movement toward the midline/to the body (bringing the arm to the body).
Abduction	Moving away from the midline. Think of someone being abducted or taken away (moving the arm away from the body).
Elevation	Scapula movement, superior movement (shoulder shrug).
Depression	Scapula movement, inferior movement (shoulder shrug).
Inversion	Lifting the medial border of the foot. Bring the sole of the foot to face inward.
Eversion	Lifting the lateral border of the foot. Bring the sole of the foot to face outward.

TRANSVERSE PLANE OF MOTION

The transverse plane passes through the body in a line parallel to the floor, dividing the body into top and bottom.

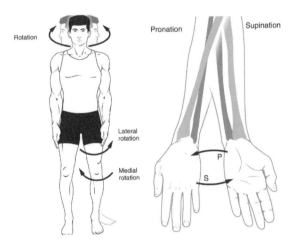

Pronation	Rotating the hand and wrist medially from the bone. If laying on the back, the hand would have the palm to the floor.
Supination	Rotating the hand and wrist laterally from the bone. If laying on the back, the palm and wrist would be facing toward the ceiling.
Horizontal adduction	The angle between two joints decreases on the horizontal plane.
Horizontal abduction	The angle between two joints increases on the horizontal plane.
Rotation	Pivoting or twisting on the axis (turning the head left or right).

MAJOR MUSCLES OF THE BODY

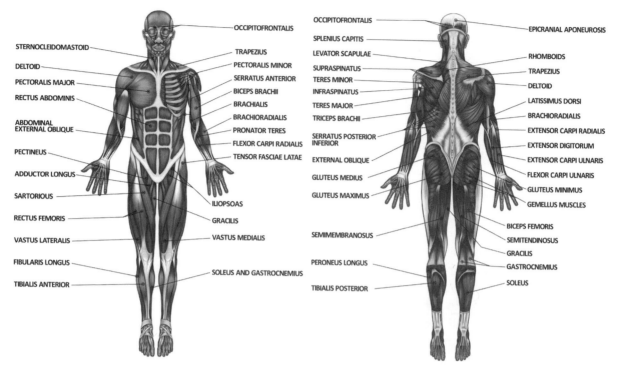

STERNOCLEIDOMASTOID
DELTOID
PECTORALIS MAJOR
RECTUS ABDOMINIS
ABDOMINAL EXTERNAL OBLIQUE
PECTINEUS
ADDUCTOR LONGUS
SARTORIOUS
RECTUS FEMORIS
VASTUS LATERALIS
FIBULARIS LONGUS
TIBIALIS ANTERIOR

OCCIPITOFRONTALIS
TRAPEZIUS
PECTORALIS MINOR
SERRATUS ANTERIOR
BICEPS BRACHII
BRACHIALIS
BRACHIORADIALIS
PRONATOR TERES
FLEXOR CARPI RADIALIS
TENSOR FASCIAE LATAE
ILIOPSOAS
GRACILIS
VASTUS MEDIALIS
SOLEUS AND GASTROCNEMIUS

OCCIPITOFRONTALIS
SPLENIUS CAPITIS
LEVATOR SCAPULAE
SUPRASPINATUS
TERES MINOR
INFRASPINATUS
TERES MAJOR
TRICEPS BRACHII
SERRATUS POSTERIOR INFERIOR
EXTERNAL OBLIQUE
GLUTEUS MEDIUS
GLUTEUS MAXIMUS
SEMIMEMBRANOSUS
PERONEUS LONGUS
TIBIALIS POSTERIOR

EPICRANIAL APONEUROSIS
RHOMBOIDS
TRAPEZIUS
DELTOID
LATISSIMUS DORSI
BRACHIORADIALIS
EXTENSOR CARPI RADIALIS
EXTENSOR DIGITORUM
EXTENSOR CARPI ULNARIS
FLEXOR CARPI ULNARIS
GLUTEUS MINIMUS
GEMELLUS MUSCLES
BICEPS FEMORIS
SEMITENDINOSUS
GRACILIS
GASTROCNEMIUS
SOLEUS

STRUCTURE OF THREE BASIC MUSCLE TYPES: STRIATED, SMOOTH, CARDIAC

Skeletal muscle is under somatic (voluntary) control and does not display myogenic activity (skeletal muscles require external stimulation to contract). They are involved in the movement of bone, support, thermoregulation, and venous return to the heart. These muscles are **striated**; the muscle fibers have alternating regions of light and dark bands. A single skeletal myocyte is cylinder-shaped and has many nuclei.

Smooth muscle is under autonomic (involuntary) control and is capable of using myogenic mechanisms to contract (independent of nervous stimulation). Smooth muscle tissue is found in the walls of hollow organs and vessels and aids in the movement of substances such as food and blood. The cells are spindle-shaped, non-striated, and uninucleate.

Like smooth muscle, cardiac muscle is under autonomic control and exhibits myogenic activity. Cardiac muscle tissue is found in the walls of the heart and is required for the pumping of blood. The cells are branched, striated, and usually uninucleate (but may have two nuclei). They are connected to each other by intercalated discs with gap junctions that allow the cells to communicate.

MUSCLE STRUCTURE AND CONTROL OF CONTRACTION

T-TUBULE SYSTEM

Transverse tubules, or **T-tubules**, are tunnel-like invaginations of the **sarcolemma**, the plasma membrane of striated muscle cells. The membranes of this system contain a high concentration of ion channels, allowing them to play an important role in muscle contraction. When an action potential propagates along the sarcolemma, the T-tubules help to depolarize the cell by carrying the impulse to the **sarcoplasmic reticulum** (SR) that surrounds the **myofibrils** in a muscle cell. The SR is a form of smooth endoplasmic reticulum that is specialized to store and release calcium ions. The t-tubules are sandwiched between two enlarged chambers of the SR called **terminal cisternae**.

This "sandwich" makes up a structure called the **triad**. When the impulse reaches the SR, the calcium channels in the SR membrane open, releasing calcium ions that ultimately cause contraction of the muscle. ATP-powered calcium pumps within the SR membrane pump Ca^{2+} back into the SR to relax the muscle.

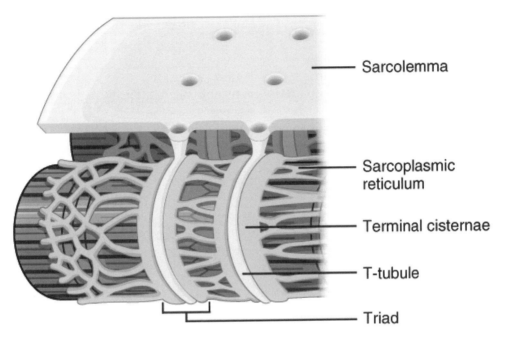

CONTRACTILE APPARATUS

The **contractile apparatus** describes a unit within muscle tissue that is specialized for contraction. The structure of the contractile apparatus is similar among striated muscle tissues and consists of a repeating unit called a **sarcomere**. Tens of thousands of these sarcomeres lie end to end to form a **myofibril**. One sarcomere is separated from another by a boundary called the **Z line**, where a network of proteins serves as a point of anchorage for **actin** (thin filaments). Six thin filaments surround a single thick myosin filament. The filaments themselves do not change length during contraction; their arrangement allows them to slide over each other when myosin heads pull on the thin filaments, causing the sarcomeres to shorten and the muscle to contract. Note that while smooth muscle cells do contain actin and myosin, the filaments are disorganized, and no sarcomeres are present.

CONTRACTILE VELOCITY OF DIFFERENT MUSCLE TYPES

There are three main types of skeletal muscle fibers: slow-twitch oxidative (SO type I), fast-twitch oxidative-glycolytic (FOG type IIa), and fast-twitch glycolytic (FG type IIb). Most muscles consist of an even blend of these fibers, but the proportions vary in certain muscles, depending on function. For example, muscles associated with maintaining posture will have a high percentage of slow-twitch fibers, while muscles in the lower legs of a sprinter will have a high percentage of fast-twitch fibers.

The characteristics of each type of fiber are summarized in the following table:

	Slow Twitch, Type I	Fast Twitch, Type IIa	Fast Twitch, Type IIb
Fiber Diameter	Smaller	Intermediate	Larger
Capillary density	High	Moderate	Low
Myoglobin Concentration / Color	High/Red	Moderate/Red-Pink	Low/White
Metabolism	High aerobic capacity, low anaerobic capacity	Both aerobic and anaerobic capabilities	Low aerobic capacity, high anaerobic capacity
Concentration of Mitochondria	High	Moderate	Low
Resistance to Fatigue	High	Moderate	Low
Contractile Velocity	Slow	Rapid	Rapid
Force Production	Low	Moderate	High
General Use	Prolonged, low-intensity aerobic activities/maintenance of posture	Moderate intensity activities, such as running	Short bursts of activity, such as sprinting or heavy lifting

REGULATION OF CARDIAC MUSCLE CONTRACTION

Cardiac muscle demonstrates myogenic activity. The pacemaker cells of the sinoatrial (SA) node of the heart generate their own action potential, which then travels to the atrioventricular (AV) node (the secondary pacemaker), the bundle of His, the bundle branches, and finally the Purkinje fibers. Gap junctions between adjacent cardiac cells facilitate the transmission of the action potential from one cell to the next. As the impulse travels through the sarcolemma of a cardiac muscle cell, voltage-gated calcium ion channels open, allowing the entry of extracellular Ca^{2+}. The inflow of Ca^{2+} triggers the release of even more Ca^{2+} from the sarcoplasmic reticulum. Calcium ions cause the cardiac muscle to contract in a similar manner to skeletal muscle cells (the sliding filament mechanism). Note that skeletal muscle cells do not generate their own action potential, and the action potential is more prolonged in cardiac cells.

While the heart is autorhythmic, the muscle contraction is further regulated by the autonomic nervous system. Sympathetic stimulation increases heart rate, while parasympathetic stimulation (the vagus nerve) decreases heart rate. The endocrine system influences heart rate as well. Epinephrine secreted from the adrenal medulla and thyroxine from the thyroid gland both increase heart rate.

OXYGEN DEBT: FATIGUE

Oxygen debt is the amount of oxygen required to restore metabolic conditions to resting levels. Muscle activity is powered by the hydrolysis of ATP. In a resting state, aerobic respiration provides enough ATP for muscles to function. Stored ATP is quickly used up during intense exercise, and a molecule called **creatine phosphate** phosphorylates ADP to produce ATP. Anaerobic respiration also supplies ATP relatively quickly, but only for a short amount of time. If oxygen is available, aerobic respiration synthesizes ATP. When oxygen levels become depleted, **lactic acid** (a byproduct of anaerobic respiration) begins to accumulate. The buildup of lactic acid, along with the depletion of ATP and oxygen, causes muscle fatigue. Lactic acid that does not remain in the muscles is brought to the liver, where it is converted into glucose. The amount of oxygen required to accomplish this task, and to replenish the levels of ATP and creatine phosphate, is called oxygen debt.

NERVOUS CONTROL

SYMPATHETIC AND PARASYMPATHETIC INNERVATION

Involuntary muscle tissues (smooth, cardiac) are innervated by motor neurons of the sympathetic and parasympathetic divisions of the autonomic nervous system. Motor pathways of the ANS consist of *two* neurons: a preganglionic and a postganglionic neuron. The cell body of a preganglionic neuron resides in the central nervous system and synapses with the cell body of one or more postganglionic neurons within an autonomic ganglion. Postganglionic nerve fibers are shorter than presynaptic fibers, and they extend to the effectors. *Pre*ganglionic neurons of both the sympathetic and parasympathetic systems release acetylcholine (ACh). *Post*ganglionic neurons of the parasympathetic division release ACh, but those of the sympathetic division release norepinephrine (NE).

In general, the sympathetic and parasympathetic systems tend to have antagonistic effects on the muscles (and glands) they innervate. The sympathetic division induces a fight or flight response, which causes heart rate and blood pressure to increase, and blood to be diverted away from the digestive system. The parasympathetic division induces a rest and digest response, which causes heart rate and blood pressure to decrease, and promotes digestion.

VOLUNTARY AND INVOLUNTARY MUSCLES

The peripheral nervous system is divided into the somatic and autonomic nervous systems. Voluntary muscles are composed of skeletal muscle tissue and are under the control of the somatic nervous system. Most voluntary muscles are connected to bone. These muscles usually contract in response to a conscious thought process, but they are also involved in certain involuntary reflexes, such as the knee jerk reflex. The motor cortex of the brain is responsible for generating most of the nerve impulses that initiate voluntary movements.

Involuntary muscles are innervated by motor neurons of the autonomic nervous system. These muscles include the smooth muscles found in the walls of hollow organs such as the intestines and blood vessels, as well as the cardiac muscle of the heart. The lower part of the brainstem called the medulla oblongata sends signals to involuntary muscles that play a role in digestion, vasodilation/vasoconstriction, heart rate, respiratory rate, and other visceral functions.

MOTOR NEURONS, NEUROMUSCULAR JUNCTION, MOTOR END PLATES

The stimulus for skeletal muscle cell contraction comes from motor neurons, and the synapse between the neuron and muscle cell is called the **neuromuscular junction**. A single motor neuron can form synapses with multiple muscle cells. The neuron and the muscle cells that it innervates are collectively called a **motor unit**. This arrangement allows a large group of cells to contract together. All the motor neurons that innervate the same muscle make up a **motor pool**.

When an action potential reaches an axon terminal, voltage-gated calcium ions in the membrane are opened, and Ca^{2+} enters. These ions bind to synaptic vesicles that store acetylcholine (ACh), causing them to fuse with the membrane and release ACh into the synaptic cleft. ACh binds to nicotinic receptors on a folded portion of the sarcolemma known as the motor end plate. The permeability of the muscle cell changes, and the cell depolarizes. The action potential is taken into the muscle cell via T-tubules, causing calcium channels in the sarcoplasmic reticulum to open. The release of calcium into the sarcoplasm causes the muscle to contract.

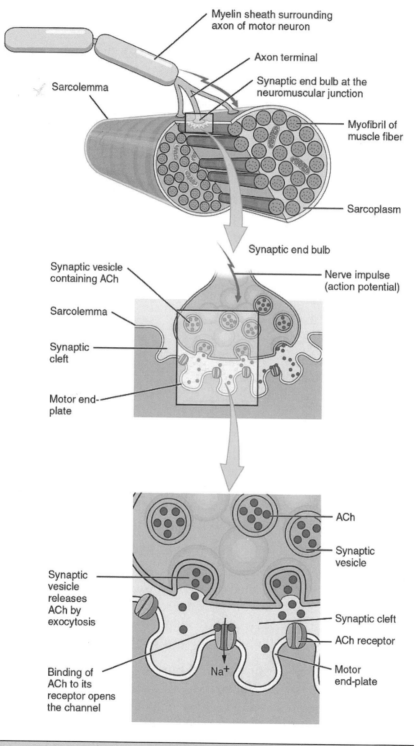

REPRODUCTIVE SYSTEM

DIFFERENCES BETWEEN MALE AND FEMALE STRUCTURES

Many of the structures within the male and female reproductive system are "homologous" to each other because they share a common developmental pathway. But these structures become specialized for different roles in reproduction.

The male reproductive system is designed to produce sperm and deliver it to the female for fertilization. Most of the male reproductive structures are external, which helps to keep the sperm at the optimal temperature. The testes produce much higher levels of testosterone than female gonads, and they produce millions of gametes per day after puberty. The male urethra is a common passageway for both urine and semen.

In contrast, the female reproductive system is designed to nurture a developing embryo. The reproductive structures are housed internally. The ovaries produce much higher levels of estrogen than male gonads. They contain all of the oocytes that they will ever have before birth, and only one is released per month during ovulation. The female urethra is not connected to the reproductive system.

MALE GENITALIA

The internal male genitalia include the epididymis, vas deferens, and accessory glands including the seminal vesicles, prostate gland, and Cowper's glands (the bulbourethral glands). The **epididymis** is a convoluted tube attached to the outside of a testicle that nourishes sperm as they finish maturing, and stores them until ejaculation. From here the sperm pass through the **vas deferens** (sperm duct), **ejaculatory duct**, and **urethra**, and exit through the penis. The **seminal vesicles** secrete fluid into the ejaculatory duct that makes up roughly 60% of the volume of semen. The contents of this mildly alkaline fluid include fructose, prostaglandins, and proteins. Secretions of the **prostate gland** (about 30% of semen volume) nourish the sperm and increase their motility. **Cowper's glands** secrete a lubricating fluid that makes up 2–5% of semen volume.

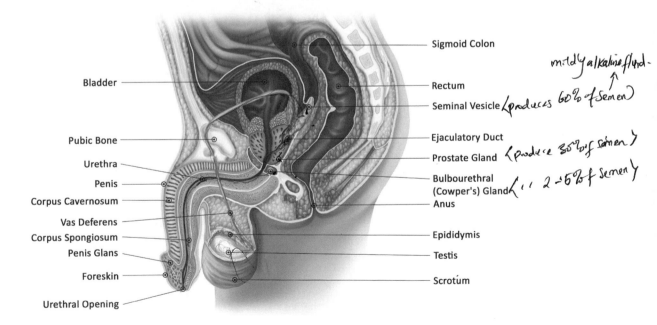

The external male genitalia include the penis and scrotum. The **penis** is the erectile organ responsible for delivering sperm to the female. It consists of three cylinders of spongy tissue: a pair of **corpora cavernosa** and the **corpus spongiosum** that surrounds the urethra. The **scrotum** is the sac that protects the sperm-producing testes and keeps them at the proper temperature.

FEMALE GENITALIA

The internal female genitalia include the ovaries, the fallopian tubes, the uterus, and the vagina. The **ovaries** produce oocytes, and also secrete sex hormones. When an oocyte is released during ovulation, it is "captured" by the **fallopian tube**, also known as the uterine tube or oviduct, which is not directly connected to the ovaries. Fertilization typically occurs in the fallopian tube, and implantation of the fertilized egg usually occurs in the endometrium of the uterus. The **uterus** is a muscular, pear-shaped organ that nourishes and protects the developing embryo. The neck of the uterus that opens to the vagina is called the **cervix**. The **vagina** is a muscular canal that receives the penis during intercourse. During childbirth, the baby passes through the vagina, also called the birth canal.

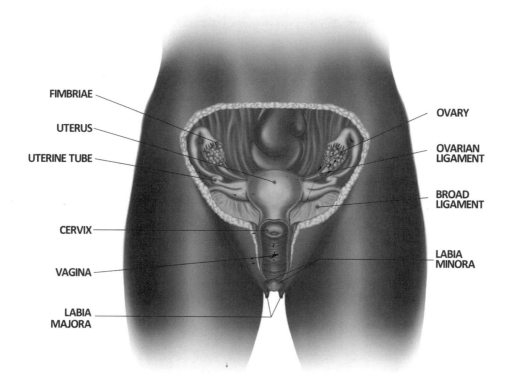

The external female genitalia include the structures of the **vulva**. These include the mons pubis, the labia majora and labia minora, Bartholin's glands, and the clitoris. The **mons pubis** is a mound of fatty tissue that lies over the pubic bone. The skin folds that form the **labia** help to protect the more delicate tissues beneath. **Bartholin's glands** produce a fluid that lubricates the vagina. The **clitoris** consists of erectile tissue full of nerve endings that contribute to sexual arousal.

GONADS

The gonads are the components of the reproductive system that produce gametes (sex cells) and secrete hormones. The male gonads are the **testes**. These structures are housed in the scrotum and encapsulated by a fibrous layer of connective tissue called the **tunica albuginea**. Thin layers of tissue extend from the tunica albuginea and divide the testes into 250 to 300 compartments called **lobules**. Each lobule contains one to four **seminiferous tubules**, the sites of spermatogenesis. The

144

epithelial lining of these tubules consists of the **spermatogenic cells** that give rise to sperm, as well as the cells that nourish them (**sustentacular cells**, also called **Sertoli cells**). **Interstitial cells** (**Leydig cells**) around the seminiferous tubules produce testosterone, which stimulates the production of sperm. The seminiferous tubules join together to form a network of channels called the **rete testis** that bring maturing sperm cells to the **efferent ducts** where they exit the testes and enter the epididymis.

The female gonads are the **ovaries**. Ovaries are oval-shaped structures that rest in slight depressions on either side of the uterus known as the **ovarian fossae**, and they are held in position by several peritoneal ligaments. Each ovary is covered by two types of tissue: a layer of simple cuboidal epithelium known as the **germinal epithelium**, and the underlying **tunica albuginea**. The ovary is subdivided into the outer cortex and the inner medulla. The **cortex** has a granular appearance due to the presence of thousands of nourishing **follicles** in various stages of development. Each of these saclike follicles contains an oocyte. Initially, the oocyte is surrounded by a single layer of **follicular cells**, but as the follicle matures, the cells give rise to a multi-layer of estrogen-producing **granulosa cells**. After ovulation, a gland called the **corpus luteum** forms, and it secretes progesterone and small amounts of estrogen. This gland disappears unless pregnancy occurs. The interior of the ovary, or **medulla**, is made of loose areolar connective tissue, and contains many blood vessels, lymphatic vessels, and nerves that enter and leave through the **hilum**.

SEXUAL DEVELOPMENT

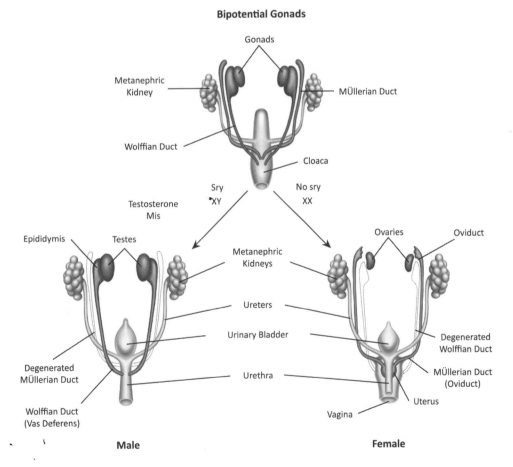

Sex determination occurs at birth; two X chromosomes will give rise to a female, and XY gives rise to a male. The SRY gene on the Y chromosomes is responsible for the development of the male reproductive organs and the repression of female reproductive organs. In the absence of the Y chromosome, the embryo will be female. **Wolffian ducts** give rise to male internal reproductive structures, and **Mullerian ducts** give rise to female internal reproductive structures. As one system develops, the other is broken down. Seven weeks after conception, the differences in external genitalia become evident. At puberty, there is a surge in development as the hypothalamus releases gonadotropin releasing hormone (GnRH). This triggers the secretion of luteinizing hormone (LH) and follicle stimulating hormone (FSH) from the anterior pituitary gland. These gonadotropins increase the production of sex hormones, which allow the male and female reproductive organs to mature. Spermatogenesis begins in males, and ovulation and menstruation begin in females. Secondary sex characteristics emerge as well. Males develop facial, axillary, and pubic hair, and the voice deepens as the larynx grows. Females develop pubic hair, begin to ovulate and menstruate, and develop wider hips.

FEMALE REPRODUCTIVE CYCLE

The female reproductive cycle is characterized by changes in both the ovaries and the uterine lining (endometrium).

The ovarian cycle has three phases: the follicular phase, ovulation, and the luteal phase. During the **follicular phase**, FSH stimulates the maturation of the follicle, which then secretes estrogen. Estrogen helps to regenerate the uterine lining that was shed during menstruation. **Ovulation**, the release of a secondary oocyte from the ovary, is induced by a surge in LH. The **luteal phase** begins with the formation of the corpus luteum from the remnants of the follicle. The corpus luteum secretes progesterone and estrogen, which inhibit FSH and LH. Progesterone also maintains the thickness of the endometrium. Without the implantation of a fertilized egg, the corpus luteum begins to regress, and the levels of estrogen and progesterone drop. FSH and LH are no longer inhibited, and the cycle renews.

The uterine cycle also consists of three phases: the proliferative phase, secretory phase, and menstrual phase. The **proliferative phase** is characterized by the regeneration of the uterine lining. During the **secretory phase**, the endometrium becomes increasingly vascular, and nutrients are secreted to prepare for implantation. Without implantation, the endometrium is shed during **menstruation**.

PREGNANCY, PARTURITION, LACTATION

Pregnancy: When a blastocyst implants in the uterine lining, it releases hCG. This hormone prevents the corpus luteum from degrading, and it continues to produce estrogen and progesterone. These hormones are necessary to maintain the uterine lining. By the second trimester, the placenta secretes enough of its own estrogen and progesterone to sustain pregnancy. The levels of estrogen continue to increase throughout pregnancy, while progesterone decreases.

Parturition: The precise mechanism for the initiation of parturition (birth) is unclear. Birth is preceded by increased levels of fetal glucocorticoids, which act on the placenta to increase estrogen and decrease progesterone. Stretching of the cervix stimulates the release of oxytocin from the posterior pituitary gland. Oxytocin and estrogen stimulate the release of prostaglandins, and prostaglandins and oxytocin increase uterine contractions. This positive feedback mechanism results in the birth of the fetus.

Lactation: During pregnancy, levels of the hormone prolactin increase, but its effect on the mammary glands is inhibited by estrogen and progesterone. After parturition, the levels of these hormones decrease, and prolactin is able to stimulate the production of milk. Suckling stimulates the release of oxytocin, which results in the ejection of milk.

INTEGUMENTARY SYSTEM
STRUCTURE

The **epidermis** is the outermost layer of skin. The keratinocytes of the stratum basale are the stem cells of the epidermis. They give rise to cells that differentiate as they move toward the surface.

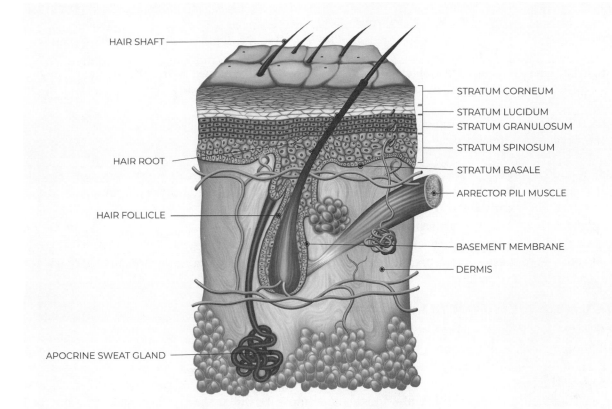

The **stratum basale** is the deepest layer of the epidermis. It usually contains just a single layer of cuboidal or columnar cells that adhere to the basement membrane. These are the most nourished cells because they are closest to the capillaries of the dermis. The **stratum spinosum** consists of eight to ten layers of spiny cells that are connected by structures called **desmosomes**. There is limited mitotic activity in the deeper portion of this layer. The **stratum granulosum** consists of two to five layers of slightly flattened cells containing granules of keratohyalin. The cells in the superficial portion of this layer lose their nuclei. The **stratum lucidum** consists of two to five layers of dead, flattened keratinocytes and is only present in the palms and the soles of feet. These cells contain **eleidin**, a translucent, water-resistant protein derived from keratohyalin. The **stratum corneum** is the most superficial layer, and it consists of 15 to 30 layers of dead, keratin-containing squamous cells. This layer helps to prevent water loss from the body.

> **Review Video: <u>Integumentary System</u>**
> Visit mometrix.com/academy and enter code: 655980

The types of cells found in the epidermis and dermis:

Epidermis Cells	Description
Keratinocytes	The most common type of cell in the epidermis, they arise from stem cells in the stratum basale. They flatten and die as they move toward the surface of the skin. They produce keratin, a fibrous protein that hardens the cell and helps make the skin water resistant.
Melanocytes	They produce melanin, a pigment that gives skin its color and protects against UV radiation.
Langerhans cells	These are antigen-presenting cells of the immune system (phagocytes). They are more common in the stratum spinosum than in any other layer of the epidermis.
Merkel cells	These cutaneous receptors detect light touch. They are located in the stratum basale.

Dermis Cells	Description
Fibroblasts	They secrete collagen, elastin, glycosaminoglycans, and other components of the extracellular matrix.
Adipocytes	These are fat cells.
Macrophages	These are phagocytic cells that engulf potential pathogens.
Mast cells	These antigen-presenting cells play a role in the inflammatory response (release histamine).

FUNCTIONS OF THE INTEGUMENTARY SYSTEM
HOMEOSTASIS, OSMOREGULATION, AND THERMOREGULATION

The skin functions in homeostasis in a variety of ways. Different types of *sensory receptors* in the skin can detect touch, pressure, temperature, and pain. This system allows the body to sense changes in the environment and to respond appropriately. As a *physical barrier*, the skin can prevent infectious microbes or harmful substances from entering the body. (Pathogens that do manage to enter are subject to a second line of defense: macrophages and other cells of the immune system.) The skin also helps to shield the body from ultraviolet radiation. When the body is exposed to the sun, melanocytes respond by increasing the production of melanin. The integumentary system has many mechanisms for *thermoregulation*, including vasoconstriction and vasodilation of superficial capillaries and sweating and evaporation. While the skin is not the primary organ involved in *osmoregulation*, it does play an important role. The skin helps prevent water loss from the underlying tissues, as well as the excessive uptake of water from outside the body. It also excretes salts and metabolic wastes such as urea and ammonia through sweat. The ducts of eccrine sweat glands reabsorb many of the sodium ions before they are lost during perspiration.

When the body is cold, it responds by contracting a small smooth muscle in the dermis called the **arrector pili**. This muscle pulls on the hair follicle, causing the hair to stand erect. When many hairs stand up simultaneously, it helps to trap a warm layer of air which has an insulating effect. However, this effect may be minimal in humans.

A better insulator comes in the form of adipose tissue. Beneath the dermis is a layer of subcutaneous tissue known as the **hypodermis** (which is considered separate from the skin). It helps to anchor the skin to the underlying organs and consists mainly of loose connective tissue, specifically adipose tissue. This layer of fat cells provides insulation from heat and cold.

SWEAT GLANDS, LOCATION IN DERMIS

There are two types of sweat glands (also called sudoriferous glands) in the body: eccrine glands and apocrine glands. The secretory portion of these glands lies in the dermis. Apocrine sweat glands tend to lie deeper in the dermis than eccrine sweat glands because eccrine sweat glands secrete sweat directly onto the skin, while the ducts of apocrine glands empty into hair follicles. Apocrine sweat glands are found only in certain regions of the body, and their function is not clear; they play no role in thermoregulation. They only activate at the onset of puberty in response to sex hormones. Eccrine glands, however, are found nearly everywhere, and the secretion and evaporation of sweat helps to cool the body. The release of sweat is regulated by the hypothalamus. When body temperature rises above normal, the hypothalamus sends signals telling the eccrine sweat glands to secrete until enough heat has been removed. Hormones play a role in the degree to which the body sweats, which may explain why men sweat more than women.

VASOCONSTRICTION AND VASODILATION IN SURFACE CAPILLARIES

When body temperature rises, arterioles in the dermis can promote heat loss by dilating in response to signals from the hypothalamus. This allows more blood to enter capillary beds near the surface of the skin, and heat is lost to the surroundings, primarily through radiation. Conduction and convection can also cool the body, assuming the surrounding temperature is cooler than the body. If the body temperature is too low, the adrenal medulla secretes the hormones epinephrine and norepinephrine, which act on the arterioles, causing them to constrict. This reduces the volume of warm blood that flows near the body's surface, minimizing heat loss at the skin surface.

PHYSICAL PROTECTION
NAILS, CALLUSES, HAIR

Nails are dense plates of hardened keratinocytes that protect the distal ends of fingers and toes. Each nail is composed of modified epidermal tissue that grows from the nail matrix. The nail itself does not have sensory receptors, but pressure can still be detected. Nails also aid in the grasping and manipulation of objects, while protecting delicate tissues beneath.

When a region of the skin experiences repeated mechanical abrasion, the stratum basale responds by increasing the rate of mitosis, which soon leads to an overdevelopment of the stratum corneum (hyperkeratosis). The buildup of dead cells forms a protective pad called a callus.

Hair provides a variety of protective functions as well. It shields the scalp from ultraviolet light, and offers some cushioning in case of injury. It also helps to insulate the skull. Hairs of the nostrils, ears, eyebrows, and eyelashes help to trap foreign particles. Hairs can also act as sensory receptors, allowing a quick response to possible injury.

PROTECTION AGAINST ABRASION, DISEASE ORGANISMS

The skin is continually subject to minor abrasions, but it is protected by the keratin-filled cells of the epidermis. The outer cells of the stratum corneum lose their connection to neighboring cells and slough off when exposed to mechanical stress. Keratinocytes, along with glycolipids produced by the stratum granulosum, form a seal that keeps harmful chemicals and pathogenic organisms from entering the body. The secretions of sweat and sebaceous glands mix together on the surface of the skin to form the **acid mantle**. The low pH of these secretions, along with antimicrobial agents and enzymes, helps to prevent infection. There are also beneficial microorganisms that populate the surface of the skin that outcompete harmful microbes. Within the layers of skin are dendritic cells and other white blood cells that are ready to engulf disease-causing organisms.

ENDOCRINE SYSTEM

The endocrine system consists of all the glands and tissues that secrete chemical messengers called hormones. The endocrine system works closely with the faster-acting nervous system to coordinate and regulate important processes including growth, development, metabolism, immune function, reproduction, response to stress, and water and electrolyte balance. In short, the endocrine system is essential for the maintenance of homeostasis in the body. When hormones are secreted into the extracellular fluid, they diffuse into the bloodstream and are carried throughout the body. Only cells with receptors that are specific to the secreted hormones are affected. This specificity allows hormones to control targeted tissues and organs, often other endocrine glands (these are called tropic hormones). Major glands of the endocrine system include the hypothalamus, pineal gland, pituitary gland, thyroid, parathyroid glands, thymus, adrenal glands, gonads, and pancreas. Certain cells within the heart, kidneys, gastrointestinal tract, and placenta also have endocrine functions.

An **endocrine gland** produces hormones and secretes them directly into the blood without the use of a duct. (*Endo* = within, *crine* = separate or secretion.) When the hormones are first released by the gland, they enter the interstitial fluid before diffusing into nearby capillaries. The circulatory system then delivers the hormones to target organs. By contrast, **exocrine glands** release non-hormone products such as sweat, oil, tears, and bile through ducts to their target locations—usually a cavity or epithelial surface inside or outside the body. Unlike hormones, exocrine products do not bind to receptors.

Hormones are molecules that bind to receptors and deliver regulatory messages. Many of these signaling molecules are steroids derived from cholesterol. These include the sex hormones and corticosteroids. The rest are non-steroids and include amines, peptides, and proteins.

HORMONE SOURCES OF THE HEAD AND NECK

The **hypothalamus** is the link between the nervous system and the endocrine system. It is located in the brain, superior to the pituitary and inferior to the thalamus. The hypothalamus communicates with the pituitary by secreting "releasing hormones" (RH) and "inhibiting hormones" (IH). Hormones of the hypothalamus include:

Hormone	Action
GnRH—gonadotropin RH	Stimulates anterior pituitary to release LH and FSH
GHRH—growth hormone RH	Stimulates anterior pituitary to release GH
GHIH—growth hormone IH (somatostatin)	Inhibits the release of GH from the anterior pituitary
TRH—thyrotropin RH	Stimulates anterior pituitary to release thyrotropin (TSH)
PRH—prolactin RH	Stimulates anterior pituitary to release prolactin
PIH—prolactin IH (dopamine)	Inhibits the release of prolactin from the anterior pituitary
CRH—corticotropin RH	Stimulates anterior pituitary to release ACTH
Oxytocin	Targets the uterus to stimulate contractions. Targets the mammary glands for milk secretion
ADH—antidiuretic hormone (vasopressin)	Targets the kidneys and blood vessels to increase water retention

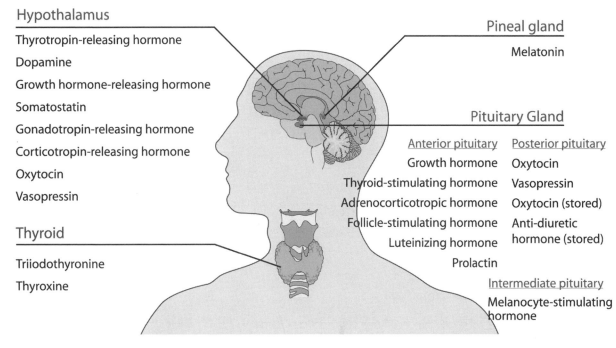

Hypothalamus

Thyrotropin-releasing hormone

Dopamine

Growth hormone-releasing hormone

Somatostatin

Gonadotropin-releasing hormone

Corticotropin-releasing hormone

Oxytocin

Vasopressin

Thyroid

Triiodothyronine

Thyroxine

Pineal gland

Melatonin

Pituitary Gland

Anterior pituitary	Posterior pituitary
Growth hormone	Oxytocin
Thyroid-stimulating hormone	Vasopressin
Adrenocorticotropic hormone	Oxytocin (stored)
Follicle-stimulating hormone	Anti-diuretic hormone (stored)
Luteinizing hormone	
Prolactin	

Intermediate pituitary

Melanocyte-stimulating hormone

Science

The **pituitary** is nicknamed the "master gland" because many of the hormones it secretes act on other endocrine glands. It is located within the sella turcica of the sphenoid bone, beneath the hypothalamus. This pea-sized gland hangs from a thin stalk called the infundibulum, and it consists of an anterior and posterior lobe, each with a different function.

Source	Hormone	Action
Pituitary gland (anterior)	TSH—thyroid stimulating hormone (thyrotropin)	Targets the thyroid—stimulates the secretion of thyroid hormones
	ACTH—adrenocorticotropic hormone	Targets the adrenal cortex—stimulates the release of glucocorticoids and mineralocorticoids
	GH—growth hormone	Targets muscle and bone—stimulates growth
	FSH—follicle stimulating hormone	Targets the gonads—stimulates the maturation of sperm cells and ovarian follicles
	LH—luteinizing hormone	Targets the gonads—stimulates the production of sex hormones; surge stimulates ovulation in females
	PRL—prolactin	Targets the mammary glands—stimulates production of milk
Pituitary gland (posterior)	Oxytocin (produced in hypothalamus; stored and released by posterior pituitary)	Targets the uterus—stimulates contractions Targets the mammary glands—stimulates milk secretion
	ADH—antidiuretic hormone (vasopressin) (produced in hypothalamus; stored and released by posterior pituitary)	Targets the kidneys and blood vessels—increases water retention

Source/Description	Hormone	Action
Pineal gland Situated between the two hemispheres of the brain where the two halves of the thalamus join.	Melatonin	Targets the brain—regulates daily rhythm (wake and sleep)
Thyroid gland Butterfly-shaped gland; the point of attachment between the two lobes is called the isthmus. The isthmus is on the anterior portion of the trachea, with the lobes wrapping partially around the trachea.	T_3—triiodothyronine	Targets most cells—stimulates cellular metabolism
	T_4—thyroxine	Targets most cells—stimulates cellular metabolism
	Calcitonin	Targets bone and kidneys—lowers blood calcium
Parathyroid gland Four small glands that are embedded in the posterior aspect of the thyroid.	PTH—Parathyroid hormone	Targets bone and kidneys—raises blood calcium

HORMONE SOURCES OF THE ABDOMEN

Source/Description	Hormone	Action
Thymus gland Located between the sternum and the heart, embedded in the mediastinum. It slowly decreases in size after puberty.	Thymosin	Targets lymphatic tissues—stimulates the production of T-cells
Pancreas The head of the pancreas is situated in the curve of the duodenum and the tail points toward the left side of the body. The pancreas is mostly posterior to the stomach.	Insulin	Targets the liver, muscle, and adipose tissue—decreases blood glucose
	Glucagon	Targets the liver—increases blood glucose
	GHIH—growth hormone IH (somatostatin)	Inhibits the secretion of insulin and glucagon
Adrenal medulla Located on top of the kidneys. The adrenal medulla is the inner part of the gland.	Epinephrine and norepinephrine	Target heart, blood vessels, liver, and lungs—increase heart rate, increase blood sugar (fight or flight response)
Adrenal cortex The adrenal cortex is the outer portion of the adrenal gland.	Mineralocorticoids (aldosterone)	Target the kidneys—increase the retention of Na^+ and excretion of K^+
	Glucocorticoids	Target most tissues—released in response to long-term stressors, increase blood glucose (but not as quickly as glucagon)
	Androgens	Target most tissues—stimulate development of secondary sex characteristics

Liver
Insulin-like growth
factor (somatomedin)
Angiotensinogen
Angiotensin
Thrombopoietin

Duodenum
Secretin
Cholecystokinin

Kidney
Renin
Erythropoietin
Calcitriol
Thrombopoietin

Stomach
Gastrin
Ghrelin
Neuropeptide Y
Somatostatin
Histamine
Endothelin

Pancreas
Insulin
Glucagon
Somatostatin
Pancreatic polypeptide

Adrenal glands
Glucocorticoids
Mineralocorticoids
Androgens

Adrenal medulla
Adrenaline
Noradrenaline
Dopamine
Enkephalin

Science

Source/Description	Hormone	Action
GI tract Cells within the mucosa of the small intestine and stomach release hormones to control much of the digestion process.	Gastrin	Targets the stomach—stimulates the release of HCl
	Secretin	Targets the pancreas and liver—stimulates the release of digestive enzymes and bile
	CCK—cholecystokinin	Targets the pancreas and liver—stimulates the release of digestive enzymes and bile
Kidneys Bean-shaped organs located in the lumbar region, one on each side of the sagittal plane.	Erythropoietin	Targets the bone marrow—stimulates the production of red blood cells
	Calcitriol	Targets the intestines—increases the reabsorption of Ca^{2+}
Heart Situated just left of the midline of the body, between the lungs	ANP—atrial natriuretic peptide	Targets the kidneys and adrenal cortex—reduces reabsorption of Na^+, lowers blood pressure
Adipose Tissue Located under the layers of skin and throughout the body.	Leptin	Targets the brain—suppresses appetite

HORMONE SOURCES OF THE REPRODUCTIVE SYSTEM

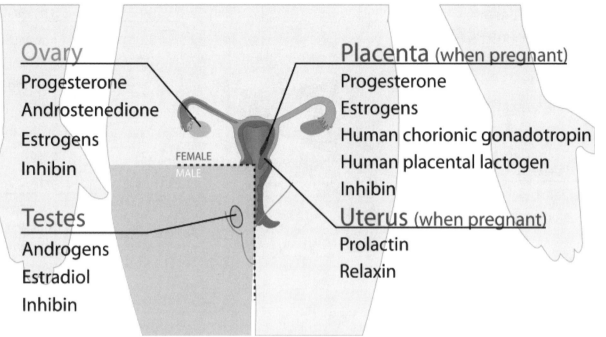

Ovary
Progesterone
Androstenedione
Estrogens
Inhibin

Testes
Androgens
Estradiol
Inhibin

FEMALE
MALE

Placenta (when pregnant)
Progesterone
Estrogens
Human chorionic gonadotropin
Human placental lactogen
Inhibin

Uterus (when pregnant)
Prolactin
Relaxin

Source/Description	Hormone	Action
Ovaries The ovaries rest in depressions in the pelvic cavity on each side of the uterus. (Note that ovaries produce testosterone in small amounts.)	Estrogen	Targets the uterus, ovaries, mammary glands, brain, and other tissues—stimulates uterine lining growth, regulates menstrual cycle, facilitates the development of secondary sex characteristics
	Progesterone	Targets mainly the uterus and mammary glands—stimulates uterine lining growth, regulates menstrual cycle, required for maintenance of pregnancy
	Inhibin	Targets the anterior pituitary—inhibits the release of FSH
Placenta Attached to the wall of the uterus during pregnancy	Estrogen, progesterone, and inhibin	(See above)
	Human chorionic gonadotropin (hCG)	Targets the ovaries—stimulates the production of estrogen and progesterone
Testes Located within the scrotum, behind the penis.	Testosterone	Targets the testes and many other tissues—promotes spermatogenesis, secondary sex characteristics
	Inhibin	(See above)

MAJOR TYPES OF HORMONES

Hormones can be broadly classified into lipid-soluble hormones (steroids) and water-soluble hormones (non-steroids). Steroid hormones are derived from cholesterol, and their base structure consists of four fused carbon rings. They are released by the adrenal cortex, testes, ovaries, and the placenta. Major types of steroid hormones include the **sex hormones** (estrogens, androgens, progesterone) and the **corticosteroids** (glucocorticoids and mineralocorticoids). Since these hormones are lipid-soluble, they can diffuse through the cell membrane and bind to the nuclear receptors that regulate transcription.

Non-steroid hormones tend to elicit faster responses than steroid hormones. They cannot diffuse into the cell and instead bind to receptors on the cell membrane, activating second-messenger systems. These hormones are classified into amines, peptides, and proteins. **Amines** are derivatives of the amino acids tyrosine or tryptophan, and include epinephrine, norepinephrine, thyroxine, and melatonin. **Peptide hormones** are short chains of amino acids. Common examples include oxytocin, somatostatin, and antidiuretic hormone. **Protein hormones** such as insulin, growth hormone, and parathyroid hormone consist of longer chains—generally over 100 amino acids. Hormones can also be **glycoproteins**. Follicle-stimulating hormone, thyroid-stimulating hormone, and luteinizing hormone all have carbohydrate attachments.

> **Review Video: Endocrine System**
> Visit mometrix.com/academy and enter code: 678939

URINARY SYSTEM
KIDNEY STRUCTURE

The kidneys are bean-shaped organs located in the lumbar region of the body that function in the filtering of blood and the excretion of wastes. Each kidney is surrounded by three protective layers of connective tissue: the **renal fascia**, the **adipose capsule**, and the innermost **renal capsule**. The capsule surrounds the outer region of the kidney called the **renal cortex**. The cortex contains many filtration units called **nephrons**, which have tubules that dip into the interior region called the **medulla**. The tubules in the medulla run parallel to each other and form striped cone-shaped masses of tissue called **medullary pyramids**. A cavity called the **renal sinus** contains the basin-like **renal pelvis**, which funnels the urine into the ureter. The **hilum** is the concave region of the kidney where the blood vessels and nerves enter and leave. Blood enters the kidney through the renal artery, which branches into smaller and smaller arteries until the blood reaches a tuft of capillaries called the **glomerulus**. Here, the blood is filtered before leaving the kidney through a network of veins that merge into the renal vein.

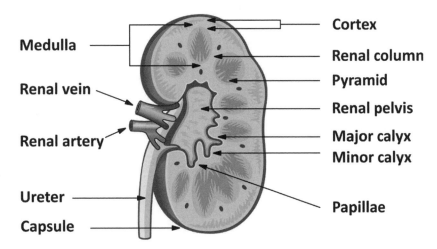

CORTEX

The renal cortex is the outer portion of the kidney, and it is the site of **ultrafiltration**: the nonspecific filtration of blood under high pressure. It is also responsible for the majority of the reabsorption of water. The cortex is very vascular and has a granular appearance due to the presence of nephrons. The renal corpuscles and the convoluted tubules of the nephrons are within the cortex (forming the **cortical labyrinth**), but the loops of Henle extend into the adjacent region known as the renal medulla. The thick, straight portions of the proximal and distal tubules, as well as the collecting ducts, form **medullary rays** that begin in the cortex and run perpendicular to the capsule. About 85% of nephrons (cortical nephrons) have short loops of Henle that extend only slightly into the medulla. The remaining 15% (juxtamedullary nephrons) have longer loops that extend deeper. Extensions of the cortex called **renal columns** dip down in between the renal pyramids of the medulla.

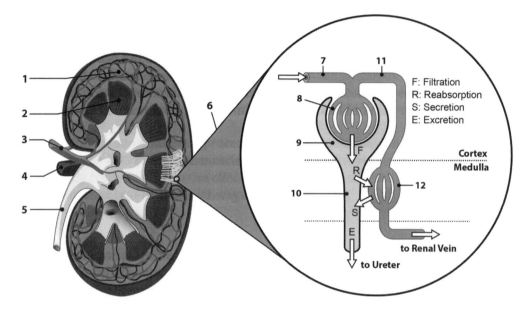

1: Renal cortex. 2: Medulla. 3: Renal artery. 4: Renal vein. 5: Ureter. 6: Nephrons. 7: Afferent arteriole. 8: Glomerulus. 9: Bowman's capsule. 10: Renal tubule. 11: Efferent arteriole. 12: Peritubular capillaries.

MEDULLA

The adrenal medulla is the inner part of the kidney, and it continues the reabsorption of water and salts that began in the cortex. These substances enter the peritubular capillaries that are associated with the nephrons. Any filtrate that is not reclaimed by the circulatory system will leave as urine.

The medulla contains cone-shaped regions of tissue called **renal pyramids** that are separated by **renal columns**. The tips of the pyramids are oriented toward the pelvis of the kidney, and the bases face the cortex. The renal pyramids contain tubules that transport renal filtrate from the renal cortex to the apex of the pyramids. At the apex is a structure called the **renal papilla** that contains ducts that allow the processed filtrate (now called urine) to pass out of the medulla to collecting chambers called **calyces**. From here the urine passes through the renal pelvis, through the ureter, and finally into the bladder.

NEPHRON STRUCTURE

The nephron is the functional unit of the kidney. Each kidney has over a million of these microscopic structures, and each one consists of two main parts: the **renal corpuscle** (which filters the blood) and the **renal tubule** (which collects and concentrates the filtrate). The renal corpuscle consists of a cup-shaped structure called **Bowman's capsule** that wraps partially around a cluster of capillaries called the **glomerulus**. The renal tubule is a looping canal that is continuous with Bowman's capsule. It consists of different regions that differ in structure and function. The **proximal convoluted tubule** begins at Bowman's capsule and then plunges into the medulla,

156

forming a u-shape called the **loop of Henle**. It then becomes the **distal convoluted tubule**, which is continuous with the **collecting duct**. The collecting duct is typically considered a separate structure and not part of the nephron.

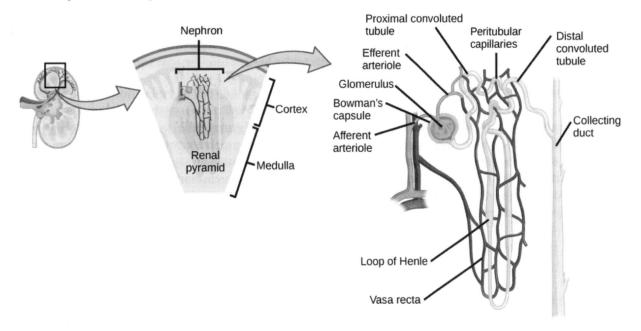

GLOMERULUS AND BOWMAN'S CAPSULE

Each renal corpuscle consists of a **glomerulus** and a **Bowman's capsule**. The glomerulus is a tangled network of blood capillaries that occupies Bowman's capsule. These fenestrated capillaries are lined with a thin layer of epithelial cells. An **afferent arteriole** takes blood to the glomerulus and an **efferent arteriole** takes it away. The smaller diameter of the efferent arteriole increases the pressure within the glomerulus, which is required for ultrafiltration. **Mesangial cells** contract to regulate blood flow, and also support the capillary network.

Bowman's capsule is a cup-like structure at the closed end of the renal tubule that encloses the glomerulus. It has an outer layer of epithelial cells that form the parietal layer, and it has a visceral layer of **podocytes** with processes called **pedicels** that wrap around the capillaries. Gaps between the pedicels (filtration slits) allow the passage of tiny molecules and ions. Together, the endothelial cells of the capillaries, the basement membrane, and the pedicels make up the **filtration membrane**. Fluid from the blood leaves the fenestrated capillaries and passes through the filtration membrane and collects in **Bowman's space** (the cavity between the two layers of Bowman's capsule). From here, the filtrate enters the renal tubule.

PROXIMAL TUBULE, LOOP OF HENLE, AND DISTAL TUBULE

The renal tubule is divided into three continuous regions: the proximal convoluted tubule, the loop of Henle, and the distal convoluted tubule. The **proximal convoluted tubule** extends from Bowman's capsule, and this coiled tube is characterized by cuboidal cells with dense microvilli that aid in reabsorption and secretion. There are only sparse microvilli in the rest of the tubule. The middle, hairpin-shaped portion of the renal tubule is called the **loop of Henle**, and it maintains a relatively high solute concentration in the medulla, which in turn assists in the reabsorption of water. The loop consists of a descending limb (which reabsorbs water) that plunges into the medulla, a U-turn that curves back toward the cortex, and an ascending limb (which reabsorbs ions). The ascending limb widens into a thick portion composed of larger epithelial cells. The loop is

157

lined with simple squamous epithelial cells, with the exception of the thick ascending limb which is lined with simple cuboidal cells. This limb becomes the **distal convoluted tubule** (also lined with cuboidal cells), which is involved in absorption and secretion, but not to the extent of the proximal convoluted tubule. It is also shorter in length.

COLLECTING DUCT

The collecting duct is the final site of reabsorption in the kidney, and it is shared by multiple nephrons. The distal tubule empties filtrate into the collecting tubule, which merges with other collecting tubules to form the collecting duct. Collecting tubules are lined with simple cuboidal epithelium, but these cells elongate to form columnar cells as they get closer to the duct. Some of these cells are **principal cells**, which reabsorb sodium ions and water (under ADH and aldosterone control). Other cells are **intercalated cells**, and they play an important role in acid-base balance and the reabsorption of sodium ions. Both these types of cells can also be found toward the end part of the distal tubule, but there are fewer microvilli than in the collecting duct. The filtrate that passes through the collecting duct enters the minor calyces at the apex of a medullary pyramid.

FORMATION OF URINE
GLOMERULAR FILTRATION

The formation of urine begins with glomerular filtration. This nonspecific filtration is driven by the hydrostatic pressure of the blood. This pressure is higher than in other capillaries because the efferent arterioles that exit the glomerulus have a smaller diameter than the afferent arterioles that enter. Water and small solutes from the blood are forced through fenestrations in the capillaries, leaving behind larger particles. The fluid must pass through the 3-layered filtration membrane before entering Bowman's space as renal filtrate. The first layer is the endothelial lining of the capillaries. Fenestrations in the capillaries prevent the passage of blood cells. The second layer is the basement membrane, which excludes plasma proteins such as albumin. The third layer is the visceral lining of Bowman's capsule. Small filtration slits between the podocytes allow only the smallest of particles to pass. The concentration of a solute in the glomerular filtrate is the same as the concentration in the blood. on average, about 1/5 of the blood is filtered, but this varies depending on the pressure.

SECRETION AND REABSORPTION OF SOLUTES

Secretion removes solutes from the blood and adds them to the filtrate, while reabsorption removes solutes from the filtrate and returns them to the blood. Solutes are moved by either primary active transport, secondary active transport, or diffusion, and water is reabsorbed by osmosis. This table outlines the functions of each region of the renal tubule and collecting duct:

Region	Role in Secretion	Role in Reabsorption
Proximal convoluted tubule	H^+, creatinine, NH_4^+, drugs, toxins—active transport	Main site of reabsorption in the kidney; 60–70% of the volume of filtrate is reclaimed in the PCT. Glucose, amino acids, vitamins, Na^+, Cl^-, K^+, Ca^{2+}, Mg^{2+}, bicarbonate, phosphate, water, urea
Loop of Henle—Descending limb	Urea	Water
Loop of Henle—Ascending limb		Na^+, Cl^-, K^+, Mg^{2+}, Ca^{2+}
Distal convoluted tubule	K^+, H^+	Cl^-, Ca^{2+}, Na^+, Water (variable permeability – opening of Na^+ channels is dependent on aldosterone)
Collecting duct	K^+, H^+	Urea, bicarbonate, Na^+, Water (variable permeability—dependent on aldosterone and ADH)

CONCENTRATION OF URINE

The concentration of urine is influenced by the high solute concentration of the medulla, and the hormones that control the permeability of the distal convoluted tubule and collecting duct.

The **countercurrent mechanism** describes the use of active transport to move solutes out of the ascending loop of Henle (which is impermeable to water) into the medullary interstitium. The osmotic gradient that is created causes water to diffuse out of the descending limb (which *is* permeable to water), concentrating the filtrate. The recycling of urea also helps to maintain a high medullary osmolarity. The descending loop of Henle and the collecting duct are both permeable to urea, but the descending limb and the distal tubule are not. Urea enters the descending loop from the interstitium, and travels through the renal tubule to the collecting duct, where it reenters the interstitium.

The concentration of urine is also regulated by hormones. The permeability of the distal convoluted tubule to sodium is dependent on aldosterone. Aldosterone promotes the reabsorption of Na^+, and since water follows the sodium, the urine becomes more concentrated. The permeability of the collecting duct is dependent on both aldosterone and ADH. ADH increases the duct's permeability by water by inserting aquaporins that allow the passage of water.

COUNTERCURRENT MULTIPLIER MECHANISM

A countercurrent system in the loop of Henle is responsible for the generation of an osmotic gradient in the medulla that promotes the reabsorption of water. The descending limb is permeable to water, but not solutes. The ascending limb is permeable to solutes, but not water. Na^+, Cl^-, and other ions are actively transported from the ascending limb into the medullary interstitium. The concentration gradient causes water to leave the descending limb by osmosis, which increases the concentration of the filtrate in the descending limb. As the filtrate moves up the ascending limb, ions are actively absorbed, raising the solute concentration in the medulla. This positive feedback loop is known as the countercurrent *multiplier* mechanism because it multiplies the concentration of the interstitial fluid as a result of the functional differences between the two limbs.

The countercurrent multiplier system is distinguished from the countercurrent *exchange* system, in which the hypertonicity of the medulla is *maintained* (not generated) by the countercurrent flow of blood in the vasa recta. As blood in the *descending* part of the vasa recta passes the *ascending* limb, it picks up ions that left the filtrate. As blood in the *ascending* vasa recta passes the *descending* limb, most of the ions diffuse back into the medulla.

STORAGE AND ELIMINATION: URETER, BLADDER, URETHRA

A **ureter** is a tubular organ that delivers urine from the kidney to the bladder for storage. The collecting ducts (the final sites of reabsorption) empty urine into the ureter, and both gravity and peristalsis move the urine into the bladder. The bladder is a bag-like organ that can store up to 600 mL of urine (though the desire to urinate begins at around 150 mL). The ureters, bladder, and superior portion of the urethra are lined with transitional epithelial tissue that allows expansion. When the organ becomes distended, the stretched epithelium appears to have fewer cell layers.

Urine is stored in the bladder until contraction of the **detrusor muscle** (the smooth muscle within the bladder wall) forces urine into the urethra. Contraction of the bladder is controlled by the parasympathetic nervous system. Stretch receptors in the bladder send impulses to the sacral region of the spinal cord. Impulses are then sent along efferent neurons to the bladder, telling it to contract. A circular smooth muscle called the internal urethral sphincter relaxes, and (if the timing

159

is appropriate) the voluntary external urethral sphincter relaxes as well. Urine flows from the bladder, through the urethra, and out of the body in a process called micturition.

MUSCULAR CONTROL: SPHINCTER MUSCLE

There are two sphincters of the urethra that delay the emptying of the bladder. The **internal urethral sphincter** (IUS) is found between the bladder and the urethra. It consists of smooth muscle and is continuous with the smooth muscle of the bladder (the detrusor muscle). The sympathetic nervous system keeps the IUS contracted until the micturition reflex is triggered. The IUS relaxes as a result of sympathetic inhibition, allowing urine to pass through. The second sphincter that controls the elimination of urine is the **external urethral sphincter** (EUS), which is made of skeletal muscle and under the control of the somatic nervous system. A conscious decision can be made to relax the EUS under appropriate circumstances. Involuntary contraction of the detrusor forces urine out of the body, and the voluntary contraction of abdominal muscles can increase the rate of flow by compressing the bladder.

> **Review Video: Urinary System**
> Visit mometrix.com/academy and enter code: 601053

ROLES IN HOMEOSTASIS
BLOOD PRESSURE

When osmoreceptors detect an increase in blood osmolality, or when baroreceptors detect a decrease in blood pressure, the pituitary gland secretes **antidiuretic hormone** (ADH). ADH stimulates the reabsorption of water in the kidney so that less water is excreted in the urine. This increases the volume and pressure of the blood.

The **renin-angiotensin-aldosterone system** (RAAS) is another mechanism by which blood pressure is regulated. When granular juxtaglomerular cells of the afferent arterioles of the kidneys detect a drop in blood pressure, they secrete an enzyme called **renin**. Renin interacts with a plasma protein called **angiotensinogen**, producing **angiotensin I**. As angiotensin I enters the capillaries of the lungs, it is acted on by another enzyme that converts it to **angiotensin II**. This hormone raises blood pressure by promoting vasoconstriction and stimulating the adrenal cortex to release **aldosterone**. Aldosterone increases the reabsorption of sodium, which increases water reabsorption, causing the blood volume and pressure to increase.

OSMOREGULATION

Osmoregulation describes the regulation of water and solute concentrations of body fluids. The primary organ involved in this process is the kidney. Dehydration or excessive salt intake will raise the osmolality of the blood. (Plasma osmolality is determined mainly by the concentrations of electrolytes, such as Na^+, Cl^-, and K^+.) When osmoreceptors in the hypothalamus detect an increase in osmolality, signals are sent to the pituitary gland to release ADH. ADH causes the collecting ducts in the kidneys to be more permeable to water, and water crosses the epithelium from the urine into the interstitium where it is returned to the blood. As a result, the blood osmolality decreases, and urine osmolality increases.

Aldosterone also plays a role in osmoregulation. When blood pressure is low, this hormone is secreted by the adrenal cortex. Aldosterone increases sodium reabsorption, which causes more water to leave the collecting tubule, thus raising blood osmolality. It also regulates the concentrations of other ions, such as potassium and chloride.

ACID–BASE BALANCE

The kidneys are key players in the maintenance of blood pH, which must be kept within a narrow range of 7.35 and 7.45. This is achieved by regulating the ratio of hydrogen ions to bicarbonate ions. (The higher the concentration of H^+ ions, the lower the pH.) Buffer systems in the body such as the phosphate, protein, and bicarbonate systems are in place to resist changes in H^+ concentration. Recall that the respiratory system helps to control pH through the bicarbonate buffer system. When carbon dioxide combines with water, carbonic acid (H_2CO_3) is formed, before dissociating into bicarbonate ions (HCO_3^-) and H^+. (Reaction: $CO_2 + H_2O \leftrightarrow H_2CO_3 \leftrightarrow HCO_3^- + H^+$.) Increasing the rate of respiration decreases the concentration of H^+, which increases pH. The reverse is true when the rate of respiration decreases. The response from the kidneys is slower, but lasts longer. As blood pH decreases, H^+ ions are excreted by the renal tubules via urine (which is now more acidic) and bicarbonate ions are retained. The intercalated cells of the late distal tubule and collecting duct can also generate new bicarbonate ions. The kidneys lower pH by reabsorbing H^+ ions and secreting bicarbonate ions.

REMOVAL OF SOLUBLE NITROGENOUS WASTE

Nitrogen-containing wastes such as ammonia, urea, uric acid, and creatinine are excreted in urine. **Ammonia** is a toxic base that is formed during the breakdown of amino acids. Enzymes in the liver convert it to a less toxic form called **urea**. There is a high concentration of urea in the medulla because the collecting ducts are permeable to it. Much of the urea enters the interstitium, and it is then reabsorbed into the descending loop of Henle. Urea is the most abundant nitrogenous waste product in the urine, but since most of it is recycled, only a small amount is eliminated in urine. The high concentration of urea in the interstitium is helpful because it promotes the reabsorption of water. **Uric acid** is another nitrogenous waste that is excreted in the urine. It is formed as a byproduct of the catabolism of purine nucleotides, and most of it is reabsorbed in the proximal tubule by active transport. Like urea, only a small percentage is excreted. **Creatinine** is produced in the muscles as a byproduct of the metabolism of creatine phosphate. It is filtered by the kidneys and excreted. Unlike urea and uric acid, creatinine is not reabsorbed by the tubules.

IMMUNE SYSTEM
INNATE (NON-SPECIFIC) VS. ADAPTIVE (SPECIFIC) IMMUNITY

Innate immunity refers to the nonspecific first line of defense against pathogens that is present at birth. There is no potential for this system to "learn" from previous pathogens or adapt to new threats. The first barriers to infection include mechanical barriers such as the skin and mucous membranes. Chemical barriers include the low pH of gastric juice, interferons that block viral replication, lysozyme in tears, and other antimicrobial proteins such as defensins, collectins, and complements. Pathogens can also be engulfed by phagocytes, or by the destruction of the infected cell by natural killer cells. Fever and inflammation can offer nonspecific protection as well. **Adaptive immunity** develops over time. It may be slow to act initially, but the "memory" of the first encounter with an **antigen** (a toxin or a molecule on the surface of a pathogen that triggers an immune response) allows for faster responses in subsequent exposures to that same antigen. The antigen is recognized as foreign, and the appropriate type of cell is selected to combat the pathogen with which it is associated. These cells are primarily lymphocytes. Depending on the type of lymphocyte, they respond to infection by producing antibodies, killing infected cells, or directing other immune responses.

ADAPTIVE IMMUNE SYSTEM CELLS

There are two main types of lymphocytes that are involved in adaptive immune responses: T-lymphocytes (T cells) and B-lymphocytes (B cells).

Science

161

T cells mature in the thymus, and are involved in cell-mediated immunity. The initial activation of T cells occurs when they encounter their specific antigen on the surface of an antigen-presenting cell (or APC). When they bind to these APCs, they proliferate and differentiate into various types of T cells. **Cytotoxic T cells** are specialized to kill infected or abnormal cells. Some cytotoxic T cells produce **memory T cells** that respond to subsequent infections. **Helper T cells** secrete cytokines that stimulate the division of T and B cells, while alerting other types of WBCs. **Regulatory (suppressor) T cells** inhibit T and B cells to stop the immune response.

B cells mature in the bone marrow and are involved in humoral-mediated immunity. The initial activation of B cells occurs when they encounter freely circulating antigens. (Many B cells require co-stimulation by a helper T cell.) After binding to specific antigens, B cells differentiate into plasma cells and memory B cells. **Plasma cells** secrete antibodies that bind to antigens. **Memory B cells** also produce antibodies, but only during a subsequent infection.

INNATE IMMUNE SYSTEM CELLS

There are various types of cells involved in innate immunity, many of which are phagocytes. **Neutrophils** account for most of the white blood cells in the bloodstream. These phagocytes are usually the first to arrive at the site of infection, and they chase pathogens using chemotaxis. **Eosinophils** regulate inflammatory responses and release chemicals that kill foreign invaders—often parasitic worms. **Mast cells** (found in connective tissues) and **basophils** (which circulate in the blood before entering tissues) both release histamine to promote inflammation and heparin to inhibit clotting. **Macrophages** (derived from monocytes, the largest leukocytes) are large WBCs that engulf debris and pathogenic microorganisms, and function as antigen presenters to effector T cells. **Dendritic cells** function in much the same way, except they activate "naive" T cells (T cells that have not yet encountered their antigen). **Natural killer cells** are not phagocytes; they destroy cells that have been infected with a pathogen by binding to them and releasing granzymes that trigger apoptosis.

Mast cell	Natural killer cell	Monocyte	Macrophage
Neutrophil	Basophil	Dendritic cell	Eosinophil
Fibroblast Cell	T Cell	B Cell	

TISSUES

The functions of the major tissues and organs that play a role in the immune system:

Tissue	Function
Bone Marrow	Produces hematopoietic stem cells that give rise to all types of blood cells, including lymphocytes. Bone marrow is the site of B cell differentiation.
Thymus	This is the site of T cell differentiation.
Spleen	Splenic cords of the red pulp contain an abundance of macrophages and lymphocytes that help to filter aged blood cells, pathogens, and debris from the blood. The white pulp is a lymphatic tissue that consists almost entirely of B and T cells, and it provides a place for these lymphocytes to proliferate.
Lymph nodes	Provide a place for lymphocytes and other WBCs to proliferate (cortex contains B cells and macrophages, medulla contains T cells). Filter the lymph of microorganisms, toxins, and wastes. B cells produce antibodies that assist in the immune response.
MALT	Mucosa-associated lymphoid tissue refers to the small clusters of lymphatic cells that are found in the tonsils, appendix, and Peyer's patches of the small intestine. T cells, B cells, and macrophages provide protection against pathogens.

LYMPHATIC SYSTEM

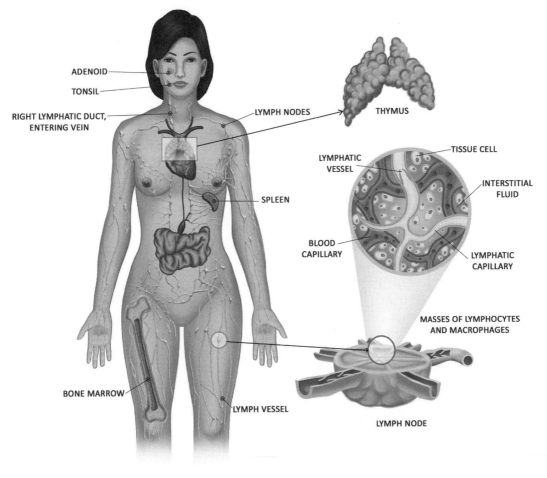

Science

STRUCTURES

The lymphatic system includes the thymus, bone marrow, tonsils, spleen, lymphatic vessels, lymph nodes, and lymph. Lymph is a clear liquid similar in composition to plasma. It is transported in one direction (toward the neck) where it is emptied into the subclavian veins. Lymph consists of white blood cells and the fluid that leaks out of the blood capillaries. Lymphatic vessels are similar in structure to veins; they have thin walls, and also have valves to prevent backflow. Their walls are more porous, however, allowing the lymph to drain into them for circulation. Lymph is moved by contractions of both smooth and skeletal muscle. Lymphatic vessels are found nearly everywhere in the body except the central nervous system and avascular tissues. The vessels are interrupted by oval-shaped masses of tissue called lymph nodes that contain lymphocytes and filter out foreign substances. The primary organs of the lymphatic system (bone marrow and thymus) produce mature lymphocytes. There are also secondary organs (such as the spleen and tonsils) that house lymphocytes. These specialized white blood cells destroy disease-causing microorganisms.

> **Review Video: Immune System**
> Visit mometrix.com/academy and enter code: 622899

CONCEPT OF ANTIGEN AND ANTIBODY

An **antigen** is a substance that elicits a response from the immune system. Antigens are usually large biomolecules (often proteins) that are identified as foreign or non-self. They can be found on the surfaces of antigenic substances such as viruses, bacteria, fungi, and pollen grains. **Foreign antigens** originate outside the body and include the examples listed above. **Self-antigens** are produced by the body and rarely initiate an immune response. They often trigger a response in other people, as seen in the rejection of transplanted tissues or organs.

Antibodies (also called immunoglobulins) are products of B cells that bind to specific antigens. The binding of an antibody to an antigen can disarm the pathogen in a variety of ways. In some cases, the pathogens **agglutinate** (clump together) before being destroyed. Antibodies can also **neutralize** the antigen by blocking its ability to attach to cells, or cause it to become insoluble and **precipitate** out of solution. Sometimes, they activate **complement**—a system of proteins that enhances the effectiveness of the immune response. Other cells of the immune system can be called to action, and phagocytosis can be enhanced in a process called **opsonization**. Antibodies also promote **inflammation** to help slow the spread of infection.

EQUALIZATION OF FLUID DISTRIBUTION AND TRANSPORT OF PROTEINS AND LARGE GLYCERIDES

One key function of the immune system is the equalization of fluid between the blood and tissues. Greater hydrostatic pressure in the blood vessels (as compared to the interstitial fluid) causes fluid to leak out of the vessels into the surrounding tissues. Porous lymphatic capillaries collect excess interstitial fluid (now called lymph) for delivery to the right and left subclavian veins. As it travels through the lymphatic system, the lymph passes through lymph nodes where it is filtered and cleansed. Eventually, it reaches either the right lymphatic duct (which drains into the right subclavian vein) or the thoracic duct (which drains into the left subclavian vein), returning fluid back into the blood. If pressure is too great in the lymphatic vessels, edema will occur as fluid leaks back into the tissues.

The lymphatic system also helps to transport certain biomolecules. The villi of the small intestine harbor specialized lymph capillaries called **lacteals** that absorb fats. These fats are transported in the form of **chylomicrons**, which give the lymph (called **chyle**) a whitish appearance. The lymphatic system is also used to return plasma proteins or cells that leaked out of the blood vessels back into the bloodstream.

PRODUCTION OF LYMPHOCYTES INVOLVED IN IMMUNE REACTIONS

The bone marrow and thymus are the "primary" lymphatic organs because they are the sites of lymphocyte production. Stem cells in the red bone marrow called **hemocytoblasts** give rise to immature lymphocytes. Lymphocytes that stay in the bone marrow differentiate into **B cells** and **natural killer (NK) cells**, and other immature lymphocytes migrate to the thymus where they differentiate into **T cells**. Lymphocytes use the bloodstream to migrate from these primary lymphatic organs to "secondary" lymphatic organs, such as the lymph nodes, spleen, and tonsils. When they make contact with antigens, the lymphocytes are activated and mature into effector cells that can participate in immune reactions.

SKELETAL SYSTEM
ADULT HUMAN SKELETON

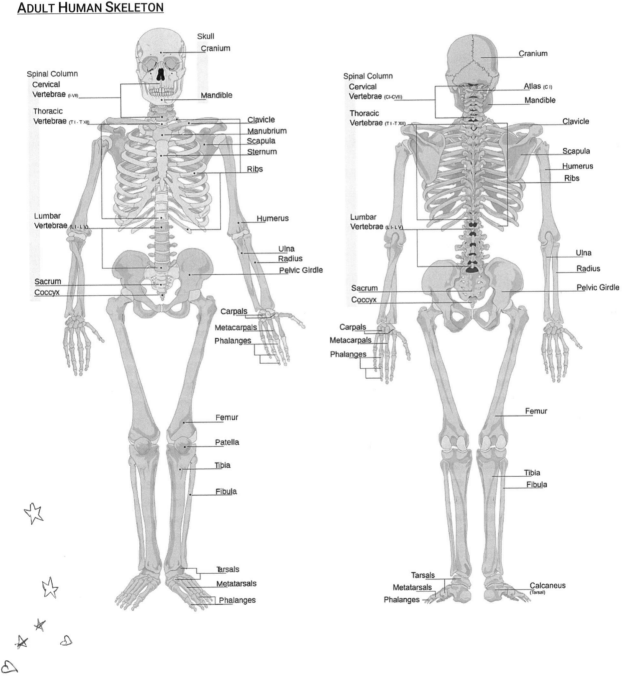

Science

165

STRUCTURE

Bones can be classified as long, short, flat, irregular, and sesamoid. **Long bones** function primarily in movement and supporting body weight. They are rod shaped and are longer than they are wide. The extremities of a long bone (**epiphyses**) are covered in articular cartilage, and they are wider than the shaft (**diaphysis**). Most of the bones of the upper and lower limbs are long bones, as are the collar bones. **Short bones** are roundish or cube-shaped. They have little to no role in movement, and instead function in support and stability. Examples of short bones include the carpals and tarsals of the wrist and ankle, respectively. **Flat bones** are flattened, thin bones that are usually curved. Their broad shape is suited for protection, as well as muscle attachment. The scapulae, sternum, ribs, ilia of the pelvic girdle, and certain cranial bones are all flat bones. **Irregular bones** have complex shapes that do not fit the classifications above, and their form is suited to their function. Examples of irregular bones include the vertebrae and many facial bones. **Sesamoid bones**, such as the kneecap, are found embedded in tendons where there is considerable mechanical stress.

> **Review Video: Skeletal System**
> Visit mometrix.com/academy and enter code: 256447

BONE STRUCTURE

Compact (or cortical) bone is the hard, dense tissue that forms the outer surfaces of bones, as well as the shafts of long bones. It consists of cylindrical structures called **osteons**, also called Haversian systems. Each osteon consists of a central **Haversian canal** that contains nerve fibers and blood vessels, and these canals connect to each other via **perforating canals** (or **Volkmann's canals**). The Haversian canal is surrounded by concentric layers of calcified **lamellae** with small spaces called **lacunae**, each of which contains an **osteocyte**. Tiny channels called **canaliculi** connect the lacunae to allow oxygen and nutrients to reach the osteocytes, and wastes to be removed.

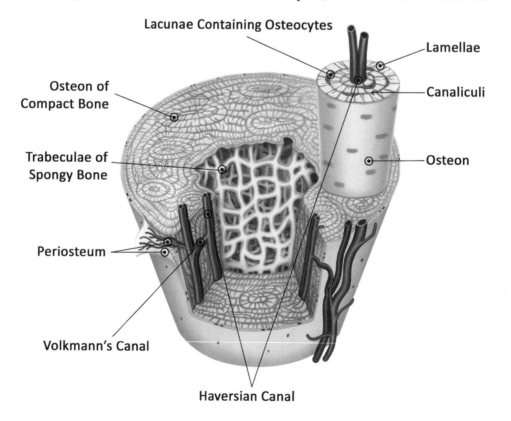

Spongy (or cancellous) bone is the porous tissue found at the ends of long bones and inside the vertebrae and flat bones. It is not as strong or abundant as compact bone, and does not contain osteons. Instead, it consists of flattened, interconnected plates called **trabeculae**. Within the spaces of the trabeculae is the **red bone marrow** that produces blood cells. There are no central canals, but osteocytes do reside in lacunae that are connected by canaliculi.

CELLULAR COMPOSITION OF BONE

Bone consists of an extracellular matrix that surrounds bone cells and functions much like reinforced concrete. The matrix consists of about 2/3 inorganic matter; mostly calcium phosphate (hydroxyapatite) with calcium carbonate and other minerals. The organic portion makes up about 1/3 of the matrix. It consists mainly of collagen, which adds strength and flexibility to the matrix, as well as ground substance proteins such as glycosaminoglycans (GAGs).

There are three types of bone cells. **Osteoblasts** (derived from osteoprogenitor cells) take calcium from the blood, and produce the matrix (including collagen fibers) that forms bone. When it is completely encased in matrix, the osteoblast differentiates into a mature bone cell called an **osteocyte**. Osteocytes are the most abundant bone cells, and they maintain the matrix by recycling calcium salts. **Osteoclasts** are large multinucleate cells that are formed by the fusion of monocytes (large white blood cells). They reside on bone surfaces and secrete acid and digestive enzymes that break down bone and return calcium to the blood.

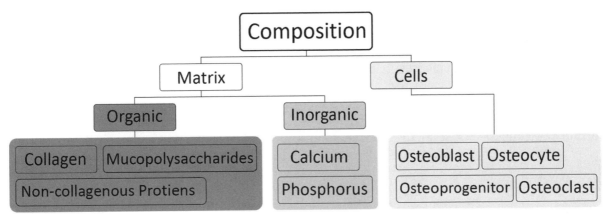

JOINT CLASSIFICATION

Joints are the locations where two or more elements of the skeleton connect. They can be classified according to structure (material holding the joint together) and function (range of motion).

Type of Joint	Structure/Material	Types/Examples
Fibrous	Held together by fibrous connective tissue	Suture: Immovable, ex: skull Gomphosis: Immovable, ex: teeth/mandible Syndesmosis: Slightly movable, ex: distal tibiofibular joint
Cartilaginous	Held together by cartilage	Synchondrosis: Hyaline cartilage, nearly immovable, ex: first rib/sternum Symphysis: Fibrocartilage, slightly movable, ex: intervertebral discs, pubic symphysis

Type of Joint	Structure/Material	Types/Examples
Synovial	The most common type of joint; characterized by a joint cavity filled with synovial fluid	Pivot: Allows rotation, ex: atlantoaxial joint Hinge: Allows movement in one plane, ex: knee Saddle: Allows pivoting in two planes and axial rotation, ex: first metacarpal/trapezium Gliding: Allows sliding, ex: carpals Condyloid: Allows pivoting in two planes but no axial rotation, ex: radiocarpal joint Ball and socket: Have the highest range of motion, ex: hip

Type of Joint	Function/Range of Motion	Examples
Synarthrosis	Immovable—either fibrous or cartilaginous	Skull sutures, teeth/mandible
Amphiarthrosis	Slight range of motion—either fibrous or cartilaginous	Intervertebral discs, distal tibiofibular joint
Diarthrosis	Moves freely—always synovial	Wrist, knee, shoulder

FUNCTIONS OF THE SKELETAL SYSTEM

STRUCTURAL RIGIDITY AND SUPPORT

The skeletal system provides a framework for the body that consists of bones, ligaments, tendons, cartilage, and other tissues. This system is essential in the support and physical protection of the body. Bones support the weight of the body, give shape to body parts, and help keep internal organs in place. Bones also serve as attachment points for muscles, allowing for body movement. Skeletal muscles connect to bones via tendons, and bones attach to each other via ligaments. Cartilage is more flexible and supports body parts such as the ear, the nose, the trachea, and various joints. The skeletal system also protects vital organs. The skull encloses the brain, the vertebrae surround the spinal cord, the thoracic cage protects the heart and lungs, and the pelvic girdle protects the inferior portion of the digestive system, the bladder, and the internal reproductive organs. Delicate bone marrow is also protected within the hollow spaces of certain bones.

CALCIUM STORAGE

Bone is a reservoir for calcium. The bone cells produce a hard acellular **matrix** composed of about 35% collagen and 65% inorganic material. Most of the inorganic matter is a type of **calcium phosphate** known as **hydroxyapatite**. Calcium is required for a number of processes, including the contraction of muscles, the conduction of a nerve impulse, and the clotting of blood. The body takes in calcium in the diet, and about 99% of absorbed calcium is stored in bones and teeth. When calcium levels are high, bone-forming cells called **osteoblasts** remove calcium from the blood and deposit it into the bone along with other components of the matrix. Eventually, these cells become surrounded by the hard, calcium-rich secretion and differentiate into mature bone cells called **osteocytes**. If blood calcium is low, cells called **osteoclasts** can break down bone and put calcium back into the blood. In a healthy individual, there is a balance between the amount of calcium deposited and the amount removed. Homeostatic imbalances result in hypercalcemia or hypocalcemia.

TYPES OF BONE FRACTURES

A bone fracture is caused when the force against the bone is greater than the bone can sustain, causing it to splinter, fracture, or break. There are multiple classifications of fractures. A **closed fracture** is when the bone breaks but does not puncture through the skin and protrude through to the outside. An **open fracture** is when the bone breaks and punctures the skin protruding to the outside of the body. A **comminuted fracture** is when the bone breaks in multiple areas. This is often seen in a trauma such as a car accident or in competitive sports. A **greenstick fracture** is when part of the bone bends and does not fully break. This is often seen in young children because the bones are flexible, softer, and still developing. A **spiral fracture** is when the bone is twisted or rotated like a corkscrew. An **avulsion fracture** is when a tendon or ligament is taxed and pulled too hard causing it to pull away and break the bone. An **oblique fracture** is a break at an angle caused by the outside force coming at a right angle to the bone. A **transverse fracture** is when the fracture is perpendicular to the shaft of the bone. A **pathological fracture** is caused by disease making the bone so weak that is may break without warning simply by putting minimal pressure on it.

CARTILAGE: STRUCTURE AND FUNCTION

Cartilage is a connective tissue with a matrix that is flexible yet resistant to stretching. Cartilage is not innervated, nor does it have a blood supply, except for the **perichondrium** that forms the surfaces of nearly all cartilage. The immature cartilage cells that secrete the matrix are called **chondroblasts**. Chondroblasts give rise to mature cells called **chondrocytes** that reside in lacunae.

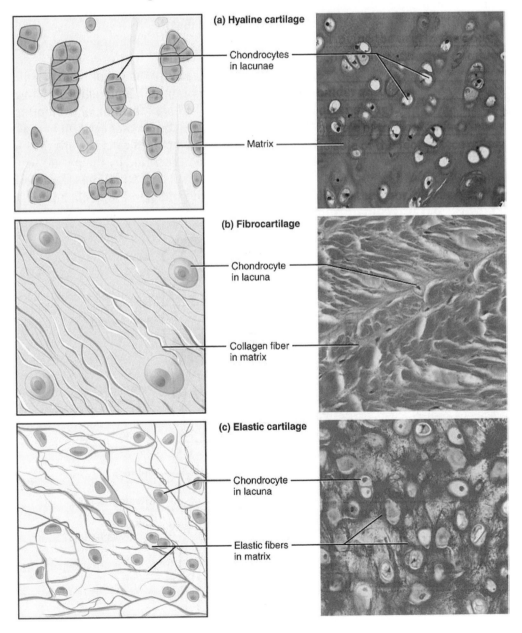

(a) Hyaline cartilage
 - Chondrocytes in lacunae
 - Matrix

(b) Fibrocartilage
 - Chondrocyte in lacuna
 - Collagen fiber in matrix

(c) Elastic cartilage
 - Chondrocyte in lacuna
 - Elastic fibers in matrix

Science

169

There are three types of cartilage: hyaline, elastic, and fibrocartilage. **Hyaline cartilage** is the most common cartilage in the body. It consists of evenly distributed collagen fibrils that explain its glassy appearance. It is found in locations that require strong support with some pliability, such as the ribs, nose, trachea, and articular surfaces. **Elastic cartilage** is similar to hyaline cartilage but is more flexible due to the presence of elastic fibers. It is found in the epiglottis and external ear. **Fibrocartilage** has collagen arranged into thick fibers, which allows it to withstand tension and compression. It is found in the jaw, in the knee, and between the vertebrae.

LIGAMENTS AND TENDONS

Ligaments connect bones to bones and help to stabilize joints. **Tendons** connect muscles to bones or other structures, such as the eyeballs, and facilitate movement. They are both composed of **dense regular connective tissue**, which consists of bundles of collagen fibers as well as elastic fibers. This gives them strength and resistance to stretching. The collagen fibers of tendons are more densely packed than those of ligaments. They are also arranged in parallel bundles, while the fibers of many ligaments are not. Tendons are tougher, but ligaments are more elastic. The yellowish color of certain ligaments results from the protein elastin.

ENDOCRINE CONTROL

The calcium-regulating hormones of the endocrine system are responsible for breaking down and reabsorbing bone tissue. The kidneys produce 1,25-hydroxyvitamin D, a biologically active form of vitamin D also known as **calcitriol**. This hormone regulates levels of calcium by promoting the absorption of dietary calcium in the intestines, which increases the level of calcium in the blood. Calcitriol also stimulates osteoclasts to break down bone, which moves calcium into the blood. When blood calcium is high, the peptide hormone **calcitonin** is secreted by the parafollicular cells of the thyroid gland. Calcitonin inhibits the activity of osteoclasts, and stimulates the activity of bone-forming osteoblasts. When blood calcium is low, parathyroid glands secrete a peptide hormone known as **parathyroid hormone (PTH)**. This increases the quantity and also the activity of osteoclasts.

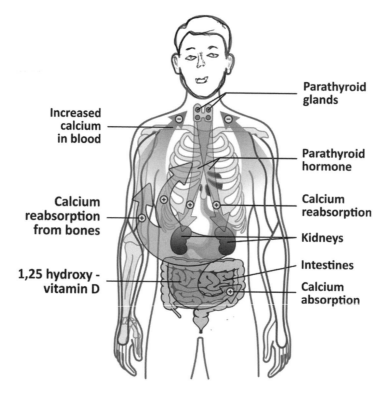

HUMAN ANATOMY AND PHYSIOLOGY CHAPTER QUIZ

1. The human body can be divided into how many primary body planes?
   a. Two
   b. Three
   c. Four
   d. Five

2. Which of the following is NOT a secondary function of the respiratory system?
   a. pH regulation of the blood
   b. Thermoregulation
   c. Speech production → larynx
   d. Heart rate regulation

3. Which of the following is produced in the mucosal lining to aid in immune defense?
   a. Immunoglobulin A +
   b. Killer T cells +
   c. Immature B cells
   d. Eosinophils

4. Which of the following is NOT part of the brain stem?
   a. Midbrain
   b. Pons
   c. Hypothalamus
   d. Medulla oblongata

5. Which of the following represents the depolarization of the atria?
   a. QRS interval
   b. T wave
   c. U wave
   d. P wave

6. Which of the following enzymes begins the digestions of polysaccharides into simpler sugars?
   a. Lipase
   b. Amylase
   c. Pepsin
   d. Cholinesterase

7. The fundus refers to which of the following?
   a. The most superior region of the stomach
   b. The region where the trachea forks into primary bronchi
   c. The thin stalk connecting the hypothalamus and the pituitary gland
   d. The outer bone of the lower leg

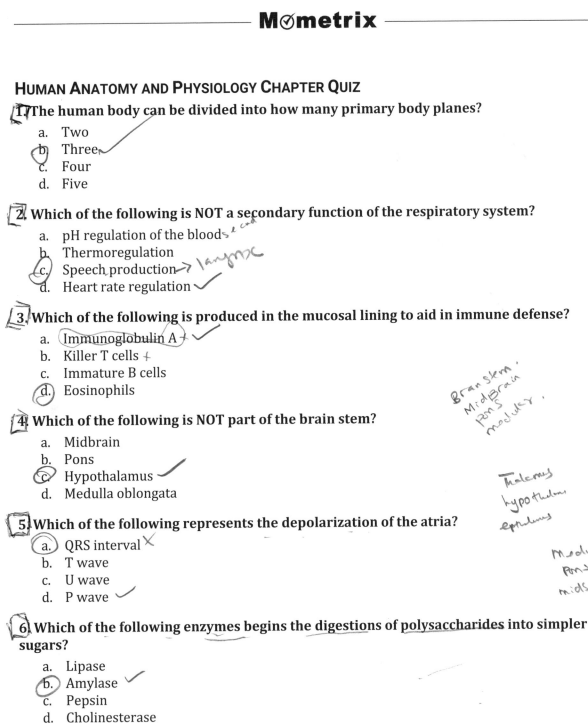

Science

8. Which of the following separates one sarcomere from another?
   a. A line
   b. D line
   c. O line
   d. Z line

9. Which of the following phases is NOT part of the ovarian cycle?
   a. Follicular phase
   b. Ovulation
   c. Proliferative phase
   d. Luteal phase

10. Where do T cells mature?
    a. Thymus
    b. Thalamus
    c. Tegmentum
    d. Thyroid

Answers for all of the chapter quiz questions can be found right before Practice Test #1.

Biology

CELLS

The cell is the basic organizational unit of all living things. Each piece within a cell has a function that helps organisms grow and survive. There are many different types of cells, and cells are unique to each type of organism. The one thing that all cells have in common is a **membrane**, which is comparable to a semi-permeable plastic bag. The membrane is composed of **phospholipids**. There are also some **transport holes**, which are proteins that help certain molecules and ions move in and out of the cell. The cell is filled with a fluid called **cytoplasm** or cytosol.

Within the cell are a variety of **organelles**, groups of complex molecules that help a cell survive, each with its own unique membrane that has a different chemical makeup from the cell membrane. The larger the cell, the more organelles it will need to live.

> **Review Video: Difference Between Plant and Animal Cells**
> Visit mometrix.com/academy and enter code: 115568

CELL STRUCTURAL ORGANIZATION

All organisms, whether plants, animals, fungi, protists, or bacteria, exhibit structural organization on the cellular and organism level. All cells contain **DNA** and **RNA** and can synthesize proteins. All organisms have a highly organized cellular structure. Each cell consists of **nucleic acids**, **cytoplasm**, and a **cell membrane**. Specialized organelles such as **mitochondria** and **chloroplasts** have specific functions within the cell. In single-celled organisms, that single cell contains all of the components necessary for life. In multicellular organisms, cells can become specialized. Different types of cells can have different functions. Life begins as a single cell whether by **asexual** or **sexual reproduction**. Cells are grouped together in **tissues**. Tissues are grouped together in **organs**. Organs are grouped together in **systems**. An **organism** is a complete individual.

DEFINING CHARACTERISTICS OF EUKARYOTIC CELLS

Cells can be classified into two main groups based on the presence or absence of a nucleus. In fact, the terms **eukaryote** and **prokaryote** mean "true kernel" and "before the kernel," respectively. The nucleus is a membrane-bound structure that encloses nearly all the genetic material of a eukaryotic cell. Eukaryotic DNA molecules wrap around associated proteins to form linear chromosomes, and the genes within them are regulated by molecules within the nucleoplasm. For this reason, the nucleus is deemed the "control center" of the cell. Eukaryotic cells are also defined by the presence of other membrane-bound organelles, including mitochondria, endoplasmic reticulum, Golgi bodies, peroxisomes, and (in animal cells) lysosomes. Ribosomes and the cytoskeleton are not enclosed by membranes and are found in both prokaryotic and eukaryotic cells. These types of cells also differ in the way that they divide. While prokaryotes reproduce by a simple process called binary fission, eukaryotes undergo a more involved method of division called mitosis. During mitosis, duplicated chromosomes are lined up along the cell's equator and split at the centromere to form two identical daughter nuclei.

> **Review Video: Eukaryotic and Prokaryotic**
> Visit mometrix.com/academy and enter code: 231438

CELL STRUCTURE

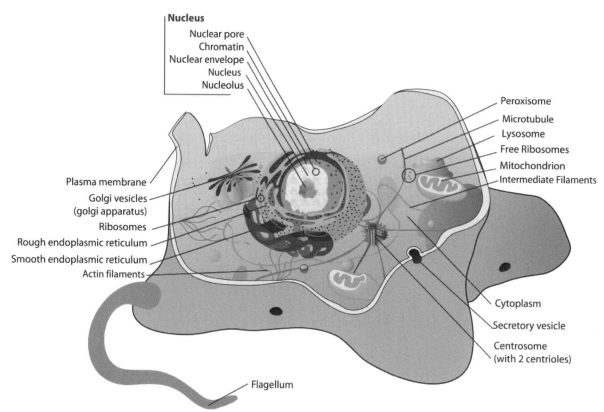

Ribosomes: Ribosomes are involved in synthesizing proteins from amino acids. They are numerous, making up about one quarter of the cell. Some cells contain thousands of ribosomes. Some are mobile and some are embedded in the rough **endoplasmic reticulum**.

Golgi complex (Golgi apparatus): This is involved in synthesizing materials such as proteins that are transported out of the cell. It is located near the nucleus and consists of layers of **membranes**.

Vacuoles: These are sacs used for storage, digestion, and waste removal. There is one large vacuole in plant cells. Animal cells have small, sometimes numerous, vacuoles.

Vesicle: This is a small organelle within a cell. It has a membrane and performs varying functions, including moving materials within a cell.

Cytoskeleton: This consists of **microtubules** that help shape and support the cell.

Microtubules: These are part of the **cytoskeleton** and help support the cell. They are made of protein.

Cytosol: This is the liquid material in the cell. It is mostly water, but also contains some floating molecules.

Cytoplasm: This is a general term that refers to cytosol and the substructures (organelles) found within the plasma membrane, but not within the nucleus.

Cell membrane (plasma membrane): This defines the cell by acting as a barrier. It keeps cytoplasm in and substances located outside the cell out. It also determines what is allowed to enter and exit the cell.

Endoplasmic reticulum (ER or RER): The two types of endoplasmic reticulum are **rough** (has ribosomes on the surface) and **smooth** (does not have ribosomes on the surface). It is a tubular network that comprises the transport system of a cell. It is fused to the nuclear membrane and extends through the cytoplasm to the cell membrane.

Mitochondrion (pl. mitochondria): These cell structures vary in terms of size and quantity. Some cells may have one mitochondrion, while others have thousands. This structure performs various functions such as generating ATP and is also involved in cell growth and death. Mitochondria contain their own DNA that is separate from that contained in the nucleus.

GOLGI APPARATUS: GENERAL STRUCTURE AND ROLE IN PACKAGING AND SECRETION

The **Golgi apparatus** consists of a series of curved, flattened sacs called cisternae. The cis face (the stack that is nearest to the ER) receives vesicles sent by the RER that contain immature proteins. The vesicles fuse with the membrane and release the proteins into the Golgi. The proteins then move from stack to stack, budding off a new vesicle which fuses with the next cisterna layer each time. During their travels, the proteins are modified by an assortment of Golgi enzymes. Proteins that were glycosylated in the ER may have some of their sugar residues removed, or more may be added. Sulfate and phosphate groups may be added as well. These "tags" influence the structure and function of the protein and also aid in the sorting and delivery of these proteins to their destinations. The proteins are packaged into vesicles that bud from the trans face (or exit face) of the Golgi. Some of these proteins are secreted from the cell through exocytosis, while others become part of the cell membrane. Still others serve as hydrolytic enzymes inside lysosomes.

LYSOSOMES: MEMBRANE-BOUND VESICLES CONTAINING HYDROLYTIC ENZYMES

Lysosomes are organelles that function in the breakdown of various substances. They bud from the Golgi apparatus and enclose hydrolytic enzymes that would damage the cell if not separated from the cytosol. These enzymes are active at a low pH of around 5, so hydrogen ions are pumped into the lysosome to maintain the acidic environment. Lysosomes play a vital role in cell homeostasis by dismantling various substrates and nonfunctioning intracellular components and recycling them in a process called autophagy. Many of the substances destined for degradation are contained in a double-membrane vesicle called an autophagosome. Lysosomes can fuse with these (and with other vesicles created by endocytosis), releasing their enzymes and digesting the contents. Other substances can be transported into the lysosome directly by crossing the membrane. If enough lysosomes are damaged, the cell undergoes apoptosis and, in cases of severe damage, necrosis. Mutations of the hydrolases within the lysosomes are associated with a number of lysosomal storage diseases, including Tay Sachs.

CYTOSKELETON

GENERAL FUNCTION IN CELL SUPPORT AND MOVEMENT

The **cytoskeleton** is a membraneless structure found in all cell types, and it is made of various types of protein fibers. In eukaryotes, the cytoskeleton has three major components: microfilaments, intermediate fibers, and microtubules. While the cytoskeleton is known for its role in cell shape and structure, it is also involved in the movement of materials within the cell and the movement of the cell itself. The cytoskeleton is dynamic and can extend and retract, allowing cells to maintain their shape or change shape as needed. The network of protein fibers stabilizes most of the organelles and also provides a "railway" for motor proteins to use to direct vesicles to their destinations. Components of the cytoskeleton help anchor the cell to neighboring cells and, in some cases, form extensions such as cilia and flagella that aid in cell movement. Cell division would be impossible without the cytoskeleton, as it is used to separate sister chromatids, and also pinches the cell into daughter cells during cytokinesis.

MICROFILAMENTS: COMPOSITION AND ROLE IN CLEAVAGE AND CONTRACTILITY

Microfilaments are the thinnest components of the cytoskeleton, averaging about 6 to 8 nm in diameter. They are composed of protein molecules called actin that join together to form two rod-like polymers which twist around each other to form flexible tension-bearing filaments. These filaments organize into either bundles or networks, and they are involved in maintaining cell shape and events like cytokinesis, muscle contraction, and movement of the cell itself.

During cytokinesis, a cleavage furrow is formed through the contraction of microfilaments. These microfilaments are organized into a ring shape which decreases in size as they contract.

The cytoplasm is constricted until the original cell pinches into two daughter cells. Microfilaments are also involved in muscle contraction. The protein myosin binds to actin filaments forming myofibrils. The two components slide past each other as the cell contracts, and the muscle shortens. Microfilaments also aid in the gross movement of a cell by elongating the plus end (actin polymerization) while shortening the minus end (actin depolymerization).

MICROTUBULES: COMPOSITION AND ROLE IN SUPPORT AND TRANSPORT

Microtubules are the thickest components of the cytoskeleton (around 25 nm in diameter). They are made of a globular protein known as tubulin, which is a dimer made of α-tubulin and β-tubulin. These dimers stack upon each other to form linear rows called protofilaments, and 13 of these protofilaments arrange themselves in a ring to form a hollow tube. Microtubules can lengthen and shorten by polymerization and depolymerization of the tubulin dimers. They extend throughout the cell, helping the cell to resist compressional forces, while also providing a framework for motor proteins to travel on. Kinesins are motor proteins that tend to "walk" toward the plus end of the microtubule and dyneins travel toward the minus end. Many of these motor proteins carry vesicles to their destinations. Microtubules are also the major components of the mitotic spindle which segregates sister chromatids during mitosis. Cilia and flagella are also formed from microtubules which group together in nine pairs that surround a central pair.

ROLE OF INTERMEDIATE FILAMENTS

Intermediate fibers are components of the cytoskeleton that are thinner than microtubules but thicker than microfilaments (about 10 nm in diameter). They are composed of over fifty types of proteins, and the types of proteins are specific to certain types of cells. For example, microfilaments made of keratin are found in epithelial cells, and microfilaments made of desmin are found in muscle cells. Lamins are proteins that form the microfilaments that line the inside portion of the nuclear envelope. Unlike their cytoskeletal counterparts, they are not polar, and they are not directly responsible for cell movement. They appear to only play a role in support. They help cells adhere to one another at cell junctions known as desmosomes, and they also help to anchor the nucleus and other organelles. Intermediate filaments are specialized to withstand tensile forces, and thereby help to prevent cell distortion under mechanical stress. They do not polymerize and depolymerize the way that microtubules and microfilaments do.

COMPOSITION AND FUNCTION OF CILIA AND FLAGELLA

Both cilia and flagella are structures made of microtubules that extend from some types of cells. In eukaryotic cells, these microtubules are doubled up into pairs, and nine doublets form a ring around a central pair (the "9 + 2" arrangement). Each cilium and flagellum is about 0.25 μm in diameter, but flagella are usually much longer than cilia. Cilia are almost always found in high numbers, while cells rarely have more than a few flagella. Both structures are able to "wave" back and forth through the action of motor proteins called dyneins.

Some cells use cilia for locomotion while cells that are fixed within a tissue may use cilia to sweep materials along the surface. Ciliated cells of the respiratory tract move mucus out of the lungs, and cells of the female reproductive tract use cilia to mobilize the egg. Some cilia can even detect signals and transmit information to the inside of the cell. When cilia move, they do so in back-and-forth strokes, much like oars on a rowboat.

Flagella move differently; they are more whip-like with an undulating, beating pattern. Unlike cilia, they are only used for locomotion. Each human sperm uses a flagellum to move, and (like cilia) they can be found in many types of protists.

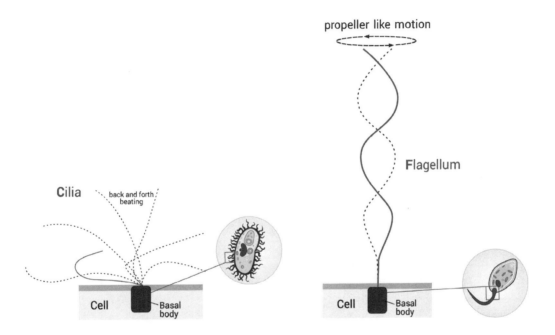

CENTRIOLES, MICROTUBULE ORGANIZING CENTERS

Centrioles are cylindrical structures that are formed from nine triplets of microtubules arranged in a circle around a hollow center. In animal cells, two perpendicular centrioles form an organelle called a **centrosome**. Other types of eukaryotic cells have simple centrosomes, but only animal cells use centrioles to organize their microtubules. Centrosomes are typically found near the nucleus, but they migrate to opposite poles of the cell during cell division. Microtubules extend from the centrioles as the plus ends grow toward the metaphase plate, forming the spindle fibers of the mitotic spindle. Polar fibers extend from one centrosome to the other, while kinetochore fibers attach to the chromosomes, pulling the sister chromatids apart during anaphase.

PLASMA MEMBRANE

GENERAL FUNCTION IN CELL CONTAINMENT

While the plasma membrane is involved in many functions (such as the regulation and transportation of materials, cell to cell recognition, and cell signaling), its most basic function is cell containment. The cell membrane is composed of a double layer of phospholipids that surrounds the cytoplasm of virtually all types of cells. The phospholipids form a fluid-like barrier that is reinforced by cholesterol and protein molecules. This barrier helps to contain the structures and molecules within the cell's interior, and also helps to maintain the desired concentrations of substances on either side of the membrane. Since the phospholipids orient themselves with their fatty acid chains pointed inward, the interior of the membrane is hydrophobic. This property causes the membrane to remain intact in its aqueous environment, while being somewhat impermeable to substances that are soluble in water (with the notable exception of nonpolar gases such as oxygen and carbon dioxide).

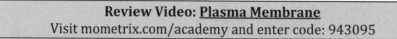

Review Video: Plasma Membrane
Visit mometrix.com/academy and enter code: 943095

PHOSPHOLIPIDS AND PHOSPHATIDES

A phospholipid consists of two nonpolar fatty acid chains bonded to a polar head made of glycerol, a phosphate group, and an organic R-group. (Phosphatides are the simplest phospholipids and lack the functional group on the phosphate.) Phospholipids are amphipathic, meaning that they have both hydrophilic (polar head) and hydrophobic (nonpolar tails) components. Because of this property, they arrange themselves into micelles or bilayers. A micelle is a small spherical structure made of a single layer of phospholipids with the tails pointed inward to form a hydrophobic core. They are used to transport lipid soluble materials. A bilayer is formed when the phospholipids assemble into parallel layers with the tails pointed in toward each other and the heads pointed out. Phospholipid bilayers surround liposomes and other vesicles, and they enclose the organelles in a eukaryotic cell. These bilayers also form cell membranes, which regulate the passage of materials into and out of all types of cells.

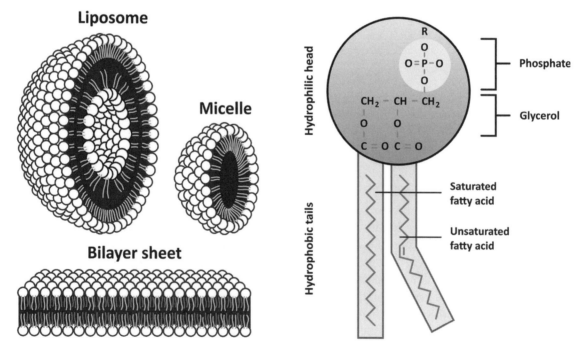

PROTEIN COMPONENTS

The proteins associated with the membrane enable most of the membrane's functions, such as the shuttling of various ions and molecules through the membrane, catalyzing reactions, joining adjacent cells, cell signaling, cellular support and stability, and cell recognition. Some of these proteins penetrate into the hydrophobic interior of the membrane, and are called **integral** proteins. **Glycoproteins** are integral proteins with an attached sugar chain that aid in cell recognition. When integral proteins extend completely through the membrane, they are called **transmembrane** proteins and are often used as receptors for cell signaling. A signal molecule (like a hormone) will bind to the receptor from the extracellular side, and relay a message to the cytoplasmic side. Transmembrane proteins are also required for transport across the membrane. Some transport proteins (called **channel** proteins) have a tunnel-like conformation that allows materials to move passively, while others (**carrier** proteins) change conformation to move materials either by active or passive transport. **Peripheral proteins** are loosely bound to either side of the membrane and often act as enzymes or receptor proteins. (Note that both of these can also be integral proteins).

OSMOSIS

Osmosis is the diffusion of water across a semipermeable membrane. The net movement of water is down its concentration gradient, meaning it will move from an area of higher water concentration to lower, or lower solute concentration to higher. Osmosis can help to restore balance when the solute cannot cross the membrane (or if it can't cross fast enough to maintain homeostasis). When the extracellular fluid has a higher solute concentration as compared to the cytoplasm, the fluid is described as **hypertonic**. Since there are fewer free water molecules surrounding the cell, the net flow of water will be *out* of the cell. When the extracellular fluid has a lower solute concentration as compared to the cytoplasm, the fluid is described as **hypotonic**. Since there are more free water molecules on the extracellular side of the membrane, the net flow of water will be *into* the cell, causing it to swell and in some cases burst. When the extracellular fluid has the same solute concentration as the cytoplasm, the fluid is described as **isotonic**, and water will move in and out of the cell at equal rates.

Science

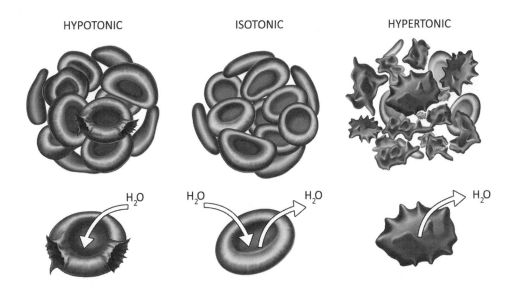

OSMOTIC PRESSURE

A **colligative property** is a property of a solution that depends only on the *amount* of solute, and not the size, mass, or chemical nature of the solute. Osmotic pressure, the minimum amount of pressure required to stop the diffusion of pure water across the membrane, is a colligative property because it is determined by the concentration of solute, as can be seen in the equation:

$$\pi = iMRT$$

- π = osmotic pressure (in atmospheres)
- i = van 't Hoff factor (the number of particles formed from one unit of solute)
- M = molar concentration
- R = ideal gas constant
- T = temperature (in Kelvin)

If a vessel is divided into two chambers by a semipermeable membrane, and pure water is placed into one chamber while a solution (such as sugar water) is placed in the other chamber, the water level will rise on the side of greater solute concentration. The diffusion of water will continue in this direction until the osmotic pressure becomes too great. The solute concentration will not have changed, but water will have moved from high to low water concentration.

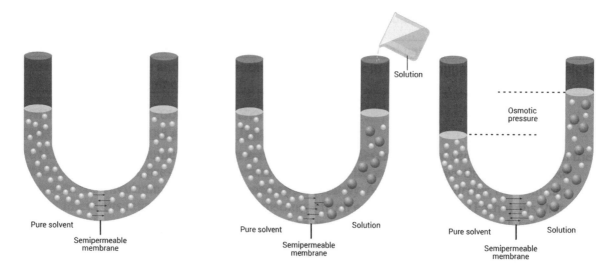

PASSIVE TRANSPORT

Passive transport is the movement of substances across a cell membrane without the input of energy. Random motion of particles will lead to the net movement of substances down their concentration gradients in a spontaneous process that leads to an increase in entropy. Simple diffusion, osmosis, and facilitated diffusion are all forms of passive transport. In simple diffusion, substances cross the membrane directly, without the aid of a transport protein. Small, nonpolar molecules such as oxygen gas, carbon dioxide, and uncharged lipids are not repelled by the hydrophobic interior of the membrane.

Osmosis is the passive transport of water across the membrane. Most polar molecules cannot use simple diffusion, but water molecules are small enough to slowly squeeze between the phospholipids. Water can also use channel proteins called aquaporins to increase the rate of osmosis. When proteins are used to transport substances down their concentration gradients, this is called **facilitated diffusion**. Large, polar, and/or charged substances require shielding from the interior of the membrane, and they may use channel or carrier proteins to assist in their transport. None of these processes require ATP, and they are driven by the difference in solute concentration.

ACTIVE TRANSPORT

In **active transport**, energy is used to move solutes into or out of the cell. In most forms of active transport, substances are pumped against their concentration gradients from areas of low to high concentration. Active transport is required for processes such as the maintenance of a membrane potential and the uptake of glucose by intestinal cells even between meals. In **primary active transport**, the pumping of solutes by a carrier protein is directly coupled to the hydrolysis of ATP. In this process, the binding of a phosphate group causes a conformational change in the protein, allowing it to transport solutes across the membrane. **Secondary active transport** relies on ATP to generate an electrochemical gradient, and it is this gradient that directly drives the active transport of a different solute. As one solute moves down its gradient, another is pumped up its gradient. When both solutes move in the same direction, it is called **symport**, and when they move in opposite directions, it is called **antiport**.

Endocytosis and **exocytosis** are types of active transport that employ vesicles to import or export substances. While these processes require ATP, they do not necessarily move solutes up their concentration gradients.

MEMBRANE CHANNELS

Membrane channels belong to a class of transport proteins that form pores to allow the passage of small, charged particles. They are specific to the solutes they transport and act as a sort of tunnel for particles of a certain size and charge. All channels move substances down their concentration gradient by facilitated diffusion, and therefore do not require energy. Unlike carrier proteins, channels interact very weakly with the solutes they transport, allowing them to move rapidly across the membrane. Channel proteins that allow the passage of water are called aquaporins, and they are always open. Without them, osmosis would occur too slowly to accommodate the needs of the cell. Ion channels, on the other hand, are usually gated; they open and close in response to various stimuli. Voltage-gated channels respond to changes in membrane potential. These types of ion channels are vital to generating electrical impulses in nerve and cardiac cells. Ligand-gated ion channels open in response to the binding of a ligand, such as a hormone or neurotransmitter. Mechanically-gated ion channels respond to a physical stimulus, such as the stretching of the membrane, and are useful in sensory tissues.

EXOCYTOSIS AND ENDOCYTOSIS

Endocytosis and exocytosis are types of vesicular transport that are used for the transport of very large particles, or bulk quantities of smaller particles. Both processes are examples of active transport because the transportation and pinching off of vesicles requires energy. (Note that particles are not necessarily moving up their concentration gradients as in other forms of active transport.) During **exocytosis**, cellular products and wastes are transported via vesicle to the cell membrane where the vesicle fuses, releasing its contents into the extracellular environment. Exocytosis is also the means by which certain membrane components (such as glycoproteins and glycolipids) become incorporated into the cell membrane. **Endocytosis** involves the ingestion of fluid, large particles, or target molecules. During this process the cell membrane folds inward, engulfing the material and pinching off into a vesicle. The ingestion of fluids is called **pinocytosis**, and it is non-specific, meaning it takes in any enzymes and nutrients that happen to be available. **Phagocytosis** is the engulfing of particles, sometimes even entire cells. Immune system cells ingest harmful bacteria by phagocytosis before destroying them. **Receptor-mediated endocytosis** is a form of endocytosis that targets certain molecules (such as LDLs, or low-density lipoproteins) that

181

are in low concentration outside the cell. These molecules bind to receptors on the cell membrane, which then invaginates to form a vesicle.

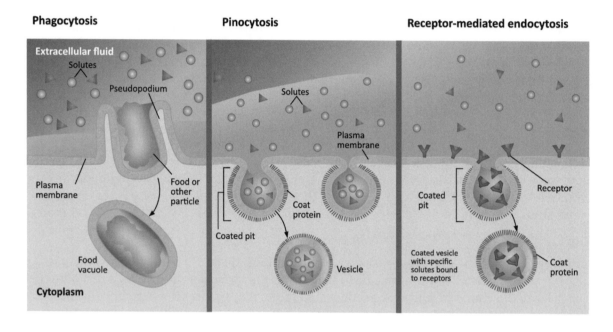

ENDOPLASMIC RETICULUM
ROUGH AND SMOOTH COMPONENTS

Both the rough and smooth endoplasmic reticulum consist of a series of continuous membranes called cisternae, but each type of ER differs in both structure and function.

The **rough ER** is continuous with the nuclear envelope, and its ribosome-studded cisternae have the appearance of flattened sacs. The ribosomes synthesize polypeptides which are then guided into the lumen of the rough ER before being modified, packaged in a vesicle, and sent to different regions within the cell, often the Golgi apparatus. The Golgi can then further modify the proteins and sort them based on their destinations. Many are shipped out of the cell via exocytosis.

The cisternae of the **smooth ER** are more tubular in shape than the rough ER, and they lack ribosomes. These membranes are continuous with the rough ER and the nucleus. Smooth ER is involved in many tasks, including the synthesis of lipids such as phospholipids and cholesterol. The smooth ER of liver cells detoxifies drugs, and the smooth ER of the muscles regulates and stores calcium ions.

ROUGH ENDOPLASMIC RETICULUM SITE OF RIBOSOMES

Secretory proteins (proteins destined to be exported from the cell) and proteins that are associated with the plasma membrane are synthesized on ribosomes that are bound to the cytoplasmic side of the rough endoplasmic reticulum. These ribosomes are not permanently fixed and will bind to sites called translocons. Ribosomes that are free in the cytosol are very similar in structure to bound ribosomes, but the proteins they produce remain in the cytosol of the cell. As a polypeptide chain is growing out of a bound ribosome during translation, the chain is fed through a tiny pore into the lumen of the rough ER, where it folds into its proper conformation. Any proteins that do not fold properly into their native shape are recycled. Enzymes in the lumen may modify proteins by covalently bonding a carbohydrate to form a glycoprotein. (The Golgi continues the

182

posttranslational modification of proteins.) Proteins that are shipped to other parts of the cell are first packaged into transport vesicles, and the vesicle will fuse with its target.

MEMBRANE STRUCTURE

The **endoplasmic reticulum** constitutes roughly half of all the plasma membrane in a cell. The membrane system of the rough ER is connected to the outer nuclear membrane, forming flattened sacs (cisternae) that connect to each other in a manner that resembles a multi-story parking garage. These helicoidal sheets are called **Terasaki ramps**. Newly synthesized proteins are packaged in transport vesicles that are coated with protein complexes that help direct each vesicle to its destination. (COPII coating proteins, for example, coat vesicles that fuse with the cis face of the Golgi apparatus.) These vesicles bud from a region of the ER known as transitional ER, where there are few ribosomes. The smooth ER lacks ribosomes altogether and has a branched tubular structure. Some of these tubules fuse with one another.

MITOCHONDRIA

Mitochondria are described as the "powerhouses" of the cell because they produce most of a cell's ATP. They have two membranes: the outer membrane, which acts a selective barrier, and the inner membrane where most of the ATP is made. The inner membrane is folded into structures called cristae, and it is within these folds that the electron transport chain of aerobic respiration is located. Between the membranes is the intermembrane space where a proton motive force is used to drive **chemiosmosis**: the synthesis of ATP. The protons that are pumped across the intermembrane space during oxidative phosphorylation re-enter the mitochondrial matrix (the interior of the mitochondrion) through the protein ATP synthase, which is located in the inner membrane. The movement of the protons powers ATP synthase, allowing it to phosphorylate ADP. Inside the matrix are ribosomes and mitochondrial DNA. This DNA carries 37 genes (in humans) that are required for normal mitochondrion function. Mitochondria also play a role in apoptosis, or programmed cell death. Proteins associated with the inner mitochondrial membrane move into the cytoplasm in response to oxidative stress and activate other proteins that begin the degradation of the cell.

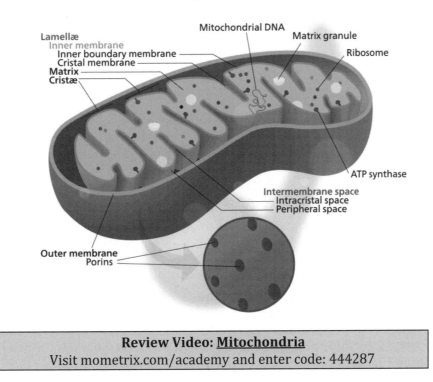

Review Video: <u>Mitochondria</u>
Visit mometrix.com/academy and enter code: 444287

SELF-REPLICATION

Mitochondria are described as semi-autonomous because each one has its own genome and ribosomes and produces many of its own proteins. They also replicate in a manner similar to that of bacteria; they copy their circular DNA molecules before undergoing fission. However, mitochondria do rely on nuclear genes to produce many of the proteins required for DNA replication and other processes. These proteins are imported from the cytosol.

While the mitochondria are not fully autonomous, it is likely that they evolved from an autonomous heterotrophic prokaryote that established a symbiotic relationship with an ancestral host cell. It was probably engulfed by the host cell (hence the double membrane) and provided that cell with ATP. (This is known as the endosymbiont theory.) Its similarity to bacteria, both in structure and manner of reproduction, suggests that mitochondria were once free-living prokaryotes.

NUCLEAR PARTS OF A CELL

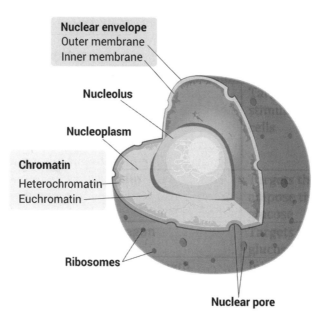

Nucleus (pl. nuclei): This is a small structure that contains the **chromosomes** and regulates the **DNA** of a cell. The nucleus is the defining structure of **eukaryotic cells**, and all eukaryotic cells have a nucleus. The nucleus is responsible for the passing on of genetic traits between generations. The nucleus contains a *nuclear envelope, nucleoplasm, a nucleolus, nuclear pores, chromatin, and ribosomes.*

Chromosomes: These are highly condensed, threadlike rods of **DNA**. Short for **deoxyribonucleic acid**, DNA is the genetic material that stores information about the plant or animal.

Chromatin: This consists of the DNA and protein that make up **chromosomes**.

Nucleolus: This structure contained within the nucleus consists of protein. It is small, round, does not have a membrane, is involved in **protein synthesis**, and synthesizes and stores **RNA (ribonucleic acid)**.

Nuclear envelope: This encloses the structures of the nucleus. It consists of inner and outer membranes made of **lipids**.

Nuclear pores: These are involved in the exchange of material between the nucleus and the **cytoplasm**.

Nucleoplasm: This is the liquid within the nucleus and is similar to cytoplasm.

COMPARTMENTALIZATION, STORAGE OF GENETIC INFORMATION

The **nucleus** stores most of a cell's genetic information. (DNA is also found in mitochondria and chloroplasts.) Nuclear DNA is enclosed by the nuclear envelope: a double membrane that is perforated with pores. These pores are made of large protein complexes that regulate the passage of materials including RNA, ribosomal subunits, proteins, ions, and signaling molecules. Enclosed in the double membrane is the nucleoplasm (a semifluid), chromatin (DNA and associated histone proteins), and a non-membranous nucleolus which produces the ribosomal subunits. The inner nuclear membrane is covered by a mesh of protein filaments called the nuclear lamina which stabilizes the nucleus while regulating events such as DNA replication and cell division. The outer membrane is continuous with the endoplasmic reticulum.

The nucleus is responsible for the storage of DNA, and is also the site of DNA replication and transcription (the synthesis of RNA). Since gene expression is regulated largely at the level of transcription, the nucleus plays an important role in coordinating the activities of the cell.

NUCLEOLUS: LOCATION AND FUNCTION

The **nucleolus** is the largest structure inside the nucleus, and it is responsible for producing ribosomal subunits. It has no membrane and is made of three regions: two thread-like fibrillar components and one granular component. The fibrillar center (FC) is where the ribosomal RNA genes are located and transcribed. The dense fibrillar center (DFC) processes the pre-rRNA, and the immature ribosomal subunits are assembled in the granular component (GC). All rRNA is synthesized in the nucleolus except the 5S-rRNA which is made in the nucleoplasm before being incorporated into ribosomal subunits. The subunits are exported from the nucleus through the nuclear pores.

The nucleolus disappears early in mitosis (prophase) and reappears in the final stage (telophase). However, it first appears as ten small units at various chromosome sites called nucleolus organizer regions (NORs) before aggregating into one structure.

NUCLEAR ENVELOPE, NUCLEAR PORES

The **nuclear envelope** is the double membrane that encloses the nucleus, separating the nucleoplasm from the cytoplasm of the cell. There is a 20–40 nm gap between the two phospholipid bilayers called the perinuclear space, and the membranes are joined at the nuclear pores. Each pore is an octagonal aqueous channel made of hundreds of proteins called nucleoporins. These proteins interact with transporter proteins called karyopherins, which shuttle large molecules like RNA and certain proteins back and forth between the nucleus and the cytoplasm. Smaller molecules and ions are able to diffuse through the pore complex without the aid of a transporter. The pores are essential for the import of the enzymes and nucleotides that are required for DNA synthesis and transcription and for the export of mRNA, tRNA, and ribosomal subunits that are required for translation.

The outer membrane of the nuclear envelope is continuous with the endoplasmic reticulum (ER), and the lumen (inner space) of the ER is open to the perinuclear space. This allows for the easy exchange of materials between the two organelles. The nucleoplasmic side of the inner membrane is lined with a network of protein filaments called the nuclear lamina which supports the nucleus, while aiding in the organization of chromatin.

Science

MITOSIS

Mitosis is the stage of the cell cycle in which the nucleus divides. It alternates with a much longer stage called interphase in which the cell performs its normal functions and prepares for division by copying organelles and duplicating chromosomes. If the cell passes the two major regulatory checkpoints of interphase, it proceeds through the four phases of mitosis, as summarized in the table below (though there will be one last checkpoint prior to anaphase). Mitosis is usually followed by cytokinesis, division of the cytoplasm, and results in two genetically identical daughter cells with the same number of chromosomes as the parent cell.

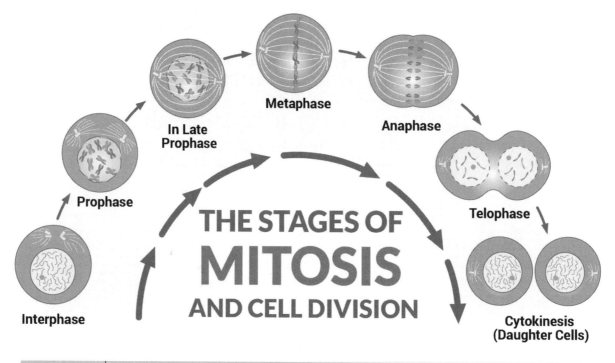

THE STAGES OF MITOSIS AND CELL DIVISION

Metaphase | In Late Prophase | Anaphase | Prophase | Telophase | Interphase | Cytokinesis (Daughter Cells)

Phase	Description
Prophase	Chromatin condenses into chromosomes The nucleolus and nuclear membrane break down The mitotic spindle begins to form
Metaphase	The spindle aligns the chromosomes along the metaphase plate
Anaphase	Sister chromatids are split at the centromere and pulled toward opposite poles
Telophase	Chromosomes uncoil A nuclear membrane forms around each set of chromosomes A nucleolus forms in each new nucleus The mitotic spindle breaks down Cytokinesis begins (it may also begin during anaphase)

Review Video: Mitosis
Visit mometrix.com/academy and enter code: 849894

At the onset of prophase, chromatin coils tightly into discrete chromosomes that are visible under a light microscope. The chromosomes resemble the shape of an "X" and have identical DNA in each sister chromatid. The sister chromatids are bound together along their entire length by protein complexes called cohesins, but by metaphase all cohesins are broken down, except those found at the centromere. As the chromatin condenses, the nuclear envelope begins to disintegrate and the nucleolus disappears. Centrosomes, the microtubule organizing centers of the cell, migrate towards opposite poles of the cell as microtubules polymerize outward. This begins the formation of the mitotic spindle, which continues until metaphase.

Protein-based structures called kinetochores form at the centromere to serve as an attachment point for the kinetochore fibers (microtubules) of the spindle. As the kinetochore microtubules attach to each chromosome at the centromere, other microtubules called polar fibers overlap at the center of the cell, never interacting with the chromosomes. By the end of prophase, the nuclear envelope has completely dissolved. This tends to be the longest stage of mitosis.

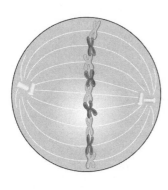

During metaphase, the centrosomes are at opposite poles of the cell, and chromosomes are positioned along an imaginary line between the two centrosomes known as the metaphase plate (sometimes called the spindle equator or equatorial plate). The kinetochore fibers lengthen or shorten as needed to line up the chromosomes, and the movement is assisted by forces exerted by motor proteins. Polar fibers continue to grow until they are sufficiently overlapped in preparation for the next stage of mitosis. Anaphase will only follow metaphase if the chromosomes are properly aligned, and every kinetochore on every sister chromatid is attached to a kinetochore fiber. Metaphase is usually shorter than prophase.

Chromosomes are at their most condensed form during anaphase. The stage begins when an enzyme known as separin cleaves the cohesins that hold sister chromatids together. The kinetochore fibers shorten as a result of depolymerization, splitting the centromeres and pulling the liberated chromosomes toward the centrosomes. As they are dragged through the cytosol, the linear chromosomes bend into a "V" shape as they trail behind the centromere. Meanwhile, the overlapping polar fibers push away from each other, causing the cell to elongate. There is now a complete set of chromosomes at each end of the cell.

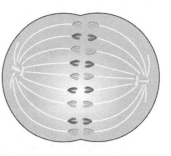

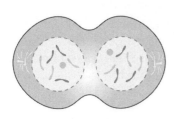

As liberated chromosomes arrive at the poles of the cell, a new nuclear membrane is formed around each group. The polar fibers continue to elongate the cell as the chromosomes uncoil and the nucleoli reform. The microtubules of the spindle are depolymerized and disappear. Cytokinesis begins during either telophase or late anaphase. A cleavage furrow forms near the site of the metaphase plate as a contractile ring of microfilaments beneath the plasma membrane begins to constrict the cell. This will continue after telophase, pinching the parent cell into two identical daughter cells.

PHASES OF THE CELL CYCLE: G_0, G_1, S, G_2, M

The **cell cycle** can be described as the life of a cell, beginning with the formation of the cell, and ending with its own division. The phases of the cycle are G_1 (first gap), S (synthesis), G_2 (second gap) and M (the mitotic phase). Many cells, however, enter a non-growing G_0 state in which the cell performs its job but does not divide. This may happen for a number of reasons, and it is not always reversible. Cells that are deficient in nutrients or growth factors may be blocked from proceeding to the S phase and only called back to the cycle when favorable conditions are restored. Mature liver cells and many adult stem cells exist in a reversible **quiescent** state, and they only divide in response to stimuli such as tissue damage. Some cells leave the cell cycle permanently. A cell with damaged DNA, for example, is likely to enter an irreversible state of **senescence**, meaning that it will cease to divide and grow. This allows the cell to avoid apoptosis (programmed cell death), but it will remain in G_0 indefinitely. Other highly differentiated cells such as nerve and cardiac muscle cells permanently leave the cell cycle because they are genetically programmed to do so.

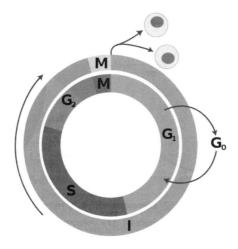

The **G_1 (first gap) phase** of the cell cycle is the first part of interphase, and it begins immediately after cell division. During this stage, the volume of the cell increases, and the metabolic activities that were inhibited during mitosis are accelerated. The cell begins the task of copying its organelles, synthesizing mRNA, tRNA, and rRNA, and producing the enzymes required for DNA replication, all while continuing to perform its given function. The time duration of this phase varies greatly, but it tends to be the longest phase of the cell cycle, averaging 6-12 hours. Some cells remain in this phase for years. Before the cell is allowed to proceed to the S phase, it is inspected at the G_1 checkpoint. It "passes" if it has grown enough and has sufficient nutrients and growth factors and if the DNA is not damaged. If it "fails" it enters the G_0 phase.

The **S (synthesis) phase** of the cell cycle falls between G_1 and G_2 of interphase. During this time (which averages 6–8 hours) each molecule of DNA is replicated, doubling the genetic content from 2n to 4n. Note that this does *not* change the ploidy of the cell; the chromosome number remains at 46. Helicases separate the two complementary strands of DNA at multiple sites along each molecule, and DNA polymerases add nucleotides at a rate of about 50 nucleotides per second. By the end of the S phase, there is an identical copy of each DNA molecule, ensuring that each daughter cell that is created during the M phase will have a complete genome. Centrosomes are duplicated during this stage as well, while transcription and protein synthesis are inhibited.

The **G_2 (second gap) phase** follows DNA replication and is the final part of interphase. It is characterized by roughly 3–4 hours of cell growth, continued replication of organelles, and protein

188

synthesis. The centrosomes that were duplicated during the S phase begin to mature as microtubules become more organized and the centrioles elongate. As it prepares for mitosis, the cell performs its usual metabolic functions, but before the cell is allowed to divide, it must pass inspection at the G_2 checkpoint. If any errors are detected in the duplicated chromosomes, the cell cycle is arrested until the DNA can be repaired. Cells that are significantly and irreparably damaged will either enter a state of senescence, or be eliminated through programmed cell death.

Mitosis (nuclear division) and cytokinesis (cytoplasmic division) together make up the **M phase** of the cell cycle. There is no growth during this phase, and normal metabolic functioning is inhibited to devote the cell's resources to the division process. During mitosis, the chromosomes condense (prophase), align along the metaphase plate (metaphase), split at the centromere and segregate (anaphase), and uncoil as a new nuclear membrane is built around each full set (telophase). Cytokinesis overlaps with the final stages of mitosis.

In animal cells, cytokinesis results from the formation of a contractile ring of actin and non-muscle myosin II filaments. This ring forms around the equator of the cell, directly beneath the plasma membrane, and parallel to the metaphase plate. Myosin is a motor protein that uses ATP to move the actin filaments, causing the ring to contract like a drawstring. As this is happening, vesicles from inside the cell fuse along the cleavage furrow to form a plasma membrane. The two cells become physically separated in a process called abscission. The M phase is the shortest phase of the cell cycle, averaging 1–2 hours.

GROWTH ARREST

Cell growth can be halted in response to signals from both inside and outside the cell. For example, most cells require anchorage to neighboring cells or substrates to proliferate. Cells that exhibit anchorage dependence usually exhibit density-dependent inhibition as well. As they become crowded, the physical constraints may stop the cells from growing. Crowding may also activate signal transduction pathways that arrest cells at certain points in the cell cycle. Growth arrest may also occur in conditions of oxidative stress, infection, or depleted levels of nutrients and/or growth factors. (Growth factors are proteins that stimulate cell growth.) Finally, any cells with damaged or incompletely replicated DNA, or chromosomes that are not properly aligned along the midline of the cell during mitosis, are arrested before they divide by checkpoint proteins. If the problem can be corrected, the cell will be allowed to progress. Cells that are too damaged will either remain in an arrested state permanently, or undergo apoptosis.

PRODUCTION AND DEVELOPMENT OF GAMETES

Gametogenesis is the process by which diploid germ cells give rise to haploid gametes (sex cells). Germ cells are produced in the early stages of embryogenesis, and migrate from the primitive streak to the gonads where they later undergo meiosis. Germ cells are distinguished from somatic cells because they can undergo both mitosis and meiosis. All other cells are restricted to mitosis, and have no potential to produce gametes. Mitosis is a single division that results in two identical cells, each with the same number of chromosomes as the parent cell. In meiosis, a germ cell undergoes two rounds of cell division (meiosis I and meiosis II). During meiosis I, homologous pairs of chromosomes exchange portions of their DNA before they are separated and distributed independently to daughter cells. These events ensure that the daughter cells are genetically unique, and the chromosome number is cut in half. The steps of meiosis II are similar to those of mitosis, and result in four haploid cells. These cells differentiate to give rise to the mature gametes that fuse during fertilization, restoring the diploid number. The production of ova and sperm is more specifically called oogenesis and spermatogenesis, respectively.

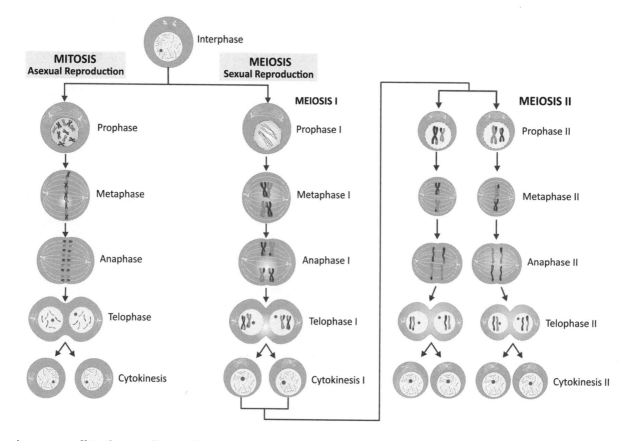

A sperm cell is the smallest of human cells, measuring about 0.05 mm in length. It has three distinct sections: the head, midpiece, and tail; its streamlined form is well suited to its function. The head contains centrioles and a compacted nucleus with tightly coiled DNA. The anterior surface of the head is capped with the **acrosome**, a Golgi-derived structure that is packed with enzymes that assist in the penetration of the zona pellucida and is therefore essential for fertilization. Between 50 and 100 mitochondria spiral around the midpiece, which is the only part of the sperm that contains any mitochondria. The ATP produced by the mitochondria powers the sliding motion of the microtubules within the tail, or **flagellum**, of the sperm, which in turn causes it to undulate. The microtubule-based core of the flagellum is called the **axoneme**, and consists of nine doublets of microtubules arranged around a central pair.

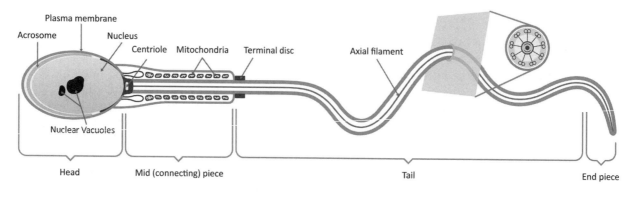

RELATIVE CONTRIBUTION TO NEXT GENERATION

When an oocyte undergoes meiosis and cytokinesis, the cytoplasm divides unequally to produce one large viable ovum. This ensures that nearly all of the resources that are required for the survival of a zygote are present. The ooplasm of the egg contains an abundance of nutrients that will sustain the zygote and later the daughter cells (blastomeres) that are produced by mitosis. All of the molecules (enzymes, RNA) needed for protein synthesis are present as well. It also contains the organelles, with the exception of the centrioles, which are degraded during oogenesis. These structures are instead donated by the sperm cell. Sperm cells do contain mitochondria, but they are left behind when the midpiece and tail are released from the head during fertilization. Any paternal mitochondria that manage to enter the egg are quickly destroyed, leaving only maternal mitochondria. Each gamete contributes 22 autosomes (non-sex chromosomes) and one sex chromosome to the zygote. The egg always contributes an X chromosome, and the sperm contributes either an X or a Y chromosome.

REPRODUCTIVE SEQUENCE: FERTILIZATION, IMPLANTATION, DEVELOPMENT, AND BIRTH

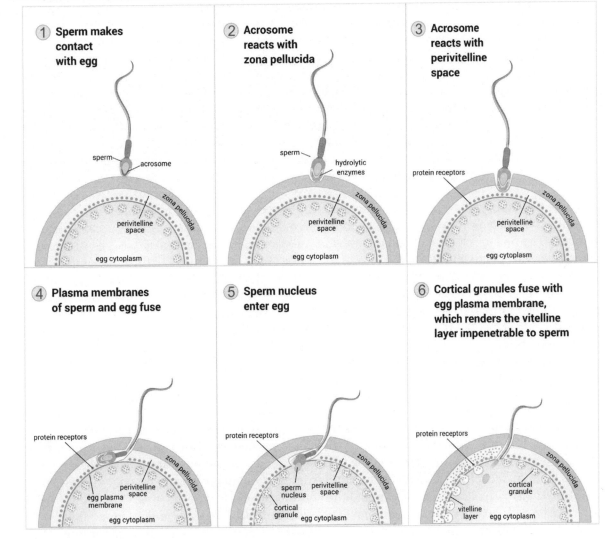

Fertilization usually occurs in the fallopian tube within 24 hours of ovulation. Of the hundreds of millions of sperm that are ejaculated, an average of 200 reach the secondary oocyte. When a sperm makes contact with the oocyte, it burrows through the corona radiata and binds to receptor proteins in the zona pellucida. The acrosome releases enzymes that allow the sperm to pass through the zona pellucida to the membrane of the oocyte. Here, actin filaments extend from the sperm to form a tubular structure called the acrosomal apparatus through which its pronucleus is passed. (The midpiece and tail are left behind.) Entry of the pronucleus stimulates the cortical reaction; enzymes from cortical granules beneath the membrane of the oocyte diffuse into the zona pellucida, causing it to harden, and preventing fertilization by more than one sperm. Another block to polyspermy is the depolarization of the oocyte membrane that occurs in response to calcium ions that are released when the sperm meets the membrane. The oocyte then divides unequally by meiosis II to produce an ovum and a nonviable polar body. The pronucleus of the sperm fuses with the pronucleus of the ovum, and a zygote (fertilized egg) is formed.

After fertilization, the zygote develops into a cluster of cells called a **morula**. The morula is pushed from the fallopian tube to the uterine cavity by peristalsis (muscle contractions) and the wave-like motions of cilia. It floats freely in the uterus for around 3 days, using uterine secretions as nourishment. The cells of the morula begin to differentiate and give rise to a blastocyst with a fluid-filled cavity and two types of cells. The inner cell mass will give rise to the embryo, and the outer trophoblasts develop into the placenta. Degeneration of the zona pellucida, followed by "zona hatching," occurs around six days after fertilization in preparation for implantation. As this transformation happens, the blastocyst secretes human chorionic gonadotropin (hCG) which stimulates the production of other hormones. These hormones help to maintain the corpus luteum (preventing menses) and prepare the endometrium for implantation. About one week after ovulation, the blastocyst (now over 200 cells) attaches to the endometrium, and outer cells of the trophoblast fuse to form large multinucleated syncytiotrophoblasts that extend like fingers (called chorionic villi) into the endometrium. Fetal blood vessels form inside these villi. About two weeks after fertilization, the blastocyst is fully implanted, and the endometrium is now called the decidua (the maternal contribution to the placenta).

During the pre-embryonic stage of development, the zygote undergoes **cleavage**, dividing mitotically to form a morula. The morula continues to divide and differentiate into a fluid-filled blastocyst. The blastocyst implants in the uterine wall, and the embryonic stage of development commences. During **gastrulation**, the cells of the embryo are reorganized to form the embryonic germ layers (ectoderm, mesoderm, and endoderm) that will produce the tissues and organs of the embryo. A neural plate derived from the ectoderm invades the mesoderm to form the neural tube in a process called **neurulation**. **Organogenesis** continues with the development of a rudimentary heart that beats at around the third week. The digestive system and other internal organs form, as well as the placenta and umbilical cord. By the end of eight weeks, the organ systems have formed and the embryo is now a fetus. During the fetal stage, development continues with the differentiation of the reproductive organs, coordinated movements of limbs, ossification of bones, and an increase of subcutaneous fat. Birth normally occurs around 40 weeks post fertilization.

The fetus must adapt quickly as it transitions from an intrauterine environment to an extrauterine environment. This transition is facilitated by hormones, notably cortisol and catecholamines. Before birth, the neonate relies on oxygen from the mother's blood, and its lungs are collapsed and fluid-filled. As labor approaches, the secretion of fluid from the fetal lungs decreases, while reabsorption increases. At birth, the lungs fill with air and the rest of the fluid leaves the lungs. This first breath triggers critical circulatory changes. Pulmonary resistance decreases, pulmonary blood flow increases, and the shunts that cause the blood to bypass the lungs and liver close or constrict. The **foramen ovale** that bypasses the lungs closes at first breath. The **ductus arteriosus**, which also bypasses the lungs, and the **ductus venosus** that bypasses the liver, both constrict at birth and close soon after. The neonate will no longer receive nourishment from the placenta and will rely on its mother's milk and stores of glycogen in the liver. The neonate must also expend energy to keep warm, and so increases its metabolic rate through muscle movements and the burning of brown fat.

TISSUES FORMED FROM EUKARYOTIC CELLS

EPITHELIAL CELLS

Epithelial cells come in a variety of shapes and functions, but they share the characteristic of being avascular. They are nourished by the diffusion of oxygen and nutrients from capillaries in the underlying layer of connective tissue called the basement membrane. Epithelial tissues are the lining and covering tissues of the body and, depending on their location, may be involved in protection, absorption, secretion, and/or filtration. These tissues are classified according to the shape and arrangement of their cells:

	Description	Name
Cell Shape	Flattened, scale-like	Squamous
	Cube-shaped	Cuboidal
	Long, thin	Columnar
Arrangement	Single layer of cells	Simple epithelia
	Appearance of multiple layers as a result of differences in cell shape and location	Pseudostratified
	Multiple layers of cells	Stratified epithelia

There are **many** types of epithelial tissues in the body. Stratified squamous epithelial tissues are found in locations that experience friction, such as the mouth, esophagus, and exterior skin. Simple columnar epithelia line the digestive tract, and harbor mucus-producing goblet cells. Simple squamous epithelia form membranes where filtration or diffusion occurs, such as the alveoli of the lungs. These are merely a few examples.

CONNECTIVE TISSUE CELLS

Connective tissues are the most abundant tissues in the body. Most connective tissues are highly vascular, the exceptions being ligaments, tendons, and cartilage. In general, they support and protect the body and are characterized by the presence of a nonliving matrix. This matrix is secreted by the cells of the connective tissue, and it consists of ground substance (water, proteins, and carbohydrates) and protein fibers such as collagen, elastin, or reticular fibers. The consistency of these connective tissues varies greatly from one tissue type to another. Blood is a connective tissue made of blood cells and plasma, and it transports oxygen, carbon dioxide, nutrients, and wastes. Adipose tissue is made of fat cells that cushion and insulate the body. Osseous tissue, or bone, consists of osteocytes surrounded by a hard matrix of calcium salts and collagen. Cartilage, like bone, is a connective tissue that provides support, but it is made of cells called chondrocytes, and is more flexible. Ligaments and tendons are made of dense fibrous connective tissue, which is made mostly of collagen fibers.

MECHANISMS OF DEVELOPMENT

CELL–CELL COMMUNICATION IN DEVELOPMENT

Cell-cell communication is crucial for the proper development of an embryo. When cells are "competent" they are able to receive signals from adjacent or nearby cells, inducing them to become a certain type of cell. (Competence is not a permanent state and may change during the course of development.) A developing cell may also secrete inducing factors of its own. Cells that secrete signal molecules are called **inducers**, and cells that differentiate in response to those signals are called **responders**. Most of these signals are growth factors that only act on cells of a specific tissue. **Autocrine** signals are self-generated; they act on the same cell that secreted them. **Paracrine**

193

signals diffuse to cells in close proximity. **Endocrine** signals enter the blood and travel to distant tissues. **Juxtacrine** signals require direct contact between cells. When the contact is made, signals from one cell bind to the receptors of another. Sometimes, two different tissues respond to each other's signals, promoting differentiation in each other. This is called **reciprocal induction**.

CELL MIGRATION

Cell migration is required for normal embryonic development; it begins during gastrulation and continues throughout life. Any errors in the migration pathway can lead to malformations, diseases, or even demise of the embryo. Migration is initiated by signaling molecules that trigger the detachment of cells from their substrate. The cell polarizes to define a leading edge, while actin filaments of the cytoskeleton polymerize to push the cell forward in a crawling motion. Rearrangement of the cytoskeleton forms flat, sheet-like projections called **lamellipodia** at the leading edge. Sometimes, finger-like projections called **filopodia** extend beyond the lamellipodia in the direction of motion. Contraction of the cell occurs when actin interacts with myosin. Chemical messengers continually influence the direction and rate of motion, ensuring that cells reach the intended site in the body at the right time. Some cells migrate individually, while others (such as epithelial and mesenchymal cells) migrate collectively.

PLURIPOTENCY: STEM CELLS

Potency describes the ability of a cell to differentiate. Totipotent cells have the greatest degree of potency which then decreases into pluripotent, multipotent, oligopotent, and finally unipotent cells, which have the least potential for differentiation. Only totipotent cells (the zygote and cells that arise after the first few divisions) have complete potency, but pluripotent stem cells still have great differentiation potential. They can develop into any cell type, with the exception of placental cells. As the zygote and subsequent blastomeres undergo cleavage, the once totipotent cells give rise to two lineages: the cells of the trophoblast, and the embryonic stem cells that give rise to the primary germ layers (the ectoderm, mesoderm, and endoderm). All of the hundreds of types of human cells stem from these germ layers; however, pluripotent cells cannot form an entire organism because they can't produce the needed placental tissues.

GENE REGULATION IN DEVELOPMENT

Differential gene expression is the mechanism for cell specialization and ultimately the development of an organism. Many factors collectively determine which genes are expressed and *when* they are expressed. In cell-cell communication, target cells detect and respond to signals (such as growth factors) released by other cells. When a signaling molecule binds to a membrane receptor, it causes a conformational change in the receptor. The signal transduction pathway continues with the phosphorylation of cytoplasmic proteins, which leads to the activation of transcription factors. Transcription factors bind to DNA and either promote or suppress gene expression.

Other strategies exist to regulate gene expression as well. **Epigenetic regulation** involves the methylation of DNA and modification of the histone proteins that it wraps around. These heritable modifications alter the structure of the chromosome. (Regions of DNA that are more condensed are less accessible to RNA polymerase.)

Regulation continues beyond the level of transcription. For example, coding regions (exons) of messenger RNA can be spliced together in different orders to produce different proteins from the same transcript. The proteins that are produced during translation may also require activation at a later time.

PROGRAMMED CELL DEATH

Programmed cell death, or **apoptosis**, is an important part of embryonic development. It is induced by signals that activate proteases called caspases. Caspases cleave certain cytoplasmic proteins, setting a series of events in motion. The cell shrinks and loses its anchorage to adjacent cells. Chromatin condenses as the cell membrane bulges out into protrusions called blebs. The DNA and organelles are broken down into fragments, and the blebs break free of the cell, taking a portion of the cytoplasm with them. The blebs, now called apoptotic bodies, are engulfed and digested by phagocytic cells. No intracellular components leak out during this process (unlike necrosis, in which an injured cell releases its contents into the surroundings).

This regulated process is used to eliminate abnormal, mispositioned, or misplaced cells. It also helps to sculpt certain structures. For example, many of the precursors to neural cells are eliminated in order to create a more direct pathway for electrical impulses. Apoptosis also helps to shape the hands and feet. If the process is incomplete, toes or fingers may be fused in a condition known as syndactyly. Sometimes, apoptosis occurs as a result of teratogenic agents, leading to malformations or fetal death.

SENESCENCE AND AGING

Senescence is a progressive decline in function as a result of biological aging. The term can be used to describe an organism as a whole, or the irreversible state of a cell that can no longer divide but remains physiologically active. Senescence can be brought on by the activation of an oncogene or the deactivation of a tumor suppressor gene, as a way to reduce the threat of cancer. This non-proliferative state can also be induced by oxidative stress, DNA damage, and telomere shortening. **Telomeres** are repetitive non-coding sequences of DNA found at the ends of chromosomes that protect the coding sequences. Every time a cell divides, the chromosomes shorten because DNA polymerase cannot replicate the end portion. Eventually the telomeres are lost and the cell must enter a state of senescence to prevent damage to important genes. An enzyme called telomerase *can* add nucleotides to these problematic end portions, but it is only found in certain types of cells, such as embryonic stem cells, germ cells, cancerous cells, and even adult stem cells (in low amounts). The proportion of senescent cells tends to increase with age, but evidence shows that senescence is also a strategy used during embryonic development to halt the growth of certain tissues, thereby helping to shape the embryo.

GENETIC MATERIAL
DNA

Chromosomes consist of **genes**, which are single units of genetic information. Genes are made up of deoxyribonucleic acid (DNA). DNA is a nucleic acid located in the cell nucleus. There is also DNA in the **mitochondria**. DNA replicates to pass on genetic information. The DNA in almost all cells is the same. It is also involved in the biosynthesis of proteins.

The model or structure of DNA is described as a **double helix**. A helix is a curve, and a double helix is two congruent curves connected by horizontal members. The model can be likened to a right-handed spiral staircase. The British scientist Rosalind Elsie Franklin is credited with taking the x-ray diffraction image in 1952 that was used by Francis Crick and James Watson to formulate the double-helix model of DNA and speculate about its important role in carrying and transferring genetic information.

> **Review Video: DNA**
> Visit mometrix.com/academy and enter code: 639552

Mometrix

DNA Structure

DNA has a double helix shape, resembles a twisted ladder, and is compact. It consists of **nucleotides**. Nucleotides consist of a **five-carbon sugar** (pentose), a **phosphate group**, and a **nitrogenous base**. Two bases pair up to form the rungs of the ladder. The "side rails" or backbone consists of the covalently bonded sugar and phosphate. The bases are attached to each other with hydrogen bonds, which are easily dismantled so replication can occur. Each base is attached to a phosphate and to a sugar. There are four types of nitrogenous bases: **adenine** (A), **guanine** (G), **cytosine** (C), and **thymine** (T). There are about 3 billion bases in human DNA. The bases are mostly the same in everybody, but their order is different. It is the order of these bases that creates diversity in people. *Adenine (A) pairs with thymine (T), and cytosine (C) pairs with guanine (G).*

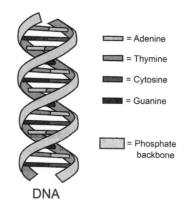

= Adenine
= Thymine
= Cytosine
= Guanine

= Phosphate backbone

DNA

Purines and Pyrimidines

The five bases in DNA and RNA can be categorized as either pyrimidine or purine according to their structure. The **pyrimidine bases** include *cytosine, thymine, and uracil.* They are six-sided and have a single ring shape. The **purine bases** are *adenine and guanine,* which consist of two attached rings. One ring has five sides and the other has six. When combined with a sugar, any of the five bases become **nucleosides**. Nucleosides formed from purine bases end in "osine" and those formed from pyrimidine bases end in "idine." **Adenosine** and **thymidine** are examples of nucleosides. Bases are the most basic components, followed by nucleosides, nucleotides, and then DNA or RNA.

Codons

Codons are groups of three nucleotides on the messenger RNA, and can be visualized as three rungs of a ladder. A **codon** has the code for a single amino acid. There are 64 codons but 20 amino acids. More than one combination, or triplet, can be used to synthesize the necessary amino acids. For example, AAA (adenine-adenine-adenine) or AAG (adenine-adenine-guanine) can serve as codons for lysine. These groups of three occur in strings, and might be thought of as frames. For example, AAAUCUUCGU, if read in groups of three from the beginning, would be AAA, UCU, UCG, which are codons for lysine, serine, and serine, respectively. If the same sequence was read in groups of three starting from the second position, the groups would be AAU (asparagine), CUU (proline), and so on. The resulting amino acids would be completely different. For this reason, there are **start and stop codons** that indicate the beginning and ending of a sequence (or frame). **AUG** (methionine) is the start codon. **UAA, UGA**, and **UAG**, also known as ocher, opal, and amber, respectively, are stop codons.

> **Review Video: Codons**
> Visit mometrix.com/academy and enter code: 978172

DNA Replication

Pairs of chromosomes are composed of DNA, which is tightly wound to conserve space. When replication starts, it unwinds. The steps in **DNA replication** are controlled by enzymes. The enzyme **helicase** instigates the deforming of hydrogen bonds between the bases to split the two strands. The splitting starts at the A-T bases (adenine and thymine) as there are only two hydrogen bonds. The cytosine-guanine base pair has three bonds. The term **"origin of replication"** is used to refer to where the splitting starts. The portion of the DNA that is unwound to be replicated is called the

196

Copyright © Mometrix Media. You have been licensed one copy of this document for personal use only. Any other reproduction or redistribution is strictly prohibited. All rights reserved. This content is provided for test preparation purposes only and does not imply an endorsement by Mometrix of any particular political, scientific, or religious point of view.

replication fork. Each strand of DNA is transcribed by an mRNA. It copies the DNA onto itself, base by base, in a complementary manner. The exception is that uracil replaces thymine.

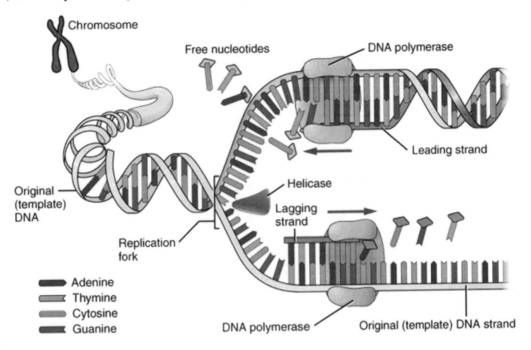

RNA

TYPES OF RNA

RNA acts as a *helper* to DNA and carries out a number of other functions. Types of RNA include ribosomal RNA (rRNA), transfer RNA (tRNA), and messenger RNA (mRNA). Viruses can use RNA to carry their genetic material to DNA. **Ribosomal RNA** is not believed to have changed much over time. For this reason, it can be used to study relationships in organisms. **Messenger RNA** carries a copy of a strand of DNA and transports it from the nucleus to the cytoplasm. **Transcription** is the process in which RNA polymerase copies DNA into RNA. DNA unwinds itself and serves as a template while RNA is being assembled. The DNA molecules are copied to RNA. **Translation** is the process whereby ribosomes use transcribed RNA to put together the needed protein. **Transfer RNA** is a molecule that helps in the translation process and is found in the cytoplasm.

DIFFERENCES BETWEEN RNA AND DNA

RNA and DNA differ in terms of structure and function. RNA has a different sugar than DNA. It has **ribose** rather than **deoxyribose** sugar. The RNA nitrogenous bases are adenine (A), guanine (G), cytosine (C), and uracil (U). **Uracil** is found only in RNA and **thymine** in found only in DNA. RNA consists of a single strand and DNA has two strands. If straightened out, DNA has two side rails. RNA only has one "backbone," or strand of sugar and phosphate group components. RNA uses the fully hydroxylated sugar **pentose**, which includes an extra oxygen compared to deoxyribose, which is the sugar used by DNA. RNA supports the functions carried out by DNA. It aids in gene expression, replication, and transportation.

Review Video: DNA vs. RNA
Visit mometrix.com/academy and enter code: 184871

GENETIC INHERITANCE
MENDEL'S LAWS

Mendel's laws are the law of segregation (the first law), the law of independent assortment (the second law), and the law of dominance (the third law). The **law of segregation** states that an organism receives half of its total number of alleles from each parent. The **law of independent assortment** states that traits are passed on randomly and are not influenced by other traits. The exception to this is linked traits. A **Punnett square** can illustrate how alleles combine from the contributing genes to form various **phenotypes**. One set of a parent's genes are put in columns, while the genes from the other parent are placed in rows. The allele combinations are shown in each cell. The **law of dominance** states that when two different alleles are present in a pair, the **dominant** one is expressed. A Punnett square can be used to predict the outcome of crosses.

> **Review Video: Punnett Square**
> Visit mometrix.com/academy and enter code: 853855

GENE, GENOTYPE, PHENOTYPE, AND ALLELE

A gene is a portion of DNA that identifies how traits are expressed and passed on in an organism. A gene is part of the **genetic code**. Collectively, all genes form the **genotype** of an individual. The genotype includes genes that may not be expressed, such as **recessive genes**. The **phenotype** is the physical, visual manifestation of genes. It is determined by the basic genetic information and how genes have been affected by their environment.

An **allele** is a variation of a gene. Also known as a trait, it determines the manifestation of a gene. This manifestation results in a specific physical appearance of some facet of an organism, such as eye color or height. For example, the genetic information for eye color is a gene. The gene variations responsible for blue, green, brown, or black eyes are called alleles. **Locus** (pl. loci) refers to the location of a gene or alleles.

> **Review Video: Genotype vs Phenotype**
> Visit mometrix.com/academy and enter code: 922853

DOMINANT AND RECESSIVE

Gene traits are represented in pairs with an upper-case letter for the dominant trait (A) and a lower-case letter for the recessive trait (a). Genes occur in pairs (AA, Aa, or aa). There is one gene on each chromosome half supplied by each parent organism. Since half the genetic material is from each parent, the offspring's traits are represented as a combination of these. A dominant trait only requires one gene of a gene pair for it to be expressed in a phenotype, whereas a recessive trait requires both genes in order to be manifested. For example, if the mother's genotype is Dd and the father's is dd, the possible combinations are Dd and dd. The dominant trait will be manifested if the genotype is DD or Dd. The recessive trait will be manifested if the genotype is dd. Both DD and dd are homozygous pairs. Dd is heterozygous.

MONOHYBRID AND DIHYBRID CROSSES

Genetic crosses are the possible combinations of alleles and can be represented using Punnett squares. A **monohybrid cross** refers to a cross involving only one trait. Typically, the ratio is 3:1 (DD, Dd, Dd, dd), which is the ratio of dominant gene manifestation to recessive gene manifestation. This ratio occurs when both parents have a pair of dominant and recessive genes. If one parent has a pair of dominant genes (DD) and the other has a pair of recessive (dd) genes, the recessive trait cannot be expressed in the next generation because the resulting crosses all have the Dd genotype.

The first monohybrid cross typically occurs between two **homozygous** parents. Each parent is homozygous for a separate allele for a particular trait. For example, in pea plants, green pods (G) are dominant over yellow pods (g). In a genetic cross of two pea plants that are homozygous for pod color, the F_1 generation will be 100% heterozygous green pods (Gg).

	g	g
G	Gg	Gg
G	Gg	Gg

If the plants with the heterozygous green pods are crossed, the resulting F_2 generation should be 50% heterozygous green (Gg), 25% homozygous green (GG), and 25% homozygous yellow (gg).

	G	g
G	GG	Gg
g	Gg	gg

A **dihybrid cross** refers to one involving more than one trait, which means more combinations are possible. The ratio of genotypes for a dihybrid cross is 9:3:3:1 when the traits are not linked. The ratio for incomplete dominance is 1:2:1, which corresponds to dominant, mixed, and recessive phenotypes. For example, in pea plants, green pods (G) are dominant over yellow pods (g), and yellow seeds (Y) are dominant over green seeds (y). In a genetic cross of two pea plants that are each homozygous for a different pod color and seed color (GGYY and ggyy), the F_1 generation will be 100% heterozygous green pods and yellow seeds (GgYy).

If these F_1 plants are crossed, the resulting F_2 generation is shown. There are nine genotypes for green-pod, yellow-seed plants: one GGYY, two GGYy, two GgYY, and four GgYy. There are three genotypes for green-pod, green-seed plants: one GGyy and two Ggyy. There are three genotypes for yellow-pod, yellow-seed plants: one ggYY and two ggYy. There is only one genotype for yellow-pod, green-seed plants: ggyy. This cross has a 9:3:3:1 ratio.

	GY	Gy	gY	gy
GY	GGYY	GGYy	GgYY	GgYy
Gy	GGYy	GGyy	GgYy	Ggyy
gY	GgYY	GgYy	ggYY	ggYy
gy	GgYy	Ggyy	ggYy	ggyy

NON-MENDELIAN CONCEPTS

CO-DOMINANCE

Co-dominance refers to the expression of *both alleles* so that both traits are shown. Cows, for example, can have hair colors of red, white, or red and white (not pink). In the latter color, both traits are fully expressed. The ABO human blood typing system is also co-dominant.

INCOMPLETE DOMINANCE

Incomplete dominance is when both the **dominant** and **recessive** genes are expressed, resulting in a phenotype that is a mixture of the two. The fact that snapdragons can be red, white, or pink is a good example. The dominant red gene (RR) results in a red flower because of large amounts of red pigment. White (rr) occurs because both genes call for no pigment. Pink (Rr) occurs because one gene is for red and one is for no pigment. The colors blend to produce pink flowers. A cross of pink flowers (Rr) can result in red (RR), white (rr), or pink (Rr) flowers.

POLYGENIC INHERITANCE

Polygenic inheritance goes beyond the simplistic Mendelian concept that one gene influences one trait. It refers to traits that are influenced by *more than one gene* and takes into account environmental influences on development.

MULTIPLE ALLELES

Each gene is made up of only two alleles, but in some cases, there are more than two possibilities for what those two alleles might be. For example, in blood typing, there are three alleles (A, B, O), but each person has only two of them. A gene with more than two possible alleles is known as a

199

multiple allele. A gene that can result in two or more possible forms or expressions is known as a polymorphic gene.

Review Video: Mendelian and Non-Mendelian Genetics
Visit mometrix.com/academy and enter code: 113159

MACROMOLECULES

Macromolecules are large and complex and play an important role in cell structure and function. The four basic organic macromolecules produced by anabolic reactions are **carbohydrates** (polysaccharides), **nucleic acids**, **proteins**, and **lipids**. The four basic building blocks involved in catabolic reactions are **monosaccharides** (glucose), **amino acids**, **fatty acids** (glycerol), and **nucleotides**.

An **anabolic reaction** is one that builds larger and more complex molecules (macromolecules) from smaller ones. **Catabolic reactions** are the opposite. Larger molecules are broken down into smaller, simpler molecules. Catabolic reactions *release energy*, while anabolic ones *require energy*.

Endothermic reactions are chemical reactions that *absorb* heat and **exothermic reactions** are chemical reactions that *release* heat.

Review Video: Macromolecules
Visit mometrix.com/academy and enter code: 220156

CARBOHYDRATE

Carbohydrates are the primary source of energy and are responsible for providing energy as they can be easily converted to **glucose**. It is the oxidation of carbohydrates that provides the cells with most of their energy. Glucose can be further broken down by respiration or fermentation by **glycolysis**. Carbohydrates are involved in the metabolic energy cycles of photosynthesis and respiration.

Structurally, carbohydrates usually take the form of some variation of CH_2O as they are made of carbon, hydrogen, and oxygen. Carbohydrates (**polysaccharides**) are broken down into sugars or glucose.

The simple sugars can be grouped into monosaccharides (glucose, fructose, and galactose) and disaccharides. These are both types of carbohydrates. Monosaccharides have one monomer of sugar and disaccharides have two. Monosaccharides (CH_2O) have one carbon for every water molecule.

A **monomer** is a small molecule. It is a single compound that forms chemical bonds with other monomers to make a polymer. A **polymer** is a compound of large molecules formed by repeating monomers. Carbohydrates, proteins, and nucleic acids are groups of macromolecules that are polymers.

Review Video: Carbohydrates
Visit mometrix.com/academy and enter code: 601714

LIPIDS

Lipids are molecules that are soluble in nonpolar solvents, but are hydrophobic, meaning they do not bond well with water or mix well with water solutions. Lipids have numerous **C–H bonds**. In this way, they are similar to **hydrocarbons** (substances consisting only of carbon and hydrogen).

The major roles of lipids include *energy storage and structural functions*. Examples of lipids include fats, phospholipids, steroids, and waxes. **Fats** (which are triglycerides) are made of long chains of fatty acids (three fatty acids bound to a glycerol). **Fatty acids** are chains with reduced carbon at one end and a carboxylic acid group at the other. An example is soap, which contains the sodium salts of free fatty acids. **Phospholipids** are lipids that have a phosphate group rather than a fatty acid. **Glycerides** are another type of lipid. Examples of glycerides are fat and oil. Glycerides are formed from fatty acids and glycerol (a type of alcohol).

> **Review Video: Lipids**
> Visit mometrix.com/academy and enter code: 269746

PROTEINS

Proteins are macromolecules formed from amino acids. They are **polypeptides**, which consist of many (10 to 100) peptides linked together. The peptide connections are the result of condensation reactions. A **condensation reaction** results in a loss of water when two molecules are joined together. A **hydrolysis reaction** is the opposite of a condensation reaction. During hydrolysis, water is added. –H is added to one of the smaller molecules and –OH is added to another molecule being formed. A **peptide** is a compound of two or more amino acids. **Amino acids** are formed by the partial hydrolysis of protein, which forms an **amide bond**. This partial hydrolysis involves an amine group and a carboxylic acid. In the carbon chain of amino acids, there is a **carboxylic acid group** (–COOH), an **amine group** (–NH$_2$), a **central carbon atom** between them with an attached hydrogen, and an attached **"R" group** (side chain), which is different for different amino acids. It is the "R" group that determines the properties of the protein.

> **Review Video: Proteins**
> Visit mometrix.com/academy and enter code: 903713

ENZYMES

Enzymes are proteins with strong **catalytic** power. They greatly accelerate the speed at which specific reactions approach equilibrium. Although enzymes do not start chemical reactions that would not eventually occur by themselves, they do make these reactions happen *faster and more often*. This acceleration can be substantial, sometimes making reactions happen a million times faster. Each type of enzyme deals with **reactants**, also called **substrates**. Each enzyme is highly selective, only interacting with substrates that are a match for it at an active site on the enzyme. This is the "key in the lock" analogy: a certain enzyme only fits with certain substrates. Even with a matching substrate, sometimes an enzyme must reshape itself to fit well with the substrate, forming a strong bond that aids in catalyzing a reaction before it returns to its original shape. An unusual quality of enzymes is that they are not permanently consumed in the reactions they speed up. They can be used again and again, providing a constant source of energy accelerants for cells. This allows for a tremendous increase in the number and rate of reactions in cells.

NUCLEIC ACIDS

Nucleic acids are macromolecules that are composed of **nucleotides**. **Hydrolysis** is a reaction in which water is broken down into **hydrogen cations** (H$^+$) and **hydroxide anions** (OH$^-$). This is part of the process by which nucleic acids are broken down by enzymes to produce shorter strings of RNA and DNA (oligonucleotides). **Oligonucleotides** are broken down into smaller sugar nitrogenous units called **nucleosides**. These can be digested by cells since the sugar is divided from the nitrogenous base. This, in turn, leads to the formation of the five types of nitrogenous bases, sugars, and the preliminary substances involved in the synthesis of new RNA and DNA. DNA and RNA have a helix shape.

Macromolecular nucleic acid polymers, such as RNA and DNA, are formed from nucleotides, which are monomeric units joined by **phosphodiester bonds**. Cells require energy in the form of ATP to synthesize proteins from amino acids and replicate DNA. **Nitrogen fixation** is used to synthesize nucleotides for DNA and amino acids for proteins. Nitrogen fixation uses the enzyme nitrogenase in the reduction of dinitrogen gas (N_2) to ammonia (NH_3).

Nucleic acids store information and energy and are also important catalysts. It is the **RNA** that catalyzes the transfer of **DNA genetic information** into protein coded information. ATP is an RNA nucleotide. **Nucleotides** are used to form the nucleic acids. Nucleotides are made of a five-carbon sugar, such as ribose or deoxyribose, a nitrogenous base, and one or more phosphates. Nucleotides consisting of more than one phosphate can also store energy in their bonds.

> **Review Video: Nucleic Acids**
> Visit mometrix.com/academy and enter code: 503931

MICROORGANISMS AND DISEASE
CYCLE OF INFECTION

The cycle of infection starts with the presence of a pathogen (a disease-causing organism) and an environment that allows it to grow and multiply. Aside from being able to grow and multiply, the conditions must allow it to be passed on (transmission) from one organism (host) to another. Transmission can be either direct or indirect. Direct transmission occurs when the infection is passed from one infected host to another. There are several different possible modes of indirect transmission. An object can become contaminated, and a person becomes infected when they touch the contaminated object (called a fomite). A vector can be employed by the pathogen, infecting an intermediate host where it can multiply and develop before being passed on to a new host. The pathogen can become airborne before finding a new host to infect. In any mode of transmission, there must be a way for the pathogen to enter the new host, and the host must be susceptible to the infection.

RESERVOIR

Medical professionals must understand all five components of the cycle of infection to prevent the spread of disease. All of these factors must be present for an infection to transpire: a **reservoir host**, **portal of exit**, **method of transmission**, **route of entrance**, and a **susceptible host**. The first aspect takes place when a microorganism (pathogen) latches onto a living host. This living host is referred to as a reservoir host and may be a human, an insect, or even an animal. A reservoir's body will offer the proper nourishment for the pathogen for it to live and/or proliferate. When humans serve as the reservoir hosts, they become carriers of the disease but are often oblivious that they have been infected and can easily transmit the disease to other people. When there is evidence of a disease in a reservoir host, one may be more aware of hand washing and other methods to prevent the spread of disease.

PORTAL OF EXIT

The second step that must take place for an infection to occur is the reservoir host providing a portal of exit. This describes the method in which the microorganism leaves the reservoir host to continue on to infect another organism, known as the susceptible host. The most prevalent avenues for exiting the body are via the mouth, nose, blood, urine, vaginal or seminal fluid, feces, and even the eyes. Often the portal of exit is the exact same as the entrance portals, which is the fourth step in the cycle of infection.

MODE OF TRANSMISSION: DROPLET

Droplet (mucous) particles may be transmitted when the reservoir host sneezes or coughs. It is known that the reservoir host does not need to be in close proximity to the susceptible host as droplet particles can travel several feet in the air. Respiratory diseases such as influenza and tuberculosis may be transmitted via a direct airborne method when the susceptible host inhales the droplets of the infected person. These types of infections may sweep through a population rapidly, so it is important to practice proper techniques to prevent airborne transmission. This includes coughing or sneezing into a tissue when possible. If a tissue is not available, one should sneeze or cough into the crook of the elbow and then perform proper hand washing. Often, patients who have a respiratory infection are asked to wear a mask to prevent the spread of infected droplets.

MODE OF TRANSMISSION: DIRECT CONTACT

Bloodborne transmission may occur by direct mode if blood from the infected reservoir host comes into contact with the susceptible host's mucous membranes or when the integrity of the skin is compromised. Healthcare workers must always practice universal precautions and utilize personal protective equipment (PPE) such as gloves, gowns, masks, eye protection, and face shields to prevent blood from reaching these mucous membranes or from getting into a cut in the skin. The most common bloodborne pathogens that may be transmitted in a healthcare setting are hepatitis B (HBV), hepatitis C (HCV), and the human immunodeficiency virus (HIV). Healthcare professionals should assume and treat all bodily fluids as if they are contaminated, and any PPE should be managed and disposed of properly. Another example of direct transmission is when a pregnant female passes on a sexually transmitted infection (STI) onto her baby via the placenta or during a vaginal delivery, such as gonorrhea, herpes, or syphilis.

MODE OF TRANSMISSION: AIRBORNE

The spread of microorganisms can take place when miniscule particles are dispersed from the respiratory system of the reservoir host and inhaled by another individual. This is known as airborne transmission. An example of airborne transmission is inhaling droplets when an infected individual coughs or sneezes. It is known that people do not need to be located right next to each other as these droplets are capable of traveling several feet following a cough or sneeze. This is a common method in which influenza, tuberculosis, or even chickenpox is spread. People may also become ill after the inhalation of bacteria or fungi within water that is contaminated. One example of this type of airborne infection is Legionnaires' disease. This is not spread from person to person but rather when somebody inhales water droplets that contain the bacteria. This is often heard of in contaminated water supplies such as in hotels, resorts, or air-conditioning systems of apartment complexes.

MODE OF TRANSMISSION: VEHICLE-BORNE FOMITE

The word *fomite* refers to any inanimate object that can spread a pathogen from one person to the next. Common examples of fomites that aid in the transmission of disease are doorknobs, drinking fountains, water glasses, pens, toys, books, and shopping carts. With these examples, it is easy to see why schools or child-care centers can readily spread germs among individuals. Note that this transmission is carried out in an indirect fashion as body membranes do not need to touch each other. Examples of vehicle-borne fomites in the medical industry could be instruments used in clinical care settings such as tools used for surgical procedures or patient care. Other examples of a vehicle-borne fomite in the medical field could be blood, biopsy specimens, or organs and tissues used for transplants or grafting material.

MODE OF TRANSMISSION: VECTOR-BORNE MECHANICAL OR BIOLOGICAL

A vector-borne method of transmission occurs when pathogens are spread from one living organism to another. **Vectors** are commonly insects that act as couriers that transport bacteria and other common pathogens from one individual to the next. Examples of vectors are mosquitoes, flies, ticks, and fleas. Mosquitoes are known for spreading West Nile virus. Flies can mechanically transmit disease as they continuously land on food and people. Infected ticks are widely known for spreading Lyme disease when they bite a person. Another disease that ticks may spread is Rocky Mountain spotted fever, which may be deadly if not diagnosed correctly. Fleas are the culprits in transferring pathogens that allow people and animals to contract the plague. Mosquitoes, ticks, and fleas tend to fall under the biological mode of transmission as they usually become infected because they feed on the blood of their hosts.

PORTAL OF ENTRY

A portal of entrance is the fourth step that must take place for an infection to occur. As the microorganism exits the reservoir host, it must have an entrance portal to infect the susceptible host. Examples of entrance portals are similar to exit routes and include any mucous membrane such as the nose, mouth, rectum, or vagina. These pathogens can also enter via the integumentary system when the skin is no longer intact. The eyes are yet another entrance portal, and conjunctivitis is a very contagious disease that is spread via this entrance method. Urinary tract infections are another common infection seen, especially in females. This occurs as bacteria from the rectum are transferred to the urethra because of the close proximity of these structures. It is important to practice proper hygiene, whether it is wiping after using the toilet or hand washing, to prevent the transfer of bacteria and other pathogens.

SUSCEPTIBLE HOST

A susceptible host is the fifth and final step in the cycle of infection. A susceptible host is an individual that is unable to fight off an infection and will enable the cycle to continue when this individual passes the pathogen onto another person. There are many factors that determine whether the susceptible host will become infected. These may include the strength of the immune system, overall health, and level of nourishment. Age is another important factor as infants and the elderly are more susceptible to certain diseases. Hygiene practices as well as living conditions are yet another determining factor that may induce an infection. For example, perhaps the host employs great hand-washing techniques but is forced to wash with water that is contaminated while living in a house with rodents and insects. Sometimes the susceptible host, regardless of how healthy he or she is, may be infected with a microorganism so potent that the host is unable to fight it off even with a strong immune system.

BACTERIA

Clinical classification of bacteria takes into account those characteristics that are helpful in identifying infectious processes:

- **Gram-positive or Gram-negative status**: Most bacteria are Gram-negative stains (red) or Gram-positive (purple) although a few cannot be identified by staining. While Gram stain isn't used to identify bacteria, it's frequently referred to clinically.
- **Taxonomic status**: Taxonomy is based on the genera and species of a bacterium, but this can be confusing because some names have changed or two names are used. Genome sequencing should standardize identification.
- **Anaerobic/aerobic status**: Some bacteria are strictly anaerobic, but very few are strictly aerobic. Those that have flexibility and can grow in either aerobic or anaerobic conditions are called *facultative*.

- **Usual environment**: Bacteria are classified according to where they usually reside as flora or where they usually cause infection.
- **Virulence factor**: Bacteria vary widely in virulence. Some are actively invasive but others only cause opportunistic infections.

GRAM-NEGATIVE BACTERIA

The cell walls of Gram-negative bacteria are characterized by red staining. The cell wall is thinner than that of Gram-positive bacteria; however, there are two separate layers to the wall: a thin inner layer of peptidoglycan (carbohydrate polymers bound by proteins), an intervening periplasmic space, and the outer membranous layer (the lipopolysaccharide layer), which produces endotoxins, making Gram-negative bacteria extremely pathogenic. A component of the outer layer is called the S-layer; it aids in adherence and protection from pathogens. The outer layer serves to protect Gram-negative organisms from antibiotics or detergents that would disrupt the inner peptidoglycan layer and provides resistance to penicillin and other compounds. Ampicillin is often able to penetrate the exterior wall, although many bacteria have become resistant to it.

Common Gram-negative cocci (round) bacteria include:

- *Neisseria gonorrhoeae*
- *Neisseria meningitides*
- *Moraxella catarrhalis*

Common Gram-negative bacilli (rods) include:

- *Haemophilus influenzae*
- *Legionella pneumophila*
- *Pseudomonas aeruginosa*
- *Escherichia coli*
- *Helicobacter pylori*

GRAM-POSITIVE BACTERIA

Gram-positive bacteria are characterized by purple staining; their cell walls tend to be thicker than those of Gram-negative bacteria. About 90% of the cell wall of Gram-positive bacteria is made of peptidoglycan (carbohydrate polymers bound by proteins). The number of peptidoglycan layers varies, but can be more than 20, making a thick-walled cell. An S-layer is attached to the peptidoglycan layer to protect the cell and aid in adherence. Gram-positive organisms tend to be easier to kill than Gram-negative because they lack the outer wall of Gram-negative organisms. They are also more sensitive to penicillin, although there are resistant strains. Peptidoglycan does not occur naturally in the human body, so it is easily recognized by the immune system as an invading organism.

Common Gram-positive cocci bacteria include:

- *Streptococcus pneumoniae*
- *Staphylococcus aureus*
- *Enterococcus*

Science

Common Gram-positive bacilli bacteria include:

- *Corynbacterium diphtheriae*
- *Listeria monocytogenes*
- *Bacillus anthracis*

BACTERIAL GROWTH

Bacterial growth generally proceeds through a series of four phases:

- **Lag phase**: Microorganisms become accustomed to their new environment. There is little to no growth during this phase.
- **Log phase**: Bacteria logarithmic, or exponential, growth begins; the rate of multiplication is the most rapid and constant.
- **Stationary phase**: The rate of multiplication slows down due to lack of nutrients and build-up of toxins. At the same time, bacteria are constantly dying so the numbers actually remain constant.
- **Death phase**: Cell numbers decrease as growth stops and existing cells die off.

VIRUSES

Viruses (virions) are sub-microscopic and generally considered non-living because they lack cell structures. Viruses consist of nucleic acid, single or double-strand DNA and/or RNA (the genome), encapsulated in a protein coating called a capsid. Some have a lipid envelope about the capsid with glycoprotein spikes. The purpose of viruses is to reproduce, but they require a host cell with a protein receptor to which a virus must bind to penetrate the cell membrane. The viral genome carries encoding that allows it to use the cell to replicate in a **lytic** or **lysogenic** cycle. In the lytic cycle, the virus forces the cell to manufacture proteins and new genomes. After new viral particles form, the cell ruptures, releasing the viruses. In a lysogenic cycle, the virus integrates the DNA of the host and as the cell replicates, the virus replicates with it. The virus remains dormant until it activates and begins a lytic cycle. Viruses that infect bacteria are **bacteriophages** (or **phages**).

> **Review Video: Viruses**
> Visit mometrix.com/academy and enter code: 984455

GENERALIZED PHAGE AND ANIMAL VIRUS LIFE CYCLES

For a virus to attach to a host cell (a process called **adsorption**), it must bind to receptor proteins. The pathway for entry of the viral genome after adsorption varies according to the type of virus, and the type of host cell. Some viruses (particularly bacteriophages) use tail fibers to attach to the host cell's receptors before injecting their genome using the tail sheath. Viruses that infect eukaryotic cells tend to enter either by receptor-mediated endocytosis or by membrane fusion. In receptor-mediated endocytosis, attachment sites on the surface of the virus bind to cell surface receptors, and cell membrane invaginates around the virus, pinching off to form a vacuole that enters the cytoplasm. Some cells mistake the virus for a desired resource, like nutrients. Enveloped viruses typically gain entry when proteins within their lipid envelope bind to receptor proteins on the cell membrane, and the envelope and membrane fuse. The virus enters, and the protein coat is degraded. If the cell does not have the specific receptor proteins used by a particular virus, then that cell cannot be infected.

Viruses depend on the biosynthetic machinery of the cell to replicate. They cannot copy their own genome, nor can they produce the proteins needed for the capsid. The host cell provides ATP, nucleotides, transfer RNA, amino acids, and most of the enzymes required for viral replication

206

(though some viral genomes contain genes that are translated into enzymes). The cell's ribosomes are redirected to translate viral proteins that are used in the assembly of progeny. The cell can no longer perform its own functions and has essentially become a virus factory.

PRIONS AND VIROIDS: SUBVIRAL PARTICLES

Prions and viroids are tiny, non-living infectious particles that are much smaller than viruses. In fact, these pathogens are nothing more than proteins and RNA molecules, respectively.

Prions are misfolded variations of normal proteins that incubate for many years before symptoms of disease begin to show. They do not replicate, but rather prompt the misfolding of other proteins, though the mechanism is not well understood. The misfolded proteins group together, triggering the formation of even more prions. The cell cannot function normally under these conditions, and animal diseases such as mad cow disease and Creutzfeldt-Jakob disease result.

Viroids are short circular molecules (approximately 250–400 nucleobases) of ssRNA that are not translated into proteins, but replicate in host plant cells. Replication requires the enzyme RNA polymerase II, and occurs either in the nucleus or in chloroplasts. Viroids cause a number of plant diseases by silencing the normal RNA of the plant, and therefore interfering with gene expression. The human disease hepatitis D is caused by a viroid-like pathogen.

FUNGI

Fungi were originally classified as plants, but they do not produce their own food through photosynthesis and must, like animals, get the food from another source. Fungi vary widely, from one-celled microorganisms to multi-celled chains that are miles long. Fungi are used to make antibiotics, but they can also cause infection and disease. Two common classifications of fungi are molds (including mushrooms) and yeast. Fungi are not motile, but some produce spores, which can be inhaled. Some, such as the yeast *Candida albicans*, are part of the normal flora of the skin but can overgrow in an opportunistic infection. As microorganisms, fungal infections can invade the sinuses, the mouth, the respiratory system, and the vagina. Antibiotics may affect the balance between bacteria and yeast, causing infection. Fungal infections include histoplasmosis, blastomycosis, and coccidioidomycosis. Fungal infections, such as *Pneumocystis jiroveci (*formerly *carinii)* pose a serious problem for the immunocompromised. Antifungal drugs are available, but systemic fungal infections are difficult to treat.

PARASITES
PROTISTS

Protists are small, eukaryotic, single-celled organisms. Although protists are small, they are much larger than prokaryotic bacteria. Protists have three general forms, which include plantlike protists, animal-like protists, and fungus-like protists. Plantlike protists are algae that contain chlorophyll and perform photosynthesis. Animal-like protists are protozoa with no cell walls that typically lack chlorophyll and are grouped by their method of locomotion. Fungus-like protists, which do not have chitin in their cell walls, are generally grouped as either slime molds or water molds. Protists may be autotrophic or heterotrophic. Autotrophic protists include many species of algae. Heterotrophic protists include parasitic, commensalistic, and mutualistic protozoa. Slime molds are heterotrophic fungus-like protists, which consume microorganisms. Some protists reproduce sexually, but most

207

reproduce asexually by binary fission. Some reproduce asexually by spores. Some reproduce by alternation of generations and require two hosts in their life cycle.

Types/Classifications	Description
Intestinal flagellates: *Giardia lamblia, Trichomonas vaginalis, Dientamoeba fragilis.* **Hemoflagellates:** *Trypanosoma, Leishmania, Trypanosoma cruzi*	Contain one or more flagella (whip-like tails), and some have an undulating membrane.
Intestinal amoebas: *Entamoeba histolytica, Balantidium coli*	Have 3 stages: amoeba, inactive cyst, and intermediate precyst. Move with pseudopodia.
Blood apicomplexa/sporozoa: *Plasmodium vivax, ovale, malariae,* and *falciparum; Isospora belli; Babesia microti, sarcocystis spp.; Cryptosporidium spp.; Toxoplasma gondii*	Spore-forming with organelle to penetrate host cell.
Microsporidia: *Encephalitozoon hellem, Enterocytozoon bieneusi, encephalitozoon intestinalis*	One-celled spore with tubular polar filament to inject sporoplasm into host where it develops.
Ciliates: *Balantidium coli*	Organism with cilia in rows/patches and 2 kinds of nuclei.

ECTOPARASITES

Ectoparasites, parasites that that live on the outside of a host, include such "bugs" as lice, fleas, ticks, mites, and scabies. Common sources are household pets whose vermin can be controlled with pesticides known to be safe to animals and humans. Precautions can be taken against encounters with ectoparasites such as ticks that carry Lyme Disease, which can be kept at bay by protectively covering the body from the waist down when walking in wooded areas. Infestations of head lice, body lice, scabies, and chiggers are common causes of rash and pruritus in children. Head lice are an annoyance, but body lice are a vector of human diseases, including typhus, relapsing fever, and trench fever. They are transmitted through infested clothing, so the best way to control outbreaks is by changing and laundering clothes and linens.

HELMINTH PARASITES

Helminths are parasitic worms that live in humans, primarily in the intestines. There are a variety of helminths, including roundworms, tapeworms, pinworms, flukes, and the worm Trichinella spiralis, which is responsible for causing trichinosis. Eggs from helminths can contaminate a variety of things, including feces, pets and other animals, water, air, food, and surfaces like toilet seats. Eggs of helminths usually enter a human via the anus, the nose, or the mouth, and they then travel to the intestines, where they hatch, grow, and multiply. The presence of helminths can be determined in most cases by examining stool samples of suspected infected individuals. Drugs known as vermifuges can be used to treat infections from helminth worms. To prevent infection from helminths, thoroughly cook meats, keep a clean kitchen and bathroom, and wash hands frequently.

MEDICAL ASEPSIS

In order to prevent or control the spread of infection, the cycle of infection must be broken. The cycle of infection refers to the conditions that allow infection to spread. These conditions (presence of pathogen, growth and reproduction, transmission to host, susceptibility of host) must all be present in order for an infection to exist. Medical asepsis (also called clean or aseptic technique) refers to cleanliness practices in a non-sterile environment. The point is to remove as many pathogens as possible from the environment and prevent the spread of those that do exist. The biggest thing that can be done in medical asepsis is the washing of hands. The basic technique of hand washing is the use of warm water, antiseptic cleaner, the removal of jewelry, and specific cleaning of fingernails. Hands should be washed before and after contact with a patient, after contact with organic materials or contaminated equipment, after removing sterile or non-sterile gloves.

SURGICAL ASEPSIS

Surgical asepsis (also called sterile technique) is a strict process of keeping an area sterile by removing any microorganisms from objects in the environment. This is done with the use of an autoclave, gas sterilization, or chemical cleaning solution. The area is them kept sterile by protecting it from contamination with the use of sterile draping, masks, caps, gowns, and gloves. Surgical asepsis should be used any time a patient is cut open for a procedure, if there is damaged skin (burns, cuts), or if a medical device is being inserted into a patient.

There are basic principles that govern surgical asepsis. They are in place to help keep an environment sterile, thus preventing and controlling the spread of infection. The most important (and basic) principle is that sterile objects remain sterile only when they come into contact with other sterile objects. No matter how clean the object it comes into contact with is, if it is not sterile, it should be considered a contaminant. If you are not sure if an object is sterile, or if the object is out of your field of view, it should be treated as contaminated.

UNIVERSAL/STANDARD PRECAUTIONS FOR PREVENTION AND CONTROL OF INFECTION

Universal (also called standard) precautions were developed in 1991 when, to help prevent and control the spread of infection, OSHA (Occupational Health Administration) and the CDC (Centers for Disease Control) mandated that every patient and specimen be treated as if it is contaminated. These precautions apply to all blood and bodily fluids (including peritoneal, amniotic, vaginal, seminal, cerebrospinal, synovial and saliva, pleural and pericardial fluids). Care should be taken when handling any of these fluids, or items contaminated with these fluids. Personal protective equipment (PPE), hand washing, and preventative measures should be employed.

MICROSCOPY

The microscope most commonly used is the **light microscope** (either monocular or binocular). This microscope uses external light or light from an internal filament that allows the light to pass upward through the specimen so that the specimen appears dark against the lighter background, although the light may be inverted, illuminating from the top, for such things as a culture in a liquid medium. **Phase contrast microscopes** that do not require staining of the specimen are used to assess cell growth, especially for organisms that are transparent with standard light microscope. The **dark field microscope** uses a special dark-field condenser that makes the specimen appear light against a dark background, useful for observing spirochetes. The **fluorescent microscope** utilizes an ultraviolet light for illumination. This microscope is used when fluorescent dye is attached to a specimen because the dye glows when exposed to ultraviolet light, useful for fluorescent antibody testing.

BIOLOGY CHAPTER QUIZ

1. Which of the following is a colligative property?

    a. Temperature

    b. Surface tension

    c. Viscosity

    d. Osmotic pressure

2. Which of the following is NOT a form of active transport?

    a. Sodium-potassium pump

    b. Endocytosis

    c. Exocytosis

    d. Osmosis

3. Which of the following is a lysosomal storage disease?

    a. Tay-Sachs

    b. Pfeiffer syndrome

    c. Myasthenia gravis

    d. Wernicke encephalopathy

4. Which of the following is NOT a pyrimidine base?

    a. Cytosine

    b. Adenine

    c. Thymine

    d. Uracil

5. Which of the following is the start codon of a messenger RNA sequence?

    a. AUG

    b. AAU

    c. UCG

    d. UAA

6. What is the probability of an offspring having a homozygous recessive trait if both parents are heterozygous for the trait?

    a. 100%

    b. 75%

    c. 50%

    d. 25%

7. Which blood type is dominant?

    a. A

    b. B

    c. O

    d. They are all co-dominant.

8. How many components comprise the cycle of infection?
   a. Three
   b. Four
   c. Five ✓
   d. Six

9. Which of the following is a gram-negative bacterium?
   a. *Corynebacterium diphtheriae*
   b. *Haemophilus influenzae* ✓
   c. *Listeria monocytogenes*
   d. *Staphylococcus aureus*

10. Who is credited with taking the x-ray diffraction image used by Watson and Crick to formulate the double-helix model of DNA?
   a. Rosalind Franklin ✓
   b. Janet Taylor
   c. Dorothy Hodgkin
   d. Barbara McClintock

Answers for all of the chapter quiz questions can be found right before Practice Test #1.

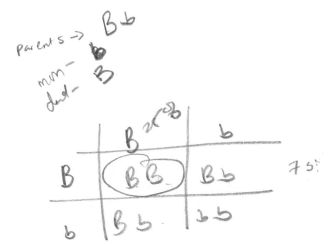

211

Chemistry

BASIC ATOMIC STRUCTURE
PIECES OF AN ATOM

All matter consists of atoms. Atoms consist of a **nucleus** and **electrons**. The nucleus consists of **protons** and **neutrons**. The properties of these are measurable; they have mass and an electrical charge. The nucleus is **positively charged** due to the presence of protons. Electrons are **negatively charged** and orbit the nucleus. The nucleus has considerably more mass than the surrounding electrons. Atoms can bond together to make **molecules**. Atoms that have an equal number of protons and electrons are electrically **neutral**. If the number of protons and electrons in an atom is not equal, the atom has a positive or negative charge and is an **ion**.

Review Video: Structure of Atoms
Visit mometrix.com/academy and enter code: 905932

MODELS OF ATOMS

Atoms are extremely small. A hydrogen atom is about 5×10^{-8} mm in diameter. According to some estimates, five trillion hydrogen atoms could fit on the head of a pin. **Atomic radius** refers to the average distance between the nucleus and the outermost electron. Models of atoms that include the proton, nucleus, and electrons typically show the electrons very close to the nucleus and revolving around it, similar to how the Earth orbits the sun. However, another model relates the Earth as the nucleus and its atmosphere as electrons, which is the basis of the term "**electron cloud**." Another description is that electrons swarm around the nucleus. It should be noted that these atomic models are not to scale. A more accurate representation would be a nucleus with a diameter of about 2 cm in a stadium. The electrons would be in the bleachers. This model is similar to the not-to-scale solar system model. In reference to the periodic table, atomic radius increases as energy levels are added and decreases as more protons are added (because they pull the electrons closer to the nucleus). Essentially, atomic radius increases toward the left and toward the bottom of the periodic table (i.e., Francium (Fr) has the largest atomic radius while Helium (He) has the smallest).

ATOMIC NUMBER

The atomic number of an element refers to the **number of protons** in the nucleus of an atom. It is a unique identifier. It can be represented as Z. Atoms with a neutral charge have an atomic number that is equal to the **number of electrons**.

ATOMIC MASS

Atomic mass is also known as the **mass number**. The atomic mass is the *total number of protons and neutrons* in the nucleus of an atom. It is referred to as "A." The atomic mass (A) is equal to the number of protons (Z) plus the number of neutrons (N). This can be represented by the equation $A = Z + N$. The mass of electrons in an atom is basically insignificant because it is so small. Atomic weight may sometimes be referred to as "**relative atomic mass**," but should not be confused with atomic mass. Atomic weight is the ratio of the average mass per atom of a sample (which can include various isotopes of an element) to 1/12 of the mass of an atom of carbon-12.

ISOTOPES

Isotopes are atoms of the same element that vary in their number of neutrons. Isotopes of the same element have the same number of protons and thus the same atomic number. They are denoted by the element symbol, preceded in superscript and subscript by the mass number and atomic number, respectively. For instance, the notations for protium, deuterium, and tritium are respectively: $_1^1H$, $_1^2H$, and $_1^3H$.

Isotopes that have not been observed to decay are **stable**, or non-radioactive, isotopes. It is not known whether some stable isotopes may have such long decay times that observing decay is not possible. Currently, 80 elements have one or more stable isotopes. There are 256 known stable isotopes in total. Carbon, for example, has three isotopes. Two (carbon-12 and carbon-13) are stable and one (carbon-14) is radioactive. **Radioactive isotopes** have unstable nuclei and can undergo spontaneous nuclear reactions, which results in particles or radiation being emitted. It cannot be predicted when a specific nucleus will decay, but large groups of identical nuclei decay at predictable rates. Knowledge about rates of decay can be used to *estimate the age of materials* that contain radioactive isotopes.

ELECTRONS

Electrons are subatomic particles that orbit the nucleus at various levels commonly referred to as **layers**, **shells**, or **clouds**. The orbiting electron or electrons account for only a fraction of the atom's mass. They are much smaller than the nucleus, are negatively charged, and exhibit wave-like characteristics. Electrons are part of the **lepton** family of elementary particles. Electrons can occupy orbits that are varying distances away from the nucleus and tend to occupy the lowest energy level they can. If an atom has all its electrons in the lowest available positions, it has a **stable** electron arrangement. The outermost electron shell of an atom in its uncombined state is known as the **valence shell**. The electrons there are called **valence electrons**, and it is their number that determines **bonding behavior**. Atoms tend to react in a manner that will allow them to fill or empty their valence shells.

CHEMICAL BONDS AND ELECTRON SHELLS

Chemical bonds involve a negative-positive attraction between an electron or electrons and the nucleus of an atom or nuclei of more than one atom. The attraction keeps the atom cohesive, but also enables the formation of bonds among other atoms and molecules. Each of the four **energy levels** (or shells) of an atom has a maximum number of electrons they can contain. Each level must be completely filled before electrons can be added to the **valence level**. The farther away from the nucleus an electron is, the more energy it has. The first shell, or K-shell, can hold a maximum of 2 electrons; the second, the L-shell, can hold 8; the third, the M-shell, can hold 18; the fourth, the N-shell, can hold 32. The shells can also have **subshells**. Chemical bonds form and break between atoms when atoms gain, lose, or share an electron in the outer valence shell. **Polar bond** refers to a covalent type of bond with a separation of charge. One end is negative and the other is positive. The hydrogen-oxygen bond in water is one example of a polar bond.

IONS

Most atoms are **neutral** since the positive charge of the protons in the nucleus is balanced by the negative charge of the surrounding electrons. Electrons are transferred between atoms when they come into contact with each other. This creates a molecule or atom in which the number of electrons does not equal the number of protons, which gives it a positive or negative charge. A **negative ion** is created when an atom gains electrons, while a **positive ion** is created when an atom loses electrons. An **ionic bond** is formed between ions with opposite charges. The resulting compound is neutral. **Ionization** refers to the process by which neutral particles are ionized into charged particles. Gases and plasmas can be partially or fully ionized through ionization.

CHEMICAL BONDS BETWEEN ATOMS

Atoms of the same element may bond together to form **molecules** or **crystalline solids**. When two or more different types of atoms bind together chemically, a **compound** is made. The physical properties of compounds reflect the nature of the interactions among their molecules. These interactions are determined by the structure of the molecules, including the atoms they consist of and the distances and angles between them.

A union between the electron structures of atoms is called **chemical bonding**. An atom may gain, surrender, or share its electrons with another atom it bonds with. Listed below are three types of chemical bonding.

- **Ionic bonding**—When an atom gains or loses electrons it becomes negatively or positively charged, turning it into an ion. An ionic bond is a relationship between two *oppositely charged ions*.
- **Covalent bonding**—Atoms that share electrons have what is called a covalent bond. Electrons shared equally have a *non-polar bond*, while electrons shared unequally have a *polar bond*.
- **Hydrogen bonding**—The atom of a molecule interacts with a hydrogen atom in the same area. Hydrogen bonds can also form between two different parts of the same molecule, as in the structure of DNA and other large molecules.

A **cation** or positive ion is formed when an atom loses one or more electrons. An **anion** or negative ion is formed when an atom gains one or more electrons.

IONIC BONDING

The transfer of electrons from one atom to another is called **ionic bonding**. Atoms that lose or gain electrons are referred to as **ions**. The gain or loss of electrons will result in an ion having a positive or negative charge. Here is an example:

> Take an atom of sodium (Na) and an atom of chlorine (Cl). The sodium atom has a total of 11 electrons (including one electron in its outer shell). The chlorine has 17 electrons (including 7 electrons in its outer shell). From this, the atomic number, or number of protons, of sodium can be calculated as 11 because the number of protons equals the number of electrons in an atom. When sodium chloride (NaCl) is formed, one electron from sodium transfers to chlorine. Ions have charges. They are written with a plus (+) or minus (−) symbol. Ions in a compound are attracted to each other because they have *opposite charges*.

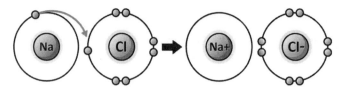

COVALENT BONDING

Covalent bonding is characterized by the sharing of one or more pairs of electrons between two atoms or between an atom and another **covalent bond**. This produces an attraction to repulsion stability that holds these molecules together.

Atoms have the tendency to share electrons with each other so that all outer electron shells are filled. The resultant bonds are always stronger than the **intermolecular hydrogen bond** and are similar in strength to ionic bonds.

Covalent bonding occurs most frequently between atoms with similar **electronegativities**. **Nonmetals** are more likely to form covalent bonds than metals since it is more difficult for nonmetals to liberate an electron. **Electron sharing** takes place when one species encounters another species with similar electronegativity. Covalent bonding of metals is important in both *process chemistry* and *industrial catalysis*.

ELECTRONEGATIVITY

Electronegativity is a measure of how capable an atom is of attracting a pair of bonding electrons. It refers to the fact that one atom exerts slightly more force in a bond than another, creating a **dipole**. If the electronegative difference between two atoms is small, the atoms will form a **polar covalent bond**. If the difference is large, the atoms will form an **ionic bond**. When there is no electronegativity, a **pure nonpolar covalent bond** is formed.

> **Review Video: Electronegativity**
> Visit mometrix.com/academy and enter code: 823348

COMPOUNDS

An **element** is the most basic type of matter. It has unique properties and cannot be broken down into other elements. The smallest unit of an element is the **atom**. A chemical combination of two or more types of elements is called a **compound**.

Compounds often have properties that are very different from those of their constituent elements. The smallest independent unit of an element or compound is known as a **molecule**. Most elements are found somewhere in nature in single-atom form, but a few elements only exist naturally in pairs. These are called **diatomic elements**, of which some of the most common are hydrogen, nitrogen, and oxygen.

Elements and compounds are represented by **chemical symbols**, one or two letters, most often the first in the element name. More than one atom of the same element in a compound is represented with a subscript number designating how many atoms of that element are present. Water, for instance, contains two hydrogens and one oxygen. Thus, the chemical formula is H_2O. Methane contains one carbon and four hydrogens, so its formula is CH_4.

NOMENCLATURE FOR ORGANIC COMPOUNDS

Alkanes, alkenes, and alkynes are organic compounds called **hydrocarbons**, which consist only of carbon and hydrogen.

Alkanes have only single bonds between their carbon atoms. Alkanes are saturated hydrocarbons because they contain as many hydrogen atoms as possible due to their single bonds. Alkanes include methane (CH_4), ethane (C_2H_6), propane (C_3H_8), and butane (C_4H_{10}).

Alkenes have at least one double bond between two of their carbon atoms. Alkenes are unsaturated hydrocarbons. Alkenes include ethene or ethylene (C_2H_4), propene (C_3H_6), 1-butene (C_4H_8), and 1-pentene (C_5H_{10}).

Alkynes have at least one triple bond between two of their carbon atoms. Like alkenes, alkynes are unsaturated hydrocarbons. Alkynes include ethyne or acetylene (C_2H_2), 1-propyne (C_3H_4), 1-butyne (C_4H_6), and 1-pentyne (C_5H_8).

The **prefixes** of hydrocarbons are based on the number of carbon atoms. These prefixes are given by the table below. For example, an alkane with one carbon atom is named methane. An alkane with two carbon atoms would be named ethane. An alkene with two carbon atoms is named ethene. An alkene with five carbon atoms is named pentene. An alkyne with four carbon atoms is named butyne. An alkyne with eight carbon atoms is named octyne.

#	Prefix	#	Prefix
1	meth-	6	hexa-
2	eth-	7	hepta-
3	prop-	8	octa-
4	but-	9	nona-
5	penta-	10	deca-

Review Video: Basics for Alkenes
Visit mometrix.com/academy and enter code: 916284

Review Video: Basics of Alkynes
Visit mometrix.com/academy and enter code: 963837

Review Video: Rules for Naming Alkanes, Alkenes, and Alkynes
Visit mometrix.com/academy and enter code: 441567

methanol

An **alcohol** is a substituted hydrocarbon compound with a hydroxyl group (–OH) bound to a saturated carbon. To name an alcohol, drop the -e from the name of the hydrocarbon and add -ol. For example, when the functional group for an alcohol replaces one hydrogen in methane, then the name is changed to methanol.

Review Video: Naming of Alcohols
Visit mometrix.com/academy and enter code: 737321

An **ether** is a substituted hydrocarbon compound containing an oxygen molecule linking two hydrocarbon groups. Ethers are named for the two hydrocarbons that flank the functional group. The root of the shorter of the two chains is named first. This is followed by *-oxy-*, which is then followed by the name of the longer chain. For example, $CH_3OCH_2CH_3$ is named methoxyethane (also commonly expressed C_3H_8O or ethyl methyl ether).

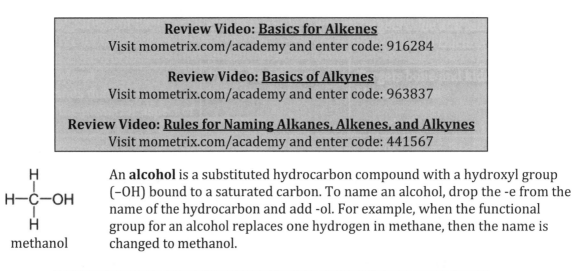

methoxyethane

An **aldehyde** is a substituted hydrocarbon compound with an oxygen molecule that is double-bound to the CH group at an end of a hydrocarbon chain. To name an aldehyde, drop the -e from the name of the hydrocarbon and add -al. For example, when the functional group for an aldehyde is substituted into methane, the aldehyde name would be methanal, also known as formaldehyde.

methanal

A **ketone** is a substituted hydrocarbon compound containing an oxygen that is double-bound to a carbon atom somewhere within the hydrocarbon chain. The difference between a ketone and an aldehyde is that in an aldehyde the =O will be at one or both ends of the hydrocarbon molecule, whereas in a ketone the =O will be somewhere other than the end of the hydrocarbon molecule. To name a ketone, drop -*e* from the name of the hydrocarbon and add -*one*. For example, when the functional group for a ketone is inserted into propane, the name is changed to propanone, which is more commonly known as acetone.

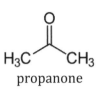
propanone

methanoic acid

Carboxylic acids are organic compounds that contain a carboxyl functional group that consists of a carbon atom double-bonded to an oxygen and single-bonded to a hydroxyl (–OH). For example, the simplest carboxylic acid is methanoic acid, also known as formic acid, HCO_2H. Fatty acids and amino acids are also examples of carboxylic acids.

Benzene is an organic compound that is an aromatic hydrocarbon. Benzene has a molecular formula of C_6H_6, where the six carbon atoms are arranged in a "ring" shaped like a hexagon. Each carbon is single-bonded to two other carbons and single-bonded to one hydrogen. The remaining valence electrons from the six carbon atoms are delocalized electrons that are shared among all the carbons in the molecule and are typically represented with alternating double bonds.

Derivatives of benzene include phenol, which is used in producing carbonates; toluene, which is used as a solvent and an octane booster in gasoline; and aniline, which is used in the production of polyurethane.

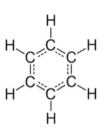
methylamine

An **amine** is a compound with a nitrogen atom that contains a lone pair of electrons and is bound to one or more hydrocarbon groups. Amines may be named in more than one way. The two most common ways are either with the prefix *amino*- or the suffix -*amine*. For example, the simplest amine is methylamine (CH_3NH_2).

PERIODIC TABLE

The periodic table is a tabular arrangement of the elements and is organized according to periodic law. The properties of the elements depend on their **atomic structure** and vary with **atomic number**. It shows periodic trends of physical and chemical properties and identifies families of elements with similar properties. In the periodic table, the elements are arranged by atomic number in horizontal rows called **periods** and vertical columns called **groups** or **families**. They are further categorized as metals, metalloids, or nonmetals. The majority of known elements are metals; there are seventeen nonmetals and eight metalloids. **Metals** are situated at the left end of the periodic table, **nonmetals** to the right and **metalloids** between the two.

A typical periodic table shows the elements' symbols and atomic number, the number of protons in the atomic nucleus. Some more detailed tables also list **atomic mass, electronegativity**, and other data. The position of an element in the table reveals its group, its block, and whether it is a representative, transition, or inner transition element. Its position also shows the element as a metal, nonmetal, or metalloid.

For the representative elements, the last digit of the **group number** reveals the number of outer-level electrons. Roman numerals for the A groups also reveal the number of outer level electrons within the group. The position of the element in the table reveals its **electronic configuration** and how it differs in atomic size from neighbors in its period or group. In this example, boron has an atomic number of 5 and an atomic weight of 10.811. It is found in group 13, in which all atoms of the group have 3 valence electrons; the group's Roman numeral representation is IIIA.

Review Video: Periodic Table
Visit mometrix.com/academy and enter code: 154828

IMPORTANT FEATURES AND STRUCTURE

The most important feature of the table is its arrangement according to **periodicity**, or the predictable trends observable in atoms. The arrangement enables classification, organization, and prediction of important elemental properties.

The table is organized in horizontal rows called **Periods**, and vertical columns called **Groups** or **Families**. Groups of elements share predictable characteristics, the most important of which is that their outer energy levels have the same configuration of electrons. For example, the highest group is group 18, the noble gases. Each element in this group has a full complement of electrons in its outer level, making the reactivity low. Elements in periods also share some common properties, but most classifications rely more heavily on groups.

CHEMICAL REACTIVITY

Reactivity refers to the tendency of a substance to engage in **chemical reactions**. If that tendency is high, the substance is said to be highly reactive, or to have **high reactivity**. Because the basis of a chemical reaction is the transfer of electrons, reactivity depends upon the presence of uncommitted electrons which are available for transfer. **Periodicity** allows us to predict an element's reactivity based on its position on the periodic table. High numbered groups on the right side of the table have a fuller complement of electrons in their outer levels, making them less likely to react. Noble gases, on the far right of the table, each have eight electrons in the outer level, with the exception of He, which has two. Because atoms tend to lose or gain electrons to reach an ideal of eight in the outer level, these elements have very low reactivity.

GROUPS AND PERIODS IN TERMS OF REACTIVITY

Reading left to right within a period, each element contains one more electron than the one preceding it. (Note that H and He are in the same period, though nothing is between them and they are in different groups.) As electrons are added, their attraction to the nucleus increases, meaning that as we read to the right in a period, each atom's electrons are more densely compacted, more strongly bound to the nucleus, and less likely to be pulled away in reactions. As we read down a group, each successive atom's outer electrons are less tightly bound to the nucleus, thus increasing their reactivity, because the principal energy levels are increasingly full as we move downward within the group. **Principal energy levels** shield the outer energy levels from nuclear attraction, allowing the valence electrons to react. For this reason, noble gases farther down the group can react under certain circumstances.

METALS, NONMETALS, AND METALLOIDS IN THE PERIODIC TABLE

The metals are located on the left side and center of the periodic table, and the nonmetals are located on the right side of the periodic table. The metalloids or semimetals form a zigzag line between the metals and nonmetals. Metals include the **alkali metals** such as lithium, sodium, and potassium and the **alkaline earth metals** such as beryllium, magnesium, and calcium. Metals also include the **transition metals** such as iron, copper, and nickel and the **inner transition metals** such as thorium, uranium, and plutonium. **Nonmetals** include the **chalcogens** such as oxygen and sulfur, the **halogens** such as fluorine and chlorine, and the **noble gases** such as helium and argon. Carbon, nitrogen, and phosphorus are also nonmetals. **Metalloids** or **semimetals** include boron, silicon, germanium, antimony, and polonium.

STATES OF MATTER

Matter refers to substances that *have mass and occupy space* (or volume). The traditional definition of matter describes it as having three states: solid, liquid, and gas. These different states are caused by differences in the distances and angles between molecules or atoms, which result in differences in the energy that binds them. **Solid** structures are rigid or nearly rigid and have strong bonds. Molecules or atoms of **liquids** move around and have weak bonds, although they are not weak enough to readily break. Molecules or atoms of **gases** move almost independently of each other, are typically far apart, and do not form bonds. The current definition of matter describes it as having four states. The fourth is **plasma**, which is an ionized gas that has some electrons that are described as free because they are not bound to an atom or molecule. However, the TEAS will only be concerned with solids, liquids, and gases.

The table below outlines the characteristic properties of the three states of matter:

State of matter	Volume/shape	Density	Compressibility	Molecular motion
Gas	Assumes volume and shape of its container	Low	High	Very free motion
Liquid	Volume remains constant but it assumes shape of its container	High	Virtually none	Move past each other freely
Solid	Definite volume and shape	High	Virtually none	Vibrate around fixed positions

The three states of matter can be traversed by the addition or removal of **heat**. For example, when a solid is heated to its melting point, it can begin to form a liquid. However, in order to transition

219

from solid to liquid, additional heat must be added at the melting point to overcome the **latent heat of fusion**. Upon further heating to its boiling point, the liquid can begin to form a gas, but again, additional heat must be added at the boiling point to overcome the **latent heat of vaporization**.

In the solid state, water is less dense than in the liquid state. This can be observed quite simply by noting that an ice cube floats at the surface of a glass of water. Were this not the case, ice would not form on the surface of lakes and rivers in those regions of the world where the climate produces temperatures below the freezing point. If water behaved as other substances do, lakes and rivers would freeze from the bottom up, which would be detrimental to many forms of aquatic life.

The lower density of ice occurs because of a combination of the unique structure of the water molecule and hydrogen bonding. In the case of ice, each oxygen atom is bound to four hydrogen atoms, two covalently and two by hydrogen bonds. This forms a roughly ordered **tetrahedral** structure that prevents the molecules from getting close to each other. As such, there are empty spaces in the structure that account for the low density of ice.

> **Review Video: <u>States of Matter</u>**
> Visit mometrix.com/academy and enter code: 742449

CHANGES IN STATES OF MATTER

A substance that is undergoing a change from a solid to a liquid is said to be **melting**. If this change occurs in the opposite direction, from liquid to solid, this change is called **freezing**. A liquid which is being converted to a gas is undergoing **vaporization**. The reverse of this process is known as **condensation**. Direct transitions from gas to solid and solid to gas are much less common in everyday life, but they can occur given the proper conditions. Solid to gas conversion is known as **sublimation**, while the reverse is called **deposition**.

Evaporation: Evaporation is the change of state in a substance from a liquid to a gaseous form at a temperature below its boiling point (the temperature at which all of the molecules in a liquid are changed to gas through vaporization). Some of the molecules at the surface of a liquid always maintain enough **heat energy** to escape the cohesive forces exerted on them by neighboring molecules. At higher temperatures, the molecules in a substance move more rapidly, increasing their number with enough energy to break out of the liquid form. The rate of evaporation is higher when more of the surface area of a liquid is exposed (as in a large water body, such as an ocean). The amount of moisture already in the air also affects the rate of evaporation—if there is a significant amount of water vapor in the air around a liquid, some evaporated molecules will return to the liquid. The speed of the evaporation process is also decreased by increased **atmospheric pressure**.

Condensation: Condensation is the phase change in a substance from a gaseous to liquid form; it is the opposite of evaporation or vaporization. When temperatures decrease in a gas, such as water vapor, the material's component molecules move more slowly. The decreased motion of the molecules enables **intermolecular cohesive forces** to pull the molecules closer together and, in water, establish hydrogen bonds. Condensation can also be caused by an increase in the pressure exerted on a gas, which results in a decrease in the substance's volume (it reduces the distance between particles). In the **hydrologic cycle**, this process is initiated when warm air containing water vapor rises and then cools. This occurs due to convection in the air, meteorological fronts, or lifting over high land formations.

CHARACTERISTIC PROPERTIES OF SUBSTANCES

INTENSIVE AND EXTENSIVE PROPERTIES

Physical properties are categorized as either intensive or extensive. **Intensive properties** *do not* depend on the amount of matter or quantity of the sample. This means that intensive properties will not change if the sample size is increased or decreased. Intensive properties include color, hardness, melting point, boiling point, density, ductility, malleability, specific heat, temperature, concentration, and magnetization.

Extensive properties *do* depend on the amount of matter or quantity of the sample. Therefore, extensive properties do change if the sample size is increased or decreased. If the sample size is increased, the property increases. If the sample size is decreased, the property decreases. Extensive properties include volume, mass, weight, energy, entropy, number of moles, and electrical charge.

PHYSICAL PROPERTIES OF MATTER

Physical properties are any property of matter that can be **observed** or **measured**. These include properties such as color, elasticity, mass, volume, and temperature. **Mass** is a measure of the amount of substance in an object. **Weight** is a measure of the gravitational pull of Earth on an object. **Volume** is a measure of the amount of space occupied. There are many formulas to determine volume. For example, the volume of a cube is the length of one side cubed (s^3) and the volume of a rectangular prism is length times width times height ($l \times w \times h$). The volume of an irregular shape can be determined by how much water it displaces. **Density** is a measure of the amount of mass per unit volume. The formula to find density is mass divided by volume ($D = m/V$). It is expressed in terms of mass per cubic unit, such as grams per cubic centimeter (g/cm^3). **Specific gravity** is a measure of the ratio of a substance's density compared to the density of water.

DENSITY

It is important to note the difference between an *object's density* and a *material's density*. Water has a density of one gram per cubic centimeter, while steel has a density approximately eight times that. Despite having a much higher material density, an object made of steel may still float. A hollow steel sphere, for instance, will float easily because the density of the object includes the air contained within the sphere.

SPECIFIC HEAT CAPACITY

Specific heat capacity, also known as **specific heat**, is the *heat capacity per unit mass*. Each element or compound has its own specific heat. For example, it takes different amounts of heat energy to raise the temperature of the same amounts of magnesium and lead by one degree. The equation for relating heat energy to specific heat capacity is $Q = mc\Delta T$, where m represents the mass of the object, and c represents its specific heat capacity.

> **Review Video: Specific Heat Capacity**
> Visit mometrix.com/academy and enter code: 736791

CONDUCTION

Heat always flows from a region of higher temperature to a region of lower temperature. If two regions are at the same temperature, there is a **thermal equilibrium** between them and there will be **no net heat transfer** between them. **Conduction** is a form of heat transfer that requires contact. Since heat is a measure of kinetic energy, most commonly vibration, at the atomic level, it may be transferred from one location to another or one object to another by contact.

CHEMICAL PROPERTIES OF MATTER

If a chemical change must be carried out in order to observe and measure a property, then the property is a **chemical property**. For example, when hydrogen gas is burned in oxygen, it forms water. This is a chemical property of hydrogen because after burning, a different chemical substance, water, is all that remains. The hydrogen cannot be recovered from the water by means of a physical change such as freezing or boiling.

> **Review Video: <u>Chemical and Physical Properties of Matter</u>**
> Visit mometrix.com/academy and enter code: 717349

OVERVIEW OF CHEMICAL REACTIONS

Chemical reactions measured in human time can take place quickly or slowly. They can take a fraction of a second or billions of years. The **rates** of chemical reactions are determined by how frequently reacting atoms and molecules interact. Rates are also influenced by the temperature and various properties (such as shape) of the reacting materials. **Catalysts** accelerate chemical reactions, while **inhibitors** decrease reaction rates. Some types of reactions release energy in the form of heat and light. Some types of reactions involve the transfer of either electrons or hydrogen ions between reacting ions, molecules, or atoms. In other reactions, chemical bonds are broken down by heat or light to form **reactive radicals** with electrons that will readily form new bonds. Processes such as the formation of ozone and greenhouse gases in the atmosphere and the burning and processing of fossil fuels are controlled by radical reactions.

> **Review Video: <u>Chemical Reactions</u>**
> Visit mometrix.com/academy and enter code: 579876

READING AND BALANCING CHEMICAL EQUATIONS

Chemical equations describe chemical reactions. The **reactants** are on the left side before the arrow and the **products** are on the right side after the arrow. The arrow indicates the **reaction** or change. The **coefficient**, or stoichiometric coefficient, is the number before the element and indicates the ratio of reactants to products in terms of moles. The equation for the formation of water from hydrogen and oxygen, for example, is $2H_2(g) + O_2(g) \rightarrow 2H_2O(l)$. The 2 preceding hydrogen and water is the coefficient, which means there are 2 moles of hydrogen and 2 of water. There is 1 mole of oxygen, which does not have to be indicated with the number 1. In parentheses, g stands for gas, l stands for liquid, s stands for solid, and aq stands for aqueous solution (a substance dissolved in water). **Charges** are shown in superscript for individual ions, but not for ionic compounds. **Polyatomic ions** are separated by parentheses so the ion will not be confused with the number of ions.

An **unbalanced equation** is one that does not follow the **law of conservation of mass**, which states that matter can only be changed, not created or destroyed. If an equation is unbalanced, the numbers of atoms indicated by the stoichiometric coefficients on each side of the arrow will not be equal. Start by writing the formulas for each species in the reaction. Count the atoms on each side and determine if the number is equal. Coefficients must be whole numbers. Fractional amounts, such as half a molecule, are not possible. Equations can be balanced by adjusting the coefficients of each part of the equation to the smallest possible whole number coefficient. $H_2 + O_2 \rightarrow H_2O$ is an example of an unbalanced equation. The balanced equation is $2H_2 + O_2 \rightarrow 2H_2O$, which indicates that it takes two moles of hydrogen and one of oxygen to produce two moles of water.

> **Review Video: <u>How to Balance a Chemical Equation</u>**
> Visit mometrix.com/academy and enter code: 341228

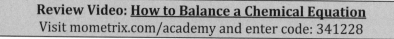

LAW OF CONSERVATION OF MASS

The Law of Conservation of Mass in a chemical reaction is commonly stated as follows:

In a chemical reaction, matter is neither created nor destroyed.

What this means is that there will always be the same **total mass** of material after a reaction as before. This allows for predicting how molecules will combine with balanced equations in which the number of each type of atom is the same on either side of the equation. For example, two hydrogen molecules combine with one oxygen molecule to form water. This is a balanced chemical equation because the number of each type of atom is the same on both sides of the arrow. It has to balance because the reaction obeys the Law of Conservation of Mass.

BASIC MECHANISMS OF REACTIONS

Chemical reactions normally occur when electrons are transferred from one atom or molecule to another. Reactions and reactivity depend on the **octet rule**, which describes the tendency of atoms to gain or lose electrons until their outer energy levels contain eight. The changes in a reaction may be in **composition** or **configuration** of a compound or substance and result in one or more products being generated which were not present in isolation before the reaction occurred. For instance, when oxygen reacts with methane (CH_4), water and carbon dioxide are the products; one set of substances ($CH_4 + O$) was transformed into a new set of substances ($CO_2 + H_2O$).

Reactions depend on the presence of a **reactant**, or substance undergoing change, a **reagent**, or partner in the reaction less transformed than the reactant (such as a catalyst), and **products**, or the final result of the reaction. **Reaction conditions**, or environmental factors, are also important components in reactions. These include conditions such as temperature, pressure, concentration, whether the reaction occurs in solution, the type of solution, and the presence or absence of catalysts. Chemical reactions are usually written in the following format:

$$Reactants \rightarrow Products$$

FIVE BASIC CHEMICAL REACTIONS
COMBINATION REACTIONS

Combination, or synthesis, reactions: In a combination reaction, two or more reactants combine to make one product. This can be seen in the equation $A + B \rightarrow AB$. These reactions are also called **synthesis** or **addition reactions**. An example is burning hydrogen in air to produce water. The equation is $2H_2(g) + O_2(g) \rightarrow 2H_2O(l)$. Another example is when water and sulfur trioxide react to form sulfuric acid. The equation is $H_2O + SO_3 \rightarrow H_2SO_4$.

DECOMPOSITION REACTIONS

Decomposition (or desynthesis, decombination, or deconstruction) reactions; in a decomposition reaction, a reactant is broken down into two or more products. This can be seen in the equation $AB \rightarrow A + B$. When a compound or substance separates into these simpler substances, the **byproducts** are often substances that are different from the original. Decomposition can be viewed as the *opposite* of combination reactions. These reactions are also called analysis reactions. Most decomposition reactions are **endothermic**. Heat needs to be added for the chemical reaction to occur. **Thermal decomposition** is caused by heat. **Electrolytic decomposition** is due to electricity. An example of this type of reaction is the decomposition of water into hydrogen and oxygen gas. The equation is $2H_2O \rightarrow 2H_2 + O_2$. Separation processes can be **mechanical** or **chemical**, and usually involve reorganizing a mixture of substances without changing their chemical nature. The separated products may differ from the original mixture in terms of chemical or physical properties. Types of separation processes include **filtration**, **crystallization**,

223

distillation, and **chromatography**. Basically, decomposition *breaks down* one compound into two or more compounds or substances that are different from the original; separation *sorts* the substances from the original mixture into like substances.

SINGLE REPLACEMENT REACTIONS

Single substitution, **displacement**, or **replacement reactions** occur when one reactant is displaced by another to form the final product (A + BC → B + AC). Single substitution reactions can be **cationic** or **anionic**. When a piece of copper (Cu) is placed into a solution of silver nitrate ($AgNO_3$), the solution turns blue. The copper appears to be replaced with a silvery-white material. The equation is $2AgNO_3 + Cu \rightarrow Cu(NO_3)_2 + 2Ag$. When this reaction takes place, the copper dissolves and the silver in the silver nitrate solution precipitates (becomes a solid), thus resulting in copper nitrate and silver. Copper and silver have switched places in the nitrate.

DOUBLE REPLACEMENT REACTIONS

Double displacement, **double replacement**, **substitution**, **metathesis**, or **ion exchange reactions** occur when ions or bonds are exchanged by two compounds to form different compounds (AC + BD → AD + BC). An example of this is that silver nitrate and sodium chloride form two different products (silver chloride and sodium nitrate) when they react. The formula for this reaction is $AgNO_3 + NaCl \rightarrow AgCl + NaNO_3$.

Double replacement reactions are **metathesis reactions**. In a double replacement reaction, the chemical reactants exchange ions but the oxidation state stays the same. One of the indicators of this is the formation of a **solid precipitate**. In acid/base reactions, an **acid** is a compound that can donate a proton, while a **base** is a compound that can accept a proton. In these types of reactions, the acid and base react to form a salt and water. When the proton is donated, the base becomes **water** and the remaining ions form a **salt**. One method of determining whether a reaction is an oxidation/reduction reaction or a metathesis reaction is that the oxidation number of atoms does not change during a metathesis reaction.

COMBUSTION REACTIONS

Combustion, or burning, is a sequence of chemical reactions involving **fuel** and an **oxidant** that produces heat and sometimes light. There are many types of combustion, such as rapid, slow, complete, turbulent, microgravity, and incomplete. Fuels and oxidants determine the **compounds** formed by a combustion reaction. For example, when rocket fuel consisting of hydrogen and oxygen combusts, it results in the formation of water vapor. When air and wood burn, resulting compounds include nitrogen, unburned carbon, and carbon compounds. Combustion is an **exothermic** process, meaning it releases energy. Exothermic energy is commonly released as heat, but can take other forms, such as light, electricity, or sound.

> **Review Video: Combustion**
> Visit mometrix.com/academy and enter code: 592219

RATE OF REACTION
ACTIVATION ENERGY

Activation energy is the minimum amount of energy that must be possessed by reactant atoms or molecules in order to react. This is due to the fact that it takes a certain amount of energy to break bonds or form bonds between atoms. Reactants lacking the activation energy required will not be able to perform the necessary breaking or forming of bonds regardless of how often they collide. Catalysts lower the activation energy of a reaction and therefore increase the rate of reaction.

REACTION MECHANISM

Often, when studying specific reactions, only the net reactions are given. Realistically, reactions take place in a series of steps or elementary reactions as shown in the reaction mechanism. **Reaction mechanisms** show how a reaction proceeds in a **series of steps**. Some steps are slow, and some are fast. Each step has its own reaction mechanism. The slowest step in the reaction mechanism coincides with the step with the greatest activation energy. This step is known as the rate-determining step.

CATALYST

A **catalyst** is a chemical that **accelerates** or speeds up a chemical reaction without being consumed or used up in the reaction. Although catalysts are not consumed or permanently changed during the process of the reaction, catalysts do participate in the elementary reaction of the reaction mechanisms. Catalysts cannot make an impossible reaction take place, but catalysts do greatly increase the rate of a reaction. Catalysts lower the **activation energy**. Because the activation energy is the minimum energy required for molecules to react, lowering the activation energy makes it possible for more of the reactant molecules to react.

> **Review Video: Catalysts**
> Visit mometrix.com/academy and enter code: 288189

FACTORS THAT AFFECT REACTION RATE

Factors that affect reaction rate include concentration, surface area, and temperature. Increasing the **concentration** of the reactants increases the number of collisions between those reactants and therefore increases the reaction rate. Increasing the **surface area of contact** between the reactants also increases the number of collisions and therefore increases the reaction rate. Finally, increasing the **temperature** of the reactants increases the number of collisions but more significantly also increases the kinetic energy of the reactants, which in turn increases the fraction of molecules meeting the activation energy requirement. With more molecules at the activation energy, more of the reactants are capable of completing the reaction.

CHEMICAL EQUILIBRIUM

A **chemical equilibrium** occurs when a reaction is reversible and the rate of the forward reaction equals the rate of the reverse reaction. The forward and reverse reactions are continually occurring, but the individual concentration of the reaction and the products do not change. The concentration of the reactants and products are not necessarily equal to each other. For this to occur, the reaction must take place in a closed system in which none of the reactants or products can escape and in which no heat is added or lost.

LE CHÂTELIER'S PRINCIPLE

Le Châtelier's principle states that when a stressor is applied to a system in equilibrium, the system will respond in such a way to at least partially offset the stressor. Stressors include increasing or decreasing the temperature, increasing or decreasing the concentration of a reactant or product, and increasing or decreasing the pressure. Systems are described as "shifting left" or "shifting right" when a stressor is applied. For example, if the temperature is increased in an equilibrium in which the forward reaction is endothermic, the system will "shift right" in order to "use up" the heat that was applied. Increasing or decreasing the pressure of an equilibrium will only cause the equilibrium to "shift" if the number of moles of gases of the reactants differs from the number of moles of gases of the products. If there are no gases in the equilibrium or if the number of moles of

225

gases of the reactants and products is equal, the change in pressure will have no effect on the equilibrium.

> **Review Video: Le Châtelier's Principle**
> Visit mometrix.com/academy and enter code: 360187

SOLUTIONS

WATER AS A SOLVENT

The important properties of water (H_2O) are *high polarity, hydrogen bonding, cohesiveness, adhesiveness, high specific heat, high latent heat, and high heat of vaporization*. It is **essential to life** as we know it, as water is one of the main constituents of many living things. Water is a liquid at room temperature. The high specific heat of water means it resists the breaking of its hydrogen bonds and resists heat and motion, which is why it has a relatively high boiling point and high vaporization point. It also resists temperature change. In its solid state, water floats. (Most substances are heavier in their solid forms.) Water is **cohesive**, which means it is attracted to itself. It is also **adhesive**, which means it readily attracts other molecules. If water tends to adhere to another substance, the substance is said to be **hydrophilic**. Because of its cohesive and adhesive properties, water makes a good solvent. Substances, particularly those with polar ions and molecules, readily dissolve in water.

> **Review Video: Properties of Water**
> Visit mometrix.com/academy and enter code: 279526

HYDROGEN BONDS

Hydrogen bonds are weaker than covalent and ionic bonds and refer to the type of attraction in an **electronegative atom** such as oxygen, fluorine, or nitrogen. Hydrogen bonds can form within a single molecule or between molecules. A water molecule is **polar**, meaning it is partially positively charged on one end (the hydrogen end) and partially negatively charged on the other (the oxygen end). This is because the hydrogen atoms are arranged around the oxygen atom in a close tetrahedron. Hydrogen is **oxidized** (its number of electrons is reduced) when it bonds with oxygen to form water. Hydrogen bonds tend not only to be weak, but also short-lived. They also tend to be numerous. Hydrogen bonds give water many of its important properties, including its high specific heat and high heat of vaporization, its solvent qualities, its adhesiveness and cohesiveness, its hydrophobic qualities, and its ability to float in its solid form. Hydrogen bonds are also an important component of *proteins, nucleic acids, and DNA*.

TERMINOLOGY FOR SOLUTIONS AND SOLUBILITY

The terms **dilute** and **concentrated** have opposite meanings. In a solution, the **solute** is dissolved in the **solvent**. The more solute that is dissolved, the more concentrated is the solution. The less solute that is dissolved, the less concentrated and the more dilute is the solution. The terms are often associated with the preparation of a stock solution for a laboratory experiment. Stock solutions are typically ordered in a concentrated solution. To prepare for use in a chemistry lab, the stock solutions are diluted to the appropriate molarity by adding a specific amount of solvent such as water to a specific amount of stock solution.

The terms *saturated, unsaturated,* and *supersaturated* are associated with solutions. In a **solution**, a **solute** is added to a **solvent**. In a saturated solution, the solute is added to the solvent until no more solute is able to dissolve. The undissolved solute will settle down to the bottom of the beaker. A solution is considered unsaturated as long as more solute is able to go into solution under ordinary conditions. The solubility of solids in liquids typically increases as temperature increases. If the temperature of a solution is increased as the solute is being added, more solute than is normally possible may go into solution, forming a supersaturated solution.

A **mixture** is made of two or more substances that are combined in various proportions. The exact proportion of the constituents is the defining characteristic of any mixture. There are two types of mixtures: homogeneous and heterogeneous. **Homogeneous** means that the mixture's composition and properties are uniform throughout. Conversely, **heterogeneous** means that the mixture's composition and properties are not uniform throughout.

A **solution** is a homogeneous mixture of substances that cannot be separated by filtration or centrifugation. Solutions are made by dissolving one or more solutes into a solvent. For example, in an aqueous glucose solution, glucose is the solute and water is the solvent. If there is more than one liquid present in the solution, then the most prevalent liquid is considered the solvent. The exact mechanism of dissolving varies depending on the mixture, but the result is always individual solute ions or molecules surrounded by solvent molecules. The proportion of solute to solvent for a particular solution is its **concentration**.

A **colloid** is a heterogeneous mixture in which small particles (<1 micrometer) are suspended, but not dissolved, in a liquid. As such, they can be separated by centrifugation. A commonplace example of a colloid is milk.

> **Review Video: Solutions**
> Visit mometrix.com/academy and enter code: 995937

CONCENTRATION OF SOLUTIONS
MOLE FRACTION, PARTS PER MILLION, PARTS PER BILLION, AND PERCENT BY MASS OR VOLUME

Concentrations can be measured in mole fractions, parts per million, parts per billion, and percent by mass or volume. **Mole fraction** (χ) is calculated by dividing the number of moles of one component by the total number of moles of all of the components of the solution. **Parts per million** (ppm) is calculated by dividing the mass of the solute in grams by the mass of the solvent and solute in grams and then multiplying the quotient by 1,000,000 ppm. **Parts per billion** (ppb) is calculated similarly, except the quotient is multiplied by 1,000,000,000 ppb. **Percent concentration** can be calculated by mass or by volume by dividing the mass or volume of the solute by the mass or volume of the solution. This quotient is a decimal that can be converted to a percent by multiplying by 100.

MOLARITY AND MOLALITY OF A SOLUTION

Molarity and molality are measures of the concentration of a solution. **Molarity** (M) is the amount of solute in moles per the amount of solution in liters. A 1.0 M solution consists of 1.0 mol of solute for each 1.0 L of solution. **Molality** (m) is the amount of solute in moles per the amount of solvent in kilograms. A 1.0 m solution consists of 1.0 mol of solute for each 1.0 kg of solvent. Often, when performing these calculations, the amount of solute is given in grams. To convert from grams of solute to moles of solute, multiply the grams of solute by the molar mass of the solute:

$$\text{Molarity (M)} = \frac{\text{moles of solute}}{\text{liters of solution}} = \frac{\text{mol}}{\text{L}}$$

$$\text{Molality (m)} = \frac{\text{moles of solute}}{\text{kilograms of solvent}} = \frac{\text{mol}}{\text{kg}}$$

> **Review Video: Mole Concept**
> Visit mometrix.com/academy and enter code: 593205

CALCULATING THE MOLARITY OF 100.0 G OF CaCl₂ IN 500.0 mL OF SOLUTION.

To use the formula molarity, you can make the necessary conversions from grams $CaCl_2$ to moles $CaCl_2$ and from 500.0 mL to liters using dimensional analysis. An alternate method of working this problem would be doing the conversions first and then substituting those values directly into the equation. Using the method of dimensional analysis and substituting the given information into the equation yields molarity $= \frac{100.0 \text{ grams } CaCl_2}{500.0 \text{ mL of solution}}$. Adding the necessary conversions using dimensional analysis yields:

$$\text{molarity} = \left(\frac{100.0 \text{ g } CaCl_2}{500.0 \text{ mL of solution}}\right)\left(\frac{\text{mol } CaCl_2}{110.98 \text{ g}}\right)\left(\frac{1,000 \text{ mL}}{L}\right) = 1.802 \text{ M}$$

PREPARING A DILUTE SOLUTION FROM A STOCK SOLUTION

In order to prepare a **dilute solution** from a **stock solution**, the molarity and the needed volume of the diluted solution as well as the molarity of the stock solution must be known. The volume of the stock solution to be diluted can be calculated using the formula $V_{stock}M_{stock} = V_{dilute}M_{dilute}$, where V_{stock} is the unknown variable, M_{stock} is the molarity of the stock solution, V_{dilute} is the needed volume of the dilute solution, and M_{dilute} is the needed molarity of the dilute solution. Solving this formula for V_{stock} yields $V_{stock} = \frac{V_{dilute}M_{dilute}}{M_{stock}}$. Then, dilute the calculated amount of stock solution (V_{stock}) to the total volume required of the diluted solution.

PASSIVE TRANSPORT MECHANISMS: DIFFUSION AND OSMOSIS

Transport mechanisms allow for the movement of substances through membranes. **Passive transport mechanisms** include simple and facilitated diffusion and osmosis. They do not require energy from the cell. **Diffusion** occurs when particles are transported from areas of higher concentration to areas of lower concentration. When equilibrium is reached, diffusion stops. Examples are gas exchange (carbon dioxide and oxygen) during photosynthesis and the transport of oxygen from air to blood and from blood to tissue. **Facilitated diffusion** occurs when specific molecules are transported by a specific carrier protein. **Carrier proteins** vary in terms of size, shape, and charge. Glucose and amino acids are examples of substances transported by carrier proteins.

Osmosis is the diffusion of water through a semi-permeable membrane from an area of lower solute concentration to one of higher solute concentration. Examples of osmosis include the absorption of water by plant roots and the alimentary canal. Plants lose and gain water through osmosis. A plant cell that swells because of water retention is said to be **turgid**.

> **Review Video: Passive Transport: Diffusion and Osmosis**
> Visit mometrix.com/academy and enter code: 642038

ACID AND BASE CHEMISTRY

pH

The **potential of hydrogen** (pH) is a measurement of the *concentration of hydrogen ions* in a substance in terms of the number of moles of H^+ per liter of solution. All substances fall between 0 and 14 on the pH scale. A lower pH indicates a higher H^+ concentration, while a higher pH indicates a lower H^+ concentration.

Pure water has a **neutral pH**, which is 7. Anything with a pH lower than pure water (<7) is considered **acidic**. Anything with a pH higher than pure water (>7) is a **base**. Drain cleaner, soap, baking soda, ammonia, egg whites, and sea water are common bases. Urine, stomach acid, citric acid, vinegar, hydrochloric acid, and battery acid are acids. A **pH indicator** is a substance that acts as a detector of hydrogen or hydronium ions. It is **halochromic**, meaning it changes color to indicate that hydrogen or hydronium ions have been detected.

> **Review Video: Overview of pH Levels**
> Visit mometrix.com/academy and enter code: 187395

ACIDS

Acids are a unique class of compounds characterized by consistent properties. The most significant property of an acid is not readily observable and is what gives acids their unique behaviors: the **ionization of H atoms**, or their tendency to dissociate from their parent molecules and take on an electrical charge. **Carboxylic acids** are also characterized by ionization, but of the O atoms. Some other properties of acids are easy to observe without any experimental apparatus. These properties include the following:

- They have a sour taste
- They change the color of litmus paper to red
- They produce gaseous H_2 in reaction with some metals
- They produce salt precipitates in reaction with bases

Other properties, while no more complex, are less easily observed. For instance, most inorganic acids are easily soluble in water and have high boiling points.

BASES

Basic chemicals are usually in aqueous solution and have the following traits: a bitter taste, a soapy or slippery texture, the capacity to restore the blue color of litmus paper which had previously been turned red by an acid, and the ability to produce salts in reaction with acids. The word **alkaline** is used to describe bases. In contrast to acids, which yield **hydrogen ions** (H^+) when dissolved in solution, bases yield **hydroxide ions** (OH^-). The Arrhenius, Bronsted-Lowry, and Lewis models used to describe acids can be inverted and used to describe bases.

Some **nonmetal oxides** (such as Na_2O) are classified as bases even though they do not contain hydroxides in their molecular form. However, these substances easily produce hydroxide ions when reacted with water, which is why they are classified as bases.

STRONG OR WEAK ACIDS AND BASES

The characteristic properties of acids and bases derive from the tendency of atoms to **ionize** by donating or accepting charged particles. The strength of an acid or base is a reflection of the degree to which its atoms ionize in solution. For example, if all of the atoms in an acid ionize, the acid is said to be **strong**. When only a few of the atoms ionize, the acid is **weak**. Acetic acid ($HC_2H_3O_2$) is a weak acid because only its O_2 atoms ionize in solution. Another way to think of the strength of an acid or base is to consider its **reactivity**. Highly reactive acids and bases are strong because they tend to form and break bonds quickly and most of their atoms ionize in the process.

> **Review Video: Strong and Weak Acids and Bases**
> Visit mometrix.com/academy and enter code: 268930

SALTS

Some properties of **salts** are that they are formed from acid base reactions, are ionic compounds consisting of metallic and nonmetallic ions, dissociate in water, and are comprised of tightly bonded ions. Some common salts are sodium chloride ($NaCl$), sodium bisulfate ($NaHSO_4$), potassium dichromate ($K_2Cr_2O_7$), and calcium chloride ($CaCl_2$). Calcium chloride is used as a drying agent, and may be used to absorb moisture when freezing mixtures. Potassium nitrate (KNO_3) is used to make fertilizer and in the manufacturing of explosives. Sodium nitrate ($NaNO_3$) is also used in the making of fertilizer. Baking soda [sodium bicarbonate ($NaHCO_3$)] is a salt, as are Epsom salts [magnesium sulfate ($MgSO_4$)]. Salt and water can react to form a base and an acid. This is called a **hydrolysis reaction**.

CHEMISTRY CHAPTER QUIZ

1. Which element has the highest atomic radius?
   a. Strontium
   b. Uranium
   c. Francium
   d. Radium

2. How do isotopes of the same element differ?
   a. They have different numbers of protons.
   b. They have different atomic numbers.
   c. They have different numbers of electrons.
   d. They have different numbers of neutrons.

3. Which of the following electron shells can hold a maximum of 32 electrons?
   a. K-shell
   b. L-shell
   c. M-shell
   d. N-shell

4. Which of the following is a substituted hydrocarbon compound containing an oxygen molecule linking two hydrocarbon groups?
   a. Aldehyde
   b. Alcohol
   c. Ether
   d. Ketone

5. Which of the following is a compound with a nitrogen atom that contains a lone pair of electrons and is bound to one or more hydrocarbon groups?
   a. Amine
   b. Benzene
   c. Carboxylic acid
   d. Thiol

6. Which of the following is NOT an extensive property?
   a. Volume
   b. Temperature
   c. Mass
   d. Electrical charge

7. Which of the following is NOT true about water?
   a. It is nonpolar.
   b. It is cohesive.
   c. It is adhesive.
   d. It has a high specific heat.

8. An object that changes color in the presence of hydrogen or hydronium ions is said to be which of the following?
   a. Piezochromic
   b. Bioluminescent
   c. Chemiluminescent
   d. Halochromic

9. Which of the following is a salt?
   a. $K_2Cr_2O_7$
   b. Li_2O
   c. HF
   d. Cl_2

10. $2AgNO_3 + Cu \rightarrow Cu(NO_3)_2 + 2Ag$ is which type of reaction?
   a. Decomposition
   b. Metathesis
   c. Combustion
   d. Single replacement

Answers for all of the chapter quiz questions can be found right before Practice Test #1.

Scientific Reasoning

METRIC SYSTEM

Using the metric system is generally accepted as the preferred method for taking measurements. Having a universal standard allows individuals to interpret measurements more easily, regardless of where they are located.

The basic units of measurement are: the **meter**, which measures length; the **liter**, which measures volume; and the **gram**, which measures mass. The metric system starts with a **base unit** and increases or decreases in units of 10. The prefix and the base unit combined are used to indicate an amount.

For example, deka is 10 times the base unit. A dekameter is 10 meters; a dekaliter is 10 liters; and a dekagram is 10 grams. The prefix hecto refers to 100 times the base amount; kilo is 1,000 times the base amount. The prefixes that indicate a fraction of the base unit are deci, which is 1/10 of the base unit; centi, which is 1/100 of the base unit; and milli, which is 1/1000 of the base unit.

SI UNITS OF MEASUREMENT

SI uses the **second** (s) to measure time. Fractions of seconds are usually measured in metric terms using prefixes such as millisecond (1/1,000 of a second) or nanosecond (1/1,000,000,000 of a second). Increments of time larger than a second are measured in minutes and hours, which are multiples of 60 and 24. An example of this is a swimmer's time in the 800-meter freestyle being described as 7:32.67, meaning 7 minutes, 32 seconds, and 67 one-hundredths of a second. One second is equal to 1/60 of a minute, 1/3,600 of an hour, and 1/86,400 of a day.

Other SI base units are the **ampere** (A) (used to measure electric current), the **kelvin** (K) (used to measure thermodynamic temperature), the **candela** (cd) (used to measure luminous intensity), and the **mole** (mol) (used to measure the amount of a substance at a molecular level). **Meter** (m) is used to measure length and **kilogram** (kg) is used to measure mass.

METRIC PREFIXES FOR MULTIPLES AND SUBDIVISIONS

The prefixes for multiples are as follows:

- deka (da), 10^1 (deka is the American spelling, but deca is also used)
- hecto (h), 10^2
- kilo (k), 10^3
- mega (M), 10^6
- giga (G), 10^9
- tera (T), 10^{12}

The prefixes for subdivisions are as follows:

- deci (d), 10^{-1}
- centi (c), 10^{-2}
- milli (m), 10^{-3}
- micro (μ), 10^{-6}
- nano (n), 10^{-9}
- pico (p), 10^{-12}

The rule of thumb is that prefixes greater than 10^3 are capitalized when abbreviating. Abbreviations do not need a period after them. A decimeter (dm) is a tenth of a meter, a deciliter (dL) is a tenth of a liter, and a decigram (dg) is a tenth of a gram. Pluralization is understood. For example, when referring to 5 mL of water, no "s" needs to be added to the abbreviation.

LAB GLASSWARE

GRADUATED CYLINDERS AND BURETTES

Graduated cylinders are used for an intermediate amount of precision. More precise than beakers and Erlenmeyer flasks but not quite as precise as volumetric flasks or pipettes, they are made of either **polypropylene** (which is shatter-resistant and resistant to chemicals but cannot be heated) or **polymethylpentene** (which is known for its clarity). They are lighter to ship and less fragile than glass.

To read a graduated cylinder, it should be placed on a flat surface and read at eye level. The surface of a liquid in a graduated cylinder forms a lens-shaped curve. The measurement should be taken from the bottom of the curve. A ring may be placed at the top of tall, narrow cylinders to help avoid breakage if they are tipped over.

A **burette**, or buret, is a piece of lab glassware used to accurately dispense liquid. It looks similar to a narrow graduated cylinder but includes a stopcock and tip. It may be filled with a funnel or pipette.

FLASKS, BEAKERS, AND PIPETTES

Two types of flasks commonly used in lab settings are **Erlenmeyer flasks** and **volumetric flasks**, which can also be used to accurately measure liquids. Erlenmeyer flasks and **beakers** can be used for mixing, transporting, and reacting, but are not appropriate for accurate measurements.

A **pipette** can be used to accurately measure small amounts of liquid. Liquid is drawn into the pipette through the bulb and a finger is then quickly placed at the top of the container. The liquid measurement is read exactly at the **meniscus**. Liquid can be released from the pipette by lifting the finger. There are also plastic disposal pipettes. A **repipette** is a hand-operated pump that dispenses solutions.

BALANCES

Unlike laboratory glassware that measures volume, **balances** such as triple-beam balances, spring balances, and electronic balances measure **mass** and **force**. An **electronic balance** is the most accurate, followed by a **triple-beam balance** and then a **spring balance**.

One part of a triple-beam balance is the **plate**, which is where the item to be weighed is placed. There are also three **beams** that have hatch marks indicating amounts and hold the weights that rest in the notches. The front beam measures weights between 0 and 10 grams, the middle beam measures weights in 100-gram increments, and the far beam measures weights in 10-gram increments.

The sum of the weight of each beam is the total weight of the object. A triple-beam balance also includes a **set screw** to calibrate the equipment and a mark indicating the object and counterweights are in balance. Analytical balances are accurate to within 0.0001 g.

REVIEW A SCIENTIFIC EXPLANATION WITH LOGIC AND EVIDENCE

DATA COLLECTION

A valid experiment must be measurable. **Data tables** should be formed, and meticulous, detailed data should be collected for every trial. First, the researcher must determine exactly what data are needed and why those data are needed. The researcher should know in advance what will be done with those data at the end of the experimental research. The data should be *repeatable, reproducible, and accurate*. The researcher should be sure that the procedure for data collection will be reliable and consistent. The researcher should validate the measurement system by performing **practice tests** and making sure that all of the equipment is correctly **calibrated** and periodically retesting the procedure and equipment to ensure that all data being collected are still valid.

SCIENTIFIC PROCESS SKILLS

Perhaps the most important skill in science is that of **observation**. Scientists must be able to take accurate data from their experimental setup or from nature without allowing bias to alter the results. Another important skill is **hypothesizing**. Scientists must be able to combine their knowledge of theory and of other experimental results to logically determine what should occur in their own tests.

The **data-analysis process** requires the twin skills of ordering and categorizing. Gathered data must be arranged in such a way that it is readable and readily shows the key results. A skill that may be integrated with the previous two is comparing. Scientists should be able to **compare** their own results with other published results. They must also be able to **infer**, or draw logical conclusions, from their results. They must be able to **apply** their knowledge of theory and results to create logical experimental designs and determine cases of special behavior.

Lastly, scientists must be able to **communicate** their results and their conclusions. The greatest scientific progress is made when scientists are able to review and test one another's work and offer advice or suggestions.

SCIENTIFIC STATEMENTS

Hypotheses are educated guesses about what is likely to occur. They provide a starting point from which to begin design of the experiment. They may be based on results of previously observed experiments or knowledge of theory and follow logically forth from these.

Assumptions are statements that are taken to be fact without proof for the purpose of performing a given experiment. They may be entirely true, or they may be true only for a given set of conditions under which the experiment will be conducted. Assumptions are necessary to simplify experiments; indeed, many experiments would be impossible without them.

Scientific models are mathematical statements that describe a physical behavior. Models are only as good as our knowledge of the actual system. Often models will be discarded when new discoveries are made that show the model to be inaccurate. While a model can never perfectly represent an actual system, it is useful for simplifying a system to allow for better understanding of its behavior.

Scientific laws are statements of natural behavior that have stood the test of time and have been found to produce accurate and repeatable results in all testing. A **theory** is a statement of behavior that consolidates all current observations. Theories are similar to laws in that they describe natural behavior, but they are more recently developed and more susceptible to being proved wrong. Theories may eventually become laws if they stand up to scrutiny and testing.

234

EVENTS AND OBJECTS
EVENTS

A **cause** is an act or event that makes something happen, and an **effect** is the thing that happens as a result of the cause. A cause-and-effect relationship is not always explicit, but there are some terms in English that signal causes, such as *since, because,* and *due to*. Terms that signal effects include *consequently, therefore, this lead(s) to.*

A *single* cause can have *multiple* effects (e.g., *Single cause*: Because you left your homework on the table, your dog eats the assignment. *Multiple effects*: As a result, you receive a failing grade, your parents do not allow you to visit your friends, you miss out on the new movie and holding the hand of a potential significant other).

A *single* effect can have *multiple* causes (e.g., *Single effect*: Alan has a fever. *Multiple causes*: An unexpected cold front came through the area, and Alan forgot to take his multi-vitamin to avoid being sick.)

An *effect* can in turn be the cause of *another effect*, in what is known as a **cause-and-effect chain**. (e.g., As a result of her disdain for procrastination, Lynn prepared for her exam. This led to her passing her test with high marks. Hence, her resume was accepted, and her application was approved.)

SCALE

From the largest objects in outer space to the smallest pieces of the human body, there are objects that can come in many different sizes and shapes. Many of those objects need to be measured in different ways. So, it is important to know which **unit of measurement** is needed to record the length or width and the weight of an object.

An example is taking the measurements of a patient. When measuring the total height of a patient or finding the length of an extremity, the accepted measure is given in meters. However, when one is asked for the diameter of a vein, the accepted measure is given in millimeters. Another example would be measuring the weight of a patient which would be given in kilograms, while the measurement of a human heart would be given in grams. The same idea for scale holds true with time as well. When measuring the lifespan of a patient, the accepted measure is given in days, months, or years. However, when measuring the number of breaths that a patient takes, the accepted measure is given in terms of minutes (e.g., breaths per minute).

SCIENTIFIC INQUIRY
SCIENTIFIC METHOD

The scientific method of inquiry is a general method by which ideas are tested and either confirmed or refuted by experimentation. The first step in the scientific method is **formulating the problem** that is to be addressed. It is essential to define clearly the limits of what is to be observed, since that allows for a more focused analysis.

Once the problem has been defined, it is necessary to form a **hypothesis**. This educated guess should be a possible solution to the problem that was formulated in the first step.

The next step is to test that hypothesis by **experimentation**. This often requires the scientist to design a complete experiment. The key to making the best possible use of an experiment is observation. Observations may be **quantitative**, that is, when a numeric measurement is taken, or they may be **qualitative**, that is, when something is evaluated based on feeling or preference. This measurement data will then be examined to find trends or patterns that are present.

From these trends, the scientist will draw **conclusions** or make **generalizations** about the results, intended to predict future results. If these conclusions support the original hypothesis, the experiment is complete, and the scientist will publish his conclusions to allow others to test them by repeating the experiment. If they do not support the hypothesis, the results should then be used to develop a new hypothesis, which can then be verified by a new or redesigned experiment.

EXPERIMENTAL DESIGN

Designing relevant experiments that allow for meaningful results is not a simple task. Every stage of the experiment must be carefully planned to ensure that the right data can be safely and accurately taken.

Ideally, an experiment should be **controlled** so that all of the conditions except the ones being manipulated are held **constant**. This helps to ensure that the results are not skewed by unintended consequences of shifting conditions. A good example of this is a placebo group in a drug trial. All other conditions are the same, but that group is not given the medication.

In addition to proper control, it is important that the experiment be designed with **data collection** in mind. For instance, if the quantity to be measured is temperature, there must be a temperature device such as a thermocouple integrated into the experimental setup. While the data are being collected, they should periodically be checked for obvious errors. If there are data points that are orders of magnitude from the expected value, then it might be a good idea to make sure that no experimental errors are being made, either in data collection or condition control.

Once all the data have been gathered, they must be **analyzed**. The way in which this should be done depends on the type of data and the type of trends observed. It may be useful to fit curves to the data to determine if the trends follow a common mathematical form. It may also be necessary to perform a statistical analysis of the results to determine what effects are significant. Data should be clearly presented.

CONTROLS

A valid experiment must be carefully **controlled**. All variables except the one being tested must be carefully maintained. This means that all conditions must be kept exactly the same except for the independent variable.

Additionally, a set of data is usually needed for a **control group**. The control group represents the "normal" state or condition of the variable being manipulated. Controls can be negative or positive. **Positive controls** are the variables that the researcher expects to have an effect on the outcome of the experiment. A positive control group can be used to verify that an experiment is set up properly. **Negative control groups** are typically thought of as placebos. A negative control group should verify that a variable has no effect on the outcome of the experiment.

The better an experiment is controlled, the more valid the conclusions from that experiment will be. A researcher is more likely to draw a valid conclusion if all variables other than the one being manipulated are being controlled.

VARIABLES

Every experiment has several **variables**; however, only one variable should be purposely changed and tested. This variable is the **manipulated** or **independent variable**. As this variable is manipulated or changed, another variable, called the **responding** or **dependent variable**, is observed and recorded. All other variables in the experiment must be carefully controlled and are usually referred to as **constants**. For example, when testing the effect of temperature on solubility of a solute, the independent variable is the temperature, and the dependent variable is the solubility. All other factors in the experiment such as pressure, amount of stirring, type of solvent, type of solute, and particle size of the solute are the constants.

SCIENTIFIC REASONING CHAPTER QUIZ

1. Which of the following correctly describes the prefix *hecto-*?
   a. 10^{-2}
   b. 10^{-1}
   c. 10^1
   d. 10^2

2. Which of the following should be used for accurately measuring a small amount of liquid?
   a. Beaker
   b. Test tubes
   c. Erlenmeyer flask
   d. Pipette

3. Which of the following is a statement of behavior that consolidates all current observations?
   a. Hypothesis
   b. Theory
   c. Model
   d. Assumption

4. A triple-beam balance measures which of the following?
   a. Volume
   b. Temperature
   c. Mass
   d. Luminous intensity

5. Which of the following prefixes indicates the largest multiple of the base unit?
   a. *Tera-*
   b. *Giga-*
   c. *Mega-*
   d. *Pico-*

Answers for all of the chapter quiz questions can be found right before Practice Test #1.

English and Language Usage

Conventions of Standard English: Spelling

COMMON RULES FOR ENGLISH SPELLING
WORDS ENDING WITH A CONSONANT

Usually, the final consonant is **doubled** on a word before adding a suffix. This is the rule for single syllable words, words ending with one consonant, and multi-syllable words with the last syllable accented. The following are examples:

- *Beg* becomes *begging* (single syllable)
- *Shop* becomes *shopped* (single syllable)
- *Add* becomes *adding* (already ends in double consonant, do not add another *d*)
- *Deter* becomes *deterring* (multi-syllable, accent on last syllable)
- *Regret* becomes *regrettable* (multi-syllable, accent on last syllable)
- *Compost* becomes *composting* (do not add another *t* because the accent is on the first syllable)

WORDS ENDING WITH Y OR C

The general rule for words ending in *y* is to keep the *y* when adding a suffix if the *y* **is preceded by a vowel**. If the word **ends in a consonant and *y*** the *y* is changed to an *i* before the suffix is added (unless the suffix itself begins with *i*). The following are examples:

- *Pay* becomes *paying* (keep the *y*)
- *Bully* becomes *bullied* (change to *i*)
- *Bully* becomes *bullying* (keep the *y* because the suffix is –*ing*)

If a word ends with *c* and the suffix begins with an *e*, *i*, or *y*, the letter *k* is usually added to the end of the word. The following are examples:

- *Panic* becomes *panicky*
- *Mimic* becomes *mimicking*

WORDS CONTAINING IE/EI OR ENDING WITH E

Most words are spelled with an *i* before *e*, except when they follow the letter *c* or sound like *a*. For example, the following words are spelled correctly according to these rules:

- *Piece, friend, believe* (*i* before *e*).
- *Receive, ceiling, conceited* (except after *c*)
- *Weight, neighborhood, veil* (sounds like *a*)

To add a suffix to words ending with the letter *e*, first determine if the *e* is silent. If it is, the *e* will be kept if the added suffix begins with a consonant. If the suffix begins with a vowel, the *e* is dropped. The following are examples:

- *Age* becomes *ageless* (keep the *e*)
- *Age* becomes *aging* (drop the *e*)

An exception to this rule occurs when the word ends in -ce or -ge and the suffix -able or -ous is added; these words will retain the letter e. The following are examples:

- *Courage* becomes *courageous*
- *Notice* becomes *noticeable*

WORDS ENDING WITH -ISE OR -IZE

A small number of words end with -ise. Most of the words in the English language with the same sound end in -ize but not all. The following are examples:

- *Advertise, advise, arise, chastise, circumcise,* and *comprise*
- *Compromise, demise, despise, devise, disguise, enterprise, excise,* and *exercise*
- *Franchise, improvise, incise, merchandise, premise, reprise,* and *revise*
- *Supervise, surmise, surprise,* and *televise*

Words that end with -ize include the following:

- *Accessorize, agonize, authorize,* and *brutalize*
- *Capitalize, caramelize, categorize, civilize,* and *demonize*
- *Downsize, empathize, euthanize, idolize,* and *immunize*
- *Legalize, metabolize, mobilize, organize,* and *ostracize*
- *Plagiarize, privatize, utilize,* and *visualize*

(Note that some words are spelled with -ise in British English, but in American English it is more common to use -ize. Examples include *symbolize/symbolise* and *baptize/baptise*.)

WORDS ENDING WITH -CEED, -SEDE, OR -CEDE

There are only three words in the English language that end with -ceed: *exceed, proceed,* and *succeed.* There is only one word in the English language that ends with -sede: *supersede.* Most other words that sound like -sede or -ceed end with -cede. The following are examples:

- *Concede, recede,* and *precede*

WORDS ENDING IN -ABLE OR -IBLE

For words ending in -able or -ible, there are no hard and fast rules. The following are examples:

- *Adjustable, unbeatable, collectable, deliverable,* and *likeable*
- *Edible, compatible, feasible, sensible,* and *credible*

There are more words ending in -able than -ible; this is useful to know if guessing is necessary.

WORDS ENDING IN -ANCE OR -ENCE

The suffixes -ence, -ency, and -ent are used in the following cases:

- The suffix is preceded by the letter c but sounds like s – *innocence*
- The suffix is preceded by the letter g but sounds like j – *intelligence, negligence*

The suffixes -ance, -ancy, and -ant are used in the following cases:

- The suffix is preceded by the letter c but sounds like k – *significant, vacant*
- The suffix is preceded by the letter g with a hard sound – *elegant, extravagance*

If the suffix is preceded by other letters, there are no clear rules. For example: *finance, abundance,* and *assistance* use the letter *a,* while *decadence, competence,* and *excellence* use the letter *e.*

WORDS ENDING IN -TION, -SION, OR -CIAN

Words ending in *-tion, -sion,* or *-cian* all sound like *shun* or *zhun.* There are no rules for which of these endings is used for words. The following are examples:

- *Action, agitation, caution, fiction, nation,* and *motion*
- *Admission, expression, mansion, permission,* and *television*
- *Electrician, magician, musician, optician,* and *physician* (note that these words tend to describe occupations)

WORDS WITH THE AI OR IA COMBINATION

When deciding if *ai* or *ia* is correct, the combination of *ai* usually sounds like one vowel sound, as in *Britain,* while the vowels in *ia* are pronounced separately, as in *guardian.* The following are examples:

- *Captain, certain, faint, hair, malaise,* and *praise* (*ai* makes one sound)
- *Bacteria, beneficiary, diamond, humiliation,* and *nuptial* (*ia* makes two sounds)

RULES FOR PLURAL FORMS

NOUNS ENDING IN -CH, -SH, -S, -X, OR -Z

When a noun ends in the letters *-ch, -sh, -s, -x,* or *-z,* an *-es* instead of a singular *s* is added to the end of the word to make it plural. The following are examples:

- *Church* becomes *churches*
- *Bush* becomes *bushes*
- *Bass* becomes *basses*
- *Mix* becomes *mixes*
- *Buzz* becomes *buzzes*

This is the rule with proper names as well; the Ross family would become the Rosses.

NOUNS ENDING IN Y OR AY/EY/IY/OY/UY

If a noun ends with a **consonant and y,** the plural is formed by replacing the *-y* with *-ies.* For example, *fly* becomes *flies* and *puppy* becomes *puppies.* If a noun ends with a **vowel and y,** the plural is formed by adding an *s.* For example, *alley* becomes *alleys* and *boy* becomes *boys.*

NOUNS ENDING IN -F OR -FE

Most nouns ending in *-f* or *-fe* are pluralized by replacing the *f* with *v* and adding *es.* The following are examples:

- *Knife* becomes *knives*
- *Self* becomes *selves*
- *Wolf* becomes *wolves*

An exception to this rule is the word *roof; roof* becomes *roofs.*

NOUNS ENDING IN O

Most nouns ending with a **consonant and o** are pluralized by adding -es. The following are examples:

- *Hero* becomes *heroes*
- *Tornado* becomes *tornadoes*
- *Potato* becomes *potatoes*

Most nouns ending with a **vowel and o** are pluralized by adding s. The following are examples:

- portfolio becomes portfolios; radio becomes radios; cameo becomes cameos.

An exception to these rules is seen with musical terms ending in *o*. These words are pluralized by adding s even if they end in a consonant and *o*. The following are examples:

- *Soprano* becomes *sopranos*
- *Banjo* becomes *banjos*
- *Piano* becomes *pianos.*

LETTERS, NUMBERS, AND SYMBOLS

Letters and numbers become plural by adding an apostrophe and *s*. The following are examples:

- The *L's* are the people whose names begin with the letter *L*.
- They broke the teams down into groups of *3's*.
- The sorority girls were all *KD's*.

COMPOUND NOUNS

A **compound noun** is a noun that is made up of two or more words; they are sometimes written with hyphens. For example, *mother-in-law* or *court-martial* are compound nouns. To make them plural, an *s* or *es* is added to the noun portion of the word. The following are examples: *mother-in-law* becomes *mothers-in-law; court-martial* becomes *courts-martial.*

EXCEPTIONS

Some words do not fall into any specific category for making the singular form plural. They are **irregular**. Certain words become plural by changing the vowels within the word. The following are examples:

- *Woman* becomes *women*
- *Goose* becomes *geese*
- *Foot* becomes *feet*

Some words change in unusual ways in the plural form. The following are examples:

- *Mouse* becomes *mice*
- *Ox* becomes *oxen*
- *Person* becomes *people*

Some words are the same in both the singular and plural forms. The following are examples:

- *Salmon*, *deer*, and *moose* are the same whether singular or plural.

COMMONLY MISSPELLED WORDS

accidentally	accommodate	accompanied	accompany	achieved
acknowledgment	across	address	aggravate	aisle
ancient	anxiety	apparently	appearance	arctic
argument	arrangement	attendance	auxiliary	awkward
bachelor	barbarian	beggar	beneficiary	biscuit
brilliant	business	cafeteria	calendar	campaign
candidate	ceiling	cemetery	changeable	changing
characteristic	chauffeur	colonel	column	commit
committee	comparative	compel	competent	competition
conceive	congratulations	conqueror	conscious	coolly
correspondent	courtesy	curiosity	cylinder	deceive
deference	deferred	definite	describe	desirable
desperate	develop	diphtheria	disappear	disappoint
disastrous	discipline	discussion	disease	dissatisfied
dissipate	drudgery	ecstasy	efficient	eighth
eligible	embarrass	emphasize	especially	exaggerate
exceed	exhaust	exhilaration	existence	explanation
extraordinary	familiar	fascinate	February	fiery
finally	forehead	foreign	foreigner	foremost
forfeit	ghost	glamorous	government	grammar
grateful	grief	grievous	handkerchief	harass
height	hoping	hurriedly	hygiene	hypocrisy
imminent	incidentally	incredible	independent	indigestible
inevitable	innocence	intelligible	intentionally	intercede
interest	irresistible	judgment	legitimate	liable
library	likelihood	literature	maintenance	maneuver
manual	mathematics	mattress	miniature	mischievous
misspell	momentous	mortgage	neither	nickel
niece	ninety	noticeable	notoriety	obedience
obstacle	occasion	occurrence	omitted	operate
optimistic	organization	outrageous	pageant	pamphlet
parallel	parliament	permissible	perseverance	persuade
physically	physician	possess	possibly	practically
prairie	preceding	prejudice	prevalent	professor
pronouncement	pronunciation	propeller	protein	psychiatrist
psychology	quantity	questionnaire	rally	recede
receive	recognize	recommend	referral	referred
relieve	religious	resistance	restaurant	rhetoric
rhythm	ridiculous	sacrilegious	salary	scarcely
schedule	secretary	sentinel	separate	severely
sheriff	shriek	similar	soliloquy	sophomore
species	strenuous	studying	suffrage	supersede
suppress	surprise	symmetry	temperament	temperature
tendency	tournament	tragedy	transferred	truly
twelfth	tyranny	unanimous	unpleasant	usage
vacuum	valuable	vein	vengeance	vigilance
villain	Wednesday	weird	wholly	

COMMONLY CONFUSED WORDS

WHICH, THAT, AND WHO

The words *which*, *that*, and *who* can act as **relative pronouns** to help clarify or describe a noun.

Which is used for things only.

> Example: Andrew's car, *which is old and rusty,* broke down last week.

That is used for people or things. *That* is usually informal when used to describe people.

> Example: Is this the only book *that Louis L'Amour wrote?*

> Example: Is Louis L'Amour the author *that wrote Western novels?*

Who is used for people or for animals that have a name.

> Example: Mozart was the composer *who wrote those operas.*

> Example: John's dog, *who is called Max,* is large and fierce.

HOMOPHONES

Homophones are words that sound alike (or similar), but they have different **spellings** and **definitions**.

TO, TOO, AND TWO

To can be an adverb or a preposition for showing direction, purpose, and relationship. See your dictionary for the many other ways use *to* in a sentence.

> Examples: I went to the store. | I want to go with you.

Too is an adverb that means *also, as well, very, or more than enough.*

> Examples: I can walk a mile too. | You have eaten too much.

Two is the second number in the series of numbers (e.g., one (1), two, (2), three (3)...)

> Example: You have two minutes left.

THERE, THEIR, AND THEY'RE

There can be an adjective, adverb, or pronoun. Often, *there* is used to show a place or to start a sentence.

> Examples: I went there yesterday. | There is something in his pocket.

Their is a pronoun that is used to show ownership.

> Examples: He is their father. | This is their fourth apology this week.

They're is a contraction of *they are.*

> Example: Did you know that they're in town?

English

KNEW AND NEW

Knew is the past tense of *know*.

> Example: I knew the answer.

New is an adjective that means something is current, has not been used, or modern.

> Example: This is my new phone.

THEN AND THAN

Then is an adverb that indicates sequence or order:

> Example: I'm going to run to the library and then come home.

Than is special-purpose word used only for comparisons:

> Example: Susie likes chips better than candy.

ITS AND IT'S

Its is a pronoun that shows ownership.

> Example: The guitar is in its case.

It's is a contraction of *it is*.

> Example: It's an honor and a privilege to meet you.

Note: The *h* in honor is silent, so the sound of the vowel *o* must have the article *an*.

YOUR AND YOU'RE

Your is a pronoun that shows ownership.

> Example: This is your moment to shine.

You're is a contraction of *you are*.

> Example: Yes, you're correct.

AFFECT AND EFFECT

There are two main reasons that **affect** and **effect** are so often confused: 1) both words can be used as either a noun or a verb, and 2) unlike most homophones, their usage and meanings are closely related to each other. Here is a quick rundown of the four usage options:

Affect (n): feeling, emotion, or mood that is displayed

> Example: The patient had a flat *affect*. (i.e., his face showed little or no emotion)

Affect (v): to alter, to change, to influence

> Example: The sunshine *affects* the plant's growth.

Effect (n): a result, a consequence

> Example: What *effect* will this weather have on our schedule?

Effect (v): to bring about, to cause to be

> Example: These new rules will *effect* order in the office.

The noun form of *affect* is rarely used outside of technical medical descriptions, so if a noun form is needed on the test, you can safely select *effect*. The verb form of *effect* is not as rare as the noun form of *affect*, but it's still not all that likely to show up on your test. If you need a verb and you can't decide which to use based on the definitions, choosing *affect* is your best bet.

HOMOGRAPHS

Homographs are words that share the same spelling, and they have multiple meanings. To figure out which meaning is being used, you should be looking for context clues. The context clues give hints to the meaning of the word. For example, the word *spot* has many meanings. It can mean "a place" or "a stain or blot." In the sentence "After my lunch, I saw a spot on my shirt," the word *spot* means "a stain or blot." The context clues of "After my lunch..." and "on my shirt" guide you to this decision.

BANK

> (noun): an establishment where money is held for savings or lending

> (verb): to collect or pile up

CONTENT

> (noun): the topics that will be addressed within a book

> (adjective): pleased or satisfied

FINE

> (noun): an amount of money that acts a penalty for an offense

> (adjective): very small or thin

INCENSE

> (noun): a material that is burned in religious settings and makes a pleasant aroma

> (verb): to frustrate or anger

LEAD

> (noun): the first or highest position

> (verb): to direct a person or group of followers

OBJECT

> (noun): a lifeless item that can be held and observed

> (verb): to disagree

PRODUCE

> (noun): fruits and vegetables

> (verb): to make or create something

English

REFUSE

>(noun): garbage or debris that has been thrown away

>(verb): to not allow

SUBJECT

>(noun): an area of study

>(verb): to force or subdue

TEAR

>(noun): a fluid secreted by the eyes

>(verb): to separate or pull apart

SPELLING CHAPTER QUIZ

1. Which of the following correctly implements the word *affect*?
- a. These new rules will affect order in the office.
- b. What affect will this weather have on our schedule?
- c. The patient had a flat affect during her examination.
- d. His narcissism had a detrimental affect on everyone around him.

2. Affect and effect would be considered which of the following?
- a. Homographs
- b. Synonyms
- c. Antonyms
- d. Homophones

3. Which of the following is a correctly spelled compound noun?
- a. Ice-cream
- b. Check-in
- c. Biology
- d. Hippopotamus

4. Which of the following singular/plural pairs is NOT correct?
- a. Woman/Women
- b. Salmon/Salmons
- c. Moose/Moose
- d. Goose/Geese

5. Which word is spelled correctly?
- a. Sacrilegious
- b. Paralell
- c. Auxillary
- d. Cemetary

Answers for all of the chapter quiz questions can be found right before Practice Test #1.

Conventions of Standard English: Punctuation

END PUNCTUATION

PERIODS

Use a period to end all sentences except direct questions, exclamations.

DECLARATIVE SENTENCE

A declarative sentence gives information or makes a statement.

> Examples: I can fly a kite. | The plane left two hours ago.

IMPERATIVE SENTENCE

An imperative sentence gives an order or command.

> Examples: You are coming with me. | Bring me that note.

PERIODS FOR ABBREVIATIONS

> Examples: 3 P.M. | 2 A.M. | Mr. Jones | Mrs. Stevens | Dr. Smith | Bill Jr. | Pennsylvania Ave.

Note: an abbreviation is a shortened form of a word or phrase.

QUESTION MARKS

Question marks should be used following a direct question. A polite request can be followed by a period instead of a question mark.

> **Direct Question**: What is for lunch today? | How are you? | Why is that the answer?

> **Polite Requests**: Can you please send me the item tomorrow. | Will you please walk with me on the track.

> **Review Video: Question Marks**
> Visit mometrix.com/academy and enter code: 118471

EXCLAMATION MARKS

Exclamation marks are used after a word group or sentence that shows much feeling or has special importance. Exclamation marks should not be overused. They are saved for proper **exclamatory interjections**.

> Example: We're going to the finals! | You have a beautiful car! | That's crazy!

> **Review Video: Exclamation Points**
> Visit mometrix.com/academy and enter code: 199367

COMMAS

The comma is a punctuation mark that can help you understand connections in a sentence. Not every sentence needs a comma. However, if a sentence needs a comma, you need to put it in the

English

right place. A comma in the wrong place (or an absent comma) will make a sentence's meaning unclear. These are some of the rules for commas:

Use Case	Example
Before a **coordinating conjunction** joining independent clauses	Bob caught three fish, and I caught two fish.
After an **introductory phrase**	After the final out, we went to a restaurant to celebrate.
After an **adverbial clause**	Studying the stars, I was awed by the beauty of the sky.
Between **items in a series**	I will bring the turkey, the pie, and the coffee.
For **interjections**	Wow, you know how to play this game.
After *yes* and *no* responses	No, I cannot come tomorrow.
Separate **nonessential modifiers**	John Frank, who coaches the team, was promoted today.
Separate **nonessential appositives**	Thomas Edison, an American inventor, was born in Ohio.
Separate **nouns of direct address**	You, John, are my only hope in this moment.
Separate **interrogative tags**	This is the last time, correct?
Separate **contrasts**	You are my friend, not my enemy.
Writing **dates**	July 4, 1776, is an important date to remember.
Writing **addresses**	He is meeting me at 456 Delaware Avenue, Washington, D.C., tomorrow morning.
Writing **geographical names**	Paris, France, is my favorite city.
Writing **titles**	John Smith, PhD, will be visiting your class today.
Separate **expressions like** *he said*	"You can start," she said, "with an apology."

Also, you can use a comma **between coordinate adjectives** not joined with *and*. However, not all adjectives are coordinate (i.e., equal or parallel).

Incorrect: The kind, brown dog followed me home.

Correct: The kind, loyal dog followed me home.

There are two simple ways to know if your adjectives are coordinate. One, you can join the adjectives with *and*: *The kind and loyal dog.* Two, you can change the order of the adjectives: *The loyal, kind dog.*

Review Video: <u>When To Use a Comma</u>
Visit mometrix.com/academy and enter code: 786797

SEMICOLONS

The semicolon is used to connect major sentence pieces of equal value. Some rules for semicolons include:

Use Case	Example
Between closely connected independent clauses **not connected with a coordinating conjunction**	You are right; we should go with your plan.
Between independent clauses **linked with a transitional word**	I think that we can agree on this; however, I am not sure about my friends.
Between items in a **series that has internal punctuation**	I have visited New York, New York; Augusta, Maine; and Baltimore, Maryland.

Review Video: How to Use Semicolons
Visit mometrix.com/academy and enter code: 370605

COLONS

The colon is used to call attention to the words that follow it. A colon must come after a **complete independent clause**. The rules for colons are as follows:

Use Case	Example
After an independent clause to **make a list**	I want to learn many languages: Spanish, German, and Italian.
For **explanations**	There is one thing that stands out on your resume: responsibility.
To give a **quote**	He started with an idea: "We are able to do more than we imagine."
After the **greeting in a formal letter**	To Whom It May Concern:
Show **hours and minutes**	It is 3:14 p.m.
Separate a **title and subtitle**	The essay is titled "America: A Short Introduction to a Modern Country."

Review Video: Colons
Visit mometrix.com/academy and enter code: 868673

PARENTHESES

Parentheses are used for additional information. Also, they can be used to put labels for letters or numbers in a series. Parentheses should be not be used very often. If they are overused, parentheses can be a distraction instead of a help.

Examples:

Extra Information: The rattlesnake (see Image 2) is a dangerous snake of North and South America.

Series: Include in the email (1) your name, (2) your address, and (3) your question for the author.

Review Video: Parentheses
Visit mometrix.com/academy and enter code: 947743

English

QUOTATION MARKS

Use quotation marks to close off **direct quotations** of a person's spoken or written words. Do not use quotation marks around indirect quotations. An indirect quotation gives someone's message without using the person's exact words. Use **single quotation marks** to close off a quotation inside a quotation.

> **Direct Quote**: Nancy said, "I am waiting for Henry to arrive."

> **Indirect Quote**: Henry said that he is going to be late to the meeting.

> **Quote inside a Quote**: The teacher asked, "Has everyone read 'The Gift of the Magi'?"

Quotation marks should be used around the titles of **short works**: newspaper and magazine articles, poems, short stories, songs, television episodes, radio programs, and subdivisions of books or websites.

Examples:

> "Rip Van Winkle" (short story by Washington Irving)

> "O Captain! My Captain!" (poem by Walt Whitman)

Although it is not standard usage, quotation marks are sometimes used to highlight **irony** or the use of words to mean something other than their dictionary definition. This type of usage should be employed sparingly, if at all.

Examples:

The boss warned Frank that he was walking on "thin ice."	Frank is not walking on real ice. Instead, he is being warned to avoid mistakes.
The teacher thanked the young man for his "honesty."	The quotation marks around *honesty* show that the teacher does not believe the young man's explanation.

> **Review Video: Quotation Marks**
> Visit mometrix.com/academy and enter code: 884918

Periods and commas are put **inside** quotation marks. Colons and semicolons are put **outside** the quotation marks. Question marks and exclamation points are placed inside quotation marks when they are part of a quote. When the question or exclamation mark goes with the whole sentence, the mark is left outside of the quotation marks.

Examples:

Period and comma	We read "The Gift of the Magi," "The Skylight Room," and "The Cactus."
Semicolon	They watched "The Nutcracker"; then, they went home.
Exclamation mark that is a part of a quote	The crowd cheered, "Victory!"
Question mark that goes with the whole sentence	Is your favorite short story "The Tell-Tale Heart"?

APOSTROPHES

An apostrophe is used to show **possession** or the **deletion of letters in contractions**. An apostrophe is not needed with the possessive pronouns *his, hers, its, ours, theirs, whose*, and *yours*.

Singular Nouns: David's car | a book's theme | my brother's board game

Plural Nouns with -*s*: the scissors' handle | boys' basketball

Plural Nouns without -*s*: Men's department | the people's adventure

> **Review Video: When to Use an Apostrophe**
> Visit mometrix.com/academy and enter code: 213068
>
> **Review Video: Punctuation Errors in Possessive Pronouns**
> Visit mometrix.com/academy and enter code: 221438

HYPHENS

Hyphens are used to **separate compound words**. Use hyphens in the following cases:

Use Case	Example
Compound numbers from 21 to 99 when written out in words	This team needs twenty-five points to win the game.
Written-out fractions that are used as adjectives	The recipe says that we need a three-fourths cup of butter.
Compound adjectives that come before a noun	The well-fed dog took a nap.
Unusual compound words that would be hard to read or easily confused with other words	This is the best anti-itch cream on the market.

Note: This is not a complete set of the rules for hyphens. A dictionary is the best tool for knowing if a compound word needs a hyphen.

> **Review Video: Hyphens**
> Visit mometrix.com/academy and enter code: 981632

DASHES

Dashes are used to show a **break** or a **change in thought** in a sentence or to act as parentheses in a sentence. When typing, use two hyphens to make a dash. Do not put a space before or after the dash. The following are the functions of dashes:

Use Case	Example
Set off parenthetical statements or an **appositive with internal punctuation**	The three trees—oak, pine, and magnolia—are coming on a truck tomorrow.
Show a **break or change in tone or thought**	The first question—how silly of me—does not have a correct answer.

ELLIPSIS MARKS

The ellipsis mark has **three** periods (...) to show when **words have been removed** from a quotation. If a **full sentence or more** is removed from a quoted passage, you need to use **four** periods to show the removed text and the end punctuation mark. The ellipsis mark should not be used at the beginning of a quotation. The ellipsis mark should also not be used at the end of a quotation unless some words have been deleted from the end of the final sentence.

Example:

"Then he picked up the groceries...paid for them...later he went home."

BRACKETS

There are two main reasons to use brackets:

Use Case	Example
Placing **parentheses inside of parentheses**	The hero of this story, Paul Revere (a silversmith and industrialist [see Ch. 4]), rode through towns of Massachusetts to warn of advancing British troops.
Adding **clarification or detail to a quotation** that is not part of the quotation	The father explained, "My children are planning to attend my alma mater [State University]."

Review Video: Brackets
Visit mometrix.com/academy and enter code: 727546

PUNCTUATION CHAPTER QUIZ

1. Which of the following correctly implements the use of parentheses?

a. The rattlesnake (see Image 2) is a dangerous snake of North and South America.
b. The rattlesnake see (Image 2) is a dangerous snake of North and South America.
c. The rattlesnake see Image (2) is a dangerous snake of North and South America.
d. The rattlesnake (see Image) (2) is a dangerous snake of North and South America.

2. Which of the following correctly describes the placement of punctuation in reference to quotations?

a. Periods and commas are put outside quotation marks; colons and semicolons go inside.
b. Periods and colons are put outside quotation marks; commas and semicolons go inside.
c. Periods and commas are put inside quotation marks; colons and semicolons go outside.
d. Periods and colons are put inside quotation marks; commas and semicolons go outside.

3. Which of the following correctly implements the use of commas?

a. He is meeting me at, 456 Delaware Avenue, Washington, D.C., tomorrow morning.
b. He is meeting me at 456 Delaware Avenue, Washington, D.C., tomorrow morning.
c. He is meeting me at 456 Delaware Avenue Washington, D.C. tomorrow morning.
d. He is meeting me at 456 Delaware Avenue, Washington, D.C. tomorrow morning.

4. Which of the following is correctly punctuated?

a. John Smith Ph. D., will be visiting your class today.
b. John Frank who is coaching the team, was promoted today.
c. "I want you to know, he began, "that I always wanted the best for you.""
d. "You can start," Jane said, "with an apology."

5. Which of the following does NOT correctly describe a rule for semicolon usage?

a. Use a semicolon between closely connected independent clauses that are not connected with a coordinating conjunction.
b. Use a semicolon between independent clauses linked with a transitional word.
c. Use a semicolon for explanations or to give a quote.
d. Use a semicolon between items in a series that has internal punctuation.

Answers for all of the chapter quiz questions can be found right before Practice Test #1.

Conventions of Standard English: Grammar

THE EIGHT PARTS OF SPEECH
NOUNS

When you talk about a person, place, thing, or idea, you are talking about a **noun**. The two main types of nouns are **common** and **proper** nouns. Also, nouns can be abstract (i.e., general) or concrete (i.e., specific).

COMMON NOUNS

Common nouns are generic names for people, places, and things. Common nouns are not usually capitalized.

Examples of common nouns:

> *People*: boy, girl, worker, manager
>
> *Places*: school, bank, library, home
>
> *Things*: dog, cat, truck, car

PROPER NOUNS

Proper nouns name specific people, places, or things. All proper nouns are capitalized.

Examples of proper nouns:

> *People*: Abraham Lincoln, George Washington, Martin Luther King, Jr.
>
> *Places*: Los Angeles, California; New York; Asia
>
> *Things*: Statue of Liberty, Earth, Lincoln Memorial

Note: When referring to the planet that we live on, capitalize *Earth*. When referring to the dirt, rocks, or land, lowercase *earth*.

GENERAL AND SPECIFIC NOUNS

General nouns are the names of conditions or ideas. **Specific nouns** name people, places, and things that are understood by using your senses.

General nouns:

> *Condition*: beauty, strength
>
> *Idea*: truth, peace

Specific nouns:

> *People*: baby, friend, father
>
> *Places*: town, park, city hall
>
> *Things*: rainbow, cough, apple, silk, gasoline

COLLECTIVE NOUNS

Collective nouns are the names for a group of people, places, or things that may act as a whole. The following are examples of collective nouns: *class, company, dozen, group, herd, team,* and *public.* Collective nouns usually require an article, which denotes the noun as being a single unit. For instance, a choir is a group of singers. Even though there are many singers in a choir, the word choir is grammatically treated as a single unit. If we refer to the members of the group, and not the group itself, it is no longer a collective noun.

Incorrect: The *choir are* going to compete nationally this year.

Correct: The *choir is* going to compete nationally this year.

Incorrect: The *members* of the choir *is* competing nationally this year.

Correct: The *members* of the choir *are* competing nationally this year.

PRONOUNS

Pronouns are words that are used to stand in for nouns. A pronoun may be classified as personal, intensive, relative, interrogative, demonstrative, indefinite, and reciprocal.

Personal: *Nominative* is the case for nouns and pronouns that are the subject of a sentence. *Objective* is the case for nouns and pronouns that are an object in a sentence. *Possessive* is the case for nouns and pronouns that show possession or ownership.

Singular

	Nominative	Objective	Possessive
First Person	I	me	my, mine
Second Person	you	you	your, yours
Third Person	he, she, it	him, her, it	his, her, hers, its

Plural

	Nominative	Objective	Possessive
First Person	we	us	our, ours
Second Person	you	you	your, yours
Third Person	they	them	their, theirs

Intensive: I myself, you yourself, he himself, she herself, the (thing) itself, we ourselves, you yourselves, they themselves

Relative: which, who, whom, whose

Interrogative: what, which, who, whom, whose

Demonstrative: this, that, these, those

Indefinite: all, any, each, everyone, either/neither, one, some, several

Reciprocal: each other, one another

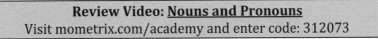

Review Video: Nouns and Pronouns
Visit mometrix.com/academy and enter code: 312073

255

VERBS

If you want to write a sentence, then you need a verb. Without a verb, you have no sentence. The verb of a sentence indicates action or being. In other words, the verb shows something's action or state of being or the action that has been done to something.

TRANSITIVE AND INTRANSITIVE VERBS

A **transitive verb** is a verb whose action (e.g., drive, run, jump) indicates a receiver (e.g., car, dog, kangaroo). **Intransitive verbs** do not indicate a receiver of an action. In other words, the action of the verb does not point to a subject or object.

> **Transitive**: She plays the piano. | John joined the crowd.

> **Intransitive**: He slept. | Sharon collapsed.

A dictionary will tell you whether a verb is transitive or intransitive. Some verbs can be transitive and intransitive.

ACTION VERBS AND LINKING VERBS

Action verbs show what the subject is doing. In other words, an action verb shows action. Unlike most types of words, a single action verb, in the right context, can be an entire sentence. **Linking verbs** link the subject of a sentence to a noun or pronoun, or they link a subject with an adjective. You always need a verb if you want a complete sentence. However, linking verbs on their own cannot be a complete sentence.

Common linking verbs include *appear, be, become, feel, grow, look, seem, smell, sound,* and *taste.* However, any verb that shows a condition and connects to a noun, pronoun, or adjective that describes the subject of a sentence is a linking verb.

Action: He sings. | Run! | Go! | I talk with him every day. | She reads.

Linking:

> Incorrect: I am.

> Correct: I am John. | That soup smells good. | Shirley felt tired.

Note: Some verbs are followed by words that look like prepositions, but they are a part of the verb and a part of the verb's meaning. These are known as phrasal verbs, and examples include *call off, look up,* and *drop off.*

> **Review Video: Action Verbs and Linking Verbs**
> Visit mometrix.com/academy and enter code: 743142

VOICE

Transitive verbs come in active or passive **voice**. If something does an action or is acted upon, then you will know whether a verb is active or passive. When the subject of the sentence is doing the action, the verb is in **active voice**. When the subject is acted upon, the verb is in **passive voice**.

> **Active**: Jon drew the picture. (The subject *Jon* is doing the action of *drawing a picture.*)

> **Passive**: The picture is drawn by Jon. (The subject *picture* is receiving the action from Jon.)

Verb Tenses

A verb **tense** shows the different form of a verb to point to the time of an action. The present and past tense are indicated by the verb's form. An action in the present, *I talk,* can change form for the past: *I talked.* However, for the other tenses, an auxiliary (i.e., helping) verb is needed to show the change in form. These helping verbs include *am, are, is | have, has, had | was, were, will* (or *shall*).

Present: I talk	Present perfect: I have talked
Past: I talked	Past perfect: I had talked
Future: I will talk	Future perfect: I will have talked

Present: The action happens at the current time.

> Example: He *walks* to the store every morning.

To show that something is happening right now, use the progressive present tense: I *am walking.*

Past: The action happened in the past.

> Example: He *walked* to the store an hour ago.

Future: The action is going to happen later.

> Example: I *will walk* to the store tomorrow.

Present perfect: The action started in the past and continues into the present or took place previously at an unspecified time

> Example: I *have walked* to the store three times today.

Past perfect: The second action happened in the past. The first action came before the second.

> Example: Before I walked to the store (Action 2), I *had walked* to the library (Action 1).

Future perfect: An action that uses the past and the future. In other words, the action is complete before a future moment.

> Example: When she comes for the supplies (future moment), I *will have walked* to the store (action completed before the future moment).

> **Review Video: Present Perfect, Past Perfect, and Future Perfect Verb Tenses**
> Visit mometrix.com/academy and enter code: 269472

Conjugating Verbs

When you need to change the form of a verb, you are **conjugating** a verb. The key forms of a verb are singular, present tense (dream); singular, past tense (dreamed); and the past participle (have dreamed). Note: the past participle needs a helping verb to make a verb tense. For example, I *have dreamed* of this day. The following tables demonstrate some of the different ways to conjugate a verb:

Singular

Tense	First Person	Second Person	Third Person
Present	I dream	You dream	He, she, it dreams
Past	I dreamed	You dreamed	He, she, it dreamed
Past Participle	I have dreamed	You have dreamed	He, she, it has dreamed

Plural

Tense	First Person	Second Person	Third Person
Present	We dream	You dream	They dream
Past	We dreamed	You dreamed	They dreamed
Past Participle	We have dreamed	You have dreamed	They have dreamed

ADJECTIVES

An **adjective** is a word that is used to modify a noun or pronoun. An adjective answers a question: *Which one? What kind?* or *How many?* Usually, adjectives come before the words that they modify, but they may also come after a linking verb.

Which one? The *third* suit is my favorite.

What kind? This suit is *navy blue*.

How many? I am going to buy *four* pairs of socks to match the suit.

ARTICLES

Articles are adjectives that are used to distinguish nouns as definite or indefinite. **Definite** nouns are preceded by the article *the* and indicate a specific person, place, thing, or idea. **Indefinite** nouns are preceded by *a* or *an* and do not indicate a specific person, place, thing, or idea. *A*, *an*, and *the* are the only articles. Note: *An* comes before words that start with a vowel sound. For example, "Are you going to get an **u**mbrella?"

Definite: I lost *the* bottle that belongs to me.

Indefinite: Does anyone have *a* bottle to share?

> **Review Video: Function of Articles**
> Visit mometrix.com/academy and enter code: 449383

COMPARISON WITH ADJECTIVES

Some adjectives are relative and other adjectives are absolute. Adjectives that are **relative** can show the comparison between things. **Absolute** adjectives can also show comparison, but they do so in a different way. Let's say that you are reading two books. You think that one book is perfect, and the other book is not exactly perfect. It is not possible for one book to be more perfect than the other. Either you think that the book is perfect, or you think that the book is imperfect. In this case, perfect and imperfect are absolute adjectives.

Relative adjectives will show the different **degrees** of something or someone to something else or someone else. The three degrees of adjectives include positive, comparative, and superlative.

The **positive** degree is the normal form of an adjective.

Example: This work is *difficult*. | She is *smart*.

The **comparative** degree compares one person or thing to another person or thing.

Example: This work is *more difficult* than your work. | She is *smarter* than me.

The **superlative** degree compares more than two people or things.

Example: This is the *most difficult* work of my life. | She is the *smartest* lady in school.

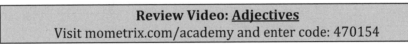

Review Video: Adjectives
Visit mometrix.com/academy and enter code: 470154

ADVERBS

An **adverb** is a word that is used to **modify** a verb, adjective, or another adverb. Usually, adverbs answer one of these questions: *When? Where? How?* and *Why?* The negatives *not* and *never* are considered adverbs. Adverbs that modify adjectives or other adverbs **strengthen** or **weaken** the words that they modify.

Examples:

He walks *quickly* through the crowd.

The water flows *smoothly* on the rocks.

Note: Adverbs are usually indicated by the morpheme *-ly*, which has been added to the root word. For instance, *quick* can be made into an adverb by adding *-ly* to construct *quickly*. Some words that end in *-ly* do not follow this rule and can behave as other parts of speech. Examples of adjectives ending in *-ly* include: *early, friendly, holy, lonely, silly*, and *ugly*. To know if a word that ends in *-ly* is an adjective or adverb, check your dictionary. Also, while many adverbs end in *-ly*, you need to remember that not all adverbs end in *-ly*.

Examples:

He is *never* angry.

You walked *across* the bridge.

Review Video: Adverbs
Visit mometrix.com/academy and enter code: 713951

Review Video: Adverbs that Modify Adjectives
Visit mometrix.com/academy and enter code: 122570

COMPARISON WITH ADVERBS

The rules for comparing adverbs are the same as the rules for adjectives.

The **positive** degree is the standard form of an adverb.

Example: He arrives *soon*. | She speaks *softly* to her friends.

The **comparative** degree compares one person or thing to another person or thing.

> Example: He arrives *sooner* than Sarah. | She speaks *more softly* than him.

The **superlative** degree compares more than two people or things.

> Example: He arrives *soonest* of the group. | She speaks the *most softly* of any of her friends.

PREPOSITIONS

A **preposition** is a word placed before a noun or pronoun that shows the relationship between an object and another word in the sentence.

Common prepositions:

about	before	during	on	under
after	beneath	for	over	until
against	between	from	past	up
among	beyond	in	through	with
around	by	of	to	within
at	down	off	toward	without

Examples:

> The napkin is *in* the drawer.

> The Earth rotates *around* the Sun.

> The needle is *beneath* the haystack.

> Can you find "me" *among* the words?

> **Review Video: Prepositions**
> Visit mometrix.com/academy and enter code: 946763

CONJUNCTIONS

Conjunctions join words, phrases, or clauses and they show the connection between the joined pieces. **Coordinating conjunctions** connect equal parts of sentences. **Correlative conjunctions** show the connection between pairs. **Subordinating conjunctions** join subordinate (i.e., dependent) clauses with independent clauses.

COORDINATING CONJUNCTIONS

The **coordinating conjunctions** include: *and, but, yet, or, nor, for,* and *so*

Examples:

> The rock was small, *but* it was heavy.

> She drove in the night, *and* he drove in the day.

CORRELATIVE CONJUNCTIONS

The **correlative conjunctions** are: *either...or* | *neither...nor* | *not only...but also*

Examples:

Either you are coming *or* you are staying.

He *not only* ran three miles *but also* swam 200 yards.

> **Review Video: Coordinating and Correlative Conjunctions**
> Visit mometrix.com/academy and enter code: 390329
>
> **Review Video: Adverb Equal Comparisons**
> Visit mometrix.com/academy and enter code: 231291

SUBORDINATING CONJUNCTIONS

Common **subordinating conjunctions** include:

after	since	whenever
although	so that	where
because	unless	wherever
before	until	whether
in order that	when	while

Examples:

I am hungry *because* I did not eat breakfast.

He went home *when* everyone left.

> **Review Video: Subordinating Conjunctions**
> Visit mometrix.com/academy and enter code: 958913

INTERJECTIONS

Interjections are words of exclamation (i.e., audible expression of great feeling) that are used alone or as a part of a sentence. Often, they are used at the beginning of a sentence for an introduction. Sometimes, they can be used in the middle of a sentence to show a change in thought or attitude.

Common Interjections: Hey! | Oh, | Ouch! | Please! | Wow!

English

GRAMMAR CHAPTER QUIZ

1. Which of the following is NOT one of the degrees of relative adjectives?

   a. Comparative
   b. Negative
   c. Positive
   d. Superlative

2. Which of the following sentences uses a linking verb?

   a. The coffee smelled delicious.
   b. I watched the sun slowly rise.
   c. Marcus had a very productive day.
   d. Sharon found a four-leaf clover.

3. In general, adverbs may modify all of the following EXCEPT

   a. Another adverb
   b. Adjectives
   c. Nouns
   d. Verbs

4. Which of the following is a correlative conjunction?

   a. Either...or
   b. After
   c. In order that
   d. Yet

5. Which one of these words is a superlative adverb?

   a. Quietly
   b. Most quietly
   c. More quietly
   d. Quietest

Answers for all of the chapter quiz questions can be found right before Practice Test #1.

Conventions of Standard English: Sentence Structure

SUBJECTS AND PREDICATES

SUBJECTS

The **subject** of a sentence names who or what the sentence is about. The subject may be directly stated in a sentence, or the subject may be the implied *you*. The **complete subject** includes the simple subject and all of its modifiers. To find the complete subject, ask *Who* or *What* and insert the verb to complete the question. The answer, including any modifiers (adjectives, prepositional phrases, etc.), is the complete subject. To find the **simple subject**, remove all of the modifiers in the complete subject. Being able to locate the subject of a sentence helps with many problems, such as those involving sentence fragments and subject-verb agreement.

Examples:

The small, red <u>car</u> is the one that he wants for Christmas.
(simple subject: car; complete subject: The small, red car)

The young <u>artist</u> is coming over for dinner.
(simple subject: artist; complete subject: The young artist)

> **Review Video: Subjects in English**
> Visit mometrix.com/academy and enter code: 444771

In **imperative** sentences, the verb's subject is understood (e.g., [You] Run to the store), but is not actually present in the sentence. Normally, the subject comes before the verb. However, the subject comes after the verb in sentences that begin with *There are* or *There was*.

Direct:

John knows the way to the park.	Who knows the way to the park?	John
The cookies need ten more minutes.	What needs ten minutes?	The cookies
By five o'clock, Bill will need to leave.	Who needs to leave?	Bill
There are five letters on the table for him.	What is on the table?	Five letters
There were coffee and doughnuts in the house.	What was in the house?	Coffee and doughnuts

Implied:

Go to the post office for me.	Who is going to the post office?	You
Come and sit with me, please?	Who needs to come and sit?	You

PREDICATES

In a sentence, you always have a predicate and a subject. The subject tells what the sentence is about, and the **predicate** explains or describes the subject.

Think about the sentence *He sings*. In this sentence, we have a subject (He) and a predicate (sings). This is all that is needed for a sentence to be complete. Most sentences contain more information, but if this is all the information that you are given, then you have a complete sentence.

Now, let's look at another sentence: *John and Jane sing on Tuesday nights at the dance hall.*

```
        subject              predicate
John and Jane   sing on Tuesday nights at the dance hall.
```

SUBJECT-VERB AGREEMENT

Verbs **agree** with their subjects in number. In other words, singular subjects need singular verbs. Plural subjects need plural verbs. **Singular** is for **one** person, place, or thing. **Plural** is for **more than one** person, place, or thing. Subjects and verbs must also share the same point of view, as in first, second, or third person. The present tense ending *-s* is used on a verb if its subject is third person singular; otherwise, the verb's ending is not modified.

> **Review Video: Subject-Verb Agreement**
> Visit mometrix.com/academy and enter code: 479190

NUMBER AGREEMENT EXAMPLES:

```
                          singular  singular
                          subject    verb
Single Subject and Verb:   Dan      calls   home.
```

Dan is one person. So, the singular verb *calls* is needed.

```
                              plural     plural
                              subject     verb
Plural Subject and Verb:  Dan and Bob   call  home.
```

More than one person needs the plural verb *call.*

PERSON AGREEMENT EXAMPLES:

First Person: I *am* walking.

Second Person: You *are* walking.

Third Person: He *is* walking.

COMPLICATIONS WITH SUBJECT-VERB AGREEMENT
WORDS BETWEEN SUBJECT AND VERB

Words that come between the simple subject and the verb have no bearing on subject-verb agreement.

Examples:

```
        singular              singular
        subject                 verb
The joy of my life returns home tonight.
```

The phrase *of my life* does not influence the verb *returns.*

singular
subject

singular
verb

The question that still remains unanswered is "Who are you?"

Don't let the phrase "*that still remains*..." trouble you. The subject *question* goes with *is*.

COMPOUND SUBJECTS

A compound subject is formed when two or more nouns joined by *and*, *or*, or *nor* jointly act as the subject of the sentence.

JOINED BY AND

When a compound subject is joined by *and*, it is treated as a plural subject and requires a plural verb.

Examples:

plural
subject

plural
verb

You and Jon are invited to come to my house.

plural
subject

plural
verb

The pencil and paper belong to me.

JOINED BY OR/NOR

For a compound subject joined by *or* or *nor*, the verb must agree in number with the part of the subject that is closest to the verb (italicized in the examples below).

Examples:

subject

verb

Today or *tomorrow* is the day.

subject

verb

Stan or *Phil* wants to read the book.

subject

verb

Neither the pen nor the *book* is on the desk.

subject

verb

Either the blanket or *pillows* arrive this afternoon.

INDEFINITE PRONOUNS AS SUBJECT

An indefinite pronoun is a pronoun that does not refer to a specific noun. Different indefinite pronouns may only function as a singular noun, only function as a plural noun, or change depending on how they are used.

English

265

ALWAYS SINGULAR

Pronouns such as *each, either, everybody, anybody, somebody,* and *nobody* are always singular.

Examples:

singular
subject

singular
verb

Each of the runners has a different bib number.

singular
verb

singular
subject

Is either of you ready for the game?

Note: The words *each* and *either* can also be used as adjectives (e.g., *each* person is unique). When one of these adjectives modifies the subject of a sentence, it is always a singular subject.

singular
subject

singular
verb

Everybody grows a day older every day.

singular
subject

singular
verb

Anybody is welcome to bring a tent.

ALWAYS PLURAL

Pronouns such as *both, several,* and *many* are always plural.

Examples:

plural
subject

plural
verb

Both of the siblings were too tired to argue.

plural
subject

plural
verb

Many have tried, but none have succeeded.

DEPEND ON CONTEXT

Pronouns such as *some, any, all, none, more,* and *most* can be either singular or plural depending on what they are representing in the context of the sentence.

Examples:

singular
subject

singular
verb

All of my dog's food was still there in his bowl.

plural
subject

plural
verb

By the end of the night, all of my guests were already excited about coming to my next party.

OTHER CASES INVOLVING PLURAL OR IRREGULAR FORM

Some nouns are **singular in meaning but plural in form**: news, mathematics, physics, and economics.

> The *news is* coming on now.

> *Mathematics is* my favorite class.

Some nouns are plural in form and meaning, and have **no singular equivalent**: scissors and pants.

> Do these *pants come* with a shirt?

> The *scissors are* for my project.

Mathematical operations are **irregular** in their construction, but are normally considered to be **singular in meaning**.

> *One plus one is* two.

> *Three times three is* nine.

Note: Look to your **dictionary** for help when you aren't sure whether a noun with a plural form has a singular or plural meaning.

COMPLEMENTS

A complement is a noun, pronoun, or adjective that is used to give more information about the subject or verb in the sentence.

DIRECT OBJECTS

A direct object is a noun or pronoun that takes or receives the **action** of a verb. (Remember: a complete sentence does not need a direct object, so not all sentences will have them. A sentence needs only a subject and a verb.) When you are looking for a direct object, find the verb and ask *who* or *what*.

Examples:

> I took *the blanket*.

> Jane read *books*.

INDIRECT OBJECTS

An indirect object is a word or group of words that show how an action had an **influence** on someone or something. If there is an indirect object in a sentence, then you always have a direct object in the sentence. When you are looking for the indirect object, find the verb and ask *to/for whom or what*.

Examples:

indirect   direct
object   object
We taught the old dog a new trick.

indirect   direct
object   object
I gave them a math lesson.

| Review Video: **Direct and Indirect Objects** |
| Visit mometrix.com/academy and enter code: 817385 |

PREDICATE NOMINATIVES AND PREDICATE ADJECTIVES

As we looked at previously, verbs may be classified as either action verbs or linking verbs. A linking verb is so named because it links the subject to words in the predicate that describe or define the subject. These words are called predicate nominatives (if nouns or pronouns) or predicate adjectives (if adjectives).

Examples:

subject   predicate
               nominative
My father is a lawyer.

subject   predicate
             adjective
Your mother is patient.

PRONOUN USAGE

The **antecedent** is the noun that has been replaced by a pronoun. A pronoun and its antecedent **agree** when they have the same number (singular or plural) and gender (male, female, or neutral).

Examples:

antecedent   pronoun
Singular agreement: John came into town, and he played for us.

antecedent   pronoun
Plural agreement: John and Rick came into town, and they played for us.

To determine which is the correct pronoun to use in a compound subject or object, try each pronoun **alone** in place of the compound in the sentence. Your knowledge of pronouns will tell you which one is correct.

Example:

Bob and (I, me) will be going.

Test: (1) *I will be going* or (2) *Me will be going*. The second choice cannot be correct because *me* cannot be used as the subject of a sentence. Instead, *me* is used as an object.

Answer: Bob and I will be going.

When a pronoun is used with a noun immediately following (as in "we boys"), try the sentence **without the added noun**.

Example:

(We/Us) boys played football last year.

Test: (1) *We played football last ye*ar or (2) *Us played football last year*. Again, the second choice cannot be correct because *us* cannot be used as a subject of a sentence. Instead, *us* is used as an object.

Answer: We boys played football last year.

> **Review Video: Pronoun Usage**
> Visit mometrix.com/academy and enter code: 666500
>
> **Review Video: What is Pronoun-Antecedent Agreement?**
> Visit mometrix.com/academy and enter code: 919704

A pronoun should point clearly to the **antecedent**. Here is how a pronoun reference can be unhelpful if it is puzzling or not directly stated.

        antecedent   pronoun

Unhelpful: Ron and Jim went to the store, and he bought soda.

Who bought soda? Ron or Jim?

        antecedent   pronoun

Helpful: Jim went to the store, and he bought soda.

The sentence is clear. Jim bought the soda.

Some pronouns change their form by their placement in a sentence. A pronoun that is a **subject** in a sentence comes in the **subjective case**. Pronouns that serve as **objects** appear in the **objective case**. Finally, the pronouns that are used as **possessives** appear in the **possessive case**.

Examples:

Subjective case: *He* is coming to the show.

The pronoun *He* is the subject of the sentence.

Objective case: Josh drove *him* to the airport.

The pronoun *him* is the object of the sentence.

Possessive case: The flowers are *mine*.

The pronoun *mine* shows ownership of the flowers.

The word *who* is a subjective-case pronoun that can be used as a **subject**. The word *whom* is an objective-case pronoun that can be used as an **object**. The words *who* and *whom* are common in subordinate clauses or in questions.

English

Examples:

He knows <u>who</u> (subject) <u>wants</u> (verb) to come.

He knows the man <u>whom</u> (object) we <u>want</u> (verb) at the party.

CLAUSES

A clause is a group of words that contains both a subject and a predicate (verb). There are two types of clauses: independent and dependent. An **independent clause** contains a complete thought, while a **dependent (or subordinate) clause** does not. A dependent clause includes a subject and a verb, and may also contain objects or complements, but it cannot stand as a complete thought without being joined to an independent clause. Dependent clauses function within sentences as adjectives, adverbs, or nouns.

Example:

<u>I am running</u> (independent clause) <u>because I want to stay in shape.</u> (dependent clause)

The clause *I am running* is an independent clause: it has a subject and a verb, and it gives a complete thought. The clause *because I want to stay in shape* is a dependent clause: it has a subject and a verb, but it does not express a complete thought. It adds detail to the independent clause to which it is attached.

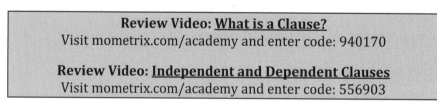

> **Review Video: What is a Clause?**
> Visit mometrix.com/academy and enter code: 940170
>
> **Review Video: Independent and Dependent Clauses**
> Visit mometrix.com/academy and enter code: 556903

TYPES OF DEPENDENT CLAUSES
ADJECTIVE CLAUSES

An **adjective clause** is a dependent clause that modifies a noun or a pronoun. Adjective clauses begin with a relative pronoun (*who, whose, whom, which,* and *that*) or a relative adverb (*where, when,* and *why*).

Also, adjective clauses come after the noun that the clause needs to explain or rename. This is done to have a clear connection to the independent clause.

Examples:

<u>I learned the reason</u> (independent clause) <u>why I won the award.</u> (adjective clause)

<u>This is the place</u> (independent clause) <u>where I started my first job.</u> (adjective clause)

An adjective clause can be an essential or nonessential clause. An essential clause is very important to the sentence. **Essential clauses** explain or define a person or thing. **Nonessential clauses** give

270

more information about a person or thing but are not necessary to define them. Nonessential clauses are set off with commas while essential clauses are not.

Examples:

essential
clause

A person who works hard at first can often rest later in life.

nonessential
clause

Neil Armstrong, who walked on the moon, is my hero.

| **Review Video: Adjective Clauses and Phrases** |
| Visit mometrix.com/academy and enter code: 520888 |

ADVERB CLAUSES

An **adverb clause** is a dependent clause that modifies a verb, adjective, or adverb. In sentences with multiple dependent clauses, adverb clauses are usually placed immediately before or after the independent clause. An adverb clause is introduced with words such as *after, although, as, before, because, if, since, so, unless, when, where*, and *while*.

Examples:

adverb
clause

When you walked outside, I called the manager.

adverb
clause

I will go with you unless you want to stay.

NOUN CLAUSES

A **noun clause** is a dependent clause that can be used as a subject, object, or complement. Noun clauses begin with words such as *how, that, what, whether, which, who,* and *why*. These words can also come with an adjective clause. Unless the noun clause is being used as the subject of the sentence, it should come after the verb of the independent clause.

Examples:

noun
clause

The real mystery is how you avoided serious injury.

noun
clause

What you learn from each other depends on your honesty with others.

SUBORDINATION

When two related ideas are not of equal importance, the ideal way to combine them is to make the more important idea an independent clause and the less important idea a dependent or subordinate clause. This is called **subordination**.

Example:

> **Separate ideas**: The team had a perfect regular season. The team lost the championship.

> **Subordinated**: Despite having a perfect regular season, *the team lost the championship.*

PHRASES

A phrase is a group of words that functions as a single part of speech, usually a noun, adjective, or adverb. A **phrase** is not a complete thought, but it adds detail or explanation to a sentence, or renames something within the sentence.

PREPOSITIONAL PHRASES

One of the most common types of phrases is the prepositional phrase. A **prepositional phrase** begins with a preposition and ends with a noun or pronoun that is the object of the preposition. Normally, the prepositional phrase functions as an **adjective** or an **adverb** within the sentence.

Examples:

prepositional
phrase

The picnic is on the blanket.

prepositional
phrase

I am sick with a fever today.

prepositional
phrase

Among the many flowers, John found a four-leaf clover.

VERBAL PHRASES

A **verbal** is a word or phrase that is formed from a verb but does not function as a verb. Depending on its particular form, it may be used as a noun, adjective, or adverb. A verbal does **not** replace a verb in a sentence.

Examples:

verb

Correct: Walk a mile daily.

This is a complete sentence with the implied subject *you*.

verbal

Incorrect: To walk a mile.

This is not a sentence since there is no functional verb.

There are three types of verbal: **participles**, **gerunds**, and **infinitives**. Each type of verbal has a corresponding **phrase** that consists of the verbal itself along with any complements or modifiers.

272

PARTICIPLES

A **participle** is a type of verbal that always functions as an adjective. The present participle always ends with *-ing*. Past participles end with *-d, -ed, -n,* or *-t*.

Examples: dance | dancing | danced
(verb | present participle | past participle)

Participial phrases most often come right before or right after the noun or pronoun that they modify.

Examples:

participial phrase
Shipwrecked on an island, the boys started to fish for food.

participial phrase
Having been seated for five hours, we got out of the car to stretch our legs.

participial phrase
Praised for their work, the group accepted the first-place trophy.

GERUNDS

A **gerund** is a type of verbal that always functions as a **noun**. Like present participles, gerunds always end with *-ing*, but they can be easily distinguished from one another by the part of speech they represent (participles always function as adjectives). Since a gerund or gerund phrase always functions as a noun, it can be used as the subject of a sentence, the predicate nominative, or the object of a verb or preposition.

Examples:

gerund
We want to be known for teaching the poor.
object of preposition

gerund
Coaching this team is the best job of my life.
subject

gerund
We like practicing our songs in the basement.
object of verb

INFINITIVES

An **infinitive** is a type of verbal that can function as a noun, an adjective, or an adverb. An infinitive is made of the word *to* and the basic form of the verb. As with all other types of verbal phrases, an infinitive phrase includes the verbal itself and all of its complements or modifiers.

English

273

Examples:

infinitive

To join the team is my goal in life.

noun

infinitive

The animals have enough food to eat for the night.

adjective

infinitive

People lift weights to exercise their muscles.

adverb

> **Review Video: Gerunds, Infinitives, and Participles**
> Visit mometrix.com/academy and enter code: 634263

APPOSITIVE PHRASES

An **appositive** is a word or phrase that is used to explain or rename nouns or pronouns. Noun phrases, gerund phrases, and infinitive phrases can all be used as appositives.

Examples:

appositive

Terriers, hunters at heart, have been dressed up to look like lap dogs.

The noun phrase *hunters at heart* renames the noun *terriers*.

appositive

His plan, to save and invest his money, was proven as a safe approach.

The infinitive phrase explains what the plan is.

Appositive phrases can be **essential** or **nonessential**. An appositive phrase is essential if the person, place, or thing being described or renamed is too general for its meaning to be understood without the appositive.

Examples:

essential

Two of America's Founding Fathers, George Washington and Thomas Jefferson, served as presidents.

nonessential

George Washington and Thomas Jefferson, two Founding Fathers, served as presidents.

ABSOLUTE PHRASES

An absolute phrase is a phrase that consists of **a noun followed by a participle**. An absolute phrase provides **context** to what is being described in the sentence, but it does not modify or explain any particular word; it is essentially independent.

Examples:

noun — The alarm   participle — ringing,   he pushed the snooze button.
absolute phrase

noun — The music   participle — paused,   she continued to dance through the crowd.
absolute phrase

PARALLELISM

When multiple items or ideas are presented in a sentence in series, such as in a list, the items or ideas must be stated in grammatically equivalent ways. In other words, if one idea is stated in gerund form, the second cannot be stated in infinitive form. For example, to write, *I enjoy reading and to study* would be incorrect. An infinitive and a gerund are not equivalent. Instead, you should write *I enjoy reading and studying*. In lists of more than two, all items must be parallel.

Example:

Incorrect: He stopped at the office, grocery store, and the pharmacy before heading home.

The first and third items in the list of places include the article *the*, so the second item needs it as well.

Correct: He stopped at the office, *the* grocery store, and the pharmacy before heading home.

Example:

Incorrect: While vacationing in Europe, she went biking, skiing, and climbed mountains.

The first and second items in the list are gerunds, so the third item must be as well.

Correct: While vacationing in Europe, she went biking, skiing, and *mountain climbing*.

> **Review Video: Parallel Construction**
> Visit mometrix.com/academy and enter code: 831988

SENTENCE PURPOSE

There are four types of sentences: declarative, imperative, interrogative, and exclamatory.

A **declarative** sentence states a fact and ends with a period.

> *The football game starts at seven o'clock.*

An **imperative** sentence tells someone to do something and generally ends with a period. An urgent command might end with an exclamation point instead.

> *Don't forget to buy your ticket.*

An **interrogative** sentence asks a question and ends with a question mark.

> *Are you going to the game on Friday?*

English

An **exclamatory** sentence shows strong emotion and ends with an exclamation point.

I can't believe we won the game!

Review Video: Functions of a Sentence
Visit mometrix.com/academy and enter code: 475974

SENTENCE STRUCTURE

Sentences are classified by structure based on the type and number of clauses present. The four classifications of sentence structure are the following:

Simple: A simple sentence has one independent clause with no dependent clauses. A simple sentence may have **compound elements** (i.e., compound subject or verb).

Examples:

single subject · single verb
Judy watered the lawn.

compound subject · single verb
Judy and Alan watered the lawn.

single subject · compound verb · compound verb
Judy watered the lawn and pulled weeds.

compound subject · compound verb · compound verb
Judy and Alan watered the lawn and pulled weeds.

Compound: A compound sentence has two or more independent clauses with no dependent clauses. Usually, the independent clauses are joined with a comma and a coordinating conjunction or with a semicolon.

Examples:

independent clause · independent clause
The time has come, and we are ready.

independent clause · independent clause
I woke up at dawn; the sun was just coming up.

Complex: A complex sentence has one independent clause and at least one dependent clause.

Examples:

dependent clause · independent clause
Although he had the flu, Harry went to work.

independent clause · dependent clause
Marcia got married, after she finished college.

Copyright © Mometrix Media. You have been licensed one copy of this document for personal use only. Any other reproduction or redistribution is strictly prohibited. All rights reserved. This content is provided for test preparation purposes only and does not imply an endorsement by Mometrix of any particular political, scientific, or religious point of view.

Compound-Complex: A compound-complex sentence has at least two independent clauses and at least one dependent clause.

Examples:

```
    independent            dependent                  independent
      clause                clause                       clause
```
John is my friend who went to India, and he brought back souvenirs.

```
    independent                    independent                dependent
      clause                         clause                     clause
```
You may not realize this, but we heard the music that you played last night.

> **Review Video: Sentence Structure**
> Visit mometrix.com/academy and enter code: 700478

Sentence variety is important to consider when writing an essay or speech. A variety of sentence lengths and types creates rhythm, makes a passage more engaging, and gives writers an opportunity to demonstrate their writing style. Writing that uses the same length or type of sentence without variation can be boring or difficult to read. To evaluate a passage for effective sentence variety, it is helpful to note whether the passage contains diverse sentence structures and lengths. It is also important to pay attention to the way each sentence starts and avoid beginning with the same words or phrases.

SENTENCE FRAGMENTS

Recall that a group of words must contain at least one **independent clause** in order to be considered a sentence. If it doesn't contain even one independent clause, it is called a **sentence fragment**.

The appropriate process for **repairing** a sentence fragment depends on what type of fragment it is. If the fragment is a dependent clause, it can sometimes be as simple as removing a subordinating word (e.g., when, because, if) from the beginning of the fragment. Alternatively, a dependent clause can be incorporated into a closely related neighboring sentence. If the fragment is missing some required part, like a subject or a verb, the fix might be as simple as adding the missing part.

Examples:

Fragment: Because he wanted to sail the Mediterranean.

Removed subordinating word: He wanted to sail the Mediterranean.

Combined with another sentence: Because he wanted to sail the Mediterranean, he booked a Greek island cruise.

RUN-ON SENTENCES

Run-on sentences consist of multiple independent clauses that have not been joined together properly. Run-on sentences can be corrected in several different ways:

Join clauses properly: This can be done with a comma and coordinating conjunction, with a semicolon, or with a colon or dash if the second clause is explaining something in the first.

Example:

> **Incorrect**: I went on the trip, we visited lots of castles.

> **Corrected**: I went on the trip, and we visited lots of castles.

Split into separate sentences: This correction is most effective when the independent clauses are very long or when they are not closely related.

Example:

> **Incorrect**: The drive to New York takes ten hours, my uncle lives in Boston.

> **Corrected**: The drive to New York takes ten hours. My uncle lives in Boston.

Make one clause dependent: This is the easiest way to make the sentence correct and more interesting at the same time. It's often as simple as adding a subordinating word between the two clauses or before the first clause.

Example:

> **Incorrect**: I finally made it to the store and I bought some eggs.

> **Corrected**: When I finally made it to the store, I bought some eggs.

Reduce to one clause with a compound verb: If both clauses have the same subject, remove the subject from the second clause, and you now have just one clause with a compound verb.

Example:

> **Incorrect**: The drive to New York takes ten hours, it makes me very tired.

> **Corrected**: The drive to New York takes ten hours and makes me very tired.

Note: While these are the simplest ways to correct a run-on sentence, often the best way is to completely reorganize the thoughts in the sentence and rewrite it.

> **Review Video: <u>Fragments and Run-on Sentences</u>**
> Visit mometrix.com/academy and enter code: 541989

DANGLING AND MISPLACED MODIFIERS

DANGLING MODIFIERS

A dangling modifier is a dependent clause or verbal phrase that does not have a clear logical connection to a word in the sentence.

Example:

                    dangling
                    modifier

Incorrect: Reading each magazine article, the stories caught my attention.

The word *stories* cannot be modified by *Reading each magazine article*. People can read, but stories cannot read. Therefore, the subject of the sentence must be a person.

                    dependent
                    clause

Corrected: Reading each magazine article, I was entertained by the stories.

Example:

                    dangling
                    modifier

Incorrect: Ever since childhood, my grandparents have visited me for Christmas.

The speaker in this sentence can't have been visited by her grandparents when *they* were children, since she wouldn't have been born yet. Either the modifier should be clarified or the sentence should be rearranged to specify whose childhood is being referenced.

                    dependent
                    clause

Clarified: Ever since I was a child, my grandparents have visited for Christmas.

                                                    dependent
                                                    clause

Rearranged: I have enjoyed my grandparents visiting for Christmas, ever since childhood.

MISPLACED MODIFIERS

Because modifiers are grammatically versatile, they can be put in many different places within the structure of a sentence. The danger of this versatility is that a modifier can accidentally be placed where it is modifying the wrong word or where it is not clear which word it is modifying.

Example:

                                            modifier

Incorrect: She read the book to a crowd that was filled with beautiful pictures.

The book was filled with beautiful pictures, not the crowd.

                                    modifier

Corrected: She read the book that was filled with beautiful pictures to a crowd.

279

Example:

modifier

Ambiguous: Derek saw a bus nearly hit a man on his way to work.

Was Derek on his way to work or was the other man?

modifier

Derek: On his way to work, Derek saw a bus nearly hit a man.

modifier

The other man: Derek saw a bus nearly hit a man who was on his way to work.

SPLIT INFINITIVES

A split infinitive occurs when a modifying word comes between the word *to* and the verb that pairs with *to*.

Example: To *clearly* explain vs. *To explain* clearly | To *softly* sing vs. *To sing* softly

Though considered improper by some, split infinitives may provide better clarity and simplicity in some cases than the alternatives. As such, avoiding them should not be considered a universal rule.

DOUBLE NEGATIVES

Standard English allows **two negatives** only when a **positive** meaning is intended. For example, *The team was not displeased with their performance*. Double negatives to emphasize negation are not used in standard English.

Negative modifiers (e.g., never, no, and not) should not be paired with other negative modifiers or negative words (e.g., none, nobody, nothing, or neither). The modifiers *hardly, barely*, and *scarcely* are also considered negatives in standard English, so they should not be used with other negatives.

SENTENCE STRUCTURE CHAPTER QUIZ

1. Which of the following is an imperative statement?

    a. John knows the way to the park.
    b. There are five letters on the table for him.
    c. Go to the post office for me.
    d. The cookies need ten more minutes.

2. Which of the following is NOT a word used to combine nouns to make a compound subject?

    a. Or
    b. Nor
    c. And
    d. Also

3. Which of the following is always singular?

    a. Each
    b. Both
    c. Several
    d. Many

4. Which of the following is the indirect object of the sentence, "I gave my mother yellow roses"?

    a. I
    b. gave
    c. my mother
    d. yellow roses

5. Which of the following is the infinitive of the sentence, "He had all the time in the world to decide what he wanted"?

    a. He had
    b. all the time in the world
    c. to decide
    d. what he wanted

Answers for all of the chapter quiz questions can be found right before Practice Test #1.

English

Knowledge of Language

USING GRAMMAR TO ENHANCE CLARITY IN WRITING

Writers must take care to use proper grammar and write clearly to help the reader understand their writing. The use of complete sentences is important to writing clearly with proper grammar, so writers should ensure that each sentence has at least a subject and a predicate. Writers must also use correct verb tenses to guide the reader through the order or time of any events described in their work. Sometimes, certain types of writing will require the use of a particular tense. For example, in academic writing, writers should use one tense consistently and are often instructed to write in the present tense. Writers should also take care with their word choice to ensure that they are communicating their message as clearly and precisely as possible. Word choice also impacts tone, so writers should pay attention to the tone their work conveys and adjust their word choice if the tone is inappropriate.

TRANSITIONS

Transitions between sentences and paragraphs guide readers from idea to idea and indicate relationships between sentences and paragraphs. Writers should be judicious in their use of transitions, inserting them sparingly. They should also be selected to fit the author's purpose—transitions can indicate time, comparison, and conclusion, among other purposes. Tone is also important to consider when using transitional phrases, varying the tone for different audiences. For example, in a scholarly essay, *in summary* would be preferable to the more informal *in short*.

When working with transitional words and phrases, writers usually find a natural flow that indicates when a transition is needed. In reading a draft of the text, it should become apparent where the flow is disrupted. At this point, the writer can add transitional elements during the revision process. Revising can also afford an opportunity to delete transitional devices that seem heavy handed or unnecessary.

> **Review Video: Transitions in Writing**
> Visit mometrix.com/academy and enter code: 233246

TYPES OF TRANSITIONAL WORDS

Time	Afterward, immediately, earlier, meanwhile, recently, lately, now, since, soon, when, then, until, before, etc.
Sequence	too, first, second, further, moreover, also, again, and, next, besides, finally
Comparison	similarly, in the same way, likewise, also, again, once more
Contrasting	but, although, despite, however, instead, nevertheless, on the one hand... on the other hand, regardless, yet, in contrast.
Cause and Effect	because, consequently, thus, therefore, then, to this end, since, so, as a result, if... then, accordingly
Examples	for example, for instance, such as, to illustrate, indeed, in fact, specifically
Place	near, far, here, there, to the left/right, next to, above, below, beyond, opposite, beside
Concession	granted that, naturally, of course, it may appear, although it is true that
Repetition, Summary, or Conclusion	as mentioned earlier, as noted, in other words, in short, on the whole, to summarize, therefore, as a result, to conclude, in conclusion
Addition	and, also, furthermore, moreover
Generalization	in broad terms, broadly speaking, in general

Mometrix

IDENTIFYING THE NARRATOR'S SETTING

When writing for a particular purpose, writers make careful choices about the diction and structure used in their writing. In narrative or informal writing, a writer may include slang or colloquialisms. These words can be used to show the reader the setting of the text if it is not stated. These terms can reveal the time period in addition to the location, as slang terms often change between each generation or decade. A writer must also make decisions that reflect the level of formality that is appropriate for his or her purpose. The inclusion of personal writing style or a particular tone can also reflect the level of formality or the writer's purpose. Detecting the level of formality can help readers narrow down the specific context of a written text, as writers will address people of different ranks or relationship to the writer with different diction and formality. Paying attention to these factors can reveal the writer's purpose and the audience for the text if these are not already clear to the reader.

INFORMAL AND FORMAL LANGUAGE

The relationship between writer and reader is important in choosing a **level of formality** as most writing requires some degree of formality. **Formal writing** is for addressing a superior in a school or work environment. Business letters, textbooks, and newspapers use a moderate to high level of formality. **Informal writing** is appropriate for *private letters, personal e-mails, and business correspondence between close associates.*

For your exam, you will want to be aware of informal and formal writing. One way that this can be accomplished is to watch for shifts in point of view in the essay. For example, unless writers are using a personal example, they will rarely refer to themselves (e.g., "*I* think that *my* point is very clear.") to avoid being informal when they need to be formal.

Also, be mindful of an author who addresses his or her audience **directly** in their writing (e.g., "Readers, *like you*, will understand this argument.") as this can be a sign of informal writing. Good writers understand the need to be consistent with their level of formality. Shifts in levels of formality or point of view can confuse readers and discount the message of an author's writing.

CLICHÉS

Clichés are phrases that have been **overused** to the point that the phrase has no importance or has lost the original meaning. The phrases have no originality and add very little to a passage. Therefore, most writers will avoid the use of clichés. Another option is to make changes to a cliché so that it is not predictable and empty of meaning.

Examples:

> When life gives you lemons, make lemonade.
> Every cloud has a silver lining.

JARGON

Jargon is a **specialized vocabulary** that is used among members of a trade or profession. Since jargon is understood by a small audience, writers tend to leave them to passages where certain readers will understand the vocabulary. Jargon includes exaggerated language that tries to impress rather than inform. Sentences filled with jargon are not precise and difficult to understand.

Examples:

> "He is going to *toenail* these frames for us." (toenailing refers to nailing at an angle)
> "They brought in a *kip* of material today." (a kip is a unit of measure equal to 1000 pounds)

SLANG

Slang is an **informal** and sometimes private language that is understood by some individuals. Slang has some usefulness, but the language can have a small audience. So, most formal writing will not include this kind of language.

Examples:

> "Yes, the event was a *blast*!" (the speaker means that the event was a great experience)
> "That attempt was an *epic fail*." (the speaker means that the attempt was a spectacular failure.)

COLLOQUIALISM

A colloquialism is a word or phrase that is found in informal writing. Unlike slang, **colloquial language** will be familiar to a greater range of people. Colloquial language can include some slang, but these are limited to contractions for the most part.

Examples:

> "Can *y'all* come back another time?" (y'all is a contraction of "you all")
> "Will you stop him from building this *castle in the air*?" (A "castle in the air" is an improbable or unlikely event.)

STYLE

Writing style can also be referred to as a writer's **voice**. When revising, writers should ensure that the style of their writing is consistent and compatible with their purpose for writing. A text's level of formality and purpose also inform how a writer conveys style, as these factors can limit word choice or the structure of a text. Writers' stylistic choices accomplish three basic effects on their audiences:

- They **communicate meanings** beyond explicitly stated meanings,
- They communicate the **author's attitude**, such as in persuasive or argumentative strategies accomplished through style, and
- They communicate or **express feelings**.

REVISING INFORMAL AND FORMAL LANGUAGE

If the purpose and audience of a text calls for the use of formal language, the writer must keep the formality of their writing in mind when revising and editing. To revise informal language, the writer must be aware of the different types of informal language to identify them in his or her writing. Additionally, the writer must be aware of alternative words and phrases that can be used to replace any informal writing. This may include changes such as simply using a more precise or formal synonym, but it also may require thinking carefully about the meaning of an informal phrase in order to rephrase it effectively. In either case, writers should be diligent and careful when revising to ensure that the formality of the piece is appropriate.

REVISING LANGUAGE FOR CULTURALLY-DIVERSE AUDIENCES

When writing for an audience that is diverse or likely to include individuals who are culturally different from the writer, the writer must respect these people as he or she considers word choice in the composition. This also applies during revising and editing, as the writer should be careful to identify and correct any clearly offensive or insensitive language. Such language may include gendered language, language that puts a person's condition or a physical attribute before the person, or language that encourages or aligns with stereotypes.

To revise gendered language, the writer can replace any words that are biased or directed toward men or women with language that includes all people. For example, *waitress* can be replaced with *server*. To revise language that names a person's condition or physical attributes before the person, people-first language can be used. For example, instead of the phrase "the blind person," a writer can use the phrase "the person who is blind" to list the individual before his or her condition or a physical attribute. Word choice that encourages a stereotype can be more complicated to revise. To revise stereotypes in writing, the writer must identify which part of their statement is prejudiced, biased, or stereotyping and identify how this is untrue. The writer must then use objective and truthful ideas and word choice to replace the inaccurate statement.

POINT OF VIEW

Point of view is the **perspective** from which writing occurs. There are several possibilities:

- **First person** is written so that the story is told by a participant or observer who is in the story and uses *I*.
- **Second person** is written directly to the reader. It is a device to draw the reader in more closely. In second person, "you," the reader, are the one taking action in the sentence.
- **Third person**, the most traditional form of point of view, is the omniscient narrator, in which the narrative voice, presumed to be the writer's, is presumed to know everything about the characters, plot, and action. Most writing uses this point of view.

> **Review Video: Point of View**
> Visit mometrix.com/academy and enter code: 383336

WELL-ORGANIZED PARAGRAPHS

After the introduction of a passage, a series of **body paragraphs** will carry a message through to the conclusion. A paragraph should be unified around a **main point**. Normally, a good **topic sentence** summarizes the paragraph's main point. A topic sentence is a general sentence that introduces the paragraph.

The sentences that follow are a **support** to the topic sentence. However, the topic sentence can come as the final sentence to the paragraph if the earlier sentences give a clear explanation of the topic sentence. Overall, paragraphs need to stay true to their main point. This means that any unnecessary sentences that do not advance the main point should be removed. Additionally, supporting details and sentences must sufficiently support the main point of the paragraph.

The **main point** of a paragraph requires adequate **development** (i.e., a substantial paragraph that covers the main point). A paragraph of only two or three sentences may not adequately cover a main point. An occasional short paragraph is fine as a **transitional device**. However, a well-developed argument will primarily consist of paragraphs with more than a few sentences.

Review Video: <u>Drafting Body Paragraphs</u>
Visit mometrix.com/academy and enter code: 724590

METHODS OF DEVELOPING PARAGRAPHS

A common method of development with paragraphs can be done with **examples**. These examples are the supporting details to the main idea of a paragraph or a passage. When authors write about something that their audience may not understand, they can provide an example to show their point. When authors write about something that is not easily accepted, they can give examples to prove their point.

Illustrations are extended examples that require several sentences. Well-selected illustrations can be a great way for authors to develop a point that may not be familiar to their audience.

Analogies make comparisons between items that appear to have nothing in common. Analogies are employed by writers to provoke fresh thoughts about a subject. These comparisons may be used to explain the unfamiliar, to clarify an abstract point, or to argue a point. Although analogies are effective *literary devices*, they should be used carefully in arguments. Two things may be alike in some respects but completely different in others.

Cause and effect is an excellent device used when the cause and effect are accepted as true. One way that authors can use cause and effect is to state the effect in the topic sentence of a paragraph and add the causes in the body of the paragraph. With this method, an author's paragraphs can have structure which always strengthens writing.

TYPES OF PARAGRAPHS

A **paragraph of narration** tells a story or a part of a story. Normally, the sentences are arranged in chronological order (i.e., the order that the events happened). However, flashbacks (i.e., beginning the story at an earlier time) can be included.

A **descriptive paragraph** makes a verbal portrait of a person, place, or thing. When specific details are used that appeal to one or more of the senses (i.e., sight, sound, smell, taste, and touch), authors give readers a sense of being present in the moment.

A **process paragraph** is related to time order (i.e., First, you open the bottle. Second, you pour the liquid, etc.). Usually, this describes a process or teaches readers how to perform a process.

Comparing two things draws attention to their similarities and indicates a number of differences. When authors **contrast**, they focus only on differences. Both comparisons and contrasts may be used point-by-point or in following paragraphs.

Reasons for starting a new paragraph include:

- To mark off the introduction and concluding paragraphs
- To signal a shift to a new idea or topic
- To indicate an important shift in time or place
- To explain a point in additional detail
- To highlight a comparison, contrast, or cause and effect relationship

PARAGRAPH LENGTH

Most readers find that their comfort level for a paragraph is *between 100 and 200 words*. Shorter paragraphs cause too much starting and stopping, and give a choppy effect. Paragraphs that are too long often test the attention span of readers. Two notable exceptions to this rule exist. In scientific or scholarly papers, longer paragraphs suggest seriousness and depth. In journalistic writing, constraints are placed on paragraph size by the narrow columns in a newspaper format.

The first and last paragraphs of a text will usually be the **introduction** and **conclusion**. These special-purpose paragraphs are likely to be shorter than paragraphs in the body of the work. Paragraphs in the body of the essay follow the subject's **outline**; one paragraph per point in short essays and a group of paragraphs per point in longer works. Some ideas require more development than others, so it is good for a writer to remain flexible. A paragraph of excessive length may be divided, and shorter ones may be combined.

COHERENT PARAGRAPHS

A smooth flow of sentences and paragraphs without gaps, shifts, or bumps will lead to paragraph **coherence**. Ties between old and new information can be smoothed by several methods:

- **Linking ideas clearly**, from the topic sentence to the body of the paragraph, is essential for a smooth transition. The topic sentence states the main point, and this should be followed by specific details, examples, and illustrations that support the topic sentence. The support may be direct or indirect. In **indirect support**, the illustrations and examples may support a sentence that in turn supports the topic directly.
- The **repetition of key words** adds coherence to a paragraph. To avoid dull language, variations of the key words may be used.
- **Parallel structures** are often used within sentences to emphasize the similarity of ideas and connect sentences giving similar information.
- Maintaining a **consistent verb tense** throughout the paragraph helps. Shifting tenses affects the smooth flow of words and can disrupt the coherence of the paragraph.

> **Review Video: How to Write a Good Paragraph**
> Visit mometrix.com/academy and enter code: 682127

English

KNOWLEDGE OF LANGUAGE CHAPTER QUIZ

1. Which of the following would NOT be considered formal writing?

    a. Private letters
    b. Business letters
    c. Textbooks
    d. Newspapers

2. Which of the following sentences contains a verb in the passive voice?

    a. The judges called the winners to the stage for their awards.
    b. Each applicant must fill out all of the forms required.
    c. He raced through the copse of trees with the grace of a deer.
    d. I was told that there would be food available at the party.

3. Which of the following refers to a phrase that has been overused to the point that it has lost the original meaning?

    a. Cliché
    b. Moot point
    c. Jargon
    d. Hyperbole

4. Which of the following refers to a comparison between items that appear to having nothing in common?

    a. Contrast
    b. Illustration
    c. Analogy
    d. Simile

5. Most writing uses which point of view?

    a. Fourth person
    b. Third person
    c. Second person
    d. First person

Answers for all of the chapter quiz questions can be found right before Practice Test #1.

Using Language and Vocabulary to Express Ideas in Writing

PRACTICE MAKES PREPARED WRITERS

Writing is a skill that continues to need development throughout a person's life. For some people, writing seems to be a natural gift. They rarely struggle with writer's block. When you read their papers, you likely find their ideas persuasive. For others, writing is an intimidating task that they endure. As you prepare for the test, believe that you can improve your skills and be better prepared for reviewing several types of writing.

A traditional way to prepare for the English and Language Usage Section is to **read**. When you read newspapers, magazines, and books, you learn about new ideas. You can read newspapers and magazines to become informed about issues that affect many people. As you think about those issues and ideas, you can take a **position** and form **opinions**. Try to develop these ideas and your opinions by sharing them with friends. After you develop your opinions, try **writing** them down as if you were going to spread your ideas beyond your friends.

Remember that you are practicing for more than an exam. Two of the most valuable skills in life are the abilities to **read critically** and to **write clearly**. When you work on evaluating the arguments of a passage and explaining your thoughts well, you develop skills that you will use for a lifetime.

ELEMENTS OF THE WRITING PROCESS

BRAINSTORMING

Brainstorming is a technique that is used to find a creative approach to a subject. This can be accomplished by simple **free-association** with a topic. For example, with paper and pen, write every thought that you have about the topic in a word or phrase. This is done without critical thinking. You should put everything that comes to your mind about the topic on your scratch paper. Then, you need to read the list over a few times. Next, look for patterns, repetitions, and clusters of ideas. This allows a variety of fresh ideas to come as you think about the topic.

FREE WRITING

Free writing is a more structured form of brainstorming. The method involves taking a limited amount of time (e.g., 2 to 3 minutes) to write everything that comes to mind about the topic in complete sentences. When time expires, review everything that has been written down. Many of your sentences may make little or no sense, but the insights and observations that can come from free writing make this method a valuable approach. Usually, free writing results in a fuller expression of ideas than brainstorming because thoughts and associations are written in complete sentences. However, both techniques can be used to complement each other.

PLANNING

Planning is the process of organizing a piece of writing before composing a draft. Planning can include creating an outline or a graphic organizer, such as a Venn diagram, a spider-map, or a flowchart. These methods should help the writer identify their topic, main ideas, and the general organization of the composition. Preliminary research can also take place during this stage. Planning helps writers organize all of their ideas and decide if they have enough material to begin their first draft. However, writers should remember that the decisions they make during this step will likely change later in the process, so their plan does not have to be perfect.

DRAFTING

Writers may then use their plan, outline, or graphic organizer to compose their first draft. They may write subsequent drafts to improve their writing. Writing multiple drafts can help writers consider different ways to communicate their ideas and address errors that may be difficult to correct without rewriting a section or the whole composition. Most writers will vary in how many drafts they choose to write, as there is no "right" number of drafts. Writing drafts also takes away the pressure to write perfectly on the first try, as writers can improve with each draft they write.

REVISING, EDITING, AND PROOFREADING

Once a writer completes a draft, they can move on to the revising, editing, and proofreading steps to improve their draft. These steps begin with making broad changes that may apply to large sections of a composition and then making small, specific corrections. **Revising** is the first and broadest of these steps. Revising involves ensuring that the composition addresses an appropriate audience, includes all necessary material, maintains focus throughout, and is organized logically. Revising may occur after the first draft to ensure that the following drafts improve upon errors from the first draft. Some revision should occur between each draft to avoid repeating these errors. The **editing** phase of writing is narrower than the revising phase. Editing a composition should include steps such as improving transitions between paragraphs, ensuring each paragraph is on topic, and improving the flow of the text. The editing phase may also include correcting grammatical errors that cannot be fixed without significantly altering the text. **Proofreading** involves fixing misspelled words, typos, other grammatical errors, and any remaining surface-level flaws in the composition.

RECURSIVE WRITING PROCESS

However you approach writing, you may find comfort in knowing that the revision process can occur in any order. The **recursive writing process** is not as difficult as the phrase may make it seem. Simply put, the recursive writing process means that you may need to revisit steps after completing other steps. Also implied in it is that there is no required order for the steps to take place. Indeed, you may find that **planning**, **drafting**, and **revising** (all a part of the writing process) can all take place at about the same time. The writing process involves moving back and forth between planning, drafting, and revising, followed by more planning, more drafting, and more revising until the writing is satisfactory.

> **Review Video: Recursive Writing Process**
> Visit mometrix.com/academy and enter code: 951611

IDENTIFYING WHEN A CITATION IS NEEDED
CITING SOURCES

While researchers should combine research with their own ideas, the information and ideas that come from outside sources should be attributed to the author of the source. When conducting research, it is helpful to record the publication information for each source so that **citations** can be easily added within the composition. Keeping a close record of the source of each idea in a composition or project is helpful for avoiding plagiarism, as both direct and indirect references require documentation.

PLAGIARISM

Understanding what is considered to be plagiarism is important to preventing unintentional plagiarism. Using another person's work in any way without proper attribution is **plagiarism**. However, it is easy to mistakenly commit plagiarism by improperly citing a source or creating a citation that is not intended for the way the source was used. Even when an honest attempt to attribute information is made, small errors can still result in plagiarized content. For this reason, it is important to create citations carefully and review citations before submitting or publishing research. When the information is the writer's own thoughts, opinions, or observations, the information does not need to be cited.

DETERMINING THE MEANING OF WORDS THROUGH STRUCTURAL ANALYSIS

An understanding of the basics of language is helpful, and often vital, to understanding what you read. The term **structural analysis** refers to looking at the parts of a word and breaking it down into its different **components** to determine the word's meaning. Parts of a word include prefixes, suffixes, and the root word. By learning the meanings of prefixes, suffixes, and other word fundamentals, you can decipher the meaning of words which may not yet be in your vocabulary.

Prefixes are common letter combinations at the beginning of words, while **suffixes** are common letter combinations at the end. The main part of the word is known as the **root**. Visually, it would look like this: prefix + root word + suffix. Look first at the individual meanings of the root word, prefix and/or suffix. Use knowledge of the meaning(s) of the prefix and/or suffix to see what information it adds to the root.

Even if the meaning of the root is unknown, one can use knowledge of the prefix's and/or suffix's meaning(s) to determine an *approximate meaning* of the word. For example, if one sees the word *uninspired* and does not know what it means, they can use the knowledge that *un-* means 'not' to know that the full word means "not inspired." Understanding the common prefixes and suffixes can illuminate at least part of the meaning of an unfamiliar word.

> **Review Video: <u>Determining Word Meanings</u>**
> Visit mometrix.com/academy and enter code: 894894

AFFIXES

Affixes in the English language are **morphemes** that are added to words to create related but different words. **Derivational affixes** form new words based on and related to the original words. For example, the affix *–ness* added to the end of the adjective *happy* forms the noun *happiness.*

Inflectional affixes form different grammatical versions of words. For example, the plural affix *–s* changes the singular noun *book* to the plural noun *books*, and the past tense affix *–ed* changes the infinitive or present tense verb *look* to the past tense *looked.*

Prefixes are affixes placed in front of words. For example, *heat* means to make hot; *preheat*, using the prefix *pre-*, means to heat in advance. **Suffixes** are affixes placed at the ends of words. The *happiness* example above contains the suffix *–ness.* **Circumfixes** add parts both before and after words, such as how *light* becomes *enlighten* with the prefix *en-* and the suffix *–en.* **Interfixes** compound words via central affixes: *speed* and *meter* become *speedometer* via the interfix *–o–.*

> **Review Video: <u>Affixes</u>**
> Visit mometrix.com/academy and enter code: 782422

PREFIXES

AMOUNT

Prefix	Definition	Examples
bi-	two	bisect, biennial
mono-	one, single	monogamy, monologue
poly-	many	polymorphous, polygamous
semi-	half, partly	semicircle, semicolon
uni-	one	uniform, unity

NEGATION

Prefix	Definition	Examples
a-	without, lacking	atheist, agnostic
in-	not, opposing	incapable, ineligible
non-	not	nonentity, nonsense
un-	not, reverse of	unhappy, unlock

TIME AND SPACE

Prefix	Definition	Examples
a-	in, on, of, up, to	abed, afoot
ab-	from, away, off	abdicate, abjure
ad-	to, toward	advance, adventure
ante-	before, previous	antecedent, antedate
anti-	against, opposing	antipathy, antidote
cata-	down, away, thoroughly	catastrophe, cataclysm
circum-	around	circumspect, circumference
com-	with, together, very	commotion, complicate
contra-	against, opposing	contradict, contravene
de-	from	depart
dia-	through, across, apart	diameter, diagnose
dis-	away, off, down, not	dissent, disappear
epi-	upon	epilogue
ex-	out	extract, excerpt
hypo-	under, beneath	hypodermic, hypothesis
inter-	among, between	intercede, interrupt
intra-	within	intramural, intrastate
ob-	against, opposing	objection
per-	through	perceive, permit
peri-	around	periscope, perimeter
post-	after, following	postpone, postscript
pre-	before, previous	prevent, preclude
pro-	forward, in place of	propel, pronoun
retro-	back, backward	retrospect, retrograde
sub-	under, beneath	subjugate, substitute
super-	above, extra	supersede, supernumerary
trans-	across, beyond, over	transact, transport
ultra-	beyond, excessively	ultramodern, ultrasonic, ultraviolet

MISCELLANEOUS

Prefix	Definition	Examples
belli-	war, warlike	bellicose
bene-	well, good	benefit, benefactor
equi-	equal	equivalent, equilibrium
for-	away, off, from	forget, forswear
fore-	previous	foretell, forefathers
homo-	same, equal	homogenized, homonym
hyper-	excessive, over	hypercritical, hypertension
in-	in, into	intrude, invade
magn-	large	magnitude, magnify
mal-	bad, poorly, not	malfunction, malpractice
mis-	bad, poorly, not	misspell, misfire
mor-	death	mortality, mortuary
neo-	new	Neolithic, neoconservative
omni-	all, everywhere	omniscient, omnivore
ortho-	right, straight	orthogonal, orthodox
over-	above	overbearing, oversight
pan-	all, entire	panorama, pandemonium
para-	beside, beyond	parallel, paradox
phil-	love, like	philosophy, philanthropic
prim-	first, early	primitive, primary
re-	backward, again	revoke, recur
sym-	with, together	sympathy, symphony
vis-	to see	visage, visible

SUFFIXES

Suffixes are a group of letters behind a root word that carry a specific meaning. Suffixes can perform one of two possible functions. They can be used to create a new word, or they can shift the tense of a word without changing its original meaning. For example, the suffix -*ability* can be added to the end of the word *account* to form the new word *accountability*. *Account* means a written narrative or description of events, while *accountability* means the state of being liable. The suffix -*ed* can be added to *account* to form the word *accounted*, which simply shifts the word from present tense to past tense.

Sometimes adding a suffix can change the **spelling** of a root word. If the suffix begins with a vowel, the final consonant of the root word must be doubled. This rule applies only if the root word has one syllable or if the accent is on the last syllable. For example, when adding the suffix -*ery* to the root word *rob*, the final word becomes *robbery*. The letter *b* is doubled because *rob* has only one syllable. However, when adding the suffix -*able* to the root word *profit*, the final word becomes *profitable*. The letter *t* is not doubled because the root word *profit* has two syllables.

Spelling is not changed when the suffixes -*less, -ness, -ly*, or -*en* are used. The only exception to this rule occurs when the suffix -*ness* or -*ly* is added to a root word ending in *y*. In this case, the *y* usually changes to *i*. For example, *happy* becomes *happily*.

Certain suffixes require that the root word be **modified**. If the suffix begins with a vowel, e.g., -*ing*, and the root word ends in the letter *e*, the *e* must be dropped before adding the suffix. For example, the word *write* becomes *writing*. If the suffix begins with a consonant instead of a vowel, the letter *e*

293

English

at the end of the root word does not need to be dropped. For example, *hope* becomes *hopeless*. The only exceptions to this rule are the words *judgment, acknowledgment,* and *argument.* If a root word ends in the letter *y* and is preceded by a consonant, the *y* is changed to *i* before adding the suffix. This is true for all suffixes except those that begin with *i*. For example, *plenty* becomes *plentiful*.

Here are some common suffixes, their meanings, and some examples of their use:

ADJECTIVE SUFFIXES

Suffix	Definition	Examples
-able (-ible)	capable of being	toler*able*, ed*ible*
-esque	in the style of, like	picturesque, grotesque
-ful	filled with, marked by	thankful, zestful
-ic	make, cause	terrific, beatific
-ish	suggesting, like	churlish, childish
-less	lacking, without	hopeless, countless
-ous	marked by, given to	religious, riotous

NOUN SUFFIXES

Suffix	Definition	Examples
-acy	state, condition	accuracy, privacy
-ance	act, condition, fact	acceptance, vigilance
-ard	one that does excessively	drunkard, sluggard
-ation	action, state, result	occupation, starvation
-dom	state, rank, condition	serfdom, wisdom
-er (-or)	office, action	teach*er*, elevat*or*, hon*or*
-ess	feminine	waitress, duchess
-hood	state, condition	manhood, statehood
-ion	action, result, state	union, fusion
-ism	act, manner, doctrine	barbarism, socialism
-ist	worker, follower	monopolist, socialist
-ity (-ty)	state, quality, condition	acid*ity*, civil*ity*, royal*ty*
-ment	result, action	refreshment, disappointment
-ness	quality, state	greatness, tallness
-ship	position	internship, citizenship
-sion (-tion)	state, result	revi*sion*, expedi*tion*
-th	act, state, quality	warmth, width
-tude	quality, state, result	magnitude, fortitude

VERB SUFFIXES

Suffix	Definition	Examples
-ate	having, showing	separate, desolate
-en	cause to be, become	deepen, strengthen
-fy	make, cause to have	glorify, fortify
-ize	cause to be, treat with	sterilize, mechanize, criticize

USING LANGUAGE AND VOCABULARY CHAPTER QUIZ

1. Which of the following is a more structured form of brainstorming?

    a. Free writing
    b. Planning
    c. Drafting
    d. Proofreading

2. Which of the following is a verb suffix?

    a. *-ism*
    b. *-fy*
    c. *-dom*
    d. *-ish*

3. Which of the following defines the miscellaneous prefix *mor-*?

    a. Away, off, from
    b. War, warlike
    c. Death
    d. Bad, poorly, not

4. Which of the following defines the noun suffix *-ation*?

    a. Act, condition, fact
    b. Action, state, result
    c. Act, manner, doctrine
    d. State, rank, condition

5. Which of the following affixes refers to the *-o-* in speedometer?

    a. Prefix
    b. Suffix
    c. Interfix
    d. Circumfix

Answers for all of the chapter quiz questions can be found right before Practice Test #1.

English

Chapter Quiz Answer Key

Reading

KEY IDEAS AND DETAILS

1. A: Summaries are often difficult to read because they omit all of the graceful language, digressions, and asides that distinguish great writing. However, an effective summary should contain much the same message as the original text. All of the significant supporting details should be included, and none of the details included should be irrelevant or insignificant.

2. A: A footnote is text at the bottom of a page which lists where facts and figures within that document page were obtained. An endnote is similar to a footnote but differs in the fact that it is listed at the end of paragraphs and chapters of a document instead of the bottom of each page of the document.

3. B: It is important to be careful to draw your conclusions from evidence directly supported in the text. This ensures you have come to a logical conclusion, which will help you determine whether you agree with the writer or not. If the author intended for the reader to draw a certain conclusion, then you can expect the arguments and details presented will lead you to that conclusion. Sometimes, several conclusions can be drawn from the same passage, but you must be careful that they are actually supported by the text.

4. B: Topic sentences should encapsulate the main idea of a text. In some textbooks and academic articles, the author will place a topic or summary sentence at the beginning of each section as a means of preparing the reader for what is to come. Research suggests that the brain is more receptive to new information when it has been prepared by the presentation of the main idea or some key words. The phenomenon is somewhat akin to the primer coat of paint that allows subsequent coats of paint to absorb more easily.

5. C: Implications are things that the author does not state directly but readers can assume based on what the author does say. In the sentence in question: *I hurried as fast as I could to class, only to find the test had already started when I arrived*, the author doesn't mention the wrong class or talk about how difficult the test is. It is safe to conclude that the author was late to class, but there isn't enough information to assume that she's late because she stayed up to late.

6. A: A line graph is a type of graph that is typically used for measuring trends over time. Bar graphs are used to illustrate numerical sets of data. Pie charts are circular graphs that are divided into sections to show how something is composed, such as the different expenses in a budget. A flow chart is a diagram that shows a workflow or process. It is typically composed of boxes (or some other shape) connected with lines and arrows to show the order in which steps occur.

CRAFT AND STRUCTURE

1. A: The claim that basketball is the best is highly subjective and unable to be conclusively proven, so it is an opinion. There are many ways someone could disagree with the claim that basketball is the best sport. They could think that maintaining constant action isn't what makes a sport great, or they could think that there is another sport that contains more action. Choices B and D are very clearly facts. It is simply true that Stephen has a meeting and that Jim's team hasn't made it to the playoffs in three years. At first glance, choice C may seem like an opinion, but it is not actually stating that orange is the best color. It is simply stating the fact that orange is Mark's favorite color.

2. C: Figurative language is language that does not mean exactly what was actually written. Literal language is language that can be taken at face value, such as statements of fact. Figurative language is often symbolic or contains implied meaning to stimulate the imagination. Exaggeration is a type of figurative language. When you compare two things, you are using figurative language. Similes and metaphors are both ways of comparing things, and both are types of figurative language commonly found in poetry.

3. B: Personification is the description of a nonhuman thing as if the item were human. It often serves to make things more comprehensible to the reader or to inspire the imagination. Choice B is the only option listed that has a nonhuman subject, so it is the only sentence listed that can contain personification. The swans are not literally dancing, but applying the word *dancing* to their movements helps the reader to imagine how beautiful they looked swimming on the surface of the water.

4. C: A simile is a figurative expression used to express comparisons, similarly to metaphors. Unlike metaphors, similes use the distancing words *like* or *as*. Choice C is the only option listed that contains this sentence construction. Specifically, "he's as stubborn *as* a mule" is the part of the sentence that contains the simile. None of the other sentences contain similes or comparisons.

5. B: Metaphors are like similes in that they are used to express comparisons, but metaphors do so in a way that allows the author to describe an item without being direct and obvious. Instead of using *like* or *as*, metaphors state that one thing *is* another thing. Choice B uses metaphor by saying that the snow *is* a quilt blanketing the small town. The other answer choices don't contain a metaphor or a comparison of any kind.

INTEGRATION OF KNOWLEDGE AND IDEAS

1. B: The bandwagon approach is the claim that an opinion is correct because it is held by the majority. Traditionalism is the belief that it is right to continue to do or believe things because that is what was done in the past. Testimonials are reviews and statements made by people to testify to the quality or worth of a product, service, person, or organization, depending on the context.

2. D: There are six major types of logical organization that are frequently used: illustrations, definitions, division/classification, comparing and contrasting, cause and effect, and problem and solution. Illustrations are extended examples used to support the thesis. Examples are the most common form of this organization. Definitions say what something is or is not. Dividing or classifying information into separate items according to their similarities is a common and effective organizing method. Comparing focuses on the similarities between things, and contrasting focuses on the differences between things. Cause and effect is a simple tool to logically understand relationships between things. Problem and solution is a simple and effective manner of logically organizing material. It is very commonly used and lucidly presents information.

3. A, B, D, E: Text evidence can take many forms, as the genre and form of a text can allude to its purpose. The context of a text may also guide the reader's predictions, conclusions, and interpretations. Evidence can most commonly be found as explicit and implicit information in a text. This information can help readers make inferences, but often, the reader will have to combine this information with their own knowledge or other information to make full conclusions, predictions, or interpretations. The author's name has no bearing on the content of their writing.

4. C: A primary source is the evidence closest to the subject being studied. An autobiography would be a primary source because it is written by the subject it is about. A bibliography is a compliation of sources, not a primary source. If you are studying a particular movie, a movie review would be a secondary source, and the movie you plan to write about would be the primary source. However, if you are using a movie as a source for real-life events, the movie would be a secondary source and documents or footage from the actual events would be primary sources.

5. D: Argumentative and persuasive passages take a stand on a debatable issue, seek to explore all sides of the issue, and aim to find the best possible solution. Argumentative and persuasive passages should not be combative or abusive. The word *argument* may remind you of two or more people shouting at each other and walking away in anger. However, an argumentative or persuasive passage should be a calm and reasonable presentation of an author's ideas for others to consider. When an author writes reasonable arguments, his or her goal is not to win or have the last word. Instead, authors want to reveal current understanding of the question at hand and suggest a solution to a problem. The purpose of argument and persuasion in a free society is to reach the best solution.

Mathematics

Answers for the math quizzes are provided immediately following the questions.

Science

HUMAN ANATOMY AND PHYSIOLOGY

1. B: There are three primary body planes: sagittal, coronal, and transverse. The sagittal plane runs parallel to the midline of the body and divides the body into right and left sections. The coronal (or frontal) plane runs vertically through the body at right angles to the midline and divides the body vertically into front and back (anterior and posterior) sections. The transverse (or horizontal) plane divides the patient's body into imaginary upper (superior) and lower (inferior or caudal) halves.

2. D: Heart rate regulation is controlled by the autonomic nervous system, not the respiratory system. Secondary functions of the respiratory system include pH regulation of the blood, thermoregulation, odor detection, and the production of speech.

3. A: All answer choices aid in immune defense, but only immunoglobulin A (IgA) is produced in the mucosal lining. These antibodies aid in immune defenses by neutralizing pathogens. T cells, B cells, and eosinophils are derived from stem cells (multipotent hematopoietic stem cells) and are produced in the bone marrow. However, T cells complete their development in the thymus.

4. C: The posterior area of the brain that is connected to the spinal cord is known as the brain stem. The midbrain, the pons, and the medulla oblongata are the three parts of the brain stem. The hypothalamus is part of the forebrain.

5. D: Each heart beat is seen as three major waves or complexes on an ECG. The heart rhythm begins in the sinoatrial node and leads to atrial depolarization. The P wave represents depolarization of the atria on an ECG. This is followed by the QRS interval, which represents depolarization of the ventricle. Next follows the ST segment and T wave, corresponding to repolarization of the ventricle. A small U wave may follow the T wave and represents further repolarization of the ventricle.

6. B: Saliva contains a variety of solutes, many of which are enzymes. Salivary amylase begins the chemical breakdown of polysaccharides into simpler sugars, lingual lipase begins the breakdown of fats, pepsin begins the breakdown of proteins, and cholinesterase begins the breakdown of acetylcholine.

7. A: The stomach itself can be divided into four main parts: the cardiac region, the fundus, the body, and the pylorus. The cardiac region is the area where food is emptied into the stomach. The fundus is the most superior region of the stomach, and the body is the largest, most central region. The body curves toward the right to form a "J" shape, with a lesser curvature and a greater curvature. It then narrows into a funnel-shaped region called the pylorus.

8. D: One sarcomere is separated from another by a boundary called the Z line, where a network of proteins serves as a point of anchorage for actin (thin filaments).

9. C: The ovarian cycle has three phases: the follicular phase, ovulation, and the luteal phase. The proliferative phase is part of the uterine cycle.

10. A: T cells mature in the thymus, and are involved in cell-mediated immunity. The initial activation of T cells occurs when they encounter their specific antigen on the surface of an antigen-presenting cell (or APC).

BIOLOGY

1. D: A colligative property is a property of a solution that depends only on the *amount* of solute, and not the size, mass, or chemical nature of the solute. Osmotic pressure, the minimum amount of pressure required to stop the diffusion of pure water across the membrane, is a colligative property because it is determined by the concentration of solute.

2. D: Osmosis is the passive transport of water across the membrane. Most polar molecules cannot use simple diffusion, but water molecules are small enough to slowly squeeze between the phospholipids. Water can also use channel proteins called aquaporins to increase the rate of osmosis.

3. A: Mutations of the hydrolases within the lysosomes are associated with a number of lysosomal storage diseases, including Tay-Sachs. Pfeiffer syndrome is a genetic disorder caused by a mutation in the FGFG genes. Myasthenia gravis is a chronic autoimmune disease where antibodies affect the communication between nerves and muscles. Wernicke encephalopathy is a degenerative brain disorder caused by a lack of vitamin B1.

4. B: The five bases in DNA and RNA can be categorized as either pyrimidine or purine according to their structure. The pyrimidine bases include cytosine, thymine, and uracil. They are six-sided and have a single ring shape. The purine bases are adenine and guanine, which consist of two attached rings.

5. A: A codon is three adjacent nucleotides and has the code for a single amino acid. There are 64 codons but 20 amino acids. For example, AAAUCUUCGU, if read in groups of three from the beginning, would be AAA, UCU, UCG, which are codons for lysine, serine, and serine, respectively. If the same sequence was read in groups of three starting from the second position, the groups would be AAU (asparagine), CUU (proline), and so on. The resulting amino acids would be completely different. For this reason, there are start and stop codons that indicate the beginning and ending of a sequence (or frame). AUG (methionine) is the start codon. UAA, UGA, and UAG are stop codons.

6. D: Genetic crosses are the possible combinations of alleles and can be represented using Punnett squares. Typically, the ratio of dominant gene manifestation to recessive gene manifestation is 3:1 (DD, Dd, Dd, dd). This ratio occurs when both parents are heterozygous, or have a dominant and recessive allele.

7. D: Co-dominance refers to the expression of both alleles so that both traits are shown. Cows, for example, can have hair colors of red, white, or red and white (not pink). In red and white cows, both traits are fully expressed. The ABO human blood typing system is also co-dominant.

8. C: Medical professionals must understand all five components of the cycle of infection to prevent the spread of disease. All of these factors must be present for an infection to transpire: a reservoir host, portal of exit, method of transmission, route of entrance, and a susceptible host.

9. B: Common gram-negative bacilli (rods) include:

- *Haemophilus influenzae*
- *Legionella pneumophila*
- *Pseudomonas aeruginosa*
- *Escherichia coli*
- *Helicobacter pylori*

10. A: The British scientist Rosalind Elsie Franklin is credited with taking the x-ray diffraction image in 1952 that was used by Francis Crick and James Watson to formulate the double-helix model of DNA and speculate about its important role in carrying and transferring genetic information.

CHEMISTRY

1. C: In reference to the periodic table, atomic radius increases as energy levels are added and decreases as more protons are added (because they pull the electrons closer to the nucleus). Essentially, atomic radius increases toward the left and toward the bottom of the periodic table (i.e., francium has the largest atomic radius while helium has the smallest).

2. D: Isotopes are atoms of the same element that vary in their number of neutrons. Isotopes of the same element have the same number of protons and thus the same atomic number. They are denoted by the element symbol, preceded in superscript and subscript by the mass number and atomic number, respectively. For instance, the notations for protium, deuterium, and tritium are respectively: ^1_1H, ^2_1H, and ^3_1H.

3. D: Each of the four energy levels (or shells) of an atom has a maximum number of electrons they can contain. Each level must be completely filled before electrons can be added to the valence level. The farther away from the nucleus an electron is, the more energy it has. The first shell, or K-shell, can hold a maximum of 2 electrons; the second, the L-shell, can hold 8; the third, the M-shell, can hold 18; and the fourth, the N-shell, can hold 32.

4. C: An ether is a substituted hydrocarbon compound containing an oxygen molecule linking two hydrocarbon groups. Ethers are named for the two hydrocarbons that flank the functional group. Both aldehydes and ketones contain a carbonyl group ($C = O$), a carbon atom that shares a double bond with an oxygen atom. Alcohols contain the hydroxy functional group (-OH).

5. A: An amine is a compound with a nitrogen atom that contains a lone pair of electrons and is bound to one or more hydrocarbon groups. Amines may be named in more than one way. The two most common ways are either with the prefix *amino-* or the suffix *-amine*. For example, the simplest amine is methylamine (CH_3NH_2).

6. B: Extensive properties depend on the amount of matter or quantity of the sample. Therefore, extensive properties do change if the sample size is increased or decreased. If the sample size is increased, the property increases. If the sample size is decreased, the property decreases. Extensive properties include volume, mass, weight, energy, entropy, number of moles, and electrical charge.

7. A: The important properties of water (H_2O) are high polarity, hydrogen bonding, cohesiveness, adhesiveness, high specific heat, high latent heat, and high heat of vaporization. Water is cohesive, which means it is attracted to itself. It is also adhesive, which means it readily attracts other molecules.

8. D: A pH indicator, or halochromic material, is a substance that acts as a detector of hydrogen or hydronium ions by changing color. Piezochromic materials change color in the presence of pressure, while bioluminescence is the production and emission of light by small living organisms. Bioluminescence is a form of chemiluminescence since a chemical reaction takes place and doesn't produce large quantities of heat.

9. A: Some properties of salts are that they are formed from acid-base reactions, are ionic compounds consisting of metallic and nonmetallic ions, dissociate in water, and are comprised of tightly bonded ions. Some common salts are sodium chloride (NaCl), sodium bisulfate ($NaHSO_4$), potassium dichromate ($K_2Cr_2O_7$), and calcium chloride ($CaCl_2$).

10. D: Single substitution, displacement, or replacement reactions occur when one reactant is displaced by another to form the final product ($A + BC \rightarrow B + AC$). Single substitution reactions can be cationic or anionic. When a piece of copper (Cu) is placed into a solution of silver nitrate ($AgNO_3$), the solution turns blue. The copper appears to be replaced with a silvery-white material. The equation is $2AgNO_3 + Cu \rightarrow Cu(NO_3)_2 + 2Ag$. When this reaction takes place, the copper dissolves and the silver in the silver nitrate solution precipitates (becomes a solid), thus resulting in copper nitrate and silver. Copper and silver have switched places in the nitrate.

SCIENTIFIC REASONING

1. D: The prefix *hecto-* refers to 100 times the base unit, while *deka-* is 10 times the base unit. Prefixes that indicate a fraction of the base unit include *deci-*, which is $\frac{1}{10}$ of the base unit and *centi-*, which is $\frac{1}{100}$ of the base unit.

2. D: A pipette can be used to accurately measure small amounts of liquid. There are several types of pipettes, including graduated, single-channel, multichannel, and disposable/transfer. Beakers, tests tubes, and Erlenmeyer flasks are used to store, mix, and heat chemicals.

3. B: A theory is a statement of behavior that consolidates all current observations. Theories are similar to laws in that they describe natural behavior, but they are more recently developed and more susceptible to being proved wrong. Theories may eventually become laws if they stand up to scrutiny and testing.

4. C: Unlike laboratory glassware that measures volume, balances such as triple-beam balances, spring balances, and electronic balances measure mass and force. An electronic balance is the most accurate, followed by a triple-beam balance and then a spring balance.

5. A: The prefixes for multiples are as follows:

- *deka-* (da), 10^1 (*deka* is the American spelling, but *deca* is also used)
- *hecto-* (h), 10^2
- *kilo-* (k), 10^3
- *mega-* (M), 10^6
- *giga-* (G), 10^9
- *tera-* (T), 10^{12}

English and Language Usage

CONVENTIONS OF STANDARD ENGLISH: SPELLING

1. C: There are two main reasons that *affect* and *effect* are so often confused: 1) both words can be used as either a noun or a verb, and 2) unlike most homophones, their usage and meanings are closely related to each other. The noun form of *affect* is rarely used outside of technical medical descriptions, so if a noun form is needed on the test, you can safely select *effect*. As a verb, *effect* means to cause to bring into being, as in choice A. The verb form of *effect* is not as rare as the noun form of *affect*, but it's still not all that likely to show up on your test. If you need a verb and you can't decide which to use based on the definitions, choosing *affect* is your best bet.

2. D: Homophones are words that sound alike (or similar) but have different spellings and definitions. A homophone is a type of homonym, which is a pair or group of words that are pronounced or spelled the same but do not mean the same thing.

3. B: A compound noun is a noun that is made up of two or more words; they are sometimes written with hyphens. *Check-in* is the only word in this list that is a correctly spelled compound word. *Ice cream* is a compound noun, but it is not spelled with a hyphen. *Baseball, mother-in-law,* and *court-martial* are all compound nouns. To make hyphenated compound nouns plural, an *s* or *es* is added to the noun portion of the word. For example, *mother-in-law* becomes *mothers-in-law,* and *court-martial* becomes *courts-martial.*

4. B: Some words are the same in both the singular and plural forms. *Salmon, deer,* and *moose* are all spelled the same whether singular or plural.

5. A: *Sacrilegious* is the only word spelled correctly. *Parallel, auxiliary,* and *cemetery* are the correct forms of the other words.

CONVENTIONS OF STANDARD ENGLISH: PUNCTUATION

1. A: Parentheses are used for additional information. Also, they can be used to put labels for letters or numbers in a series. In this sentence, "see image 2" is the additional information that should be in parentheses. Answer choices B and C don't put the entire phrase in parentheses. Choice D incorrectly splits the phrase into two parenthetical statements instead of one.

2. C: Periods and commas are put *inside* quotation marks. Colons and semicolons are put *outside* the quotation marks. Question marks and exclamation points are placed inside quotation marks when they are part of a quote. When the question or exclamation mark goes with the whole sentence, the mark is left outside of the quotation marks.

3. B: Choice B correctly follows the comma rules for writing addresses. Choice A puts an extra comma between "at" and "456." Choice C neglects to place a needed comma between "Avenue" and "Washington." Choice D neglects to place a comma after "D.C."

4. D: Choice D correctly uses commas to separate expressions like *he said* and *she said* that come after a quote. Choice A is missing a comma after John Smith and before his title. Choice B contains the nonessential modifier "who coaches the team," which must have a comma both before and after it. Finally, choice C is missing closing quotation marks after "I want you to know" and has an extra set of quotation marks at the very end of the sentence.

5. C: Choices A, B, and D are all rules for semicolon usage. The semicolon is used to connect major sentence pieces of equal value. Semicolons are used between closely connected independent clauses not connected with a coordinating conjunction, between closely connected independent clauses linked with a transitional word, and between items in a series with internal punctuation. Choice C is actually a rule for colons, which can be used for explanations or to give a quote.

CONVENTIONS OF STANDARD ENGLISH: GRAMMAR

1. B: Relative adjectives will show the different degrees of something or someone to something else or someone else. The three degrees of relative adjective are positive, comparative, and superlative.

2. A: All of the sentences except the one in choice A use action verbs. Linking verbs equate the subject of a sentence to a noun or pronoun, or they link a subject with a descriptive adjective. Common linking verbs include *appear*, *be*, *become*, *feel*, *grow*, *look*, *seem*, *smell*, *sound*, and *taste*. However, any verb that shows a condition and connects to a noun, pronoun, or adjective that describes the subject of a sentence can be a linking verb.

3. C: An adverb is a word that is used to modify a verb, adjective, or another adverb. Usually, adverbs answer one of these questions: *When? Where? How?* and *Why?* The negatives *not* and *never* are considered adverbs. Adverbs that modify adjectives or other adverbs strengthen or weaken the words that they modify. Adjectives, not adverbs, are used to modify nouns.

4. A: Conjunctions join words, phrases, or clauses, and they show the connection between the joined pieces. Coordinating conjunctions connect equal parts of sentences. You can remember coordinating conjunctions with the acronym FANBOYS: *for*, *and*, *nor*, *but*, *or*, *yet*, and *so*. Correlative conjunctions show the connection between pairs, between words that *correlate* with each other. The correlative conjunctions are: *either...or | neither...nor | not only...but also*.

5. B: Superlative adverbs compare the actions of one item to a group. If the new student sings the *most quietly* out of all the choir students, she is at the upper level of quiet compared to all the other students. *Quietly* is the positive form, or the standard form, of this adverb. *More quietly* is the comparative form. This form is used to compare the actions of two items or people. For example: the new student sings *more quietly* than her friend. Finally, *quietest* is a superlative adjective, not an adverb. This would be used to describe a person, not her actions: the new student is the *quietest*.

CONVENTIONS OF STANDARD ENGLISH: SENTENCE STRUCTURE

1. C: Imperative sentences are requests or commands such as, "Go to the post office for me." In imperative sentences, the verb's subject is understood (e.g., [You] Run to the store), but is not actually present in the sentence. Choices A, B, and D are all declarative sentences, which means that they simply state facts.

2. D: A compound subject is formed when two or more nouns joined by *and*, *or*, or *nor* jointly act as the subject of the sentence.

3. A: Pronouns such as *each*, *either*, *everybody*, *anybody*, *somebody*, and *nobody* are always singular.

4. C: An indirect object is a word or group of words that show how an action had an influence on someone or something. If there is an indirect object in a sentence, then you always have a direct object in the sentence. It can be easy to look at a sentence like this one and assume that *my mother* is the direct object and that *yellow roses* is the indirect object. However, the speaker isn't giving his mother, he is giving roses to his mother. To find the indirect object, identify the verb and ask *to/for whom, or what.*

indirect   direct
object   object

I gave my mother yellow roses.

5. C: An infinitive is a type of verbal that can function as a noun, an adjective, or an adverb. An infinitive is made of the word *to* and the basic form of the verb. As with all other types of verbal phrases, an infinitive phrase includes the verbal itself and all of its complements or modifiers.

infinitive

He had all the time in the world to decide what he wanted.

adjective

KNOWLEDGE OF LANGUAGE

1. A: The relationship between writer and reader is important in choosing a level of formality as most writing requires some degree of formality. Formal writing is for addressing a superior in a school or work environment. Business letters, textbooks, and newspapers use a moderate to high level of formality. Informal writing is appropriate for private letters, personal emails, and business correspondence between close associates.

2. D: Choice D contains a verb in the passive voice. A verb is in the passive voice when the subject is the recipient of an action. In choice D, the speaker is not the one doing the telling, but was told by someone else. In the other three answer choices the subject is the one doing the action, so these sentences are all in the active voice.

3. A: *Clichés* are phrases that have been overused to the point that the phrase has no importance or has lost the original meaning. The phrases have no originality and add very little to a passage. A *moot point* is a fact that is not relevant to the current topic. *Jargon* is technical or specialized vocabulary used by people in a certain field or profession. *Hyperbole* is overstating or exaggerating claims.

4. C: Analogies make comparisons between items that appear to have nothing in common. Analogies are employed by writers to provoke fresh thoughts about a subject. These comparisons may be used to explain the unfamiliar, to clarify an abstract point, or to argue a point. Contrast emphasizes the difference between two items or claims. An illustration is an extended example used to elaborate on a point. Finally, a simile is a figurative expression that uses the words *like* or *as* to compare one thing to something else.

5. B: Most writing is in the third person point of view. Point of view is the perspective from which writing occurs. The third person point of view is from the writer's perspective, or by someone outside of the story. The second person point of view is written as though the reader is the main character; it uses *you* instead of *I, he, she,* or *they*. The first person is told by someone in the story and uses the pronoun *I*. There is no such thing as the fourth person.

USING LANGUAGE AND VOCABULARY TO EXPRESS IDEAS IN WRITING

1. A: Free writing is a more structured form of brainstorming. The method involves taking a limited amount of time (e.g., 2 to 3 minutes) to write everything that comes to mind about the topic in complete sentences. Usually, free writing results in a fuller expression of ideas than brainstorming because thoughts and associations are written in complete sentences. However, both techniques can be used to complement each other. Planning involves making a plan for what you will write. Drafting is actually writing the paper or text. Proofreading is the last step in the writing process, where you simply check for typos, misspellings, and things of that nature.

2. B: The only verb suffix in this list is *-fy*, which means to make or cause to have. Choice A, *-ism*, is a noun suffix that signifies a doctrine cause or theory as in *communism*, or an act, practice, or process as in *criticism*. Choice C, *-dom*, is also a noun suffix and can mean state or fact of being, realm, or jurisdiction as in *kingdom*. Choice D, *-ish* is actually an adjective suffix that means of, relating to, or being as in *childish* or *bookish*.

3. C: The prefix *mor-* means death. This can be seen in words like *mortal* and *mortuary*. "Away, off, and from" are meanings of the prefix *for-* as in *foretell* and *forgive*. The prefix *belli-* means war, or warlike. Finally, "bad, poorly, and not" are possible meanings for the prefixes *mal-* and *mis-*.

4. B: The noun suffix *-ation* is correctly defined with "action, state, or result" as in *vacation* and *interpretation*. "Act, condition, fact" is the definition for the suffix *-ance* as in *independence*. "Act, manner, and doctrine" is the correct definition for the suffix *-ism* as in *capitalism*. "State, rank, or condition" are meanings for the suffix *-dom* as in *freedom* and *serfdom*.

5. C: Prefixes are affixes placed in front of words. For example, *heat* means to make hot, and *pre-* means before. *Preheat* means to heat in advance. Suffixes are affixes placed at the ends of words. For example, *happiness* contains the suffix *–ness.* Circumfixes add parts both before and after words, such as how *light* becomes *enlighten* with the prefix *en-* and the suffix *–en.* Interfixes create compound words via central affixes: *speed* and *meter* become *speedometer* via the interfix *–o–*.

Quiz Answers

Practice Test Answer Sheets

For your convenience, we have created a set of printable answer sheets to use when taking the practice tests in this book. Incorporated into each answer sheet is a subscore guide that will show you how well you did on each subsection of the test. For instance, within the Reading test, it will highlight which questions relate to the subsections of Key Ideas and Details, Craft and Structure, and Integration of Knowledge and Ideas. Don't worry though; it doesn't show you the answers. You'll have to look in the back of the book for those.

Visit this link to download and print off a copy:
mometrix.com/academy/teas-7-answer-sheets/

306

TEAS Practice Test #1

Reading

1. Which of the following would best support the argument that people cause global climate change?

    a. The average global temperature has increased 1.5 degrees Fahrenheit since 1880.
    b. Common greenhouse gases include carbon dioxide and water vapor.
    c. Most of the greenhouse gases today come from burning things like coal and other fossil fuels for energy.
    d. The average person breathes out about 1.0 kg of carbon dioxide every day, while the average cow produces about 80 kg of methane.

The next three questions are based on the following information.

    The Dewey Decimal Classes

        000 Computer science, information, and general works
        100 Philosophy and psychology
        200 Religion
        300 Social sciences
        400 Languages
        500 Science and mathematics
        600 Technical and applied science
        700 Arts and recreation
        800 Literature
        900 History, geography, and biography

2. Lise is doing a research project on the various psychological theories that Sigmund Freud developed and on the modern response to those theories. To which section of the library should she go to begin looking for research material?

    a. 100
    b. 200
    c. 300
    d. 900

3. During her research, Lise discovers that Freud's theory of the Oedipal complex was based on ancient Greek mythology that was made famous by Sophocles' play *Oedipus Rex*. To which section of the library should she go if she is interested in reading the play?

    a. 300
    b. 400
    c. 800
    d. 900

Mometrix

4. Also during her research, Lise learns about Freud's Jewish background, and she decides to compare Freud's theories to traditional Judaism. To which section of the library should she go for more information on this subject?

- a. 100
- →b. 200 ✓
- c. 800
- d. 900

5. Consider the following scenario:

> Mara is conducting a study that will examine the ideas of middle school teachers concerning the usage of iPhones in the classroom. She interviews all teachers who teach a computer software course.

Which of the answer choices best describes the appropriateness of Mara's data sample?

- →a. The sample is biased because it only includes teachers who are immersed in the technology field. ✓
- b. The sample is biased because the sample size is too small.
- c. The sample is biased because the sample size is too large.
- d. The sample is not biased and is appropriate for the study.

6. Follow the instructions below to transform the starting word into a different word.

- Start with the word ESOTERICT   SORT
- Remove both instances of the letter E from the word
- Remove the letter I from the word
- Move the letter T from the middle of the word to the end of the word
- Remove the letter C from the word

What new word has been spelled?

- a. SECT
- → b. SORT ✓
- c. SORE
- d. TORE

7. Consider the statement below:

> Literacy rates are lower today than they were fifteen years ago. Then, most people learned to read through the use of phonics. Today, whole language programs are favored by many educators.

Assuming this statement is true, which of the answer choices is a logical conclusion?

- a. Whole language is more effective at teaching people to read than phonics.
- →b. Phonics is more effective at teaching people to read than whole language. ✓
- c. Literacy rates will probably continue to decline over the next 15 years.
- d. The definition of what it means to be literate is much stricter now.

The next four questions are based on the following passage.

The Bermuda Triangle

The area known as the Bermuda Triangle has become such a part of popular culture that it can be difficult to separate fact from fiction. The interest first began when five Navy planes vanished in 1945, officially attributed to "causes or reasons unknown." The explanations about other accidents in the Triangle range from the scientific to the supernatural. Researchers have never been able to find anything truly mysterious about what happens in the Bermuda Triangle, if there even is a Bermuda Triangle. What is more, one of the biggest challenges in considering the phenomenon is deciding how much area actually represents the Bermuda Triangle. Most consider the Triangle to stretch from Miami out to Puerto Rico and to include the island of Bermuda. Others expand the area to include all of the Caribbean islands and to extend eastward as far as the Azores, which are closer to Europe than they are to North America.

The problem with having a larger Bermuda Triangle is that it increases the odds of accidents. There is near-constant travel, by ship and by plane, across the Atlantic, and accidents are expected to occur. In fact, the Bermuda Triangle happens to fall within one of the busiest navigational regions in the world, and the reality of greater activity creates the possibility for more to go wrong. Shipping records suggest that there is not a greater than average loss of vessels within the Bermuda Triangle, and many researchers have argued that the reputation of the Triangle makes any accident seem out of the ordinary. In fact, most accidents fall within the expected margin of error. The increase in ships from East Asia no doubt contributes to an increase in accidents. And as for the story of the Navy planes that disappeared within the Triangle, many researchers now conclude that it was the result of mistakes on the part of the pilots who were flying into storm clouds and simply got lost.

8. Which of the following describes this type of writing?
- a. Narrative
- b. Persuasive
- c. Expository
- d. Technical

9. Which of the following sentences is most representative of a summary sentence for this passage?
- a. The problem with having a larger Bermuda Triangle is that it increases the odds of accidents.
- b. The area that is called the Bermuda Triangle happens to fall within one of the busiest navigational regions in the world, and the reality of greater activity creates the possibility for more to go wrong.
- c. One of the biggest challenges in considering the phenomenon is deciding how much area actually represents the Bermuda Triangle.
- d. Researchers have never been able to find anything truly mysterious about what happens in the Bermuda Triangle, if there even is a Bermuda Triangle.

10. With which of the following statements would the author most likely agree?

    a.   There is no real mystery about the Bermuda Triangle because most events have reasonable explanations.

    b.   Researchers are wrong to expand the focus of the Triangle to the Azores, because this increases the likelihood of accidents.

    c.   The official statement of "causes or reasons unknown" in the loss of the Navy planes was a deliberate concealment from the Navy.

    d.   Reducing the legends about the mysteries of the Bermuda Triangle will help to reduce the number of reported accidents or shipping losses in that region.

11. Which of the following should the writer consult for more detailed information about the Bermuda Triangle?

    a.   An encyclopedia entry about the Bermuda Triangle

    b.   Travel journal entries from a ship captain who sailed the area frequently

    c.   A brochure for a resort located in the Bermuda Triangle

    d.   A biography of someone who disappeared in the Bermuda Triangle

12. Which of the following is a primary source?

    a.   A report of an original research experiment

    b.   An academic textbook's citation of research

    c.   A quotation of a researcher in a news article

    d.   A website description of another's research

The next two questions are based on the following chart.

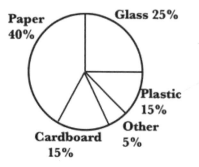

13. A recycling company collects sorted materials from its clients. The materials are weighed and then processed for re-use. The chart shows the weights of various classes of materials that were collected by the company during a representative month. Which of the following statements is NOT supported by the data in the chart?

    a.   Paper products, including cardboard, make up a majority of the collected materials.

    b.   One quarter of the materials collected are made of glass.

    c.   More plastic is collected than cardboard.

    d.   Plastic and cardboard together represent a larger portion of the collected materials than glass bottles.

14. Which of the following would most likely be sorted into the "other" category?

a. A cereal box
b. A soda bottle
c. A soda can
d. Bubble wrap

15. Archie says, "Northerners eat bland food." The most precise definition of this statement is...

a. A stereotype
b. An inference
c. A bias
d. A generalization

16. Which of the following best provides detailed support for the claim that "seatbelts save lives"?

a. A government website containing driving accident information
b. A blog developed by one of the largest car companies in the world
c. An encyclopedia entry on the seatbelt and its development
d. A social media post from a famous race car driver

17. Consider the following scenario:

The latest movie by a certain director gets bad reviews before it opens in theatres. Consequently, very few people go to the movie and the director is given much less money to make his next movie, which is also unsuccessful.

Which of the answer choices presents a valid inference based on this scenario?

a. This director makes terrible movies.
b. The general public does not pay attention to movie reviews.
c. The movie reviewers were right about the first movie.
d. Movie reviewers exert influence on the movie quality.

The next four questions are based on the following graphic.

Table 1. Consumer Price Index for All Urban Consumers (CPI-U): U.S. city average, by expenditure category and commodity and service group

(1982-84=100, unless otherwise noted)

Item and group	Relative importance, December 2008	Unadjusted indexes		Unadjusted percent change to June 2009 from—		Seasonally adjusted percent change from—		
		May 2009	June 2009	June 2008	May 2009	Mar. to Apr.	Apr. to May	May to June
Expenditure category								
All items	100.000	213.856	215.693	-1.4	0.9	0.0	0.1	0.7
All items (1967=100)	-	640.616	646.121	-	-	-	-	-
Food and beverages	15.757	218.076	218.030	2.2	.0	-.2	-.2	.1
Food	14.629	217.826	217.740	2.1	.0	-.2	-.2	.0
Food at home	8.156	215.088	214.824	.8	-.1	-.6	-.5	.0
Cereals and bakery products	1.150	252.714	253.008	3.0	.1	-.7	-.2	.0
Meats, poultry, fish, and eggs	1.898	203.789	204.031	.6	.1	.0	-.9	-.2
Dairy and related products [1]	.910	196.055	194.197	-7.1	-.9	-1.3	-.5	-.9
Fruits and vegetables	1.194	274.006	272.608	-1.9	-.5	.0	-1.0	1.1
Nonalcoholic beverages and beverage materials	.982	162.803	162.571	2.7	-.1	-1.0	-.1	.1
Other food at home	2.022	191.144	191.328	4.1	.1	-.8	-.1	.0
Sugar and sweets	.300	196.403	197.009	6.2	.3	-.5	.0	.2
Fats and oils	.241	200.679	201.127	2.5	.2	-1.4	-.7	.6
Other foods	1.481	205.587	205.654	3.9	.0	-.8	.0	-.2
Other miscellaneous foods [1] [2]	.433	122.838	122.224	3.2	-.5	.4	.0	-.5
Food away from home [1]	6.474	223.023	223.163	3.8	.1	.3	.1	.1
Other food away from home [1] [2]	.314	155.099	155.841	4.0	.5	.4	.0	.5
Alcoholic beverages	1.127	220.005	220.477	3.1	.2	-.1	.3	.2
Housing	43.421	216.971	218.071	.1	.5	-.1	-.1	.0
Shelter	33.200	249.779	250.243	1.3	.2	.2	.1	.1
Rent of primary residence [3]	5.957	249.069	249.092	2.7	.0	.2	.1	.1
Lodging away from home [2]	2.478	135.680	138.318	-6.9	1.9	.5	.1	.3
Owners' equivalent rent of primary residence [3] [4]	24.433	256.875	256.981	1.9	.0	.1	.1	.1
Tenants' and household insurance [1] [2]	.333	120.728	121.083	1.7	.3	-.1	.0	.3
Fuels and utilities	5.431	206.358	212.677	-8.1	3.1	-1.7	-1.3	-.8
Household energy	4.460	183.783	190.647	-10.8	3.7	-2.2	-1.8	-1.0
Fuel oil and other fuels	.301	225.164	232.638	-40.3	3.3	-2.1	-3.1	2.0
Gas (piped) and electricity [3]	4.159	189.619	196.754	-7.8	3.8	-2.2	-1.7	-1.2
Water and sewer and trash collection services [2]	.971	159.517	159.831	6.2	.2	.6	.6	.4
Household furnishings and operations	4.790	129.644	129.623	1.6	.0	.0	.0	.0
Household operations [1] [2]	.781	149.468	149.995	1.3	.4	-.1	-.9	.4
Apparel	3.691	121.751	118.799	1.5	-2.4	-.2	-.2	.7
Men's and boys' apparel	.923	117.146	112.849	.7	-3.7	-1.7	.4	-.5
Women's and girls' apparel	1.541	109.460	106.455	2.1	-2.7	.2	-.1	1.6
Infants' and toddlers' apparel	.183	114.142	113.915	2.1	-.2	1.3	-1.6	2.2
Footwear	.688	127.519	125.515	1.6	-1.6	.4	.1	.2
Transportation	15.314	175.997	183.735	-13.2	4.4	-.4	.8	4.2
Private transportation	14.189	171.757	179.649	-13.3	4.6	-.3	.9	4.5
New and used motor vehicles [2]	6.931	92.701	93.020	-.6	.3	.4	.5	.4
New vehicles	4.480	135.162	135.719	.9	.4	.4	.5	.7
Used cars and trucks	1.628	122.650	124.323	-8.6	1.4	-.1	1.0	.9
Motor fuel	3.164	193.609	225.021	-35.2	16.2	-2.6	2.7	17.2
Gasoline (all types)	2.964	193.727	225.526	-34.6	16.4	-2.8	3.1	17.3
Motor vehicle parts and equipment [1]	.382	134.347	134.270	5.0	-.1	.1	-.2	-.1
Motor vehicle maintenance and repair [1]	1.188	242.488	242.683	4.1	.1	.2	-.1	.1
Public transportation	1.125	228.878	232.540	-12.1	1.6	-.8	-1.0	-.5

18. On a seasonally adjusted basis, which of the following decreased by the greatest percentage between April and May of 2009?

    a. Gasoline
    b. Fuel oil and other fuels
    c. Infants' and toddlers' apparel
    d. Fruits and vegetables

19. According to the organization of the table, which of the following expense categories is not considered to be a component of the "Food at Home" category?
    a. Cereals and bakery products
    b. Fats and oils
    c. Other miscellaneous foods
    d. Alcoholic beverages

20. Which expenditure category was the most important in December of 2008?
    a. Housing
    b. Food and beverages
    c. Apparel
    d. Transportation

21. Which apparel category increased by the greatest percentage between May and June of 2009?
    a. Men's and boy's apparel
    b. Women's and girls' apparel
    c. Infants' and toddlers' apparel
    d. Footwear

The next question refers to the following image.

Starting Image

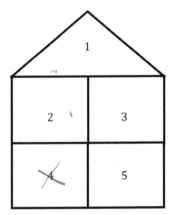

Start with the shape pictured above. Follow the directions to alter its appearance.

- Rotate section 1 90° clockwise and move it to the right side, against sections 3 and 5.
- Remove section 4.
- Move section 2 immediately above section 3.
- Swap section 2 and section 5.
- Remove section 5.
- Draw a circle around the shape, enclosing it completely.

22. Which of the following does the shape now look like?

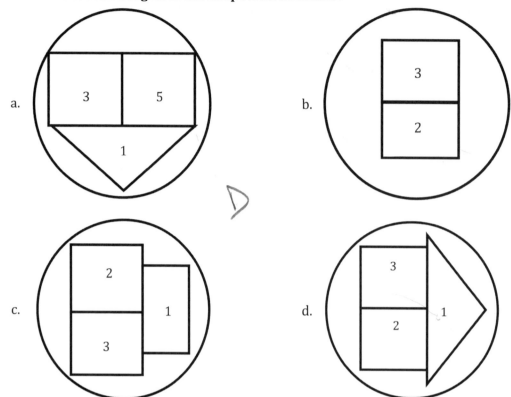

23. Anna is planning a trip to Bretagne, or Brittany, in the northwestern part of France. Since she knows very little about it, she is hoping to find information about hiking trails, beaches, restaurants, and accommodations. Which of the following guides will be the best for her to review?

    a. *The Top Ten Places to Visit in Brittany*, published by a non-profit organization in Bretagne looking to draw tourism to the region

    b. *Getting to Know Nantes: Eating, Staying, and Sightseeing in Brittany's Largest City*, published by the French Ministry of Tourism

    c. *Hiking Through Bretagne: The Best Trails for Discovering Northwestern France*, published by a company that specializes in travel for those wanting to experience the outdoors

    d. *The Complete Guide to Brittany*, published by a travel book company that publishes guides for travel throughout Europe

The next three questions are based on the following statements.

    Lisa Grant: "Schools should make students wear uniforms. Everyone would look the same. Students would be able to respect each other based on their ideas and character because they would no longer be judged by their appearance."

    Vivian Harris: "Students should not have to wear uniforms. Clothing is an important part of self-expression. Taking away that method of expression is suppressing that student's rights."

24. **What is one idea that the students above seem to agree on, based on their statements?**
    a. Students should be allowed to express themselves through apparel.
    b. Schools should give students a certain amount of respect.
    c. Students should focus more on school than on appearance.
    d. Schools would violate students' basic rights by enforcing a dress code.

25. **Which of the following statements could NOT provide support for BOTH arguments?**
    a. A number of local school districts have recently implemented dress codes.
    b. School administrators have been in talks with parents over the issue of uniforms.
    c. Students have reported that school uniforms are costly and typically ill-fitting.
    d. Several groups of students have been organized to discuss uniform dress codes.

26. **Which of the following would be an effective primary source to support Vivian Harris's argument?**
    a. A study showing that fewer students are bullied at schools that require uniforms
    b. An article describing the negative of uniforms in American schools
    c. An interview with a local principal who regrets implementing uniform requirements
    d. A persuasive essay written by Vivian that includes statistics and quotes from psychological studies and other students that support her position

The next four questions are based on the following passage.

Dear Students:

The scores for the essay exam have been posted in the online course grade book. By now, many of you have probably seen your grade and are a little concerned, since this accounts for 70% of your final grade. (And if you're not concerned, you should be—at least a bit!) At the beginning of the semester, I informed the class that I have a strict grading policy and that all scores will stand unquestioned. With each class comes a new challenge, however, and as any good instructor will tell you, sometimes the original plan has to change. As a result, I propose the following options for students to make up their score:

1. I will present the class with an extra credit project at the next course meeting. The extra credit project will be worth 150% of the point value of the essay exam that has just been completed. While I will not drop the essay exam score, I will give you more than enough of a chance to make up the difference and raise your overall score.
2. I will allow each student to develop his or her own extra credit project. This project may reflect the tenor of option number 1 (above) but will allow the student to create a project more in his or her own line of interest. Bear in mind, however, that this is more of a risk. The scoring for option number 2 will be more subjective, depending on whether or not I feel that the project is a successful alternative to the essay exam. If it is, the student will be awarded up to 150% of the point value of the essay exam.
3. I will provide the class with the option of developing a group project. Students may form groups of 3 to 4 and put together an extra credit project that reflects a stronger response to the questions in the essay exam. This extra credit project will also be worth 150% of the point value of the essay exam. Note that each student will receive an equal score for the project, so there is a risk in this as well. If you are part of a group in which you do most of the work, each member of the group will receive equal credit for it. The purpose of the group project is to allow students to work together and arrive at a stronger response than if each worked individually.

Test #1

315

If you are interested in pursuing extra credit to make up for the essay exam, please choose <u>one</u> of the options above. No other extra credit opportunities will be provided for the course.

Good luck!

Dr. Edwards

27. Which of the following describes this type of writing?
   a. Technical
   b. Narrative
   c. Persuasive
   d. Expository

28. Which of the following best describes the instructor's purpose in writing this email to his students?
   a. To berate students for the poor scores that they made on the recent essay exam
   b. To encourage students to continue working hard in spite of failure
   c. To give students the opportunity to make up the bad score and avoid failing the course
   d. To admit that the essay exam was likely too difficult for most students

29. Which of the following quotes offers the best summary for the instructor's motive in sending the email to the students?
   a. By now, many of you have probably seen your grade and are a little concerned. (And if you're not concerned, you should be—at least a bit!)
   b. With each class comes a new challenge, however, and as any good instructor will tell you, sometimes the original plan has to change.
   c. The purpose of the group project is to allow students to work together and arrive at a stronger response than if each worked individually.
   d. At the beginning of the semester, I informed the class that I have a strict grading policy and that all scores will stand unquestioned.

30. Based on the passage, which of the following is the most logical conclusion?
   a. The professor will offer another extra credit project later in the semester.
   b. Students who choose two extra-credit options will be given double the extra credit.
   c. Students who choose the third option will receive one quarter of the offered extra credit.
   d. Students are most likely to earn maximum extra credit by choosing the first option.

The next five questions are based on the following excerpt.

In the United States, where we have more land than people, it is not at all difficult for persons in good health to make money. In this comparatively new field there are so many avenues of success open, so many vocations which are not crowded, that any person of either sex who is willing, at least for the time being, to engage in any respectable occupation that offers, may find lucrative employment.

Those who really desire to attain an independence, have only to set their minds upon it, and adopt the proper means, as they do in regard to any other object which they wish to accomplish, and the thing is easily done. But however easy it may be found to make money, I have no doubt many of my hearers will agree it is the most difficult thing in the world to keep it. The road to wealth is, as Dr. Franklin truly says, "as plain as the road to the mill." It consists simply in expending less than we earn; that seems to be a very simple problem. Mr. Micawber, one of those happy creations of the genial Dickens, puts the case in a strong light when he says that to have annual income of twenty pounds, per annum, and spend twenty pounds and sixpence, is to be the most miserable of men; whereas, to have an income of only twenty pounds, and spend but nineteen pounds and sixpence, is to be the happiest of mortals.

Many of my hearers may say, "we understand this; this is economy, and we know economy is wealth; we know we can't eat our cake and keep it also." Yet I beg to say that perhaps more cases of failure arise from mistakes on this point than almost any other. The fact is, many people think they understand economy when they really do not.

—Excerpted from *The Art of Money-Getting* by P.T. Barnum

31. Which of the following statements best expresses the main idea of the passage?
 a. Getting a job is easier now than it ever has been before.
 b. Earning money is much less difficult than managing it properly.
 c. Dr. Franklin advocated getting a job in a mill.
 d. Spending money is the greatest temptation in the world.

32. What would this author's attitude likely be to a person unable to find employment?
 a. Descriptive
 b. Conciliatory
 c. Ingenuous
 d. Incredulous

33. What is the best definition of *economy* as it is used in this passage?
 a. Exchange of money, goods, and services
 b. Delegation of household affairs
 c. Efficient money management
 d. Less expensive

34. Which word best describes the author's attitude toward those who believe they understand money?
 a. Supportive
 b. Incriminating
 c. Excessive
 d. Patronizing

35. This passage is most likely taken from a(n) _____.
 a. Self-help manual
 b. Autobiography
 c. Epistle
 d. Novel

The next question refers to the following graphic.

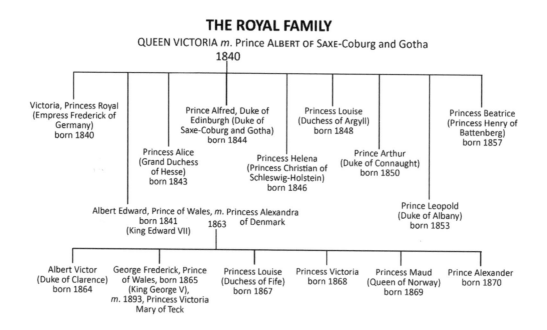

THE ROYAL FAMILY

36. In what way is the family tree organized?
  a. The oldest generation at the bottom, and the youngest generation at the top.
  b. The youngest children on right and the oldest children on the left.
  c. The youngest children on the left and the oldest children on the right.   X B
  d. The grandparents (Queen Victoria and Prince Albert) are on the top, followed by their children, grandchildren, and great-grandchildren on the bottom layers.

The next three questions are based on this passage.

As a plunger is depressed, air inside the wide rubber cup is pushed out. This depression action forms a strong, airtight seal around the top of a clogged pipe and the plunger cup is held fast by the air pressure of the user. Continued plunging—pressing down on the plunger—causes an increase in pressure inside the clogged pipe and will usually force out whatever may be causing the clog.

37. What word best describes the organization of this passage?
  a. Modeling
  b. Hypothesizing
  c. Explaining
  d. Observing

38. As used in the passage, what does the word "depressed" most nearly mean?
  a. Very unhappy
  b. Decreased appreciably
  c. Exhaled hard
  d. Pushed down

39. Which word in the passage shows that the plunger is depressed and air is pushed out at the same time?

a. Out
b. Continued
c. As
d. Causes

The next two questions are based on this passage.

The classic opera *Madame Butterfly* was written by Giacomo Puccini. In the opus, an American naval officer stationed in Japan falls in love with Butterfly, a Japanese woman. He returns to America but promises to come back to marry her. When the soldier does return to Japan three years later, he is accompanied by his American wife. Shocked and humiliated, Butterfly stabs herself. She dies in the soldier's arms as he begs her to forgive him.

40. This passage describes characters' feelings in *Madame Butterfly* as all of the following EXCEPT:

a. Romantic
b. Poignant
c. Tragic
d. Musical

41. What is the purpose of the italicized text in the passage?

a. To show Madame Butterfly's thoughts
b. To emphasize an idea
c. To format a heading
d. To indicate the title of the opera

The next four questions are based on this passage.

Journalists often use a recording device to capture the audio transcript of an interview with a subject. The recording device is thought of as a reliable and efficient way to ensure that all important parts of the interview have been archived, which is something that may be complicated for a journalist to do by hand. Besides being difficult to execute quickly, legibly, and efficiently, taking notes by hand can distract the journalist from the interview subject's body language, non-verbal cues, or other subtle information that can go unnoticed when the journalist is not fully concentrating on the person talking. These missed cues (for example, noticing that the tough-guy interview subject closed his eyes and trembled slightly when he talked about his recently departed mother) could mean that the opportunity for an interesting perspective in the article is lost.

Relying on a recording device is not without troubles, however. Most journalists can quickly relate stories of disappointments they or co-workers have endured due to problems with equipment. For instance, a journalist may not notice low batteries until it is too late. As a result, a portion of an interview can be lost without any way to reclaim it. The machine's volume can be accidentally left too low to hear the subject on later playback, the recorder may be accidentally switched off during the interview, and any number of other unplanned and unexpected electronic malfunctions can occur to sabotage the recording. While recording device problems may not occur often, even a rate of once a year can be extremely problematic for a writer. Some glitches may be unrealized until hours later when the journalist is prepared to work with the recording.

Most experienced journalists do not rely solely on technology when they are interviewing a subject for an article. Instead, as the recording device creates an audio record of the interview, journalists will simultaneously record their own notes by hand. This dual-note method means that most of the time, a wise journalist has two good resources to use as he or she writes the article draft.

42. According to the passage, which of the following are reasons an audio recording device can be superior to taking notes by hand during an interview? (Select all that apply.)

    a.   A recording device may be low on batteries without the journalist noticing.

    b.   Efficient, legible note-taking is a difficult skill to master.

    c.   The journalist has to look away from the interview subject to write notes.

    d.   Recording devices capture only what is said, ignoring non-verbal cues.

    e.   Taking notes by hand does not require any advanced technology.

43. Which of the following are examples of body language or non-verbal cues as described in the passage? (Select all that apply.)

    a.   A surprised look

    b.   Rubbing hands together

    c.   A quiet answer

    d.   An angry expression

    e.   A trembling voice

    f.   A nodding head

44. Which statement from the passage best supports the conclusion that taking notes and recording audio during an interview is a good practice for journalists?

    a.   Journalists often use a recording device to capture the audio transcript of an interview with a subject.

    b.   Relying on a recording device is not without troubles, however.

    c.   As a result, a portion of an interview can be lost without any way to reclaim it.

    d.   This dual-note method means that most of the time, a wise journalist has two good resources to use as he or she writes the article draft.

45. Which title is the best choice for this passage?

    a.   "The Art of Writing Notes"

    b.   "Conducting an Interview"

    c.   "Recording an Interview"

    d.   "Problems with Interviews"

Mathematics

We now have video explanations for every math question in this practice test. Visit **mometrix.com/academy/teas-math-videos/** or scan this QR code to access these videos.

SCAN HERE

1. Which of the following best describes the data represented by this scatterplot?

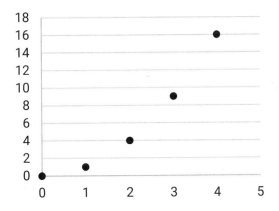

a. This is a linear association with a positive correlation between bivariate data.
b. This is a linear association with a negative correlation between bivariate data.
→ c. This is a nonlinear association between bivariate data. ✓
d. There is no association between the bivariate data.

2. If Stella's current weight is 56 kilograms, which of the following is her approximate weight in pounds? (Note: 1 kilogram is approximately equal to 2.2 pounds.)

→ a. 123 pounds ✓
b. 110 pounds
c. 156 pounds
d. 137 pounds

3. Solve for x: $2x + 4 = x - 6$.

a. $x = -12$
→ b. $x = 10$
c. $x = -16$
d. $x = -10$ ✓

4. A farmer plans to install fencing around a certain field. If each side of the hexagonal field is 320 feet long and fencing costs $1.75 per foot, how much will the farmer need to spend on fencing material to fence the perimeter of the field?

$3,360 ✓

321

Test #1

5. Erma has her eye on two sweaters at her favorite clothing store, but she has been waiting for the store to offer a sale. This week, the store advertises that all clothing purchases, including sweaters, come with an incentive: 25% off a second item of equal or lesser value. One sweater is $50 and the other is $44. If Erma purchases the sweaters during the sale, what will she spend?

    a. $79
    b. $81
    c. $83
    d. $85

6. A woman wants to stack two small bookcases beneath a window that is $26\frac{1}{2}$ inches from the floor. The larger bookcase is $14\frac{1}{2}$ inches tall. The other bookcase is $8\frac{3}{4}$ inches tall. How tall will the two bookcases be when they are stacked together?

    a. 12 inches tall
    b. $23\frac{1}{4}$ inches tall
    c. $35\frac{1}{4}$ inches tall
    d. 41 inches tall

7. Four more than a number, x, is 2 less than $\frac{1}{3}$ of another number, y. Which of the following algebraic equations correctly represents this sentence?

    a. $x + 4 = \frac{1}{3}y - 2$
    b. $4x = 2 - \frac{1}{3}y$
    c. $4 - x = 2 + \frac{1}{3}y$
    d. $x + 4 = 2 - \frac{1}{3}y$

8. Margery is planning a vacation, and she has added up the total potential cost. Her round-trip airfare will cost $572. Her hotel cost is $89 per night, and she will be staying at the hotel for five nights. She has allotted a total of $150 for sightseeing during her trip, and she expects to spend about $250 on meals. As she books the hotel, she is told that she will receive a discount of 10% off the price of $89 for each additional night after the first night she stays there. Taking this discount into consideration, what is the amount that Margery expects to spend on her vacation?

    a. $1,328.35
    b. $1,373.50
    c. $1,381.40
    d. $1,417.60

322

9. Given the double bar graph shown below, which of the following statements is true?

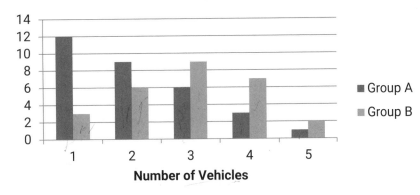

Number of Vehicles Owned

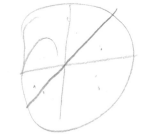

a. Group A is negatively skewed, while Group B is approximately normal.
b. Group A is positively skewed, while Group B is approximately normal.
→ c. Group A is approximately normal, while Group B is negatively skewed.
d. Group A is approximately normal, while Group B is positively skewed.

10. After a hurricane struck a Pacific island, donations began flooding into a disaster relief organization. The organization provided the opportunity for donors to specify where they wanted the money to be used, and the organization provided four options. When the organization tallied the funds received, they allotted each to the designated need. Reviewing the chart below, what percentage of the funds was donated to support construction costs?

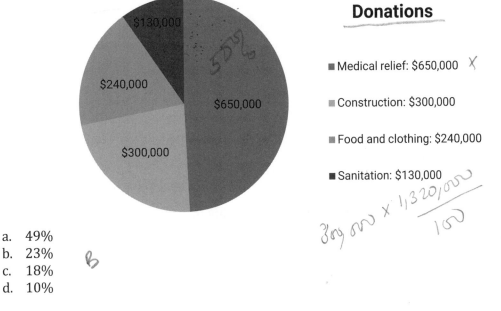

Donations

■ Medical relief: $650,000

■ Construction: $300,000

■ Food and clothing: $240,000

■ Sanitation: $130,000

a. 49%
b. 23%
c. 18%
d. 10%

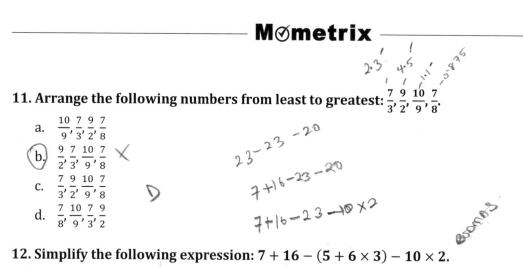

M⊘metrix

11. Arrange the following numbers from least to greatest: $\frac{7}{3}, \frac{9}{2}, \frac{10}{9}, \frac{7}{8}$.

    a. $\frac{10}{9}, \frac{7}{3}, \frac{9}{2}, \frac{7}{8}$

    b. $\frac{9}{2}, \frac{7}{3}, \frac{10}{9}, \frac{7}{8}$

    c. $\frac{7}{3}, \frac{9}{2}, \frac{10}{9}, \frac{7}{8}$

    d. $\frac{7}{8}, \frac{10}{9}, \frac{7}{3}, \frac{9}{2}$

12. Simplify the following expression: $7 + 16 - (5 + 6 \times 3) - 10 \times 2$.

    a.   −42

    b.   −20

    c.   23

    d.   20

13. Which of the following best describes the relationship of this set of data?

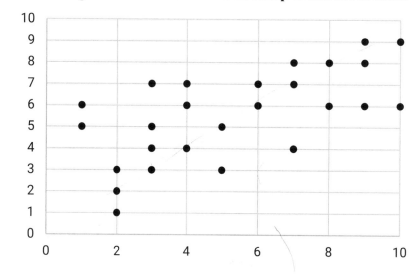

    a.   High positive correlation

    b.   Low positive correlation

    c.   Low negative correlation

    d.   No correlation

14. A patient requires a 30% decrease in the dosage of his medication. His current dosage is 340 mg. What will his dosage be after the decrease?

    a.   70 mg

    b.   238 mg

    c.   270 mg

    d.   340 mg

15. A rectangle has a width of 9 inches and a length of 15 inches. If the rectangle is enlarged by a scale factor of $\frac{3}{2}$, **what is the perimeter of the dilated rectangle?**

    _____ inches

Copyright © Mometrix Media. You have been licensed one copy of this document for personal use only. Any other reproduction or redistribution is strictly prohibited. All rights reserved.
This content is provided for test preparation purposes only and does not imply an endorsement by Mometrix of any particular political, scientific, or religious point of view.

16. The table below shows the average amount of rainfall Houston receives during the summer and autumn months.

Month	Rainfall (inches)
June	5.35
July	3.18
August	3.83
September	4.33
October	4.5
November	4.19

What percentage of rainfall received during this timeframe is received during the month of October?

   a. 13.5%
   b. 15.1%
   c. 16.9%
   d. 17.7%

17. Gordon purchased a television when his local electronics store had a sale. The television was offered at 30% off its original price of $472. What was the sale price that Gordon paid?

   a. $141.60
   b. $225.70
   c. $305.30
   d. $330.40

18. Robert is planning to drive 1,800 miles on a cross-country trip. If his car gets 30 miles to the gallon and his tank holds 12 gallons of gas, how many tanks of gas will he need to complete the trip?

   _5_ tanks

19. While at the local ice-skating rink, Cora went around the rink 27 times total. She slipped and fell 20 of the 27 times she skated around the rink. What approximate percentage of the times around the rink did Cora *not* slip and fall?

   a. 37%
   b. 74%
   c. 26%
   d. 15%

20. Joshua has to earn more than 92 points on the state test in order to qualify for an academic scholarship. Each question is worth 4 points, and the test has a total of 30 questions. Let x represent the number of test questions. Which of the following inequalities can be solved to determine the number of questions Joshua must answer correctly?

   a. $4x < 30$
   b. $4x < 92$
   c. $4x > 30$
   d. $4x > 92$

Test #1

21. Susan decided to celebrate getting her first nursing job by purchasing a new outfit. She bought a dress for $69.99 and a pair of shoes for $39.99. She also bought accessories for $34.67. What was the total cost of Susan's outfit, including accessories?

$ 144.65

The next two questions are based on the following information:

Mrs. McConnell's Classroom

Eye Color	Number of Students
Brown	14 0.14
Blue	9 0.09
Hazel	5 0.05
Green	2 0.02

22. Approximately what percentage of students in Mrs. McConnell's classroom have either hazel or green eyes?
  a. 23%
  b. 30%
  c. 47%
  d. 77%

23. What is the ratio of students with brown eyes to students with green eyes?
  a. 1:2
  b. 3:1
  c. 1:5
  d. 7:1

24. During week 1, Nurse Cameron worked 5 shifts. During week 2, she worked twice as many shifts as she did during week 1. During week 3, she added 4 shifts to the number of shifts she worked during week 2. Which equation below describes the number of shifts Nurse Cameron worked during week 3?
  a. Shifts $= (2)(5) + 4$
  b. Shifts $= (4)(5) + 2$
  c. Shifts $= 5 + 2 + 4$
  d. Shifts $= (5)(2)(4)$

25. Consider a bag that has 3 orange blocks, 5 green blocks, and 4 purple blocks. If you pull an orange block out, what is the probability of consecutively pulling two more orange blocks, without replacement, from those that remain in the bag?
  a. $\frac{1}{3}$
  b. $\frac{1}{55}$
  c. $\frac{2}{81}$
  d. $\frac{31}{110}$

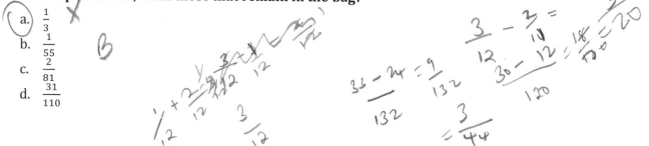

26. 9.5% of the people in a town voted for a certain proposition in a municipal election. If the town's population is 51,623, about how many people in the town voted for the proposition?

    a. 3,000
    b. 5,000
    c. 7,000
    d. 10,000

27. A charter bus driver drove at an average speed of 65 mph for 305 miles. If he stops at a gas station for 15 minutes, then drives another 162 miles at an average speed of 80 mph, how long will it have been since he began the trip?

    a. 0.96 hours
    b. 6.44 hours
    c. 6.69 hours
    d. 6.97 hours

28. Using the chart below, which equation describes the relationship between x and y?

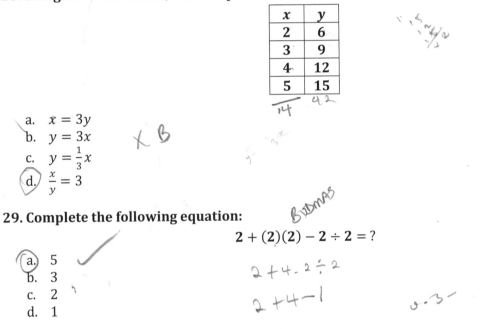

x	y
2	6
3	9
4	12
5	15

    a. $x = 3y$
    b. $y = 3x$
    c. $y = \frac{1}{3}x$
    d. $\frac{x}{y} = 3$

29. Complete the following equation:

$$2 + (2)(2) - 2 \div 2 = ?$$

    a. 5
    b. 3
    c. 2
    d. 1

30. A can has a radius of 1.5 inches and a height of 3 inches. Which of the following best represents the volume of the can?

    a. 17.2 in^3
    b. 19.4 in^3
    c. 21.2 in^3
    d. 23.4 in^3

31. A study about anorexia was conducted on 100 patients. Within that patient population 70% were women, and 10% of the men were overweight as children. How many male patients in the study were NOT overweight as children?

    a. 3
    b. 10
    c. 27
    d. 30

32. What is the independent variable in the graph below?

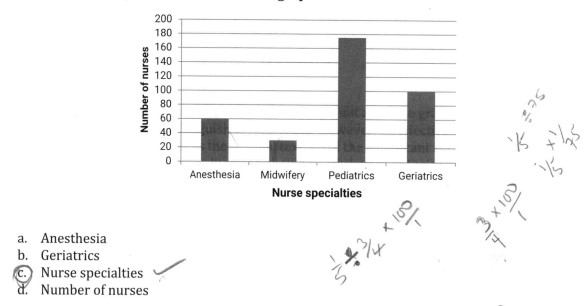

a. Anesthesia
b. Geriatrics
c. Nurse specialties ✓
d. Number of nurses

33. University Q has an extremely competitive nursing program. Historically, $\frac{3}{4}$ of the students in each incoming class major in nursing, but only $\frac{1}{5}$ of those who major in nursing actually complete the program. If this year's incoming class has 100 students, how many students will complete the nursing program?

a. 75
b. 20
c. 15 ✓
d. 5

34. What kind of association does the scatter plot show?

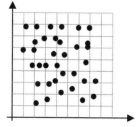

a. Linear, positive
b. Linear, negative
c. Quadratic
d. No association

35. The number of flights a flight attendant made per month is represented by the line graph below.

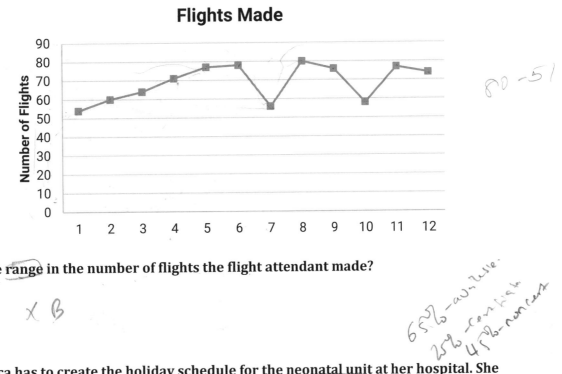

Flights Made

What is the range in the number of flights the flight attendant made?

    a. 20
    b. 25
    c. 29
    d. 32

36. Veronica has to create the holiday schedule for the neonatal unit at her hospital. She knows that 35% of the staff members will not be available because they are taking vacation days during the holiday. Of the remaining staff members who will be available, only 20% are certified to work in the neonatal unit. What percentage of the total staff is certified and available to work in the neonatal unit during the holiday?

    a. 7%
    b. 13%
    c. 65%
    d. 80%

37. Which of the following describes a graph that represents a directly proportional relationship?

    a. The graph has a slope of 2,500 and a y-intercept of 250.
    b. The graph has a slope of 1,500 and a y-intercept of −150.
    c. The graph has a slope of 2,000 and a y-intercept of 0.
    d. The graph has a slope of −1,800 and a y-intercept of −100.

38. As part of a study, a set of patients will be divided into three groups: $\frac{4}{15}$ of the patients will be in Group Alpha, $\frac{2}{5}$ of the patients will be in Group Beta, and $\frac{1}{3}$ of the patients will be in Group Gamma. Order the groups from smallest to largest, according to the number of patients in each group.

    a. Group Alpha, Group Beta, Group Gamma
    b. Group Alpha, Group Gamma, Group Beta
    c. Group Gamma, Group Alpha, Group Beta
    d. Group Gamma, Group Beta, Group Alpha

329

Test #1

Science

1. Chemical C is a catalyst in the reaction between chemical A and chemical B. What is the effect of chemical C?

    a. Chemical C increases the rate of the reaction between A and B. A

    b. Chemical C decreases the rate of the reaction between A and B.

    c. Chemical C initiates the reaction between A and B.

    d. Chemical C converts A from a base to an acid.

Refer to the following for questions 2–3:

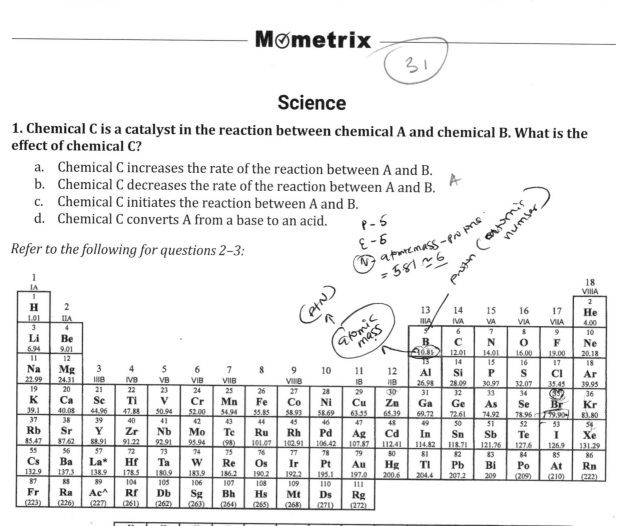

P - 5
E - 5
N → atomic mass - protons
= 381 ≈ 6

Note: The row labeled with * is the lanthanide series, and the row labeled with ^ is the actinide series.

2. On average, how many neutrons does one atom of bromine (Br) have?

    a. 35

    b. 44.90 ✓

    c. 45

    d. 79.90

3. On average, how many protons does one atom of zinc (Zn) have?

    a. 30 ✓

    b. 35

    c. 35.39

    d. 65.39 ✗

4. A scientific study has over 2,000 data points. Which of the following methods is most likely to help the researcher gain usable information from the data?

    a. Use statistical analysis to understand trends in the data. ✓

    b. Look at each individual data point and try to create a trend.

    c. Eliminate 90% of the data so that the sample size is more manageable.

    d. Stare at the data until a pattern pops out.

5. Which of the following accurately describes the path of blood through the heart?

a. Blood enters the heart through the pulmonary vein, into the right atrium, through the tricuspid valve to the right ventricle. ✗

b. Once the right ventricle is full, blood exits into the pulmonary artery and then empties into the left ventricle.

c. After traveling through the lungs, oxygenated blood enters into the left atrium, then through the mitral valve to the left ventricle. ✓

d. Once the left ventricle is full, the left tricuspid valve shuts, the ventricle contracts, and blood exits through the aorta.

6. Which of the statements below accurately list a component along with its function? (Select all that apply.)

a. Collagen is a fatty compound that creates a padding between bones and other structures.

b. Hemoglobin is a protein in the blood that facilitates the carrying of oxygen.

c. Lymph is tissue that forms into nodes through which blood is filtered and cleaned. ·   B & D

d. An antigen is a substance that stimulates the production of antibodies. ✗

7. Which of the statements below list the correct function of the digestive system organ? (Select all that apply.)

a. The large intestine reabsorbs water into the body to form solid waste.

b. The duodenum is the part of the small intestine in which acids, fat, and sugar are absorbed.

c. The liver produces bile, which aids digestion by emulsifying fats after they have passed through the stomach.

d. The ileum functions to recover vitamins, salts, and nutrients from the chyme before it   ACID
passes into the large intestine.

e. The jejunum receives chyme from the stomach and is the site where most chemical digestion occurs.

f. The gallbladder produces insulin to assist in the transport of sugars from the blood to the organs.

8. Which pattern below best describes the elements listed in the table?

Element	Atomic number	Approximate atomic weight
H	1	1
He	2	4
Li	3	7
Be	4	9

a. The elements are arranged in order by weight, with H being the heaviest atom and Be being the lightest atom.

b. The elements are arranged in order by electron charge, with H having the most electrons and Be having the fewest electrons.

c. The elements are arranged in order by protons, with H having the most protons and Be having the fewest protons.

d. The elements are arranged in order by protons, with H having the fewest protons and Be having the most protons. ✓

331

9. Based on the following evidence, what is the most likely reason that spoiled food left out in the open often contained fly larvae?

Many years ago, people believed that flies were created from spoiled food because spoiled food that was left out in the open often contained fly larvae. So a scientist placed fresh food in a sealed container for an extended period of time. The food spoiled, but no fly larvae were found in the food that was sealed.

a. The spoiled food evolved into fly larvae.
b. Since the food was left out in the open, flies would lay eggs in the food.
c. Fly larvae were spontaneously generated by the spoiled food.
d. People only imagined they saw fly larvae in the spoiled food.

10. How do DNA and RNA function together as part of the human genome?

a. DNA carries genetic information from RNA to the cell cytoplasm.
b. RNA carries genetic information from DNA to the cell cytoplasm.
c. DNA and RNA carry genetic information from the cell nucleus to the cytoplasm.
d. DNA and RNA do not interact within the cell.

11. Which statement most accurately compares and contrasts the structures of DNA and RNA?

a. Both DNA and RNA have 4 nucleotide bases. Three of the bases are the same, but the fourth base is thymine in DNA and uracil in RNA.
b. Both DNA and RNA have the same 4 nucleotide bases. However, the nucleotides bond differently in the DNA when compared to RNA.
c. Both DNA and RNA have 6 nucleotide bases. However, the shape of DNA is a triple helix and the shape of RNA is a double helix.
d. Both DNA and RNA have a double helix structure. However, DNA contains 6 nucleotide bases and RNA contains 4 nucleotide bases.

12. Fill in the blanks in the following sentence:

Enzymes are _____ molecules that serve as _____ for certain biological reactions.

a. complex; suppressors
b. acidic; triggers
c. small; targets
d. large; catalysts

13. What type of molecules are enzymes?

a. Water molecules
b. Protein molecules
c. Tripolar molecules
d. Inorganic molecules

14. Which blood vessel carries oxygenated blood back to the heart?

a. Pulmonary vein
b. Pulmonary artery
c. Aorta
d. Superior vena cava

15. Mrs. Jones's class is conducting an experiment. They will substitute artificial sweetener for sugar in a cookie recipe to determine the effect on the overall color of the baked cookies. Which of the following should be included in the instructions for the experiment?

a. When preparing the batch that includes artificial sweetener, 20% more water should be included since artificial sweetener requires more water to dissolve than sugar.
b. The bake temperature should be decreased from 425° to 400° on the batch that uses artificial sweetener since the recipe indicates that sugar may take longer to bake.
c. The batch with artificial sweetener should be baked on a stainless steel sheet, while the batch with sugar should be baked on a nonstick sheet, since sugar is stickier when dissolved.
d. Ingredient proportions, bake time, bake temperature, and cookie sheet material should all be kept the same between the two batches of cookies to avoid confounding factors.

16. An atom has 5 protons, 5 neutrons, and 6 electrons. What is the electric charge of this atom?

a. Neutral
b. Positive
c. Negative
d. Undetermined

17. How many different types of tissue are there in the human body?

a. 4
b. 6
c. 8
d. 10

18. Of the following, the blood vessel containing the least-oxygenated blood is the:

a. Aorta
b. Vena cava
c. Pulmonary artery
d. Femoral vein

Refer to the following for questions 19–20:

A student is conducting an experiment using a ball that is attached to the end of a string, forming a pendulum. The student pulls the ball back so that it is at an angle to its resting position. As the student releases the ball, it swings forward and backward. The student measures the time it takes the ball to make one complete period. A period is defined as the time it takes the ball to swing forward and back again to its starting position. This is repeated using different string lengths.

19. The student formed the following hypothesis:

Lengthening the string of the pendulum increases the time it takes the ball to make one complete period.

What correction would you have the student make to the hypothesis?

a. Turn it into an "if/then" statement.
b. Change "increases" to "will increase."
c. Switch the order of the sentence so that the phrase about the period comes first, and the phrase about the string's length is last.
d. No corrections are needed.

20. What would be an appropriate control variable for this experiment?

    a.   The period
    b.   The length of the string
    c.   The mass of the ball
    d.   The color of the ball

21. Which of the following components of the human integumentary system is the deepest?

    a.   Stratum basale
    b.   Epidermis
    c.   Hypodermis
    d.   Dermis

22. Two nursing students will be completing a scientific experiment measuring the mass of chewed gum after one-minute chewing increments. Which lab equipment will the students most likely use?

    a.   Triple beam balance
    b.   Anemometer
    c.   Hot plate
    d.   Microscope

23. Which of the following is an example of the location and function of cartilage in the body?

    a.   The dense connective tissue that makes up the majority of the structural skeleton
    b.   The supportive pads that provide cushioning at joints, such as between the vertebrae of the spinal cord
    c.   The connective structure made of fibrous collagen that connects muscles and bones, such as the connection of the patella to the quadriceps
    d.   The layer beneath the skin and on the outside of internal organs that provides cushioning and protection

24. Which of the following best describes a plane that divides the body into upper and lower portions?

    a.   Coronal
    b.   Transverse
    c.   Oblique
    d.   Median

25. Which of the following is NOT an element of the respiratory system?

    a.   Ribs
    b.   Trachea
    c.   Diaphragm
    d.   Alveoli

26. A substance is only considered acidic if it has a pH less than what?

    a.   12
    b.   9
    c.   7
    d.   4

27. What function do ribosomes serve within the cell?

    a. Ribosomes are responsible for cell movement.
    b. Ribosomes aid in protein synthesis.
    c. Ribosomes help protect the cell from its environment.
    d. Ribosomes have enzymes that help with digestion.

28. Which of the following best describes one of the roles of RNA?

    a. Manufacturing the proteins needed for DNA
    b. Creating the bonds between the elements that compose DNA
    c. Sending messages about the correct sequence of proteins in DNA
    d. Forming the identifiable double helix shape of DNA

29. In the suburban neighborhood of Northwoods, there have been large populations of deer, and residents have complained about them eating flowers and garden plants. What would be a logical explanation for the large increase in the deer population over the last two seasons?

    a. There has been an increase in the quantity of food sources in surrounding areas.
    b. The population of a natural predators in Northwoods has decreased.
    c. Deer have migrated from surrounding areas.
    d. There has been a recent increase in hunting licenses sold.

Refer to the following for questions 30–31:

B = allele for brown eyes; b = allele for green eyes

	B	b
B	BB	Bb
b	Bb	bb

30. Which word describes the allele for green eyes?

    a. Dominant
    b. Recessive
    c. Homozygous
    d. Heterozygous

31. What is the probability that the offspring produced will have brown eyes? Round your answer to the nearest whole percentage.

    75 %

32. What type of chemical bond connects the oxygen and hydrogen atoms in a molecule of water?

    a. Static bond
    b. Aquatic bond
    c. Ionic bond
    d. Covalent bond

Test #1

33. Which of the following substances is NOT a product of respiration?
  a. Carbon dioxide
  b. Water
  c. Oxygen
  d. ATP

34. Which of the following statements correctly describes the function of a physiological structure?
  a. The trachea connects the throat and the stomach, encouraging food to follow this path through contractions.
  b. The esophagus is the cylindrical portion of the respiratory tract that joins the larynx with the lungs.
  c. The diaphragm is a muscle that controls the height of the thoracic cavity, decreasing the height on contraction and increasing the height on relaxation, causing expiration.
  d. The epiglottis covers the trachea during swallowing, preventing food from entering the airway.

35. Which of the following choices best describes the location of the trachea in relation to the esophagus?
  a. Lateral
  b. Anterior
  c. Posterior
  d. Dorsal

36. Which of the following statements describes a chemical property of water?
  a. Water has a pH of 1.
  b. A water molecule contains 2 hydrogen atoms and 1 oxygen atom.
  c. A water molecule contains 2 oxygen atoms and 1 hydrogen atom.
  d. The chemical formula for water is HO_2.

37. Where are the parathyroid glands located?

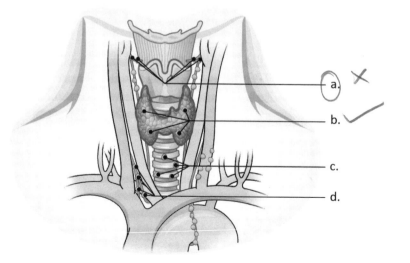

38. What functions do genes serve in the relationship between parents and offspring?

   a. Genes enable hereditary information to be passed from parents to offspring.
   b. Genes prohibit hereditary information from being passed from parents to offspring.
   c. Genes enable environmental factors to affect parents and offspring.
   d. Genes serve no function in the relationship between parents and offspring.

39. Which statement below correctly describes the movement of molecules in the body and/or in relation to the external environment?

   a. Osmosis is the movement of a solution from an area of low solute concentration to an area of high solute concentration.
   b. Diffusion is the process in the lungs by which oxygen is transported from the air to the blood.
   c. Dissipation is the transport of molecules across a semipermeable membrane from an area of low concentration to high concentration, requiring energy.
   d. Reverse osmosis is the movement of molecules in a solution from an area of high concentration to an area of lower concentration.

40. Which of the following describes one responsibility of the integumentary system?

   a. Distributing vital substances (such as nutrients) throughout the body
   b. Blocking pathogens that cause disease
   c. Sending leaked fluids from the cardiovascular system back to the blood vessels
   d. Storing bodily hormones that influence gender traits

41. A triple beam balance would show which units of measurement?

   a. Liters
   b. Grams
   c. Meters
   d. Gallons

42. Which of the following body systems controls fluid loss, protects deep tissues, and synthesizes vitamin D?

   a. The skeletal system
   b. The muscular system
   c. The lymphatic system
   d. The integumentary system

43. The process of changing from a liquid to a gas is called _____.

   a. freezing
   b. condensation
   c. vaporization
   d. sublimation

44. Which part of the cell provides energy for cellular functions?

   a. Nucleus
   b. Cell membrane
   c. Mitochondria
   d. Cytoplasm

Test #1

45. Which of the following statements accurately characterizes the relationship between genes and chromosomes?

   a. Each gene contains multiple chromosomes. ✗

   b. Each chromosome contains multiple genes. B

   c. Genes and chromosomes are two words for the same thing.

   d. Genes and chromosomes are not the same thing, but always occur in equal numbers.

46. Which of the following characteristics is part of a person's genotype?

   a. Brown eyes that appear hazel in the sunlight

   b. The CFTR gene, which causes cystic fibrosis ✓ B

   c. Black hair that grows rapidly

   d. Being a fast runner ✗

47. Which of the following quantities do _catalysts_ alter to control the rate of a chemical reaction?

   a. Substrate energy ✗ B

   b. Activation energy

   c. Inhibitor energy

   d. Promoter energy

48. Which of the following best describes a function carried out by the circulatory system and the integumentary system working together?

   a. Removal of excess heat from body ✓

   b. Hormonal influence on blood pressure

   c. Regulation of blood's pressure and volume

   d. Development of blood cells within marrow

49. Which of the following activities are consistent with the scientific method? (Select all that apply.)

   a. Observe the data, noting potential outliers, and then analyze the results. ✗ ADE

   b. Research to make sure no one else has ever experimented based on the same hypothesis.

   c. Conduct an experiment and then formulate a hypothesis that fits the results.

   d. Communicate the results of an experiment that did not confirm the hypothesis.

   e. Develop a new hypothesis based on a conclusion from a previous experiment.

50. What lab equipment would most likely be used to precisely measure the volume of a liquid solution?

   a. Flask

   b. Triple beam balance ✗ C

   c. Graduated cylinder

   d. Test tube

English and Language Usage

1. Which of the following represents a correct plural form of the word *syllabus*?

  a. Syllabus
  b. Syllaba
  c. Syllabi
  d. Syllabis

2. Which of the following types of language is acceptable in a research paper?

  a. Colloquialisms
  b. Contractions
  c. Relative pronouns
  d. Second-person point of view

3. *Bi*, *re*, and *un* are:

  a. Suffixes, appearing at the beginning of base words to change their meaning
  b. Suffixes, appearing at the end of base words to enhance their meaning
  c. Prefixes, appearing at the beginning of base words to emphasize their meaning
  d. Prefixes, appearing at the beginning of base words to change their meaning

4. Which of the following sentences shows the correct use of quotation marks?

  a. Grady asked Abe, 'Did you know that an earthquake and a tsunami hit Messina, Italy, in 1908?'
  b. Grady asked Abe, "Did you know that an earthquake and a tsunami hit Messina, Italy, in 1908"?
  c. Grady asked Abe, "Did you know that an earthquake and a tsunami hit Messina, Italy, in 1908?"
  d. Grady asked Abe, " 'Did you know that an earthquake and a tsunami hit Messina, Italy, in 1908'?"

5. *Therefore*, *because*, and *accordingly* are examples of which type of signal words?

  a. Emphasis words
  b. Compare/contrast words
  c. Cause-and-effect words
  d. Temporal sequencing words

6. Which of the following provides the best definition for the prefix *trans-* as used in the underlined word in the sentence below?

  Most of the window was heavily covered with dirt, but one spot in the corner had been carefully cleaned so that the outside light brilliantly shone through this part of the translucent pane.

  a. Across
  b. Beautiful
  c. Change
  d. Different

7. Which of the following is essential in the concluding statement of an argument?

    a. The introduction of new points that might lead to future arguments

    b. A summary of the argument that clearly reinforces its main points

    c. A brief explanation of other perspectives on the topic

    d. A short metaphor to help the main idea be more memorable to the audience

8. Which of the following is an example of revision?

    a. Typing the first draft of an essay

    b. Reading sentences for clarity and making necessary changes

    c. Creating a list of all sources used within the essay

    d. Mapping out possible topics and subtopics

9. Which of the following words contains an exception to a spelling rule?

    a. Unclear

    b. Memorize

    c. Noticeable

    d. Grieved

10. What transition should be added to the beginning of sentence 2 below?

    (1) I zoned out in class, turned work in late, talked out in class, and handed in assignments after the due date. (2) Mr. Shanbourne just nodded.

    a. Surprisingly

    b. Actually

    c. Furthermore

    d. Instead

11. The following words all end in the same suffix, -ism: *polytheism, communism, nationalism*. Considering the meaning of these three words, which of the following best correlates to the meaning of the suffix?

    a. A doctrine

    b. A condition

    c. A characteristic

    d. A state of being

12. What is the most effective way to rewrite the following sentence?

    She is saying that some of the students are wearing to school is being distracting and inappropriate.

    a. Some of the outfits students wear to school, she is saying, are distracting and not appropriate.

    b. The outfits are distracting and inappropriate, she says, that students wear to school.

    c. She says that some of the outfits that students wear to school are distracting and inappropriate.

    d. She says that it is distracting and inappropriate that students wear outfits to school.

13. Which of the following is an example of a correctly punctuated sentence?

a. Beatrice is very intelligent, she just does not apply herself well enough in her classes to make good grades. ✗

b. Beatrice is very intelligent: she just does not apply herself well enough in her classes to make good grades. ✗

c. Beatrice is very intelligent she just does not apply herself well enough in her classes to make good grades. ✗

d. Beatrice is very intelligent; she just does not apply herself well enough in her classes to make good grades. ✓

14. Which of the following is NOT a prewriting strategy?

a. Brainstorming ✗
b. Visual mapping of ideas ✗
c. Asking questions ✗
d. Organizing writing into paragraphs ✓

15. Which of the following is a compound sentence?

a. Tabitha and Simon started the day at the zoo and then went to the art museum for the rest of the afternoon. ✗

b. Tabitha and Simon started the day at the zoo, and then they went to the art museum for the rest of the afternoon. ✓

c. After starting the day at the zoo, Tabitha and Simon then went to the art museum for the rest of the afternoon. ✗ complex sentence

d. Tabitha and Simon had a busy day, because they started at the zoo, and then they went to the art museum for the rest of the afternoon. ✗

16. Which of the following makes a correction to an error in this sentence?

The family sprinted through the airport, worryed they would miss their flight.

a. "family" should be "families"
b. "worryed" should be "worried" ✓
c. "airport," should be "airport;"
d. "their" should be "there"

17. Which of these examples of communications would call for use of formal language? (Select all that apply.)

a. An email to the dean of admissions ✓
b. A resume cover letter ✓
c. A letter to a congressperson advocating for a policy position ✓
d. A text to your study group proposing a meeting time change ✗
e. An incident report to be filed with human resources ✓
f. An email to a colleague asking for a favor ✗

18. Which of the following sets of words correctly fill in the blanks in the sentence below?

We cannot allow the budget cuts to _____ the plans to improve education; the futures of _____ children are at stake.

a. effect; your ✗
b. affect; you're ✗
c. effect; you're ✗
d. affect; your ✓

341

19. Which of the basic elements of the writing process should be completed before the first draft is written?

a. Prewriting ✓
b. Revising
c. Conferencing
d. Editing

20. Which of the following sentences contains an incorrect use of capitalization?

a. For Christmas, we are driving to the South to visit my grandmother in Mississippi. ✗
b. Last year, we went to East Texas to go camping in Piney Woods. ✗
c. Next month, we will visit my Aunt Darla, who lives just East of us. ✓
d. When my sister-in-law Susan has her baby, I will take the train north to see her. ✗

21. Which of the following sentences is grammatically correct?

a. Krista was not sure who to hold responsible for the broken window. ✗
b. Krista was not sure whom was responsible for the broken window. ✗
c. Krista was not sure whom to hold responsible for the broken window. ✓
d. Krista was not sure on who she should place responsibility for the broken window. ✗

22. Which of the following sentences would be classified as informal language?

a. I'm counting on you to finish this before the deadline. ✗
b. The deadline presented by the CEO is non-negotiable. ✗
c. Every member of the department must meet the deadline. ✗
d. The time period prior to the deadline is extremely significant. ✗

23. Which of the following pieces of information would NOT support a thesis about the importance of hands-on learning in early education?

a. Building structures with blocks helps develop fine-motor skills. ✗
b. Using modeling clay helps strengthen small finger and hand muscles. ✗
c. Learning to take good notes helps young students become better listeners. ✓
d. Hopscotch helps children develop coordination and even counting skills. ✗

24. Which of the following sentences contains a correct example of subject-verb agreement?

a. All of the board members are in agreement on the issue. ✓
b. Each of the students were concerned about the test scores for the final exam.
c. Neither of the children are at home right now. ✗
d. Any of the brownie recipes are perfect for the bake sale.

25. Which of the following choices is NOT an appropriate way to express an opinion in a formal debate?

a. There are still many arguments concerning the nature of space-time, including whether Einstein's theory of relativity is applicable in every natural situation. ✗
b. The study of climate science is an ever-evolving field, but it is important to recognize that the tools being utilized have been tested in other fields. ✗
c. Energy independence is an important topic that needs to be addressed in a thoughtful, careful manner that considers the far-reaching impact of any proposed changes. ✗
d. It is the height of hypocrisy to acknowledge that global warming is a problem and then still tool around in a gas-guzzling vehicle. ✓

26. Which of the following is a simple sentence?
    a. Phillippa walked the dog, and Primula gave the dog a bath.
    b. Phillippa walked and bathed the dog, and Primula helped.
    c. Phillippa walked the dog, while Primula gave the dog a bath.
    d. Phillippa and Primula walked the dog and gave the dog a bath.

27. Which of the following lists elements of the prewriting portion of the writing process?
    a. Researching, outlining, editing
    b. Preparation, referencing sources, drafting
    c. Planning, brainstorming, outlining
    d. Drafting, researching, referencing sources

28. What does the prefix *poly-* mean in the word *polygon*?
    a. Few
    b. Several
    c. None
    d. Many

29. What are the five basic elements of the writing process?
    a. Prewriting, drafting, conferencing, revision, editing
    b. Brainstorming, outlining, writing, peer-review, researching
    c. Researching, prewriting, writing, brainstorming, conferencing
    d. Prewriting, writing, revising, researching, proofreading

30. Julia is writing an essay about the influence of technology on interpersonal relationships. Which of the following sentences would NOT be a relevant supporting detail?
    a. Studies show that the more teenagers engage in social media, the less they engage with their peers.
    b. College students study and work on homework an average of 4-6 hours a day.
    c. Use of technology such as smartphones can lead to a lack of engagement in conversations.
    d. Some psychologists think that watching TV activates the same part of the brain as having an in-depth conversation.

31. Which of the following transitional words or phrases can be used to indicate contrast? (Select all that apply.)
    a. Regardless
    b. Furthermore
    c. Subsequently
    d. Similarly
    e. On the other hand
    f. Moreover

32. Which of the following sentences uses proper capitalization?
    a. Last Summer, my family went on a trip to Niagara Falls in New York.
    b. Last summer, my family went on a trip to niagara falls in New York.
    c. Last summer, my family went on a trip to Niagara Falls in New York.
    d. Last Summer, my family went on a trip to Niagara Falls in new york.

33. The following words share a common Greek-based suffix: *anthropology*, *biology*, *cosmetology*, *etymology*, **and** *genealogy*. **What is the most likely meaning of the suffix** *-logy*?

 a. Record
 b. Study ✓
 c. Science
 d. Technique

34. Which of the answer choices best combines the following four sentences into two sentences?

> I'm usually good about keeping track of my keys. I lost them. I spent hours looking for them. I found them in the freezer.

 a. I lost my keys, even though I'm usually good about keeping track of them. I found them in the freezer and spent hours looking for them. ✗
 b. I spent hours looking for my keys and found them in the freezer. I had lost them, even though I'm usually good about keeping track of them. ✓
 c. I'm usually good about keeping track of my keys, but I lost them. After spending hours looking for them, I found them in the freezer. ✓
 d. I'm usually good about keeping track of my keys, but I lost them in the freezer. I had to spend hours looking for them. ✗

35. Which of the following suffixes is NOT commonly used to form a noun from some other part of speech?

 a. *–ation* ✗   *Comm*
 b. *–ness* ✗
 c. *–ity*
 d. *–ize* ✓

36. Which of the answer choices is an effective revision of the ambiguous sentence below?

> Tanya told her sister to tell her boyfriend Joe to call her as soon as he got home.

 a. "Tanya," said her sister, "Tell Joe to call your boyfriend as soon as Joe gets home."
 b. Her sister told her boyfriend Joe to call Tanya as soon as she got home.
 c. Tanya's sister was told by her, "Joe should call me as soon as he gets home."
 d. Tanya said to her sister, "Tell your boyfriend Joe to call me as soon as he gets home." ✓

37. Which of the following sentences shows the correct way to separate the items in the series?

 a. These are actual cities in the United States: Unalaska, Alaska; Yreka, California; Two Egg, Florida; and Boring, Maryland. ✓
 b. These are actual cities in the United States: Unalaska; Alaska, Yreka; California, Two Egg; Florida, and Boring; Maryland.
 c. These are actual cities in the United States: Unalaska, Alaska, Yreka, California, Two Egg, Florida, and Boring, Maryland.
 d. These are actual cities in the United States: Unalaska Alaska, Yreka California, Two Egg Florida, and Boring Maryland.

Answer Key and Explanations for Test #1

Reading

1. C: This choice shows how greenhouse gases are released from burning coal and other fuels, which people need for power. Choices A, B, and D are facts, but don't show a relationship to the main idea.

2. A: Since Lise's project is on Sigmund Freud's psychological theories, publications about psychology would be good research material for her to start with. The Dewey Decimal System groups publications about philosophy and psychology in the 100s. To find information on Freud's psychological theories, Lise should go to class 100. Choice B is the 200s, which includes materials related to religion. Choice C is the 300s, which includes materials related to social sciences. Choice D is the 900s, which includes biographies and materials related to history and geography. While any of these subjects may become relevant to Lise's project as she researches, they are not the subjects she should research first. Choice A, the 100s, is the best answer.

3. C: Lise is looking for a play, which is considered a literary work, or literature. According to the Dewey Decimal System, literature is found in the 800s, so Lise should consult the 800s section. Choice A, the 300s, includes books on the social sciences; choice B, the 400s, includes books on languages; and choice D, the 900s, includes biographies and books about history and geography. While some books in these sections may mention *Oedipus Rex*, a copy of the play will not be found in these sections. The 800s is the best section for Lise to consult to read the play.

4. B: Lise is looking for information about Judaism, which is a religion. Materials about religion are found in the 200s, so Lise should look there to learn more about Judaism. Choice A is the 100s, which includes material about philosophy; choice C is the 800s, which includes literature; and choice D is the 900s, which includes biographies and material on history and geography. While Judaism may be relevant to materials from these sections, publications in the 200s will be the best sources for Lise to learn more information about Judaism.

5. A: The sample is biased because the study wishes to examine all middle school teachers' ideas regarding usage of iPhones in the classroom, while the sample only represents ideas of those teachers teaching technology courses.

6. B: The word SORT results from following all of the provided directions. Choice A fails to remove the E and C, choice C fails to remove the E, and choice D fails to remove the E and move the T.

7. B: It can be concluded that phonics is a more effective way to learn to read for two reasons. First, the passage states that literacy rates are lower now than they were 15 years ago, meaning that more people knew how to read 15 years ago. Second, the passage states that phonics was the main way people learned how to read 15 years ago. Based on these two facts, it can be concluded that phonics is more effective at teaching people to read. Choice A says that whole language programs are more effective, so it is incorrect. The passage does not include any information that can be used to predict future literacy rates, nor does it suggest that the definition of literate has changed, so choices C and D are also incorrect.

8. C: The passage is expository because it communicates information about the mysteries of the Bermuda Triangle and what researchers have studied and now believe. The author includes facts to inform the reader, which is the goal of expository writing. The passage does not tell a story or

345

describe one event, so it is not a narrative. The passage also does not seek to lead the reader to take action or accept a particular conclusion, so this passage is not persuasive. The passage also does not give technical information and does not aim to help the reader understand a technical concept, so this passage is not technical.

9. D: This sentence is the best summary statement for the entire passage because it clearly describes what the author is saying about the results of studies on the Bermuda Triangle. Each paragraph in the passage includes details that support the statement that researchers have never found anything truly mysterious about the Bermuda Triangle. Choices A, B, and C are all details found in the passage, but none of these answer choices give a summary of the whole passage. Each of these answer choices support the statement in choice D, as do the rest of the details in the passage. Choice D is the best summary of these choices.

10. A: Of all the sentences provided, this is the one with which the author would most likely agree. The passage suggests that most of the "mysteries" of the Bermuda Triangle can be explained in a reasonable way. The passage mentions that some expand the Triangle to the Azores, but this is a point of fact, and the author makes no mention of whether or not this is in error. The author quotes the Navy's response to the disappearance of the planes, but there is no reason to believe the author questions this response. The author raises questions about the many myths surrounding the Triangle, but at no point does the author claim that these myths are to blame for the accidents that fall "within the expected margin of error."

11. B: A collection of travel journal entries from someone who frequently traveled the Bermuda Triangle is the most likely of these choices to provide detailed information. Choice A would provide useful information, but this information is not likely to go into much detail. Choice C would likely include many details, but it would only contain information about a very small section of the Bermuda Triangle. Choice D could include details about the Bermuda Triangle, but these details would also only describe a limited section of the area and would be given through a narrow perspective.

12. A: When a researcher has conducted an original experiment and reports the results, findings, and associated conclusions in a research report, that report is considered a primary source. Academic textbooks, journal articles, articles in other periodicals, and authoritative databases may all be primary sources. When an academic textbook cites research by others, that citation is considered a secondary source as it refers to information originally presented by others. When a news article quotes a researcher's writing, that is also a secondary source, as is a description given on a website of another person's research.

13. C: The chart shows that plastic and cardboard materials both comprise 15% of the collected materials, and therefore it is incorrect to say that there is more plastic than cardboard. They are present in equal quantities.

14. C: Soda cans are made from aluminum, which is a type of metal. Since metal is not a category specifically listed on the chart, a soda can would be sorted into the "Other" category. Choice A would be sorted into either the "Paper" or "Cardboard" category, choice B would be sorted into either the "Glass" or "Plastic" category, and choice D would be sorted into the "Plastic" category. Since choice C is the only option made from a material that is not represented on the chart, it is the correct answer.

15. A: The statement reflects a stereotype. A stereotype is an assumption or generalization made about everybody in an identified group. A bias impacts one's opinion. Biases can be informed by stereotypes, but they are not stereotypes themselves. Generalizations apply to a great many subjects, not just to the characteristics of a specific group of people. An inference is a conclusion based on available evidence rather than on an overt statement of fact. For example, if Archie said, "That man is from the North, so he must like bland food," he would be making an inference based on his stereotype of people from the North. Therefore, stereotype is the most precise definition of the statement.

16. A: A government website would publish credible data on seatbelt usage, such as how many people are wearing seatbelts when accidents occur and how many of them survive. Choice B is likely to include information that is related to a particular brand of cars and may not be relevant to the topic. Choice C would have reliable information related to the topic, but would most likely not contain many useful details about this particular claim. Choice D would most likely contain only a few details that could be used to support the claim and may not be credible.

17. D: The passage says that the poor reviews of the first movie caused the film to have low attendance. This resulted in low funding for the next movie, which may have caused it to be of low quality, as it also failed. This supports the inference that movie reviewers influence movie quality, making choice D correct. The actual quality of the first movie is not mentioned in the passage, so neither choice A or choice C is a valid inference. Choice B is incorrect because the reviews clearly affected whether members of the general public attended the movie.

18. B: This information can be found in the second column from the right. Fuel oil and other fuels decreased by 3.1% during this period. Gasoline increased by 3.1%. The other commodities decreased, but by lesser amounts.

19. D: In the table, components of each category are shown by indentation under the name of the category itself. There may be sub-categories within each category that are further indented. All of the choices are indented under "Food at Home" except for "Alcoholic Beverages," which is a separate category.

20. A: Read this from the second column in the table, "Relative Importance December 2008." These numbers represent the average percentage of household budgets that are spent on the expenditure category. The greatest number, 43.421%, is on the row corresponding to housing.

21. C: The column showing seasonally adjusted percent changes from May to June shows that infants' and toddlers' apparel increased by 2.2%. Women's and girls' apparel and footwear also increased, but they increased by smaller percentages. Men's and boys' apparel decreased from May to June.

22. D: Choice D is the only option that correctly follows the instructions in the question. Sections 4 and 5 are removed, section 1 is placed on the right side along sections 3 and 2, and there is a circle drawn around the entire shape. Choice A places section 1 in the wrong location, unnecessarily moves section 3, and fails to switch sections 2 and 5. Choice B incorrectly removes section 1 altogether. Choice C changes the shape of section 1 to a rectangle and reverses sections 2 and 3.

23. D: Anna is ultimately looking for a good all-around guidebook for the region. *The Top Ten Places to Visit in Brittany* might have some useful information, but it will not provide enough details about hiking trails, beaches, restaurants, and accommodations. *Getting to Know Nantes* limits the information to one city, and Anna's destination in Brittany is not identified. *Hiking Through Bretagne* limits the information to one activity. These three guidebooks might offer great supplemental information, but *The Complete Guide to Brittany* is most likely to offer all the information that Anna needs for her trip.

Test #1

24. B: Both of the speakers are arguing over how uniforms will affect students, though they are going about it in different ways. Choices A and D are details mentioned in Vivian Harris's argument, but they contradict the points made in Lisa Grant's argument. Choice C could align with Lisa Grant's argument, but neither student's argument suggests that students should focus more on school.

25. C: This detail would only really support the argument against wearing school uniforms, as it introduces evidence that shows that uniforms are not always a preferable option. The other three choices could all appear as details in support of either side of the argument, since each detail is objective and neutral.

26. C: Choice C is a primary source that would contain information relevant to Vivian's argument. Choice A is a primary source, but it includes information that is contrary to Vivian's argument. Choice B supports Vivian's position, but articles are secondary sources, so it is incorrect. Choice D could be a secondary or tertiary source, but it is not a primary source. It would also be ineffective for Vivian to use a source she wrote herself to support her own argument, so choice D is incorrect.

27. A: Technical passages focus on presenting specific information and have a tone of formality. They also usually prompt a response from their recipient. Expository passages reveal information to the reader. This passage does give information, but the information is specific, technical, and meant to prompt action from the students receiving the email. Therefore, choice A, technical, is the best answer. Narrative writing focuses on telling a story, and the passage offers no indication of this. Persuasive writing attempts to persuade the reader to agree with a certain position; the instructor offers the students information and advice but leaves the decision up to each student.

28. C: Choice C fits the tone of the passage best. The instructor is simply offering students the chance to make up the exam score (which is worth 70% of their grade) and thus avoid failing the course. The instructor does not berate students at any point, nor does the instructor admit that the exam was too difficult. Additionally, the instructor offers encouragement to the students should they choose to complete an extra credit project, but that is not the primary purpose of this email.

29. B: This question asks for the best summary of the instructor's motive. In the opening paragraph, the instructor notes that his original grading plan has to change to reflect the exam scores. Because they were low, he now wants to give students a chance to make up for their low scores. Choice B thus summarizes his motive effectively by stating that he recognizes the need for a change in the policy. The instructor introduces his email with the notes about the scores being posted, but given the information that is provided in the message, this is not the sole motive for his writing, so choice A is incorrect. Choice C limits the motive to the details about the group project, but the instructor provides three options. Choice D overlooks the instructor's further note about how the grading policy sometimes has to bend to reflect circumstances.

30. D: The professor is designing the project in option one, so this project is guaranteed to be an acceptable alternative to the essay exam. The professor encourages students to choose this option, as the other two options may not yield projects that are acceptable alternatives. If students choose options two or three, there is a chance they may not be eligible for the entire 150% of the point value the professor is offering. The professor states that there will be no additional extra credit opportunities and emphasizes that each student may only choose one extra-credit option, so choices A and B are incorrect. Option three states that each student will receive equal credit, but it does not state that the 150% of the point value will be divided among the students, so choice C is incorrect.

31. B: The author asserts that earning money is easy, but what often challenges people is managing money. This is the main idea of the passage. Choice B says that earning money is less difficult than managing money, so it is correct. Getting a job and the temptation to spend money are both mentioned in the passage as details. However, neither of these are the main idea, so choices A and D are both incorrect. The quote from Franklin does not advocate for working at a mill and does not summarize the main idea, so choice C is also incorrect.

32. D: The author seems to believe that there are plenty of lucrative jobs for everyone, so he or she would doubt that a person really could not find employment. This makes choice D the best choice, as *incredulous* means to struggle to believe something. *Descriptive* means describing, *conciliatory* means satisfying or appeasing, and *ingenuous* means innocent. None of these terms describe the attitude of the author, so choices A, B, and C are incorrect.

33. C: In this passage, the author is speaking of money management on a personal or household level. In this context, economy refers to efficient money management, so choice C is correct. While this definition of economy is relevant to households, it is not related to delegation within a household, making choice B incorrect. Economy in the context of the exchange of money, goods, and services is more applicable beyond personal or household finances, so choice A is incorrect. This passage uses economy to describe wise money management, not simply goods that are less expensive than others, so choice D is incorrect.

34. D: The author suggests that many people who believe they understand economy in fact do not, and that he or she has a better understanding of economy than such people. The best choice to describe this attitude is patronizing, which means to offer help in a way that is condescending. The author is offering information that is helpful, but presents it in a way that is critical. The author's writing does not encourage or blame those who misunderstand economy, so the author's attitude is not supportive or incriminating. The author's attitude is also not conveyed excessively, so choice C is also incorrect.

35. A: The passage is written to inform the reader about making and managing money, which is an appropriate topic for a self-help manual. The passage is not describing the author's life, so it is not likely to be an excerpt from an autobiography. It is also written in an impersonal tone, so it is also not likely to be from an epistle, or a letter. Finally, the passage is nonfictional, so it is not taken from a novel.

36. B: This is the correct answer because the birthdates show that the youngest children are on the right and their older siblings are on the left side of the family tree. Choice A is incorrect because Queen Victoria and Prince Albert are the oldest generation, and they are at the top of the family tree. Choice C is incorrect because the youngest children are on the left, not the right (the reader can see this by looking at the birthdates). Choice D is partially correct because Queen Victoria and Prince Albert are at the top of the family tree, but the family tree does not show great-grandchildren. Although it looks like there are more than three layers, the middle layers all show Queen Victoria and Prince Albert's children.

37. C: The passage describes what happens when a plunger is used to clear a clogged pipe and why this process works. This is best described as an explanation. While the passage does describe a chain of events, it also explains why these events happen, meaning that the passage as a whole is not an observation. The passage is also simply explaining how plungers work, not providing an example or modeling the use of a plunger. Hypothesizing means to propose an unproven idea. The passage does not propose something unproven, so this is incorrect.

38. D: "Depressed" is used in the passage to describe how a plunger is pushed down to make it work. "Very unhappy" is not an action, and it is also not logical for the plunger to be decreased, so choices A and B can be eliminated. The passage also says that when the plunger is depressed, air moves. If the user exhaled on the plunger, this would not cause the air inside the cup to move, so choice C is incorrect.

39. C: *As* is the only word of these choices that indicates that two or more events are happening simultaneously. *Out* is a preposition, and it does not indicate the sequence of events. *Continued* can describe the duration of an event, but it does not show the order of events. *Causes* can indicate the order of events, as an event that causes an effect must occur first, but it does not show that two events happened at the same time.

40. D: Although this passage describes an opera, the feelings experienced by the characters would not be considered musical. The passage does mention that the American officer falls in love with Butterfly, so it is reasonable to describe the characters' feelings as romantic. *Poignant* and *tragic* both refer to feelings of intense emotional distress, which are expressed through both Butterfly and the officer's reactions at the end of the passage. These terms clearly describe the characters' feelings, making *musical* the correct answer.

41. D: The passage is describing the events of an opera titled *Madame Butterfly*. The opera title is given in the first sentence of the passage, and since an opera is a major work, its title should be italicized in typed text. The first sentence simply gives the name of the opera and the writer, it does not introduce an important idea or a section heading, so choices B and C are incorrect. None of the character's thoughts or dialogue are quoted in the passage, so choice A is also incorrect.

42. B, C: The passage mentions advantages and disadvantages to both processes. Note-taking is described as being difficult to do efficiently and legibly, and it carries with it the necessity for frequently looking away from the interview subject. Choices A and E, on the other hand, are reasons that note-taking may be superior to audio recording. Technology can fail unexpectedly, causing information to be lost. Choice D alludes to a potential drawback of both methods, namely that non-verbal cues may be missed.

43. A, B, D, F: In the passage, the first paragraph gives two examples of body language when it describes an interview subject closing his eyes and trembling slightly. A surprised look, rubbing hands together, an angry expression, and a nodding head are all examples of body language or non-verbal cues that could be missed if the journalist is looking down to take notes instead of looking at the interview subject. A quiet answer would be heard rather than seen, as would a trembling voice.

44. D: Choice D states that wise journalists both record audio and take hand-written notes during interviews so that they have a backup resource in case the recording or notes are not reliable. Choice A simply states the purpose of recording devices but does not give enough information to support the conclusion that journalists should both record audio and take notes. Choices B and C show that recording audio is not always reliable, but neither of these choices shows why it is a good practice.

45. C: "Recording an Interview" is relevant to each section of the passage. The passage includes details related to writing notes, but since this is not the main idea, choice A is not the best choice. Recording an interview is only one part of interviewing, so choice B is too broad for this passage. The passage also only talks about problems that occur when taking notes, not problems with interviews in general, so choice D is also not the best title.

Mathematics (Video Explanations Available)

We now have video explanations for every math question in this practice test. Visit **mometrix.com/academy/teas-math-videos/** or scan this QR code to access these videos.

SCAN HERE

1. C: The data points in this scatter plot form a curve. This is a nonlinear association. Therefore, choice C is correct.

2. A: To find the correct answer, multiply Stella's weight in kilograms by the conversion factor for kilograms to pounds.

$$\frac{56 \text{ kg}}{1} \times \frac{2.2 \text{ lb}}{1 \text{ kg}} = 123.2 \text{ lb} \approx 123 \text{ lb}$$

3. D: Begin by subtracting 4 from both sides, then subtract x from both sides:

$$2x + 4 - 4 = x - 6 - 4$$
$$2x = x - 10$$
$$2x - x = x - 10 - x$$
$$x = -10$$

4. 3,360: A hexagonal field has 6 sides. Each side is 320 feet long, so multiply 320 by 6 to get the perimeter of the field: $320 \times 6 = 1,920$ feet. At \$1.75 per foot, the perimeter fence will cost $1,920 \times 1.75 = \$3,360$.

5. C: Erma's sale discount will be applied to the less expensive sweater, so she will receive the \$44 sweater for 25% off. This amounts to a discount of \$11, so the cost of the sweater will be \$33. Added to the cost of the \$50 sweater, which is not discounted, Erma's total is \$83.

6. B: Add to solve. The height of the window from the floor is not needed in this equation. It is extra information. You only need to add the heights of the two bookcases. Convert the fractions so that they have a common denominator. After you add, simplify the fraction.

$$14\frac{1}{2} + 8\frac{3}{4} = 14\frac{2}{4} + 8\frac{3}{4}$$
$$= 22\frac{5}{4}$$
$$= 23\frac{1}{4}$$

7. A: The expression "Four more than a number, x" can be interpreted as $x + 4$. This is equal to "2 less than $\frac{1}{3}$ of another number, y," or $\frac{1}{3}y - 2$. Thus, the equation is $x + 4 = \frac{1}{3}y - 2$.

8. C: Start by adding up the costs of the trip, excluding the hotel cost: $\$572 + \$150 + \$250 = \$972$. Then, calculate what Margery will spend on the hotel. The first of her five nights at the hotel will cost her \$89. For each of the other four nights, she will get a discount of 10% per night, or \$8.90.

Test #1

This discount of $8.90 multiplied by the four nights is $35.60. The total she would have spent on the five nights without the discount is $445. With the discount, the amount goes down to $409.40. Add this amount to the $972 for a grand total of $1,381.40.

9. B: Data is said to be positively skewed when there are a higher number of lower values, indicating data that is skewed right. An approximately normal distribution shows an increase in frequency, followed by a decrease in frequency, of approximately the same rate.

10. B: Start by locating the section of the pie chart that represents construction. It looks close to a quarter of the pie chart, which means that it is probably 23%, but you can verify by adding up the numbers. The total amount of all donations is about $1.3 million and the amount given for construction is $0.3 million: $\frac{0.3}{1.3} \approx 0.231 \approx 23\%$.

11. D: Turn the fractions into mixed numbers to see the amounts more clearly. The result is that $\frac{7}{8}$ is smaller than $\frac{10}{9}$, or $1\frac{1}{9}$, which is smaller than $\frac{7}{3}$, or $2\frac{1}{3}$, which is smaller than $\frac{9}{2}$, or $4\frac{1}{2}$.

12. B: Simplify this expression by using the order of operations (PEMDAS). First, simplify the parentheses. Remember, the order of operations has to be followed within parentheses, so multiply before you add.

$$7 + 16 - (5 + 6 \times 3) - 10 \times 2$$

$$7 + 16 - (5 + 18) - 10 \times 2$$

$$7 + 16 - 23 + 10 \times 2$$

Then, simplify the multiplication.

$$7 + 16 - 23 - 20$$

Finally, add and subtract from left to right.

$$7 + 16 - 23 - 20 = -20$$

13. B: Since the points in this scatterplot tend to be rising, this is a positive correlation. However, since the points are not clustered to resemble a straight line, this is a low positive correlation.

14. B: The patient's dosage must decrease by 30%, so calculate 30% of 340:

$$(0.30)(340 \text{ mg}) = 102 \text{ mg}$$

Now subtract the 30% decrease from the original dosage.

$$340 \text{ mg} - 102 \text{ mg} = 238 \text{ mg}$$

15. 72: The width of the enlarged rectangle is equal to the product of 9 in and $\frac{3}{2}$, or 13.5 in. The length of the enlarged rectangle is equal to the product of 15 in and $\frac{3}{2}$, or 22.5 in. $P_{rect} = 2w + 2l$. Thus, the perimeter is equal to $2 \times 13.5 \text{ in} + 2 \times 22.5 \text{ in} = 72 \text{ in}$.

16. D: The total rainfall is 25.38 inches. Thus, the ratio $\frac{4.5}{25.38}$, represents the percentage of rainfall received during October. $\frac{4.5}{25.38} \approx 0.177$, or 17.7%.

17. D: The television is 30% off its original price of $472. 30% of $472 is $141.60. To find the sale price, subtract the amount saved from the original price, $472 − $141.60 = $330.40. Thus, Gordon paid $330.40 for the television.

18. 5: First, determine how many miles can be driven on one tank of gas by multiplying the numbers of gallons in a tank by the miles per gallon:

$$\frac{12 \text{ gallons}}{1 \text{ tank}} \times \frac{30 \text{ miles}}{1 \text{ gallon}} = 360 \text{ miles/tank}$$

Next, divide the total miles for the trip by the number of miles driven per tank of gas to determine how many total tanks of gas Robert will need:

$$1{,}800 \text{ miles} \div \frac{360 \text{ miles}}{1 \text{ tank}} = \frac{1{,}800 \text{ miles}}{1} \times \frac{1 \text{ tank}}{360 \text{ miles}} = 5 \text{ tanks}$$

19. C: Cora did *not* fall 7 out of 27 times, or $\frac{7}{27}$. To find the solution, divide 7 by 27 to convert this fraction to a decimal.

$$7 \div 27 \approx 0.26$$

To convert a decimal to a percent, simply multiply the number by 100, which moves the decimal point two places to the right, and add a percent sign to the end. Therefore, 0.26 converted to a percentage is 26%. This means that Cora did *not* slip and fall 26% of the time.

20. D: In order to determine the number of questions Joshua must answer correctly, consider the number of points he must earn. Joshua will receive 4 points for each question he answers correctly, and x represents the number of questions. Therefore, Joshua will receive a total of $4x$ points for all the questions he answers correctly. Joshua must earn more than 92 points. Therefore, to determine the number of questions he must answer correctly, solve the inequality $4x > 92$.

21. 144.65: To determine the total cost of Susan's outfit, add the costs of all her purchases.

$$\$69.99 + \$39.99 + \$34.76 = \$144.65$$

22. A: To find the total number of students, add all 4 values together: $14 + 9 + 5 + 2 = 30$. The total number of students with either green or hazel eyes is $5 + 2 = 7$. To convert the fraction into a percentage, use a proportion:

$$\frac{7}{30} = \frac{x}{100}$$

From here, cross multiply.

$$700 = 30x$$

Finally, divide both sides of the equation by 30.

$$x = 23.3$$

Therefore, approximately 23% of her students have either hazel or green eyes.

23. D: There are 14 students with brown eyes and 2 students with green eyes. So, the ratio of blue-eyed students to green-eyed students is $14:2$, which simplifies to $7:1$.

24. A: During week 1, Nurse Cameron worked 5 shifts.

$$\text{Shifts for week } 1 = 5$$

During week 2, she worked twice as many shifts as she did during week 1.

$$\text{Shifts for week } 2 = (2)(5)$$

During week 3, she added 4 shifts to the number of shifts she worked during week 2.

$$\text{Shifts for week } 3 = (2)(5) + 4$$

25. B: There are a total of $3 + 4 + 5 = 12$ blocks in the bag to start. After you take out an orange one, there are 11 left, 2 of which are orange. So, the probability of taking another orange one out is $\frac{2}{11}$. Getting the last orange one would then have a probability of $\frac{1}{10}$. Since both events are required to meet the criteria of "pulling two more orange blocks," they are multiplied. The probability is then $\frac{2}{11} \times \frac{1}{10} = \frac{2}{110} = \frac{1}{55}$.

26. B: The number of people who voted for the proposition is 9.5% of 51,623. If we only require an approximation, we can round 9.5% to 10% and 51,623 to 50,000. Then 9.5% of 51,623 is about 10% of 50,000, or $(0.1)(50,000) = 5,000$.

27. D: To calculate the total time taken, divide the distance driven by the speed it was driven at:

$$305 \text{ mi} \div 65 \text{ mph} = 305 \text{ miles} \times \frac{1 \text{ hour}}{65 \text{ miles}} = 4.69 \text{ hours}$$

$$162 \text{ mi} \div 80 \text{ mph} = 162 \text{ miles} \times \frac{1 \text{ hour}}{80 \text{ miles}} = 2.03 \text{ hours}$$

Convert the minutes spent at the gas station to hours: $15 \text{ min} \times \frac{1 \text{ hour}}{60 \text{ minutes}} = 0.25 \text{ hours}$.

Find the total time taken on the trip by summing all the times: $4.69 + 2.03 + 0.25 = 6.97$ hours.

28. B: The chart indicates that each x-value must be tripled to equal the corresponding y-value, so $y = 3x$. One way you can determine this is by plugging corresponding pairs of x and y into the answer choices.

29. A: Apply the order of operations to solve this problem. Multiplication and division are computed first from left to right. Then addition and subtraction are computed next from left to right.

$$2 + (2)(2) - 2 \div 2 = 2 + 4 - 2 \div 2$$
$$= 2 + 4 - 1$$
$$= 6 - 1$$
$$= 5$$

30. C: The volume of a cylinder may be calculated using the formula $V = \pi r^2 h$, where r represents the radius of the circular base and h represents the height. Substituting 3.14 for π, 1.5 for r, and 3 for h gives $V = (3.14)(1.5 \text{ in})^2 (3 \text{ in})$, which simplifies to $V \approx 21.2 \text{ in}^3$.

31. C: Since 70% of the patients in the study were women, 30% of the patients were men. Calculate the number of male patients by multiplying 100 by 0.30.

$$(100)(0.30) = 30$$

Of the 30 male patients in the study, 10% were overweight as children, so 90% were not overweight. Multiply 30 by 0.90 to get the final answer.

$$(30)(0.90) = 27$$

32. C: The variables are the objects the graph measures. In this case, the graph measures the nurse specialties and the number of nurses for each specialty. The dependent variable changes with the independent variable. Here, the number of nurses depends on the particular nurse specialty. Therefore, the independent variable is nurse specialties.

33. C: If the incoming class has 100 students, then $\frac{3}{4}$ of those students will major in nursing.

$$(100)\left(\frac{3}{4}\right) = 75$$

So, 75 students will major in nursing but only $\frac{1}{5}$ of that 75 will complete the nursing program.

$$(75)\left(\frac{1}{5}\right) = 15$$

Therefore, 15 students will complete the program.

34. D: The points do not show any trend line or trend curve at all, so there is no association in the scatter plot.

35. B: The line graph shows the largest number of flights made during a month as 79 with the smallest number of flights made during a month as 54. The range is equal to the difference between the largest number of flights and smallest number of flights: $79 - 54 = 25$. Therefore, the range is equal to 25.

36. B: Since 35% of the staff will take vacation days, only $100\% - 35\% = 65\%$ of the staff is available to work. Of the remaining 65%, only 20% are certified to work in the neonatal unit. Therefore multiply 65% by 20% using these steps:

Convert 65% and 20% into decimals by dividing both numbers by 100.

$$\frac{65}{100} = 0.65 \text{ and } \frac{20}{100} = 0.20$$

Now multiply 0.65 by 0.20 to get:

$$(0.65)(0.20) = 0.13$$

Test #1

Now convert 0.13 to a percentage by multiplying by 100.

$$(0.13)(100) = 13\%$$

37. C: A graph that has a y-intercept of 0 indicates a directly proportional relationship because the starting value is 0, and no amount is added to, or subtracted from, the term containing the slope.

38. B: Compare and order the rational numbers by finding a common denominator for all three fractions. The least common denominator for 3, 5, and 15 is 15. Now convert the fractions with different denominators into fractions with a common denominator.

$$\frac{4}{15} = \frac{4}{15}$$

$$\frac{2 \times 3}{5 \times 3} = \frac{6}{15}$$

$$\frac{1 \times 5}{3 \times 5} = \frac{5}{15}$$

Now that all three fractions have the same denominator, order them from smallest to largest by comparing the numerators.

$$\frac{4}{15} < \frac{5}{15} < \frac{6}{15}$$

Since $\frac{4}{15}$ of the patients are in Group Alpha, this group has the smallest number of patients. The next largest group has $\frac{5}{15}$ of the patients, which is Group Gamma. The largest group has $\frac{6}{15}$ of the patients, which is Group Beta.

Science

1. A: A catalyst increases the rate of a chemical reaction without becoming part of the net reaction. Therefore, chemical C increases the rate of the reaction between A and B. The catalyst does not change the chemicals within the reaction or initiate the reaction itself.

2. B: To determine the average number of neutrons in one atom of an element, subtract the atomic number from the average atomic mass. For bromine (Br), subtract its atomic number (35) from its average atomic mass (79.90) to find the average number of neutrons, 44.90.

3. A: The number of protons is the same for every atom of a given element and is the element's atomic number. The atomic number of zinc (Zn) is 30.

4. A: The researcher should use statistical analysis to understand trends in the data. Different statistics tools can help manage and examine large data sets. The researcher would probably miss important correlations by looking at the individual data points, and eliminating most of the data would defeat the purpose of conducting the study. Simply staring at the data would not be helpful.

5. C: Blood returns to the heart from both the inferior and superior vena cava, entering into the right atrium, through the tricuspid valve, and into the right ventricle. Once the right ventricle is full, the tricuspid valve closes, and upon heart contraction, the blood is pumped through the pulmonary artery, becoming oxygenated in the lungs. The blood returns to the heart from the lungs through the pulmonary vein, into the left atrium, through the mitral valve, and into the left ventricle. When the left ventricle is full, the mitral valve closes, and the heart contracts and distributes the newly oxygenated blood throughout the body through the aortic valve and into the aorta.

6. B, D: An antigen is any substance perceived by the immune system as dangerous. When the body senses an antigen, it produces an antibody. Collagen is one of the components of bone, tendon, and cartilage. It is a spongy protein that can be turned into gelatin by boiling. Hemoglobin is a protein in red blood cells that carries oxygen. In order for the blood to carry enough oxygen to the cells of the body, there has to be a sufficient amount of hemoglobin. Lymph is a near-transparent fluid that performs a number of functions in the body: it removes bacteria from tissues, replaces lymphocytes in the blood, and moves fat away from the small intestine. Lymph nodes are the structures that filter the lymph and work to neutralize undesirable substances.

7. A, C, D: One of the large intestine's main functions is the reabsorption of water into the body to form solid waste. It also allows for the absorption of vitamin K, biotin, and electrolytes. The liver produces bile, which aids in digestion. Bile is primarily stored in the gallbladder before it enters the digestive tract. The ileum, the final segment of the small intestine, extracts the last of the nutrients from the chyme. The duodenum (not the jejunum) is the first section of the small intestine, and it receives chyme from the stomach, further digesting it with the help of enzymes released by the gallbladder. The jejunum (not the duodenum) is the portion of the small intestine in which amino acids, fatty acids, and sugars are absorbed. The pancreas (not the gallbladder) releases insulin to assist in the removal and transport of sugar in the body.

8. D: The atomic number equals the number of protons in an atom (and, in a neutral atom, the number of electrons). Since Be has an atomic number of 4, it has 4 protons and 4 electrons. H has the fewest protons and electrons, as denoted by its atomic number of 1.

9. B: Based on the evidence, the most likely explanation for fly larvae in the spoiled food is that flies laid their eggs in the food. When the food was left out in the open, the flies had access to it and laid their eggs. However, when the food was in a sealed container, the flies could not lay their eggs in the food. Hence, the spoiled food in the sealed container had no fly larvae.

10. B: DNA is the primary carrier of genetic information in most cells. RNA serves as a messenger that transmits genetic information from DNA to the cytoplasm of the cell.

11. A: Both DNA and RNA are made up of 4 nucleotide bases. Both DNA and RNA contain cytosine, guanine, and adenine. However, DNA contains thymine and RNA contains uracil. Choice B is incorrect because DNA and RNA do not have the same 4 nucleotides, and choices C and D are incorrect because neither DNA nor RNA contains 6 nucleotides. Furthermore, DNA has a double helix structure, and RNA has a single helix structure.

12. D: Enzymes are large molecules that serve as catalysts for certain biological reactions. Enzymes are complex but they do not suppress reactions. Enzymes can be triggered or targeted by biological reactions. While they are often connected to acidic processes, enzymes themselves are not acidic.

13. B: Enzymes are protein molecules produced by living organisms. Enzymes serve as catalysts for certain biological reactions.

14. A: Generally speaking, veins carry deoxygenated blood and arteries carry oxygenated blood, but there are exceptions. The pulmonary veins carry oxygenated blood from the lungs to the left side of the heart, and the pulmonary arteries carry deoxygenated blood from the right side of the heart to the lungs. The aorta takes oxygenated blood away from the left side of the heart and distributes it throughout the body. The superior vena cava returns unoxygenated blood back to the right side of the heart, to then be distributed through the lungs and reoxygenated.

15. D: In order to be valid and repeatable, an experiment must be designed to measure only the effect from the stated independent variable. In this case, the independent variable is the type of sweetener to be used. Modifying other aspects of the experiment, such as the ingredient proportions, the bake time and temperature, or the material of the sheet on which the cookies are baked, will render the experiment invalid for its stated purpose. For example, if the bake temperature were decreased for one of the batches, it would be impossible to say with certainty how much of the color difference was due to the different sweetener and how much was due to the different bake temperature.

16. C: The atom is negatively charged. Neutrons have no charge. Protons have positive charge, and electrons have negative charge that is equal in magnitude. Because the atom has more electrons than protons, the atom has a negative charge.

17. A: There are four different types of tissue in the human body: epithelial, connective, muscle, and nerve. *Epithelial* tissue lines the internal and external surfaces of the body. It is like a sheet, consisting of squamous, cuboidal, and columnar cells. They can expand and contract, like on the inner lining of the bladder. *Connective* tissue provides the structure of the body, as well as the links between various body parts. Tendons, ligaments, cartilage, and bone are all examples of connective tissue. *Muscle* tissue is composed of tiny fibers, which contract to move the skeleton. There are three types of muscle tissue: smooth, cardiac, and skeletal. *Nerve* tissue makes up the nervous system; it is composed of nerve cells, nerve fibers, neuroglia, and dendrites.

18. C: The pulmonary artery carries oxygen-depleted blood from the heart to the lungs, where CO_2 is released and the supply of oxygen is replenished. This blood then returns to the heart through the pulmonary vein, and is carried through the aorta and a series of branching arteries to the capillaries, where the bulk of gas exchange with the tissues occurs. Oxygen-depleted blood returns to the heart through branching veins (the femoral veins bring it from the legs) into the vena cava, which carries it again to the heart. Since the pulmonary artery is the last step before replenishment of the blood's oxygen content, it contains the blood which is the most oxygen depleted.

19. A: A formalized hypothesis written in the form of an if/then statement can then be tested. A statement may make a prediction or imply a cause/effect relationship, but that does not necessarily make it a good hypothesis. In this example, the student could rewrite the statement in the form of an if/then statement such as, "If the length of the string of the pendulum is varied, then the time it takes the ball to make one complete period changes." This hypothesis is testable, and doesn't simply make a prediction or a conclusion. The validity of the hypothesis can then be supported or disproved by experimentation and observation.

20. C: A control or controlled variable is a factor that could be varied, but for testing purposes should remain the same throughout all experiments, otherwise, it could affect the results. In this case, if the mass of the ball was changed, it could also affect the length of the period. The length of the string is meant to be an independent variable, one that is changed during experiments to observe the results upon the dependent variable, which is the variable (or variables) that are affected. In this case, the period would be the dependent variable.

21. C: The epidermis is the surface layer of skin, and the stratum basale is the deepest layer of the epidermis. The dermis is a layer of connective tissue immediately beneath the epidermis. The hypodermis, while not a layer of skin, is part of the integumentary system located just below the dermis.

22. A: A triple beam balance would be used to measure the mass (in grams) of the gum in this experiment. An anemometer is used to measure wind speed. A hot plate is used to heat liquids. A microscope is used to magnify microscopic particles or organisms.

23. B: The pads that support the vertebrae are made up of cartilage. Cartilage, a strong form of connective tissue, cushions and supports the joints. Cartilage also makes up the larynx and the outer ear. Bone is a form of connective tissue that makes up the majority of the skeleton. It includes both organic and inorganic substances. Tendons connect the muscles to other structures of the body, typically bones. Tendons can increase and decrease in length as the bones move. Fat is a combination of lipids; in humans, fat forms a layer beneath the skin and on the outside of the internal organs.

24. B: The transverse plane separates the body into upper and lower portions. An oblique plane is any plane that goes through the body at any angle other than horizontal or vertical. The midsagittal or median plane divides the body into equal right and left portions. The frontal or coronal plane separates the body into anterior and posterior sections.

25. A: The respiratory system uses the lungs, diaphragm, trachea, alveoli, and bronchi to help the body distribute oxygen and remove carbon dioxide. While the ribs contain and protect many of these elements, the ribs are part of the musculoskeletal system, which is responsible for providing structure, stability, and protection to the internal organs.

26. C: The number 7 on the pH scale is the "breaking point" between basic and acidic. Solutions with a pH above 7 are considered basic, while solutions with a pH below 7 are considered acidic. For instance, milk, with a pH of 6.5, is actually considered acidic. Bleach, with a pH of 12.5, is considered basic.

27. B: Ribosomes are organelles that help synthesize proteins within the cell. Cilia and flagella are responsible for cell movement. The cell membrane helps the cell maintain its shape and protects it from the environment. Lysosomes have digestive enzymes.

28. C: RNA has several roles, one of which is to act as a messenger and deliver information about the correct sequence of proteins in DNA. The ribosomes do the actual manufacturing of the proteins. Hydrogen, oxygen, and nitrogen work to create the bonds within DNA. The double-stranded sugar-phosphate backbone of DNA helps form its double helix shape, while RNA is only single-stranded.

29. B: A decrease in a natural predator, such as wolves, coyotes, bobcats, or wild dogs, would allow the population to become out of control. When a population of deer has increased, there would be a natural decrease in deer food sources in surrounding areas. Although deer have been known to share developed human habitats, this is often forced by reduced territory and food sources. An increase in hunting licenses would be used by local officials to try to control the population, helping to decrease the number of adults of breeding age.

30. B: Recessive alleles are represented by lowercase letters, while dominant alleles are represented by uppercase letters. Organisms that are homozygous for a trait have two identical alleles (BB or bb), while those that are heterozygous for a trait have two different alleles (Bb).

31. 75: Dominant genes are always expressed when both alleles are dominant (BB) or when one is dominant and one is recessive (Bb). In this case, $\frac{3}{4}$ or 75% will have brown eyes.

32. D: A covalent bond is one in which atoms share valence electrons. Within a water molecule, one oxygen atom and two hydrogen atoms share valence electrons to yield the H_2O structure.

33. C: In respiration, a human inhales air (oxygen), and then produces energy (ATP) and exhales carbon dioxide and water vapor. While oxygen is a main component of the respiratory system's process, it is not produced by the respiratory system. Rather, it is utilized and distributed throughout the body, and then what is not absorbed, is exhaled back into the environment.

34. D: The epiglottis covers the trachea during swallowing, thus preventing food from entering the airway. The trachea, also known as the windpipe, is a cylindrical portion of the respiratory tract that joins the larynx with the lungs. The esophagus connects the throat and the stomach. When a person swallows, the esophagus contracts to force the food down into the stomach. Like many other structures in the digestive and respiratory systems, the esophagus secretes mucus for lubrication. The diaphragm is a muscle that controls the height of the thoracic cavity, increasing the height on contraction (inspiration), and decreasing the height on relaxation (expiration).

35. B: The trachea is anterior or ventral to the esophagus. The trachea is separated from the esophagus by the epiglottis, which is a flap of cartilage that covers one while the other is in use. The trachea's proximal portion is connected to the larynx, and the distal portion splits off into the right and left bronchi.

36. B: A water molecule contains 2 hydrogen atoms and 1 oxygen atom. Therefore, the chemical formula for water is H_2O. Also, the pH of water is 7.

37. B: The parathyroid glands are located on the lateral lobes of the thyroid gland in the neck, on the posterior aspect. They are part of the endocrine system. When the supply of calcium in blood diminishes to unhealthy levels, the parathyroid glands motivate the secretion of a hormone that encourages the bones to release calcium into the bloodstream. The parathyroid glands also regulate the amount of phosphate in the blood by stimulating the excretion of phosphates in the urine.

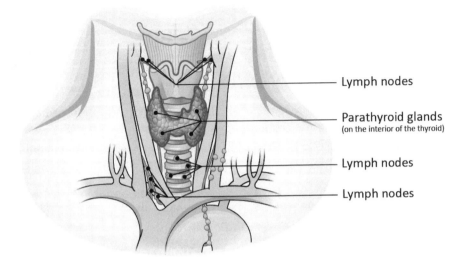

38. A: Genes store hereditary information and thus allow hereditary traits to be passed from parents to offspring. Genes do not prohibit hereditary transmission. Environmental factors like (temperature or light cycles) can determine what genes are expressed or not expressed, but not the other way around.

39. B: In the lungs, oxygen is transported from the air to the blood through the process of diffusion, in which molecules passively move from an area of high concentration to low concentration. Specifically, the alveolar membranes withdraw the oxygen from the air in the lungs into the bloodstream. Osmosis is the passive movement of a fluid, especially water, from an area of low solute concentration to an area of higher solute concentration through a permeable membrane. Reverse osmosis is the active transport of water opposite the concentration gradient, from an area of high solute concentration to low solute concentration. Dissipation is a more general reference of the spread or loss of energy.

40. B: The integumentary system includes skin, hair, and mucous membranes, all of which are responsible—in part, at least—for blocking disease-causing pathogens from entering the bloodstream. The circulatory system distributes vital substances through the body, and the lymphatic system sends leaked fluids from the cardiovascular system back to the blood vessels. The reproductive system stores bodily hormones that influence gender traits.

41. B: All the answers are part of the International System of Units (SI), with the exception of gallons. Liters measure volume, and meters measure length. Grams are a unit of measurement for the weight of an object, which would be measured on the triple beam balance.

42. D: The skin is a part of the integumentary system, along with the hair, nails, and glands. The skin controls fluid loss, protects deep tissues, and synthesizes vitamin D. The skeletal system gives the body its supporting structure, protects vital organs, assists muscles in body movement, stores calcium, and produces red blood cells. The muscular system maintains posture, collaborates with the bones in body movement, uses energy, and generates heat. The lymphatic system contains white blood cells, which aid in immune responses, and retrieves fluids leaked from capillaries.

361

43. C: Vaporization is the process of changing from a liquid to a gas. For instance, water vaporizes when boiled to create steam. Freezing is the process of changing from a liquid to a solid. Condensation describes changing from a gas to a liquid, and sublimation is the process of changing from a solid to a gas.

44. C: Mitochondria are often called the "powerhouse" of the cell because they provide energy for the cell to function. The nucleus is the control center for the cell. The cell membrane surrounds the cell and separates the cell from its environment. Cytoplasm is the thick fluid within the cell membrane that surrounds the nucleus and contains organelles.

45. B: Each chromosome contains many genes, which are the basic unit of heredity. Each gene consists of a number of DNA base pairs, ranging from thousands to hundreds of thousands of base pairs. A human chromosome is a single strand of DNA, which is usually tightly coiled. Human chromosomes average more than 100 million base pairs that encode between 200 and 2,000 genes.

46. B: The genotype describes a person's genetic makeup. The phenotype describes a person's observable characteristics. Among the choices, the CFTR gene refers to genetic makeup, while the other choices all describe traits that are observable.

47. B: Catalysts alter the activation energy during a chemical reaction and therefore control the rate of the reaction. The substrate is the actual surface that enzymes use during a chemical reaction (and there is no such term as *substrate energy*). Inhibitors and promoters participate in the chemical reaction, but it is the activation energy that catalysts alter to control the overall rate as the reaction occurs.

48. A: The integumentary system (i.e., the skin, hair, mucous membranes, etc.) coordinates with the circulatory system to remove excess heat from the body. The superficial blood vessels (those nearest the surface of the skin) dilate to allow the heat to exit the body. The hormonal influence on blood pressure is the result of the relationship between the circulatory system and the endocrine system. The urinary system is responsible for assisting in the regulation of blood's pressure and volume. The skeletal system is responsible for assisting in the development of blood vessels within the marrow.

49. A, D, E: Experiments are frequently conducted multiple times by different experimenters (B) to verify that the results are consistent. According to the principles of the scientific method, it is imperative that the hypothesis be established prior to the experiment (C), since the experiment is designed to test the hypothesis. As the experiment is conducted, data is observed and later analyzed to report results. If the results do not support the hypothesis, that is acceptable and may still be reported, since it is often informative. Once an experiment is complete, the information gained from it can be used to develop a new hypothesis to test.

50. C: A graduated cylinder would be the best equipment to accurately measure the volume of a liquid solution due to its fine measurement increments and precise manufacturing. Flasks and test tubes are used as reaction or storage vessels. Some of them may have volume markings, but they are not designed for accurate measurement. While it could be possible to calculate volume from a known density and the weight found by a triple beam balance, it is not a common method.

English and Language Usage

1. C: The word *syllabi* is the most common plural form of *syllabus* (although *syllabuses* is also correct). The other answer choices reflect incorrect plural forms. In English, words are normally pluralized by adding *–s* or *–es* to the end of a word, as in *car/cars* and *dish/dishes*. Irregular plural forms break this rule and follow different patterns. Words that come from Greek or Latin follow some distinctive patterns and are frequently used in mathematical or scientific language, as is the case for the word *syllabus.*

Singular Form	Singular Example	Plural Form	Plural Example
–us	Syllabus	*–i*	Syllabi
–is	Thesis	*–es*	Theses
–on	Phenomenon	*–a*	Phenomena
–um	Curriculum	*–a*	Curricula
–x	Index	*–ces* or *–xes*	Indices

2. C: Research papers are formal exercises that should not include several types of speech used in informal spoken settings. Colloquialisms are nonstandard forms of language, such as *ain't*, or slang, like *dude*. Contractions represent the words as they sound in speech, so *do not* is formal, whereas *don't* is informal. Relative pronouns are necessary in grammar. In the phrase "The boy who I met...," *who* is a relative pronoun. The second-person point of view is when the writer tells the audience something directly, such as a direct imperative, like "You should do this." This is normally inappropriate for a research paper, as it makes the paper too informal by removing distance between the reader and the subject, often sacrificing clarity in the process.

3. D: Suffixes appear at the end of words. Prefixes are attached to the beginning of words to change their meanings. *Un+happy, bi+monthly,* and *re+examine* include prefixes that change the meanings of the words to which they are attached. Suffixes usually act in a grammatical function, changing the part of speech or plurality of a word. A couple examples are *-s*, which makes most nouns plural and *-ly*, which signifies that an adjective is being changed into an adverb, such as *sad/sadly*.

4. C: Choice C is correct because the quotation is ordinary speech (requiring double quotes). Since the speech itself is a question, the question mark belongs inside the quotation marks. Choice A correctly places the question mark inside the quotation marks, but the use of single quotes is incorrect for standard quotations. Choice B is incorrect because it places the question mark outside the quotation marks. Choice D uses nested quotation marks, which are unnecessary in this case, since the sentence presents only one quotation.

5. C: Signal words give the reader hints about the purpose of a particular passage. Some signal words are concerned with comparing or contrasting, some with cause and effect, some with temporal sequencing (the order in which things happen), some with physical location, and some with a problem and its solution. To determine the function of a signal word, it is often best to test it in a sentence. For instance, "I stopped eating hot dogs because they give me indigestion." In this sentence, the word *because* connects the outcome ("I stopped eating hot dogs") to a cause (indigestion). The words *therefore*, *because*, and *accordingly* are used when describing cause-and-effect relationships.

6. A: The given sentence describes a mostly dirty window with a part of it that has been cleaned so that the light can shine in. The word *translucent* indicates that light can pass through something or, put another way, can go across to the other side. The prefix *trans-* refers to going across, and the root *lucent* refers to light.

7. B: The key to an effective concluding statement is a concise summary of the argument's main points. Such a conclusion leaves the audience with a clear and organized understanding of the argument. The introduction of new points would weaken the argument by straying from the main point at the last minute. Introducing other perspectives would work against the argument's effectiveness. Metaphors can help to make an idea more comprehensible, but they would normally be used before the conclusion, and they are not essential in any case.

8. B: The act of making changes to words or sentences in an essay is revision. Revising is the last step of the writing process. The other choices refer to activities that fall within the prewriting or writing stages of the writing process.

9. C: Normally, when a word ending with *e* gets a suffix that starts with a vowel, the final *e* is dropped (for example, *make* + *ing* = *making*). However, *noticeable* is an exception to this and the final *e* is not dropped.

10. A: The transition *surprisingly* indicates that the reaction was unexpected. The speaker not turning his or her work in on time and talking out in class would most predictably result in getting in trouble with the teacher. The other answer choices do not make as much sense to coordinate these two sentences.

11. A: The three words given are all ideologies, such as a type of religion or political viewpoint. The suffix *-ism* here suggests a doctrine that is followed, whether that be the doctrine of polytheism (a religious doctrine), communism (a social doctrine), or nationalism (a political doctrine). The suffix *-ia* often denotes a condition, as in *anemia* and *hysteria*. The suffix *-ness* often denotes a characteristic, as in *kindness* and *sadness*. The suffixes *-sion* and *-ance* can denote a state of being, as in *confusion* and *acceptance*. There are many suffixes with varying meanings in English, so sometimes the best way to learn their meanings is to find similar words and compare them to get a working definition.

12. C: Sentences are often easiest to understand when they first give the subject (the noun that is performing an action), then the verb (the action), and finally the object (the noun that is receiving the action). Only choices C and D follow this order, giving the subject (*She*), then the verb (*says*), and then the object (what she is saying). Only choice C keeps the original meaning; choice D implies that she does not like any outfits at all. The original sentence does also follow subject-verb-object order, but it is missing the word *outfits* and has other problems as well.

13. D: The semicolon correctly joins the two sentences. Answer choice A is incorrect, because it uses a comma splice to join two independent clauses. (To join two independent clauses, a comma needs to be accompanied by a coordinating conjunction.) The colon in answer choice B is incorrect because the information in the second clause does not clearly define or explain the previous clause. Answer choice C is incorrect because it offers no punctuation to separate the two independent clauses and thus creates more confusion than clarity.

14. D: Organizing writing into paragraphs is done either during the writing process, or afterward, in the revision stage. It is not a prewriting strategy. Choices A, B, and C describe steps that are used during the prewriting process to gather or organize information.

15. B: Answer choice B contains two independent clauses that are joined with a comma and the coordinating conjunction *and*. Answer choice A, though it contains a compound subject and a compound verb, is still a simple sentence. Answer choice C opens with a dependent clause, so it is a complex sentence. Answer choice D is a compound-complex sentence because it includes a dependent clause as well as two independent clauses.

16. B: The word *worryed* is misspelled because it does not follow the spelling rule of changing the final *y* to an *i* when adding a suffix. The second part of this sentence needs to match the past tense form of the first verb in the sentence, *sprinted*. In order to accomplish this, *worry* should be added to the suffix *-ed*, so the *y* must become an *i*, spelling *worried*.

17. A, B, C, E: Determining the context of a situation is important when considering whether or not formal language is necessary. The examples among the answer choices that would call for formal language involve admission to college, applying for a job, petitioning an elected official, and filing paperwork with an employer that would be stored long-term. These situations are less personal and have higher stakes than an email to a work colleague or a text to several fellow students, so they have a different standard of formality.

18. D: The word *affect* is a verb in this context and is the correct usage within the sentence. The word *effect* is generally used as a noun and is usually more passive than the word *affect*. In this sentence, budget cuts threaten to affect the plans, which would have an effect on the futures of the children. The possessive pronoun *your* also correctly modifies *children*, so answer choice D is correct. All other answer choices incorrectly apply the words to the sentence.

19. A: Prewriting must occur before drafting. Conferencing refers to collaborating with others so they may critique the draft or offer suggestions to improve it. Revising and editing both refer to changes a writer makes to a draft to improve it. Since choices B, C, and D are meant to help a writer improve a draft, they cannot be completed before the first draft is written.

20. C: The word *east* in answer choice C is simply a directional indication and does not need to be capitalized in the context of the sentence. All other uses of capitalization are correct in the context of the sentences. The word *South* should be capitalized when it refers to a region of the United States (as indicated by the mention of Mississippi and by the use of the determiner *the*). The word *East* should be capitalized when it refers to a specific area, such as a region of Texas. And the word *north* does not need to be capitalized when it is simply a directional indication (as in answer choice D).

21. C: The word *who* should be used as the subject of a sentence, the noun that is performing the action. The word *whom* should be used to indicate the object of the sentence, or the noun that is being acted upon. Choice C correctly uses the objective case, as Krista is holding someone responsible. The word *whom* is correct in this place, as it refers to the object of the sentence, the person being held responsible. Choices A and D do not use this form correctly, so they are incorrect. Choice B uses a different sentence structure, using a noun clause, "whom was responsible," but incorrectly uses the objective case, *whom*. Noun clauses need to be evaluated separately from the rest of the sentence to determine whether to use the subjective or objective case. In this sentence, we will insert a placeholder noun to help evaluate the noun clause: "[Jimmy] was responsible for the broken window." In this form, it is easier to see that the noun clause should use the word *who*, as in the subjective case.

22. A: Informal language is more casual and personal than formal language. In this example, the presence of the first-person pronoun *I*, as well as the colloquialism *counting on you*, indicate the use of informal language. The other choices do not contain first-person pronouns, colloquialisms, phrasal verbs, or slang.

23. C: Taking notes is not an example of a hands-on learning activity, and therefore would not be an effective supportive detail. Choices A, B, and D each mention an activity in which a child would be directly engaging in learning, whereas note-taking is a more passive activity.

Test #1

24. A: The pronoun *all* is plural, so it requires the plural verb *are*. The pronouns *each* and *neither* are singular and require singular verbs (not provided in answer choices B and C). The pronoun *any* can be either singular or plural depending on the context of the sentence. In this case, *any* suggests a singular usage, so answer choice D is incorrect with the plural verb.

25. D: In a formal debate, participants are expected to make their points using precise formal language. Key things to be avoided are contractions, colloquialisms, and first-person references. Choices A, B, and C are good representations of the sort of language that might be used in a formal debate. By contrast, choice D employs two colloquialisms, *tool around* and *gas-guzzling*, which would not be appropriate in a formal setting.

26. D: A simple sentence only has one clause, which means that there is one subject, the person doing the action, and one predicate, with one or more actions performed by the subject. While answer choice D is arguably the longest of the four sentences, it is actually a simple sentence. It contains a compound subject and a compound predicate, but because it represents only one independent clause it still functions as a simple sentence. Choices A and B contain two independent clauses and are thus compound sentences. Choice C contains a dependent clause, so it is a complex sentence.

27. C: Making a writing plan, brainstorming possible topics or subtopics, and creating an outline that the essay will follow are all elements that happen during the prewriting portion of the writing process. During prewriting, writers begin to think about how they want to explore a topic or argument in an essay. Prewriting is the first stage of the writing process, and it lays the groundwork for the actual writing which will take place.

28. D: The prefix *poly-* means "many." A strategy for solving this question is to compare *polygon* with similar words, such as pentagon and octagon. If you know that a pentagon has five sides and an octagon has eight sides and that both are polygons, it makes the most sense that *poly-* would mean many. Words that use the prefix *poly-* tend to be technical and difficult, such as *polynomial* or *polytheism*, so trying to compare other uses of the prefix are not as likely to be successful as looking at the root word.

29. A: The five basic elements of the writing process are prewriting, conferencing, writing, editing, and revising. Choices B, C, and D contain steps within those five elements.

30. B: This is the only choice that does not directly relate to the topic. Choices A, C, and D each connect to the idea of technology influencing relationships.

31. A, E: *Regardless* and *on the other hand* are transitional words/phrases that indicate contrast between the preceding ideas and the ones that are to follow. *Regardless* would commonly be used when the writer has just acknowledged a competing idea and is about to explain why that competing idea does not weaken his or her own argument. *On the other hand* may be used more neutrally to simply introduce a competing idea. *Furthermore* is a transitional word that indicates a logical continuation. *Subsequently* is a transitional word that indicates a temporal relationship. *Similarly* is a transitional word indicating comparison.

32. C: This is the best choice because *summer* is not a proper noun, but *Niagara Falls* and *New York* are proper nouns and require capitalization.

33. B: The suffix *-logy* usually means the study of something. The meaning of this suffix can only be derived from these word examples if the definition of one or more is known already. *Anthropology* means the study of humans, *biology* is the scientific study of life, *cosmetology* is the study of cosmetic techniques, *etymology* is the study of the origin of word meanings, and *genealogy* is the study of family history. Some of these words, such as *etymology* and *genealogy*, could suggest a meaning of *record*, as in choice A, but this is not fitting for words such as *cosmetology*. Likewise, some of these are sciences, but *study* is still a better fit, as *science* conventionally means a more specific form of study with experimentation and does not fit as well with *etymology* or *genealogy*. Finally, *cosmetology* is the only one of these that directly relates to techniques, as indicated by choice D. Study is the best fit for the entire collection of words.

34. C: Choice C offers the most effective combination of the sentences, with the use of the conjunction *but* and the dependent clause starting with *after*. All other answer choices result in choppy or unclear combinations of the four sentences. When combining sentences, it is important to use effective transitions and sequencing of ideas. In this case, the correct answer kept the sequence of events in order: losing the keys, looking for the keys, and finding them. The statement "I'm usually good about keeping track of my keys" is not an event in the sequence, but it serves well as an introduction at the beginning. Choice D made effective use of ordering and transitions, but it omitted the fact that the speaker found the keys, leaving ambiguity in the resulting sentence.

35. D: The suffix *–ation* commonly forms nouns from verbs, for example, *converse* to *conversation, confront* to *confrontation, revoke* to *revocation,* and *celebrate* to *celebration*. The suffix *–ness* commonly forms nouns from adjectives, for example, *happy* to *happiness, kind* to *kindness,* and *dark* to *darkness*. The suffix *–ity* also forms nouns from adjectives, for example, *formal* to *formality, sensitive* to *sensitivity,* and *gay* to *gaiety*. But the suffix *–ize* commonly forms verbs from nouns or adjectives, for example, *final* to *finalize, crystal* to *crystallize,* and *idol* to *idolize.*

36. D: The sentence in choice D is the only revision that expresses a possible meaning of the original sentence while both eliminating the pronoun-antecedent ambiguity and remaining idiomatic, or natural, in its expression. The sentence in choice A eliminates the ambiguity and is idiomatic, but the meaning is not compatible with the original. The sentence in choice B is ambiguous, and its meaning is also not compatible with the original. The sentence in choice C does not sound natural, and it loses information (that Joe is the boyfriend).

37. A: Semicolons are used to separate items in a series when those items contain internal commas, such as in a listing of cities and states. Choice A correctly demonstrates this. Choice B places the semicolon between the city and its state, instead of between each city and state pair, and this is incorrect. A comma is always used to separate a single instance of a city and a state. Choice C separates the items in the series with commas, but this creates confusion for the reader, since there are already commas between each city and its state. Choice D places commas between each item in the series, but fails to include the necessary comma between each city and its state.

TEAS Practice Test #2

Reading

The next four questions are based on the following passage.

As little as three years before her birth, few would have thought that the child born Princess Alexandrina Victoria would eventually become Britain's longest reigning monarch, Queen Victoria. She was born in 1819, the only child of Edward, Duke of Kent, who was the fourth son of King George III. Ahead of Edward were three brothers, two of whom became king but none of whom produced a legitimate, surviving heir. King George's eldest son, who was eventually crowned King George IV, secretly married a Catholic commoner, Maria Fitzherbert, in 1783. The marriage was never officially recognized, and in 1795, George was persuaded to marry a distant cousin, Caroline of Brunswick. The marriage was bitter, and the two had only one daughter, Princess Charlotte Augusta. She was popular in England where her eventual reign was welcomed, but in a tragic event that shocked the nation, the princess and her stillborn son died in childbirth in 1817.

Realizing the precarious position of the British throne, the remaining sons of King George III were motivated to marry and produce an heir. The first in line was Prince Frederick, the Duke of York. Frederick married Princess Frederica Charlotte of Prussia, but the two had no children. After Prince Frederick was Prince William, the Duke of Clarence. William married Princess Adelaide of Saxe-Meiningen, and they had two sickly daughters, neither of whom survived infancy. Finally, Prince Edward, the Duke of Kent, threw his hat into the ring with his marriage to Princess Victoria of Saxe-Coburg-Saalfeld. The Duke of Kent died less than a year after his daughter's birth, but the surviving Duchess of Kent was not unaware of the future possibilities for her daughter. She took every precaution to ensure that the young Princess Victoria was healthy and safe throughout her childhood.

Princess Victoria's uncle, William, succeeded his brother George IV to become King William IV. The new king recognized his niece as his future heir, but he did not necessarily trust her mother. As a result, he was determined to survive until Victoria's eighteenth birthday to ensure that she could rule in her own right without the regency of the Duchess of Kent. The king's fervent prayers were answered: he died June 20, 1837, less than one month after Victoria turned eighteen. Though young and inexperienced, the young queen recognized the importance of her position and determined to rule fairly and wisely. The improbable princess who became queen ruled for more than sixty-three years, and her reign is considered to be one of the most important in British history.

1. What is the author's likely purpose in writing this passage about Queen Victoria?
   a. To persuade the reader to appreciate the accomplishments of Queen Victoria, especially when placed against the failures of her forebears.
   b. To introduce the historical impact of the Victorian Era by introducing to readers the queen who gave that era its name.
   c. To explain how small events in history placed an unlikely princess in line to become the queen of England.
   d. To indicate the role that King George III's many sons played in changing the history of England.

2. Based on the context of the passage, the reader can infer that this information is likely to appear in which of the following types of works?

    a. A scholarly paper

    b. A mystery ✗   ✗   d

    c. A fictional story ✗

    d. A biography

3. Which of the following shows the correct chronological order of events from the passage?

    a. Princess Charlotte Augusta died, Princess Alexandrina Victoria was born, King George IV married Maria Fitzherbert, King George IV married Caroline of Brunswick

    b. Princess Alexandrina Victoria was born, King George IV married Maria Fitzherbert, King George IV married Caroline of Brunswick, Princess Charlotte Augusta died ✓

    c. King George IV married Maria Fitzherbert, King George IV married Caroline of Brunswick, Princess Charlotte Augusta died, Princess Alexandrina Victoria was born

    d. King George IV married Caroline of Brunswick, Princess Charlotte Augusta died, King George IV married Maria Fitzherbert, Princess Alexandrina Victoria was born

4. Which of the following could be considered a theme of the passage?

    a. Anyone can become royalty.

    b. People should only marry for advantage.

    c. Queen Victoria was a fair, but unlikely, queen. ✓

    d. Even the most unlikely events can happen.

5. If an author argues that children like strawberries more than any other fruit, what would be the best evidence to support her argument?

    a. A diary written by one child ✗

    b. An interview from a kindergarten teacher

    c. An article about strawberries from a school paper ✗

    d. A survey of 500 children that supports the author's theory ✓

6. Which of the answer choices gives the best definition for the underlined word in the following sentence?

    Adelaide attempted to <u>assuage</u> her guilt over the piece of cheesecake by limiting herself to salads the following day.

    a. Increase

    b. Support

    c. Appease ✓

    d. Conceal

7. Which of the following statements represents the BEST way to evaluate the information in a source?

    a. Make an educated guess about the source's accuracy. ✗

    b. Assume any printed source is completely accurate. ✗

    c. Get in touch with the person who wrote the source.

    d. Check it against information in one or more other sources. ✓

Test #2

The next three questions are based on the following chart.

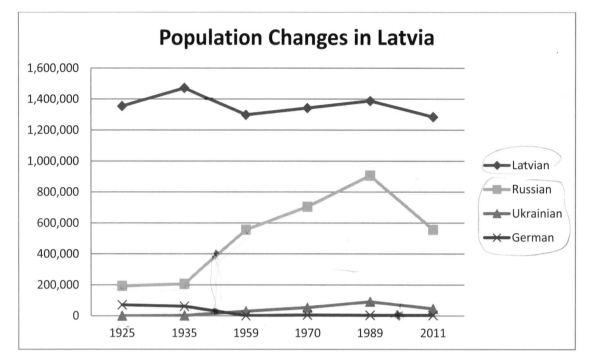

Population Changes in Latvia

8. Between 1925 and 1991, Latvia was part of the Soviet Union. Since 1991, the population of which ethnic group in Latvia appears to have decreased the most?

　　a.　Latvian
　　b.　Russian
　　c.　Ukrainian
　　d.　German

9. After World War II ended in 1945, large numbers of non-Latvian workers entered the country, primarily to work at construction jobs. Among these non-Latvian ethnic groups, the increase in workers represented a population percentage shift of less than one percent before 1945 to more than three percent by the time of the Soviet Union's collapse. Which ethnic group shown on the chart best represents this shift?

　　a.　Latvian
　　b.　Russian
　　c.　Ukrainian
　　d.　German

10. Which ethnic group's population had the least change after the end of World War II?

　　a.　Latvian
　　b.　Russian
　　c.　Ukrainian
　　d.　German

The next five questions are based on the following passage.

　　In the United States, the foreign language requirement for high school graduation is decided at the state level. This means the requirement varies, with some states deciding to forego a foreign language requirement altogether (www.ncssfl.org). It is necessary that these states reconsider their position and amend their requirements to reflect compulsory completion of a course of one or more foreign languages. Studying a foreign language has become increasingly important for the global economy. As technology continues to make international business relations increasingly easy, people need to keep up by increasing their communication capabilities. High school graduates with foreign language credits have been shown to have an increased college acceptance rate. In addition, students who have mastered more than one language typically find themselves in greater demand when they reach the job market. Students who did not study a foreign language often find themselves unable to obtain a job at all.

11. What is the main idea of this passage?
   a. Studying a foreign language will help graduating students find jobs after high school.
   b. Studying a foreign language should be a mandatory requirement for high school graduation.
   c. Studying a foreign language helps students gain an understanding of other cultures.
   d. Studying a foreign language is essential if a student hopes to get into college.

12. Which of the following statements represents the best summary of the claims made in this passage?
   a. Studying a foreign language is important if you want to graduate from high school and get a job.
   b. Studying a foreign language is important for the global economy because of the technological advances that have been made in international communications.
   c. Studying a foreign language is important for the global economy, college acceptance rates, and becoming a sought-after candidate in the job market.
   d. Studying a foreign language is important for college acceptance rates and obtaining a job after college.

13. Which of the following statements represents an exaggerated claim in support of the argument presented in this passage?
   a. In the United States, the foreign language requirement for high school graduation is decided at the state level.
   b. Studying a foreign language has become increasingly important for the global economy.
   c. High school graduates with foreign language credits have been shown to have an increased college acceptance rate.
   d. Students who did not study a foreign language often find themselves unable to obtain a job at all.

14. Which of the following would be a useful source of information to determine the validity of the argument presented in this passage?
   a. A survey of high school students' preferences with regard to foreign language requirements
   b. A comparison of the correlation between a second language introduced at home and subsequent college acceptance rates
   c. A survey that asks parents to select the foreign language they would like their children to study in high school
   d. A comparison of the correlation between high school students' study of a foreign language and subsequent college acceptance rates

Test #2

371

15. Which of the following would be the best concluding statement for this passage?

a. States should consider how important foreign languages are for the global economy when making their policies regarding foreign language requirements for graduation from high school.

b. Policies regarding a foreign language requirement for graduation from high school should take into account the importance of foreign languages for the global economy and the correlation between foreign languages and increased college acceptance rates and employment opportunities.

c. High school graduation requirements should include a foreign language class because of the influence knowledge of a second language has on college acceptance rates.

d. Policies regarding a foreign language requirement for graduation from high school should take into account how difficult it is to obtain a job in today's economy for those who do not have knowledge of more than one language.

The next question is based on the following information.

> LOOKING FOR ROOMMATE – CLEAN HOUSE / QUIET AREA / CLOSE TO UNIVERSITY
> Need one more female roommate for 3-bd house w/in walking distance of univ. Current occupants quiet, house clean/smoke-free. No pets. Long-term applicants preferred. Rent: $800/mo. Utilities/internet included. Avail: Aug 15. Call Florence at 985-5687, or send an email to f.carpenter@email.com.

16. Florence receives a number of calls about the roommate advertisement. Of the individuals described below, who seems like the best applicant?

a. Frances is a research assistant in the science department; she has a Yorkshire terrier.
b. Adelaide works in the humanities department; she is looking for a three-month rental.
c. Cosette is allergic to cigarette smoke; she needs a quiet place to study.
d. Felix is a graduate student in the history department; he doesn't have a car.

17. Which of the following would be the best source to begin developing a position about civil rights for an oral debate?

a. A blog created by a proponent of civil rights
b. An interview with someone who took part in a civil rights march
c. A history textbook detailing civil rights
d. A speech by a famous civil rights leader

18. Consider the following scenario:

Nora is preparing a large research project for the end of the term, and the instructor has required that all students make sure they are using reliable, scholarly resources in their papers. Nora will have to research numerous topics spanning science, medicine, economics, and more.

Which of the following resource options would be considered reliable, scholarly sources for Nora? (Select all that apply.)

a. The Bureau of Labor Statistics (bls.gov)
b. Wikipedia (wikipedia.org)
c. The Royal Society of Chemistry (rsc.org)
d. The National Institutes of Health (nih.gov)
e. The Sierra Club (sierraclub.org)

19. The year listed with each country is when the nation gained independence. Which of the following conclusions is true?

a. The nations of North America were also fighting for independence at the same time as nations in South America.
b. France lost most of its control in the New World because of these revolutions. ✗
c. Nations on the west coast gained independence first.
d. South America had many revolutions in the first three decades of the 19th century. ✗

The next three questions are based on the following passage.

For lunch, she likes ham and cheese (torn into bites), yogurt, raisins, applesauce, peanut butter sandwiches in the fridge drawer, or any combo of these. She's not a huge eater. Help yourself too. Bread is on counter if you want to make a sandwich.

It's fine if you want to go somewhere, just leave us a note of where you are. Make sure she's buckled and drive carefully! Certain fast-food places are fun if they have playgrounds and are indoors. It's probably too hot for the playground, but whatever you want to do is fine. Take a sippy cup of water and a diaper wherever you go. There's some money here for you in case you decide to go out for lunch with her.

As for nap, try after lunch. She may not sleep, but try anyway. Read her a couple of books first, put cream on her mosquito bites (it's in the den on the buffet), then maybe rock in her chair. Give her a bottle of milk, and refill as needed, but don't let her drink more than $2\frac{1}{2}$ bottles of milk or she'll throw up. Turn on music in her room, leave her in her crib with a

Test #2

dry diaper and bottle to try to sleep. She likes a stuffed animal too. Try for 30–45 minutes. You may have to start the tape again. If she won't sleep, that's fine. We just call it "rest time" on those days that naps won't happen.

20. To whom is this passage probably being written?

    a. A mother
    b. A father
    c. A babysitter
    d. A nurse

21. Which of the following details from the passage best supports the conclusion that the little girl is no older than three years old?

    a. For lunch, she likes ham and cheese (torn into bites), yogurt, raisins, applesauce, peanut butter sandwiches in the fridge drawer, or any combo of these.
    b. It's fine if you want to go somewhere, just leave us a note of where you are.
    c. As for nap, try after lunch. She may not sleep, but try anyway.
    d. Turn on music in her room, leave her in her crib with a dry diaper and bottle to try to sleep.

22. What is the first thing the instruction say to do to get the young girl to sleep?

    a. Give her a stuffed animal.
    b. Read her a couple of books.
    c. Rock her in her chair.
    d. Play music in her room.

The next four questions are based on the following passage.

In 1603, Queen Elizabeth I of England died. She had never married and had no heir, so the throne passed to a distant relative: James Stuart, the son of Elizabeth's cousin and one-time rival for the throne, Mary, Queen of Scots. James was crowned King James I of England. At the time, he was also King James VI of Scotland, and the combination of roles would create a spirit of conflict that haunted the two nations for generations to come.

The conflict developed as a result of rising tensions among the people within the nations, as well as between them. Scholars in the 21st century are far too hasty in dismissing the role of religion in political disputes, but religion undoubtedly played a role in the problems that faced England and Scotland. By the time of James Stuart's succession to the English throne, the English people had firmly embraced the teachings of Protestant theology. Similarly, the Scottish Lowlands was decisively Protestant. In the Scottish Highlands, however, the clans retained their Catholic faith. James acknowledged the Church of England and still sanctioned the largely Protestant translation of the Bible that still bears his name.

James's son King Charles I proved himself to be less committed to the Protestant Church of England. Charles married the Catholic Princess Henrietta Maria of France, and there were suspicions among the English and the Lowland Scots that Charles was quietly a Catholic. Charles's own political troubles extended beyond religion in this case, and he was beheaded in 1649. Eventually, his son King Charles II would be crowned, and this Charles is believed to have converted secretly to the Catholic Church. Charles II died without a legitimate heir, and his brother James ascended to the throne as King James II.

James was recognized to be a practicing Catholic, and his commitment to Catholicism would prove to be his downfall. James's wife Mary Beatrice lost a number of children during their infancy, and when she became pregnant again in 1687 the public became concerned. If James had a son, that son would undoubtedly be raised a Catholic, and the English people would not stand for this. Mary gave birth to a son, but the story quickly circulated that the royal child had died and the child named James's heir was a foundling smuggled in. James, his wife, and his infant son were forced to flee; and James's Protestant daughter Mary was crowned the queen.

In spite of a strong resemblance to the king, the young James II was generally rejected among the English and the Lowland Scots, who referred to him as "the Pretender." But in the Highlands the Catholic princeling was welcomed. He inspired a group known as *Jacobites*, to reflect the Latin version of his name. His own son Charles, known affectionately as Bonnie Prince Charlie, would eventually raise an army and attempt to recapture what he believed to be his throne. The movement was soundly defeated at the Battle of Culloden in 1746, and England and Scotland have remained ostensibly Protestant ever since.

23. **Which of the following sentences contains an opinion on the part of the author?**
    a. James was recognized to be a practicing Catholic, and his commitment to Catholicism would prove to be his downfall.
    b. James' son King Charles I proved himself to be less committed to the Protestant Church of England.
    c. The movement was soundly defeated at the Battle of Culloden in 1746, and England and Scotland have remained ostensibly Protestant ever since.
    d. Scholars in the 21st century are far too hasty in dismissing the role of religion in political disputes, but religion undoubtedly played a role in the problems that faced England and Scotland.

24. **Which of the following is a logical conclusion based on the information that is provided within the passage?**
    a. Like Elizabeth I, Charles II never married and thus never had children.
    b. The English people were relieved each time that James II's wife Mary lost another child, as this prevented the chance of a Catholic monarch.
    c. Charles I's beheading had less to do with religion than with other political problems that England was facing.
    d. Unlike his son and grandsons, King James I had no Catholic leanings and was a faithful follower of the Protestant Church of England.

25. **Which of the following best describes the organization of the information in the passage?**
    a. Cause-effect
    b. Chronological sequence
    c. Problem-solution
    d. Comparison-contrast

26. **Which of the following best describes the author's intent in the passage?**
    a. To persuade
    b. To entertain
    c. To express feeling
    d. To inform

375

Test #2

The next two questions are based on the following information.

Dear library patrons:

To ensure that all visitors have the opportunity to use our limited number of computers, we ask that each person restrict himself or herself to 30 minutes on a computer. For those needing to use a computer beyond this time frame, there will be a $3 charge for each 15-minute period.

We thank you in advance for your cooperation.

Pineville Library

27. Which of the following is a logical conclusion that can be derived from the announcement above?
   a. The library is planning to purchase more computers but cannot afford them yet.
   b. The library is facing budget cuts and is using the internet fee to compensate for them.
   c. The library has added the fee to discourage patrons from spending too long on the computers.
   d. The library is offsetting its own internet service costs by passing on the fee to patrons.

28. Raoul has an upcoming school project, and his own computer is not working. He needs to use the library computer, and he has estimated that he will need to be on the computer for approximately an hour and a half. How much of a fee can Raoul expect to pay for his computer use at the library?
   a. $6
   b. $9
   c. $12
   d. $15

The next five questions are based on the following passage.

Global warming and the depletion of natural resources are constant threats to the future of our planet. All people have a responsibility to be proactive participants in the fight to save Earth by working now to conserve resources for later. Participation begins with our everyday choices. From what you buy to what you do to how much you use, your decisions affect the planet and everyone around you. Now is the time to take action.

When choosing what to buy, look for sustainable products made from renewable or recycled resources. The packaging of the products you buy is just as important as the products themselves. Is the item minimally packaged in a recycled container? How did the product reach the store? Locally grown food and other products manufactured within your community are the best choices. The fewer miles a product traveled to reach you, the fewer resources it required.

You can continue to make a difference for the planet in how you use what you bought and the resources you have available. Remember the locally grown food you purchased? Don't pile it on your plate at dinner. Food that remains on your plate is a wasted resource, and you can always go back for seconds. You should try to be aware of your consumption of water and energy. Turn off the water when you brush your teeth, and limit your showers to five minutes. Turn off the lights, and don't leave appliances or chargers plugged in when not in use.

Together, we can use less, waste less, recycle more, and make the right choices. It may be the only chance we have.

29. What is the author's tone?

a. The author's tone is optimistic.
b. The author's tone is pessimistic.
c. The author's tone is matter-of-fact.
d. The author's tone is angry.

30. Why does the author say it is important to buy locally grown food?

a. Buying locally grown food supports people in your community.
b. Locally grown food travels the least distance to reach you and therefore uses fewer resources.
c. Locally grown food uses less packaging.
d. Locally grown food is healthier for you because it has been exposed to fewer pesticides.

31. What does the author imply will happen if people do not follow his suggestions?

a. The author implies we will run out of resources in the next 10 years.
b. The author implies water and energy prices will rise sharply in the near future.
c. The author implies global warming and the depletion of natural resources will continue.
d. The author implies local farmers will lose their farms.

32. What is the best definition of the underlined word in the selection below, taken from the third paragraph of the passage?

You should try to be aware of your <u>consumption</u> of water and energy.

a. Using the greatest amount
b. Illness of the lungs
c. Using the least amount
d. Depletion of goods

33. Which of the following is one way the author specifies that a person can try to be aware of their consumption of water and energy?

a. Food that remains on your plate is a wasted resource, and you can always go back for a second helping.
b. Locally grown food and other products manufactured within your community are the best choices.
c. Don't leave appliances or chargers plugged in when not in use.
d. Participation begins with our everyday choices.

34. Which of the following statements would be LEAST relevant in a formal essay about artist Salvador Dalí?

a. Although his works are famed for their dream-like qualities, Dalí executed them with realism reminiscent of the Renaissance masters.
b. Salvador Dalí's eccentricity extended beyond his artwork, affecting the strange public persona he created, which can be witnessed in his numerous television appearances.
c. I've always found Dalí's painting *The Persistence of Memory* to be really disturbing for some reason.
d. Although Salvador Dalí is best known for his paintings, he also was active in cinema and collaborated with such filmmakers as Luis Bunuel and Alfred Hitchcock.

Test #2

35. Which of the answer choices gives the best definition of the underlined word in the following sentence?

Finlay flatly refused to take part in the piano recital, so his parents had to <u>cajole</u> him with the promise of a trip to his favorite toy store.

a. Prevent
b. Threaten
c. Insist
d. Coax

36. Your teacher has assigned you a research project on ancient Persian culture. Which of the following sources would be a good starting point that provides the most accurate information?

a. The Wikipedia "Persian Culture" entry
b. "All Cool Persian Stuff," a blog written by a scientist
c. *An Overview of Persian Society*, a book written by a historian
d. "Uncovering the Secrets of Persia," a two-page magazine article about lost temples

37. Which of the following sentences uses the word "smart" with a negative connotation, rather than a positive connotation or simply the word's denotation?

a. Eliot's teacher said he was not quite gifted, but too smart for a general class.
b. Eliot was smart to have studied the day before the test; he got a good grade.
c. Eliot was identified by his teacher as one of the smart students in her classes.
d. Eliot got into trouble when he gave a smart answer to his teacher's question.

The next four questions are based on the following information.

The Dewey Decimal Classes

000 Computer science, information, and general works
100 Philosophy and psychology
200 Religion
300 Social sciences
400 Languages
500 Science and mathematics
600 Technical and applied science
700 Arts and recreation
800 Literature
900 History, geography, and biography

38. Jorgen is doing a project on the ancient Greek mathematician and poet Eratosthenes. In his initial review, Jorgen learns that Eratosthenes is considered the first person to calculate the circumference of the earth, and that he is considered the first to describe geography as it is studied today. To which section of the library should Jorgen go to find one of the early maps created by Eratosthenes?

a. 100
b. 300
c. 600
d. 900

378

39. Due to his many interests and pursuits, Eratosthenes dabbled in a variety of fields, and he is credited with a theory known as the sieve of Eratosthenes. This is an early algorithm used to determine prime numbers. To which section of the library should Jorgen go to find out more about the current applications of the sieve of Eratosthenes?

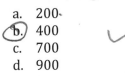

    a. 000
    b. 100
    c. 400
    d. 500

40. One ancient work claims that Eratosthenes received the nickname "beta" from those who knew him. This is a word that represents the second letter of the Greek alphabet, and it represented Eratosthenes's accomplishments in the many areas that he studied. To which section of the library should Jorgen go to learn more about the letters of the Greek alphabet and the meaning of the word "beta"?

    a. 200
    b. 400
    c. 700
    d. 900

41. Finally, Jorgen learns that Eratosthenes was fascinated by the story of the Trojan War, and that he attempted to determine the exact dates when this event occurred. Jorgen is unfamiliar with the story of the fall of Troy, so he decides to look into writings such as *The Iliad* and *The Odyssey* by Homer. To which section of the library should Jorgen go to locate these works?

    a. 100
    b. 200
    c. 700
    d. 800

42. Which of the following is a primary source that would be relevant to a biography about Jules Verne?

    a. Articles about Jules Verne written after his death
    b. Reviews of Jules Verne's works
    c. Film adaptations of Jules Verne's works
    d. Letters exchanged by Jules Verne and a close friend

43. Which of the following is NOT a way that theme is conveyed in nonfiction text?

    a. Through events
    b. Through word choice
    c. Through imagery
    d. Through meter

Test #2

The next question is based on the following passage.

One component of good story writing is showing and not telling. Showing can be achieved through descriptions of settings, events, and characters' appearances, words, and actions to show what is happening in the story rather than directly telling information as though the story is being narrated by the writer:

It was a cold and rainy morning. The first track meet of the season was scheduled for that day.

Instead of telling the reader information this way, it's often better to show the information. For example, the characters can show information through their words and actions:

Marissa shivered as she stood next to Jessica on the side walk. "Why didn't I bring my coat?" Marissa whined. "It's going to feel like this on the bus, too! And why does it have to rain the morning of our first track meet?"

"I know. I hope it isn't cancelled. I really wanted to see how my meet times were looking. I want to move up to a varsity slot so bad." Jessica huddled close to Marissa and craned her neck to look down the street. She glanced at her watch and frowned.

By having the two characters show the information, the reader has jumped right into the story and learned about the characters in the first few sentences.

44. What is the purpose of the italicized text in the passage?
- a. To distinguish dialogue from the rest of the passage
- b. To distinguish the examples of narrative writing from the rest of the passage   *B*
- c. To format a title of a major work
- d. To show the characters' inner thoughts

45. Which of the following is a primary source that would contain the most useful information for a research paper over the effects different family structures have on children?
- a. An article that includes quotes from people who grew up in single-parent homes
- b. An autobiography written by a person whose parents are divorced
- c. A study that examines the mental health of children from a variety of family structures
- d. A census that reflects the number of households that have a nuclear family structure

Mathematics

We now have video explanations for every math question in this practice test. Visit **mometrix.com/academy/teas-math-videos-2/** or scan this QR code to access these videos.

1. Curtis is taking a road trip through Germany, where all distance signs are in metric. He passes a sign that states the city of Dusseldorf is 45 kilometers away. Approximately how far is this in miles?

    a.   42 miles
    b.   37 miles
    c.   28 miles
    d.   16 miles

2. A man decided to buy new furniture from Futuristic Furniture for $2,600. Futuristic Furniture gave the man two choices: pay the entire amount in one payment with cash, or pay $1,000 as a down payment and $120 per month for two full years in the financing plan. If the man chooses the financing plan, how much more would he pay?

    a. $1,480 more
    b. $1,280 more
    c. $1,600 more
    d. $2,480 more

3. Given the histograms shown below, which of the following statements is true?

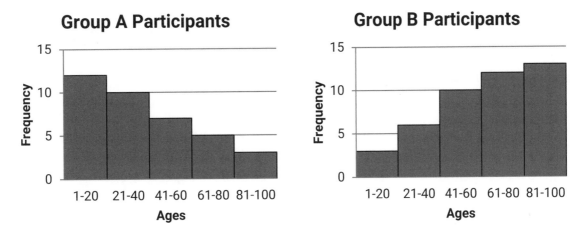

    a.   Group A is skewed left and has a mean age that is less than the mean age of Group B.
    b.   Group A is skewed right and has a mean age that is more than the mean age of Group B.
    c.   Group B is skewed left and has a mean age that is more than the mean age of Group A.
    d.   Group B is skewed right and has a mean age that is less than the mean age of Group A.

Test #2

4. Veronica decided to celebrate her promotion by purchasing a new car. The base price for the car was $40,210. She paid an additional $3,015 for a surround sound system and $5,218 for a maintenance package. What was the total price of Veronica's new car?

    a. $50,210
    b. $48,443
    c. $43,225
    d. $40,210

5. Which of the following is equivalent to $-8 + (17 - 9) \times 4 + 7$?

    a. 11
    b. 31
    c. 28
    d. 80

6. What statement best describes the rate of change?

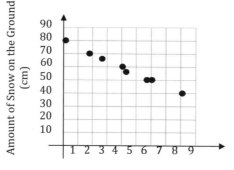

    a. Every day the snow melts about 10 centimeters.
    b. Every day the snow melts about 5 centimeters.
    c. Every day the snow on the ground increases by about 10 centimeters.
    d. Every day the snow on the ground increases by about 5 centimeters.

7. How many milligrams are in 5 grams?

    _____mg

8. There are $\frac{80 \text{ mg}}{0.8 \text{ mL}}$ of acetaminophen in concentrated infant drops. If the proper dosage for a four-year-old child is 240 mg, how many milliliters should the child receive?

    a. 0.8 mL
    b. 1.6 mL
    c. 2.4 mL
    d. 3.2 mL

9. On a highway map, the scale indicates that 1 inch represents 45 miles. If the distance on the map is 3.2 inches, how far is the actual distance in miles?

    _____mi

10. Given the double bar graph shown below, which of the following statements is true?

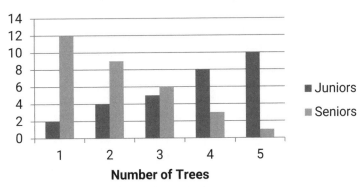

Number of Trees Planted

a. The number of trees planted by the Juniors is skewed right, while the number of trees planted by the Seniors is approximately normal.

b. The number of trees planted by the Juniors is skewed left, while the number of trees planted by the Seniors is skewed right.

c. The number of trees planted by the Juniors is skewed right, while the number of trees planted by the Seniors is skewed left.

d. The number of trees planted by the Juniors is approximately normal, while the number of trees planted by the Juniors is skewed right.

11. In the 2008 Olympic games, the semifinal heat for the women's 200m event had the following results:

Time (in seconds)
22.33
22.50
22.50
22.61
22.71
22.72
22.83
23.22

What was the mean time for the women who ran this 200m event?

a. 22.50 sec
b. 22.66 sec
c. 22.68 sec
d. 22.77 sec

12. A patient requires a 30% increase in the dosage of her medication. Her current dosage is 270 mg. What will her dosage be after the increase?

a. 81 mg
b. 270 mg
c. 300 mg
d. 351 mg

Test #2

The next two questions are based on the following information.

Kyle bats third in the batting order for the Badgers baseball team. The table shows the number of hits that Kyle had in each of 7 consecutive games played during one week in July.

Day of the Week	Number of Hits
Monday	1
Tuesday	2
Wednesday	3
Thursday	1
Friday	1
Saturday	4
Sunday	2

13. What is the mode of the numbers in the distribution shown in the table?

    a. 1
    b. 2
    c. 3
    d. 4

14. What is the mean of the numbers in the distribution shown in the table?

    a. 1
    b. 2
    c. 3
    d. 4

15. The graph below shows the weekly church attendance among residents in the town of Ellsford, with the town having five different denominations: Episcopal, Methodist, Baptist, Catholic, and Orthodox. Approximately what percentage of church-goers in Ellsford attend Catholic churches?

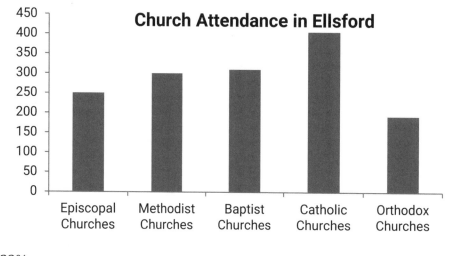

    a. 23%
    b. 28%
    c. 36%
    d. 42%

16. Lauren must travel a distance of 1,480 miles to get to her destination. She plans to drive approximately the same number of miles per day for 5 days. Which of the following is a reasonable estimate of the number of miles she will drive per day?

    a. 240 miles
    b. 260 miles
    c. 300 miles
    d. 340 miles

17. Based on their prescribing habits, a set of doctors was divided into three groups: $\frac{1}{3}$ of the doctors were placed in Group X because they always prescribed medication. $\frac{5}{12}$ of the doctors were placed in Group Y because they never prescribed medication. $\frac{1}{4}$ of the doctors were placed in Group Z because they sometimes prescribed medication. Order the groups from largest to smallest, according to the number of doctors in each group.

    a. Group X, Group Y, Group Z
    b. Group Z, Group Y, Group X
    c. Group Z, Group X, Group Y
    d. Group Y, Group X, Group Z

18. Solve for x:

$$3(x - 1) = 2(3x - 9)$$

_____

19. During January, Dr. Lewis worked 20 shifts. During February, she worked three times as many shifts as she did during January. During March, she worked half the number of shifts she worked during February. Which equation below describes the number of shifts Dr. Lewis worked in March?

    a. Shifts $= 20 + 3 + \frac{1}{2}$
    b. Shifts $= (20)(3)\left(\frac{1}{2}\right)$
    c. Shifts $= (20)(3) + \frac{1}{2}$
    d. Shifts $= 20 + (3)\left(\frac{1}{2}\right)$

20. A book has a width of 2.5 decimeters. What is the width of the book in centimeters?

    a. 0.25 centimeters
    b. 25 centimeters
    c. 250 centimeters
    d. 0.025 centimeters

21. Simplify the following expression:

$$\frac{5}{9} \times \frac{3}{4}$$

    a. $\frac{5}{12}$
    b. $\frac{8}{13}$
    c. $\frac{20}{27}$
    d. $\frac{47}{36}$

Test #2

The next question is based on the following information.

Profile of Staff at Hospital X and Hospital Y
(Total Staff: 433)

Hospital X (250)		Hospital Y (183)
Profession		
74	Doctor	55
121	Registered Nurse	87
14	Administrator	9
15	Maintenance	11
6	Pharmacist	5
4	Radiologist	2
2	Physical Therapist	2
1	Speech Pathologist	1
13	Other	11
Gender		
153	Male	93
97	Female	90
Age		
24	Youngest	22
73	Oldest	77
Ethnicity		
51	African American	42
50	Asian American	27
45	Hispanic American	35
47	Caucasian	37
57	Other	42
Years on Staff		
64	0–5	32
63	5–10	41
57	10–15	67
47	15–20	30
14	20–25	19
5	More than 25	5
Number of Patient Complaints		
202	0	161
43	1–4	21
5	5–10	1
0	More than 10	0

22. Which percentage is greatest?

a. The percentage of Asian Americans to staff as a whole at Hospital X
b. The percentage of staff members who have been on staff 10–15 years to staff as a whole at Hospital X
c. The percentage of doctors to staff as a whole at Hospital X and Hospital Y
d. The percentage of staff with 1–4 complaints to staff as a whole at Hospital Y

23. How many centimeters are in 7 meters?

    a. 0.07 cm
    b. 0.7 cm
    c. 70 cm
    d. 700 cm

24. Evaluate the expression: $3 - 3^3 + (3 \times 3 - 3)^3$

    a. 210
    b. 192
    c. 84
    d. 12

25. The number of houses Amelia has sold per year over the past ten years is listed below:

$$42, 36, 39, 45, 11, 47, 38, 41, 44, 34$$

Which of the following measures will most accurately reflect the number of houses she sold per year?

    a. Mean
    b. Median
    c. Mode
    d. Range

26. If Leonard bought 2 packs of batteries for x amount of dollars, how many packs of batteries could he purchase for $5.00 at the same rate?

    a. $10x$
    b. $\dfrac{2}{x}$
    c. $2x$
    d. $\dfrac{10}{x}$

27. Which of the following is listed in order from greatest to least?

    a. $2\frac{1}{4}, \frac{32}{5}, \frac{4}{5}, -5, -2$
    b. $\frac{32}{5}, 2\frac{1}{4}, \frac{4}{5}, -2, -5$
    c. $-5, -2, \frac{32}{5}, \frac{4}{5}, 2\frac{1}{4}$
    d. $\frac{32}{5}, 2\frac{1}{4}, \frac{4}{5}, -5, -2$

28. Dr. Lee saw that 30% of all his patients developed an infection after taking a certain antibiotic. He further noticed that 5% of that 30% required hospitalization to recover from the infection. What percentage of Dr. Lee's patients were hospitalized after taking the antibiotic?

    a. 1.5%
    b. 5%
    c. 15%
    d. 30%

Test #2

29. Olga drew the regular figure shown here. She painted part of the figure a light color and part of it a darker color. She left the rest of the figure white.

Which of the following equations best models the part of the figure Olga left white?

a. $1 - \frac{1}{3} - \frac{1}{3} = \frac{1}{3}$

b. $1 - \frac{1}{6} - \frac{1}{6} = \frac{2}{3}$

c. $1 - \frac{1}{6} - \frac{1}{2} = \frac{1}{3}$

d. $1 - \frac{1}{2} - \frac{1}{3} = \frac{2}{3}$

30. A farmer had about 150 bags of potatoes on his trailer. Each bag contained from 23 to 27 pounds of potatoes. Which is the best estimate of the total number of pounds of potatoes on the farmer's trailer?

a. 3,000
b. 3,700
c. 4,100
d. 5,000

31. Curtis measured the temperature of water in a flask in his science class. The temperature of the water was 35 °C. He carefully heated the flask so that the temperature of the water increased about 2 °C every 3 minutes. Approximately how much had the temperature of the water increased after 20 minutes?

a. 10 °C
b. 13 °C
c. 15 °C
d. 35 °C

32. John's Gym charges its members according to the equation $C = 40m$, where m is the number of months and C represents the total cost to each customer after m months. Ralph's Recreation Room charges its members according to the equation $C = 45m$. What relationship can be determined about the monthly cost to the members of each company?

a. John's monthly membership fee is equal to Ralph's monthly membership fee.
b. John's monthly membership fee is more than Ralph's monthly membership fee.
c. John's monthly membership fee is less than Ralph's monthly membership fee.
d. No relationship between the monthly membership fees can be determined.

33. On a floor plan drawn at a scale of 1: 100, the area of a rectangular room is 30 cm². What is the actual area of the room?

a. 30,000 cm²
b. 300 m²
c. 3,000 m²
d. 30 m²

34. Juan wishes to compare the percentages of time he spends on different tasks during the workday. Which of the following representations is the most appropriate choice for displaying the data?

    a. Line plot
    b. Bar graph
    c. Line graph
    d. Pie chart

35. Adrian measures the circumference of a circular picture frame with a radius of 3 inches. Which of the following is the best estimate for the circumference of the frame?

    a. 12 inches
    b. 16 inches
    c. 18 inches
    d. 24 inches

36. A certain exam has 30 questions. A student gets 1 point for each question he gets right and loses half a point for a question he answers incorrectly; he neither gains nor loses any points for a question left blank. If C is the number of questions a student gets right and B is the number of questions he leaves blank, which of the following represents his score on the exam?

    a. $C - \frac{1}{2}B$
    b. $C - \frac{1}{2}(30 - B)$
    c. $C - \frac{1}{2}(30 - B - C)$
    d. $(30 - C) - \frac{1}{2}(30 - B)$

37. Prizes are to be awarded to the best pupils in each class of an elementary school. The number of students in each grade is shown in the table, and the school principal wants the number of prizes awarded in each grade to be proportional to the number of students. If there are twenty prizes, how many should go to fifth-grade students?

Grade	1	2	3	4	5
Students	35	38	38	33	36

    a. 5
    b. 4
    c. 7
    d. 3

38. When the sampling distribution of means is plotted, which of the following is true?

    a. The distribution is approximately normal.
    b. The distribution is positively skewed.
    c. The distribution is negatively skewed.
    d. There is no predictive shape to the distribution.

Test #2

Science

1. Which of the following is NOT part of the circulatory system?
- (a.) Kidneys
- b. Heart
- c. Blood
- d. Blood vessels

2. What is the cellular function of cilia and flagella?
- (a.) Cilia and flagella are responsible for cell movement. ✓
- b. Cilia and flagella synthesize proteins.
- c. Cilia and flagella help protect the cell from its environment.
- d. Cilia and flagella have enzymes that help with digestion.

3. Which of the following elements is considered a transition metal?

1																	2 a.
3	4 b.											5	6	7	8	9	10
11	12											13	14	15	16 c.	17	18
19	20	21	22	23	24	25	26	27	28	29	30 d.	31	32	33	34	35	36
37	38	39	40	41	42	43	44	45	46	47	48	49	50	51	52	53	54
55	56	*	72	73	74	75	76	77	78	79	80	81	82	83	84	85	86
87	88	**	104	105	106	107	108	109	110	111	112	113	114	115	116	117	118

	57	58	59	60	61	62	63	64	65	66	67	68	69	70	71
*															
**	89	90	91	92	93	94	95	96	97	98	99	100	101	102	103

4. Where does gas exchange occur in the human body?
- (a.) Alveoli ✓
- b. Bronchi
- c. Larynx
- d. Pharynx

5. In your garden, you have noticed that the tomato plants on the north side of your house are growing better than those on the west side, and you have decided to figure out why. They are both planted in the same soil, and they are watered at the same time during the week. Over the course of a week, you begin to measure the amount of sunlight that hits each side of the house and determine that the north side receives more light because the sunlight is blocked on the west side by the house's shadow for much of the day. What is the name of the factor in your observations that affected the tomato plants' growth?
- a. The hypothesis
- b. The independent variable ✓
- c. The dependent variable
- d. The conclusion

6. **Which of the following is most different from the others?**

 (a.) Thyroid
 b. Stomach
 c. Intestines
 d. Pancreas.

7. **A vaccination is a way of acquiring which type of immunity?**

 a. Passive natural immunity +
 b. Active natural immunity
 (c.) Active artificial immunity
 d. Passive artificial immunity +

8. **Which of the following stimulates adaptive immunity?**

 a. Peptides
 (b.) Phagocytes
 c. Prions.
 d. Platelets.

9. **Which structure controls the hormones secreted by the pituitary gland?**

 (a.) Hypothalamus
 b. Adrenal gland
 c. Testes.
 d. Pancreas.

The next two questions are based on the following information.

Let B represent the dominant allele for a full head of hair, and let b represent the recessive allele for male-pattern baldness. The following Punnett square represents the offspring of two people with recessive genes for baldness.

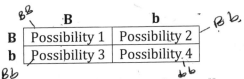

	B	b
B	Possibility 1	Possibility 2
b	Possibility 3	Possibility 4

10. **According to the Punnett square, which selection includes all outcomes that would produce an offspring with male-pattern baldness?**

 a. Possibility 1
 (b.) Possibility 4
 c. Possibilities 1, 2, and 3
 d. Possibilities 2, 3, and 4

11. **According to the Punnett square, which selection includes all outcomes that would produce an offspring with a full head of hair?**

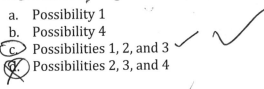

 a. Possibility 1
 b. Possibility 4
 (c.) Possibilities 1, 2, and 3
 (d.) Possibilities 2, 3, and 4

Test #2

12. Two isotopes of the same element have different numbers of:
    a. Electrons
    b. Protons
    (c.) Neutrons
    d. Nuclei

$2 + 4$

13. An atom has 2 protons, 4 neutrons, and 2 electrons. What is the approximate atomic mass of this atom?
    a. 2
    b. 4
    (c.) 6 ✓
    d. 8

14. A researcher wants to investigate the relationship between family income and quality of medical care. Which statement provides the best reason to conduct this investigation?
    a. The researcher can identify cheap medical care to recommend to low-income families.
    b. The investigation can help target healthy people so that they can remain healthy.
    (c.) Results of this investigation may identify a group of people who do not receive quality medical care and these people could receive better medical treatments.
    d. There is no reason to conduct this investigation.

15. The hydrogen bonds between its molecules make water a good:
    a. Solvent for lipids
    b. Participant in replacement reactions
    c. Surface for small particles and living organisms to move across
    (d.) Solvent for polysaccharides such as cellulose

16. Which part of the cell serves as the control center for all cell activity?
    (a.) Nucleus
    b. Cell membrane ✗
    c. Cytoplasm
    d. Mitochondria energy

17. Which of the following is a constant?
    (a.) The number of protons in an oxygen atom
    b. The temperature at which iron ore will melt
    c. The human population size
    d. The time the sun rises each day

18. Women were more likely to die in childbirth in the 18th century than in the 21st century. What is a possible explanation for why women are less likely to die in childbirth in the present age?
    a. Doctors are better equipped to perform cesarean sections.
    b. Doctors have more tools to monitor mothers during childbirth, so complications can be detected much earlier.
    c. Doctors wash their hands well to avoid transferring germs and infections.
    (d.) All of the statements above offer reasonable explanations for decreases in mortality during childbirth.

19. Which of the following does not contain blood vessels?
    a. Hyperdermis †
    b. Hypodermis·
    c. Dermis
    d. Epidermis.

20. Which of the following is not a type of muscle tissue?
    a. Skeletal
    b. Smooth
    c. Cardiac
    d. Adipose

21. Which of the following is considered an intensive property?
    a. Mass
    b. Weight
    c. Volume
    d. Density

22. The average life expectancy at birth in the United States at the beginning of the 21st century was about 75 years. The average life expectancy at birth in the middle of the 19th century was only about 40 years. Which of the following factors are likely to have, contributed to the longer life expectancy in the 21st century? (Select all that apply.)
    a. The human body has evolved to become more resilient to its environment.
    b. There have been numerous advances in medical technology and treatments.
    c. Higher standards of basic cleanliness have helped people avoid illness.
    d. The creation of vaccines has nearly eliminated certain diseases that were once deadly.
    e. Genetic disorders have been largely eliminated from the population.

B, C, D

23. The chart below shows the average snowfall in inches for a town on Michigan's Upper Peninsula during the months November through April.

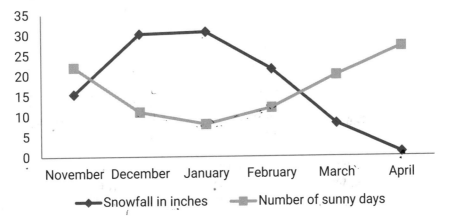

Which of the following can be concluded based on the information that is provided in the. chart?
    a. April is not a good month to go skiing in the Upper Peninsula.
    b. Snowfall blocks the sunshine and reduces the number of sunny days.
    c. The fewest sunny days occur in the months with the heaviest snowfall.
    d. The number of sunny days only increases after November.

C

Test #2

393

24. In order to be included in the formation of a scientific conclusion, evidence must be:
    a. Quantitative
    b. Reproducible
    c. Obvious
    d. All of the above

25. Which of the following does not exist in RNA?
    a. Uracil
    b. Thymine
    c. Cytosine
    d. Guanine

26. Which of the following is FALSE regarding the use of qualitative and quantitative data in scientific research?
    a. Quantitative data is collected through numerical measurements.
    b. Quantitative data is more accurate than qualitative data.
    c. Qualitative data is focused on perspectives and behavior.
    d. Qualitative data is collected through observation and interviews.

27. What kind of bond connects sugar and phosphate in DNA?
    a. Hydrogen
    b. Ionic
    c. Covalent
    d. Overt

28. All of the following are components of the genitourinary system EXCEPT:
    a. The kidneys.
    b. The urethra.
    c. The rectum
    d. The bladder

The next two questions are based on the following information.

Let T represent the dominant allele for a person being tall, and let the t allele represent a person being short. Additionally, the B allele corresponds to black hair, and the b allele corresponds with red hair. The genes of a tall person with red hair (Ttbb) are crossed with a short person with black hair (ttBb). Now consider the Punnett square below.

	Tb	Tb	tb	tb
tB	Possibility 1	Possibility 2	Possibility 3	Possibility 4
tb	Possibility 5	Possibility 6	Possibility 7	Possibility 8
tB	Possibility 9	Possibility 10	Possibility 11	Possibility 12
tb	Possibility 13	Possibility 14	Possibility 15	Possibility 16

29. What are the characteristics of a person with the genotype from Possibility 1?
    a. Short with black hair
    b. Short with red hair
    c. Tall with black hair
    d. Tall with red hair

30. Which of the following possibilities would produce a short offspring with black hair?
    a. Possibility 13
    b. Possibility 10
    c. Possibility 7
    d. Possibility 4

31. All of the following are parts of the respiratory system EXCEPT the:
    a. Trachea
    b. Bronchi
    c. Esophagus
    d. Larynx

32. The table below contains information from the periodic table of elements.

Element	Atomic number	Approximate atomic weight
B	5	11
C	6	12
N	7	14
O	8	16

Which pattern below best describes the masses of the elements listed in the table?
    a. The elements are listed in random order, C being the heaviest element and N being the lightest element.
    b. The elements are listed in decreasing order, B being the heaviest element and O being the lightest element.
    c. The elements are listed in increasing order, B being the lightest element and O being the heaviest element.
    d. All the elements weigh the same, so the order is irrelevant.

33. The majority of nutrient absorption occurs in the:
    a. Mouth
    b. Stomach
    c. Small intestine
    d. Large intestine

34. Which of the following items is a true statement about the immune system?
    a. The immune system is controlled by the hypothalamus.
    b. The immune system filters toxins out of the blood.
    c. The immune system stimulates the production of blood cells in response to infections.
    d. The immune system helps the body avoid, detect, and eliminate infections.

35. What is the smallest unit that can encode for a trait?
    a. A codon
    b. A gene
    c. A nucleotide
    d. A chromosome

36. Long bones are one of the five major types of bone in the human body. Which of the following bones are long bones? (Select all that apply.)
- a. Sacrum ✗
- b. Clavicle ✗
- c. Patella ✗
- d. Ulna
- e. Fibula
- f. Humerus

37. Which of the following is true regarding T cells?
- a. They are only seen in those with leukemia. ✗
- b. They are a specialized type of red blood cell. ✗
- c. They mature in the thyroid.
- d. They play a role in the immune response.

38. If a biologist is describing the physical and visible expression of a genetic trait, which of the following is he or she referring to?
- a. Phenotype
- b. Allele
- c. Gamete
- d. Genotype

39. What type of bond is formed when electrons are transferred between atoms?
- a. Transfer bond
- b. Static bond
- c. Covalent bond
- d. Ionic bond

40. Which type of cell secretes antibodies?
- a. Bacterial cells
- b. Viral cells
- c. Lymph cells
- d. Plasma cells

41. Which of the following structures have the lowest blood pressure?
- a. Arteries
- b. Arterioles
- c. Venules
- d. Veins

42. If an organism is AaBb, which of the following combinations in the gametes is NOT possible?
- a. AB ✓
- b. aa
- c. aB ✓
- d. Ab ✓

396

43. **Which of the following statements is NOT true of most metals?**
    a. They are good conductors of heat.
    b. They are gases at room temperature.
    c. They are ductile.
    d. They make up the majority of elements on the periodic table.

44. **The adrenal glands are part of the:**
    a. Immune system
    b. Endocrine system
    c. Lymphatic system
    d. Respiratory system

45. **What is the name of a condition where the heart rate is 118 beats per minute (bpm)?**
    a. Tachycardia
    b. Apnea
    c. Bradycardia
    d. Tachypnea

46. **A dietitian wants to convince a patient to lose weight. Which statement below best communicates a scientific argument that justifies the need for weight loss?**
    a. Losing weight can lower blood pressure, increase energy level, and promote overall health.
    b. Society tends to treat overweight people unfairly.
    c. Members of the opposite sex are more interested in people who maintain a healthy weight.
    d. Losing weight is easy to do.

47. **A researcher is studying the response of bacteria to a certain chemical. In three experiments, the bacteria swim towards the chemical, and in one experiment the bacteria swim away from it. What would be the most appropriate next step for the researcher?**
    a. Report only the first three experiments.
    b. Report all the experiments, but refrain from making any conclusions.
    c. Repeat the experiment several more times and apply a statistical analysis to the data.
    d. Repeat the experiment, adding a new chemical to determine its effect on the bacteria.

48. **Which of the following is NOT one of the major types of bones in the human body?**
    a. Dense bone
    b. Long bone
    c. Short bone
    d. Irregular bone

49. **Which statement below best describes the process of condensation?**
    a. Condensation is the process of changing from a gas to a liquid.
    b. Condensation is the process of changing from a liquid to a gas.
    c. Condensation is the process of changing from a solid to a liquid.
    d. Condensation is the process of changing from a solid to a gas.

397

Test #2

50. Using the graph below, what conclusion can be made about the students' scores?

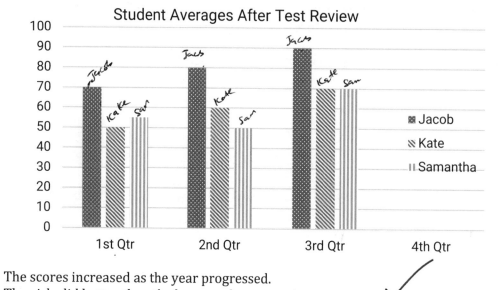

Student Averages After Test Review

- (a) The scores increased as the year progressed.
- b. The girls did better than the boys on the test each quarter. ✗
- c. The test was about math. ✗
- d. The scores were heavily impacted by the test reviews that were provided. ✗

English and Language Usage

1. Which of the following follows the rules of capitalization?

- a. Dashiell visited his Cousin Elaine on Tuesday.
- b. Juniper sent a card to Uncle Archibald, who has been unwell.
- c. Flicka and her Mother spent the day setting up the rummage sale.
- d. Lowell and his twin Sister look alike but have very different personalities.

2. Based on the word choices in the following sentence, which of the following is the most likely meaning of the prefix *per-*?

The barista poured water onto the coffee grounds until the water fully permeated the grounds and percolated into the glass vessel below.

- a. Across
- b. By
- c. With
- d. Through

Read the following excerpt from *The Great Gatsby* by F. Scott Fitzgerald and answer the question that follows.

"My dear," she told her sister in a high, mincing shout, "most of these fellas will cheat you every time. All they think of is money. I had a woman up here last week to look at my feet, and when she gave me the bill you'd of thought she had my appendicitis out."

3. Which of the following literary devices is present in the excerpt?

  a. Personification
  b. Synecdoche
  c. Metaphor
  d. Colloquialism

4. Which of the following sentences is most correct in terms of style, clarity, and punctuation?

  a. The possible side effects of the medication that the doctor had prescribed for her was a concern for Lucinda, and she continued to take the medication.
  b. The medication that the doctor prescribed had side effects concerning Lucinda who continued to take it.
  c. Lucinda was concerned about side effects from the medication that her doctor had prescribed, so she continued to take it.
  d. Although Lucinda was concerned about the possible side effects, she continued to take the medication that her doctor had prescribed for her.

5. Javier is writing a persuasive essay about the role of government in education. He has outlined his paper, written a draft, and revised his draft. Which of the following steps in the writing process has NOT been completed?

  a. Brainstorm topics
  b. Research reliable sources
  c. Write a second draft
  d. Select a topic

6. The word *capacity* functions as which part of speech in the following sentence?

  Irish politician Constance Markiewicz was the first woman elected to the British House of Commons, but she never served in that capacity due to her activity in forming the Irish Republic.

  a. Verb
  b. Noun
  c. Adverb
  d. Pronoun

7. Which of the following sentences represents the best style and clarity of expression?

  a. Without adequate preparation, the test was likely to be a failure for Zara.
  b. The test was likely to be a failure for Zara without adequate preparation.
  c. Without adequate preparation, Zara expected to fail the test.
  d. Zara expected to fail the test without adequate preparation.

8. What does the prefix *circum-* mean in the word *circumference?*

  a. Beyond
  b. After
  c. Around
  d. Before

399

9. Which of the following sentences demonstrates the correct use of an apostrophe?

   a. Lyle works for the courthouse, and among his responsibilities is getting the jurors meal's.
   b. Lyle works for the courthouse, and among his responsibilities is getting the juror's meals.
   c. Lyle works for the courthouse, and among his responsibilities is getting the jurors' meals.
   d. Lyle works for the courthouse, and among his responsibilities is getting the jurors meals'.

10. Which of the following would belong in a formal speech?

   a. We all need to work together to make this school better. First, we need to organize a list of our issues. Then we need to form small groups to discuss them and find solutions. Finally, we need to implement those solutions.
   b. Our purpose is to work together to improve the quality of education at this school. Ideally, we need to organize a list of our issues. Secondly, we need to form small groups to discuss them and find solutions. Then, we need to implement some solutions.
   c. We all got to work together to make this school much better than before. First, we need to say what is on our mind. We got to form small groups to discuss them and find solutions. And, we need to talk about those solutions.
   d. It is possible for us to talk about the problems in school and solve them. Of course, we need to organize a list of our issues. For example, we should form small groups to discuss them and find solutions. Finally, we need to implement those solutions.

11. Which of the following sentences demonstrates correct use of an apostrophe?

   a. In one version of the story, there are seven fairy's invited to the christening, while in another version there are twelve fairy's.
   b. Some historians' believe that the number twelve represents the shift from a lunar year of thirteen months to a solar year of twelve months.
   c. Other historians claim that the symbolism in the fairy tale is more about nature and the shifting season's.
   d. Regardless of its meaning, the fairy tale remains popular and has been immortalized in Tchaikovsky's music for the ballet.

12. Which of the following is NOT an example of a phrase that might be found within the transition sentence of a paragraph?

   a. In the same way
   b. Research proves that
   c. Another reason for this is
   d. As a result

13. Which of the following sentences contain proper subject-verb agreement? (Select all that apply.)

   a. Neither Jeanne nor Pauline like the dinner options on the menu.
   b. The issues that the council is discussing today concerns the local property tax rate.
   c. The faculty of the math department were unable to agree on the curriculum changes.
   d. Both Clara and Don feels that they need to be more proactive in checking on the contractors.
   e. If either Pablo or Julio is willing to accept the position, we will be fully staffed.

Mometrix

14. Which of the following statements would require a citation?

    a. The rate of increase in gasoline prices is unprecedented.
    b. I saw on the news that gas prices are increasing.
    c. *Economic Times* reported that gas prices are up 11% from last month.
    d. My friend and I were shocked about how much gas cost when we filled up yesterday.

15. What is the most effective way to combine the two sentences below?

    German cuisine is known for its hearty meat and potato dishes. Families often enjoy a rich Sunday dinner of roast meat, potatoes, and cabbage.

    a. German cuisine is known for its hearty meat and potato dishes but families often enjoy a rich Sunday dinner of roast meat, potatoes, and cabbage.
    b. German cuisine is known for its hearty meat and potato dishes, but families often enjoy a rich Sunday dinner of roast meat, potatoes, and cabbage.
    c. German cuisine is known for its hearty meat and potato dishes and families often enjoy a rich Sunday dinner of roast meat, potatoes and cabbage.
    d. German cuisine is known for its hearty meat and potato dishes, and families often enjoy a rich Sunday dinner of roast meat, potatoes, and cabbage.

16. Which of the following is a simple sentence?

    a. Ben likes baseball, but Joseph likes basketball.
    b. It looks like rain; be sure to bring an umbrella.
    c. Although he was tired, Edgar still attended the recital.
    d. Marjorie and Thomas planned an exciting trip to Maui.

17. Which of the following actions should NOT take place during the revising, editing, and proofreading steps of the writing process?

    a. Improving word choice
    b. Replacing irrelevant or weak sentences
    c. Identifying sentences that require citations
    d. Determining the argument the composition will defend

18. When writing a letter to the school board of a public school, which of the following greetings would be most appropriate?

    a. Dearest School Board,
    b. To Whom it May Concern,
    c. Dear Sir and/or Ma'am,
    d. Hello all,

19. Which of the following sentences represents a homophone error?

    a. Their decision to stay home was vindicated when they heard about what happened.
    b. Jane was given a prescription for aural paste to put on her mouth ulcers.
    c. The team from Cincinnati led the league in scoring last year.
    d. What effect will this new legislation have on hospital policy?

Test #2

Read the following sentences, adapted from *Alice's Adventures in Wonderland* by Lewis Carroll, and answer the question that follows:

I.   There was not a moment to be lost: away went Alice like the wind, and was just in time to hear it say, as it turned a corner, "Oh my ears and whiskers, how late it's getting!"

II.   There were doors all round the hall, but they were all locked; and Alice went all the way down one side and up the other, trying every door.

III.   Alice looked up, but it was all dark overhead; before her was another long passage, and the White Rabbit was in sight, hurrying down it.

IV.   She was close behind it when she turned the corner, but the Rabbit was no longer to be seen: she found herself in a long, low hall, which was lit up by a row of lamps hanging from the roof.

20. Which of the following choices shows the best chronological order for the sentences within the paragraph?

a. IV, II, I, III
b. III, IV, II, I
c. I, II, III, IV
d. III, I, IV, II

21. Choose the sentence that most effectively follows the conventions of standard written English:

a. Wilbur and Orville Wright were two brothers, and they tested their prototype airplane on a beach in Kitty Hawk, North Carolina.
b. The two brothers, Wilbur and Orville Wright, tested their prototype airplane on a beach in Kitty Hawk, North Carolina.
c. Testing their prototype airplane on a beach in Kitty Hawk, North Carolina, were the two brothers, Wilbur and Orville Wright.
d. The beach in Kitty Hawk, North Carolina was where the two brothers, Wilbur and Orville Wright, came and tested their prototype airplane.

22. Joann has brainstormed, created an outline, and completed research for a major term paper. Which of the following is the next step she should complete in the writing process?

a. Editing
b. Publishing
c. Proofreading
d. Drafting

23. If the word *antibacterial* describes a substance that kills bacteria, you can infer that the prefix *anti-* means:

a. Original to
b. Against
c. Before
d. Under

24. Which of the following is the most likely setting of the scenario below?

> Walking along the Thames, Julianna saw a sign advertising a fish and chips shop. Since she felt a bit peckish, she made her way over to the queue.

a. Chicago, United States
b. Vienna, Austria
c. Tokyo, Japan
d. London, England

25. **Which of the following words functions as a pronoun in the sentence below?**

> Anne-Charlotte and I will be driving together to the picnic this weekend.

a. Be
b. This
c. Together
d. I

26. **Which of the sentences below contain a correctly spelled plural noun? (Select all that apply.)**

a. She spends an hour making lunches each morning.
b. Be careful; there are dangerous gass in this area.
c. I've heard there are beautiful wolfs at the local zoo.
d. Not many people own house's in this area.
e. Merry Christmas from the Baldwins!
f. It was a week's work to mow all the neighborhood's lawns.

27. **Which of the answer choices best explains the purpose of the parentheses in the sentence?**

> The Hapsburg rule of the Austro-Hungarian Empire effectively ended with the reign of Franz Joseph I (1848–1916).

a. To offer brief commentary on the subject matter being discussed
b. To modify or qualify the statement that came immediately before
c. To identify information that was located using another source
d. To set off useful information that does not fit the flow of the sentence

28. **Which of the following is NOT an effective brainstorming strategy?**

a. Making a list of possible topics/subtopics
b. Daydreaming until inspiration strikes
c. Freewriting, then reading over what you wrote
d. Asking yourself who, what, where, when, why, and how

Test #2

29. In the words *proactive, progress,* and *projecting, pro-* is a(n) _____ that means _____.

    a. suffix; good, on top of, or over
    b. prefix; before, forward, or front
    c. affix; after, behind, or in back of
    d. prefix; against, under, or below

30. Maria's topic sentence is "My family throws elaborate holiday celebrations." Which of the following would be the best supporting detail to follow that sentence?

    a. Holidays are just a waste of everyone's time and money, in my opinion.
    b. First, we decide who will host the holiday dinner and when the celebration will take place.
    c. My household includes five people, but my extended family includes over thirty people.
    d. Afterwards, we all help clean up and then relax by continuing to chat with each other.

31. Which of the following is a complex sentence?

    a. Milton's favorite meal is spaghetti and meatballs, along with a side salad and garlic toast.
    b. Before Ernestine purchases a book, she always checks to see if the library has it.
    c. Desiree prefers warm, sunny weather, but her twin sister Destiny likes a crisp, cold day.
    d. Ethel, Ben, and Alice are working together on a school project about deteriorating dams.

32. By examining the parts of each word, determine which of the following words refers to "a drug that removes feeling or sensation."

    a. Hyperalgesia
    b. Subcranial
    c. Hypoglycemic
    d. Anaesthetic

33. Which transitional word would be the best option to represent the logical link between these two sentences?

> I often have heard arguments claiming that complete freedom of speech could lead to dangerous situations.
> Without complete freedom of speech, can it truly be said that we live in a free society?

    a. However
    b. Therefore
    c. So
    d. Supposedly

34. Which of the following is a simple sentence?

    a. Following the French and Indian War, Spain gave up Florida to England.
    b. England returned part of Cuba to Spain, while France gave up part of Louisiana.
    c. France lost most of its Caribbean islands, and England gained dominance over them.
    d. Because every nation lost something, no clear victor was declared.

35. Which of the following pairs of words includes a suffix that makes the second word have a different meaning than the first?

    a. fort; fortification
    b. mount; dismount
    c. flee; fleeing
    d. fame; famous

36. Which of the following demonstrates correct punctuation?

a. Graham still needs the following items for his class: a sable brush, soft pastels, a sketchbook, and an easel.

b. Graham still needs the following items for his class, a sable brush, soft pastels, a sketchbook, and an easel.

c. Graham still needs the following items for his class: a sable brush; soft pastels; a sketchbook; and an easel.

d. Graham still needs the following items for his class – a sable brush; soft pastels; a sketchbook; and an easel.

37. Which of the answer choices best combines the following sentences?

The French and Indian War was not an isolated war in North America. It was part of a larger war that Europe was fighting. Europeans called it the Seven Years' War.

a. The French and Indian War did not occur in North America but was rather a small part of the larger European war known as the Seven Years' War.

b. What Europeans called the Seven Years' War was called the French and Indian War in North America. It was part of a larger war that Europe was fighting.

c. The French and Indian War was not an isolated war in North America but was rather part of a larger war that Europe was fighting, known among Europeans as the Seven Years' War.

d. While North America was fighting the French and Indian War, the Europeans were fighting a much larger war known as the Seven Years' War.

Answer Key and Explanations for Test #2

Reading

1. C: The author actually notes in the last paragraph that Victoria was an "improbable princess who became queen" and the rest of the passage demonstrates how it was a series of small events that changed the course of British succession. The passage is largely factual, so it makes little sense as a persuasive argument. The author mentions the Victorian Era, but the passage is more about Queen Victoria's family background than it is about the era to which she gave her name. And the passage is more about how the events affected Victoria (and through her, England) than it is about the direct effect that George III's sons had on English history.

2. D: This passage is most likely to belong in some kind of biographical reference about Queen Victoria. A scholarly paper would include more analysis instead of just fact. The information in the passage does not fit the genre of mystery at all. And since the passage recounts history, it is not a likely candidate for a fictional story.

3. C: The passage states that King George IV married Maria Fitzherbert in 1783 and then later married Caroline of Brunswick in 1795. King George and Caroline's daughter, Charlotte Augusta, died in 1817. Queen Victoria was born in 1819. Choice C gives the correct chronology of these events. Though the passage does not use many signal words to show the order of these events, it does provide the year that some of these events occurred and recounts the events in a logical order.

4. D: Only choice D is conveyed throughout this passage. The passage describes the true, but unlikely events that led up to the reign of Queen Victoria. While it was unlikely that Victoria would become the queen, she was born into royalty, so the passage does not support choice A. While King George IV was persuaded to marry for advantage, this is just one detail in the passage, so choice B is not a theme conveyed by the whole passage. Choice C is supported by the passage, but this statement is too specific to be a theme. Themes must be universally applicable, and choice C is an observation specific to Queen Victoria.

5. D: It is not reasonable to extrapolate from the opinion of one child to children in general, so choice A is incorrect. Choice B is also not a valid choice because a kindergarten teacher would only know the food preferences of their own students, which is a small sample size. Choice C, an article in a school paper, only gives us the opinion of the author, not children in general, just like choice A. The survey, choice D, has the greatest number of participants, so it will be the most accurate in reporting what fruit children like best.

6. C: To assuage is to lessen the effects of something. In this case, Adelaide is trying to lessen the guilt over eating a piece of cheesecake. The context of the sentence also suggests that she feels sorry for eating it and wants to compensate the following day. Choice D is the second-best option, as it still conveys a negative feeling about her guilt; however, the context indicates that she changed her behavior the next day. If concealment of her guilt was all Adelaide wanted, she would have tried to hide or forget that she ate cheesecake, not try to make up for it. Choices A and B are not supported by the context as they would indicate the opposite of what Adelaide was attempting to accomplish.

7. D: One should not assume that a source is accurate just because it is printed. It is also unwise to simply guess a source's accuracy. Getting in touch with the author of the source will not tell you if it is accurate. The author is likely biased and not an objective judge of the accuracy of their own writing. The best way to evaluate the accuracy of the information in a source is to check it against other sources on the same topic. If other credible sources verify it, the information is likely trustworthy.

8. B: The Russian population of Latvia decreased the most since 1991. The Latvian population decreased slightly, but not to the same degree. The Ukrainian population decreased by an even smaller percentage since 1991. The German population remained relatively unchanged between 1991 and 2011.

9. C: On the chart, the only ethnic group that represents approximately one percent of the population after World War II and approximately three percent by 1991 is the Ukrainian population. The Latvian and Russian populations represent much larger percentages of the total population of Latvia. The German population decreased significantly during this time period.

10. D: The passage states that World War II ended in 1945. The chart shows that the German population began falling in 1935, so there is a slight decrease from 1945 to 1959. While the Ukrainian population's net change was small, it did rise and fall more than the German population's net change. The Latvian and Russian populations fluctuated much more than the German population did over the entire period reflected on the chart, including after 1945.

11. B: The passage argues that high schools should require that students study a foreign language and gives reasons to support this argument. Choice B accurately describes the main idea of the passage. The passage does say that studying a foreign language is helpful for college acceptance and finding a job, but neither of these points are the main idea of the passage. They are both supporting details. The passage does not say that studying a foreign language will help students gain an understanding of other cultures.

12. C: The passage includes claims that studying a foreign language is helpful for participating in the global economy, being accepted into college, and being a desirable candidate for various jobs. These points are summarized in choice C, making it the best summary of the passage. The passage argues that studying a foreign language should be mandatory, but it does not claim that studying a foreign language is currently essential to high school graduation, so choice A is incorrect. Choices B and D represent claims made in the passage, but do not include all of the claims made.

13. D: Although students may find knowledge of a foreign language helpful for obtaining a job, it is clearly an exaggeration to claim that students who did not study a foreign language are unemployable. Choice A simply lists a fact that can be verified, so it cannot be an exaggeration. Choices B and C include statements that the importance of knowing a foreign language and the acceptance rates for students who have studied a foreign language have increased. These statements simply describe the direction of a trend, so while they can be incorrect, they cannot be exaggerations.

14. D: Choice D can confirm the author's claim that high school graduates who studied a foreign language are more likely to be accepted to college, so it is correct. Choices A and C would provide information regarding the opinions of students and parents, but not actual evidence regarding the influence of studying a foreign language on future success. Choice B specifies a second language taught at home, whereas the passage focuses specifically on a foreign language taught in high school.

15. B: Choice B emphasizes the passage's argument and includes a summary of the main supporting details used to defend it. This makes choice B the best conclusion. Choices A, C, and D each emphasize the passage's main argument, but each one only mentions one supporting detail. These are not effective conclusions, so they are incorrect.

Test #2

16. C: Only Cosette fits the description in the ad. She is allergic to cigarette smoke, so she most likely does not smoke. She needs a quiet place to study in a house that is advertised as having quiet occupants. Cosette's need to be close to the university is also implied, since she is likely going to be studying for classes. Frances has a dog, and this is unacceptable, according to the ad. Adelaide is looking for a short-term lease, and the current occupants prefer a long-term renter. Felix is male, and the current occupants are looking for a female renter.

17. C: All of these are good sources to use while developing a position on civil rights; nonetheless, first you must first familiarize yourself with an overview of the issue. A history textbook probably would be the most comprehensive and the least affected by personal opinion. Speeches, interviews, and blogs are great next steps in the research process, but these choices may prove too subjective to provide a necessary overview of the issue.

18. A, C, D: The Bureau of Labor Statistics is part of the US Department of Labor responsible for compiling and publishing employment-related statistics in the United States. The Royal Society of Chemistry is a UK-based professional society dedicated to the advancement of the chemical sciences. The National Institutes of Health is part of the US Department of Health and Human Services. All of these would be considered reliable scholarly sources for a research project. While Wikipedia may be a good place to learn about many things, it is not considered a reliable scholarly source. The Sierra Club is a political advocacy organization dedicated to environmental preservation. Even though information obtained from the Sierra Club may be accurate, the organization's bias rules it out as a reliable scholarly source.

19. D: Ten nations received independence in the first thirty years of the nineteenth century, so choice D is correct. Choice A is incorrect because the American Revolution was fought during the latter 1770s and early 1780s. This was decades before the independence movements in South America. France did not have many possessions in South America, and the graphic gives no information about French control in South America, so choice B is incorrect. Some nations on the west coast were among the last to gain independence, so choice C is also incorrect.

20. C: The directions in the passage are clearly instructions for how to take care of a little girl, so this is probably written for a babysitter. A mother or father would most likely not need this information written down in such detail. A nurse would need more information about how to medically care for the child, rather than information about how to entertain the child or settle her down for a nap.

21. D: The need for a dry diaper and a bottle are the best indications that the child is no older than three years old. Many children, but by no means all, are potty trained by the time they are four years old. Also, most children no longer drink from bottles by the age of four. Of the details presented, this makes choice D the best answer to the question. Choice A does not necessarily support the conclusion that the little girl is no older than three years old; children of any age could enjoy the foods that are listed. Choice B does not support the conclusion either, as the babysitter would still probably need to leave a note regardless of the child's age. Children of any age may also nap, so choice C is not the best answer.

22. B: The first instruction for getting the young girl to take a nap is to read her a couple of books. The passage says "read her a couple of books first." The signal word *first* shows that reading is the first thing the babysitter should try. After this instruction, the passage says "them maybe rock her in her chair," so choice C is the second thing the babysitter should try. Choice D is a later step in these instructions. Choice A is not an instruction given in the passage, as the passage simply states that the girl "likes a stuffed animal."

23. D: Only the sentence in choice D indicates an unsupported opinion on the part of the author. The author's use of phrases like "far too hasty" and "undoubtedly" make the information in this sentence subjective to the author, since it cannot be proven whether the scholars' dismissal is too hasty or whether religion's role in the situation is unable to be doubted. All other sentences in the passage offer support or an explanation that is factual and able to be confirmed.

24. C: The author actually says, "Charles's own political troubles extended beyond religion in this case, and he was beheaded in 1649." This would indicate that religion was less involved in this situation than in other situations. There is not enough information to infer that Charles II never married; the passage only notes that he had no legitimate children. (In fact, he had more than ten illegitimate children by his mistresses.) While the chance of a Catholic king frightened many in England, it is reaching beyond logical inference to assume that people were relieved when the royal children died. Finally, the author does not provide enough detail for the reader to assume that James I had no Catholic leanings. The author only says that James acknowledged the Church of England and approved a Protestant translation of the Bible.

25. B: The passage is composed in a chronological sequence with each king introduced in order of reign, so choice B is correct. While some of the events in the passage may have a cause-and-effect relationship, the organization of the overall passage is not cause and effect. The passage also does not seek to introduce problems and solutions, so choice C is incorrect. While the people mentioned in the passage are compared and contrasted, these comparisons do not dictate the organization of the passage, so choice D is incorrect.

26. D: The passage is largely informative in focus, and the author provides extensive details about this period in English and Scottish history. There is little in the passage to suggest persuasion, and the tone of the passage has no indication of a desire to entertain. Additionally, the passage is historical, so the author avoids expressing feelings and instead focuses on factual information (with the exception of the one opinion statement).

27. C: The only logical conclusion that can be made based on the announcement is that the library has applied a fee to computer usage beyond 30 minutes to discourage patrons from spending too much time on the computers. There is nothing in the announcement to suggest that the library plans to add more computers. The announcement mentions a limited number of computers, but there is no indication that there are plans to change this fact. The announcement makes no mention of the library's budget, so it is impossible to infer that the library is facing budget cuts or that the library is compensating for budget cuts with the fee. Similarly, the announcement says nothing about the library's internet costs, so it is impossible to conclude logically that the library is attempting to offset its own internet fees.

28. C: Raoul will need the computer for a total of 90 minutes. The first 30 minutes are free, so Raoul will need to be prepared to pay for 60 minutes. This is equal to four intervals of 15 minutes. Each 15-minute interval costs $3, so Raoul will need to pay $12 for his computer usage at the library.

29. C: The author states what he believes to be the current state of the planet's environment and makes practical suggestions for making better use of its resources in the future, so choice C is correct. The author does not express expectations for improvement or regression, nor does the author condemn, complain, or make accusations in his descriptions.

30. B: As the passage states: "Locally grown food and other products manufactured within your community are the best choices. The fewer miles a product traveled to reach you, the fewer resources it required." This is summarized by choice B. The passage does not mention whether

Test #2

buying locally grown food supports community members, uses less packaging, or is healthier to eat, so choices A, C, and D are incorrect.

31. C: The author describes global warming and the depletion of natural resources as constant threats and makes suggestions that can slow or prevent the effects of these threats. This implies that if the author's suggestions are not followed, then these threats will continue. The author does not mention running out of resources in a specific time period, the cost of water and energy, or the possibility of hardship for local farmers.

32. D: The passage states: "You should try to be aware of your consumption of water and energy." The passage then gives examples for decreasing one's use of water and energy. The contexts of these sentences indicate that consumption means the depletion of goods. The passage instructs readers to be aware of their consumption of water and energy, but it does not suggest anything about using the greatest or least amount of water and energy. There also is no information about an illness of the lungs in the passage, so consumption does not refer to lung disease in this context.

33. C: To reduce water and energy, the author suggests that the reader turn off the water when brushing his or her teeth, limit showers to five minutes, turn off lights, and unplug appliances and chargers that are not being used. Choice C includes an item from this list, so it is correct. Choices A and B are statements related to conserving other types of resources, and choice D is a statement that applies to general conservation practices.

34. C: Choice C includes an opinion about one of Dalí's works, rather than information about Salvador Dalí, so it is irrelevant to the essay. Additionally, it is written in first person, which makes it inappropriate for a formal essay. Choices A, B, and D include insightful information about the essay's subject and are all appropriate for a formal work.

35. D: In the context of the sentence, it appears that Finlay's parents are attempting to *coax* him by promising a trip to his favorite toy store. Choice A makes little sense, as the sentence indicates Finlay's parents want him to participate in the recital. Choice B might work, but the promise of a trip to the toy store seems more like a reward than a punishment. Choice C makes no sense when added to the sentence in place of the word *cajole*.

36. C: *An Overview of Persian Society*, a book written by a historian, would be the best starting point. While the other sources may have reliable information, a book on the research topic is usually a good place to start. Books typically get researched by the author and then vetted by a team of editors. Choice A, a Wikipedia entry, may not contain accurate information, as anyone can edit such an entry without verifying their sources or credibility. A blog may contain accurate information, but the blog listed in choice B is not written by an expert in the field, so the book by the historian is a better choice. The subject of the article in choice D is too narrow, as it only looks at part of the research topic, so it is not a good starting point for this research project.

37. D: This use of "smart" has a negative connotation: "a smart answer" here means a disrespectful or impertinent one. This is evident from the sentence context ("Eliot got into trouble"). The word "smart" has a literal denotation meaning intelligent or competent. "Smart" also has a positive connotation meaning wise or judicious. The context "he got a good grade" informs this use: Eliot was smart to have studied, meaning he used good judgment when he prepared, evidenced by the positive outcome.

38. D: To find early maps by one of the first people to study geography, Jorgen should consult the 900 section of the library, which contains works of history, geography, and biography. Jorgen is not likely to find maps in books from the 100 section, which includes works on philosophy and psychology; the 300 section, which includes works on social sciences; or the 600 section, which includes works on technical and applied science.

39. D: The sieve of Eratosthenes is a mathematical tool, so Jorgen should go to the science and mathematics section. While the sieve might be used in certain computer applications, there is no specific indication of this. As a result, answer choice D is a better option than answer choice A. Also, Jorgen has no reason to check the philosophy and psychology or languages sections to find out more about a mathematical topic.

40. B: Section 400 is the section on languages, so it is a good place to look for more information about the letters of the Greek alphabet. Jorgen would be unlikely to find anything useful in the sections on religion, arts and recreation, or history, geography, and biography.

41. D: Section 800 features works of literature, so that is the best place for Jorgen to begin looking for *The Iliad* and *The Odyssey*. The philosophy and psychology section will likely contain references to these works, but Jorgen would still have to go to the literature section to obtain the works themselves. The same thing can be said about the religion and the arts and recreation sections.

42. D: Choice D is the only choice that would include information directly from the subject of the research paper. Choices A and B would provide secondhand information about Jules Verne. Choice C could be a primary source in some contexts, but it would not be in this case because it is not Jules Verne's original work, as it would have been heavily adapted. Additionally, choice C would not be relevant to a paper on Verne's life.

43. D: Meter is the only one of these options that is not found in nonfiction texts. Events can be described in a variety of texts, including works of nonfiction. Word choice is important to all types of text. Imagery may be used in fiction much more often than it is in nonfiction, but it can certainly be used in both. Choices A, B, and C may all help communicate theme in nonfiction passages. Meter is not a feature of nonfiction text, so choice D is the best choice.

44. B: The italicized paragraphs are examples of narrative writing used to exemplify the difference between showing and telling. There is description and dialogue included in the italicized paragraphs, so choice A is incorrect. No major works are named in this passage, and the characters' inner thoughts are not explicitly narrated, so choices C and D are incorrect.

45. C: Choice C would contain the most useful information, as the focus of the study directly relates to the topic of the research paper. Additionally, choice C is a primary source, as studies usually involve someone's analysis of data they gathered, so it is comprised of their original work. Choice A is a secondary source. Choices B and D are primary sources, but they both offer limited information and focus on one small aspect of the research topic. Choice C includes information about multiple aspects of the topic, so it is more useful.

Test #2

Mathematics (Video Explanations Available)

We now have video explanations for every math question in this practice test. Visit **mometrix.com/academy/teas-math-videos-2/** or scan this QR code to access these videos.

1. C: To solve this question, you must know that there are approximately 1.609 kilometers in 1 mile. We are given a distance in kilometers and asked to convert it to miles. To do this, use conversion fractions. Make sure the units you are given are in the denominator of your conversion fraction and the units you are wanting are in the numerator. This will cancel out the units you are given and leave you with the units you are looking for.

$$\frac{45 \text{ km}}{1} \times \frac{1 \text{ mi}}{1.609 \text{ km}} \approx 27.97 \text{ mi}$$

Therefore, Dusseldorf is approximately 28 miles away.

2. B: Multiply $120 by 24 months (a full two years) to get $2,880. Add $1,000 for the down payment to get $3,880. Find the difference between the entire amount all at once ($2,600) and the amount paid in the plan ($3,880). To find the difference, you subtract. The difference shows that $1,280 more is paid with the financing plan.

3. C: Group B is skewed left since there are more participants in the older age groups. With more elderly participants, the mean age for Group B will be higher. One way to think about skew is which way the thin "tail" of values is pointing. In this case it is to the left. Since there is a whole set of values in that direction not just a point or two, they aren't outliers, but they do have a marked effect on the statistics of the data that should be noted. The way it is indicated is to say the data is skewed left.

4. B: To determine the total cost of Veronica's new car, add all her expenditures.

$$\$40,210 + \$3,015 + \$5,218 = \$48,443$$

5. B: The order of operations requires evaluation of the expression inside the parentheses as a first step. Thus, the expression can be re-written as $-8 + 8 \times 4 + 7$. Now, the order of operations next requires all multiplication and division to be computed as they appear from left to right. Thus, the expression can be written as $-8 + 32 + 7$. Finally, the addition may be computed as it appears from left to right. The expression simplifies to $24 + 7$, or 31.

6. B: This scatter plot shows a 10 cm decrease in the amount of snow on the ground about every 2 days. If we are interested in approximately how much snow melts in one day, divide 10 cm by 2. Therefore, the snow melts approximately 5 cm each day.

7. 5,000: There are 1,000 milligrams in 1 gram. Therefore, to find the number of milligrams in 5 grams, multiply 1,000 by 5: $1,000 \times 5 = 5,000$.

8. C: Divide the mg the child should receive by the number of mg in 0.8 mL to determine how many 0.8 mL doses the child should receive: $\frac{240}{80} = 3$. Multiply the number of doses by 0.8 to determine how many mL the child should receive: $3 \times 0.8 = 2.4$ mL.

9. 144: This problem can be solved by using a proportion. We are told that 1 inch represents 45 miles, and we are asked for the actual distance if the highway on the map measures 3.2 inches. Make sure to set the proportions equal to each other and have the same units in the numerators and the same units in the denominators.

$$\frac{1 \text{ in}}{45 \text{ miles}} = \frac{3.2 \text{ in}}{x \text{ miles}}$$

Cross multiply to solve for x:

$$x = (45)(3.2) = 144 \text{ miles}$$

10. B: The number of trees planted by the Juniors is skewed left, with more individuals with high numbers of trees planted. The number of trees planted by the Seniors is skewed right, with more individuals with lower numbers of trees planted. The direction associated with the skew is always where the "tail" is pointing. These points have a strong impact on the mean and other statistics of the data because they don't fit with the main grouping of datapoints.

11. C: The mean is found by adding up all the values and dividing by the number of values. To determine the mean time for this event, add up all 8 event times (181.42) and then divide that value by the number of times (8): $\frac{181.42}{8} = 22.6775 \approx 22.68$ sec.

12. D: The patient's dosage must increase by 30%, so calculate 30% of 270:

$$(0.30)(270 \text{ mg}) = 81 \text{ mg}$$

Now, add the 30% increase to the original dosage.

$$270 \text{ mg} + 81 \text{ mg} = 351 \text{ mg}$$

13. A: The mode is the number that appears most often in a set of data. If no item appears most often, then the data set has no mode. In this case, Kyle achieved 1 hit a total of three times, 2 hits twice, 3 hits once, and 4 hits once. 1 hit occurred the most times, therefore the mode of the data set is 1.

14. B: The mean, or average, is the sum of the numbers in a data set divided by the total number of items. This data set contains seven items, one for each day of the week. The total number of hits that Kyle had during the week is the sum of the numbers in the right-hand column, or 14. This gives: Mean $= \frac{14}{7} = 2$.

15. B: Adding up the number of church-goers in Ellsford results in about 1,450 residents who attend a church in the town each week. There are approximately 400 people in Ellsford who attend a Catholic church each week. Calculate the percentage of church-goers who attend Catholic churches by dividing the number of people who attend a Catholic church by the number of people who attend church. $\frac{400}{1,450} \approx 0.276$, which can be converted to a percentage by moving the decimal point two places to the right and adding a percent sign to the end. This makes the percentage 27.6%, or approximately 28%.

16. C: The number of miles Lauren must drive can be rounded to 1,500; 1,500 miles divided by 5 days equals 300 miles per day. Thus, a reasonable estimate for the number of miles driven per day is 300.

17. D: Compare and order the rational numbers by finding a common denominator for all three fractions. The least common denominator for 3, 12, and 4 is 12. Now convert the fractions with different denominators into fractions with the same denominator.

$$\frac{1 \times 4}{3 \times 4} = \frac{4}{12}$$

$$\frac{5}{12} = \frac{5}{12}$$

$$\frac{1 \times 3}{4 \times 3} = \frac{3}{12}$$

Now that all three fractions have the same denominator, order them from largest to smallest by comparing the numerators.

$$\frac{5}{12} > \frac{4}{12} > \frac{3}{12}$$

Since $\frac{5}{12}$ of the doctors are in Group Y, this group has the largest number of doctors. The next largest group has $\frac{4}{12}$ of the doctors, which is Group X. The smallest group has $\frac{3}{12}$ of the doctors, which is Group Z.

18. 5: The following steps can be used to solve for x:

$3(x - 1) = 2(3x - 9)$	Distribute.
$3x - 3 = 6x - 18$	Subtract $3x$ from both sides.
$-3 = 3x - 18$	Add 18 to both sides.
$15 = 3x$	Divide both sides by 3.
$5 = x$	

19. B: During January, Dr. Lewis worked 20 shifts.

$$\text{Shifts for January} = 20$$

During February, she worked three times as many shifts as she did during January.

$$\text{Shifts for February} = (20)(3)$$

During March, she worked half the number of shifts she worked in February.

$$\text{Shifts for March} = (20)(3)\left(\frac{1}{2}\right)$$

20. B: One decimeter equals 10 centimeters, so to find the number of centimeters in 2.5 decimeters, multiply 2.5 by 10. $2.5 \times 10 = 25$, so there are 25 centimeters in 2.5 decimeters.

21. A: When multiplying fractions, multiply the terms straight across the fraction: $\frac{5}{9} \times \frac{3}{4} = \frac{15}{36}$. Then, simplify the fraction. Since 15 and 36 are both multiples of 3, divide each term by 3 to reach the final result: $\frac{5}{12}$.

22. C: To find each percentage, divide the first number by the second number, then multiply by 100. The percentage in answer A is $\left(\frac{50}{250}\right) \times 100 = 20\%$, the percentage in answer B is $\left(\frac{57}{250}\right) \times 100 = 22.8\%$, the percentage in answer C is $\frac{74+55}{433} \times 100 = \left(\frac{129}{433}\right) \times 100 = 29.8\%$, and the percentage in answer D is $\left(\frac{21}{183}\right) \times 100 = 11.5\%$. Therefore, the percentage of doctors to staff as a whole at Hospital X and Hospital Y (29.8%) is the greatest.

23. D: The prefix, *centi-*, means 100th. In this case,

$$1 \text{ m} = 100 \text{ cm}$$

Therefore,

$$(7)(1 \text{ m}) = (7)(100 \text{ cm})$$

$$7 \text{ m} = 700 \text{ cm}$$

24. B: To evaluate the expression, follow the order of operations, starting with the parentheses. Be sure to follow the order of operations even inside the parentheses.

$$3 - 3^3 + (3 \times 3 - 3)^3 = 3 - 3^3 + (9 - 3)^3 = 3 - 3^3 + (6)^3$$

Then, evaluate the exponents.

$$3 - 3^3 + 6^3 = 3 - 3 \times 3 \times 3 + 6 \times 6 \times 6 = 3 - 27 + 216$$

Now, perform the addition and subtraction in order from left to right.

$$3 - 27 + 216 = -24 + 216 = 192$$

25. B: The outlier of 11 would skew the data if the mean or range were used. Therefore, the median is the most appropriate measure for reflecting the number of houses she sold per year. This data set does not have a mode, so mode is not the most appropriate.

26. D: Set the relationship up, and solve for the number of packs.

$$\frac{2}{x} = \frac{\text{packs}}{5}$$

Cross multiply.

$$10 = x(\text{packs})$$

Divide both sides by x.

$$\frac{10}{x} = \text{packs}$$

Test #2

27. B: The rational numbers can be compared by converting $\frac{32}{5}$ to a mixed number. $\frac{32}{5} = 6\frac{2}{5}$, and we now have all the information we need to order the numbers. By looking at the whole number parts, we can see that $6\frac{2}{5} > 2\frac{1}{4} > \frac{3}{4}$. Now, we evaluate the negative numbers. Negative numbers with seemingly larger values are actually smaller because they represent a greater distance from 0; therefore, $-2 > -5$. If we convert $6\frac{2}{5}$ back to $\frac{32}{5}$, we will get the list: $\frac{32}{5}, 2\frac{1}{4}, \frac{4}{5}, -2, -5$.

28. A: Dr. Lee noticed that 5% of 30% of his patients were hospitalized. So, multiply 30% by 5% using these steps:

Convert 30% and 5% into decimals by dividing both numbers by 100.

$$\frac{30}{100} = 0.30 \text{ and } \frac{5}{100} = 0.05$$

Now multiply 0.30 by 0.05 to get

$$(0.30)(0.05) = 0.015$$

Now convert 0.015 to a percentage by multiplying by 100.

$$(0.015)(100) = 1.5\%$$

29. C: To answer this question, notice that this figure is a regular hexagon, having 6 equal sides and angles. The part painted darker can be represented by $\frac{1}{6}$. The part painted lighter is clearly $\frac{1}{2}$, which is equivalent to $\frac{3}{6}$. The whole figure is represented by the number 1. So, the white part can be found by subtracting $1 - \frac{1}{6} - \frac{3}{6} = \frac{2}{6}$, which is equivalent to $\frac{1}{3}$. Therefore, the equation, $1 - \frac{1}{6} - \frac{1}{2} = \frac{1}{3}$ best models the part of the figure Olga left white.

30. B: 3,700 is the only answer between the minimum number of potatoes that could have been on the trailer, $150 \times 23 = 3,450$, and the maximum number of potatoes that could have been on the trailer, $27 \times 150 = 4,050$. Another method that could be used to answer this question is to multiply 25, the number halfway between 23 and 27, by 150. The product, 3,750, is very near the correct answer.

31. B: The water temperature increased by about 2 °C every 3 minutes, or $\frac{2}{3}$ of a degree Celsius every minute. Multiplying the increase in degrees per minute by the total number of minutes yields:

$$\frac{2 \,°C}{3 \text{ min}} \times 20 \text{ min} = \frac{40}{3}, \text{ or } 13.33°$$

Since the problem asks for the increase in temperature and not the total temperature that results after the increases, 13 °C is the closest to our answer.

32. C: In both equations, the coefficient of m is the rate of change. In this problem, the rate of change represents the customer's monthly cost. Therefore, the customers at John's Gym pay $40 per month, and the customers at Ralph's Recreation Room pay $45 per month. Thus, John's monthly membership fee is less than Ralph's monthly membership fee.

33. D: Since there are 100 cm in a meter, on a 1: 100 scale drawing, each centimeter represents one meter. Therefore, an area of one square centimeter on the drawing represents one square meter in actuality. Since the area of the room in the scale drawing is 30 cm², the room's actual area is 30 m².

Another way to determine the area of the room is to write and solve an equation, such as this one: $\frac{l}{100} \times \frac{w}{100} = 30$ cm^2, where l and w are the dimensions of the actual room.

$$\frac{lw}{10,000} = 30 \text{ cm}^2$$

$$\text{Area} = 300,000 \text{ cm}^2$$

Since this is not one of the answer choices, convert cm^2 to m^2:

$$300,000 \text{ cm}^2 \times \frac{1 \text{ m}}{100 \text{ cm}} \times \frac{1 \text{ m}}{100 \text{ cm}} = 30 \text{ m}^2$$

34. D: Pie charts are the best way to display data when looking at percentages of a whole. Line plots and bar graphs are useful for seeing the distribution of data. Line graphs are most often used to show how data changes over time.

35. C: The circumference of a circle can be found by using the formula, $C = 2\pi r$. Since the radius is equal to 3 inches. Substituting a value of 3 inches for r and estimating pi to be 3, gives an approximate circumference of 18 inches.

36. C: If the exam has 30 questions and the student answered C questions correctly and left B questions blank, then the number of questions the student answered incorrectly must be $30 - B - C$. He gets one point for each correct question, or $1 \times C = C$ points, and loses $\frac{1}{2}$ point for each incorrect question, or $\frac{1}{2}(30 - B - C)$ points. Therefore, one way to express his total score is $C - \frac{1}{2}(30 - B - C)$.

37. B: First, determine the proportion of students in Grade 5. Since the total number of students is 180, this proportion is $\frac{36}{180} = 0.2$, or 20%. Then, determine the same proportion of the total prizes, which is 20% of 20, or $0.2 \times 20 = 4$. Therefore, 4 prizes should go to the fifth-grade students.

38. A: When plotting the sampling distribution of means, the distribution is always approximately normal. As the number of random samples increases, the plotting of the means approaches a normal distribution.

Science

1. A: The circulatory system circulates materials throughout the entire body. The heart, blood, and blood vessels are part of the circulatory system. The kidneys, however, are part of the urinary system.

2. A: Cilia and flagella are responsible for cell movement. Ribosomes are organelles that help synthesize proteins within the cell. The cell membrane helps the cell maintain its shape and protects it from the environment. Lysosomes have digestive enzymes.

3. D: Element 30 is zinc. Elements in groups 3-12 are considered transition metals.

1 H																	2 He
3 Li	4 Be											5 B	6 C	7 N	8 O	9 F	10 Ne
11 Na	12 Mg											13 Al	14 Si	15 P	16 S	17 Cl	18 Ar
19 K	20 Ca	21 Sc	22 Ti	23 V	24 Cr	25 Mn	26 Fe	27 Co	28 Ni	29 Cu	30 Zn	31 Ga	32 Ge	33 As	34 Se	35 Br	36 Kr
37 Rb	38 Sr	39 Y	40 Zr	41 Nb	42 Mo	43 Tc	44 Ru	45 Rh	46 Pd	47 Ag	48 Cd	49 In	50 Sn	51 Sb	52 Te	53 I	54 Xe
55 Cs	56 Ba	*	72 Hf	73 Ta	74 W	75 Re	76 Os	77 Ir	78 Pt	79 Au	80 Hg	81 Tl	82 Pb	83 Bi	84 Po	85 At	86 Rn
87 Fr	88 Ra	**	104 Rf	105 Db	106 Sg	107 Bh	108 Hs	109 Mt	110 Ds	111 Rg	112 Cn	113 Uut	114 Fl	115 Uup	116 Lv	117 Uus	118 Uuo

*	57 La	58 Ce	59 Pr	60 Nd	61 Pm	62 Sm	63 Eu	64 Gd	65 Tb	66 Dy	67 Ho	68 Er	69 Tm	70 Yb	71 Lu
**	89 Ac	90 Th	91 Pa	92 U	93 Np	94 Pu	95 Am	96 Cm	97 Bk	98 Cf	99 Es	100 Fm	101 Md	102 No	103 Lr

4. A: Gas exchange occurs in the alveoli, the tiny air sacs on the interior of the lungs. The bronchi are large cartilage-based tubes of air; they extend from the end of the trachea into the lungs, where they branch apart. The larynx, which houses the vocal cords, is positioned between the trachea and the pharynx; it is involved in swallowing, breathing, and speaking. The pharynx extends from the nose to the uppermost portions of the trachea and esophagus. In order to enter these two structures, air and other matter must pass through the pharynx.

5. B: The independent variable was the amount of light that was given to the plants, which could have been manipulated by the experimenter by moving the plants. The dependent variable was tomato plant growth. No hypothesis or conclusion were clearly stated in this experiment, but we could infer that getting more sunlight makes tomato plants grow better.

6. A: The pancreas, intestines, and stomach all play important roles in the digestive system. The thyroid is part of the endocrine system. It secretes hormones that help regulate the heart rate, blood pressure, body temperature, and metabolism.

7. C: A vaccination is a way of acquiring active artificial immunity, where an antigen is deliberately introduced into an individual to stimulate the immune system. Vaccines contain dead or dying pathogens that are not enough to cause an infection, but allow the immune system to "remember" the pathogen and become immune to it.

8. B: Phagocytes are specialized white blood cells that kill pathogens and initiate an immune response. They display the ingested pathogen to the B cells, or memory cells, which help the body "remember" the pathogen in the future.

9. A: The hypothalamus controls the hormones secreted by the pituitary gland. This part of the brain maintains the body temperature and helps to control metabolism. The adrenal glands, which lie above the kidneys, secrete steroidal hormones, epinephrine, and norepinephrine. The testes are the male reproductive glands, responsible for the production of sperm and testosterone. The pancreas secretes insulin and a fluid that aids in digestion.

10. B: The complete Punnett square is shown below.

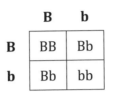

Because male-pattern baldness is a recessive gene, the offspring would need the bb gene combination in order to inherit this trait. Possibility 4 corresponds to the bb gene combination.

11. C: Because a full head of hair is dominant, the offspring would need a B allele present in the gene combination in order to inherit this trait. Therefore, any offspring with the B allele (Possibilities 1, 2, and 3) will have a full head of hair.

12. C: Isotopes are atoms of the same element with different atomic masses. Since they are of the same element, they must have equal numbers of protons. Therefore, to have different atomic masses (number of protons plus neutrons), they must have different numbers of neutrons. The number of electrons depends on the atom's ionization state; if both isotopes are electrically neutral, they will have the same number of electrons. Isotopes cannot differ in the number of nuclei; every atom has one nucleus (though that nucleus may contain numerous protons and neutrons).

13. C: The atomic mass of an atom is approximately equal to the number of protons plus the number of neutrons. The weight of the electrons has little effect on the overall atomic mass.

14. C: Conducting this investigation may reveal a group of people who need higher-quality medical care. The investigation is not specifically about the cost of medical care, though that is a related idea. Helping healthy people to stay healthy is important, but helping those with poor medical care is more critical.

15. C: The hydrogen bonds between water molecules cause water molecules to attract each other (negative pole to positive pole) and "stick" together. This gives water a high surface tension, which allows small living organisms, such as water striders, to move across its surface. Since water is a polar molecule, it readily dissolves other polar and ionic molecules, such as carbohydrates and amino acids. Polarity alone is not sufficient to make something soluble in water, however; for example, cellulose is polar but its molecular weight is so large that it is not soluble in water.

16. A: The nucleus is the control center for the cell. The cell membrane surrounds the cell and separates the cell from its environment. Cytoplasm is the thick fluid within the cell membrane that surrounds the nucleus and contains organelles. Mitochondria are often called the powerhouse of the cell because they provide energy for the cell to function.

Test #2

17. A: An atom is defined by its number of protons; oxygen has 8 protons. The temperature at which iron ore will melt (B) varies depending on several factors, including pressure. The human population size (C) has been changing ever since humans first inhabited the earth. The time the sun rises (D) varies according to the time of year and the location of the observer.

18. D: Decreased mortality during childbirth could be explained by any or all of the statements presented. Safer cesarean sections, health monitoring tools, and hand washing could all improve a woman's chances of surviving childbirth.

19. D: Humans have three layers of skin called: epidermis, dermis, and hypodermis. Epidermis is the top layer of the skin, the dermis is the second layer, and the hypodermis, which includes fatty tissue, makes up the bottom layer. The epidermis does not contain blood vessels, and hyperdermis is not a standard biological term.

20. D: Skeletal, smooth, and cardiac are all types of muscle tissue. Adipose tissue, or body fat, is not.

21. D: Intensive properties do not depend on the amount of matter that is present. Mass, weight, and volume do depend on the amount of matter that is present, and are considered extensive properties. Density does not depend on the amount of matter that is present, and is therefore considered an intensive property.

22. B, C, D: Improved medical care, better cleanliness, and vaccines to eliminate deadly diseases could all help explain the dramatic increase in life expectancy in just 150 years. The human body has not been observed to have evolved over that time period in any meaningful way. Genetic disorders have not been largely eliminated; rather, they are one of the leading causes of infant mortality in the United States.

23. C: The chart shows two specific changes: snowfall levels from November to April and sunny days from November to April. Based on the chart alone, the only information that can be determined is that the fewest sunny days coincide with the months that have the heaviest snowfall. Anything further reaches beyond the immediate facts of the chart and moves into the territory of requiring other facts. As for answer choice D, the number of sunny days decreases in December and January.

24. B: Evidence used to make a scientific conclusion must be reproducible, meaning the same results would occur again and again if an experiment was repeated. For example, the boiling point of water (at a given air pressure) always remains the same, regardless of where, when, or how many times it is measured. Evidence used to make scientific conclusions can be quantitative or qualitative, making (A) incorrect, and evidence doesn't have to be obvious to be valid, making (C) an incorrect choice. Since (A) and (C) are incorrect, (D) is also incorrect.

25. B: The nitrogenous base thymine does not exist in RNA, but does exist in DNA. The bases of RNA are uracil, cytosine, guanine, and adenine.

26. B: The two types of measurement important in science are quantitative (when a numerical result is used) and qualitative (when descriptions or qualities are reported). Qualitative data is collected through observation and interviews, and focuses on the informant's behavior and perspectives. Qualitative and quantitative data are equally important in scientific research. When combined and analyzed together, they can provide a full picture of the question at hand. Additionally, both qualitative and quantitative data can be accurate or skewed by bias; therefore, both should be thoroughly analyzed.

27. C: The sugar and phosphate in DNA are connected by covalent bonds. A covalent bond is formed when atoms share electrons. It is very common for atoms to share pairs of electrons. Hydrogen bonds are used in DNA to bind complementary bases together, such as adenine with thymine or guanine with cytosine. An ionic bond is created when one or more electrons are transferred between atoms. Ionic bonds, also known as electrovalent bonds, are formed between ions with opposite charges. There is no such thing as an overt bond in chemistry. The exam will require you to understand and have some examples of these different types of bonds.

28. C: The genitourinary system is responsible for removing waste from the body through urine. Components include two kidneys, two ureters that drain the urine from the kidney to the bladder, and the urethra, which drains urine from the bladder out of the body. The rectum is the last section of the large intestine, and is part of the digestive system.

29. C: The complete Punnett square is shown below.

	Tb	Tb	tb	tb
tB	TtBb	TtBb	ttBb	ttBb
tb	Ttbb	Ttbb	ttbb	ttbb
tB	TtBb	TtBb	ttBb	ttBb
tb	Ttbb	Ttbb	ttbb	ttbb

Possibility 1 corresponds to a person with the TtBb genotype, which means the person is tall with black hair.

30. D: Possibility 4 corresponds to the ttBb genotype, which is short with black hair. The other possibilities that would express that phenotype are 3, 11, and 12.

31. C: The esophagus is the only structure that is not part of the respiratory system. It is part of the digestive system. The larynx houses the voice box; it also acts as a passageway for air to travel into the lungs. The trachea connects the larynx to the lungs. The trachea splits into the right and left bronchi, which divide into smaller passageways called the bronchioles.

32. C: The atomic weight tells the mass of the element. In the table, B is the lightest element, weighing 11 atomic mass units, and O is the heaviest element, weighing 16 atomic mass units.

33. C: Food enters the digestive system through the mouth and proceeds down to the stomach after mastication by the teeth. Once the food is in the stomach, enzymes are secreted that begin to digest the specific substances in the food (proteins, carbohydrates, etc.). Next, the food passes through to the small intestine, where the nutrients are absorbed, and then into the large intestine, where extra water is absorbed.

34. D: The main function of the immune system is to help the body avoid, detect, and eliminate infections. The immune system is comprised of many different elements that receive signals from various hormone pathways, but the hypothalamus is not one of them. Toxins are filtered out of the blood in the kidneys as part of the urinary system. The kidneys are also the source of erythropoietin, the hormone that stimulates blood cell production.

35. B: A gene will encode a polypeptide, which is eventually folded to form a biologically functional protein and is the minimum requirement for a trait. Genes are made of DNA and thus carry the hereditary information that gets passed down from parents to offspring. Some genes contain the

Test #2

421

information needed to create proteins through the process of transcription and translation. The types of traits visible in an organism depend on whether certain proteins are produced. For example, certain genes code for proteins that help make pigments or colors.

36. B, D, E, F: Long bones are bones that are longer than they are wide. The long bones in the human body are the clavicle, the arm bones (humerus, radius, and ulna), the leg bones (femur, tibia, and fibula), and some of the hand and foot bones (metacarpals, metatarsals, and phalanges). The sacrum, which is part of the pelvis, is a flat bone, and the patella, or kneecap, is a sesamoid bone.

37. D: T cells are a specialized type of white blood cell that play an important role in the immune response of all humans. They help destroy pathogens in the body and initiate the body's immune response to fight the infection. T cells are produced in the bone marrow, but they mature in the thymus gland.

38. A: The physical expression of a gene—such as hair color—is the phenotype. The genotype is the basic genetic code. An allele is one of two or more alternative gene forms that generally arise via mutation, and are located in the same part of a chromosome. A gamete is a germ cell (female or male) that can unite with the opposite-sex germ cell in the process of zygote formation in sexual reproduction.

39. D: Ionic bonds are formed when electrons are transferred between atoms. For instance, the sodium and chlorine atoms in salt have ionic bonds because electrons are transferred from sodium to chlorine.

40. D: Plasma cells secrete antibodies. These cells, also known as plasmacytes, are located in lymphoid tissue. Antibodies are only secreted in response to a particular stimulus, usually the detection of an antigen in the body. Antigens include bacteria, viruses, and parasites.

41. D: Of the given structures, veins have the lowest blood pressure. Veins carry oxygen-poor blood from the outlying parts of the body to the heart. An artery carries oxygen-rich blood from the heart to the peripheral parts of the body. An arteriole extends from an artery to a capillary. A venule is a tiny vessel that extends from a capillary to a larger vein.

42. B: It is impossible for an AaBb organism to have the aa combination in the gametes. It is impossible for each letter to be used more than one time, so it would be impossible for the lowercase a to appear twice in the gametes. Gametes are germ cells involved in sexual reproduction.

43. B: Metals are usually solids at room temperature, while nonmetals are usually gases at room temperature.

44. B: The adrenal glands are part of the endocrine system. They sit on the kidneys and produce hormones that regulate salt and water balance and influence blood pressure and heart rate.

45. A: Tachycardia is a faster-than-normal heart rate (>100 bpm) while at rest. A healthy adult heart normally beats 60 to 100 times a minute when a person is at rest. Bradycardia is a slower-than-normal (<60 bpm) heart rate while at rest. Apnea is the absence of respirations, while tachypnea is the presence of rapid respirations (>20 breaths per minute).

46. A: A scientific argument should discuss outcomes that are objective and measurable, such as blood pressure, energy level, and overall health. The other choices present arguments that are subjective and based on emotions instead of facts.

47. C: By repeating the experiment, the researcher could determine whether the instance of the bacteria swimming away from the chemical was simply due to chance. Observing the same results would allow the researcher to make conclusions with more certainty, and statistical analysis would help determine the significance of the data. Researchers must report all data (A), and reaching a conclusion is a vital part of any experiment (B). Adding a new chemical would completely change the experiment, so it would not be helpful (D).

48. A: The human body has five types of bones: long bones, short bones, irregular bones, flat bones, and sesamoid bones. While bones may be dense, this is not a major category of bones in the body.

49. A: Condensation is the process of changing from a gas to a liquid. For instance, gaseous water molecules in the air condense to form liquid raindrops. Vaporization describes changing from liquid to gas. Melting is the process of changing from solid to liquid, and sublimation describes changing from solid to gas.

50. A: The graph reflects student scores for each quarter. The trend that can be seen in the graph is an increase in scores as the year progressed. The graph title mentions a test review, but there is not enough information about that to know if that is the reason for the scores changing.

English and Language Usage

1. B: Answer choice B correctly capitalizes *Uncle Archibald*, where *Uncle Archibald* is used as one whole name, which makes it a proper noun. If the sentence said "her uncle Archibald," then *uncle* would remain lowercase. In choice A, the word *cousin* needs no capitalization, because it is used to describe Elaine but is not used as part of her name. Similarly, *mother* and *sister* (choices C and D) do not need to be capitalized unless they are used in place of a name.

2. D: The prefix *per-* means *through*, which can be deduced from two words in the example sentence: *permeated* and *percolated*. To permeate means to spread throughout, which is implied by the sentence. As the barista pours water on top, the grounds would get wet. The context uses the clue *fully*, which gives us a picture of how the water and the grounds interact—that is, that the water went *through*. One way of restating the actions of the sentence might be to say that the barista poured water *through* the grounds, as indicated by the prepositions *onto, into,* and *below*. This gives us a strong idea of the process of percolation, which means for a fluid to pass or filter through a porous substance.

3. D: The informal phrases and words in this excerpt are an example of colloquialism. Colloquialism is a literary device used to make characters and dialogue more realistic and to help establish a setting for the story. In this example, the word *fellas* and the phrase *you'd of* help create a more lifelike character.

4. D: Choice D correctly arranges the ideas to most effectively reflect the meaning of the sentence. Choice A has several problems; for instance, it should use but instead of and because Lucinda is taking the medication in spite of her concerns. Choice B also has several problems; for instance, it's unclear whether concerning Lucinda means about Lucinda or causing Lucinda concern. Choice C is the second-best choice; its only problem is that it should use but instead of so.

5. B: Researching reliable sources is a significant portion of the writing process. The other choices refer to elements that have already been accomplished based on the description of Javier's progress.

6. B: The word *capacity* is a noun because it is a thing, so choice B is correct. Adverbs are usually single words that modify the meaning of a verb and are usually indicated by the suffix *-ly*, as in *quickly* or *sloppily.* Verbs are action words. Pronouns are words that stand in for nouns.

7. C: Choice C summarizes the ideas within the sentence simply and clearly, and it correctly links *adequate preparation* to Zara and not to the test. Choice A is clumsy because the phrase *without adequate preparation* seems like it is modifying *the test*, when it should describe Zara's preparation. Choice B also creates a dangling modifier with the phrase *without adequate preparation*, so it cannot be correct. Similarly, in choice D, this phrase is a dangling modifier that makes the flow of thought awkward instead of clear.

8. C: *Circumference* is the measure around a circle, so it is reasonable to conclude that *circum-* means *around. Post-* is a prefix for *after. Pre-* is a prefix for *before.* There are several prefixes for *beyond*, such as *trans-*, *hyper-*, and *extra-.*

9. C: This sentence implies multiple jurors who possess multiple meals, so the correct answer must demonstrate *jurors* as a plural possessive and *meals* as a plural word that is not possessive. When a plural word is made possessive, the standard rule is to place the apostrophe after the final *s*, as in *jurors'.* Choice C correctly demonstrates this. Choices A and D incorrectly add the possessive apostrophe to *meals* instead of *jurors.* Choice B incorrectly places the possessive apostrophe before the final *s*, as in *juror's*, which indicates only a single juror.

10. A: This answer provides an example of formal speech, lays out the steps to a solution in a concise manner, and utilizes the correct transition words. Choice B uses the transition words *ideally*, *secondly*, and *then*, which do not form a clear sequence like *first*, *then*, and *finally* in choice A. Choice C uses nonstandard and informal language, such as the past tense *got to* in place of *need to* or *have to.* Choice D uses a variety of transition phrases between thoughts that do not necessarily fit the context. As it is used in the third sentence, the phrase *for example* is a non sequitur, meaning that it does not follow the thought pattern of the previous statement, which said they need to organize a list.

11. D: Answer choice D correctly uses an apostrophe to indicate the possessive element within the sentence. Answer choice A incorrectly changes the plural word *fairies* into the possessive word *fairy's.* Similarly, answer choice B makes the plural *historians* possessive, and answer choice C makes the plural *seasons* possessive by changing it to the singular possessive *season's.* None of these words is possessive in the context of their respective sentences, so only answer choice D is correct.

12. B: Transition sentences signal to the reader that a new paragraph with a different focus is about to begin. These phrases are often found at the end of a paragraph, near or within the concluding statement. Choice B appears to belong in a sentence that will expound on an idea, not one which will transition to a new idea.

13. C, E: *Faculty* as used in choice C is a plural noun, which requires a plural verb. In a sentence that has a compound subject using an *either/or* or *neither/nor* structure, the verb must agree with the closer of the two parts of the subject. Choice E does this correctly, while choice A does not. In choice B, the subject *issues* is separated from the verb *concerns* by a relative clause, but they must still agree. As for choice D, a compound subject joined by *and* is always treated as plural.

14. C: Citations are necessary anytime writers incorporate research, words, data, ideas, or information that is not their own. In this case, choice C contains data that belongs to the *Economic Times*' publication. Using it to corroborate their claim without a proper citation would be plagiarism.

15. D: A comma and the conjunction *and* are required to combine the sentences, as the combined sentence contains two independent clauses. *And* is a better choice than *but* because the second sentence is a continuation of the first rather than a contradiction. Choices A and B are incorrect because the conjunction *but* doesn't fit the meaning of the sentences, as the two clauses do not disagree with each other. Choice A is also missing the required comma. Choice C uses the correct conjunction, *and*, but is missing the comma.

16. D: Choice D has a compound subject, but is still a simple sentence. A compound subject is where two nouns act together as the subject of a clause. In this case, *Marjorie and Thomas* act together as the subject of the sentence. Choice A is a compound sentence, as it is composed of two independent clauses. Choice B consists of two independent sentences that are correctly joined by a semicolon. The semicolon stands in the place of a conjunction, making a sentence with two independent clauses. Choice C contains a dependent clause, so it is a complex sentence.

17. D: The composition cannot be written until the topic or argument has been determined, so choice D is correct. Revising, editing, and proofreading help writers improve drafts of the composition. Choices A, B, and C are all tasks that are part of revising and editing, so these choices are incorrect.

18. B: The correct choice of greeting would be choice B. The other choices contain language which is too informal or too familiar for a professional communication. Overly personal words such as *dearest* are not appropriate for communications regarding business, especially with a group of people.

19. B: The sentence in choice B incorrectly uses the word *aural* (meaning related to the ears) instead of *oral* (meaning related to the mouth). In choice A, *their* is used correctly as a third-person plural possessive pronoun. In choice C, *led* (past tense of *lead*) is correct rather than *lead* (the metal). In choice D, *effect* (a noun meaning result) is used correctly rather than *affect* (most commonly a verb).

20. D: The sequence which constructs the paragraph chronologically is choice D. Correctly ordered, the paragraph would read: *Alice looked up, but it was all dark overhead; before her was another long passage, and the White Rabbit was in sight, hurrying down it. There was not a moment to be lost: away went Alice like the wind, and was just in time to hear it say, as it turned a corner, "Oh my ears and whiskers, how late it's getting!" She was close behind it when she turned the corner, but the Rabbit was no longer to be seen: she found herself in a long, low hall, which was lit up by a row of lamps hanging from the roof. There were doors all round the hall, but they were all locked; and Alice went all the way down one side and up the other, trying every door.*

21. B: Choice B is the best version of the sentence, as it lays out the subjects, action, and location in a clear, straightforward way. The other choices also follow the rules of English, but they are not as effective. Choice A takes a single idea (the Wright brothers tested their airplane at Kitty Hawk) and splits it into two statements, which may be slightly awkward to read. Choices C and D put the subject (the Wright brothers) at the middle or end of the sentence, whereas it is simpler to have the subject at the beginning of the sentence unless there is a reason not to.

22. D: Joann has brainstormed and has an outline and research, so she is ready to begin drafting her paper. Brainstorming, outlining, and research are all parts of prewriting, which prepares the writer for drafting. Choices A and C occur after drafting. Editing and proofreading are steps used to improve drafts. If a draft has not been written yet, these steps cannot occur. Choice B is publishing, which is the very last part of the writing process. Publishing occurs when the composition has been written and sufficiently edited, revised, and proofread. Without a draft, publishing cannot occur. Choice D is the best next step.

23. B: The antibacterial agent goes against what enables the bacteria to live. If something that is antibacterial kills bacteria, then it would not be original to it. While an antibacterial substance could be under bacteria or come before bacteria, these meanings are not supported by the given definition of *antibacterial*, as neither of these qualities would imply that the substance kills bacteria.

24. D: The setting for this scenario is London, England. The key words *Thames*, *fish and chips*, *peckish*, and *queue* help readers determine that the setting for this sentence is London. Being aware of types of language, including differences in dialect, is a helpful tool when evaluating setting. In this case, knowing that the River Thames is located in England is helpful but not necessary to determine the setting.

25. D: In this sentence, choice A is a helping verb, choice B is an adjective, choice C is an adverb, and choice D is a pronoun.

26. A, E, F: The plural noun in choice A is *lunches*, which follows the rule of adding *-es* to the end of a singular noun that ends in *-s*, *-ss*, *-sh*, *-ch*, *-x*, or *-z*. The plural noun in choice E is *Baldwins*. Last names are pluralized by added an *-s* or *-es* to the end. The plural noun in choice F is *lawns*. Nouns are never pluralized with an apostrophe or with an *-ss*. Nouns that end in *-lf* are typically pluralized by changing the *f* to a *v* and adding *-es*.

27. D: The parenthetical statement includes information that is useful—in this case, the years of Franz Joseph I's reign—but does not fit within the flow of the sentence. The writer has chosen to include the years of Franz Joseph I's reign in parentheses, instead of using a dependent clause along the lines of "...the reign of Franz Joseph I, who ruled from 1848 to 1916." The parentheses provide information that the reader would likely want to know without interrupting the flow of the sentence.

28. B: While daydreaming and waiting for inspiration is what many people do when brainstorming, it is not an effective prewriting strategy. The other choices are ways to get the creative part of the brain moving and help writers begin the task of writing.

29. B: The prefix *pro-*, from Latin, means *before*, *earlier*, *prior to*; *for* or *forward*; or *front*. Prefixes come at the beginnings of words; suffixes come at the ends of words. Prefixes and suffixes are types of affixes.

30. B: Choice B is the best of these choices. The word *first* shows that this sentence describes the beginning of Maria's family's process for planning holiday celebrations. This is an appropriate detail to follow Maria's introductory sentence. Choices A and C are not clearly relevant to the topic sentence. While these may be important details later, neither of these sentences should follow the topic sentence. Choice D should be included later in the composition, as the word *afterwards* shows that the described step occurs later.

31. B: A complex sentence contains a single independent clause in addition to a dependent clause. Choice B opens with the dependent clause *Before Ernestine purchases a book* and ends with the independent clause *she always checks to see if the library has it*. Choice A is a simple sentence, as it has no dependent clause. Choice C is a compound sentence because it has two independent clauses. Choice D is also a simple sentence, although it has a compound subject.

32. D: The prefix *an-* means *without* or *lacking*, and the root word *aesthetic* refers to feeling or sensation, so taken together, this word refers to something that removes feeling or sensation. The prefix *hyper-* indicates that something is increased or elevated rather than removed (in this case, sensitivity to pain). The prefix *sub-* means *below* or *under*, while the root *cranial* refers to the skull. The prefix *hypo-* indicates that something is reduced or diminished, which could work here, but the root *glycemic* refers to blood sugar as opposed to sensation.

33. A: The first sentence introduces an argument against complete freedom of speech. The second sentence makes a statement in favor of it. The second sentence opposes the first one, so the two sentences should be linked with the transitional word *however*.

34. A: A simple sentence is one in which there is only one clause: a single independent clause. A compound sentence is one in which there are two or more independent clauses, and a complex sentence is one in which there is at least one dependent clause. Of the options listed, only choice A contains a simple sentence because, while the sentence includes an opening phrase, it has only one clause. The sentences in choices B and D each contain a dependent clause, while the sentence in choice C contains two independent clauses.

35. D: *Fame* is a noun that refers to high popularity or awareness of a person, thing, or group. *Famous* is an adjective that refers to a person, thing, or group to describe them as having fame. *Fame* and *famous* are different parts of speech, so they are used differently and have distinct meanings. Choice A is *fort* and *fortification*. A fort is like a military base or a stronghold. *Fortification* has a couple of meanings, but one of its meanings is the same as the meaning of *fort*. Choice B is *mount* and *dismount*. This pair includes a root word and the root word with a prefix added. While the meaning does change from the root word, this is due to the addition of a prefix, not a suffix. Choice C is *flee* and *fleeing*. To flee is to run away from something. *Fleeing* is simply the present participle form of *flee*, so the meaning of these words is the same.

36. A: Choice A includes all of the correct elements of punctuation needed to make this sentence clear and readable. In particular, there is a colon after the phrase "the following items for his class"; this indicates that a series of items will be listed. As these items do not contain internal commas, they may be separated by commas, so the rest of the punctuation in choice A is correct. Choice B uses a comma instead of a colon in front of the introductory phrase, making the series of items difficult to distinguish. Choice C uses semicolons instead of commas between the items in the series. The semicolons are not necessary, and make the sentence more confusing to read instead of clearer. Choice D uses a dash, which is not a correct way to introduce a series of items.

37. C: Choice C combines all of the information in the passage into a single coherent sentence. Choice A states that the French and Indian War did not occur in North America, which contradicts the original sentences. Choice B contains correct information, but is choppy rather than fluid and coherent. Choice B is also more than one sentence, and it lacks the style and clarity of choice C. Choice D contains correct information, but it fails to explain—as stated in the original passage— that the French and Indian War was actually part of the larger Seven Years' War. Choice D implies that the French and Indian War was unrelated to the Seven Years' War, which contradicts the passage.

Four Additional Practice Tests

In addition to the two practice tests printed in this book, we have **four more TEAS 7 practice tests** available to be taken in online interactive format. To access them, please visit our bonus page by scanning the QR code to the right or by navigating there directly: **mometrix.com/bonus948/teas7**

How to Overcome Test Anxiety

Just the thought of taking a test is enough to make most people a little nervous. A test is an important event that can have a long-term impact on your future, so it's important to take it seriously and it's natural to feel anxious about performing well. But just because anxiety is normal, that doesn't mean that it's helpful in test taking, or that you should simply accept it as part of your life. Anxiety can have a variety of effects. These effects can be mild, like making you feel slightly nervous, or severe, like blocking your ability to focus or remember even a simple detail.

If you experience test anxiety—whether severe or mild—it's important to know how to beat it. To discover this, first you need to understand what causes test anxiety.

Causes of Test Anxiety

While we often think of anxiety as an uncontrollable emotional state, it can actually be caused by simple, practical things. One of the most common causes of test anxiety is that a person does not feel adequately prepared for their test. This feeling can be the result of many different issues such as poor study habits or lack of organization, but the most common culprit is time management. Starting to study too late, failing to organize your study time to cover all of the material, or being distracted while you study will mean that you're not well prepared for the test. This may lead to cramming the night before, which will cause you to be physically and mentally exhausted for the test. Poor time management also contributes to feelings of stress, fear, and hopelessness as you realize you are not well prepared but don't know what to do about it.

Other times, test anxiety is not related to your preparation for the test but comes from unresolved fear. This may be a past failure on a test, or poor performance on tests in general. It may come from comparing yourself to others who seem to be performing better or from the stress of living up to expectations. Anxiety may be driven by fears of the future—how failure on this test would affect your educational and career goals. These fears are often completely irrational, but they can still negatively impact your test performance.

> **Review Video: <u>3 Reasons You Have Test Anxiety</u>**
> Visit mometrix.com/academy and enter code: 428468

Elements of Test Anxiety

As mentioned earlier, test anxiety is considered to be an emotional state, but it has physical and mental components as well. Sometimes you may not even realize that you are suffering from test anxiety until you notice the physical symptoms. These can include trembling hands, rapid heartbeat, sweating, nausea, and tense muscles. Extreme anxiety may lead to fainting or vomiting. Obviously, any of these symptoms can have a negative impact on testing. It is important to recognize them as soon as they begin to occur so that you can address the problem before it damages your performance.

> **Review Video: 3 Ways to Tell You Have Test Anxiety**
> Visit mometrix.com/academy and enter code: 927847

The mental components of test anxiety include trouble focusing and inability to remember learned information. During a test, your mind is on high alert, which can help you recall information and stay focused for an extended period of time. However, anxiety interferes with your mind's natural processes, causing you to blank out, even on the questions you know well. The strain of testing during anxiety makes it difficult to stay focused, especially on a test that may take several hours. Extreme anxiety can take a huge mental toll, making it difficult not only to recall test information but even to understand the test questions or pull your thoughts together.

> **Review Video: How Test Anxiety Affects Memory**
> Visit mometrix.com/academy and enter code: 609003

Effects of Test Anxiety

Test anxiety is like a disease—if left untreated, it will get progressively worse. Anxiety leads to poor performance, and this reinforces the feelings of fear and failure, which in turn lead to poor performances on subsequent tests. It can grow from a mild nervousness to a crippling condition. If allowed to progress, test anxiety can have a big impact on your schooling, and consequently on your future.

Test anxiety can spread to other parts of your life. Anxiety on tests can become anxiety in any stressful situation, and blanking on a test can turn into panicking in a job situation. But fortunately, you don't have to let anxiety rule your testing and determine your grades. There are a number of relatively simple steps you can take to move past anxiety and function normally on a test and in the rest of life.

> **Review Video: How Test Anxiety Impacts Your Grades**
> Visit mometrix.com/academy and enter code: 939819

Physical Steps for Beating Test Anxiety

While test anxiety is a serious problem, the good news is that it can be overcome. It doesn't have to control your ability to think and remember information. While it may take time, you can begin taking steps today to beat anxiety.

Just as your first hint that you may be struggling with anxiety comes from the physical symptoms, the first step to treating it is also physical. Rest is crucial for having a clear, strong mind. If you are tired, it is much easier to give in to anxiety. But if you establish good sleep habits, your body and mind will be ready to perform optimally, without the strain of exhaustion. Additionally, sleeping well helps you to retain information better, so you're more likely to recall the answers when you see the test questions.

Getting good sleep means more than going to bed on time. It's important to allow your brain time to relax. Take study breaks from time to time so it doesn't get overworked, and don't study right before bed. Take time to rest your mind before trying to rest your body, or you may find it difficult to fall asleep.

> **Review Video: <u>The Importance of Sleep for Your Brain</u>**
> Visit mometrix.com/academy and enter code: 319338

Along with sleep, other aspects of physical health are important in preparing for a test. Good nutrition is vital for good brain function. Sugary foods and drinks may give a burst of energy but this burst is followed by a crash, both physically and emotionally. Instead, fuel your body with protein and vitamin-rich foods.

Also, drink plenty of water. Dehydration can lead to headaches and exhaustion, especially if your brain is already under stress from the rigors of the test. Particularly if your test is a long one, drink water during the breaks. And if possible, take an energy-boosting snack to eat between sections.

> **Review Video: <u>How Diet Can Affect your Mood</u>**
> Visit mometrix.com/academy and enter code: 624317

Along with sleep and diet, a third important part of physical health is exercise. Maintaining a steady workout schedule is helpful, but even taking 5-minute study breaks to walk can help get your blood pumping faster and clear your head. Exercise also releases endorphins, which contribute to a positive feeling and can help combat test anxiety.

When you nurture your physical health, you are also contributing to your mental health. If your body is healthy, your mind is much more likely to be healthy as well. So take time to rest, nourish your body with healthy food and water, and get moving as much as possible. Taking these physical steps will make you stronger and more able to take the mental steps necessary to overcome test anxiety.

Mental Steps for Beating Test Anxiety

Working on the mental side of test anxiety can be more challenging, but as with the physical side, there are clear steps you can take to overcome it. As mentioned earlier, test anxiety often stems from lack of preparation, so the obvious solution is to prepare for the test. Effective studying may be the most important weapon you have for beating test anxiety, but you can and should employ several other mental tools to combat fear.

First, boost your confidence by reminding yourself of past success—tests or projects that you aced. If you're putting as much effort into preparing for this test as you did for those, there's no reason you should expect to fail here. Work hard to prepare; then trust your preparation.

Second, surround yourself with encouraging people. It can be helpful to find a study group, but be sure that the people you're around will encourage a positive attitude. If you spend time with others who are anxious or cynical, this will only contribute to your own anxiety. Look for others who are motivated to study hard from a desire to succeed, not from a fear of failure.

Third, reward yourself. A test is physically and mentally tiring, even without anxiety, and it can be helpful to have something to look forward to. Plan an activity following the test, regardless of the outcome, such as going to a movie or getting ice cream.

When you are taking the test, if you find yourself beginning to feel anxious, remind yourself that you know the material. Visualize successfully completing the test. Then take a few deep, relaxing breaths and return to it. Work through the questions carefully but with confidence, knowing that you are capable of succeeding.

Developing a healthy mental approach to test taking will also aid in other areas of life. Test anxiety affects more than just the actual test—it can be damaging to your mental health and even contribute to depression. It's important to beat test anxiety before it becomes a problem for more than testing.

Review Video: Test Anxiety and Depression
Visit mometrix.com/academy and enter code: 904704

Study Strategy

Being prepared for the test is necessary to combat anxiety, but what does being prepared look like? You may study for hours on end and still not feel prepared. What you need is a strategy for test prep. The next few pages outline our recommended steps to help you plan out and conquer the challenge of preparation.

STEP 1: SCOPE OUT THE TEST

Learn everything you can about the format (multiple choice, essay, etc.) and what will be on the test. Gather any study materials, course outlines, or sample exams that may be available. Not only will this help you to prepare, but knowing what to expect can help to alleviate test anxiety.

STEP 2: MAP OUT THE MATERIAL

Look through the textbook or study guide and make note of how many chapters or sections it has. Then divide these over the time you have. For example, if a book has 15 chapters and you have five days to study, you need to cover three chapters each day. Even better, if you have the time, leave an extra day at the end for overall review after you have gone through the material in depth.

If time is limited, you may need to prioritize the material. Look through it and make note of which sections you think you already have a good grasp on, and which need review. While you are studying, skim quickly through the familiar sections and take more time on the challenging parts. Write out your plan so you don't get lost as you go. Having a written plan also helps you feel more in control of the study, so anxiety is less likely to arise from feeling overwhelmed at the amount to cover.

STEP 3: GATHER YOUR TOOLS

Decide what study method works best for you. Do you prefer to highlight in the book as you study and then go back over the highlighted portions? Or do you type out notes of the important information? Or is it helpful to make flashcards that you can carry with you? Assemble the pens, index cards, highlighters, post-it notes, and any other materials you may need so you won't be distracted by getting up to find things while you study.

If you're having a hard time retaining the information or organizing your notes, experiment with different methods. For example, try color-coding by subject with colored pens, highlighters, or post-it notes. If you learn better by hearing, try recording yourself reading your notes so you can listen while in the car, working out, or simply sitting at your desk. Ask a friend to quiz you from your flashcards, or try teaching someone the material to solidify it in your mind.

STEP 4: CREATE YOUR ENVIRONMENT

It's important to avoid distractions while you study. This includes both the obvious distractions like visitors and the subtle distractions like an uncomfortable chair (or a too-comfortable couch that makes you want to fall asleep). Set up the best study environment possible: good lighting and a comfortable work area. If background music helps you focus, you may want to turn it on, but otherwise keep the room quiet. If you are using a computer to take notes, be sure you don't have any other windows open, especially applications like social media, games, or anything else that could distract you. Silence your phone and turn off notifications. Be sure to keep water close by so you stay hydrated while you study (but avoid unhealthy drinks and snacks).

Also, take into account the best time of day to study. Are you freshest first thing in the morning? Try to set aside some time then to work through the material. Is your mind clearer in the afternoon or evening? Schedule your study session then. Another method is to study at the same time of day that you will take the test, so that your brain gets used to working on the material at that time and will be ready to focus at test time.

STEP 5: STUDY!

Once you have done all the study preparation, it's time to settle into the actual studying. Sit down, take a few moments to settle your mind so you can focus, and begin to follow your study plan. Don't give in to distractions or let yourself procrastinate. This is your time to prepare so you'll be ready to fearlessly approach the test. Make the most of the time and stay focused.

Of course, you don't want to burn out. If you study too long you may find that you're not retaining the information very well. Take regular study breaks. For example, taking five minutes out of every hour to walk briskly, breathing deeply and swinging your arms, can help your mind stay fresh.

As you get to the end of each chapter or section, it's a good idea to do a quick review. Remind yourself of what you learned and work on any difficult parts. When you feel that you've mastered the material, move on to the next part. At the end of your study session, briefly skim through your notes again.

But while review is helpful, cramming last minute is NOT. If at all possible, work ahead so that you won't need to fit all your study into the last day. Cramming overloads your brain with more information than it can process and retain, and your tired mind may struggle to recall even previously learned information when it is overwhelmed with last-minute study. Also, the urgent nature of cramming and the stress placed on your brain contribute to anxiety. You'll be more likely to go to the test feeling unprepared and having trouble thinking clearly.

So don't cram, and don't stay up late before the test, even just to review your notes at a leisurely pace. Your brain needs rest more than it needs to go over the information again. In fact, plan to finish your studies by noon or early afternoon the day before the test. Give your brain the rest of the day to relax or focus on other things, and get a good night's sleep. Then you will be fresh for the test and better able to recall what you've studied.

STEP 6: TAKE A PRACTICE TEST

Many courses offer sample tests, either online or in the study materials. This is an excellent resource to check whether you have mastered the material, as well as to prepare for the test format and environment.

Check the test format ahead of time: the number of questions, the type (multiple choice, free response, etc.), and the time limit. Then create a plan for working through them. For example, if you have 30 minutes to take a 60-question test, your limit is 30 seconds per question. Spend less time on the questions you know well so that you can take more time on the difficult ones.

If you have time to take several practice tests, take the first one open book, with no time limit. Work through the questions at your own pace and make sure you fully understand them. Gradually work up to taking a test under test conditions: sit at a desk with all study materials put away and set a timer. Pace yourself to make sure you finish the test with time to spare and go back to check your answers if you have time.

After each test, check your answers. On the questions you missed, be sure you understand why you missed them. Did you misread the question (tests can use tricky wording)? Did you forget the information? Or was it something you hadn't learned? Go back and study any shaky areas that the practice tests reveal.

Taking these tests not only helps with your grade, but also aids in combating test anxiety. If you're already used to the test conditions, you're less likely to worry about it, and working through tests until you're scoring well gives you a confidence boost. Go through the practice tests until you feel comfortable, and then you can go into the test knowing that you're ready for it.

Test Tips

On test day, you should be confident, knowing that you've prepared well and are ready to answer the questions. But aside from preparation, there are several test day strategies you can employ to maximize your performance.

First, as stated before, get a good night's sleep the night before the test (and for several nights before that, if possible). Go into the test with a fresh, alert mind rather than staying up late to study.

Try not to change too much about your normal routine on the day of the test. It's important to eat a nutritious breakfast, but if you normally don't eat breakfast at all, consider eating just a protein bar. If you're a coffee drinker, go ahead and have your normal coffee. Just make sure you time it so that the caffeine doesn't wear off right in the middle of your test. Avoid sugary beverages, and drink enough water to stay hydrated but not so much that you need a restroom break 10 minutes into the test. If your test isn't first thing in the morning, consider going for a walk or doing a light workout before the test to get your blood flowing.

Allow yourself enough time to get ready, and leave for the test with plenty of time to spare so you won't have the anxiety of scrambling to arrive in time. Another reason to be early is to select a good seat. It's helpful to sit away from doors and windows, which can be distracting. Find a good seat, get out your supplies, and settle your mind before the test begins.

When the test begins, start by going over the instructions carefully, even if you already know what to expect. Make sure you avoid any careless mistakes by following the directions.

Then begin working through the questions, pacing yourself as you've practiced. If you're not sure on an answer, don't spend too much time on it, and don't let it shake your confidence. Either skip it and come back later, or eliminate as many wrong answers as possible and guess among the remaining ones. Don't dwell on these questions as you continue—put them out of your mind and focus on what lies ahead.

Be sure to read all of the answer choices, even if you're sure the first one is the right answer. Sometimes you'll find a better one if you keep reading. But don't second-guess yourself if you do immediately know the answer. Your gut instinct is usually right. Don't let test anxiety rob you of the information you know.

If you have time at the end of the test (and if the test format allows), go back and review your answers. Be cautious about changing any, since your first instinct tends to be correct, but make sure you didn't misread any of the questions or accidentally mark the wrong answer choice. Look over any you skipped and make an educated guess.

At the end, leave the test feeling confident. You've done your best, so don't waste time worrying about your performance or wishing you could change anything. Instead, celebrate the successful completion of this test. And finally, use this test to learn how to deal with anxiety even better next time.

> **Review Video: 5 Tips to Beat Test Anxiety**
> Visit mometrix.com/academy and enter code: 570656

Important Qualification

Not all anxiety is created equal. If your test anxiety is causing major issues in your life beyond the classroom or testing center, or if you are experiencing troubling physical symptoms related to your anxiety, it may be a sign of a serious physiological or psychological condition. If this sounds like your situation, we strongly encourage you to seek professional help.

Additional Bonus Material

Due to our efforts to try to keep this book to a manageable length, we've created a link that will give you access to all of your additional bonus material:

mometrix.com/bonus948/teas7